Irish Peasants
Violence & Political Unrest
1780–1914

Irish Peasants
Violence & Political Unrest
1780–1914

Edited by
Samuel Clark & James S. Donnelly, Jr.

THE UNIVERSITY OF WISCONSIN PRESS

Published 1983

The University of Wisconsin Press
114 North Murray Street
Madison, Wisconsin 53715

Published in Great Britain by
Manchester University Press
Oxford Road, Manchester M13 9PL

First Printing

Printed in the United States of America

For LC CIP information see the colophon

ISBN 0-299-09370-0

To the memory of
Bill Feingold
1932–81

Contents

Editors and Contributors

Paul Bew
   Lecturer in modern history, Queen's University of Belfast

John W. Boyle
   Professor of history, University of Guelph, Ontario

Samuel Clark
   Associate professor of sociology, University of Western Ontario

David Dickson
   Lecturer in modern history, Trinity College, Dublin

James S. Donnelly, Jr.
   Professor of history, University of Wisconsin-Madison

William L. Feingold
   Late associate professor of history, Bellevue College, Bellevue, Nebraska

David S. Jones
   Lecturer in political science, National University of Singapore

Líam Kennedy
   Lecturer in economic and social history, Queen's University of Belfast

David W. Miller
   Professor of history, Carnegie-Mellon University, Pittsburgh, Pennsylvania

Paul E. W. Roberts
   Postgraduate student, University of Leeds

Brian M. Walker
   Lecturer in political science, Queen's University of Belfast

Frank Wright
   Lecturer in political science, Queen's University of Belfast

Acknowledgments

The first acknowledgment must go to the contributors, who had to endure two fastidious editors. We certainly gave them more trouble than they gave us.

For their kind permission to consult or quote from material which is in their ownership or possession, or of which they own the copyright, the contributors wish to thank the following: the Duke of Abercorn; Major-General Sir Allan Adair, Bt.; the Earl of Belmore; Messrs. Carleton, Atkinson & Sloan; the Marquess of Downshire; Messrs. P. A. Duffy & Co.; the Trustees of the Greer Estate; Her Majesty the Queen; the Marquess of Hertford; Captain Peter S. Montgomery; John Moore, Esq.; Lord O'Hagan; Denis O'Neill, Esq., C.B.; the late T. G. F. Paterson; Lord Redesdale; the Earl of Rosse; the Marquess of Salisbury; the Bodleian Library; the British Library Board; the Secretary of the Cork Archives Council; the County and Diocesan Archivist, Gloucestershire Record Office; the Director and Trustees of the National Library of Ireland; the National Trust of the United Kingdom; the Public Record Office of England; the Deputy Keeper of the Records, Public Record Office of Ireland; the Deputy Keeper of the Records, Public Record Office of Northern Ireland; the Council of the Royal Irish Academy; the Keeper of State Papers, State Paper Office, Dublin; the Head of the Archives Department, University College, Dublin; and the Head of the Department of Irish Folklore, University College, Dublin.

We would also like to thank Kevin McQuillan, Theda Skocpol, and Donald Von Eschen, who read portions of our introductions and gave us helpful comments. The University of Western Ontario and the University of Wisconsin-Madison provided financial assistance and clerical services; our principal typist, Anita Olson, performed marvelous labors, and to her we are especially grateful. The publication of the book has been made possible by a large grant from the Graduate School of the University of Wisconsin-Madison.

The book is dedicated to one of our contributors, whose death has torn a gaping hole in our lives. It is small recognition for his devotion to the study of Irish history and for the fellowship which we shared with him and which is now gone forever.

Abbreviations

B.F.P.	*Ballymoney Free Press*
B.M.N.	*Belfast Morning News*
B.N.L.	*Belfast Newsletter*
C.S.O.	Chief Secretary's Office
E.H.R.	*English Historical Review*
F.J.	*Freeman's Journal* (Dublin)
H.C.	House of Commons
H.L.	House of Lords
I.F.C.	Irish Folklore Commission
I.H.S.	*Irish Historical Studies*
N.L.I.	National Library of Ireland, Dublin
P.R.O.	Public Record Office of England, London and Kew
P.R.O.I.	Public Record Office of Ireland, Dublin
P.R.O.N.I.	Public Record Office of Northern Ireland, Belfast
R.I.A.	Royal Irish Academy, Dublin
R.P.	Registered papers
S.O.C.P.	State of the country papers
S.P.O.	State Paper Office, Dublin
Studia Hib.	*Studia Hibernica*
U.C.D.	University College, Dublin
W.E.U.O.	*Weekly Examiner and Ulster Observer* (Belfast)

Note: For other abbreviations used in footnotes, see "Rules for contributors to Irish Historical Studies" in *Irish Historical Studies*, supplement I (Jan. 1968).

Irish Peasants
Violence & Political Unrest
1780–1914

ATLANTIC OCEAN

Coleraine
Letterkenny
LONDONDERRY
LONDONDERRY
ANTRIM
DONEGAL
Ballymena
Strabane
Carrickfergus
TYRONE
LOUGH Antrim
Mountjoy
NEAGH
BELFAST
Dungannon
Lisburn
Benburb
D O W N
Armagh
ULSTER
Enniskillen
Downpatrick
Sligo
FERMANAGH
ARMAGH
Newry
Ballina
SLIGO
MONAGHAN
CONNACHT
Cavan
Dundalk
MAYO
LEITRIM
Boyle
Castlebar
CAVAN
LOUTH
Westport
ROSCOMMON
LONGFORD
Drogheda
Claremorris
Roscommon
Clifden
Tuam
MEATH
GALWAY
Mullingar
Athlone
GALWAY
WESTMEATH
Ballinasloe
DUBLIN
Loughrea
KING'S
Tullamore
KILDARE
DUBLIN
LEINSTER
Wicklow
CLARE
QUEEN'S
WICKLOW
Ennis
Nenagh
Arklow
Kilrush
TIPPERARY
CARLOW
LIMERICK
Kilkenny
WEXFORD
LIMERICK
Cashel
Enniscorthy
KILKENNY
New Ross
Clonmel
Tralee
MUNSTER
WATERFORD
Wexford
Dingle
Mallow
WATERFORD
Killarney
Dungarvan
KERRY
CORK
CORK
Youghal
Bantry

IRISH SEA

LEGEND

—— COUNTY
---- PROVINCE

N

0   10   20   30 mi.

0   20   40 km.

55°

54°

53°

52°

10°   8°

CARTOGRAPHIC LABORATORY, UNIVERSITY OF WISCONSIN – MADISON

Ireland

General Introduction

For the student of the Irish experience, agrarian movements, rural sectarianism, and popular political unrest in the period from the late eighteenth to the early twentieth centuries are subjects that deserve particular attention at the present time. This volume, which undertakes to pull together divergent strands of current research on these topics and to initiate the process of fitting them into larger conceptual frameworks, will, we hope, prove to be more than merely a convenient compendium of individual works. To some extent, such a collection of essays yields a varied picture of seemingly unconnected developments. In a broader sense, however, the very act of assembling a diverse set of works like these serves to aid in the identification of general questions and issues that should be of paramount concern in Irish studies.

We have grouped the essays into three sections in accordance with our perception of the major historical problems which Irish scholars have faced in studying agrarian society and popular politics in Ireland. In the first section are those works that seek to understand the nature of traditional rural collective action during the late eighteenth and early nineteenth centuries. The second consists of the fruits of research on the very distinctive patterns of collective action in the province of Ulster. And the third comprises studies of various facets of the modernization of rural collective action in Ireland during the late nineteenth and early twentieth centuries. Not all the essays in this volume fall perfectly into only one of these categories, but we have been able to organize them roughly on this basis. At the beginning of each section we have provided a brief historical introduction to help to orient the nonspecialized reader

3

and to tie together the individual contributions. These contributions themselves examine quite specific topics; in most cases they are empirical studies
heavily based on primary sources. As a rule, we endeavored to obtain
works focusing on relatively neglected subjects in Irish agrarian history,
such as the impact of taxation, rural sectarianism, agrarian politics in
Ulster, agricultural laborers, and the cleavage between graziers and small
farmers. Better-known subjects, such as the tithe war, the Tenant League,
and the land war, have been wholly or largely set aside, not because we
deny their importance, but because they have received a disproportionate
share of attention in existing works. The present book hopes to contribute
to the expansion of Irish historiography into new areas of inquiry.

Some of our contributors are traditional in their approaches; when
we commissioned their essays, we made no attempt to force them to
address larger theoretical issues. Yet we have consciously sought to produce a volume that will be useful not just to Irish specialists but also
to historians, sociologists, political scientists, and anthropologists interested in the study of agrarian peoples and their collective action. All
of the articles in this book have relevance to broad questions posed by
students of peasant movements, even if this relevance is not always made
explicit.

To facilitate the integration of Irish social history with general theoretical issues, this introduction is devoted to surveying some of the principal questions that students of peasant movements have been trying to
answer. We shall consider three of the issues that have dominated the
literature in this field:

1. What impact does modernization have on peasant societies? Does
   it increase the likelihood of peasant movements?
2. How do peasants become mobilized into collective action? What
   are the major obstacles to their mobilization? What social factors tend to promote their mobilization?
3. How are differences in agrarian social structure related to peasant movements? What classes or types of peasants have the most
   revolutionary potential?

What follows is a review of recent literature that seeks to answer these
questions. We shall also indicate some of the ways in which Irish peasants conform to or differ from the general patterns.

Modernization

There is a highly diverse body of literature which treats the effect of
modernization on peasant societies. Until recently, it was generally held
that modernization increases the probability of unrest among peasants

by helping to overcome their parochialism, thereby exposing them to new, more egalitarian and democratic influences, making them politically more conscious and active, or raising their expectations.[1] Although some of these arguments can still find highly credible proponents,[2] it is now common to take a less positive view of the effect of modernization on peasants. Today, for example, we often find scholars saying that modernization has steadily drawn peasants into a new economic system that poses threats to which they were not exposed in more traditional societies. The market is not, of course, an entirely new reality for peasants, but the extent of their involvement and the scope of the markets in which they participate have expanded enormously over the past several hundred years. The result, so the argument goes, is that peasants have become more dependent on distant economic forces beyond their control and are subject to price fluctuations that are more violent and less predictable than was traditionally the case. The greater commercialization that accompanies market participation also makes peasants more reliant on money. They become less self-sufficient, so that losses of income constitute threats to their survival in a way that was never true before, especially if the new economic forces also undermine secondary subsistence resources, that is, alternative supplies of food or income which previously enabled peasants to survive when their principal crop failed. Rural uprisings have often been explained, at least in part, as a consequence of the deprivation suffered by peasants in such hazardous economic circumstances, and perhaps also as a result of their determination to restore an earlier economic system.[3] Modernization frequently entails as well a loss of traditional rights

1. One or more of these arguments can be found in E. M. Rogers, *Modernization among peasants: the impact of communication* (New York, 1969); J. C. Davies (ed.), *When men revolt and why* (New York, 1970); T. R. Gurr, *Why men rebel* (Princeton, 1970); K. W. Deutsch, "Social mobilization and political development" in *American Political Science Review*, lv, no. 3 (Sept. 1961), pp. 493–514.

2. Emmanuel Le Roy Ladurie, "Révoltes et contestations en France de 1675 à 1788" in *Annales: Économies, Sociétés, Civilisations*, xxix, no. 1 (Jan.–Feb. 1974), pp. 6–22; J. S. Migdal, *Peasants, politics, and revolution: pressures toward political and social change in the third world* (Princeton, 1974); T. W. Margadant, *French peasants in revolt: the insurrection of 1851* (Princeton, 1979), especially pp. 55, 79, 106–7.

3. E. R. Wolf, *Peasant wars of the twentieth century* (New York, 1969); Jean Chesneaux, *Peasant revolts in China, 1840–1949* (London, 1973), pp. 66, 79; Shepard Forman, "Disunity and discontent: a study of peasant political movements in Brazil" in *Journal of Latin American Studies*, iii, pt. 1 (May 1971), pp. 3–24; Migdal, *Peasants, politics, and revolution*, pp. 52–5; J. C. Scott, *The moral economy of the peasant: rebellion and subsistence in southeast Asia* (New Haven, 1976); Nicos Mouzelis, "Greek and Bulgarian peasants: aspects of their sociopolitical situation during the interwar period" in *Comparative Studies in Society and History*, xviii, no. 1 (Jan. 1976), pp. 85–105; Margadant, *French peasants in revolt*, especially pp. 55, 81, 103.

to common land, of a minimum food supply, or of security of tenure.[4] And modernization has also been blamed for rapid population growth, which can have devastating effects on peasant standards of living.[5]

A closely related set of arguments in the general literature on peasant movements claims that modernization uproots peasants and weakens traditional institutions that have served both to control them and to support their way of life. These traditional institutions may consist of communal ties among peasants, which can provide succor during economic crises and a means by which country people are integrated into the existing order. The breakdown of traditional organizations, or the attempt to defend such organizations against breakdown, has frequently been cited as an underlying cause of peasant unrest.[6] A variation on this line of thinking is that modernization disrupts social ties between elites and peasants, and thereby removes a major social constraint on peasant revolt. The best-known writer to make this argument is Barrington Moore, Jr. Borrowing a page from de Tocqueville, Moore suggested that modernization may disrupt the social exchange binding traditional landed elites and peasants by removing from the hands of these elites important functions which they had previously performed, such as providing protection, administering justice, and furnishing relief in hard times. When these functions are transferred to a central government, local elites are deprived of the traditional rationale for their exactions from the peasantry. It is true that vertical ties between traditional elites and peasants are sometimes maintained in spite of modernization. When this happens, there is a tendency, according to Moore, toward fascist or rightist regimes. But in most cases modernization weakens the bonds between the peasantry and the old elite.[7]

4. On the problems of food supply, see the well-known essay by E. P. Thompson, "The moral economy of the English crowd in the eighteenth century" in *Past & Present*, no. 50 (Feb. 1971), pp. 76–136. For an example of loss of rights to common land, see Margadant, *French peasants in revolt*, pp. 43–6.

5. Chesneaux, *Peasant revolts in China*, p. 14; Migdal, *Peasants, politics, and revolution*, pp. 92–103.

6. George Rudé, *The crowd in history: a study of popular disturbances in France and England, 1730–1848* (New York, 1964), p. 156; Wolf, *Peasant wars*, especially pp. 276–302; Chesneaux, *Peasant revolts in China*, pp. 10, 18, 41, 70, 82–3; Migdal, *Peasants, politics, and revolution*, pp. 173–81; Charles Tilly, "Revolutions and collective violence" in F. I. Greenstein and Nelson Polsby (ed.), *Handbook of political science* (Reading, Mass., 1975), pp. 497–8; Daniel Chirot and Charles Ragin, "The market, tradition, and peasant rebellion: the case of Romania in 1907" in *American Sociological Review*, xl, no. 4 (Aug. 1975), p. 429; Michael Adas, *Prophets of rebellion: millenarian protest movements against the European colonial order* (Chapel Hill, N.C., 1979), pp. 42, 77–8.

7. Barrington Moore, Jr., *Social origins of dictatorship and democracy: lord and peasant in the making of the modern world* (Boston, 1966), especially pp. 453–83. See also

Many writers who adopt this perspective also suggest ways in which the exploitation of peasants may become intensified under the impact of modernization. Rising costs faced by traditional landed elites may force them to squeeze a larger surplus out of the peasantry; the traditional landed elite may become more commercially oriented, or it may be replaced by a bourgeois elite whose relationship to the peasantry is more formal and mercenary; or the growing power of a centralized state or colonial regime may impose heavier fiscal and military burdens on peasant populations.[8] Modernization usually entails greater contact with state or imperial officialdom. The extension of bureaucratic controls into rural areas and the exposure of peasants to state officials (e.g., tax collectors, district administrators, and agricultural advisers) have been crucial ingredients in the modernization of peasant societies.[9]

Class differentiation among peasants in modernizing societies has attracted considerable attention. It is a subject that has always interested Marxists. Today most writers accept that agricultural commercialization transforms agrarian class structures. Though disagreement persists about the nature of this transformation, there is a general recognition that several different patterns of change are possible.[10] The position perhaps most often taken is that modernization accentuates class differentiation and gives rise to three distinct classes within the agrarian population: (1) a "rural bourgeoisie" whose members have successfully entered the market economy and employ wage labor; (2) a middle peasantry consisting of independent smallholders who are partially involved in the market economy; and (3) poor peasants, landless or almost so, who are forced to sell their labor, usually to members of the rural bourgeoisie or to large landowners.[11] There has been some debate over which of these three classes has the most revolutionary potential, and we shall return to this question later. At this point it may simply be noted that many writers believe the middle peasantry to be a doomed social class, whose members will

Chesneaux, *Peasant revolts in China*, pp. 81–2; Migdal, *Peasants, politics, and revolution*, pp. 103–6; Adas, *Prophets of rebellion*, pp. 62–3.

8. One or more of these arguments can be found in Moore, *Social origins;* Le Roy Ladurie, "Révoltes et contestations"; Charles Tilly, "Reflections on the history of European state-making" in Charles Tilly (ed.), *The formation of national states in western Europe* (Princeton, 1975); Scott, *Moral economy.*

9. Migdal, *Peasants, politics, and revolution*, pp. 92, 106–7.

10. Ibid., pp. 156–71.

11. Kathleen Gough, "Peasant resistance and revolt in south India" in *Pacific Affairs*, xli, no. 4 (Winter 1968–9), pp. 526–44; Hamza Alavi, "Peasants and revolution" in Ralph Miliband and John Saville (ed.), *The socialist register, 1965* (New York, 1965), pp. 241–77; H. A. Landsberger, "Peasant unrest: themes and variations" in H. A. Landsberger (ed.), *Rural protest: peasant movements and social change* (London, 1974), pp. 15–17.

inevitably become proletarianized and join the ranks of poor peasants. When middle peasants participate in agrarian movements, they do so, it is said, in an effort to resist this inexorable historical process.[12]

All the works which we have been discussing imply that social unrest increases in peasant societies experiencing modernization. Some writers, however, would challenge this notion, or they would at least insist that what is more important is the way in which the character of social unrest changes under the impact of modernization. There are a variety of views about the qualitative changes that can occur.[13] Most theories of this kind contain an underlying evolutionary assumption that with modernization peasant protest becomes less "primitive," more sophisticated, better organized, and perhaps more forward-looking and less defensive.[14] Charles Tilly maintains that the character of collective action in western Europe has changed over the past several centuries in three principal ways: (1) it has become more often national rather than local; (2) it has become less reactive (i.e., defending old rights) and more proactive (i.e., making new demands); and (3) it has become less communal and more associational in its organizational structure.[15]

Now let us turn to Irish peasants. Many of the above ideas about the impact of modernization have appeared in the Irish literature, though in most cases not consciously derived from the writings that we have discussed. One example is the notion of a persistent degeneration in social relations between elites and peasants in Ireland during the early modern and modern periods. It has been argued that the massive transfers in land-ownership during the seventeenth century caused a deterioration in landlord-tenant relations; the new owners were presumably more commercialized and impersonal than those whom they replaced, and they demanded cash rents from their tenants. Yet the contention has also been heard that these landlords of the seventeenth and eighteenth centuries were more indulgent and less exacting in their relations with tenants than those of the early nineteenth century. Especially during the economic

12. Gough, "Peasant resistance"; Wolf, *Peasant wars*, pp. 291–2; D. F. Ferguson, "Rural/urban relations and peasant radicalism: a preliminary statement" in *Comparative Studies in Society and History*, xviii, no. 1 (Jan. 1976), pp. 106–18.

13. David Sabean, "The communal basis of pre-1800 peasant uprisings in western Europe" in *Comparative Politics*, viii, no. 3 (Apr. 1976), pp. 355–64; Margadant, *French peasants in revolt*, p. 339.

14. E. J. Hobsbawm, *Primitive rebels: studies in archaic forms of social movements in the 19th and 20th centuries* (Manchester, 1959); Rudé, *Crowd in history*; Chesneaux, *Peasant revolts in China*, especially pp. 86–9, 151–3.

15. Charles Tilly, *From mobilization to revolution* (Reading, Mass., 1978), especially pp. 143–71. See also Charles Tilly, Louise Tilly, and Richard Tilly, *The rebellious century, 1830–1930* (Cambridge, Mass., 1975), especially pp. 17–23.

downturn that followed the French revolutionary and Napoleonic wars, landowners sought to tighten the management of their properties, with the result that they became more demanding and less tolerant of the loose practices commonly permitted on estates in the eighteenth century and during the wartime prosperity. Relations are said to have deteriorated even further during and after the famine. In particular, it was common in the postfamine years to single out for rebuke the "new" landowners who bought property under the incumbered-estates acts of 1849 and 1858. These new owners were said to be bourgeois men, more mercenary than prefamine proprietors and less flexible in administering their estates, the implication being that this disruption of landlord-tenant relations contributed to the agrarian upheaval or land war of 1879–82. Thus the assertion has repeatedly been made that the landlords of one era were more demanding and impersonal than those of the preceding era.

Other arguments have also been advanced about Irish peasants that parallel themes found in the general literature. The resistance of prefamine cottiers and small farmers to the breakup of joint tenancies, to the conversion of tillage land into pasture, to the consolidation of holdings, and to other landlord "improvements" can be used to illustrate the opposition of Irish peasants to modernization and their determination to defend traditional practices. The land war of 1879–82 has been explained as a consequence of rising expectations. The Irish rural population experienced rising expectations in the postfamine years as a result of unprecedented prosperity in agriculture, particularly in the livestock sector. When expectations of continued improvement in living standards were grievously disappointed by the agricultural depression of the late 1870s, great numbers of farmers rose in revolt. Even though the discontent felt at this time was not without precedent, the theory of rising expectations does help to explain why the downturn of 1877–80 gave rise to so much disaffection and why the land war occurred when it did.

Contributors to this collection also frequently deal with facets of the Irish experience that illustrate arguments found in the broader literature on peasant movements. David Dickson calls attention to the importance of popular opposition to taxation in the 1790s, a time when sentiment against the established order and the authority of the state ran high. David Miller, in his essay on the Armagh disturbances of 1784–95, puts forward the hypothesis that these conflicts originated in a breakdown of traditional social relations in Armagh society. Specifically, he points to a possible breakdown in social control within the family, especially the Protestant family, the source of which lay in the development of domestic linen weaving and in the independence given to adolescent males by cash wages. He also considers the proposition that the troubles stemmed

from a breakdown in the social control previously exercised by the landed
elite over the Protestant population.

In recent years the subject of class differences within Irish rural society has also received explicit attention from scholars. It is treated in four
articles in the present volume, those by Paul E. W. Roberts, William
L. Feingold, John W. Boyle, and David S. Jones. Roberts focuses on the
acute class conflict among Irish peasants in the early decades of the nineteenth century. Feingold analyzes class differences in support for the Land
League. Boyle examines the much-neglected subject of agricultural laborers in the last half of the nineteenth century. And Jones contends that
increased agricultural commercialization and the expansion of the livestock market after 1850 led to the development of a distinct and socially
aloof class of graziers, a group whose economic interests and mode of
living put them at odds with other members of agrarian society.

We can also perceive a change in the character of rural collective action in Ireland that is consistent with some of the general theories, especially with Tilly's model of the transformation of collective action in
western Europe. In Ireland the major change occurred between the late
eighteenth and early nineteenth centuries on the one hand, and the late
nineteenth and the twentieth centuries on the other. This is not to say
that in the first period all rural collective action was local, reactive, and
communal, while in the second it all became national, proactive, and
associational. What happened was much more complex, involving in
each period a mixture of forms of collective action. The development
of national proactive movements with associational features began in
Ireland in the late eighteenth century and developed further from the
1820s to the 1840s with the great O'Connellite movements and the tithe
war. In the same period, however, we can also find an enormous number of small rural combinations, often locally and communally based,
and primarily defensive in their objectives. There were also a significant
number of regional peasant movements of impressive magnitude, such
as those described by Roberts and James S. Donnelly, Jr., in their essays
for this collection. In the late nineteenth century, by contrast, local and
communal collective action declined in significance (though it did not
disappear entirely, especially in the northeast, where sectarian clashes
of this kind persist to the present day). Even the regional movements
that could be found before the famine had few equivalents after 1850.
What emerged as the predominant form of collective action in the last
half of the nineteenth century was the large associational movement stak-
ing new claims to a share of power at the national level—the Home
Rule League, the Land League, and the National League.

While recognizing these highly important changes in the character of collective action in Ireland during the nineteenth century, we are skeptical about the argument that peasant movements become less primitive, more sophisticated, and better organized as a result of modernization. Such ideas, we suspect, represent the biases of writers who live in highly urbanized and industrialized societies, and who have become accustomed to thinking of organization solely in modern associational terms. We shall encounter this problem again when we discuss peasant mobilization.

Studying the Irish experience leads us to question other arguments in the general literature as well. We shall mention two of them. First, we are somewhat dismayed by the tendency of numerous scholars to idealize earlier periods of time, or at least to assume that conditions deteriorate in peasant societies under the impact of modernization. Admittedly, in many societies modernization has indeed intensified exploitation, increased hardship, or undermined traditional values among peasants. But it has not always done so, and any theory of peasant movements which assumes that it always does will inevitably be unsatisfactory. Certainly, such a theory would not cover the case of Ireland, where modernization added to hardship in the first half of the nineteenth century but reduced it during the last half.

Second, we would like to caution against the assumption that modernization and the peasantry are antithetical. This notion underlies many writings on peasants. Yet it ignores the fact that peasant societies as we know them have evolved as part of processes which we normally identify with modernization, such as capitalism and state-making.[16] While these processes may ultimately destroy peasantries, they certainly have not had this effect in western Europe until recently, and in most parts of the world the destruction of the peasantry has hardly begun. One of the defining characteristics of a peasant — the extraction of a significant portion of his produce by nonagrarian social groups — became more pronounced in western Europe at a very early stage in the development of capitalism and has grown with capitalism ever since. The peasant population in this part of the world has been actively engaged for several centuries in producing goods for national and even international markets, both agricultural and nonagricultural. In numerical terms the link between peasants and modernization has been even more obvious. There is still some debate about causal factors, but there is no doubt about what happened. The development of capitalism and the formation of national states in western Europe between 1600 and 1900 generally coincided with an increase in the size of the peasant population, not only in absolute num-

16. Charles Tilly, "Peasants against capitalism and the state: a review essay" in *Agricultural History*, lii, no. 3 (July 1978), pp. 407–16.

bers but in many places even in proportion to the rest of the society. In most areas the decline in the size of peasant populations (proportionately at first, and eventually in absolute terms) did not begin until well into the nineteenth century. Even then, it could not generally be said that peasants were forced off the land and replaced by large-scale agribusinesses. The small family farm — combining subsistence tillage with commercial production and employing little or no wage labor — did not disappear in the late nineteenth century. In many parts of western Europe it remained the predominant form of agricultural organization and became further integrated into the capitalist economy.[17] Also, in many places it adapted to modern political institutions in a way that insured its persistence into the twentieth century.[18] The survival of the small peasantry in Ireland serves as a good illustration of these processes.

Mobilization

The preceding review of literature on the effect of modernization has avoided drawing an important distinction. Most studies of social unrest, especially peasant unrest, explicitly or implicitly make one of two opposing assumptions. The first is that unrest results from social disorganization or disruption; such an assumption is generally known as a breakdown theory. Alternatively, it is believed that unrest occurs when organized collectivities become engaged in struggles to defend or advance their interests; an assumption of this kind is usually called a mobilization or solidarity theory. This well-known theoretical distinction is discussed later in this volume by Miller, who attempts to combine the two approaches in order to explain collective violence in Ulster in the closing decades of the eighteenth century. Most scholars whose writings we have reviewed above belong to the first school; they take it for granted that modernization generates social unrest by disrupting traditional society economically, politically, or socially. But not all of them do so. A significant number of authors we have cited recognize that peasant revolt is possible only if peasants are organized. Yet can peasants become organized? Do they themselves have the capacity for effective political mobilization? This is one of the most enduring questions in the study of peasant societies.

One very widespread point of view is that peasants are inherently incapable of effective political action. Many reasons have been given to support this proposition. First, it is frequently claimed that peasants are

17. Harriet Friedmann, "World market, state, and family farm: social bases of household production in the era of wage labor" in *Comparative Studies in Society and History*, xx, no. 4 (Oct. 1978), pp. 545–86.
18. Margadant, *French peasants in revolt*, especially p. 338.

highly individualistic. In most cases they work in family units, and it is difficult to persuade them to join forces with other peasant households, from whom they are economically distinct and perhaps geographically separated.[19] Second, peasants are parochial; their social and mental horizons do not extend much beyond their kinship groups and villages.[20] Third, peasants are uneducated, indeed generally illiterate; they also lack political experience since they are normally excluded from formal political processes.[21] Fourth, peasants are tied to their landholdings and to a fixed work routine; they do not have the free time, mobility, or flexibility necessary for organizing political activity.[22] Fifth, peasants are often fragmented by regional, ethnic, religious, or class divisions.[23] And finally, peasants are by nature conservative and hesitant to take risks.[24] Many scholars hold that, for these and other reasons, peasant mobilization is problematic. It can occur, but only under special conditions. If these conditions do not obtain, peasant discontent is spent in unorganized protest — what one writer calls "spontaneous, amorphous action," or what another describes as "expressive, 'primary,' noninstrumental violence."[25] A prevalent image of peasant revolt is that it results from sheer desperation, when wretched people are driven to the breaking point by ruthless oppression and unbearable exploitation. It then bursts forth without ideology, discipline, or organization.

Those who take this position would acknowledge that peasant rebellion may achieve some degree of organization if the discontented are united

19. The best-known statement of this view is that of Marx. See *The Eighteenth Brumaire of Louis Bonaparte* (New York, 1963), pp. 123–4. See also Wolf, *Peasant wars*, pp. 289–90; James Petras and Maurice Zeitlin, "Agrarian radicalism in Chile" in Rodolfo Stavenhagen (ed.), *Agrarian problems and peasant movements in Latin America* (New York, 1970), p. 522.

20. Rogers, *Modernization among peasants;* Adas, *Prophets of rebellion*, p. 81.

21. Wolf, *Peasant wars*, pp. 289–90; Adas, *Prophets of rebellion*, p. 80.

22. Wolf, *Peasant wars*, pp. 289–90; J. S. Saul and Roger Woods, "African peasantries" in Teodor Shanin (ed.), *Peasants and peasant societies* (Harmondsworth, 1971), p. 105; Adas, *Prophets of rebellion*, p. 81; Migdal, *Peasants, politics, and revolution*, p. 21; Chesneaux, *Peasant revolts in China*, p. 70. But elsewhere in *Peasant revolts in China*, Chesneaux maintains that peasants are more independent than industrial workers (p. 156).

23. Teodor Shanin, "Peasantry as a political factor" in Shanin, *Peasants and peasant societies*, p. 255; Landsberger, "Peasant unrest," pp. 53–5.

24. R. A. White, "Mexico: the Zapata movement and the revolution" in H. A. Landsberger (ed.), *Latin American peasant movements* (Ithaca, 1969), p. 123; Rogers, *Modernization among peasants;* Petras and Zeitlin, "Agrarian radicalism in Chile," p. 522; Paul Stirling, "A Turkish village" in Shanin, *Peasants and peasant societies*, p. 46.

25. H. A. Landsberger, "The role of peasant movements and revolts in development" in Landsberger, *Latin American peasant movements*, p. 36; Shanin, "Peasantry as a political factor," p. 258. See also Chesneaux, *Peasant revolts in China*, pp. 14, 22, 84–5, 152–3. Chesneaux refers to the "sporadic, scattered, and ephemeral character" of Chinese uprisings, but his accounts of specific revolts do not always bear out this generalization.

by common beliefs, such as nationalist or religious sentiments.[26] The millenarian movement, in which people are united by a shared expectation of deliverance, is considered the prototype of this sort of peasant collective action.[27] The most accepted view is that millenarian movements tend to emerge in those societies where more advanced forms of organization have not yet developed.[28] Secret societies, though they are incapable of mobilizing great numbers of people, may also help peasants to achieve some measure of cohesion.[29]

Yet both millenarian movements and secret societies have been generally regarded as comparatively primitive forms of peasant protest. It has been repeatedly argued that the most successful peasant movements acquire effective organization and political leverage through the help of nonpeasant leaders. Traditionally, this outside leadership may have come from rural elites, but in the past century or more it has typically come from urban groups.[30] Peasant mobilization is also facilitated if for some reason the strength of ruling elites is weakened. A number of scholars have pointed out that peasant movements tend to be most successful when the class against whom peasants are revolting is being challenged at the same time by other groups in the society or is experiencing a general decline in its power.[31] These writers quite properly insist that peasant revolts cannot be understood without studying the larger national and even international context in which they occur. It is especially important to investigate whether peasants are tightly bound to the established order or possess what Eric Wolf has called tactical power or leverage, giving them sufficient independence to engage in collective action in their own interests.[32]

The experience of Irish peasants illuminates some of these themes. They were certainly fragmented by sharp cleavages, including regional

26. John Iliffe, "The organisation of the Maji Maji rebellion" in *Journal of African History*, viii, no. 3 (1967), pp. 495–512; Chesneaux, *Peasant revolts in China*, pp. 28, 127; Anthony Oberschall, *Social conflict and social movements* (Englewood Cliffs, N.J., 1973), pp. 142–3; Landsberger, "Peasant unrest," pp. 53–5.

27. Norman Cohn, *The pursuit of the millennium: revolutionary millenarians and mystical anarchists of the middle ages* (rev. ed., New York, 1970); Adas, *Prophets of rebellion*.

28. The best-known statement of this view can be found in Peter Worsley, *The trumpet shall sound: a study of "cargo" cults in Melanesia* (2nd ed., New York, 1968).

29. Chesneaux, *Peasant revolts in China*, pp. 18, 84.

30. G. C. Alroy, *The involvement of peasants in internal wars* (Princeton, 1966); Wolf, *Peasant wars*, p. 294; Chesneaux, *Peasant revolts in China*, especially pp. 16, 55, 151–3, 162; Roderick Aya, *The missed revolution: the fate of rural rebels in Sicily and southern Spain, 1840–1950* (Amsterdam, 1975), p. 122; Ferguson, "Rural/urban relations."

31. Landsberger, "Role of peasant movements," p. 23; Aya, *Missed revolution*.

32. Wolf, *Peasant wars*, pp. 290–3; Aya, *Missed revolution*; Theda Skocpol, *States and social revolutions: a comparative analysis of France, Russia, and China* (Cambridge, 1979).

and class divisions, but above all, of course, by religious division. The second section of the present volume contains three essays that examine political and social unrest in the province of Ulster. Implicitly or explicitly, these contributions reveal the obstacles created by sectarian cleavage to the mobilization of peasants against their landlords. Miller describes and seeks to explain the wave of sectarian violence that erupted in County Armagh after 1785, and that superseded less sectarian patterns of unrest that had predominated earlier. Paul Bew and Frank Wright explore the complex interaction between the land question and denominational allegiances in northern politics in the postfamine period. And Brian M. Walker focuses more closely on Ulster county elections in the years 1868–86. The latter two essays show that the land question had far more impact in Ulster than has generally been recognized. Their authors then demonstrate why agrarian radicalism in the north was eventually overwhelmed by sectarian conflict.

Yet if denominational divisions inhibited alliances between Catholics and Protestants against the Irish landed elite, by the same token religious affiliation formed an effective base for separate collective action by each of the two religious groups. Indeed, given that the Irish landed elite was predominately Protestant, religious loyalty among Catholics provided a major source of integration which repeatedly facilitated the mobilization of peasants in defense of their interests. In spite of its undeniably divisive effect in most of Ulster, the net impact of the religious cleavage was to support rather than to impede collective action among Irish peasants. An especially striking illustration is the Rockite movement of 1821–4, treated by Donnelly in his essay for our collection. This movement shows how Catholic aspirations to overthrow Protestant domination could facilitate the organization of peasants in an effective agrarian challenge to the established order. The Rockites are not the only example of the mobilizing potential of religious ties. Both the tithe war of the early 1830s and the land war of 1879–82 relied heavily on the strong sense of identity shared by Catholics.

The Irish case gives little support to the view that peasants are incapable of political organization. The magnitude of prefamine agrarian rebellion — an impressive succession of regional movements punctuating every decade between 1760 and 1840 — indicates the capacity of Irish peasants for effective action without external assistance. Roberts's contribution on the great feud between the lower-class Caravats and the middle-class Shanavests is especially interesting in this regard. He demonstrates clearly that even poor peasants were able to organize themselves in a broadly based movement independently of rural or urban middle-class leadership. The Caravats were not unusual in this regard.

Most prefamine rural collective action occurred without the help of the urban middle class. Moreover, when middle-class townsmen did ally with rural people in collective action, as they did in the great national movements, their role was inevitably a complex one. Although they often performed leadership roles, it is not at all clear that they were functionally necessary for rural political organization in Ireland. Nor is it true that they always served the welfare of peasants, as Líam Kennedy shows in his contribution to this volume.

Rather than assuming that urban assistance is functionally necessary for peasant movements, it is more useful to explore the ways in which social processes give peasants the "leverage" of which Wolf speaks. Forces which diminish the power of the landed elite and strengthen that of the peasantry facilitate the mobilization of the latter in their own interests, regardless of the particular groups involved. Ireland offers a good illustration of this general phenomenon. Challenges to established authority in Ireland by the Catholic church, by Catholic political movements, and above all by nationalist movements served to weaken the position of the Protestant landowning class and provided ideologies as well as organizational structures that facilitated peasant opposition. It is no accident that the greatest peasant movements in Irish history—the Defender movement of the 1790s, the tithe war of the early 1830s, and the land war of 1879–82—all occurred at times when the Catholic or nationalist challenge to the Protestant ascendancy was at a high point.

Peasant Typologies

A third theoretical approach to the study of agrarian movements endeavors to classify peasants into various types and then to generalize about the kind of collective action to be expected from each one. It is possible to identify two versions of this perspective: the first approach emphasizes class divisions within peasant populations, while the second seeks primarily to construct a typology of peasant economies.

We have referred already to some of the literature on class differentiation in peasant societies and noted the view that modernization poses the greatest threat to the "middle peasantry." Although it is usually found that large, commercialized farmers have the most political skills and experience,[33] and that poor peasants are the most rebellious,[34] Wolf and others have argued that the middle peasantry has the greatest revolution-

33. Landsberger, "Role of peasant movements," p. 39.
34. "Review of meeting: rural-development panel seminar on peasants, land reform, and revolutionary movements" in *Peasant Studies Newsletter*, iv, no. 1 (Jan. 1975), pp. 15–16; Ronald Waterbury, "Non-revolutionary peasants: Oaxaca compared to Morelos in

ary potential. The reason is not that middle peasants are more revolutionary in spirit; on the contrary, they are the most conservative and tradition-bound of the peasant classes. Nevertheless, for this very reason they tend to be the most resistant to social change and can be provoked into the strongest reaction against it. It has also been argued that middle peasants have more tactical leverage than poor peasants, and that they have greater contact with urban society and therefore more access to urban ideas and leadership.[35]

To what extent have Irish peasants conformed to this general pattern? Naturally, much depends on how one defines the middle peasantry. In his contribution to our volume Feingold classifies farmers who were entitled to vote in poor-law elections into three categories: large, middling, and small. He finds the greatest support for the Land League among large and small farmers, and the least support among the middling group. It is necessary to understand, however, that this ranking does not include poor peasants because only those with holdings valued at £4 or more were entitled to vote for poor-law guardians. A slightly different classification is necessary in order to sort out the entire agrarian population. For the sake of discussion, our suggestion would be that rich peasants in the Irish context were "large farmers," generally with over 30 acres of good land. At the other end of the scale, the poor peasants were those members of the agricultural labor force who had little or no land, and who were consequently obliged to work for someone else. They include prefamine cottiers and the wage laborers whose unenviable lot Boyle discusses in his contribution to this collection. Middle peasants were those in between. They were the "small farmers" of Ireland, in most cases holding from 5 to 20 acres of land. They differ, however, in an important respect from Wolf's middle peasants: Wolf generally restricts this term to peasants who own their land, whereas relatively few peasants in Ireland were proprietors until the twentieth century.

In any case, if we ask which class or classes of peasants were the most active in agrarian protest in Ireland between 1780 and 1914, we find it difficult to single out one particular group. The class that was the most rebellious varied from one period to another and even from one movement to another. At the risk of oversimplifying a complex subject, we will offer two general hypotheses. First, in the period before the great famine the numerical predominance of agricultural laborers and small

---

the Mexican revolution" in *Comparative Studies in Society and History*, xvii, no. 4 (Oct. 1975), p. 438.

    35. Alavi, "Peasants and revolution"; Wolf, *Peasant wars*, pp. 291–2; Ferguson, "Rural/urban relations."

farmers in the rural population, together with their acute sense of oppression and very real grievances, meant that these groups figured most prominently in agrarian movements. After the famine the proportional decline in the number of agricultural laborers helped to change the character of agrarian collective action. It came to reflect the interests of large and small farmers, to the neglect of the concerns of agricultural laborers. Our second hypothesis is that the social composition of movements tended to vary with the economic conditions that gave rise to them. During the prefamine period collective action that was sparked by severe agricultural depression generally involved large and small farmers as well as agricultural laborers. Agrarian movements that arose in times of seeming prosperity, when land values were rising, were usually dominated by the poorest social classes.

The remaining set of theoretical writings to be considered are those that endeavor to construct a typology of peasant economies. A well-known work of this kind is a comparative study by Jeffery Paige.[36] He explicitly rejects Wolf's thesis that landowning middle peasants have the most revolutionary potential. He classifies peasant economies into four types according to sources of income and hypothesizes a particular form of collective action for each type. The greatest revolutionary potential, says Paige, is to be found in societies where elites extract their wealth from land and most peasants derive their income from wages, paid either in money or in kind. There are two reasons for this. First, because of their dependence on land, elites in this kind of economy are unable and unwilling to grant political or economic concessions to peasants. In other types of agrarian systems where elites earn income from capital, they can afford to make economic concessions in order to defuse peasant opposition. Second, in societies where peasants draw income from wages, they generally become, for a number of reasons, more conscious of class and better organized than in societies where peasant earnings come directly from the land. It is the combination of intransigent elites and class-conscious agricultural wage earners that is most likely to give rise to a peasant revolution, according to Paige.

This conclusion is supported by other studies,[37] but curiously enough, it is not altogether consistent with an earlier work by Arthur Stinchcombe which provided the inspiration for Paige's theory. In a highly influential article published in 1961, Stinchcombe identified five basic types of agrarian economy: (1) the manorial or hacienda system;

---

36. J. M. Paige, *Agrarian revolution: social movements and export agriculture in the underdeveloped world* (New York, 1975).

37. See, e.g., Petras and Zeitlin, "Agrarian radicalism in Chile."

(2) family-size tenancy; (3) family smallholding; (4) plantation agriculture; and (5) capitalist extensive agriculture with wage labor, which he refers to as the "ranch."[38]

In the first system peasants live on very small holdings devoted mostly to subsistence crops and at the same time work as laborers on large agricultural enterprises operated by landowners. The kind of economic structure that Stinchcombe has in mind in this case has never prevailed in Ireland. The closest thing to it was the practice of laborers and small farmers working on large farms. The employers in this case, however, were for the most part middle-class tenant farmers rather than upper-class landowners. Also, the farms on which laborers and small farmers were employed in Ireland were very much smaller than Stinchcombe's manors or haciendas.

When Stinchcombe turns to the family-size tenancy, however, he provides a conceptual tool that is extremely helpful for understanding agrarian unrest in Ireland. In the family-size tenancy the operative unit is the family enterprise, but property rights rest with rentier capitalists. In Stinchcombe's view this system can become politically explosive for a number of reasons: the rentier class and the peasantry are involved in a zero-sum conflict (i.e., a gain for one party is usually at the expense of the other); severe conflict can arise over the distribution of risks in the enterprise (each party seeks to force the other to bear most of the risks); the social bond between landlord and tenant is usually weak because the rentier class is often absentee and generally does little more than collect rents through an agent; peasants of different class positions are able to unite on the basis of a common opposition to this rentier class; and finally, tenants are aware that they can get along without landlords and inevitably attempt to do so. This theoretical type describes almost precisely the kind of system in which many peasants found themselves in Ireland during the nineteenth century. Although only a minority of the rural population occupied family-size tenancies before the famine, this kind of enterprise came to predominate in the postfamine period and goes a long way toward explaining the land war of 1879–82.

Eventually, family-size tenancy in Ireland gave way to Stinchcombe's third type of enterprise, in which family farms are owned by their occupiers. As Stinchcombe points out, this evolution transforms entirely the kind of collective action that one can expect. Peasants are no longer engaged in a zero-sum conflict with a landowning class. Instead, they now focus their collective efforts on improving their position in credit and

38. A. L. Stinchcombe, "Agricultural enterprise and rural class relations" in *American Journal of Sociology*, lxvii, no. 2 (Sept. 1961), pp. 165–76.

commodity markets. As a result, collective action in family-smallholding systems becomes anti-urban. This transition is clearly visible in Ireland. Around 1900 or even earlier, people began to realize that the battle with landlords would eventually be won by Irish farmers, and consequently the alliance between townsmen and farmers, which had been so close in the days of the land war, showed signs of disintegration. The two issues over which they became most divided were credit and cooperatives. In his essay in this volume Kennedy describes the quarrel over cooperatives and the general advantages enjoyed by townsmen in this conflict.

Although plantation agriculture has never been common in Ireland, a variant of Stinchcombe's fifth type, the ranch, has come to occupy a growing proportion of the land ever since the great famine of the late 1840s. The essential feature of the ranch is that it requires large amounts of land and low inputs of labor. There is no pressure to recruit, maintain, or exploit great numbers of peasants. On the contrary, the economic pressure of ranching operates to force peasants off the land. In Ireland, therefore, as Jones argues in his provocative essay for our collection, the economics of ranching brought it into direct conflict with the family-size holding, which had become the dominant form of agricultural enterprise in the country. The story of this conflict — its economic foundation and historical evolution — has been a relatively neglected subject in Irish agrarian history.

Is it, in the end, vital that historians of Ireland know what scholars have been saying about other peasant societies? We think it is. The social development of Ireland was very much a part of the enormous transformation resulting from the rise of world capitalism. How peasantries have expanded under this economic system, how their societies and cultures have been affected, how and under what conditions they have mobilized, and what differences have existed among peasants in their responses — these are questions which Irish specialists cannot avoid because the Irish experience took place in the context of the larger transformation. Indeed, the central role played by England in world capitalism has meant that the social upheaval which all peasantries have undergone or are now undergoing was experienced very early and acutely by the Irish. The great expansion and then brutal contraction of the Irish rural population in the eighteenth and nineteenth centuries, as well as the massive migration of Irish peasants to urban industrial centers in widely separated parts of the world, bear witness to the sensitive place that Irish country people came to occupy at a relatively early point in the evolution of world capitalism. Thus, in our view, there are especially compelling reasons for scholars investigating the Irish past to set their research into larger theoretical frameworks in order to advance our understanding of both the Irish experience and the peasant experience in general.

I

THE TRADITION OF VIOLENCE

Introduction

Ireland became almost synonymous with rebellion during the late eighteenth and early nineteenth centuries. Every decade between 1760 and 1840 was punctuated by at least one major outbreak of rural discontent. Though these upheavals generally lacked regional organization, they were regional in the sense that the participants pursued broadly similar aims over wide areas of the country. Effective repression was difficult for the government to achieve, largely because the rebels usually adopted clandestine forms of collective action. Some regional movements — the Oakboys of 1763, the Houghers of 1778-9, the Ribbonmen of 1819-20 — were of short duration and had a life measured only in months. But others — the Rightboys of 1785-8, the Rockites of 1821-4 — endured for several years. And in the 1790s a staggering series of popular protests erupted in the Irish countryside, which were not purely agrarian or economic in aim, and which culminated in a vast revolutionary effort dedicated to the establishment of a separatist republic.

All these movements, taken together, left scarcely any part of Ireland untouched. Yet in certain regions, especially the west midlands, the south, and the southeast, agrarian rebellion occurred so often that it became a deep-seated tradition. It acquired customary features — uniforms or special dress, quasi-military organization, oaths of secrecy and loyalty, codes of approved behavior, rituals of intimidation and punishment — all reappearing again and again until the 1840s. That decade was the first since the 1750s in which no regional agrarian revolt took place in Ireland.[1]

1. No comprehensive study of Irish agrarian movements and rural violence in the late

During that long span of time Irish peasants compiled a record of collective protest probably unequaled anywhere else in Europe.

Individual agrarian rebellions usually had specific causes, such as a depression in agricultural prices, a series of bad harvests, a sharp and sudden rise in the level of rents, or a new fiscal imposition by the state. But the magnitude of Irish agrarian disorder can only be explained by taking account of broader economic and social developments. The most important of these was the rapid demographic expansion which began in the middle of the eighteenth century and continued, apparently at a steady pace (though with certain marked regional variations), until the end of the Napoleonic wars. Only then did the rate of population growth finally slacken. According to the most recent estimates, the total population rose from less than 2.5 million in 1753 to 4.4 million in 1791 and reached 6.8 million by 1821. The slower rate of demographic expansion during the 1820s and 1830s still boosted the population of the country to almost 8.2 million by the time of the 1841 census. Other European countries also experienced striking increases in population over roughly the same period, but the secular rate of growth in Ireland was certainly exceptional by contemporary European standards.[2]

---

eighteenth and early nineteenth centuries has yet appeared, but the following works bearing on this subject may be noted: M. R. Beames, "Peasant movements: Ireland, 1785–95" in *Journal of Peasant Studies*, ii, no. 4 (July 1975), pp. 502–6; Beames, "Rural conflict in pre-famine Ireland: peasant assassinations in Tipperary, 1837–1847" in *Past & Present*, no. 81 (Nov. 1978), pp. 75–91; R. E. Burns, "Parsons, priests, and the people: the rise of Irish anticlericalism, 1785–1789" in *Church History*, xxxi, no. 2 (June 1962), pp. 151–63; G. E. Christianson, "Secret societies and agrarian violence in Ireland, 1790–1840" in *Agricultural History*, xlvi, no. 4 (Oct. 1972), pp. 369–84; Samuel Clark, *Social origins of the Irish land war* (Princeton, 1979), pp. 65–104; J. S. Donnelly, Jr., "The Whiteboy movement, 1761–5" in *I.H.S.*, xxi, no. 81 (Mar. 1978), pp. 20–54; Donnelly, "The Rightboy movement, 1785–8" in *Studia Hib.*, nos. 17–18 (1977–8), pp. 120–202; Marianne Elliott, "The origins and transformation of early Irish republicanism" in *International Review of Social History*, xxiii, pt. 3 (1978), pp. 405–28; Robert Kee, *The green flag: a history of Irish nationalism* (London, 1972), pp. 54–145; Lecky, *Ire.*, ii, 1–51; iii, 212–25, 385–92, 419–21; Joseph Lee, "The Ribbonmen" in T. D. Williams (ed.), *Secret societies in Ireland* (Dublin and New York, 1973), pp. 26–35; G. C. Lewis, *On local disturbances in Ireland, and on the Irish church question* (London, 1836); Oliver MacDonagh, *Ireland: the union and its aftermath* (rev. ed., London, 1977), pp. 144–50; Sailbheastar Ó Muireadhaigh, "Na Carabhait agus na Sean-Bheisteanna" in *Galvia*, viii (1961), pp. 4–20; Ó Muireadhaigh, "Buachaillí na carraige, 1820–25" in *Galvia*, ix (1962), pp. 4–13; George Rudé, *Protest and punishment: the story of the social and political protesters transported to Australia, 1788–1868* (Oxford, 1978), pp. 27–41, 71–81, 103–12; Maureen Wall, "The Whiteboys" in Williams, *Secret societies*, pp. 13–25. See also the works by Macintyre and O'Donoghue cited in fn. 11.

2. Stuart Daultry, David Dickson, and Cormac Ó Gráda, "Eighteenth-century Irish population: new perspectives from old sources" in *Journal of Economic History*, xli, no. 3

Controversy surrounds the causes of this tremendous spurt in the population of Ireland, but its impact on the shape of the agrarian class structure is not in doubt. The paramount change was the multiplication of laborers and cottiers. The statistical data bearing on this development are imperfect in various ways, but the broad picture is clear. Joseph Lee has calculated that by 1845 cottiers (holders of less than 5 acres) and laborers had come to outnumber farmers, large and small, by almost two to one. And if small farmers (holders of 5 to 15 acres) are ranked with laborers and cottiers, the people in these three categories were more than four times as numerous as the elite of larger farmers (holders of over 15 acres) on the eve of the great famine.[3] More recently, it has been estimated that landless laborers and landholding laborers constituted 56 percent of the adult-male agricultural work force in 1841. If small farmers (i.e., those holding 20 acres of land or less) are included, then the three categories of the rural poor accounted for over 75 percent of all adult males in the agricultural sector of the economy.[4] Though it is impossible to state precisely the relative proportions of laborers, cottiers, and farmers in 1750, there is universal agreement that right up to the great famine population growth was heavily concentrated at the lower end of the rural class structure.

The population explosion and the attendant transformation in the social structure would have been impossible without an enormous addition to the food supplies of the country.[5] But even with the increase in food supplies (oats as well as potatoes), the population grew so rapidly that there was almost constant tension over the mismatch between needs and resources. Some scholars have been impressed by the comparative rarity of food riots in Ireland during the late eighteenth and early nineteenth centuries, in contrast to their frequency in England and France.[6] This contrast is significant. In Ireland the equivalent of the food disturbance was the forcible turning up of pasture so as to make more land available for the cultivation of potatoes. This tactic was usually accompanied by systematic efforts to regulate by popular fiat the price of "conacre" (land rented seasonally by laborers to grow their potatoes). Collective action aimed at lowering the price of conacre and increasing its availability was often a localized affair, unconnected with widespread upheavals, but it was also a recurrent feature of re-

(Sept. 1981), pp. 621–8. See also W. E. Vaughan and A. J. Fitzpatrick (ed.), *Irish historical statistics: population, 1821–1971* (Dublin, 1978), p. 3.

3. Joseph Lee, *The modernisation of Irish society, 1848–1918* (Dublin, 1973), p. 2.
4. Clark, *Social origins*, p. 114.
5. Connell, *Population*, pp. 86–162.
6. See, e.g., Rudé, *Protest and punishment*, p. 57.

gional agrarian rebellions from the beginning of the cycle in the early 1760s.[7]

The magnitude of Irish agrarian rebellion is to be explained not only by an underlying subsistence crisis but also, somewhat paradoxically, by the commercialization of agriculture. In the first instance commercialization of the Irish agricultural economy depended upon the expansion of demand abroad, either in Britain or elsewhere in Europe, or in the overseas colonies of the European powers. During the seventeenth and early eighteenth centuries Britain and the rest of Europe were self-sufficient in grain, except of course in years of harvest failure. As long as this situation persisted, the only promising line of advance for Irish agriculture was a concentration on livestock and livestock products. But even this path long offered only limited opportunities. In most of continental Europe domestic supplies were usually sufficient to satisfy the demand for beef and butter, especially since continental grain growers, faced with low prices in years of normal or above-average harvests, increasingly shifted to pastoral products. Colonial demand was no more reliable. The exportation of Irish salted provisions to the colonies was essentially a function of the rate of settlement in the West Indies and North America. Even though Irish exports of salted beef did rise rapidly in the late seventeenth century, the colonial market was not yet exerting a major impact on Irish agriculture.

For most of the seventeenth century England was by far the best customer for the products of Irish grasslands. In 1665 almost three-fourths of all Irish exports went to England, and cattle, sheep, wool, tallow, and hides accounted for as much as 70 percent of the English share. But this was on the eve of a drastic alteration in the structure of Anglo-Irish trade. Under a statute passed at Westminster in 1666, the British market was closed to cattle, sheep, beef, butter, and pork from Ireland. From this blow Irish cattle raising did not recover for half a century. Irish beef producers eventually found substitute outlets in the English and French West Indies, but only at extremely low prices. Because returns were so disappointing, beef-cattle production stagnated. Irish dairy farmers, on the other hand, fared much better. Butter exports to the continent (chiefly to France) expanded very rapidly at least until the late 1680s, and sheep farming continued to be remunerative because of the generally strong demand for wool in England. Thus the late seventeenth century saw a large-scale shift within the Irish agricultural economy away from the

7. Donnelly, "Whiteboy movement," pp. 33–4; Lee, "Ribbonmen," pp. 28, 30; Clark, *Social origins*, pp. 71–3. See also M. R. Beames, "Cottiers and conacre in pre-famine Ireland" in *Journal of Peasant Studies*, ii, no. 3 (Apr. 1975), pp. 352–4.

raising of cattle to the rearing of sheep and the production of butter. But this switch — a change of emphasis on the pastoral side — probably did not entail a great expansion in the total area of grassland, and no evidence of popular resistance to the change has yet come to light.[8]

While the modest commercialization of agriculture that occurred in the seventeenth century was accommodated without major social disruption, the renewal of the process after 1730 led eventually to intense social strains. The years from 1700 to 1730 were a period of almost unrelieved agricultural stagnation because of sluggish external demand. But from the 1730s on, agricultural production, exports, and prices began a long-sustained advance that persisted (apart from short-term interruptions) through the French revolutionary and Napoleonic wars. At first, export-market opportunities favored continued concentration on pastoral products. From the 1720s on, colonial demand intensified, initially in the French West Indies and later in the English colonies as well. Salted beef was especially wanted, and by the 1760s and 1770s two-thirds to three-fourths of all the beef exported annually from Ireland went to the English colonies or to France for its overseas possessions. Along with graziers, dairy farmers also expanded output in response to the lusty development of the transatlantic trade. Besides the butter that they shipped directly to the new world, Irish merchants sent a high proportion of their supplies to Spain and Portugal for reexport to colonial destinations. And when colonial demand for Irish butter and beef slackened in the closing decades of the century, the British market hungrily absorbed the surplus.

Indeed, as the century progressed, the British market exerted increasing influence over the structure and output of the entire Irish economy, industrial as well as agricultural. By 1800 over 85 percent of all Irish exports went to Britain, as compared with 46 percent a hundred years earlier. Throughout the eighteenth century linen textiles dwarfed the agricultural exports. At the end of the 1750s as much as 80 percent of Irish exports to Britain (by value) consisted of linen cloth and yarn. But after 1760 the relative position of linen declined somewhat, initially as a result of the readmission of Irish cattle and provisions to the British market and subsequently because of the growing exports of grain, meal, and flour to Britain. At first, Ireland's own burgeoning population was the chief stimulus to the increased cultivation of grain, but after 1780

8. On Irish agriculture and trade in the second half of the seventeenth century, see Cullen, *Anglo-Ir. trade*, pp. 29–44; idem, *An economic history of Ireland since 1660* (London, 1972), pp. 7–25; idem, "Economic trends, 1660–91" in T. W. Moody, F. X. Martin, and F. J. Byrne (ed.), *A new history of Ireland*, vol. iii: *early modern Ireland, 1534–1691* (Oxford, 1976), pp. 387–407.

Britain's swelling food requirements became the main driving force behind the extension of the area devoted to corn crops in Ireland, an extension that persisted in all likelihood right up to the great famine. It was
in the late eighteenth century, then, that there began a historic shift from
pastoral to tillage commodities within the Irish agricultural economy.
British needs were the primary determinant of the shift, encouraging
within Ireland the growth of population, the subdivision of holdings,
and the transformation of the agrarian class structure.[9]

Population growth and the commercialization of Irish agriculture contributed to agrarian rebellion in a number of ways, but perhaps the most
striking illustration of the links between these phenomena is provided
by tithes, the most persistent of all agrarian grievances until the late 1830s.
From 1735 to 1823 livestock and livestock products were wholly or largely
exempt from liability to tithes. With minor exceptions the burden of supporting the clergy of the Protestant Church of Ireland — the established
church — fell on landholders engaged in tillage. In Ireland, where the
mass of tithe payers were either Catholics or Presbyterians, the likelihood
of religious objections to payment could never be discounted, but in general, opposition was economically motivated. As long as the Irish agricultural economy remained predominantly pastoral, with tillage designed
mostly to satisfy subsistence needs, no great popular outcry about tithes
was heard. But once the shift toward tillage gathered momentum, as
population increased at home and as consumer demand in Britain raised
Irish grain prices, the clamor against tithes grew shrill.

Given the peculiar incidence of tithes in Ireland, the conversion of
grassland (largely or completely tithe-free) to the production of grain
resulted automatically in the imposition of a clerical tax. Moreover, potatoes were titheable (at the highest rates per acre) throughout Munster
and in parts of Leinster, whereas elsewhere in Ireland there was little
or no clerical tax on this subsistence crop of the rural poor. Thus in the
south a clear line of association connected demographic expansion, potato cultivation by the poor, and the strenuous opposition of laborers
and cottiers to the heavy tithe on potatoes. At the same time commercial
tillage farmers everywhere deeply resented the tithes on wheat, barley,
and oats. It was precisely their resentment, in the early stages of the
switch to corn growing, that sparked the outbreak of one agrarian rebellion in County Kilkenny in 1769 and another in County Cork in 1785.[10]

During the early nineteenth century, which saw a vast expansion of

9. For the Irish economy in the eighteenth century, see Cullen, Anglo-Ir. trade, pp.
45–74; idem, Economic history, pp. 26–99.
10. Donnelly, "Rightboy movement," pp. 126, 149–63.

the area under corn, a somewhat different twist was given to the connection between commercialization and popular opposition to tithes. With its agricultural economy now almost exclusively dependent on the British market, particularly with respect to grain, Ireland was exposed to the full force of the British postwar price deflation and to violent fluctuations in prices. Sharp downward plunges in corn prices occurred between 1813 and 1816, from 1819 to 1822, and again in the early 1830s. Each of these plunges provoked a major agrarian rebellion, and in each of these rebellions the issue of tithes figured prominently.[11]

There were, of course, other grievances besides tithes, as demonstrated by the first three contributions to our collection. Paul Roberts's examination of the Caravat and Shanavest movements, principally between 1806 and 1811, is a highly instructive case study showing how the transformation of the agrarian class structure and the commercialization of agriculture together produced intense class conflict between large farmers and the rural poor. Such conflict was especially likely to occur in times of agricultural prosperity, that is, when land values were rising sharply. The reasons for this association are best seen against the background of tenurial arrangements. Though the land was owned by a relatively small elite numbering perhaps fewer than 10,000 aristocrats and gentry, their estates were generally sublet to such a degree that for the majority of rural dwellers, their landlord was not the proprietor of the soil but rather a large farmer. Such a farmer might sublet part of his holding to small tenants at a stipulated rent; he might give cabins and plots of ground to laborers, who would pay rent for these by working for him at a stated wage; or he might let some of his land in conacre to laborers for the growing of a crop of potatoes. Thus it was usually the large farmer, rather than the proprietor or his agent, who directly controlled access to both land and employment.

Into this complex tenurial system the commercialization of agriculture and demographic expansion injected a pronounced element of inequality. Large farmers were mostly leaseholders, with extended tenure at a fixed rent for the term of the lease. Before the 1790s terms of three lives or thirty-one years, whichever lasted longer, were quite common, though shorter terms (one life or twenty-one years) probably predominated thereafter. Small farmers and especially cottiers, on the other

11. Lee, "Ribbonmen," pp. 27–8. See also Patrick O'Donoghue, "The tithe war, 1830–1833" (M.A. thesis, University College, Dublin, 1961); idem, "Causes of the opposition to tithes, 1830–38" in *Studia Hib.*, no. 5 (1965), pp. 7–28; idem, "Opposition to tithe payments in 1830–31" in *Studia Hib.*, no. 6 (1966), pp. 69–98; idem, "Opposition to tithe payment in 1832–3" in *Studia Hib.*, no. 12 (1972), pp. 77–108; Angus Macintyre, *The Liberator: Daniel O'Connell and the Irish party, 1830–1847* (London, 1965), pp. 167–200.

hand, were usually tenants at will. As a result, the impact of the steep secular rise in land values that began shortly before 1750 and persisted until 1813 was unevenly distributed. The rents paid by small farmers and cottiers for their holdings, and even more the rents paid by landless laborers for conacre ground, generally moved in line with the strong upward trend in agricultural prices. But the rents paid by leaseholding large farmers could not be adjusted until their agreements expired. Many of them, having taken a lease for three lives or thirty-one years before 1790, escaped any rise in rent at all during the protracted French wars, despite dramatic increases in agricultural prices. It was partly the desire for a reversal of this inequality, or for its mitigation, that prompted wide sections of the rural poor to join the Caravat bands of east Munster in the first decade or so of the nineteenth century. Their movement had noticeable similarities to other agrarian upheavals, such as the Whiteboys of 1761–5, the Defenders of 1795, and the Threshers of 1806–7, which also erupted in periods of sharply rising land values.

Certain additional attributes of wartime prosperity explain other features of the class conflict between the Caravat poor and well-to-do Shanavest farmers. Hostility to migrant laborers, or spalpeens, and their employers did not originate with the Caravats; it was a long-standing grievance, and by no means confined to better times. Yet it was a particularly explosive issue at this juncture because of the increasing dimensions of migrant labor. With the rapid expansion of labor-intensive tillage farming in east Munster during the later stages of the French wars, the influx of spalpeens from west Munster for the grain and potato harvests assumed proportions that local laborers found especially threatening to their economic position. This Caravat grievance was associated with the wider problem of inflation. During the French wars real wages generally failed to keep pace with the rise in both food prices and conacre rents. Consequently, laborers and cottiers often became victims of the narrowing margin between what they had to pay for food or land and the means they possessed for doing so.[12]

Even though class conflict between the rural poor and large farmers and graziers intensified after 1790, the violent rivalry between Caravats and Shanavests should not be regarded as the paradigm of the agrarian upheavals that marked the early nineteenth century. The three greatest upheavals — the Caravat Whiteboys of 1813–16, the Rockites of 1821–4, and the tithe war of the early 1830s — all displayed a substantial degree of cohesion across social-class lines within the agrarian population. There

12. For Irish agricultural prices and production in wartime, see R. D. Crotty, *Irish agricultural production: its volume and structure* (Cork, 1966), pp. 19–23, 276–7, 283–4.

were two main reasons for this cohesion. First, tithes constituted a major grievance in all three movements, and on this issue all nonelite social groups were united in demanding redress. Second, severe slumps in agricultural prices sparked these three movements. As previously noted, outbreaks of discontent in prosperous times tended to be dominated by the rural poor and to be directed primarily against large farmers and graziers. On the other hand, movements that arose in periods of severe agricultural depression mobilized not only elements of the rural poor but also many large farmers or their sons over the issues of eviction and land rents in general. At such times the sense of oppression and the will to combat it were not restricted to the rural poor but moved up the social scale to embrace that formerly affluent minority of large farmers — at once tenants and landlords — who stood far above the mere peasantry.

An especially deep popular conviction of oppression lay behind the millenarian and sectarian features of the Rockite movement of 1821–4, examined by James Donnelly in the third essay in this section. Given the Protestant character of the Irish state and the virtual Protestant monopoly of landownership, together with a lively Catholic folk memory which cast Protestants in the roles of confiscators and persecutors, it is hardly surprising that lower-class Catholics should have conceived of the millennium as the destruction of Protestantism. Although the rural poor frequently regarded large Catholic farmers as their immediate oppressors in an economic sense, they also tended to see the Protestant church and state, or the local representatives of this regime, as the ultimate source of both their general degradation and some of their specific grievances. Even larger Catholic farmers were not immune to millennial beliefs and sectarian passions, though the apocalyptic mentality seems to have been most pervasive among the rural poor. Indeed, if there was ever a society that was ripe for the acceptance of millennial dreams of deliverance from oppression and imperial domination, it was Catholic Ireland in the thirty years before the great famine.

By no means all Irish agrarian movements of this period, however, were heavily imbued with millennial convictions. Millenarianism was not a significant force among the Threshers, the Caravat Whiteboys, or the Terry Alts. Yet it would be wrong to think that agrarian movements unencumbered by millenarian baggage were somehow more rational, sophisticated, or effective than rural revolts in which millennial dreams were abundantly present.[13] As the Rockite movement shows, Irish peas-

---

13. For a view that stresses the rationality of Irish agrarian protest, almost to the exclusion of millenarian consciousness, see Patrick O'Farrell, "Millenialism, messianism, and utopianism in Irish history" in *Anglo-Irish Studies*, ii (1976), pp. 45–68.

ant protest could combine a high degree of organization and considerable effectiveness in achieving economic objectives with a strong current of millenarianism. Indeed, it can be argued that by fostering solidarity among Catholic country people, the prophecies of Protestant doom in 1825 significantly blunted class conflict between large farmers and the rural poor. As in other cultures where political power and wealth rested in the hands of a small elite, and where religious or ethnic cleavages were salient, millennial visions played an integrative role among non-elite social groups whose material interests were often in conflict.[14]

Just as the Rockite movement was strengthened rather than weakened by millenarianism, so too was the campaign for Catholic emancipation, especially at its inception in 1824. A noted social anthropologist contends that all millenarian movements "ultimately result either in the emergence of secular political organization or turn into cults of passive resignation."[15] In the concluding section of his essay Donnelly shows how the widespread belief in Pastorini's prophecies contributed to the rise of Daniel O'Connell's campaign for the admission of Catholics to Parliament. It appears that the cult of Pastorini was well suited to becoming a significant organizational and ideological dynamic of a modern political mass movement.

Millennial hopes of deliverance, primarily through an invasion of Ireland by the French, had also served as a potent stimulus to collective action during the 1790s.[16] But as David Dickson shows in the first essay in this section, Irish radicals and revolutionaries could exploit a broad range of practical grievances, among which taxes came to possess unaccustomed importance. In one form or another the issue of taxation figured in the list of complaints during most of the agrarian upheavals of the late eighteenth and early nineteenth centuries. But with rare exceptions this question was relegated to a distinctly subordinate position by the greater urgency of other popular concerns, especially tithes, rents, and evictions. Even in the 1790s these grievances tended to overshadow that of taxation. Yet, as Dickson demonstrates, the insistent fiscal demands of both defense against invasion and Irish participation in the war abroad led to a substantial increase in the overall tax burden. At certain times and in particular regions of the country new taxes or changes in fiscal policy deeply alienated the affected population from the government. Indeed, though Dickson's claims for the significance of the tax question

14. On the integrative role of millenarian cults, see Peter Worsley, *The trumpet shall sound: a study of "cargo" cults in Melanesia* (2nd ed., New York, 1968), pp. 227–43.
15. Ibid., p. 236. See also ibid., pp. xlii–xlviii.
16. D. W. Miller, "Presbyterianism and 'modernization' in Ulster" in *Past & Present*, no. 80 (Aug. 1978), pp. 74–84; J. S. Donnelly, Jr., "Propagating the cause of the United Irishmen" in *Studies*, lxix, no. 273 (Spring 1980), pp. 15–20.

among the events that paved the way to 1798 are modest enough, it is clear that this issue loomed larger in the popular mind during the 1790s than ever before.

The raising of a costly militia in 1793, followed by its augmentation two years later, resulted in perhaps the largest single addition to the tax burden. Though the tax increase that the militia entailed was not the only reason for furious popular opposition to the force, economic objections exerted much influence in provoking the antimilitia uprisings of 1793.[17] These disturbances constituted an important turning point in the history of Irish rural protest and in the official response to it. Well over 200 persons lost their lives in fighting or demonstrating against the implementation of the militia act of 1793. In the succession of agrarian rebellions that punctuated the three decades from 1760 to 1790, the insurgents had been far more cautious of sacrificing themselves in battles or skirmishes with the forces of the crown. By the same token military parties and the magistrates who led them had been far less inclined to inflict lethal gunfire on crowds and agrarian bands. By 1793, however, the mutual circumspection which had previously been a marked feature of confrontations between the ruling class and various sorts of rebels seemed to be giving way to a new era in which both sides readily courted a maximum of violence.[18] The intense rural violence of the early nineteenth century was not, of course, derived merely from the events of the 1790s, but the legacy of that decade was weighty indeed.

17. For the implementation of the militia act of 1793, see Sir Henry McAnally, *The Irish militia, 1793–1816: a social and military study* (Dublin and London, 1949), pp. 28–51.

18. Thomas Bartlett, "An end to moral economy: the Irish militia disturbances of 1793" (forthcoming).

1 *David Dickson*

Taxation and Disaffection in Late Eighteenth-Century Ireland

Tax revolts have had a long history. Grievances about taxation and tribute have formed the basis of tactical class and regional alliances against imperial and central authorities probably as long as coins have been minted. Resentment against a crushing load of public charges has traditionally been assigned a high place among the causes of peasant rebellion. Certainly, the explanation of peasant furies in terms of something as comprehensible as overtaxation has had a perennial appeal to lawyers and others among the propertied classes, including many a historian. Even now, with our much fuller understanding of the complexity and diversity of peasant societies of the ancien régime, the nature and level of taxation is still recognized as having been one of the chief determinants of rural social stability. C. S. L. Davies has recently suggested that differing levels of popular taxation, particularly noticeable in the seventeenth century, go a long way toward accounting for the relative infrequency of peasant revolt in early modern England in contrast with the greater incidence of rebellion in France.[1]

In most preindustrial European societies the fiscal demands of the state and other public authorities that the peasant household had to meet were overshadowed by seigneurial dues, services, and rents as well as by ecclesiastical tithes. The mix varied enormously, both spatially and temporally,

An earlier draft of this essay was given as a paper to L. M. Cullen's economic and social history seminar in Trinity College, Dublin. I am grateful for the comments and criticisms made on that occasion.
1. C. S. L. Davies, "Peasant revolt in France and England: a comparison" in *Agricultural History Review*, xxi, pt. 2 (1973), pp. 125–6.

reflecting the political economy of different societies, but there was clearly no simple correlation between the composition of peasant obligations to state, seigneur, and clergy on the one hand, and the articulation of peasant grievances on the other. The state might receive the smallest share of the peasant surplus, but if that share was growing in relative terms, or if it had to be rendered in cash while those of others could be paid in kind, or if it was collected in a particularly arbitrary manner, then the demand of the state was likely to be seen as the least tolerable burden. Furthermore, even where the nobility was exempt from taxation, opposition to the tax collector was usually the grievance that would do most to unite local society at all levels.

There was nevertheless a relationship between the fiscal demands of the state and the course of popular agitation. In the eighteenth century, despite the rising costs of war, most governments in western Europe imposed a relatively less onerous burden than they had during the previous century. Economic expansion, tighter administrative control by governments over the tax gatherer, and the associated trend toward relatively more indirect taxation as well as a greater diversity of taxes all helped to soften the demands of the state in the countryside. These factors partly explain the much-reduced incidence of peasant disturbances in the first half of the eighteenth century. In France the grievances that lay behind riots and local agitation in the generation before the revolution were far more concerned with seigneurial demands and encroachments or with the behavior of those who controlled the grain trade than with the exactions of the agents of the tax farmers used by the monarchy.[2] Yet with the onset of the revolution the tax collector once again became a major object of popular fury and served, as revolutionary organizers like Babeuf recognized, to unite town and country, consumer and producer, in a common program against a common enemy.[3]

In Britain the financial crises of the late seventeenth century led to a system of state borrowing by means of a permanent funded debt, an arrangement which gave far greater flexibility when spending escalated in wartime. Related to this was a decline in the role of direct taxation. The hearth and poll taxes did not survive the Glorious Revolution, and

2. Henry Kamen, *The iron century: social change in Europe, 1550–1660* (London, 1971), pp. 353–7; Emmanuel Le Roy Ladurie, "Rural revolts and protest movements in France from 1675 to 1788" in R. C. Rosbottom (ed.), *Studies in eighteenth-century culture*, v (Madison, Wis., 1976), pp. 423–42; William Doyle, *The old European order, 1660–1800* (Oxford, 1978), pp. 108–9, 119–20; George Rudé, *Europe in the eighteenth century: aristocracy and the bourgeois challenge* (London, 1972), pp. 242–8.

3. R. B. Rose, "Tax revolt and popular organization in Picardy, 1789–91" in *Past & Present*, no. 43 (May 1969), pp. 92–108.

a land tax, imposed in 1697–8, was to remain the only major eighteenth-century direct exaction by the state. Even this charge fell only on land-lords, at rates that were not adjusted during the century. Excise taxes, which had expanded rapidly after their introduction in 1644, rose more modestly in relation to national income during the eighteenth century. Yet by the 1780s indirect taxation — excise plus customs duties — contributed a much larger share of total state revenue in Britain than in France. Indeed, the overall tax burden as a proportion of the value of physical output was possibly higher in Britain. Taxation was certainly collected more efficiently and more invisibly than in France, and, ironically, it may also have been more regressive in its effects.[4]

In Ireland the situation was, at first sight, quite similar to that in Britain. Government revenues, drawn largely from customs duties and excise, grew during the eighteenth century in line with the economy, but the overall level of taxation remained low. Public income in the years 1782–93 did not exceed £1.4 million annually, or less than one-quarter of British per capita levels.[5] Customs duties and excise on a small group of consumption goods — alcohol, sugar, tea, and tobacco — then accounted for three-fifths of the Irish government's total revenue.[6] More than in Britain, customs duties levied at the ports formed the central element in government receipts. Many contemporaries were struck by the low level of Irish taxation, and W. E. H. Lecky, in his history of eighteenth-century Ireland, contrasted the burden of land rents and tithes with the lightness of direct, parliamentary taxation, though he did assert that local taxation (i.e., county cess) had been "often scandalously excessive."[7] There was, however, one direct charge which affected most of the population — the hearth tax. This unpopular impost survived in Ireland a century and

4. Edward Hughes, *Studies in administration and finance, 1558–1825* (Manchester, 1934), pp. 168–75; Peter Mathias, *The first industrial nation: an economic history of Britain, 1700–1914* (London, 1969), pp. 39–42; Peter Mathias and Patrick O'Brien, "Taxation in Britain and France, 1715–1810: a comparison of the social and economic incidence of taxes collected for the central governments" in *Journal of European Economic History*, v, no. 3 (Winter 1976), pp. 601–50.

5. A. J. Fitzpatrick, "The economic effects of the French revolutionary and Napoleonic wars on Ireland" (Ph.D. thesis, University of Manchester, 1973), pp. 6, 23; O'Brien, *Econ. hist. Ire., 18th cent.*, p. 331; Mathias, *First industrial nation*, p. 41. See also *Minutes of evidence, up to the 28th March 1895, taken before her majesty's commissioners appointed to inquire into the financial relations between Great Britain and Ireland, with appendices*, p. 370 [C 7720-I], H.C. 1895, xxxvi, 5.

6. Fitzpatrick, "Economic effects," pp. 7–8.

7. Lecky, *Ire.*, iii, 398–9. See also Arthur Young, *A tour of Ireland . . . made in the years 1776, 1777, 1778 . . .* (2nd ed., 2 vols., Dublin, 1780), ii, 226; Wakefield, *Account of Ire.*, i, 598; Froude, *Ire.*, ii, 4.

a quarter longer than it did in England. Since 1706 collection of hearth money had been the responsibility of a distinct department under the revenue commissioners, and the tax remained at the fixed rate of 2s. per hearth until 1795. Officially, only poor widows and disabled beggars were exempt from paying it, but the margin of indulgence had grown considerably before the criterion of exemption was changed by two statutes of 1793 and 1795. Beginning in 1795 all householders in single-hearth dwellings — at least 85 percent of total habitations — were excused from the tax.[8]

Despite the modest fiscal demands of the central government, in the years leading up to the rebellion of 1798, "tax" was one of the three or four economic grievances regularly mentioned in subversive literature and by observers of the revolutionary activities of the United Irishmen and the Defenders. The regulation of rents, wages, and above all tithes had been major issues during Whiteboy and Rightboy agitations over the previous thirty years.[9] County cess had also featured intermittently among popular complaints, and a reduction in hearth money had been one of the less vocal demands of the Rightboys in 1786 and 1787.[10] It might seem that since hearth money was no longer levied on the vast majority of households after the statutory reform of 1795, the inclusion of tax as one of the grievances in the revolutionary ferment of 1795–8 was no more than an afterthought.

There are, however, some grounds for believing that the tax issue was in reality a matter of great popular concern during the mid and late 1790s. The parliamentary session that followed the 1793 modification of hearth money saw the introduction of a tax on leather, the first of several new excise taxes which were to be felt by most of the population, if not by the very poor. The coming of war in 1793 led to a considerable increase in the Irish budget, with much of the new expenditure going for domestic defense against both invasion and internal rebellion. In the first years of the war the government's financial needs were met by raising funds locally through the Bank of Ireland, but borrowing through London intermediaries became increasingly important, and by the end of the decade most of the Irish national debt was in English hands.[11]

8. The administrative evolution of hearth money is more fully discussed in a paper by Stuart Daultrey, David Dickson, and Cormac Ó Gráda, "Hearth tax, household size, and Irish population change, 1672–1821" in *R.I.A. Proc.*, lxxxii, sec. C, no. 6 (Dec. 1982), pp. 126–7, 134–9.

9. Lecky, *Ire.*, ii, 18–28; J. S. Donnelly, Jr., "The Whiteboy movement, 1761–5" in *I.H.S.*, xxi, no. 81 (Mar. 1978), pp. 34–7, 41.

10. J. S. Donnelly, Jr., "The Rightboy movement, 1785–8" in *Studia Hib.*, nos. 17–18 (1977–8), pp. 176–7.

11. Wakefield, *Account of Ire.*, ii, 278.

But taxation levels were soon affected, as they had to be adjusted to meet interest charges and to cover shortfalls in the yield of existing taxes. A financial crisis finally developed in the early months of 1797, in the wake of the unsuccessful French invasion and at a time of commercial crisis in Ireland and Britain.

Two provisions of the Irish budget for that year caused shock waves in the countryside that went beyond what even opposition critics of the chancellor of the exchequer had predicted. These were the imposition of substantially heavier salt duties and the withdrawal of all bounties (i.e., subsidies) on the inland and coastal carriage of grain to Dublin. Recently, Thomas Powell has argued that the impact of the elimination of these transport subsidies on County Wexford, the center of the malt trade supplying the Dublin market, was critical in disrupting the local economy and in promoting revolutionary organization in affected districts.[12] In what follows, the issue will be examined in a wider context, first by charting the evolution of official attitudes to direct and indirect taxation, then by surveying changes in the real burden of taxation before 1798, and finally by evaluating what in national terms were the social and political effects of those changes.

Principles and Policy

The structure of Irish government revenue that had evolved earlier in the eighteenth century was not permanently affected by the financial embarrassments of the administration in the early 1770s or during the American war, and there was no major fiscal innovation in the decade of peace after 1783. The size of the national debt, which had almost doubled in the later stages of the American war, was the focus of parliamentary attention for a time, and to halt its further growth a new malt duty was introduced along with other measures in 1785.[13] The buoyancy of the economy in the subsequent eight years insured a rising tax yield (see table 1.1), and most reforms in revenue administration may have contributed to the same result. This improved budgetary situation provided the financial base that allowed greatly increased parliamentary expenditure for public works as well as for grants and subsidies to manufacturers and promoters. Revenue from customs and import excise remained

12. Thomas Powell, "An economic factor in the Wexford rebellion of 1798" in *Studia Hib.*, no. 16 (1976), pp. 140–57.

13. O'Brien, *Econ. hist. Ire., 18th cent.*, pp. 329–40. The introduction of the malt duty was a measure specifically designed to counter the illicit distiller (E. B. Maguire, *Irish whiskey: a history of distilling, the spirit trade, and excise controls in Ireland* [Dublin, 1973], pp. 138–46).

TABLE 1.1
Trends in Customs and Excise, 1785–1805

Year	Customs and import excise (100 = £913,311)	Inland excise (100 = £356,450)
1785/6	100	100
1786/7	94	93
1787/8	105	101
1788/9	95	124
1789/90	97	128
1790/1	99	149
1791/2	95	141
1792/3	87	134
1793/4	78	143
1794/5	102	165
1795/6	107	204
1796/7	90	202
1797/8	92	228
1798/9	137	229
1799/1800	191	228

SOURCE: *Minutes of evidence, up to the 28th March 1895, taken before her majesty's commissioners appointed to inquire into the financial relations between Great Britain and Ireland, with appendices*, pp. 370, 372 [C 7720-I], H.C. 1895, xxxvi, 5.

ahead of that from inland excise, but, as table 1.2 shows, the difference was diminishing; together, they eclipsed the contribution of assessed taxes (i.e., hearth money, the carriage tax, quit rents, and so on).

No opposition critic in this period of heightened parliamentary activity challenged the basic framework of cheap government financed mainly by taxes on consumables, especially alcohol. The "commercial propositions" of 1785, which would have led to a reduction and standardization of duties in Anglo-Irish trade, might have caused, if successful, rapid changes in Irish tax policy. The propositions apart, there were only three major issues relating to finance and taxation that repeatedly attracted parliamentary attention in the 1780s and 1790s: first, the question of changing the structure of alcohol taxation; second, the movement to reform hearth money; and third, the issue of taxing absentee landowners. Of the three, the debates concerning duties on spirits, beer, and their raw material were by far the most complex, for there were several discrete issues involved. One was the desirability of a tax structure that would encourage the Irish brewing and distilling industries against imported ales, wines, brandy, and rum. Another was the growing problem of countering illicit distillation and the smuggling of foreign spirits into the country. And a third was the argument over the consumption of domestic spirits and whether or not they should be discouraged through

TABLE 1.2
Inland Excise as a Percentage of Customs
and Import Excise, 1785–1816

Years	Percentage
1785/6 to 1789/90	43.4
1790/1 to 1794/5	61.9
1795/6 to 1799/1800	69.1
1811/12 to 1815/16	111.4

SOURCE: See table 1.1.

heavy taxation, and the drinking of beer favored, in the hope that this step would curb the perceived growth in popular drunkenness.

Between 1779, when major modifications occurred in the distillery laws, and 1795, when beer was relieved of any excise charge, parliamentary debate took place against a background of shifting relative prices of the different kinds of alcohol and changing technologies of production. Economic circumstance, political pressure, and administrative convenience together dictated the alterations in tax levels, but the contribution of alcohol (including malt) to government revenue remained fairly constant throughout the 1780s and 1790s, when it formed upwards of one-third of total income.[14] The authorities sought greater efficiency in tax collection and in the licensing of producers and vendors. They also levied an increasing proportion of alcohol duties on malt on the assumption that tax evasion was more difficult at that stage in the production process. But the victory of Irish ale, porter, and grain spirits over imported wine, rum, and porter was a consequence of deeper economic influences; excise legislation adjusted to this situation and was not its progenitor. The continuing importance of alcohol taxes to the state explains the enormous official effort and resources expended to collect them. Legislative refinements appeared session after session; increasingly severe penal sanctions were laid on the illicit activities of maltsters, distillers, and smugglers; and attempts at enforcement were intensified through the expansion of both revenue and military manpower.[15]

Change in the levying of hearth money was frequently mooted. At the beginning of the 1790s, revelations about corruption among officials in the hearth-money department prompted talk of reform. Henry Grattan included the impost as one of the several areas of the revenue requiring amendment in 1783, and in the following years his brother-in-law, G. P. Bushe, one of the revenue commissioners, greatly improved the

14. Fitzpatrick, "Economic effects," pp. 7–8.
15. Ibid., p. 10; Maguire, *Whiskey*, pp. 88, 126–64; A. P. W. Malcomson, *John Foster: the politics of the Anglo-Irish ascendancy* (Oxford, 1978), pp. 106–7.

department's efficiency by dismissing fraudulent officers and in effect
increasing salaries by means of bonus payments linked to higher yields.
At the time of the Rightboy movement in the mid-1780s several attempts
were made in Parliament to limit the proportion of households obliged
to pay the tax. The recorded debate on this question in 1788 reveals some
of the underlying assumptions concerning the equity and functions of
direct taxation.[16] The chief proposers of a radical change in the 2s. tax,
which would have exempted all those with houses and lands worth 30s.
or less per annum, were Thomas Conolly and John O'Neill. They argued
that for a substantial portion of those having to pay the tax, the yearly
cash demand was an unreasonable burden, particularly at a time when
the treasury was in a healthy state. "Our poor countrymen," Conolly
maintained, "are sufficiently taxed by their situation in life—they procure us bread and fight his [majesty's] battles."[17] Grattan developed the
same point: "The man who has but five pounds in the world . . . ought
not to pay hearth money. . . . What benefit does the state confer on such
a man that it should have a right to tax him? In what property do your
laws protect such a man . . . who has nothing except the labour which
he gives the state . . . ?"[18] Those without an interest in property were
beyond the reach of the state. If they were little affected by indirect taxation, that in Grattan's view only confirmed the impropriety of imposing a direct tax on them.

Since the proposals for reform would have had a relatively small impact on the exchequer in these years of rising yields, the official defense
of the status quo was not made on fiscal grounds. Instead, defenders argued that hearth money, being equivalent to four days' wages of a laborer,
was a light burden, and that the proposed exemption, based on the valuation of one's holding, would prove very awkward to implement. They
also expressed the fear that hearth-money reform would prove the thin
edge of the wedge, opening the way in popular expectations to a regulation of tithes and possibly even of rents.[19] Nevertheless, there was an official inquiry to determine what loss in revenue could be expected if all
those with holdings worth 30s. or less a year were exempted; the results
suggested that very few existing taxpayers had holdings of such little
value.[20] The most ingenious justification for retaining a universal hearth
tax was that given by the chancellor of the exchequer some years later

16. *Parl. reg. Ire.*, viii (1788), pp. 397–406; O'Brien, *Econ. hist. Ire., 18th cent.*, pp.
332–3.
17. *Parl. reg. Ire.*, viii (1788), p. 402.
18. Ibid., p. 406.
19. Ibid., p. 399.
20. For Bushe's statement in the House of Commons in 1793, see *Dublin Evening Post*
(hereafter cited as *D.E.P.*), 7 Feb. 1793.

and recorded by Lord Carysfort in a private memorandum in the early 1790s. While admitting that the tax caused distress to some, the chancellor reportedly maintained that "it was necessary to make them [i.e., the people] *feel* that there was a government over them." The implication was that direct taxation made visible the contract between the state and its subjects. Carysfort was evidently unconvinced by such an argument, believing that the popularity which a government could obtain by hearth-money reform would, if properly managed, yield greater benefits, while the revenue loss would be minimal.[21]

Major reform of the hearth tax was finally carried in 1793. One-hearth householders with less than £10 in personal property, or with houses and lands worth £5 or less, were henceforth deemed exempt from the tax.[22] The measure was apparently a consequence of parliamentary pressure in the previous session; the modification of the window tax in Britain giving total relief to poorer householders had led to calls in the Irish Parliament for similar "liberality" in the light of Ireland's healthy finances. The chancellor had refused, but a parliamentary committee was established under the de facto chairmanship of Bushe.[23] In his report to the Commons in February 1793 Bushe rejected opposition demands that the hearth tax should be lifted from all one-hearth households and be increased on all others. He pointed out that the many urban householders in the latter category would be hard pressed by extra taxation, while many farmers in one-hearth houses were well able to face the hearth-money collector. Bushe warned that "to relieve those persons from the tax would be a fiction, for the excises you would [have to] impose would affect them more."[24] Bushe's successful proposal to divide the one-hearth householders into two groups, those above and those below £5 in annual valuation, was intended to discriminate between the two rural classes that he identified, the laboring poor, who had every reason to be exempted, and the farmers, who were sufficiently affluent to be consumers of excised goods.[25] The impost on multiple-hearth houses was raised slightly in 1793, and total revenue from the hearth tax fell during the following two years by only 11 percent.[26] This unexpectedly modest decline stemmed partly, it seems, from the fact that the new procedures

21. *Calendar of the manuscripts of J. B. Fortescue,* iii (H.M.C., London, 1899), pp. 549–50.

22. 33 Geo. 3, c. 14.

23. *D.E.P.,* 17 Mar. 1792; "Report of the commissioners appointed to inquire into the state of the duties of hearth money" in *Commons' jn. Ire.,* xv (1792–4), appendix, pp. cccxxxi–xxxviii.

24. *D.E.P.,* 7 Feb. 1793.

25. *D.E.P.,* 7, 16 Feb. 1793.

26. For hearth-tax trends before 1801, see *Evidence, financial relations comm.,* p. 370.

for obtaining exemption were too cumbersome. Many householders apparently continued to pay the tax even though they were legally entitled to claim exemption. Therefore, in the 1795 budget, freedom from hearth tax was extended to *all* one-hearth householders, as the opposition had earlier demanded. The chancellor of the exchequer described it as a "more manly measure" of reform than that of 1793, and the decision received exaggerated acclaim in Parliament.[27] As Bushe was dead by that stage, there was apparently no one willing to champion selective one-hearth taxation or to resist the chancellor's logic for raising further the tax on multiple-hearth houses.[28] Certainly, as a universal direct tax, it had been too costly to the exchequer, even when efficiently collected. The hearth-tax department, however, remained a major branch of the revenue establishment, since responsibility for the collection of the other assessed taxes, which were becoming increasingly important, rested with the officers of that section. By the turn of the century their primary concern had become the enumeration of carriages, male servants, and, from 1799, windows.[29]

The third controversy over taxation that periodically agitated Parliament and literate public opinion was whether a major source of the government's revenue should come from a tax imposed on the incomes of absentee landowners. Apart from hearth money, the nonresident proprietor contributed nothing to the Irish exchequer and clearly benefited from the predominantly indirect character of Irish taxation. The demand for an absentee tax usually emanated from the more "patriotic" M.P.s, but the resounding defeat of such a proposal even when, as in 1773, the viceroy Lord Harcourt himself promoted the idea at a time of financial difficulty, only demonstrated the strength of vested interests, English and Irish, against a tax of this kind.[30] It was put forward on several occasions after 1773 in the Irish Commons and became a major radical demand during the 1790s. Owing to the financial crisis of 1797, the proposal resurfaced and secured considerable parliamentary backing. Though government supporters again resisted it successfully, they now had to use practical arguments about the difficulties of implementing such a tax quickly rather than the old legal and constitutional defense of the 1770s.[31]

27. *Parl. reg. Ire.*, xv (1795), pp. 108, 110.

28. 35 Geo. 3, c. 1.

29. *Third report of the commissioners appointed to inquire into fees, gratuities, perquisites, and emoluments in public offices in Ireland*, p. 4, H.C. 1806–7 (1), vi, 1. For the relative importance of the assessed taxes, see *Papers relating to the income, expenditure, commerce, and trade of Ireland*, p. 30, H.C. 1834 (194), xii, 207.

30. Lecky, *Ire.*, ii, 90, 113, 119, 122, 130–2.

31. *Parl. reg. Ire.*, xvi (1796–7), pp. 383–403; Lecky, *Ire.*, iv, 7–8; Bolton, *Ir. act of union*, pp. 47–9.

Numerous other expedients, even that of an income tax, were canvassed during the somewhat frenzied budget debates of 1797. The actual
decisions of that parliamentary session mark a turning point in Irish fiscal history. Many of the old taxation issues dropped from sight permanently, and the urgent problems of increasing current revenue at a time
of commercial crisis dominated discussion. The government was now
entering a period lasting nearly two decades during which the sheer weight
of wartime financial obligations on the Irish exchequer completely dictated the evolution of its fiscal policy. The actual measures brought forward in 1797 were not, it seems, the result of careful preparation; at
least one of the chancellor of the exchequer's proposals in the Commons —
the sanctioning of a new loan under exceptionally attractive terms —
surprised even a fellow "cabinet" member, John Foster, and had to be
amended.[32] Three budgets previously, the chancellor had declared that
"taxes must operate on the bulk of the people, [although] he would relieve
them as much as possible by taxing the luxuries of life."[33] Until the budget of 1797 he had largely kept his word. Apart from the leather tax,
the new burdens probably did not have much effect on the rural majority. Progovernment pamphleteers in 1796 and 1797 were convinced that
the low level of taxation experienced by the Irish countryman in contrast
to his French counterpart was still a propaganda point worth publi-
cizing.[34] But the 1797 budget weakened their case substantially.

No defense other than the current crisis induced by the war was used
to excuse the new duties on salt. Opposition speakers in Parliament were
quick to draw comparisons with the notorious gabelle in France and to
note its fate at the hands of revolutionaries there.[35] It was argued that
direct taxation would be preferable to such an impost, which, as one
speaker suggested, "would remind the wretched peasant every time he
sat down to his miserable morsel that he was taxed for the support of
property, in which he had but a small share, and for the support of a
constitution which afforded him but few blessings."[36] As for the withdrawal of the bounties on the inland and coastal corn trade, the administration presented it as a move likely to affect landed gentlemen more
than the poor. Opponents of the measure placed greater emphasis on the

32. *Parl. reg. Ire.*, xvi (1796–7), pp. 360, 378; Lecky, *Ire.*, iv, 5–7; Kiernan, *Finan. admin.*, pp. 302–3.

33. *Faulkner's Dublin Journal* (hereafter cited as *F.D.J.*), 13 Feb. 1794. For remarks by the chancellor of the exchequer, see *F.D.J.*, 18 Feb. 1794.

34. *A letter to his excellency Earl Camden on the present causes of discontent, by a yeoman* (Dublin, 1796), p. 18; *To the tradesmen, farmers, shopkeepers, and country people in general of the kingdom of Ireland* (Dublin, 1797), pp. 8–9.

35. *F.D.J.*, 23, 25 Feb. 1797.

36. *Parl. reg. Ire.*, xvi (1796–7), p. 341.

political folly of such a change in policy rather than on its economic impact or its social inequity. And in spite of apocalyptic warnings from M.P.s
with interests in the leading tillage counties, the decision to cancel the
subsidies went through Parliament in the spring of 1797, with a saving
to the exchequer calculated at £80,000, a sum close to the expected yield
of the new salt duties.[37]

The Tax Burden

There is little doubt that the major part of the increased burden of
indirect taxes during the 1790s, as in the later stages of the French wars,
was borne by middle-income groups and urban wage earners — that is,
by those who were regular consumers of alcohol, sugar, and tea. For
the rural masses, only the enlarged duties or taxes on salt, leather, and
tobacco are likely to have affected consumption.[38] Given the absence
of comprehensive retail-price series for items such as leather, legal whiskey, beer, and tobacco, it is difficult to assess the importance of changes
in taxation and other elements of fiscal policy. Trends in the per capita
consumption of alcohol certainly cannot be calculated until more is known
about the scale of illicit distilling and the pace of population growth
in this period. What is clear, however, is that tithe rates and current
rent levels rose sharply between the mid-1780s and 1797. As a result,
the share of the rural smallholder's surplus taken by taxation was most
probably declining until 1797. Indeed, for many small farmers in tillage
areas, the increase in grain prices in the early and mid-1790s gave a decided boost to their retained incomes, and those tenants with old leases
held at relatively low rents could afford to widen their consumption of
traded commodities. The position of the cottier-laborer in the early war
years was less satisfactory, since rents for conacre (i.e., potato ground)
were moving ahead of contracted wages, though the sharp rise in pig
and pork prices partly offset this squeeze. Urban industrial employment
was badly dislocated in the recession of 1792–3 as well as during the
crisis of 1796–7, and excise increases such as those on malt in 1794 and
1795 probably hit artisan households with particular force. Yet apart
from them, the fiscal changes before 1797 were perhaps little more than
a minor irritant, despite predictions of hardship by parliamentary critics, one of whom challenged the leather tax in 1795 by asking "whether

37. *Parl. reg. Ire.*, xv (1795), p. 103; xvi (1796–7), pp. 422–6, 442–3, 459; *F.D.J.*, 23
Feb. 1797. For John Beresford's unfavorable views on the taxes of 1797 and the problems
of finding any alternative means of raising revenue, see Bolton, *Ir. act of union*, p. 47.
    38. See Fitzpatrick, "Economic effects," pp. 23–4.

it is fair to pretend an indulgence to the poor by easing them of two-shillings hearth money while we lay four shillings upon brogues."[39]

The budgetary measures of 1797 undoubtedly pinched more deeply, both because they were more sweeping in themselves and because they were introduced at a time of wider economic difficulties. The salt duty alone, Edward Tighe estimated, "would take three shillings per year from the peasant and was therefore . . . a more oppressive tax than that on hearths." Import duties on salt by the bushel were raised from 4d. to 2s. per bushel, and on rock salt from 1s. 1d. to £3 per ton.[40] The effects of this adjustment on consumers can be judged by the fact that legislation to control the price of salt in retail markets had to be enacted later in the parliamentary session (37 Geo. 3, c. 18). At the same time the duties on unrefined sugar were raised by a sixth and those on French wines by a fifth.

Far more serious in their economic impact were the withdrawal of subsidies on the carriage of grain and the introduction of new restrictions on the licensing of maltings. The latter measure prohibited the granting of a license to all malthouses with cisterns having a capacity of less than 25 barrels. It apparently had traumatic effects on the malt trade in areas such as County Wexford, the south midlands, and the northwest, where malting was an important, though highly dispersed, activity.[41] Meanwhile, the termination of the inland corn bounties aggravated the downswing in grain prices, especially those of barley, and seemed to threaten the viability of many smaller flour mills.[42] The collapse in grain prices during the course of 1797 led to greatly increased tension over tithes in tillage districts, for tithe notes (i.e., promises to pay twelve months hence) had been widely passed in the autumn of 1796 in the false expectation of continued high prices. When collection was attempted in the autumn of 1797 and the following winter, violent resistance to tithe farmers and proctors spread through such areas as west Waterford and east Cork.[43]

39. *Parl. reg. Ire.*, xv (1795), p. 106. The marked rise in inland-excise revenue in 1794/5 and 1795/6 (see table 1.1) resulted mainly from the doubling of malt duties.

40. *Parl. reg. Ire.*, xvi (1796–7), p. 358; 37 Geo. 3, c. 3.

41. See "An account of the number of malthouses at present licensed in Ireland . . . " in *Commons' jn. Ire.*, xvi (1795–6), appendix, pp. ccccxix–xlii. For the revenue commissioners' disquiet about the effects of the malt duties, see Richard Annesley to Edward Cooke, 7 July 1797 (P.R.O.I., Customs and excise administration papers, 1A/43/5, no. 78).

42. The negative impact on the inland grain and flour trades, however, was short-lived. See William Tighe, *Statistical observations relative to the county of Kilkenny. . .* (Dublin, 1802), p. 289; L. M. Cullen, "Eighteenth-century flour milling in Ireland" in *Irish Economic and Social History*, iv (1977), pp. 24–5.

43. Thomas Knowlton to John Heaton, 13 Sept., 4 Oct. 1797 (P.R.O.N.I., Devonshire MSS, T.3158); *New Cork Evening Post* (hereafter cited as *N.C.E.P.*), 5, 26 Oct., 13 Nov.

Yet another unpopular development in the spring of 1797 was the ending of the convertibility of Bank of Ireland notes into gold, a move that followed directly after similar action by the Bank of England. This step appears to have led to a rapid fall in the amount of specie in circulation and to a reduction in the volume of commercial transactions.[44] General acceptance of the new monetary situation was a gradual process; in the interim, economic activity at all levels was dampened.

The fiscal policies of the central government also affected trends in those taxes imposed by local authorities during the 1790s. County cess, the most important of these, reflected the size of presentments as fixed at the half-yearly county assizes. It had always been a small charge levied on every "plowland"; surveys and applotments dating from the seventeenth century were still being used in the late eighteenth century as the basis of assessment in nearly every county. In those counties for which information survives, budgets were rising after 1785, especially in the late 1780s and from 1795 to 1796, as table 1.3 illustrates.

In the absence of comprehensive records of county presentments, it is not certain what caused this growth in spending. The most important factors were probably: (1) increased road and bridge building in the expansionary years of the late 1780s; (2) the establishment in certain counties of local police forces under the legislation of 1787; and (3) county obligations arising from the various militia acts of 1793 and 1795. The sharpest recorded rise during the late 1780s occurred in County Cork, where the budget increased by about 60 percent between 1786 and 1790; Cork was one of the counties that implemented the new police act, which was a consequence of the Rightboy agitation.[45] The new police establishment was generally unpopular. According to one west Cork land agent in 1794, it "adds 10s. a plowland to the burdens of the farmers and they [i.e., the subconstables] don't do duty . . . ; they extort liquor and fees, etc., tho' they are paid by the county, and they sho[ul]d get but £12 a y[ea]r inst[ea]d of £24. . . ."[46]

The further growth of county budgets in the mid-1790s was mainly prompted by novel charges stemming from the formation of the militia.

1797, 26 Mar. 1798; [de Latocnaye], *Rambles through Ireland by a French emigrant* (2 vols., Cork, 1798), i, 94–5n.

44. For predictions as to the effects of restricting the acceptability of notes other than those of the Bank of Ireland, see John Beresford to Edward Cooke, 7 Mar. 1797 (P.R.O.I., Customs and excise administration papers, 1A/43/5, no. 73).

45. 27 Geo. 3, c. 40. See S. H. Palmer, "The Irish police experiment: the beginnings of modern police in the British isles, 1788–1795" in *Social Science Quarterly*, lvi, no. 3 (Dec. 1975), pp. 418–21; Donnelly, "Rightboy movement," p. 192.

46. Diary of Robert Day, 1794 (R.I.A., MS 12 W 14, p. 30). See also Thomas Garde to John Heaton, 4 Dec. 1792 (P.R.O.N.I., Devonshire MSS, T.3158).

TABLE 1.3
Trend of County Cess in Nineteen Counties and
Counties of Cities, 1786–1800 (100 = £102,199)

Year	Trend
1786	100
1787	108
1788	117
1789	123
1790	130
1791	132
1792	137
1793	133
1794	142
1795	146
1796	162
1797	148
1798	161
1799	175
1800	202

SOURCE: *Appendix to minutes of evidence taken before her majesty's commissioners of inquiry into the state of the law and practice in respect to the occupation of land in Ireland*, no. 70, pp. 178–9, pt. iv [672], H.C. 1845, xxii, 1.

Under the militia act of 1793 (33 Geo. 3, c. 22) and the militia-augmentation act of 1795 (35 Geo. 3, c. 8), counties that failed to enroll their statutory quota of militia privates were required to make a specific payment for every man short; £10 per man was the county liability under the 1795 act.[47] Even more costly was the obligation imposed on counties by the revised militia-families act of 1795 (35 Geo. 3, c. 2), which was designed to provide maintenance for the dependents of militiamen who moved with these recruits from their native county.[48] In 1795, 1796, and 1797 a number of counties presented large sums for militia families at the prescribed rates, amounting to about £10 a year for a household in which the dependents consisted only of wife and children.[49] Subsequent legislation was more restrictive, as the cost of the 1795 act proved heavy for some counties, especially in Connacht and Munster, though there was suspicion that maintenance claims may have been inflated by militia colonels or by interested parties serving on the grand juries.[50] In Kerry, where

47. Sir Henry McAnally, *The Irish militia, 1793–1816: a social and military study* (Dublin and London, 1949), pp. 74–5.
48. Ibid., pp. 49, 266–70.
49. Ibid., pp. 268–70.
50. Ibid., pp. 268–71. See "Returns made by treasurers of counties . . ." in *Commons' jn. Ire.*, xviii (1799), appendix, pp. ccvii–xxv.

claims for dependents' allowances were most numerous, they absorbed about 26 percent of the overall county budget in 1796 and 1797.[51]

For most families, even at the end of the 1790s, the total burden of taxes — direct, indirect, and local — can rarely have amounted to more than a few percent of the value of gross household production. Taxes of all kinds together took less than tithe, much less than rent. Yet there are several reasons why such bald assertions may understate the real weight of the tax burden. First, every tax rise necessitated an increased outlay of cash for those affected, and this in an environment where, for laboring households at least, cash income and cash transactions were extremely limited. Part of the hostility to hearth money and tithe occurred precisely because they were demands that were normally settled only in cash. Second, there was often an invisible supplementary impost attached to locally collected taxes. Illicit fees and gratuities were sought by revenue officials and petty constables, whose salaries had not been adjusted, or had been insufficiently adjusted, to allow for late eighteenth-century inflation. Lastly, with specific regard to cess, the archaic mode of applotting the county rate meant that the burden was very unevenly distributed between areas of old and new settlement, both within plowlands and between one plowland and another.

The Social and Political Impact

A number of decisions taken by the Irish administration in the years before 1798 can thus be seen to have made a substantial, if subordinate, contribution to the increasing economic strains and tensions within the rural economy. Yet the initial spread of disaffection from the government had occurred at a time of rising farm incomes, not of rural depression. The transformation of the United Irishmen from a reformist into a revolutionary association by 1795, and the evolution of rural Defenderism away from its restricted sectarian beginnings, coincided with a series of generally adequate harvests and favorable prices. Until 1795 the regulation of tithes, wages, and conacre rents had always been the specific objects of Whiteboy-type movements in the south, and the economic goals of rural Defenderism in Leinster and Connacht were much the same; grievances

51. "Returns made by treasurers," appendix, p. ccxiii; *Appendix to minutes of evidence taken before her majesty's commissioners of inquiry into the state of the law and practice in respect to the occupation of land in Ireland*, no. 70, pp. 178–9, pt. iv [672], H.C. 1845, xxii, 1. See also Robert Day to earl of Glandore, 2 Aug. 1796: "The militia-family tax has oppressed and disaffected this county [i.e., Kerry] more than all the other burdens it sustains, and if anything can shake its steady loyalty and good temper, it is that wanton, partial, and unnecessary measure . . . ." (N.L.I., Talbot-Crosbie MSS, P.C. 188).

were overwhelmingly local and specific, even if some of the campaigns were regional in scope. Clearly, a new element was introduced when Jacobin symbolism began to appear in agrarian agitation by about 1795. The radical literature of urban United Irish societies was reaching the schoolmaster activists in some rural areas, and through them, was beginning to influence the language used in publicized threats and demands.[52] Yet the problem for the United Irish leaders, once they had committed themselves to securing the military assistance of France and to preparing for a general uprising in the country, was to translate their political goal of an independent democratic republic into a formula attractive to a heterogeneous rural society that was largely illiterate and "prepolitical." It was necessary but hardly sufficient for urban republicans to argue that a democratic administration would abolish tithes and restrain rents; neither grievance was immediately associated in the popular mind with the current government. In the case of tithes, the enemy in the eyes of most country people seems to have been the tithe farmer or proctor, not the established church or its clergy as such. Even the great groundswell of anti-Protestant feeling after 1795 was essentially a reaction to Orange outrages in the north and to the rumors of further Orange retribution to come, not a widening of the tithe issue.

The self-defined task of the United Irishmen after 1795 was to develop and communicate a set of arguments that would convince the "mass of associations" constituting Defenderism[53] and, in Munster, the former Rightboy organizers and the potential activists to accept United leadership and discipline for their mutual benefit. The political goal of transforming the constitution would only appear directly relevant to the less literate ranks of rural society if it could be demonstrated that prevailing agrarian grievances flowed from the actions of the current administration and Parliament. The more the policies of government were felt at the local level and the more distasteful these were, the greater the opportunity for United Irish propagandists to focus popular anger on the existing administration and to demonstrate the superiority of nationwide revolutionary political action over localized, economically motivated agitation against particular targets.

Of course, the particular targets favored over the years had sometimes included servants of the state. Certain hearth-money collectors regularly

---

52. Diary of Robert Day, 1794, pp. 22–3; *N.C.E.P.*, 7 Apr. 1794; J. G. O. Kerrane, "The background to the 1798 rebellion in County Meath" (M.A. thesis, University College, Dublin, 1971), pp. 33–5, 54–7, 66.

53. W. J. MacNeven, *Pieces of Irish history illustrative of the condition of the Catholics of Ireland, of the origin and progress of the political system of the United Irishmen, and of their transactions with the Anglo-Irish government* (New York, 1807), pp. 118–19.

traveled with escorts for protection, and not without reason, as Thomas
Wray, inspector general of hearth money, discovered while conducting
a survey in County Cork in 1791, when the house in which he was staying was set on fire. In 1793 four local people were killed in an affray
in County Sligo when distresses for nonpayment of hearth money were
being levied.[54] Harsh, arbitrary, or corrupt behavior on the part of local
officers was probably the most frequent cause of such disturbances.

In the more restricted sphere of maritime smuggling, violent conflict
had become increasingly common during the previous generation. Yet,
even if this violence significantly shaped the political attitudes of those
directly concerned, the smuggling trade involved relatively few communities.[55] On the other hand, the growth in illicit distilling during the 1780s
and 1790s had far more inflammatory effects, especially in the outer cres-
cent of Ulster, that is, in Donegal and the border counties of south Ulster
and the north midlands, where the output of small-scale distilling enterprises seems to have risen dramatically. Bloody encounters between distillers and revenue officers became more frequent beginning in the late
1780s, a consequence of rising duties on spirits, changes in the distillery
laws, and the greater availability of firearms. In one notorious incident
in 1795 near Mohill, Co. Leitrim, about a dozen revenue men, who had
apparently been extracting protection money, were killed when they went
to seize a still and pot ale; the distillers' supporters also suffered heavy
casualties in a later reprisal for the murders.[56] Rising communal resentment against such local officers was almost inevitable; the growing numbers employed in the inland-revenue departments and their increasingly
varied duties made them much more visible as the relative importance
of inland excise in total tax receipts continued to expand. The more frequent use of regular troops and militia to assist them in the field was
both a symptom and a cause of the new climate of violence that had
emerged by the mid-1790s.

What especially intensified antigovernment sentiment was the raising
of the militia in the summer of 1793. The recruitment of some 15,000

    54. *Hibernian Chronicle* (hereafter cited as *Hib. Chron.*), 20 Oct. 1791; *Cork Gazette*,
16 Nov. 1791; *F.D.J.*, 30 Mar. 1793; *Third rep., fees comm.*, p. 21. See also *F.D.J.*, 25 Jan.
1794.
    55. L. M. Cullen, "The smuggling trade in Ireland in the eighteenth century" in *R.I.A.
Proc.*, lxvii, sec. C, no. 5 (Mar. 1969), pp. 160, 165–6, 172, 175.
    56. Edward Hay to Earl Fitzwilliam, 21 June 1795 (Fitzwilliam MSS, N.L.I. microfilm
p. 5641; *F.D.J.*, 28 Apr., 5 May 1795. See also the chapter on illicit distilling in K. H.
Connell, *Irish peasant society: four historical essays* (Oxford, 1968), especially pp. 30–2,
36–42; David Dickson, "The barony of Inishowen in the century before the famine" (B.A.
thesis, University of Dublin, 1969), pp. 23–4.

men from within the country into militia regiments having a preponderance of Catholics in the noncommissioned ranks was a new departure in military policy. Almost from the first rumors of compulsory enlistment by ballot, a striking series of disturbances erupted, affecting at least sixteen counties. Public posting of the lists of able-bodied men whose names were to be balloted triggered off numerous clashes, and the occasion of the ballot itself often provoked popular reaction. Heavy casualties among the insurgents were reported from some encounters — nineteen killed near Ballinafad, Co. Roscommon, fourteen at Dingle, Co. Kerry, twenty-six at Bruff, Co. Limerick — and such carnage at the hands of the regular troops seems to have been remembered long after amendments to the initial militia act had reduced friction.[57]

The formation of the new militia was, as all could see, a consequence of the outbreak of war with France in February 1793. In Ireland the opening of hostilities coincided with soaring potato and bread prices, caused by a bad harvest in 1792, and with a serious business depression. The resulting distress was severe in rural manufacturing households as well as among urban workers, and some food riots occurred.[58] Conservatives were inclined to blame the popular unrest on subversive radicals. One anti-Jacobin pamphleteer in Cork city asserted that "the friends of the people" were linking food shortages to the international crisis, inflaming "the deluded minds of the peasantry by aggravating their wants and exaggerating any little occasional scarcity . . . ; they take occasion also to irritate them against the government by insinuating that the war is the source of their calamities."[59] But contrary to what government supporters feared, the wave of urban and agrarian disturbances in 1793 and early 1794 was not significantly influenced or inflamed by radical political propaganda. Efforts to link economic grievances specifically with the administration made some headway thereafter, however, as rumors of war taxes circulated, and as food prices remained high. In addition, local hostility toward revenue officers, whether stirred up by their forays against illicit distillers or by their enforcement of the excise laws regulating maltsters and alcohol retailers, was being harnessed for political ends,

57. Diary of Robert Day, 1794, pp. 34–5; Edward Cooke to [?], 27 June 1793 (P.R.O., HO/100/44, f. 184); *Finn's Leinster Journal*, 29 May–1 June, 29 June–3 July, 20–24 July 1793; Kerrane, "Meath," pp. 12, 44–6; Lecky, *Ire.*, iii, 216–18; McAnally, *Militia*, pp. 32–7. In some counties confrontation occurred in 1795 over the balloting for additional militia. For instance, in April of that year there were disturbances at Five Mile House, Co. Westmeath, where a large crowd gathered to prevent a ballot; sixteen persons were reportedly killed in three separate fights with the militia and with a magistrates' posse (*F.D.J.*, 14 Apr. 1795).

58. See, e.g., *Hib. Chron.*, 22 Nov. 1792.

59. *A hint to the Jacobins of Great Britain and Ireland* (Cork, 1793), p. 20.

at least in Ulster.[60] The French émigré de Latocnaye noted a conversation with a young United Irish supporter he had met in a cabin near Coleraine, Co. Derry, during his travels in the summer of 1796: "I was really surprised to hear all this talk about equality, fraternity, and oppression. After a little I asked him what was the oppression of which he complained. He named taxes on wine and beer, and when I asked him if he ever drank the one or the other, he said . . . it was very hard on those who had to pay, with more nonsense of this kind."[61] By this stage, with the insurrection act in force and a number of areas placed under martial law, some communities needed little propagandizing to appreciate how oppressive the servants of the crown—in the form of the regular army and the militia—could be. Even though most of the country was not directly affected by "disarming" campaigns until late in 1797, a hardening of rural hostilities against the administration and its agents could already be detected. The convergence of the new taxes, the cancellation of the grain-carriage bounties, the collapse in corn prices, the contraction of specie in circulation, and, in some counties, the escalation of cess rates—all played into the hands of the United Irishmen. The precise degree to which those events marked a sea change in the political attitudes of illiterate farmers, cottiers, and laborers must remain a matter of speculation, but that there were major repercussions throughout the country seems clear from the reports of local observers. Of course, they were generally hostile witnesses and possibly inclined to misinterpret the state of popular sentiment, but the similarity of comments by correspondents in widely dispersed parts of the country is suggestive.

From Aughnacloy on the Tyrone-Monaghan border, for example, an area where rural United Irish organization already existed,[62] the beleaguered local postmaster reported in March 1797 that the general object, as he understood it, of oaths and combinations was parliamentary reform, and that the two specific grievances which he heard most often mentioned were the imposition of the salt duties and the failure of the proposed absentee tax. Earlier in the same month a magistrate in neighboring Cavan listed the grievances currently leading to the formation

60. Rev. Brendan McEvoy, "The United Irishmen in Co. Tyrone" in *Seanchas Ardmhacha*, iii (1959), pp. 292–3. For links between distilling and the United Irishmen in 1797, see Fitzmaurice Caldwell to revenue commissioners, 29 May 1797 (S.P.O., Rebellion papers, 620/30/266); Kerrane, "Meath," p. 100; Lecky, *Ire.*, iv, 10.

61. De Latocnaye, *A Frenchman's walk through Ireland, 1796–7*, trans. John Stevenson (Belfast, 1917), pp. 204–5.

62. Edward Moore to John Lees, 30 Mar. 1797 (S.P.O., Rebellion papers, 620/29/142); McEvoy, "Tyrone" (1959), p. 301; McEvoy, "The United Irishmen in Co. Tyrone" in *Seanchas Ardmhacha*, iv (1960–1), pp. 4–5.

of United Irish societies in both his county and Fermanagh as the "price of lands, unequal taxation, illegal fees, nonresidence of clergy and landlords, and the whole of the revenue laws as they now stand."[63] From west Donegal in April the Church of Ireland rector of Killaghtee warned Dublin Castle that "since my last [letter] the principles of the United Irishmen, from the discontents for the salt duty, have flashed like lightening [*sic*] in my whole parish. . . ."[64]

From County Cork came reports of a marked shift in rural attitudes away from the passivity of late 1796, when the French had appeared in Bantry Bay, to the ferment of the following summer. The north Cork agent of the earl of Egmont informed his employer in June 1797 that "many who seemed well affected last winter are now very much the contrary . . . ; the taking off the bounty on land carriage to Dublin and the late duty on salt have been a great means of perverting the minds of the lower order of the Irish."[65] William Warren, who resided at Lisgoold in east Cork, suggested in a pamphlet later in the year that the turning point had been the decreased circulation of specie, which had "alienated more than one-half of the people's affections from its government"; he castigated the administration for its failure to take more energetic measures to counter the collapse of credit and business activity, for the unemployment and distress of artisans had led them into forming "associations and conspiracies to annihilate the constitution."[66]

Thus the growing burden of Ireland's contribution, in both human and financial terms, to the war with France helped to deepen the domestic crisis in the first half of 1797. The administration's decisions caused such a spontaneous shock in the countryside because they had severe economic implications for a great many people, and because they came at a time of increased popular receptivity to rumor and fears. Yet it would be fanciful to label the rising a year later as a tax revolt, even though excise

63. Irwin Johnston to Thomas Pelham, 5 Mar. 1797 (S.P.O., Rebellion papers, 620/29/23). Johnston's inventory of grievances can be compared to one found in the possession of a Tyrone United Irishman in 1795. According to the document, United Irish goals included the abolition of tithes, hearth money, tolls at fairs, church cess, and government pensions; certain excise laws were to be repealed, and "no plundering revenue officers" were to be allowed. The aim of reformed county grand juries was to be "good roads and low cess" (McEvoy, "Tyrone" [1959], pp. 292–3).

64. Rev. Patrick Morgan to [?], 15 Apr. 1797 (S.P.O., Rebellion papers, 620/29/264). The price of salt would of course have been a particularly sensitive issue in this fishing district.

65. John Purcell to earl of Egmont, 3 June 1797, holographic copy (Cork Archives Council, Ryan-Purcell MSS). See also Lecky, *Ire.*, iv, 134.

66. William Warren, *A political and moral pamphlet* . . . (Cork, 1797), pp. 13, 113–15. Warren also argued against the new taxes (ibid., p. 117).

duties on whiskey and tobacco were raised sharply in March 1798. Admittedly, revenue officials were special objects of vengeance in some districts during the rebellion, but the circumstances surrounding such incidents are not always clear.[67] On the whole, however, exploitation of the unpopular fiscal measures of 1797 by the revolutionaries seems to have had a tactical rather than a strategic importance, except perhaps in parts of Ulster. The narrow base of United Irish organization in the larger southern towns (apart from Dublin), and the more pressing concerns of military preparation meant that relatively little political capital was made of the antagonism felt toward the government and the war by those who sold grain, consumed salt, or were otherwise involved in the marketplace. By the beginning of 1798 the issue of tithes had probably eclipsed the more novel grievances of the previous year. Despite the nearly universal impact of increased salt duties and of further excises on whiskey and tobacco, it was opposition to tithes and fear of Orangemen, yeomen, and regular troops that united rural communities, and they did so more effectively than any fiscal issue could have done.[68]

The evolution of Irish taxation in the 1790s had repercussions beyond the rising and the act of union. In spite of enormous growth in military expenditure during the Napoleonic period, very little extra revenue was gathered by means of direct taxation. The window tax, introduced in 1799, applied only to households with seven or more windows, thus leaving the great majority of the population unaffected. Attempts to install a land or an income tax were repelled. With regard to items of popular consumption, only the increased excise and duty on tobacco (from 8d. Irish per pound in 1798 to 3s. 2d. in 1815) and the heightened excise on whiskey (from 2s. 6d. Irish per gallon in 1799 to 6s. 1½d. in 1815) were likely to have been widely noticed. Government tax revenue rose by approximately 6 percent a year between 1801 and 1815, and along with

67. The excise on tobacco was raised by two-thirds and that on Irish spirits by one-third in 1798 (see table 1.1 for the overall effects). The informer Leonard McNally claimed that the new tax of that year on male servants decidedly radicalized this group in Dublin (Thomas Pakenham, *The year of liberty: the great Irish rebellion of 1798* [London, 1969], p. 37). For comments on the fate of revenue officers during the rebellion, see *Some observations on the original and recent and present state of the excise establishment, and on the laws and regulations of the excise of Ireland* (Dublin, 1815), pp. 35–6.

68. Marianne Elliott, "The origins and transformation of early Irish republicanism" in *International Review of Social History*, xxiii, pt. 3 (1978), pp. 409–10, 417–20, 426–7. The links connecting the wars, increased taxation, unemployment, and rural revolt can be studied in the very different context of southern Italy, where peasant risings in the 1790s were anti-French (Patrick Chorley, *Oil, silk, and enlightenment: economic problems in eighteenth-century Naples* [Naples, 1965], pp. 81–2; Jacques Godechot, *The counter-revolution: doctrine and action, 1789–1804*, trans. Salvator Athanasio [London, 1972], pp. 328–37).

expanded income from the "old reliables," a number of adjustments in the duties on stamps, sugar, and tea helped to boost tax receipts from £2.5 million in 1801/2 to £6.1 million in 1815/16. Local cess also increased sharply, county budgets approximately doubling over the same period.

Yet in the eyes of the administration Irish finances were increasingly perilous in these years. The growth of the Irish national debt outpaced the rise in tax receipts, and toward the end of the wars the cost of servicing the debt alone consumed nearly 85 percent of current revenue.[69] The underlying difficulty was the apparent incapacity or unwillingness of Irish consumers to bear a growing burden of indirect taxation, for the yields from heavily taxed commodities began to decline far sooner than in Britain. Thus Irish chancellors of the exchequer had to resort to borrowing much more extensively than their British counterparts in order to meet military and debt-service obligations.[70] The problem arose partly from the administrative inadequacies of the revenue establishment as the demands on it multiplied. But the various forms of popular resistance to heightened taxation — smuggling and evasion, intimidation or the threat of it, constant reference to tax as a grievance in periods of general agitation — helped to constrain the growth of current revenue, chiefly by restricting the flexibility of fiscal policy.[71] Admittedly, there were few positive popular victories over the appetite of the state. The drastic modification of hearth money constituted the only clear-cut reform that relieved poorer households. And in the final analysis it was probably the somewhat different patterns of income distribution and consumption in Ireland that gave rise to the peculiar difficulties of the Irish exchequer throughout the Napoleonic period. The growing tax burden had to fall disproportionately on middle-income groups and artisans.[72] For some of their descendants overtaxation was to be one of the great catchcries when the union came under attack.

69. *Evidence, financial relations comm.*, p. 372. See also Fitzpatrick, "Economic effects," pp. 25-8.

70. Malcomson, *Foster*, pp. 98-9n.

71. Robert Shipkey, "Problems in alcohol production and controls in early nineteenth-century Ireland" in *Hist. Jn.*, xvi, no. 2 (1973), pp. 295-300.

72. Fitzpatrick, "Economic effects," p. 34. Another major constraint in the period between the union and consolidation of the national debts in 1817 was simply the obligation on Irish chancellors of the exchequer to follow as far as possible British treasury precedent and practice. John Foster, Irish chancellor of the exchequer between 1804 and 1806, could see very little room for maneuver when discussing a successor's budget problems in 1815, "believing as I do that by the fair interpretation of the act of union you can tax nothing more highly here than in Great Britain, and believing also that everything here is already taxed nearly as high" (John L. Foster to William Vesey Fitzgerald, 1 May 1815, N.L.I., Vesey Fitzgerald MSS, Letter book of William Vesey Fitzgerald, 1815, MS 7840, pp. 167-8). I am grateful to A. P. W. Malcomson for drawing my attention to this correspondence.

BIBLIOGRAPHY

Contemporary sources

Manuscript material
Cork Archives Council
    Ryan-Purcell MSS.
National Library of Ireland, Dublin
    Fitzwilliam MSS: Edward Hay to Earl Fitzwilliam, 21 June 1795 (Microfilm
        p. 5641; original in Leeds City Library).
    Talbot-Crosbie MSS (P.C. 188).
    Vesey Fitzgerald MSS: Letter book of William Vesey Fitzgerald, 1815 (MS
        7840).
Public Record Office, London
    Home Office papers: Irish civil correspondence, June–Aug. 1793 (HO/100/
        44).
Public Record Office of Ireland, Dublin
    Customs and excise administration papers (1A/43/5).
Public Record Office of Northern Ireland, Belfast
    Chatsworth MSS (photocopies of originals in Chatsworth House, Derbyshire).
Royal Irish Academy, Dublin
    Diary of Robert Day, 1794 (MS 12 W 14).
State Paper Office, Dublin
    Rebellion papers.

Published manuscript collections
Calendar of the manuscripts of J. B. Fortescue, iii (Historical Manuscripts Com-
    mission, London, 1899).

Contemporary publications
I. Parliamentary proceedings, reports, speeches, statutes, etc.
    The statutes at large passed in the parliaments held in Ireland, 1310–1800,
        20 vols. (Dublin, 1789–1800).
    Journals of the House of Commons of the kingdom of Ireland, 1613–1800, 19
        vols. (Dublin, 1796–1800).
    *The parliamentary register, or history of the proceedings and debates of the
        House of Commons of Ireland*, 1781–97, 17 vols. (Dublin, 1782–1801).
    *Third report of the commissioners appointed to inquire into fees, gratuities,
        perquisites, and emoluments in public offices in Ireland*, H.C. 1806–7 (1)
        vi, 1.
    Papers relating to the income, expenditure, commerce, and trade of Ireland,
        H.C. 1834 (194), xli, 207.
    *Appendix to minutes of evidence taken before her majesty's commissioners
        of inquiry into the state of the law and practice in respect to the occupa-
        tion of land in Ireland*, pt. iv [672], H.C. 1845, xxii, 1.

Minutes of evidence, up to the 28th March 1895, taken before her majesty's commissioners appointed to inquire into the financial relations between Great Britain and Ireland, with appendices [C 7720-I], H.C. 1895, xxxvi, 5.

II. Newspapers
Cork Gazette, 1791–7.
Dublin Evening Post, 1791–8.
Faulkner's Dublin Journal, 1793–7.
Finn's Leinster Journal (Kilkenny), 1793.
Hibernian Chronicle (Cork), 1791–8.
New Cork Evening Post, 1792–8.

III. Other contemporary publications
A hint to the Jacobins of Great Britain and Ireland (Cork, 1793).
[de Latocnaye]. *Rambles through Ireland by a French emigrant*, 2 vols. (Cork, 1798).
[de Latocnaye]. *A Frenchman's walk through Ireland, 1796–7*, trans. John Stevenson (Belfast, 1917).
A letter to his excellency Earl Camden on the present causes of discontent, by a yeoman (Dublin, 1796).
MacNeven, W. J. *Pieces of Irish history illustrative of the condition of the Catholics of Ireland, of the origin and progress of the political system of the United Irishmen, and of their transactions with the Anglo-Irish government* (New York, 1807).
Some observations on the original and recent and present state of the excise establishment, and on the laws and regulations of the excise of Ireland (Dublin, 1815).
Tighe, William. *Statistical observations relative to the county of Kilkenny . . .* (Dublin, 1802).
To the tradesmen, farmers, shopkeepers, and country people in general of the kingdom of Ireland (Dublin, 1797).
Wakefield, Edward. *An account of Ireland, statistical and political*, 2 vols. (London, 1812).
Warren, William. *A political and moral pamphlet addressed to the lord lieutenant and people of Ireland* (Cork, 1797).
Young, Arthur. *A tour in Ireland with general observations on the present state of the kingdom made in the years 1776, 1777, 1778, and brought down to the end of 1779*, 2 vols. (2nd ed., Dublin, 1780).

Later works

Writings in Irish studies
Bolton, G. C. *The passing of the Irish act of union* (Oxford, 1966).
Connell, K. H. *Irish peasant society: four historical essays* (Oxford, 1968).
Cullen, L. M. "The smuggling trade in Ireland in the eighteenth century" in *Proceedings of the Royal Irish Academy*, lxvii, sec. C, no. 5 (Mar. 1969), pp. 149–75.

Cullen, L. M. "Eighteenth-century flour milling in Ireland" in *Irish Economic and Social History*, iv (1977), pp. 5–25.

Daultrey, Stuart; Dickson, David; and Ó Gráda, Cormac. "Hearth tax, household size, and Irish population change, 1672–1821" in *Proceedings of the Royal Irish Academy*, lxxxii, sec. C, no. 6 (Dec. 1982), pp. 125–81.

Dickson, David. "The barony of Inishowen in the century before the famine" (B.A. thesis, University of Dublin, 1969).

Donnelly, J. S., Jr. "The Rightboy movement, 1785–8" in *Studia Hibernica*, nos. 17–18 (1977–8), pp. 120–202.

Donnelly, J. S., Jr. "The Whiteboy movement, 1761–5" in *Irish Historical Studies*, xxi, no. 81 (Mar. 1978), pp. 20–54.

Elliott, Marianne. "The origins and transformation of early Irish republicanism" in *International Review of Social History*, xxiii, pt. 3 (1978), pp. 405–28.

Fitzpatrick, A. J. "The economic effects of the French revolutionary and Napoleonic wars on Ireland" (Ph.D. thesis, University of Manchester, 1973).

Froude, J. A. *The English in Ireland in the eighteenth century*, 3 vols. (London, 1882).

Kerrane, J. G. O. "The background to the 1798 rebellion in County Meath" (M.A. thesis, University College, Dublin, 1971).

Kiernan, T. J. *History of the financial administration of Ireland to 1817* (London, 1930).

Lecky, W. E. H. *A history of Ireland in the eighteenth century*, 5 vols. (London, 1892).

McAnally, Sir Henry. *The Irish militia, 1793–1816: a social and military study* (Dublin and London, 1949).

McEvoy, Brendan. "The United Irishmen in Co. Tyrone" in *Seanchas Ardmhacha*, iii (1959), pp. 282–314; iv (1960), pp. 1–32.

Maguire, E. B. *Irish whiskey: a history of distilling, the spirit trade, and excise controls in Ireland* (Dublin, 1973).

Malcomson, A. P. W. *John Foster: the politics of the Anglo-Irish ascendancy* (Oxford, 1978).

O'Brien, George. *Economic history of Ireland in the eighteenth century* (Dublin, 1918).

Pakenham, Thomas. *The year of liberty: the great Irish rebellion of 1798* (London, 1969).

Palmer, S. H. "The Irish police experiment: the beginnings of modern police in the British isles, 1788–1795" in *Social Science Quarterly*, lvi, no. 3 (Dec. 1975), pp. 410–24.

Powell, Thomas. "An economic factor in the Wexford rebellion of 1798" in *Studia Hibernica*, no. 16 (1976), pp. 140–57.

Shipkey, Robert. "Problems in alcohol production and controls in early nineteenth-century Ireland" in *Historical Journal*, xvi, no. 2 (1973), pp. 291–302.

Other writings in social science

Chorley, Patrick. *Oil, silk, and enlightenment: economic problems in eighteenth-century Naples* (Naples, 1965).

Davies, C. S. L. "Peasant revolt in France and England: a comparison" in *Agricultural History Review*, xxi, pt. 2 (1973), pp. 122–34.

Doyle, William. *The old European order, 1660–1800* (Oxford, 1978).

Godechot, Jacques. *The counter-revolution: doctrine and action, 1789–1804*, trans. Salvator Athanasio (London, 1972).

Hughes, Edward, *Studies in administration and finance, 1558–1825* (Manchester, 1934).

Kamen, Henry. *The iron century: social change in Europe, 1550–1660* (London, 1971).

Le Roy Ladurie, Emmanuel. "Rural revolts and protest movements in France from 1675 to 1788" in R. C. Rosbottom (ed.), *Studies in eighteenth-century culture*, v (Madison, Wis., 1976), pp. 423–42.

Mathias, Peter. *The first industrial nation: an economic history of Britain, 1700–1914* (London, 1969).

Mathias, Peter, and O'Brien, Patrick. "Taxation in Britain and France, 1715–1810: a comparison of the social and economic incidence of taxes collected for the central governments" in *Journal of European Economic History*, v, no. 3 (Winter 1976), pp. 601–50.

Rose, R. B. "Tax revolt and popular organization in Picardy, 1789–91" in *Past & Present*, no. 43 (May 1969), pp. 92–108.

Rudé, George. *Europe in the eighteenth century: aristocracy and the bourgeois challenge* (London, 1972).

2 *Paul E. W. Roberts*

Caravats and Shanavests: Whiteboyism and Faction Fighting in East Munster, 1802–11

I

Small farmers and rural laborers in prefamine Ireland thought of themselves as one distinct class — as "the poor." Most laborers were in fact small farmers of a kind, receiving their wages in land, renting conacre plots, or holding bona fide farms of up to about 10 acres. For their part, small farmers were sometimes reduced to supplementary laboring, and their surplus sons often became laborers. Shared poverty and shared grievances cemented the bond.[1]

Their most direct economic relationships tended to be with the rural middle class, by which I mean the medium and larger farmers, and such people as publicans, millers, and shopkeepers. These were the main employers, traders in food, and monopolizers of land. For most laborers and many small farmers they were also their immediate landlords as a result of various forms of subletting.

Beginning in the mideighteenth century, relations between these two classes became increasingly strained under the pressure of rapid economic and demographic growth. The most spectacular manifestation of this conflict was Whiteboyism — outbreaks of agrarian terrorism that repeatedly

---

1. This class consciousness is particularly apparent in Whiteboy notices, which habitually deal with both small farmers' and laborers' grievances although they speak only of "the poor." Hundreds of these notices are preserved in the State of the country papers, series 1 and 2 (S.P.O.), a collection of documents relating to Irish unrest from 1796 to 1831. These are mostly letters from country gentlemen and military officers to the central government and constitute the basic source for this essay.

Area of the Caravat and Shanavest Movements

swept parts of Ireland between 1760 and 1845, primarily aimed at re-
dressing the economic grievances of the poor and thus mainly directed
against the middle class.[2]

This period also saw a marked increase in faction fighting, a term which
refers to pitched battles between feuding bands at fairs and other public
gatherings. The older feuds were largely territorial, but the new fighting
often reflected more modern tensions, such as power conflicts between
kinship-based mafias led by ambitious members of the middle class.[3]

II

In 1806 a new faction feud erupted in east Munster between two large
combinations styling themselves the Caravats (*Carabhaití*) and Shanavests (*Sean-Bheisteanna*), or the Cravats and Old Waistcoats. It was quite
unlike previous feuds, which in their geographical range were usually
confined to a few parishes or perhaps a barony. Between 1806 and 1811
the Caravat-Shanavest conflict seriously disturbed large areas of Tipperary, Waterford, Kilkenny, Limerick, and Cork, began to spread into
Queen's County, Carlow, and Wexford, and briefly touched Clare, Kerry,
and Kildare—eleven counties in all. Its violence was unprecedented. Traditional faction fights were ritualized, relatively restrained, and generally fought with sticks. The clashes between Caravats and Shanavests
were ruthless free-for-alls involving firearms and frequent deaths. But
most striking of all, the feud itself was overshadowed by a related Whiteboy outbreak. The feud was in fact a novel extension of the struggle between the Whiteboys and the rural middle class, and its unique scale and
violence reflected its roots in the supralocal and bitter loyalties of class.

The Caravats were primarily a Whiteboy organization. They were a
kind of primitive syndicalist movement whose aim was apparently to absorb as many of the poor as possible into a network of autonomous local
gangs, each exercising thoroughgoing control over its local economy, and
the whole adding up to a generalized alternative system. This was not
drastically different from previous Whiteboy movements, with the important exception that the Caravats do not seem to have tried to enroll

2. Good introductions to this neglected subject are J. S. Donnelly, Jr., "The Rightboy
movement, 1785–8" in *Studia Hib.*, nos. 17–18 (1977–8), pp. 120–202; idem, "The Whiteboy movement, 1761–5" in *I.H.S.*, xxi, no. 81 (Mar. 1978), pp. 20–54; Maureen Wall, "The
Whiteboys," and Joseph Lee, "The Ribbonmen" in T. D. Williams (ed.), *Secret societies
in Ireland* (Dublin and New York, 1973), pp. 13–35.

3. Faction fighting has received little scholarly attention. The observations here are
based on my own research. For a nonanalytical account, see Patrick O'Donnell, *The Irish
faction fighters of the 19th century* (Dublin, 1975).

members of the middle and upper classes. They set class limits to the regulation of grievances shared with such groups, and they displayed an intense hostility to the middle class as a whole, not simply to specific offenders against their laws. In Caravatism one detects a definite heightening of class consciousness among the poor, and Shanavestism shows that this phenomenon was not confined to the poor alone.[4]

The Shanavests were an unprecedented middle-class anti-Whiteboy movement formed specifically to combat the Caravats. They seem to have combined vigilantism and informing with the propagation of an ideological alternative to Whiteboyism, namely, nationalism. This political orientation was not accidental. Irish nationalism in this period was primarily a middle-class ideology. It was perhaps the only force capable of creating an effective collective movement out of this somewhat fragmented social group, and it obviously lent itself to condemnation of Whiteboys as enemies of national unity.

To the authorities the feud was a total mystery. Indeed, it has never been satisfactorily explained. In part, this reflects the participants' remarkable code of silence, steadfastly maintained before all forms of authority, from parish priests to judges.[5] But it reflects too the peculiar mixture of ignorance, indifference, and paranoia with which the Irish ruling class related to the world below them. One looks in vain through their writings for even an intelligent opinion as to the cause of the feud; most observers made no comment, some confessed themselves perplexed, and a few alleged that it was all a pretense concealing a general popish conspiracy.[6] Indeed, many observers assumed that the Caravats' Whiteboy activity was purely incidental, and some even believed that both factions were Whiteboys. These assumptions have been echoed ever since.[7] Yet the most

4. Earlier movements were also dominated by the poor and their grievances but were not as socially exclusive in their composition. See Donnelly, "Rightboys," pp. 126–7, 137–8; idem, "Whiteboys," pp. 30–44.

5. See, e.g., Randall Kernan, *A report of the trials of the Caravats and Shanavests at the special commission for the several counties of Tipperary, Waterford, and Kilkenny* . . . (Dublin, 1811), pp. 29–33 (hereafter cited as *Special commission*). Those questioned by the judges as to the cause of the feud included the nephew of the Shanavests' founder. After much prevarication he declared that it was all "a foolish dispute about May balls."

6. See, e.g., Lord Whitworth, "A statement of the nature and extent of the disturbances which have recently prevailed in Ireland" in *Annual Register, 1816* (London, 1817), p. 403 (hereafter cited as Whitworth, "Disturbances"); *Minutes of evidence taken before the select committee appointed to inquire into disturbances in Ireland* . . . , p. 113, H.L. 1825 (37), clxxxviii, 165 (hereafter cited as *Select committee on disturbances, 1825*); S.P.O., S.O.C.P.1, 1277/58–62, 64, 79.

7. See, e.g., Whitworth, "Disturbances," p. 403; General J. Lee, 1 July 1810; Brigade-Major H. Croker, 28 Sept. 1810 (S.P.O., S.O.C.P.2, 1810/36); W. G. Broehl, *The Molly*

cursory glance at the sources shows that the Caravats were far more active as Whiteboys than as feudists, and a thorough scrutiny of the surviving records reveals not one Shanavest agrarian outrage.[8]

Only two worthwhile statements on the nature of the feud have in
fact been found, both collected from oral tradition in the midtwentieth
century. One simply tells us that it "arose out of a land dispute in the
Cashel region,"[9] but the other is rather more detailed: "The parties originated in County Tipperary with a big farmer who had a falling out with
some of his smaller neighbours and farm labourers. . . . Whatever happened, several of the working class were hanged, and their friends became bitter enemies of the [richer] element in their midst, and these in
turn got up against their poorer neighbours and so spread the evil."[10]
Six of the "working class" were in fact hanged, but tradition concentrates
on the death of one in particular.

III

In the winter of 1805–6 a man named Nicholas Hanley was hanged
at Clonmel before a violent crowd of enthusiastic admirers and bitter
enemies. The latter were led by Patrick Connors, nicknamed "Paudeen
Gar" (Sharp Paddy) and noted for his battered old waistcoat, or "shanavest." Hanley was nicknamed after his elegant cravat, or "caravat." According to tradition, Connors called out a sneering pun on Hanley's nickname and its cant meaning (the hangman's rope). Hanley retorted with
a cutting comment on Connors's old waistcoat, and this exchange gave
rise to the formation of the two factions. Certainly, the execution of Hanley seems to have acted as a catalyst, and the factions took their names,
emblems, and inspiration from these two men and their sartorial spe-
cialities. But two gangs led by Hanley and Connors had been fighting

---

Maguires (Cambridge, Mass., 1964), p. 19; Galen Broeker, *Rural disorder and police reform
in Ireland, 1812–36* (London and Toronto, 1970), p. 16. The only existing study of the
movement is Sailbheastar Ó Muireadhaigh, "Na Carabhait agus na Sean-Bheisteanna"
in *Galvia*, viii (1961), pp. 4–20. He makes no attempt to explain the feud and assumes
that Whiteboy activity was incidental and involved both factions.

8. I refer here to the original movement from 1806 to 1811. There are a few instances
of Shanavest Whiteboyism after 1811 in certain fringe areas (see section X of this essay).
Before 1811 the only recorded incident remotely resembling a Shanavest agrarian outrage
was their posting of a Whiteboy-type notice, probably over a private quarrel (Kernan,
Special commission, pp. 39–40).

9. Folklore of Clonmel, 1941 (Department of Irish Folklore, U.C.D., I.F.C., MS 1127,
p. 92).

10. Folklore of Callan, 1948 (U.C.D., I.F.C., MS 1240, p. 157).

for some time, and the Caravat-Shanavest feud was actually an extension of this earlier conflict.[11]

Between 1802 and 1805 there had been a major Whiteboy outbreak in southeast Tipperary. The normal modus operandi was a nocturnal raid on the victim's home by about a dozen armed men, who frequently committed savage violence, savage even by Whiteboy standards. One woman was slain simply as a warning to her husband to quit his farm; in a similar case several children were badly beaten. Killing was almost casual. No less than twelve murders and six or seven attempted murders are recorded, and there had apparently been many more.[12]

As far as we can tell, most victims were comfortable Catholic farmers, and their commonest offense was "land grabbing" — taking land over the heads of the occupying tenants at the end of their term.[13] But it was not just specific offenders who suffered. The Whiteboys also robbed arms and commandeered horses, levied contributions to "the cause," committed several robberies, and abducted farmers' daughters. Even in these ancillary activities the medium and larger farmers suffered most.[14]

The Whiteboys were said to be small farmers and laborers, and of

11. U.C.D., I.F.C., MS S538, p. 235; MS S637, pp. 57–8; MS 1127, p. 92; MS 1240, pp. 82, 157; S.P.O., S.O.C.P.1, 1121/61; Kernan, *Special commission*, p. 31; O'Donnell, *Faction fighters*, pp. 23–5; John Banim, "John Doe" in *Tales of the O'Hara family, part III* (Belfast, 1846), p. 32; *Select committee on disturbances, 1825*, p. 113; *Minutes of evidence before the select committee of the House of Lords appointed to examine into the nature and extent of the disturbances which have prevailed in those districts of Ireland now subject to the provisions of the insurrection act . . .* , p. 110, H.L. 1825 (35), cxc, 1 (hereafter cited as *Select committee . . . insurrection act, 1825*). Caravats and Shanavests actually sported cravats and old waistcoats at fights. These are usually described as white, the traditional color of popular celebration (and revolt), though there are references to cravats in red, green, and even black silk.

12. Our knowledge of the movement is heavily dependent on rough statistics compiled by a few magistrates more than two years after the violence began (S.P.O., S.O.C.P.1, 1031/72). Their lists all conclude with such statements as these: "Murders and flogging matches are so frequent and notorious they need not be mentioned," and "I omit a long list of murders, abductions, mail robberies, and horse stealing." Even so, the lists reveal a state of extreme unrest.

13. This statement is based on an analysis of every recorded outrage in S.O.C.P.1 and 2, 1802–5. Several laborers and dairymen were also attacked, the former as Kerrymen or informers, the latter probably for reducing the number of conacre lettings. Only two gentlemen seem to have been attacked, in their capacity as dairy farmers.

14. The levying of contributions was a way of furnishing the means to buy ammunition and to support imprisoned comrades. Abductions were a peculiar form of social banditry. The women were forced to marry poor men, who thus (they hoped) gained their dowries. See S.P.O., S.O.C.P.1, 1031/72; 1192/6; 1207/71; 1406/3–4; Sir G. C. Lewis, *On local disturbances in Ireland, and on the Irish church question* (London, 1836), pp. 295–6.

seventeen whose status is known, all but one were laborers.[15] The exception was a gentleman: Thomas Mandeville, scion of a "most ancient family," notorious highwayman, and now a Whiteboy captain.[16] Another gentleman called Butler was marginally involved, a hanger-on with a taste for exotic drinking companions.[17] These two men were drawn from that thriving rural underworld where Whiteboys, bandits, smugglers, and the like happily rubbed shoulders and frequently shared personnel. Their involvement serves as a reminder that Whiteboyism was not an inevitable reaction to popular grievances, but a reaction molded by a particular culture, one with a strong tradition of lawlessness, which was by no means the exclusive preserve of the poor.[18]

The Whiteboys of southeast Tipperary seem to have evolved between 1802 and 1805 from a loose series of ad hoc combinations into an organized federation of distinct parish gangs, coordinating their activities and assuming a collective name—the Moyle Rangers. One man probably played a key role in this transformation. The Rangers were so personally identified with him that, with his capture, the unrest simply and abruptly ceased. This was "Caravat" Hanley.[19]

Hanley's peculiar ascendancy seems to have reflected sheer charisma. The few glimpses we get of him suggest an archetypal popular hero—a flamboyant dandy who strutted about by day openly sporting a blunderbuss and a brace of pistols, and who died coolly trading insults with Paudeen Gar and ostentatiously throwing his cravat to the mob.[20] One sus-

---

15. S.P.O., S.O.C.P.1, 1031/69, 76; U.C.D., I.F.C., MS 1240, p. 157.

16. L. H. Jephson, 4 Nov. 1805 (S.P.O., S.O.C.P.2, 1805/31); S.P.O., S.O.C.P.1, 1025/46–7; 1026/30–1, 37; 1031/62–84.

17. L. H. Jephson, 4 Nov. 1805 (S.P.O., S.O.C.P.2, 1805/31); R. E. Butler, 20, 24 Aug. 1807 (S.P.O., S.O.C.P.2, 1807/33); S.P.O., S.O.C.P.1, 1120/80.

18. Mandeville and Butler both became spies and played a major role in breaking up the movement. Some sort of animosity existed between them: Mandeville burned Butler's house in 1807. Their subsequent careers are obscure, though reports from Tipperary and Waterford between 1810 and 1815 include several references to crimes committed by gentlemen named Mandeville and Butler. The offenses ranged from involvement with factionists to the murder of creditors. Of course, Mandeville and Butler were common surnames among the local gentry, but the references perhaps involve more than a coincidence (S.P.O., S.O.C.P.1, 1275/17; 1277/74; 1540/42, 53–53A; 1559/68, 76, 78, 85; 1566/25; 1775/5; 1835/46–9; 1959/28).

19. S.P.O., S.O.C.P.1, 1026/18, 31; 1031/72, 76–77, 79, 81; L. H. Jephson, 4 Nov. 1805 (S.P.O., S.O.C.P.2, 1805/31); Kernan, Special commission, p. 31; O'Donnell, Faction fighters, p. 24. The river Moyle runs through the heart of the disturbed district. Since local volunteer and yeomanry corps were often styled rangers, including companies formed to hunt Whiteboys in the eighteenth century, there was a certain defiant humor in the name Moyle Rangers.

20. S.P.O., S.O.C.P.1, 1031/76; Select committee on disturbances, 1825, p. 113.

pects that he was responsible for the particular audacity which marked some of the Whiteboys' exploits. For example, they committed a whole series of mail robberies at the same two villages on the Clonmel-Cashel road, sometimes on successive nights.[21] Moreover, the villages were Clerahan and Lowesgreen, where many of the Whiteboys actually lived; they were operating literally on their own doorsteps.[22] An eyewitness account of one robbery survives. The solitary passenger described the gang as both "shabby" and brutal, with one exception. While the rest of the gang were forcing the dying guard to crawl into a snow-filled ditch and debating whether or not to murder the helpless driver, a remarkably well-dressed man pranced around the witness like a caricature chapbook highwayman, scorning to steal his paltry 15s., returning him his watch and hat (it was not passengers, but "his majesty's coach" that the man wanted to rob), and ordering the gang to treat the passenger with more respect ("as witness was a gentleman"). This was probably Hanley. The witness was particularly struck by his "fashionable" red cravat.[23]

So much for "Caravat" Hanley, apparently the leading figure in a particularly savage Whiteboy war and in the creation of a formidable Whiteboy federation, a man abundantly possessed of the kind of flamboyance and audacity traditionally idolized by the poor — qualities symbolized in his nickname. But who was "Paudeen Gar" Connors, and why did he and his friends bear Hanley such intense hatred?

Connors was the leader of a powerful faction: "Paudeen Gar's Boys." They were apparently drawn from the class which had borne the brunt of the Whiteboy onslaught, and many of them had suffered personally. The known members were Patrick Shea, a prosperous farmer, notorious land grabber, and the Whiteboys' first and repeated victim; one Griffiths, a farmer and grabber who was murdered by Hanley himself; Stephen Blake, a farmer who narrowly escaped death when Griffiths was slain; and several milesmen, that is, part-time policemen responsible for the roads at night, and like most petty functionaries, probably drawn from the middle class.[24] Connors himself was a milesman as well as a publican and a big farmer. Indeed, he may have been responsible for the roads around Clerahan, which could not have helped him to love Hanley.[25]

21. S.P.O., S.O.C.P.1, 1025/46–7, 53–4, 61; 1026/21, 24–8; 1030/91; 1031/64, 67, 77A, 80; Brigade-Major R. Crawford, 24 Feb. 1805 (S.P.O., S.O.C.P.2, 1805/31).
22. S.P.O., S.O.C.P.1, 1026/25, 38; 1031/76–8.
23. Information of T. Quinlan, 19 Jan. 1803, enclosed in R. Lane, 19 Jan. 1803 (S.P.O., S.O.C.P.1, 1025/46).
24. S.P.O., S.O.C.P.1, 1031/68–79; L. H. Jephson, 4 Nov. 1805 (S.P.O., S.O.C.P.2, 1805/31); Kernan, *Special commission*, p. 31; O'Donnell, *Faction fighters*, p. 24.
25. S.P.O., S.O.C.P.1, 1026/38; Folklore of Fethard (U.C.D., I.F.C., MS 1127, pp.

Many factions were mafias pursuing private gain and collective power. This was probably true of Connors's gang, given the number of grabbers and petty officials belonging to it. Certainly, Connors was a typical mafia chief.[26] Unlike most such groups, however, it was apparently based not on kinship but on political allegiance. It was a nationalist organization. Connors planned to lead the Tipperary rebellion if the French landed, and his "boys" were the nucleus of his army.[27] This fact explains the group's wide middle-class base. And because of its composition the group was uniquely placed to give organized expression to general anti-Whiteboy feeling. It was in practice as much an anti-Whiteboy organization as anything else, fighting them at fairs and informing against them. Indeed, it was some of Connors's followers who actually prosecuted Hanley.[28]

Connors's role in all of this is particularly interesting because it parallels that of Hanley. Like Hanley, Connors seems to have embodied many of the aspirations and virtues of his class, and like Hanley, his nickname and mode of dress seem to have symbolized something of his special qualities. As a publican, big farmer, policeman, faction boss, and political leader, he was the epitome of middle-class success; "Gar" implies a man noted for the bourgeois virtues of dourness and cunning.[29] Can one not see in his battered old waistcoat a symbol of hard work and thrift, worn with as much pride as Hanley's elegant cravat?

Like all class conflict, the war between the Moyle Rangers and Paudeen Gar's Boys was more than an economic struggle. One can discern here the clash of two different moral and cultural worlds, and the rival leaders seem to have personified many of the different values and aspirations of each. This was reflected in their evocative nicknames and dress, which is surely the reason why tradition places such emphasis on an exchange of insults about clothes at Hanley's execution, and why the factions automatically seized on cravats and old waistcoats as their rival

---

70–2); Folklore of Lisronagh (U.C.D., I.F.C., MS S568, p. 22); Folklore of Callan (U.C.D., I.F.C., MS 1240, p. 157); O'Donnell, *Faction fighters*, p. 24. Connors lived at Giant's Grave, about three miles from Clerahan.

26. See the article on factions in *Tipperary Vindicator*, 18 June 1845; U.C.D., I.F.C., MS 1244, p. 472; U.C.D., I.F.C., MS 782, pp. 273–83; S.P.O., S.O.C.P.1, 1193/12; 1567/17; 1717/27; 1723/1–2; 1837/34.

27. S.P.O., S.O.C.P.1, 1026/38; Warrant for the arrest of Patrick Connors of Giant's Grave, and of John and Denis, his sons, for treasonable practices, 29 Oct. 1804 (S.P.O., S.O.C.P.2, 1804/31).

28. S.P.O., S.O.C.P.1, 1026/38; 1031/68–79; Kernan, *Special commission*, p. 31.

29. Ó Muireadhaigh interprets "Gar" as *Geárr*, or "short." But *Geárr* usually means short in time or space, as in "a short while." "Short Paddy" would surely be "Paudeen Beg" (*Paídín Beag*). I agree with O'Donnell, who interprets it as *Géar*, meaning "sharp," in the sense of "dour" and "cunning."

emblems. And it was no doubt the archetypal quality of this conflict and its chief protagonists that gave it such a hold on the imaginations of people elsewhere, with such dramatic consequences.

IV

The Caravat and Shanavest movements made their public debut in the autumn of 1806. South Tipperary had been quiet for almost a year after Hanley's death, but the tranquillity ended abruptly in September 1806 with a new wave of faction fighting, followed in October by reports that a mysterious new "combination oath" had been widely taken in a region stretching from east Limerick through south Tipperary into east Waterford.[30] From its content and area of circulation this was undoubtedly the Caravat oath, and within weeks there was an almost simultaneous upsurge of Whiteboy violence throughout the region, commencing, rather appropriately, with yet another mail robbery at Clerahan.[31]

The disturbances were most intense in Tipperary and Waterford, in certain areas which were to remain the chief strongholds of the two movements until their apparent suppression in 1811. During this period a distinct and cohesive heartland evolved around these initial centers: more or less the baronies of Middlethird, Slievardagh, and Iffa and Offa in Tipperary; the east and west Decies, the Suir valley, and Gaultiere in Waterford; and the south and midwest fringes of Kilkenny. This was not the full extent of the Caravat and Shanavest movements, as has generally been assumed. They existed from the start in east Limerick, west Tipperary, and probably north Cork, affected at least eleven counties, and survived into the present century.[32] But it was in this heartland from 1806 to 1811 that the disturbances were most severe, it was here that allegiances were most open and fervent, and only here did the two movements visibly monopolize Whiteboy and faction violence. This area and period provide the focus of this essay, and for the moment we are concerned only with the Caravats.

The heartland of the movement can be divided into several distinct subregions. The most disturbed was the old Moyle Rangers' territory of southeast Tipperary. From the start Caravat activity here was concentrated around the three main towns of Clonmel, Cashel, and Fethard

30. S.P.O., S.O.C.P.1, 1080/6, 30; Brigade-Major R. Crawford, 1 Nov. 1806; General J. Floyd, 1 Dec. 1806; Brigade-Major J. Rogers, 4 Dec. 1806 (S.P.O., S.O.C.P.2, 1806/32).

31. S.P.O., S.O.C.P.1, 1080/27, 35; 1091/76, 78, 80–1; 1120/91–2; 1121/1, 14, 21; Brigade-Major R. Crawford, 1 Nov. 1806; General J. Floyd, 1 Dec. 1806; General Meyrick, 1 Dec. 1806; Brigade-Major J. Ormsby, 1 Dec. 1806; Brigade-Major J. Rogers, 4, 29 Dec. 1806, 4 Jan. 1807 (S.P.O., S.O.C.P.2, 1806–7/32).

32. See sections IX and X of this essay.

as well as the smaller towns of Ardfinnan and Mullinahone, but by mid-1808 it had also spread northward into the colliery district near Killenaule and Ballingarry, and southwestward into the country around the textile center of Clogheen.[33] The participants seem to have been drawn mainly from the towns themselves, though there were distinct gangs based in the villages of Newinn and Clerahan near Clonmel and of Ardmayle near Cashel, while a gang from the mountainous district around Araglin was involved in activities near Clogheen, and several small villages about Newcastle and Ardfinnan were apparently particular Caravat strongholds.[34] By mid-1808 the unrest had also spread into west Kilkenny, but disturbances here were rather sporadic, largely confined to the vicinity of Callan, Kilmanagh, and Kilmaganny, and mainly the work of emissaries from Tipperary,[35] though local gangs centered on the town of Callan and on the Windgap quarries had become quite formidable by 1810.[36]

There were three distinct regions of Caravat activity in County Waterford. Initially, western Decies was the most important. From 1806 to 1809 a particularly energetic gang based on a cluster of hill villages where the Knockmealdowns meet the Comeraghs (Knockboy, Tooraneena, Lackandarra, Sleadycastle, Ballinamult) terrorized and proselytized both their own area and the rich agricultural district to the south, around the ports of Cappoquin and Dungarvan and the village of Aglish, from which the movement spread southward to Ardmore.[37] Despite the formation of local groups in and near these various settlements, the suppression of the original Knockboy gang in 1809 quieted the whole region.[38]

33. S.P.O., S.O.C.P.1, 1080/35; 1121/2; 1207/63; 1120/82, 88; 1188/26, 28, 52–3, 56; 1193/10; General J. Floyd, 1 Dec. 1806; Brigade-Major J. Ormsby, 1 Dec. 1806 (S.P.O., S.O.C.P.2, 1806/32); T. Prendergast, 6, 14 May 1808 (S.P.O., S.O.C.P.2, 1808/34).

34. S.P.O., S.O.C.P.1, 1188/54, 56; 1193/9–10, 12; 1230/48; 1404/7; 1406/2, 14–15; Brigade-Major J. Ormsby, 13, 14 Mar. 1808; J. Homan, 21 Mar. 1808 (S.P.O., S.O.C.P.2, 1808/34); "Secret" to E. Trevor, 20 Feb. 1809 (S.P.O., S.O.C.P.2, 1809/36); General J. Lee, 21 Sept., 1 Oct. 1810; Sir J. Carden, 24 Dec. 1810 (S.P.O., S.O.C.P.2, 1810/37).

35. Brigade-Major J. Ormsby, 13, 14 Mar. 1808; E. Elliot, 20 Mar. 1808; J. Homan, 21 Mar. 1808; J. Strangeways, 20 June 1808 (S.P.O., S.O.C.P.2, 1808/34).

36. S.P.O., S.O.C.P.1, 1275/7–27; 1381/49–50, 56; "Secret" to E. Trevor, 20 Feb. 1809 (S.P.O., S.O.C.P.2, 1809/36); J. B. Elliot, 9 July 1810 (S.P.O., S.O.C.P.2, 1810/37); J. Strangeways, 3 Jan. 1811 (S.P.O., S.O.C.P.2, 1811/38); U.C.D., I.F.C., MS S852, pp. 199–200.

37. S.P.O., S.O.C.P.1, 1091/81; 1121/14, 61; Brigade-Major J. Rogers, 4 Jan. 1807 (S.P.O., S.O.C.P.2, 1807/32); Rogers, 14 Dec. 1807 (S.P.O., S.O.C.P.2, 1807/34); Commander of the Forces Office, 7, 8, 9, 27 Oct. 1807 (S.P.O., S.O.C.P.2, 1807/34); E. Elliot, Nov.–Dec. 1808; Brigade-Major B. Gahan, 30 Nov., 8, 14 Dec. 1808 (S.P.O., S.O.C.P.2, 1808/35).

38. S.P.O., S.O.C.P.1, 1227/1–34; 1230/67–82; 1277/10, 87–110; Brigade-Major B. Gahan, 30 Nov. 1808 (S.P.O., S.O.C.P.2, 1808/35); R. Usher, 13 July 1809; General N.

The second region in County Waterford followed the line of the Suir and the Carrick-Waterford road. Despite a mild beginning, by 1809 this was the most disturbed area of the county. The gangs seem to have been based largely on centers of textile industry: the town of Carrick, its suburb Carrickbeg, the neighboring village of Cregg, and the little towns of Portlaw and Kilmeadan. Their activities were heavily concentrated in the rich agricultural district between Portlaw and Waterford city, with occasional forays being made on the Kilkenny side of the river.[39] In the winter of 1809–10 the movement spread into Gaultiere barony, east of the city. Little is known about its strongholds here, but they probably included the Harristown area and the suburbs of Waterford.[40]

Eastern Decies formed the final (and apparently the quietest) region. Disturbances commenced around the market town of Kilmacthomas, spreading southward in the summer of 1807 through Kill and Ballylaneen to the mining area around Bunmahon and Stradbally.[41] To judge from the pattern elsewhere, these towns were probably the local Caravat strongholds.

The overall pattern reflects one simple fact: Caravat grievances stemmed from the workings of the agricultural market economy. The heartland as a whole was the most developed and prosperous area of Munster, noted for its superb land, numerous large farms and demesnes, local industries, and thriving commercial agriculture.[42] Within it, unrest was clearly concentrated around the main towns and larger (especially industrial) villages, that is, closest to the market where commercial agriculture was most developed. This was where land was most valuable and rents were highest, where middlemen and the export trade inflated the price of food, and where the poorest and most desperate

Waller, 1 Aug. 1809 (S.P.O., S.O.C.P.2, 1809/36); Usher, 8 Apr. 1810 (S.P.O., S.O.C.P.2, 1810/37).

39. S.P.O., S.O.C.P.1, 1026/20; 1188/59; 1207/71; 1228/10; 1277/87–110; Brigade-Major J. Rogers, 1 Mar. 1807 (S.P.O., S.O.C.P.2, 1807/33); E. Elliot, 20 Mar. 1808 (S.P.O., S.O.C.P.2, 1808/34); Brigade-Major B. Gahan, 4 Apr. 1809; General N. Waller, 1 May 1809; Brigade-Major J. Ormsby, 1 Aug. 1809 (S.P.O., S.O.C.P.2, 1809/36); R. Willcocks, 30 Jan. 1810; H. Cole, 10 June 1810; D. Mahon, 14 June 1810; Elliot, 23, 24 June, 11 Dec. 1810; Ormsby, 1 Aug. 1810 (S.P.O., S.O.C.P.2, 1810/37).

40. S.P.O., S.O.C.P.1, 1277/87–9; 1387/72–81; Brigade-Major B. Gahan, 1 Feb., 17 Nov. 1810 (S.P.O., S.O.C.P.2, 1810/37).

41. S.P.O., S.O.C.P.1, 1080/27; 1180/27; 1188/61; Brigade-Major J. Rogers, 4 Dec. 1806 (S.P.O., S.O.C.P.2, 1806/32); Rogers, 31 Aug. 1807; R. T. Carew, 13 Aug. 1807 (S.P.O., S.O.C.P.2, 1807/33); Carew, 22 Oct. 1808 (S.P.O., S.O.C.P.2, 1808/35); General H. Wyngard, 4 Apr. 1809 (S.P.O., S.O.C.P.2, 1809/36).

42. T. W. Freeman, *Pre-famine Ireland: a study in historical geography* (Manchester, 1957), pp. 203–17; J. E. Bicheno, *Ireland and its economy, being the result of observations made in a tour through the country in the autumn of 1829* (London, 1830), pp. 13–17, 20.

congregated in search of work.[43] Even the Knockboy and Araglin moun-
taineers conducted their operations mostly around towns.

It is particularly striking how far most of the known gangs were actually based *in* these towns and villages. The movement was in fact dominated by agricultural day laborers, who were heavily concentrated within
such communities, and by certain groups of industrial workers.[44] The
latter were most evident in the many gangs drawn from small industrial
communities — the Windgap quarries, the Slievardagh collieries, and the
Suir textile villages. But the affected towns tended to be those with some
industry too, and industrial workers often joined these gangs, as they
did at Carrick, where the boatmen and cloth workers were notorious
Caravats.[45]

The important role of day laborers is hardly surprising. They were
the most depressed rural class. As for industrial workers, they frequently
rented smallholdings and in slack times sought farm work.[46] Given the
intensity of agrarian problems around their communities, their participation also makes sense. Nevertheless, some of these workers were relatively
prosperous, and it is odd that they should have been so heavily involved,
compared with such depressed groups as farm servants and cottiers. The
Suir valley cloth industry was certainly in the throes of a major slump,
but elsewhere local industries seem to have been thriving, and though
information on wages and conditions is hard to obtain, the Windgap
quarrymen, Slievardagh colliers, and Carrick boatmen were almost certainly highly paid. In Kilkenny and Kildare quarrymen and boatmen
earned 1s. 1d. a day plus food, while colliers earned from 1s. 1d. to 2s.

43. William Tighe, *Statistical observations relative to the county of Kilkenny made
in the years 1800 & 1801* (Dublin, 1802), pp. 425–6; James Hall, *Tour through Ireland,
particularly the interior and least known parts, containing an accurate view of the parties, politics, and improvements in the different provinces* . . . (2 vols., London, 1813),
i, 132; W. S. Mason, *A statistical account or parochial survey of Ireland, drawn up from
the communications of the clergy* (3 vols., Dublin, 1814–19), i, 117; A. Atkinson, *The Irish
tourist: in a series of picturesque views, travelling incidents, and observations statistical,
political, and moral* . . . (Dublin, 1815), p. 625; Freeman, *Pre-famine Ireland*, pp. 5, 20,
24, 53.

44. Brigade-Major B. Gahan, 23 Jan. 1809 (S.P.O., S.O.C.P.2, 1809/36); W. G. Paul,
29 Apr. 1811 (S.P.O., S.O.C.P.2, 1811/38); W. Izod, 7 Jan. 1813 (S.P.O., S.O.C.P.2, 1813/39);
S.P.O., S.O.C.P.1, 1381/56); R. Willcocks, State of the Tipperary peasantry (Peel papers,
B.L., Add. MS 40202, ff. 286–7); Freeman, *Pre-famine Ireland*, pp. 5, 20, 24.

45. S.P.O., S.O.C.P.1, 1386/42); Folklore of Clogheen (U.C.D., I.F.C., MS S562, p.
302); Tighe, *Kilkenny*, pp. 538–57; Hall, *Tour*, i, 113–52; Mason, *Statistical account*, i,
119–20; Freeman, *Pre-famine Ireland*, pp. 203–17; Edward Wakefield, *An account of Ireland, statistical and political* (2 vols., London, 1812), ii, 772.

46. S.P.O., S.O.C.P.1, 1557/23; 1954/37; U.C.D., I.F.C., MS S585, p. 89; MS 1210,
p. 156; Tighe, *Kilkenny*, pp. 540–1.

2d. a day. This compares to a farm laborer's normal wage of from 6d. to 10d. a day — and day laborers did not even have regular work.[47] The gangs did not draw their members simply from the most aggrieved groups. Rather, they tended to emerge in areas of concentrated settlement, often among groups involved in collective work, all of which made it easier to organize. Thus industrial workers were heavily involved, while farm servants and cottiers, dispersed on their employers' holdings, were not.[48] This also explains the otherwise rather strange pattern of small-farmer participation. Although their grievances were most intense in the developed areas near the towns, small farmers here were not heavily engaged. Yet they were the backbone of a series of gangs drawn from the remote hill districts around Newcastle, Araglin, and Knockboy. The difference was that small farmers near the towns tended to live on dispersed holdings, whereas these upland districts were areas of intense clachan settlement and widespread collective tenure. Small farmers here lived in village communities, often holding their land in common and periodically redividing it to insure a rough equality.[49]

A closer look suggests that most gangs were in fact based on distinct laborers' and small farmers' ghettoes — tightly knit and somewhat independent communities, often with a collectivist economic base, whose structure positively encouraged group action and a lawless spirit, and which usually had long-standing reputations for both.[50] These were the sprawling cabin slums on the edges of towns, like the notorious squatter settlements on the commons of Callan and Ardmore;[51] similar concentrations of the ultrapoor in nearby villages, like "wretched" Newinn and "peculiarly disaffected" Clerahan;[52] self-contained industrial villages, like

47. S.P.O., S.O.C.P.1, 1406/18; Tighe, *Kilkenny*, pp. 41, 52–72, 80–1, 94, 102, 141, 473–504, 538–58; Wakefield, *Ireland*, ii, 208–29; Hall, *Tour*, i, 67–8; Mason, *Statistical account*, i, 119–20; Atkinson, *Irish tourist*, p. 441.

48. Of course, farm servants, cottiers, and people from areas of dispersed settlement sometimes participated. This is only to be expected, given the dynamic recruiting policy of the main gangs. See S.P.O., S.O.C.P.1, 1026/20; 1188/56; 1381/56; 1386/10, 52.

49. S.P.O., S.O.C.P.1, 1031/84; 1121/52; 1230/63; 1387/55; 1559/32, 41; U.C.D., I.F.C., MS S572, pp. 530–1; Desmond McCourt, "The rundale system in Ireland" (Ph.D. dissertation, Queen's University, Belfast, 1950), pp. 75–81, 89, 306; *Arthur Young's tour in Ireland (1776–1779)*, ed. A. W. Hutton (2 vols., London, 1892), i, 458–9, 462.

50. Thus the centers of Caravatism had often been centers of earlier Whiteboy movements (S.P.O., S.O.C.P.1, 1188/57; 1381/67; 1406/14; 1721/65; Donnelly, "Rightboys," pp. 130–1, 136; idem, "Whiteboys," pp. 20–6).

51. S.P.O., S.O.C.P.1, 1381/56; 1719/1; Brigade-Major J. Ormsby, 14 Mar. 1808 (S.P.O., S.O.C.P.2, 1808/34); Freeman, *Pre-famine Ireland*, pp. 200–1.

52. Brigade-Major R. Crawford, 10 Apr. 1804 (S.P.O., S.O.C.P.1, 1026/25); R. Willcocks, 1 Dec. 1820 (S.P.O., S.O.C.P.1, 2186/27).

"lawless" Ballingarry and "that nest of robbers" Carrickbeg;[53] and wild hill clachans, communities of poor farmers remote from authority and lacking resident gentlemen, like Araglin (an "armed fastness" and "an asylum for fugitives and deserters") and Knockboy ("for ages past, notorious for insubordination").[54]

V

The Caravats' principal tactic was the nocturnal raid by perhaps a dozen men, usually armed, mounted, and disguised with blackfaces or women's clothes.[55] Sundays and holidays were favored raiding times, and winter was the preferred season.[56] Offenders were considered entitled to three warnings, normally threatening notices accompanied by escalating attacks on property. In one typical case the Caravats resorted to the digging of a grave, the killing of a sheep, and the burning of a house.[57] If such warnings were disregarded, personal violence followed, usually a severe beating with gun butts, spades, or sticks. Recorded instances of more serious violence are confined to six or seven murders and a handful of notable atrocities — a gang rape, the burning of a house with the inhabitants inside, and one or perhaps two cases where the victim's ears were cut off.[58]

The movement was based on a series of small local gangs, many of which were active long before the organization of the Caravats. These were apparently informal affinity groups, bound by ties of kinship, community, and friendship. The original Knockboy gang was typical. It consisted of about a dozen young men, all neighbors, several apparently related (they included two Foley brothers, two Connorses, and two

53. O. Latham, 7 Apr. 1808 (S.P.O., S.O.C.P.1, 1193/10); P. Power, 15 Feb. 1811 (S.P.O., S.O.C.P.1, 1026/20).

54. Brigade-Major B. Gahan, 8 Dec. 1808 (S.P.O., S.O.C.P.1, 1188/65); T. Prendergast, 25, 26 Apr. 1812 (S.P.O., S.O.C.P.1, 1406/14–15).

55. In a few cases the raiders were undisguised or simply turned up their collars. Surprisingly, the records contain not one reference to the traditional Whiteboy uniform of a white shirt worn over the clothes.

56. See S.P.O., S.O.C.P.1, 1031/68, 72, 76; 1277/19; 1386/87; 1387/61–5.

57. S.P.O., S.O.C.P.1, 1121/14; 1193/12, 14; 1387/49; E. Lee, 3 Jan. 1810 (S.P.O., S.O.C.P.2, 1810/37).

58. These figures have been compiled from S.O.C.P.1 and 2, Oct. 1806–Jan. 1811, and refer to agrarian punishments only. The Caravats also killed several people for refusing arms, horses, or bridles, and burned another family in their home in pursuit of a private quarrel (see fn. 69). A further five or six murders may have been agrarian but are inadequately documented.

Hogans), and probably active under an alternative local name (the Quilts) from about 1801.[59]

New recruits were bound to these parent bodies, and the different gangs to each other, by a standard oath of allegiance and solidarity. This is the fullest recorded version: "To be true to each other and to our friends, to attend all meetings when warned, no cause to excuse absence but sickness, of which sufficient proof must be [given], to keep all secrets, to suffer death rather than betray each other or whatever may be seen or heard relating to our cause, and to stand by each other at all fairs and patrons."[60] Apart from this oath, both local and supralocal organization seems to have remained essentially informal. There is no evidence of committees, delegates, officers, or similar structures. Members generally came from the same neighborhood, age group, sex, and class; peer-group ties made elaborate organization unnecessary. The movement was sustained by sheer enthusiasm and by a deep sense of common purpose and identity embodied in symbols rather than institutions — the Caravat name itself, the neckcloth badge, and the pseudonym John Doe, which was used by most Caravat captains and appeared regularly on Caravat notices.[61]

Informality did not preclude efficiency, perseverance, and an impressive degree of supralocal cooperation, for which Caravatism was notable. Nor did it prevent the emergence of recognized leaders. The local

59. S.P.O., S.O.C.P.1, 1121/61; 1188/54; 1230/74–80; 1277/91; 1404/13; Commander of the Forces Office, 8, 9 Oct. 1807; Brigade-Major J. Rogers, 14 Dec. 1807 (S.P.O., S.O.C.P.2, 1807/34); R. Usher, 13 July 1809 (S.P.O., S.O.C.P.2, 1809/36); Usher, 8 Apr. 1810 (S.P.O., S.O.C.P.2, 1810/37). "Quilts" apparently meant "cats" ("as they work by night"). Some other gangs used alternative and possibly older names too. In east Tipperary and west Kilkenny the Caravats often called themselves John Does; around Clogheen, Caravats and Shanavests sometimes fought as Parkers and Farmers; and in the Carrick-Clonmel area the Shanavests may sometimes have used the name St. Peter's Corps (S.P.O., S.O.C.P.1, 1121/49; 1193/14; 1404/13; T. Prendergast, 14 May 1808 [S.P.O., S.O.C.P.2, 1808/34]).

60. Commander of the Forces Office, 8 Oct. 1807 (S.P.O., S.O.C.P.2, 1807/34). This version comes from County Waterford in 1807. Though other reports merely summarize or partially reproduce the oath, the wording usually tallies closely. Thus the initial oath of October 1806 was summed up as "to be true to each other on every occasion, particularly quarrels at fairs." See S.P.O., S.O.C.P.1, 1121/49; 1207/63; 1277/22; Brigade-Major R. Crawford, 1 Nov. 1806 (S.P.O., S.O.C.P.2, 1806/32); Brigade-Major B. Gahan, 30 Nov. 1808 (S.P.O., S.O.C.P.2, 1808/35).

61. "John Doe" was a standard pseudonym in the heartland long before the formation of the Caravats. That its use was virtually confined to this region suggests the existence of a definite collective consciousness among its Whiteboys even before 1806. It is of course a well-known "everyman" pseudonym. It was employed in this period in legal documents, and its adoption by Whiteboys shows their usually defiant humor. See Banim, "John Doe," p. 34; S.P.O., S.O.C.P.1, 1020/42, 44; 1025/56–8; 1031/76; 1080/27; 1188/28, 61; 1193/14; 1228/8; 1381/55; 1406/22; 1554/9.

gangs were fairly democratic; it was noted of one group that all its members had "equal commands."[62] But inevitably the most experienced, daring, and charismatic individuals came to wield the greatest influence. These men were especially important on the supralocal level. The most notorious of them sometimes assumed control of combined gangs at faction fights. The best known were John Brian ("Captain Wheeler") of the Gaultiere gang; Pierce Nowlan ("Captain Flogger") of Portlaw; Paddy Callaghan ("Captain Cutter"), who led the combined east Decies gangs at one fight; and Thomas Foley of the Knockboy gang, who came closest to being an overall chief. Foley was to have led the entire Caravat strength at a showdown with the Shanavests at Kilgobnet fair in 1808, but it never took place.[63]

The chief common denominator of the Caravat captains was their extravagant personalities, manifested in colorful nicknames, in theatrical public behavior, and sometimes in outrageous personal lives. "Captain Wheeler" had three wives and murdered an entire family to gain a fourth.[64] Flamboyance was also displayed in their elegant and expensive clothing, to which there are several references.[65] Yet they seem to have been uniformly men of the poorest class: Foley was probably a poor hill farmer; Brian and Callaghan were itinerant spalpeens, the lowest form of laborer; the leaders of the Kilmeadan gang were a spalpeen and a small farmer.[66] Clearly, Hanley was not the only proletarian Beau Brummell in Munster.

The available evidence suggests that membership was confined exclusively to the poor. Of five general assessments of the composition of the movement in the main sources, two indicate "labourers," two "the lowest class," and one "the class of day labourers and small farmers . . . , the dregs of the people."[67] Of thirty-six individual Caravats whose status is known, no less than twenty-one were laborers; there were also eight farmers, three military deserters, a carpenter, a postboy, a tailor, and a sur-

62. W. Fenge, 11 Dec. 1814 (S.P.O., S.O.C.P.1, 1566/91).

63. S.P.O., S.O.C.P.1, 1121/61; 1188/58; 1277/94–6, 103; Commander of the Forces Office, 8, 9 Oct. 1807 (S.P.O., S.O.C.P.2, 1807/34). Clearly, Brian and Callaghan were noted stick fighters. A "wheel" was a provocative display by a leader or champion before a faction fight, and a stroke of a faction stick was called a cut.

64. See fn. 69.

65. See, e.g., S.P.O., S.O.C.P.1, 1121/61; Brigade-Major J. Ormsby, 14 Mar. 1808 (S.P.O., S.O.C.P.2, 1808/34).

66. S.P.O., S.O.C.P.1, 1121/61; 1277/96, 98. Yet another spalpeen apparently exerted particular influence over the Fethard gang (S.P.O., S.O.C.P.1, 1193/12, 14).

67. T. Prendergast, 14 May 1808; J. B. Elliot, 22 May 1808 (S.P.O., S.O.C.P.2, 1808/34); Brigade-Major B. Gahan, 23 Jan. 1809; General J. Lee, 1 July 1810 (S.P.O., S.O.C.P.2, 1809–10/36); R. Willcocks, 18 Apr. 1810 (S.P.O., S.O.C.P.1, 1277/46).

veyor. Seven of the farmers came from mountain clachans and were almost certainly smallholders, while the eighth was actually described as a small farmer; soldiers were generally drawn from the very poor; and all the other occupations were lower-class.[68]

It was not simply a class movement, however. Hundreds of individual Caravats are named in contemporary documents: all were male, with one exception. A certain Joan Lacy was said to have "considerable influence" over the east Waterford Caravats. Her influence was sufficient to persuade a party to murder the lover who had jilted her and to kill his entire family as well. But she did not take part in the raid herself, a fact which speaks volumes.[69] There is less documentation for age, but it is equally consistent. Three Tipperary leaders were described as "young men"; an English traveler was disturbed by the "youthful appearance" of Caravat prisoners; there is a reference to another convict's "extreme youth"; and there are general references to the Caravats as "the deluded young people," "the young men," and "young men and labourers."[70] Specific ages were mentioned in only three cases, but they indicate just what "young" meant: a sixteen-year-old robber of arms, an eighteen-year-old murderer, and "Captain Wheeler," a veritable geriatric at "26 to 30."[71] The Caravats were not simply the poor; they were the young male poor.

VI

Caravatism was the product of the wartime agricultural boom of 1793–1813. Increased demand for food meant higher prices and farm profits and thus rising land values and rents. This situation obviously favored

68. These figures have been compiled from S.O.C.P.1 and 2, Oct. 1806–Jan. 1811, and Kernan, *Special commission*. Several documents dated after January 1811 also refer to the composition of the movement. They confirm its social exclusiveness and the predominance of laborers. See, e.g., S.P.O., S.O.C.P.1, 1381/56; 1389/1; 1404/13; 1406/22; W. G. Paul, 29 Apr. 1811 (S.P.O., S.O.C.P.2, 1811/38); W. Izod, 7 Jan. 1813 (S.P.O., S.O.C.P.2, 1813/39). In Carrick (and possibly elsewhere) some publicans patronized the movement, for fairly obvious reasons. It is doubtful if they can be regarded as members. One mustered a party to help him elope with his girl friend, but this was probably the nearest any of them came to Whiteboy activity (S.P.O., S.O.C.P.1, 1386/42; L. H. Jephson, 27 Feb. 1808; E. Elliot, 20 Mar. 1808 [S.P.O., S.O.C.P.2, 1808/34]).

69. Joan's ex-lover was John Collins. John Brian ("Captain Wheeler") was in love with Collins's wife: Joan and Brian therefore plotted together to destroy Collins, his sister, and his brothers by burning them in their house (S.P.O., S.O.C.P.1, 1277/94–6; 1387/1–87).

70. Commander of the Forces Office, 27 Oct. 1807 (S.P.O., S.O.C.P.2, 1807/34); General J. Lee, 1 July 1810 (S.P.O., S.O.C.P.2, 1810/36); Kernan, *Special commission*, pp. 55–6; Atkinson, *Irish tourist*, p. 426.

71. S.P.O., S.O.C.P.1, 1277/94; 1406/27; Lord Shannon, 13 May 1810 (S.P.O., S.O.C.P.2, 1810/37).

market producers, retailers, and the landlords of tenancies unprotected by leases — in other words, the medium and larger farmers, shopkeepers, publicans, and so forth. But the boom occurred at the expense of consumers and leaseless tenants, that is, most laborers and many small farmers. They faced inflated rents and prices, while population growth insured that there was little increase in real wages or employment.[72] The prosperity also took place at the expense of small farmers holding old leases, because expiry often meant the canting of their land to the highest bidders, usually to bigger commercial farmers, people with the incentive and the spare capital to expand their acreage. To some extent large farmers themselves suffered from rent inflation and canting, but to a much lesser degree. It was hardly in a landlord's interest to oust thriving tenants, who in any case were cushioned by their wartime profits. It was the subsistence and near-subsistence farmers who could not afford the new market rents.[73]

The Caravats attempted to reduce food prices as well as the rents of the poor and sometimes sought to raise wages by compelling obedience to stipulated rates.[74] They opposed inflationary market practices by attacking farmers and retailers who hoarded food to force up prices, bought it to resell at a profit, or exported it from the local area. Occasionally, they simply compelled farmers to give food to needy neighbors.[75] They interfered to help small tenants distrained for arrears of rent by hiding or rescuing their property and by victimizing the landlords or people who bought distrained goods.[76] They attacked herds and dairymen and

72. S.P.O., S.O.C.P.1, 1080/6; John Trotter, *Walks through Ireland in the years 1812, 1814, and 1817, described in a series of letters to an English gentleman* (London, 1819), pp. 16–17; Sir John Carr, *The stranger in Ireland, or a tour in the southern and western part of that country in the year 1805* (London, 1806), p. 503; L. M. Cullen, *An economic history of Ireland since 1660* (London, 1972) pp. 100–4.

73. Trotter, *Walks*, p. 21; Carr, *Stranger*, p. 519; Whitworth, "Disturbances," p. 404; Brigade-Major J. Ormsby, 30 Apr. 1809 (S.P.O., S.O.C.P.2, 1809/36). Numerous Caravat attacks on grabbers are recorded in S.O.C.P.1 and 2, but only three reports actually state the size of the disputed holdings — 14, 8, and "a few" acres. As for the grabbers, most are simply described as "farmers," but for nine we have more precise information: four were gentlemen farmers, one was "a wealthy farmer," two held more than one farm, one employed several men, and one was a yeoman. In short, all nine appear to have been relatively well-to-do.

74. Brigade-Major J. Ormsby, 13 Mar. 1808 (S.P.O., S.O.C.P.2, 1808/34); Brigade-Major B. Gahan, 10 May, 30 Nov. 1808 (S.P.O., S.O.C.P.2, 1808/35); Gahan, 28 June 1810 (S.P.O., S.O.C.P.2, 1810/37); General H. Wyngard, 3 Nov. 1810 (S.P.O., S.O.C.P.2, 1810/36); Kernan, *Special commission*, pp. 9–10.

75. S.P.O., S.O.C.P.1, 1404/4–19; Brigade-Major B. Gahan, 10 May, 30 Nov. 1808 (S.P.O., S.O.C.P.2, 1808/35); Gahan, 28 June 1810 (S.P.O., S.O.C.P.2, 1810/37).

76. S.P.O., S.O.C.P.1, 1026/20; 1230/82; 1387/23–6, 37, 43, 60, 65; R. T. Carew, 13

injured plantations to force more conacre into circulation, and they mounted a particularly sustained campaign against "strangers," that is, itinerant and immigrant laborers from Cork and Kerry, whose competition lowered wages and inflated rents.[77] Above all, they waged an unrelenting war against the grabbers of canted smallholdings.[78]

This all-embracing regulation amounted to the imposition of an alternative economic system and was in fact seen as a coherent system of "laws," a term frequently on Caravat lips.[79] Against the free market in land, labor, and goods it asserted the principle that economic life should be rigorously controlled in accordance with wider social objectives, specifically, to guarantee land and food to the poor. Caravat regulation was indeed class conscious. There is only one recorded case in which they interfered to help a large farmer adversely affected by rising rents and canting, and he bribed them to intervene. Moreover, the relationship was strained from the start, despite the farmer's attempts to present himself as a defender of the poor, and despite the particular notoriety of the grabber who had taken his land. The relationship began to collapse when the farmer tried to dispense with the customary three warnings, and the affair ended with his first refusing to pay up and then murdering the Caravats' spokesman.[80] They were champions of the poor only, and of the poor generally, not just of their own members or over a few grievances. Indeed, though the bulk of their activity was concerned with the major economic grievances outlined above, they were prepared to press any popular complaint, no matter how local or petty. Thus they were involved in enclosure and tithe disputes near Clogheen and Ardfinnan, and in part of Waterford they acted against the impounding of trespassing livestock. They even attacked one man for wife beating.[81]

Aug. 1807; Brigade-Major J. Rogers, 31 Aug. 1807 (S.P.O., S.O.C.P.2, 1807/33); Brigade-Major J. Ormsby, 1 Nov. 1810; General H. Wyngard, 3 Nov. 1810 (S.P.O., S.O.C.P.2, 1810/36); Kernan, *Special commission*, pp. 56–8.

77. S.P.O., S.O.C.P.1, 1188/28, 52, 54, 57; 1230/73; 1277/87; Brigade-Major B. Gahan, 30 Nov. 1808 (S.P.O., S.O.C.P.2, 1808/35); General J. Floyd, 25 July 1810 (S.P.O., S.O.C.P.2, 1810/37).

78. Brigade-Major B. Gahan, 10 May 1808; J. Strangeways, 20 June 1808 (S.P.O., S.O.C.P.2, 1808/34–5); Gahan, 4 Apr. 1809; Brigade-Major J. Ormsby, 30 Apr. 1809; Brigade-Major R. Bushe, 1 Aug. 1810 (S.P.O., S.O.C.P.2, 1809–10/36); M. Kennedy, 3 Jan. 1810; H. Cole, 10 June 1810 (S.P.O., S.O.C.P.2, 1810/37). Though the precise importance of each issue varied from area to area and period to period, attacks on grabbers seem to have absorbed most Caravat energy, closely followed by the regulating of rents and the banishing of strangers.

79. S.P.O., S.O.C.P.1, 1406/15; Brigade-Major J. Ormsby, 13 Mar. 1808 (S.P.O., S.O.C.P.2, 1808/34).

80. S.P.O., S.O.C.P.1, 1193/12, 14.

81. S.P.O., S.O.C.P.1, 1230/63; 1404/13; Brigade-Major B. Gahan, 10 May 1808 (S.P.O.,

As the Gaultiere gang told potential recruits, the aim was simply "to better
the condition of the poor."[82]

A closer look at their activities reveals much about the deeper ideas
and aspirations of the peasantry. It is interesting that this movement,
though dominated by laborers, was obsessed with the preservation of
small farms and with laborers' rents and tenancies rather than their
wages. Perhaps this orientation confirms one witness's claim that there
was a widespread desire among the Tipperary peasantry to divide the
land equally among everyone and to create a society of independent subsistence farmers.[83] Attacks on food exporters and strangers were an obvious way to improve wages and to lower rents and prices, but they
probably reflected a conscious preference for a small-scale economy too.
As one threatening notice put it, "let every parish live in itself."[84] This
attitude explains why they attacked strangers rather than their employers (even when the latter were present and helpless), often voicing such
sentiments as "get back to your own country."[85] Their great bête noire
was the callous greed of the middle class, which sought to monopolize
essential resources and to profit from scarcity. Hence the particular hostility to forestallers and hoarders, who deliberately created scarcity and
inflation, and the orientation of violence against land grabbers rather
than the landlords who canted the land; it was the actual grabbers who
were consciously monopolizing the basic source of subsistence. They were
"a parcel of rascals" who "deserve to be hanged or shot for turning away
poor people from their ground"; they already "had enough" without "robbing the poor." One gang said of a frequent victim, "There is not a spot
of ground between here and Kilkenny that he would not take if he was
let alone."[86] This disgust at middle-class greed is a persistent theme of
Caravat notices, and there is more than a hint of an outraged sense of
proper social hierarchy in the scornful references to "potato eaters" and
"vagabonds" presuming to "make riches."[87]

As the main employers and landlords of the poor, as land grabbers

S.O.C.P.2, 1808/35); marquis of Ely, 22 Nov. 1810 (S.P.O., S.O.C.P.2, 1810/37); Kernan,
Special commission, pp. 21–3, 33–6.

82. Brigade-Major B. Gahan, 29 Jan. 1810 (S.P.O., S.O.C.P.1, 1277/87).

83. *Third report of evidence from the select committee on the state of the poor in
Ireland . . .* , pp. 549–51, H.L. 1830 (14), cclxxxvi, 1.

84. E. Carte, 3 June 1815 (S.P.O., S.O.C.P.1, 1717/15).

85. S.P.O., S.O.C.P.1, 1188/57; 1386/20; H. Cole, 10 June 1810 (S.P.O., S.O.C.P.2,
1810/37).

86. Brigade-Major J. Rogers, 4 Jan. 1807 (S.P.O., S.O.C.P.2, 1807/32); Lord Ikerrin,
30 Aug. 1808 (S.P.O., S.O.C.P.1, 1193/12).

87. Major J. Wills, 24 Apr. 1816 (S.P.O., S.O.C.P.1, 1771/79); E. Wilson, 10 Sept. 1815
(S.P.O., S.O.C.P.1, 1722/3).

and dealers in food, the better-off farmers and other middle-class elements inevitably bore the brunt of Caravat violence. An analysis of recorded regulatory attacks shows no less than fifty on farmers (as far as we can tell, usually richer farmers), nine on other middle-class elements (millers, publicans, yeomen, policemen, a priest), and seven on gentlemen as farmers, as opposed to only three on gentlemen as landlords, six on gentlemen for unspecified reasons, and twelve on laborers or other employees.[88] That the Caravats were hostile toward a class was particularly evident in their ancillary operations. Arms raids were socially indiscriminate, and the class bias of abductions was inherent in the nature of the crime. But their raids to borrow horses, exact contributions, and to rob, seem to have been deliberately aimed at the middle class as a group.[89] Moreover, attacks on such people were often wantonly violent, in stark contrast to the generally polite arms raids on gentlemen. Rich farmers were sometimes murdered for refusing arms, horses, or bridles. Two were so badly bullied by parties which had come for their horses that they died of fright. One County Waterford gang terrorized the "rich respectable farmers" for months in a series of robberies accompanied by brutal beatings with broken spades.[90] Small wonder that a group of magistrates summed up the movement as a sustained attempt to "deter the industrious farmer from advancing himself."[91]

VII

Most Caravat activity was the work of the local gangs in isolation. When they did function as a movement (i.e., cooperate), the aim was usually expansion of the movement itself: enlisting fresh recruits and converting new areas. Some observers believed that the Caravats intended

88. S.O.C.P.1 and 2, Oct. 1806–Jan. 1811. In addition, two gentlemen were attacked as active magistrates, four laborers or employees as informers, and four workers as proxy victims in place of their employers. Many observers noted the antifarmer orientation of the movement. See, e.g., S.P.O., S.O.C.P.1, 1227/26; 1277/92; R. Creaghe, 17 Sept. 1810 (S.P.O., S.O.C.P.2, 1810/37).

89. S.P.O., S.O.C.P.1, 1277/92; "Secret" to E. Trevor, 20 Feb. 1809; Brigade-Major J. Ormsby, 1 Aug. 1810 (S.P.O., S.O.C.P.2, 1809–10/36). Attitudes to robbing varied. One gang actually turned in another for "degrading the character of Caravats" by robbery. Besides committing ordinary robberies, the Tipperary Caravats maintained their traditional predilection for mail robberies. There were also regular bandits in the area, notably the gang led by Edward Brennan ("Brennan-on-the-Moor") in south Tipperary and north Cork in early 1809.

90. S.P.O., S.O.C.P.1, 1230/48; 1277/92; Brigade-Major J. Ormsby, 14 Mar. 1808; J. Homan, 21 Mar. 1808 (S.P.O., S.O.C.P.2, 1808/34); H. Cole, 10 June 1810; D. Mahon, 14 June 1810 (S.P.O., S.O.C.P.2, 1810/37).

91. Lord Ikerrin, 2 June 1813 (S.P.O., S.O.C.P.2, 1813/39).

to absorb the entire young male poor, and in much of Waterford and south Tipperary they may have come close to achieving this.[92] There were no apparent geographical limits to such ambitions; the successful establishment of the movement in one area was followed by raiding into the next. They intended, it seems, to bring about an all-embracing union of the poor and the general imposition of their alternative system.

Particularly impressive were the persistent attempts of the main gangs to convert new districts to their laws and to stimulate the formation of local groups. Some of the Waterford gangs seem to have been primarily concerned with these aims, such as the Carrick-area Caravats around Waterford city and the Knockboy gang in the Cappoquin-Dungarvan region.[93] In west Kilkenny most disturbances were in fact the work of Tipperary emissaries until late 1810. The unrest began with raids by the combined Fethard and Mullinahone gangs in the Callan and Kilmaganny areas in the spring of 1808. They attacked several grabbers and informed local people that they had "come to introduce new laws among them."[94] Shortly thereafter, another Tipperary band attacked several people around Kilmanagh and left a notice from "Sir John Doe, governor of Munster," warning that "my rules in the County Tipperary must stand good in the County Kilkenny."[95] Further south, evictions on the Bessborough estate led to the joint intervention of the Carrick and Windgap gangs. As he departed from one grabber's house, the Carrick leader exclaimed, "Did you suppose there were no Caravats in this country?"[96] When a local movement finally blossomed, the Tipperary boys simply extended their operations into north and east Kilkenny.[97]

Much effort and organization went into these activities. Raiders covered impressive distances, considering that they often had to rendezvous, steal horses, reach their destination, attack offenders or recruit new members, and ride back, all in one night. Journeys totaling 30 to 60 miles were normal; Kilmaganny is 30 miles from Fethard and 15 from Mullinahone, and Waterford city is 15 miles from Carrick. A Caravat party surprised by soldiers near Holycross in 1810 consisted of men from Newinn,

92. S.P.O., S.O.C.P.1, 1230/50; General N. Waller, 26 Oct. 1807 (S.P.O., S.O.C.P.2, 1807/34); Brigade-Major B. Gahan, 30 Nov. 1808 (S.P.O., S.O.C.P.2, 1808/35).
93. See section IV of this essay.
94. S.P.O., S.O.C.P.1, 1193/9, 12, 14; Brigade-Major J. Ormsby, 13, 14 Mar. 1808; J. Homan, 21 Mar. 1808 (S.P.O., S.O.C.P.2, 1808/34).
95. J. Strangeways, 20 June 1808 (S.P.O., S.O.C.P.2, 1808/34).
96. Brigade-Major J. Ormsby, 1 Aug. 1810 (S.P.O., S.O.C.P.2, 1810/36); J. B. Elliot, 9 July 1810 (S.P.O., S.O.C.P.2, 1810/37); Kernan, *Special commission*, pp. 65–87.
97. S.P.O., S.O.C.P.1, 1275/18; 1381/42, 45, 48, 51–2; H. Wyngard, 4 Jan. 1811 (S.P.O., S.O.C.P.2, 1811/37). With respect to the domination of Kilkenny unrest by emissaries from Tipperary, see also S.P.O., S.O.C.P.1, 1228/8–10; 1230/79; 1275/16; 1277/19.

15 miles away, and Clonmel, 30 miles away.[98] Such operations often mobilized considerable numbers, who then split into smaller raiding parties at their destination. The first raids from Tipperary into Kilkenny involved large bands of 300 to 400 men, while the Holycross party was estimated at 150, and another in County Waterford at no fewer than 3,000.[99] Perhaps most striking of all is the patience that the Caravats displayed — the dogged persistence with which they battered away at areas like west Kilkenny for years, and the careful explanation of their aims before tendering the oath. Indeed, it is possible that they rarely resorted to compulsion to gain recruits. There is certainly little evidence that they practiced the kind of wholesale forcible enrollment, often involving entire communities, favored by many Whiteboy movements.[100]

Recruiters did not rely on nocturnal tactics alone. Fairs and other public gatherings offered unparalleled opportunities for winning adherents, and both factions, particularly the Caravats, attended them like military recruiting parties. They paraded in force, firing shots and yelling slogans, sometimes led by musicians, and afterward dispersed to the pubs to explain their aims and administer their oath. After Ballykerogue fair in 1807 many Caravats stayed behind for days to enlist new members.[101] When both factions assembled at the same fair, violence inevitably erupted. And both often did gather, if only to thwart the other side. Of course, known Caravats and Shanavests were going to clash at public assemblies anyway; they were going to attend in numbers for protection; and given the special intensity of class hatreds, the subsequent fights were bound to be extremely bitter. But the close association of Caravat-Shanavest faction fights with recruiting efforts explains much of the unprecedented frequency, violence, and organization of these encounters.

Fights probably took place at most fairs and other large public gatherings in south Tipperary throughout the period 1806–11. Encounters were apparently just as frequent in County Waterford during 1807 and 1808, and in west Kilkenny during 1810. Hundreds of men usually took part, sometimes thousands, and in 1808 the Caravats challenged the Shanavests to an Armageddon at Kilgobnet fair in Waterford, which was to

98. General J. Lee, 21 Sept., 1 Oct. 1810 (S.P.O., S.O.C.P.2, 1810/37); Kernan, *Special commission*, pp. 26–8.

99. Commander of the Forces Office, 27 Oct. 1807; Brigade-Major J. Ormsby, 13, 14 Mar. 1808 (S.P.O., S.O.C.P.2, 1807–8/34).

100. S.P.O., S.O.C.P.1, 1121/49; 1230/50; 1277/87. One County Waterford report, however, speaks of attacks on "all those who refuse to take the oath" (Brigade-Major B. Gahan, 30 Nov. 1808 [S.P.O., S.O.C.P.2, 1808/35]).

101. S.P.O., S.O.C.P.1, 1121/61; 1275/17; 1277/52, 79; O. Latham, 17 July 1810 (S.P.O., S.O.C.P.2, 1810/37).

have pitted the entire strength of both factions. It was prevented by the military after faint hearts on both sides secretly disclosed the plan.[102] A whole new range of lethal weaponry was brought into play during these years. The traditional faction stick was replaced by the ash plant weighted with lead and called a *clogh alpeen*. This was supplemented by ingenious homemade swords and spears and by whatever firearms could be mustered. Particularly favored was the sawed-off shotgun, easily concealed and deadly at close quarters.[103] Some smiths developed a profitable sideline in making and repairing weapons; deserters and veterans were enlisted to give military training.[104] The robbery of arms became a veritable mania, especially in the weeks before a major fight. Parties entered the homes of absent parsons and gentlemen on Sunday mornings and fair days; guns were wrested from marching soldiers, sentries, lone sportsmen, and travelers; and in November 1810 the Caravats held up the Cork mail coach near Cashel simply to steal the guards' arms.[105] Not surprisingly, most fights ended in several deaths; as many as twenty people were killed at the May fair of Golden in 1807.[106] Altogether, literally hundreds must have died.

VIII

Information on the Shanavests is sparse, though consistent. They seem to have been formed at about the same time as the Caravats, in the autumn of 1806. The little that is known of the confederating bands suggests that Shanavestism was originally based on the remnants of the United Irish movement, and that the Caravat-Shanavest conflict absorbed several existing feuds between Whiteboys and middle-class political-cum-

102. S.P.O., S.O.C.P.1, 1188/58, 62; 1207/63; 1277/79; 1386/81, 88; E. Elliot, 27, 28 Dec. 1808 (S.P.O., S.O.C.P.2, 1808/35); Brigade-Major R. Bushe, 1 Aug. 1810 (S.P.O., S.O.C.P.2, 1810/36).

103. S.P.O., S.O.C.P.1, 1121/34, 49, 61; 1228/8; 1277/10; 1381/56; T. Prendergast, 14 May 1808; J. B. Elliot, 5 Dec. 1807 (S.P.O., S.O.C.P.2, 1807–8/34); Brigade-Major R. Crawford, 28 Nov. 1808 (S.P.O., S.O.C.P.2, 1808/35).

104. S.P.O., S.O.C.P.1, 1188/54; 1193/12; 1230/69–70; 1386/14, 17, 24; 1387/38; Brigade-Major R. Crawford, 28 Nov. 1808 (S.P.O., S.O.C.P.2, 1808/35).

105. S.P.O., S.O.C.P.1, 1188/55; 1207/65, 73; 1228/16; 1230/48, 50; 1275/14; 1277/52–6, 64–6, 68–72, 76, 81–9; General H. Wyngard, 4 Oct. 1809 (S.P.O., S.O.C.P.2, 1809/36); J. Strangeways, 3 Jan. 1811 (S.P.O., S.O.C.P.2, 1811/38); Kernan, *Special commission*, pp. 7–19.

106. S.P.O., S.O.C.P.1, 1227/27; J. Trail, 3 Aug. 1807; Sergeant A. Moore, 15 Dec. 1807 (S.P.O., S.O.C.P.2, 1807/33–4); Brigade-Major R. Crawford, 29 Feb. 1808 (S.P.O., S.O.C.P.2, 1808/35); General J. Lee, 1 July 1810; R. Sadleir, 5 Dec. 1810 (S.P.O., S.O.C.P.2, 1810/36–7).

vigilante groups.[107] In most places, however, Shanavest bodies were no doubt formed later, in direct response to Caravat activity.[108]

It is not clear how extensive the Shanavest movement was. The groups around Knockboy, Ardfinnan, Carrick, Fethard, Mullinahone, Ballingarry, Whitechurch, and Modeligo are the only ones definitely known, though there must have been others.[109] These districts were Caravat strongholds too, and only near Whitechurch and Modeligo do the Shanavests seem to have dominated, though they certainly held their own in the vicinity of Ballingarry. They were clearly the weaker of the two movements and usually lost on the faction field. This is not surprising. As the party of the poor, the Caravats were almost inevitably more numerous.[110]

The organization of the Shanavests was probably more formal than that of the Caravats. The Whitechurch gang, for example, was led by a committee of fourteen.[111] One faction actually entered the names of new recruits in books at Modeligo pattern in 1807; it was probably the Shanavests, as this was one of their stronger districts.[112] Of their supralocal organization only a few things are known: they had an oath and elaborate passwords on the United Irish model;[113] they were capable of effective mass mobilization for fights; and Paudeen Gar remained some sort of overall leader, though perhaps a purely symbolic one.[114]

Also known are the occupations of twenty-eight members: a carpenter,

---

107. Between 1802 and 1805 there was an upsurge of faction fighting in many areas soon to be affected by the Caravat-Shanavest conflict; it was characterized by the same novel ultraviolence. A little is known about three of these feuds; all pitted Whiteboys against nationalists, and all were absorbed by the Caravat-Shanavest conflict. See section III of this essay (Moyle Rangers versus Paudeen Gar's Boys) and section X (Blakes versus Quaids; Dingers versus Dowsers). See also S.P.O., S.O.C.P.1, 1021/3, 1026/6 (north Cork, 1802–4); 1030/66, 1091/40 (Callan, 1804–6); S. Prendergast, 23 Mar. 1806 (S.P.O., S.O.C.P.2, 1806/32) (east Limerick, 1805–6).

108. See, e.g., Brigade-Major J. Rogers, 30 Aug. 1807; Commander of the Forces Office, 9 Oct. 1807 (S.P.O., S.O.C.P.2, 1807/33–4).

109. S.P.O., S.O.C.P.1, 1188/56; 1230/9, 48; 1386/4, 42; J. Homan, 21 Mar. 1808, E. Elliot, Nov.–Dec. 1808; C. F. Musgrave, 30 Nov. 1808 (S.P.O., S.O.C.P.2, 1808/34–5); Brigade-Major B. Gahan, 23 Jan., 4 Apr. 1809 (S.P.O., S.O.C.P.2, 1809/36); U.C.D., I.F.C., MS S637, pp. 57–8.

110. S.P.O., S.O.C.P.1, 1188/53, 62; 1193/10; 1384/16; 1386/44, 48, 51, 61; U.C.D., I.F.C., MS S562, pp. 204–9.

111. E. Elliot, 28 Nov., 4 Dec. 1808 (S.P.O., S.O.C.P.2, 1808/35).

112. Brigade-Major J. Rogers, 30 Aug. 1807 (S.P.O., S.O.C.P.2, 1807/33).

113. S.P.O., S.O.C.P.1, 1120/81; 1230/47; 1382/60; 1723/1–2; 1771/6.

114. J. Homan, 21 Mar. 1808 (S.P.O., S.O.C.P.2, 1808/34); Kernan, *Special commission*, p. 31; *Historical notices of the several rebellions, disturbances, and illegal associations in Ireland from the earliest period to the year 1822* . . . (Dublin, 1822), p. 49.

a yeoman, a policeman, four laborers, and twenty-one farmers. The policeman and nineteen of the farmers were leaders; of these nineteen, fourteen made up the Whitechurch committee and were described as belonging to "the first class of farmers, worth £200 a year." This pattern stands in stark contrast to the proletarian Caravats and their spalpeen leadership, though it is interesting that the Shanavests enlisted some laborers. Presumably, these included strangers seeking protection and others who simply adhered to the party of their employers or of richer relatives. In certain districts political consciousness was undoubtedly an important factor in enabling the Shanavests to attract support from laborers. Shanavest strength in Modeligo and Ballingarry lay in the traditional nationalism of sections of the local poor, including many of the Ballingarry miners.[115]

The main practical function of the Shanavests was probably vigilantism. Apart from faction fighting and arms raids, their only recorded crimes were a series of murders and assaults directed against prominent Caravats.[116] The only Shanavest arms raid well documented in contemporary sources was a spectacular sweep through the Portlaw-Kilmeadan area; it involved several gangs who talked as if they were disarming the district rather than arming themselves. Since this was a notable Caravat stronghold, they probably were.[117] These murders and assaults, and the apparent disarming of a district, had no Caravat parallels, and it is interesting that they all occurred by day, as if the Shanavests believed that their violence was somehow less illegal.

A magistrate who interrogated the Whitechurch committee found its members adamant that their only aim was "to defend themselves against the Caravats."[118] They had every reason to do so. For years — even before the formation of the Caravats — the richer farmers of this district had been liable to serious Whiteboy violence, involving repeated invasions by the Knockboy gang in support of the local Whiteboys.[119] Shanavest domination temporarily brought peace, but within days of meekly

115. These figures have been compiled from S.O.C.P.1 and 2, Oct. 1806–Jan. 1811. For the Whitechurch committee, see E. Elliot, 4 Dec. 1808 (S.P.O., S.O.C.P.1, 1188/62); Elliot, Nov.–Dec. 1808 (S.P.O., S.O.C.P.2, 1808/35). For Modeligo and Ballingarry, see U.C.D., I.F.C., MS S562, pp. 204–9; MS S637, pp. 57–8; Sir Richard Musgrave, *Memoirs of the different rebellions in Ireland from the arrival of the English* . . . (Dublin, 1801), app. xi, pp. 32, 49.

116. S.P.O., S.O.C.P.1, 1188/56; 1230/48; 1386/51; 1409/34; J. Homan, 21 Mar. 1808 (S.P.O., S.O.C.P.2, 1808/34).

117. S.P.O., S.O.C.P.1, 1230/67–8.

118. E. Elliot, 4 Dec. 1808 (S.P.O., S.O.C.P.1, 1188/62).

119. See S.P.O., S.O.C.P.1, 1018/23; 1020/10, 43–8, 52B; 1031/82; 1091/78, 81; 1121/14 (1799–1806); S.O.C.P.2, 31–452 (1801). See also fn. 37.

surrendering their arms to a magistrate, the Shanavests were again subjected to raids from Knockboy. The local Whiteboys were able to grow
unchecked, and by 1815 the Whitechurch Caravats were one of the most
formidable gangs in County Waterford.[120]
    All these examples of vigilantism occurred in the winter of 1808–9.
Subsequently, the Shanavests seem to have resorted to the cruder tactic
of informing. At least one major prosecution of Caravats at the special
commission of 1811 was pursued by admitted Shanavests. One of them
made a habit of such activities, for in 1815 he applied to the government
for a reward as a long-standing and frequent informer.[121] The four men
who prosecuted the Knockboy gang in 1809 may have been Shanavests
too. All came from around Knockboy, where the Shanavests certainly
maintained a rival presence, and there is evidence linking three of the
four with an underground political movement; one was arrested in Clare
in 1817 as the emissary of a nationalist organization, and the other two
were former United Irishmen, still known locally as "the two croppies,"
one of whom had been prosecuted as recently as 1808 for possessing arms
illegally.[122] Perhaps the Shanavests were also responsible for an anonymous letter that named the leaders of the Kilmeadan Caravats; it bore
the suspiciously patriotic pseudonym "John Irishman."[123]

IX

    It may seem odd that many people felt the need for an anti-Whiteboy
secret society. Why did they not rely on the state for protection? Presumably, the political and religious alienation of the middle class from the
state inclined them to look to their own resources. This alienation was
particularly intense in Tipperary and Waterford in the years following
1798. People who had endured the indiscriminate white terror of Thomas
Judkin Fitzgerald and Sir Richard Musgrave were not going to turn to
authority for protection. On the contrary, they were likely to be responsive to nationalist ideas; the situation, in fact, was particularly ripe for
the emergence of a movement like the Shanavests. In addition, there were
serious limits to the ability of any contemporary state to offer protection
when faced with the solidarity of whole communities and the absence
of an effective police force. The fate of informers is particularly instructive. One of the witnesses against the Knockboy gang had to be kept in

protective custody for seven years. Witnesses before the commission of
1811 were repeatedly attacked, and three were still under military guard
in 1813. Two more had left the area, one for a government job in Dublin, where he was desperately unhappy.[124]

In Ireland the inherent weaknesses of the contemporary state were
greatly aggravated by the peculiar attitudes of the gentry. The pattern
was the same in most agrarian outbreaks: some gentlemen do not seem
to have cared what was going on, others were too scared to resist, and
some basically sympathized with the Whiteboys. The few activists among
the gentry were too often anti-Catholic paranoids who scarcely differentiated between the Whiteboys and their victims, and terrorized the population indiscriminately. Thus agrarian disturbances that could have been
contained at their onset were frequently allowed to reach a level where
the central government had little choice but to intervene.

By 1810 it was clear that such a point had been reached in east Munster.
In many areas gangs had been stirring every night for months.[125] Most
fairs were disrupted by pitched battles, and there were frequent brawls
and murders in pubs and on the highways.[126] Thousands of young men
had been sworn in, and the whole popular culture of the region infected;
there were Caravat and Shanavest pubs, mummers' teams, wren-boys,
songs, and dance tunes.[127] Most ominous of all, the expansion of both
movements had become increasingly vigorous and successful. During the
winter of 1809–10 Caravatism finally spread into Gaultiere, and by the
following summer local Caravat and Shanavest groups had blossomed
at last in west Kilkenny.[128] In the same period came the first definite
reports of the two movements in west Tipperary, east Limerick, and

124. S.P.O., S.O.C.P.1, 1230/80; 1277/91, 98–9, 102; 1386/52; 1387/6, 29, 38, 45, 53;
1540/20–55; 1834/49.

125. S.P.O., S.O.C.P.1, 1275/8, 13; 1277/89; General H. Wyngard, 4 Oct. 1809, 3 Nov.
1810; Brigade-Major J. Ormsby, 4 Sept. 1810 (S.P.O., S.O.C.P.2, 1809–10/36); R. Creaghe,
17 Sept. 1810; O. Latham, 29 Dec. 1810 (S.P.O., S.O.C.P.2, 1810/37).

126. S.P.O., S.O.C.P.1, 1188/56; 1230/48; 1227/19; J. Homan, 21 Mar. 1808 (S.P.O.,
S.O.C.P.2, 1808/34); J. Strangeways, 3 Jan. 1811 (S.P.O., S.O.C.P.2, 1811/38).

127. S.P.O., S.O.C.P.1, 1275/21; 1386/42; J. Evans, Apr. 1810 (S.P.O., S.O.C.P.2,
1810/37); U.C.D., I.F.C., MS S563, pp. 171–3; O'Donnell, Faction fighters, pp. 24, 48–9,
65; Ó Muireadhaigh, "Na Carabhait," pp. 11–12. Many Caravat and Shanavest tunes are
still popular among traditional musicians: e.g., "The high caul cap," "The Coolrus reel,"
"The old vest and cravat" (or "John Doe"), "The Caravat jig" (better known as "The rakes
of Kildare"), and "The Shanavest jig" (better known as "Donnybrook fair" or "Joy of my
life").

128. S.P.O., S.O.C.P.1, 1275/7–27; 1277/87; General J. Lee, 1 July 1810; Brigade-Major
J. Ormsby, 4 Sept. 1810 (S.P.O., S.O.C.P.2, 1810/36); E. Littlehales, 13 June 1810; Lord
Ikerrin, 11 June 1810; J. B. Elliot, 9 July 1810 (S.P.O., S.O.C.P.2, 1810/37).

north Cork, their first forays into north Tipperary, and even some evidence of isolated Shanavest activity in Kerry.[129] By late 1810 Tipperary
raiders had touched Killaloe on the Clare side of the Shannon, the first
signs of the conflict had appeared in the Queen's County-Kilkenny border region, Caravat emissaries had penetrated east Kilkenny, and in early
1811 there were vague reports of both movements from the long disturbed Wexford-Carlow border country.[130] In January 1811 Caravatism
even touched Kildare, where a band of Tipperary spalpeens, annoyed
at the posting of a reward by some people whom they had robbed, issued
a rival notice directed against "land jobbers" and "their glittering gold"
and signed "Cornet Caravat."[131]

The heartland of the movement was flooded with soldiers. By December 1810 there were more troops in the region than in 1798, patrolling
the roads, attending fairs, and sweeping whole districts for arms and
offenders.[132] The government considered imposing the insurrection act
and martial law, but rejected this course in favor of sending stipendiary
magistrates and professional spies to prepare for a major special commission;[133] it opened on 1 February 1811. Forty men from the three counties
of Tipperary, Waterford, and Kilkenny were tried: twenty of them were
sentenced to be executed, and seventeen to be transported, flogged, or
imprisoned, while only three were acquitted.[134] After the free hand enjoyed by the factions for years, the effect was dramatic. The original

129. See section X of this essay; see also S.P.O., S.O.C.P.1, 1230/47; General H. Wyngard,
4 Oct. 1809 (S.P.O., S.O.C.P.2, 1809/36); General J. Lee, 21 Sept., 1 Oct. 1810 (S.P.O.,
S.O.C.P.2, 1810/37). In north Kerry a magistrate seized a copy of a Shanavest-type oath,
political and sectarian in nature and forbidding involvement in Whiteboy activity. It had
apparently been introduced from County Limerick, where there was of course a Shanavest
presence, and it employed the traditional east Munster pseudonym "John Doe" — the only
case I have found of its use outside south Tipperary, west Kilkenny, and Waterford. Though
the pseudonym was usually associated with the Caravats, there is no reason why the Shanavests should not have adopted this customary regional name.
130. S.P.O., S.O.C.P.1, 1275/18; 1381/6-7, 42-5, 48, 51-2, 54-5; 1382/39-50, 60, 73,
79, 82-3; Colonel J. Vandeleur, 19 Oct. 1810; H. Wyngard, 4 Jan. 1811 (S.P.O., S.O.C.P.2,
1810-11/37); T. Prior, 15 Jan. 1811 (S.P.O., S.O.C.P.2, 1811/38).
131. S.P.O., S.O.C.P.1, 1381/27-9, 31-5.
132. General J. Floyd, 8 Aug. 1810; "Letters relative to military aid" (S.P.O., S.O.C.P.2,
1810/37); Kernan, *Special commission*, p. 14.
133. S.P.O., S.O.C.P.1, 1275/16; 1277/80, 110; R. Willcocks, 23 Nov. 1810; General
H. Wyngard, 3 Dec. 1810; bishop of Elphin, 2 Oct. 1810 (S.P.O., S.O.C.P.2, 1810/37).
134. S.P.O., S.O.C.P.1, 1386/4; Whitworth, "Disturbances," pp. 402-3; Kernan, *Special
commission*, passim. Inevitably, the prisoners were mostly Caravats, charged with various
Whiteboy offenses. As far as one can tell, only two Shanavests were tried, and one of them
was acquitted.

Caravat-Shanavest outbreak collapsed. Yet this was far from the end of the two movements.

X

The Caravat and Shanavest movements had existed from the start in a distinct second region: west Tipperary, east Limerick, and northeast Cork. Unfortunately, they were extremely clandestine in this second region, one reason for excluding it from our study so far. One cannot even be sure precisely what areas were affected or when. Yet it is probable that both movements were stronger and more extensive here than has been realized.

The situation is clearest in west Tipperary. The two movements could be found around the villages of Bansha and Cappaghwhite from an early date. The initial oath of 1806 was reported from both districts, and they were persistently disturbed afterward, even if no document mentions either movement by name until 1816.[135] Reports of new oaths and faction fighting suggest that the conflict reached Tipperary town and the Golden-Dundrum area in 1807, though there were no further reports of violence and no mention of either movement by name until 1810.[136] In the winter of 1809–10 both movements certainly spread into the Newport-Killaloe district.[137] Since other parts of west Tipperary were quiet, this was probably the full extent of Caravat-Shanavest penetration.

In Limerick and Cork the situation is more obscure. Written sources contain no direct reference to the existence of either movement before 1809 or outside two small areas close to the Tipperary border—around Pallas, Kilteely, Knocklong, and Caherconlish in Limerick, and around Doneraile, Charleville, and Mitchelstown in Cork.[138] But since the oath

135. S.P.O., S.O.C.P.1, 1120/81; 1121/2; 1771/6; Brigade-Major R. Crawford, 1 Nov. 1806; General J. Floyd, 1 Dec. 1806 (S.P.O., S.O.C.P.2, 1806/32); General H. Wyngard, 28 Dec. 1809 (S.P.O., S.O.C.P.2, 1809/36). The Shanavests may have been stronger than usual around Bansha and Cappaghwhite because of the popular appeal of nationalism there.

136. S.P.O., S.O.C.P.1, 1120/81; 1277/53–6, 65–6, 70–2; 1279/11; 1386/49, 88; J. Trail, 3 Aug. 1807 (S.P.O., S.O.C.P.2, 1807/33); General J. Floyd, 8 Aug. 1810; R. Sadleir, 5 Dec. 1810; N. Wayland, 10 Aug. 1810 (S.P.O., S.O.C.P.2, 1810/37); Select committee on disturbances, 1825, p. 113.

137. S.P.O., S.O.C.P.1, 1277/45–7; J. Evans, [?] Apr., 11 Apr. 1810; Colonel J. Vandeleur, 19, 31 Oct. 1810 (S.P.O., S.O.C.P.2, 1810/37); General J. Affleck, 1 Oct. 1810 (S.P.O., S.O.C.P.2, 1810/36).

138. S.P.O., S.O.C.P.1, 1277/22; 1385/2–3; Brigade-Major H. Croker, 28 Sept. 1810; General J. Floyd, 1 Dec. 1810 (S.P.O., S.O.C.P.2, 1810/36); Lewis, Disturbances, p. 203; W. R. Le Fanu, Seventy years of Irish life (London, 1893), p. 33; O'Donnell, Faction fighters, pp. 48–9.

of 1806 was widely taken in Limerick, and was probably taken in Cork, it seems that the conflict was present from the start.[139] Exactly where the oath was sworn is unknown, but there was a parallel upsurge of Whiteboyism and new-style ultraviolent factionism over much of east Limerick and north Cork, extending as far west as Croom. This upsurge was viewed in official quarters as a series of purely local feuds and unrelated Whiteboy outbreaks. But oral tradition in the Croom area confirms that in this district at least, it marked the introduction of the infant Caravat and Shanavest movements. The new organizations apparently absorbed a long-standing feud similar to that between the Moyle Rangers and Paudeen Gar's Boys, this one pitting the Blakes, a notorious Whiteboy clan, against the Quaids, who were rich farmers, United Irishmen, and anti-Whiteboy vigilantes.[140] Moreover, while reports only occasionally refer to Caravats and Shanavests by name, there is no specific mention of other Whiteboy, faction, or underground political organizations anywhere in east Limerick, north Cork, or west Tipperary between 1806 and 1818. And yet disturbances were of a scale usually associated with a major regional movement. Two other names do crop up, but, like the Blakes and Quaids, these appear to have been Caravat or Shanavest aliases. There are several references from various districts in this region, as far apart as Newport, Golden, Doneraile, and Kilteely, to Whiteboys styling themselves Blue Belt Boys. This was apparently a regional name for the Caravats. It occurred only in areas and periods of Caravat activity, and several accounts directly identified the Blue Belts with the Caravats.[141] In 1807 a new group called the Liberty Rangers was reported from Cappaghwhite and Tipperary town. Given the evidence of Caravat and Shanavest penetration of both districts at this time, and the political overtones of the designation, possibly parodying the Moyle Rangers, this was probably a local name for the Shanavests.[142] The evidence is limited, but it certainly raises the possibility that there was Caravat-Shanavest domination of unrest in this region from an early date.

The development of the two movements after 1811, both here and elsewhere, is even more obscure. There is no doubt of their continued

---

139. See section IV of this essay; see also Commander of the Forces Office, 27 Oct. 1807 (S.P.O., S.O.C.P.2, 1807/34).

140. S.P.O., S.O.C.P.1, 1020/24–5; 1080/32A; 1091/26; S. Prendergast, 23 Mar. 1806; Commander of the Forces Office, 3 Nov. 1806; General J. Floyd, 8 Dec. 1806 (S.P.O., S.O.C.P.2, 1806/32); U.C.D., I.F.C., MS S506, pp. 381–4, 448–9, 516–17; MS S525, pp. 131–2.

141. S.P.O., S.O.C.P.1, 1385/2; 1836/19; J. Evans, 11 Apr. 1810; E. Littlehales, 13 June 1810; J. B. Elliot, 9 July 1810; N. Wayland, 10 Aug. 1810 (S.P.O., S.O.C.P.2, 1810/37).

142. S.P.O., S.O.C.P.1, 1120/81.

existence. In south Tipperary and west Kilkenny the impact of the special commission was devastating. For several years the only disturbances here were the bandit activities of those on the run. But both movements persisted much as before in County Waterford, and the Caravats even expanded into southeast Cork. Around 1812 and 1813 the feud suddenly erupted again in those areas proselytized (usually with little apparent impact) between 1809 and 1811, and by 1815 there were even signs of its revival in south Tipperary. By the 1820s the Caravats and Shanavests probably extended through much of Tipperary, Waterford, east Limerick, east Cork, south Queen's County, as well as north and west Kilkenny; they had also made inroads into Carlow, Wexford, King's County, and perhaps west Limerick and north Kerry. The two movements appear to have maintained some sort of presence in most of these areas at least up to the famine. But only between 1811 and 1816 in Waterford, east Cork, and the Queen's County-Kilkenny border region was this presence obvious. Elsewhere both movements were now so clandestine that the authorities were hardly aware of their continued existence. The names Caravat and Shanavest sometimes appeared in official correspondence, but they were thought to reflect only isolated and insignificant survivals.[143] By compiling scattered information, particularly from oral tradition, a different picture begins to emerge.

It seems that open feuding was largely pursued under a series of regional names. Between 1809 and 1811 the two factions had penetrated north Tipperary, absorbing a major local feud, which dated back to 1804, between Whiteboys and a nationalist faction. In 1815 those involved either adopted new names or resurrected their original labels. The local Caravats now usually called themselves Dowsers, while the Shanavests called themselves Dingers, though they sometimes fought as Ryans versus Dwyers or as Bootashees versus Bogboys.[144] From 1818 until the famine a major feud between two factions styling themselves the Three Year Olds and Four Year Olds persistently disturbed large areas of Tipperary, Limerick, and Cork; the feud may even have penetrated into north Kerry. According to tradition, this feud was a conscious revival of the Caravat and Shanavest movements, involving the same people and the continued secondary use of the older names. Tradition has less to say about the nature of the feud, but the Caravat Three Year Olds

143. See S.P.O., S.O.C.P.1, 1406/22–3; 1721/42; 1761/38.

144. S.P.O., S.O.C.P.1, 1277/58–9; 1386/17; 1721/42, 89; 1722/53; 1723/1–2; 1960/5, 10, 14, 19; General H. Wyngard, 4 Oct. 1809 (S.P.O., S.O.C.P.2, 1809/36); General J. Lee, 21 Sept., 1 Oct. 1810 (S.P.O., S.O.C.P.2, 1810/37); Lewis, *Disturbances*, pp. 288–9. The leader of the Dinger-Shanavests was called "Bootashee" Ryan.

apparently remained Whiteboys.[145] Between 1811 and 1813 the White-boys of the Wexford-Carlow border country federated with the Caravats but retained their original name of Moll Doyle's Children. When the Shanavests organized here, they fought under an older name too: Pau-deen Gar's Men.[146] In County Waterford, Caravats and Shanavests some-times fought as Polleens and Gows, though the original names remained more popular.[147] The use of aliases in these cases inevitably raises suspi-cions about the possible Caravat-Shanavest connections of other feuds in east Munster and south Leinster between 1811 and 1845. In fact, there are prima facie grounds for investigating all the major ones. For exam-ple, the Coffees and Ruskavellas of Limerick and northwest Tipperary occupied more or less those areas where the Caravats and Shanavests had been reported by name in the years 1809–11, and the Ruskavellas appear to have been Whiteboys.[148] The Black Hens and Magpies of north Tipperary operated around Borrisoleigh, where there were occasional reports of Caravats and Shanavests; again, the Black Hens were prob-ably Whiteboys.[149] The famous feud between the Whitefeet and Black-feet in the late 1820s and early 1830s raged through parts of Queen's County and Kilkenny (where the last major disturbances had been the Caravat and Shanavest movements of 1811–16), and through the south-ern portion of King's County (where a Caravat oath was certainly circu-lating in the 1820s). Tradition indicates that the feud pitted an insurgent Whiteboy movement against a middle-class nationalist and vigilante organization.[150]

Until more research is done, we can only speculate on the real extent of the later Caravat and Shanavest movements, and on their relation-ship to these feuds and to the Whiteboy and underground political un-rest, which tended to rise and fall in the same districts at the same times. At present we cannot even be sure how far the later manifestations of

145. O'Donnell, *Faction fighters*, pp. 24–5, 48–9; U.C.D., I.F.C., MS S505, p. 164; MS S506, pp. 326–30, 360, 394–8, 509; MS S507, pp. 93, 120, 209.

146. S.P.O., S.O.C.P.1, 1381/6; 1382/60, 73, 79, 82–3; 1559/27; Brigade-Major O. Moore, 10 Sept. 1813 (S.P.O., S.O.C.P.2, 1813/40); *Historical notices*, p. 49; Broehl, *Molly Maguires*, p. 26.

147. U.C.D., I.F.C., MS S637, pp. 57–8.

148. Lewis, *Disturbances*, pp. 107, 288; Le Fanu, *Seventy years*, pp. 33–7. Interest-ingly enough, one of the Shanavest leaders in west Tipperary and east Limerick in 1811 was called Coffee (S.P.O., S.O.C.P.1, 1386/88).

149. S.P.O., S.O.C.P.1, 1277/58–9; U.C.D., I.F.C., MS S544, p. 219; MS S538, p. 235; MS S551, p. 212; Lewis, *Disturbances*, p. 107.

150. U.C.D., I.F.C., MS 98, pp. 162–6; MS 700, p. 275; MS S831, p. 527; MS S833, p. 50; MS 1240, pp. 82, 161, 299–300; *Select committee . . . insurrection act, 1825*, pp. 105–10.

the two movements conformed to the battle lines of the original feud. On the one hand, when reports mention Caravats by name, it is generally as Whiteboys, and when they mention Shanavests, it is usually as nationalists.[151] The Dowsers, Moll Doylists, and Whitefeet were primarily Whiteboys, and so probably were the Three Year Olds, Ruskavellas, and Black Hens; the Dingers and Blackfeet were nationalists. On the other hand, commonsense suggests that various factors may eventually have weakened the social base of the feud, especially outside the original heartland. Families must have risen and fallen in the social scale while retaining their initial faction allegiances. Nationalism gained ground among the poor between 1815 and 1845. And the worsening economic condition of the rural middle class after 1813 created a more fertile soil for cooperation across class divisions. Indeed, as early as 1816 Shanavest Whiteboys had emerged around Bansha and Castlecomer, where the popular appeal of nationalism had gained the movement a serious following among the poor.[152]

The development of the two movements after 1845 presents the historian with even greater problems. What information there is comes almost entirely from the sparsely recorded oral traditions of a vanishing generation. These tell us that in parts of Tipperary, Waterford, and Kilkenny people were fighting as Caravats and Shanavests long after the famine, even into the twentieth century.[153] But how extensive these survivals were, and how far they retained the character of the original feud, is almost impossible to determine. Accounts from the Ballingarry and Callan districts suggest that by the late nineteenth century the feud had degenerated into a series of hereditary family hatreds bearing little relationship to the social and political divisions of the period.[154] Yet in County Waterford an old man told Ó Muireadhaigh in the 1960s of how he had seen Caravats acting against grabbers at the turn of the century.[155] This essay has, I hope, answered some of the important questions surrounding the

151. See the State of the country papers for Waterford, Cork, Kilkenny, and Queen's County, 1811–16, when these counties saw major Whiteboy unrest under the Caravat banner. See also S.P.O., S.O.C.P.1, 1559/60; 1771/6; 1960/14.

152. S.P.O., S.O.C.P.1, 1712/20–1; 1771/6. The Castlecomer situation is not totally clear. In north Kilkenny and south Queen's County several maverick gangs, mostly bandits dabbling in Whiteboyism, adopted the names Caravat and Shanavest, often using both simultaneously. The Castlecomer Shanavest Whiteboys may have been such a band. Nevertheless, the Shanavests did have a mass base among the politically conscious Castlecomer miners, and the area was the scene of persistent agrarian disorder. See S.P.O., S.O.C.P.1, 1381/45; 1382/39–50; 1554/36–47; 1563/1–24; 1761/36–8; 1953/2–3, 28.

153. U.C.D., I.F.C., MS 1240, pp. 17, 144, 157; MS S562, pp. 163, 204–9; MS 259, pp. 656–7; MS S637, pp. 57–60; Ó Muireadhaigh, "Na Carabhait," p. 20.

154. U.C.D., I.F.C., MS 1240, pp. 17, 157; MS S562, pp. 163, 204–9.

155. Ó Muireadhaigh, "Na Carabhait," p. 20.

original Caravat-Shanavest conflict of 1806–11, but a number of intriguing questions clearly remain.

BIBLIOGRAPHY

Contemporary sources

Manuscript material
British Library, London
    Peel papers (Add. MS 40202).
Department of Irish Folklore, University College, Dublin
    Irish Folklore Commission MSS 98, 259, 700, 782, 1127, 1210, 1240, 1244,
        S505, S506, S507, S525, S536, S538, S544, S551, S562, S563, S568, S572,
        S585, S637, S831, S833, S852.
State Paper Office, Dublin
    State of the country papers, series 1 and 2 (1799–1820).

Contemporary publications
I. Parliamentary papers (in chronological order)
    *Minutes of evidence taken before the select committee appointed to inquire
        into the disturbances in Ireland, in the last session of parliament, 13 May–18
        June 1824,* H.L. 1825 (37), clxxxviii, 165.
    *Minutes of evidence taken before the select committee of the House of Lords
        appointed to examine into the nature and extent of the disturbances which
        have prevailed in those districts of Ireland which are now subject to the
        provisions of the insurrection act, and to report to the House, 18 May–23
        June 1824,* H.L. 1825 (35), cxc, 1.
    *Third report of evidence from the select committee on the state of the poor
        in Ireland, minutes of evidence, 8 June–7 July, with an appendix of
        documents and papers, and likewise a general index,* H.L. 1830 (14),
        cclxxxvi, 1.

II. Newspapers and periodicals
    Annual Register, 1816 (London, 1817).
    Tipperary Vindicator (Nenagh), 18 June 1845.

III. Other contemporary publications
    Atkinson, A. *The Irish tourist: in a series of picturesque views, travelling
        incidents, and observations, statistical, political, and moral, on the character
        and aspect of the Irish nation* (Dublin, 1815).
    Banim, John. "John Doe" in *Tales of the O'Hara family, part III* (Belfast, 1846).
    Bicheno, J. E. *Ireland and its economy, being the result of observations made
        in a tour through the country in the autumn of 1829* (London, 1830).
    Carr, Sir John. *The stranger in Ireland, or a tour in the southern and western
        part of that country in the year 1805* (London, 1806).

Hall, James. *Tour through Ireland, particularly the interior and least known parts, containing an accurate view of the parties, politics, and improvements in the different provinces, with reflections and observations on the union of Britain and Ireland, the practicability and advantages of a telegraphic communication between the two countries, and other matters of importance*, 2 vols. (London, 1813).

Historical notices of the several rebellions, disturbances, and illegal associations in Ireland from the earliest period to the year 1822, and a view of the actual state of the country, and of the events generating or connected with its past disturbances and present discontented and demoralized situation, with suggestions for the restoration and maintenance of tranquility and for promoting the national prosperity and happiness (Dublin, 1822).

Kernan, Randall. *A report of the trials of the Caravats and Shanavests at the special commission for the several counties of Tipperary, Waterford, and Kilkenny, before the Right Hon. Lord Norbury and the Right Hon. S. O'Gready, commencing at Clonmel on Monday, February 4th, 1811 . . .* (Dublin, 1811).

Le Fanu, W. R. *Seventy years of Irish life* (London, 1893).

Lewis, Sir G. C. *On local disturbances in Ireland, and on the Irish church question* (London, 1836).

Mason, W. S. *A statistical account or parochial survey of Ireland, drawn up from the communications of the clergy*, 3 vols. (Dublin, 1814–19).

Musgrave, Sir Richard. *Memoirs of the different rebellions in Ireland from the arrival of the English, with a particular detail of that which broke out the XXIIId of May, MDCCXCVIII, the history of the conspiracy which preceded it, and the characters of the principal actors in it* (Dublin, 1801).

Tighe, William. *Statistical observations relative to the county of Kilkenny made in the years 1800 & 1801* (Dublin, 1802).

Trotter, John. *Walks through Ireland in the years 1812, 1814, and 1817, described in a series of letters to an English gentleman* (London, 1819).

Wakefield, Edward. *An account of Ireland, statistical and political*, 2 vols. (London, 1812).

Young, Arthur. *Arthur Young's tour in Ireland (1776–1779)*, ed. A. W. Hutton, 2 vols. (London, 1892).

Later works

Writings in Irish studies

Broehl, W. G. *The Molly Maguires* (Cambridge, Mass., 1964).

Broeker, Galen. *Rural disorder and police reform in Ireland, 1812–36* (London and Toronto, 1970).

Cullen, L. M. *An economic history of Ireland since 1660* (London, 1972).

Donnelly, J. S., Jr. "The Rightboy movement, 1785–8" in *Studia Hibernica*, nos. 17–18 (1977–8), pp. 120–202.

Donnelly, J. S., Jr. "The Whiteboy movement, 1761–5" in *Irish Historical Studies*, xxi, no. 81 (Mar. 1978), pp. 20–54.

Freeman, T. W. *Pre-famine Ireland: a study in historical geography* (Manchester, 1957).

McCourt, Desmond. "The rundale system in Ireland" (Ph.D. dissertation, Queen's University, Belfast, 1950).

O'Donnell, Patrick. *The Irish faction fighters of the 19th century* (Dublin, 1975).

Ó Muireadhaigh, Sailbheastar. "Na Carabhait agus na Sean-Bheisteanna" in *Galvia*, viii (1961), pp. 4–20.

Williams, T. D. (ed.). *Secret societies in Ireland* (Dublin and New York, 1973).

3 James S. Donnelly, Jr.

Pastorini and Captain Rock: Millenarianism and Sectarianism in the Rockite Movement of 1821–4

I

During the last twenty or thirty years social scientists have abundantly demonstrated the importance of millenarian beliefs and collective action based on such beliefs in the culture of disparate societies in nearly all parts of the world and in many historical eras. Scholars have also shown that millennialism is an exceedingly complex social phenomenon. At different times the millennium itself has been invested by believers with a great variety of meanings. The agencies considered capable of bringing about the millennium have been both personal (such as living prophets or messiahs) and impersonal (such as unknown kings and dead ancestors), as well as internal or external to a society. Some forms of Christian millenarianism have held that Christ's second coming will precede the millennial period; these fall into the category of premillennialism. Other forms have placed the second advent at the expiration of the millennial period and thus are kinds of postmillennialism. As ideologies of social change, some types of millenarianism have been revolutionary, whereas others have been reformist. Millennial beliefs have appealed to educated or unlearned people, or to both at once, to sections of the middle and upper strata of society or to the lower strata, or again to both at once. Numerous millenarian cults have remained passive in relation to the world around them, but others have become active, turning into, supporting, supplanting, or being absorbed by large-scale social protests or revolutionary movements of a secular character.[1]

1. See especially Peter Worsley, *The trumpet shall sound: a study of "cargo" cults in*

102

Area of the Rockite Movement

Amid all this variety a number of uniformities exist. Scholarly recognition of the extraordinary geographical and temporal diffusion of millennial cults has prompted considerable discussion about general patterns of causation. Although it is invariably admitted that no particular set of social conditions guarantees that a millenarian movement will arise, there is broad, though not universal, agreement on a sociopsychological interpretation of the genesis of activist millennial cults. According to this widely prevailing view, certain kinds of events, social situations, or social processes — specifically, those producing intense individual and collective anxiety, insecurity, and frustration — are especially conducive to the formation and growth of activist millenarian movements.[2]

Among the antecedent predisposing or causative circumstances identified by various scholars, three are of particular relevance to the Irish

Melanesia (2nd ed., New York, 1968), pp. ix–lxix, 221–56; George Shepperson, "The comparative study of millenarian movements" in S. L. Thrupp (ed.), *Millennial dreams in action: studies in revolutionary religious movements* (Schocken Books paperback ed., New York, 1970), pp. 44–52.

2. Norman Cohn, "Medieval millenarism: its bearing on the comparative study of millenarian movements" in Thrupp, *Millennial dreams*, p. 42. See also J. F. C. Harrison, *The second coming: popular millenarianism, 1780–1850* (London and New Brunswick, N.J., 1979), pp. 207–30.

millenarian phenomena considered in this essay. First, disaster or the fear
of catastrophe, such as famine, epidemic disease, or massacre, has been
a recurrent cause of millennial cults that have mobilized masses of people. Second, millenarian movements are likely to emerge in those agrarian societies where peasants are effectively excluded from the political
apparatus of the state and lack secular political organizations of their
own to defend or advance their common interests. And third, activist
millennial cults have tended to flourish in colonial countries, especially
during the early stages of the imposition of imperial regimes or after the
indigenous peoples have incurred repeated defeats in their efforts to resist
foreign domination through secular military or political means.[3] "Central to this form of millenarism," one historian has declared, "is the belief
that the oppressors are about to be cast down, even annihilated, with
the help of supernatural beings."[4]

British imperial domination of Ireland was far from being in its initial
phases during the early decades of the nineteenth century. But in this
period Irish millenarianism was in some respects closely akin to that often
found in colonial contexts, perhaps partly because the savage suppression of the 1798 rebellion and, later, the fall of Napoleon — who was surely
a messianic figure in Ireland — made British rule seem impervious to overthrow by human effort alone. In a provocative and often penetrating
recent article, however, Patrick O'Farrell has attributed the weakness
of millennialism in Ireland before and after 1800 to the strength of anti-
English feeling among the Catholic population. In O'Farrell's opinion
hatred of England and of the English (or Anglo-Irish) in Ireland was a
secular substitute for millennial visions in popular Irish Catholic culture.[5]
Apparently because his general notion of what constitutes millenarianism
is far too specific and restrictive, O'Farrell fails to see that the very hostility
he recognizes as perdurable was at times capable of becoming the keystone
of an Irish Catholic millennialism. The hatred of Catholics for Protestants
and "the English" entered heavily into the millenarian dreams widespread
in Ireland during the revolutionary 1790s.[6] It did so again under different

3. Worsley, *Trumpet*, pp. 227–43; Cohn, "Medieval millenarism," pp. 40–1; Cohn, *The pursuit of the millennium: revolutionary millenarians and mystical anarchists of the middle ages* (rev. ed., New York, 1970), pp. 281–6 and passim.

4. Cohn, "Medieval millenarism," p. 41. See also Michael Adas's excellent study, *Prophets of rebellion: millenarian protest movements against the European colonial order* (Chapel Hill, N.C., 1979).

5. Patrick O'Farrell, "Millenialism, messianism, and utopianism in Irish history" in *Anglo-Irish Studies*, ii (1976), pp. 53–4.

6. J. S. Donnelly, Jr., "Propagating the cause of the United Irishmen" in *Studies*, lxix, no. 273 (Spring 1980), pp. 15–20.

circumstances and in a novel form around 1820. At that time the prophecy on which popular Catholic attention chiefly focused did not herald an imminent second advent. Instead, it was postmillennial; Christ's second coming was not to occur until long after the arrival of a millennium conceived as the obliteration of Protestant heresy and, by extension, the destruction of the Protestant church and state in Ireland.[7] Of course, Irish Catholic country people associated the prospective fulfillment of this prophecy, and similar ones current at the same time, with abolishing economic injustices and taking revenge for historic wrongs. But O'Farrell misleads when he claims that the destruction of Protestantism "was envisaged more as a time of retribution, an end to quite concrete grievances, than the dawning of a new era."[8] In fact, retribution, deliverance from grievances, and the new epoch went hand in hand, all being viewed as integral to the millennium long overdue.

Was there persistent millenarian content to the long succession of regional agrarian revolts in Ireland during the late eighteenth and early nineteenth centuries? Scholars have given a resounding negative to this question. O'Farrell has dismissed millennialism as seemingly irrelevant to agrarian agitation before the great famine: "In the century following the 1760s the popular rebellious elements in Ireland were too remote from their nominal religion, too ignorant of its content, and too consistently opposed by its ministers to entertain any idea of setting their protests in a religious context."[9] Much more guardedly, Joseph Lee has observed, "No genuine millenarian movements, endemic in most peasant societies, swept the Irish countryside, despite attempts to disseminate Pastorini's prophecies in the 1820s."[10] With good reason both O'Farrell and Lee insist on the rational attitudes and behavior of Irish agrarian rebels: O'Farrell refers to "the reactionary pragmatic realism of the Whiteboy phase of Irish turbulence — the 1760s to the 1830s," while Lee stresses the rebels' "limited, concrete, pragmatic programme," the "relentless realism" of the Whiteboy mind.[11] Indeed, in O'Farrell's view the very pervasiveness and effectiveness of agrarian secret societies in prefamine Ireland was one important reason for the lack of resort to millennial ideologies or cults.[12] And as a general explanation of the absence of genuine millenarian movements, O'Farrell's contention is highly persuasive. It constitutes a

7. See below, section III.
8. O'Farrell, "Millenialism," p. 52.
9. Ibid., p. 47.
10. Joseph Lee, "The Ribbonmen" in T. D. Williams (ed.), *Secret societies in Ireland* (Dublin and New York, 1973), p. 33.
11. O'Farrell, "Millenialism," p. 50; Lee, "Ribbonmen," p. 33.
12. O'Farrell, "Millenialism," pp. 49–50.

significant contribution to the comparative study of millennialism in peasant societies.

Yet if the capacity for effective self-defense helps to explain why millenarianism appealed less to Irish country people between 1760 and 1840 than it has to peasants in other countries at various times, the contrast should not be drawn too sharply. Lee and O'Farrell both assume that activist millennial movements, or revolts strongly influenced by millennial ideas, have arisen more often than the facts indicate. It is extremely doubtful that millenarian movements are "endemic in most peasant societies," as Lee alleges.[13] Norman Cohn and other scholars have shown that the medieval West produced numerous millennial cults in both rural and urban settings.[14] In a relatively small number of instances, now perhaps almost too well known, the millennial ideas of the cults spilled over into social protest and rebellion. But as Sylvia Thrupp has written, "In the vast majority of the many hundreds of medieval peasant revolts and urban revolutions on record there is no evidence of any millennial influence."[15]

If it is incorrect to assume that protest movements in peasant societies have regularly been infused with millenarian beliefs, there is also no certainty that when millennial ideas do penetrate the consciousness of those engaged in revolt, the apocalyptic notions displace whatever limited and realistic goals the rebels may earlier have had. At times revolutionary millenarians have no doubt succeeded in substituting their boundless salvationist dreams for the restrained objectives with which social movements have commenced, but on other occasions millennial doctrines, though present, have not become the actual charter of collective action.[16] A particular millenarian vision permeated the Rockite movement of 1821–4, but the immediate goals of the Rockites were not boundless or wildly unrealistic. Nor did the unusual prevalence of apocalyptic notions diminish the practical effectiveness of these agrarian rebels. The realization of their pragmatic aims depended on human agency, while the destruction of Protestantism was seen to hinge mostly on supernatural intervention — certainly a sensible division of labor under the circumstances.

Though millennial ideas did not provide the Rockite movement with a program of action, they served other important purposes. Such beliefs

13. Lee, "Ribbonmen," p. 33.

14. Cohn, *Pursuit of millennium*, passim. See also the essays by Cohn, Howard Kaminsky, and Donald Weinstein in Thrupp, *Millennial dreams*, pp. 31–43, 166–203.

15. S. L. Thrupp, "Millennial dreams in action: a report on the conference discussion" in Thrupp, *Millennial dreams*, p. 23.

16. Cohn, *Pursuit of millennium*, pp. 198–222, 234–51, 284–5; idem, "Medieval millenarism," pp. 37–9. But see also Worsley, *Trumpet*, pp. xxxix–xlii.

helped to rally Catholic country people to the Rockite cause, and to confirm them in their allegiance in the face of severe government repression, by presenting the Protestant establishment in church and state as a doomed edifice on the verge of annihilation. Millennial ideas also performed an additional function. They assisted in integrating within the same movement Catholics whose material interests frequently clashed, namely, landless laborers and cottiers on the one hand and the larger farmers on the other.[17] Acceptance of the prophesied ruin of Protestantism was concentrated among the lowest strata of Catholic rural society, but many middling and some substantial farmers also gave credence to this millennial vision. Though a shared belief in Protestant oppression and its impending destruction was not enough to obliterate class conflict between the Catholic poor and the larger Catholic farmers, anti-Protestant millennialism almost certainly reduced the sharpness of such antagonism.

II

Part of the reason why students of Irish history have undervalued the important role of millenarianism and sectarianism in providing an organizational and ideological basis for the Rockite movement may be that the negative testimony of certain contemporaries has been given far too much weight. A considerable number of contemporaries belonging to the middle and upper classes strongly resisted the notion that anti-Protestant animus figured prominently in the mentality of Rockites or motivated their behavior. Thus a gentleman in the Churchtown district, reporting to Dublin Castle in April 1822 that nearly the whole of County Cork had once again become tranquil, declared flatly that "there was not at any time the slightest tincture of hostility to the government nor any of the spirit of religious bigotry pervading the mass of the community in this county."[18] Although few Protestant clergymen would have credited the Catholic farmers and laborers among whom they lived with quite so much religious tolerance, even some parsons derided the idea that Protestants were considered enemies by the Rockites. Using commonsensical logic, the Rev. John Orpen pointed out in March 1822 that many of his Catholic neighbors had "suffered severely" at Rockite hands, while he — a parson, a small tithe-owner, the occupant of an unguarded house, and a zealous magistrate — had been left unmolested.[19] Even the

17. For a discussion of the integrative function of millennial cults, see Worsley, *Trumpet*, pp. 227–43.
18. Wills G. Crofts to William Gregory, 26 Apr. 1822 (S.P.O., S.O.C.P.1, 2345/65).
19. Rev. John E. Orpen to William Gregory, 4 Mar. 1822 (S.P.O., S.O.C.P.1, 2345/10).

receipt of "a terrible denunciation of Capt[ai]n Rock's vengeance if I persevered in having divine service for the soldiers in Kanturk barracks" failed to shake Orpen's convictions on this point. After mentioning the threat in May 1823, he also observed that "outrages appear in this part of the country to be committed with equal severity on every class, rank, & description of persons. The poorest labourer who infringes on Capt[ain] Rock's laws is treated with as much vengeance as the Protestant gentleman who has the audacity to demand a portion of his rent."[20]

Catholics of superior social status often expressed similar views even more insistently. To them, the anti-Rockite pulpit oratory of priests and their edifying speeches at public executions gave the lie to charges that the agrarian rebels aimed at the destruction of Protestantism and the ascendancy of Catholicism. As the *Dublin Evening Post*, a Catholic paper whose columns were filled with news about the Rockite movement, boasted in February 1822, "There has been scarcely a barony meeting through the counties of Cork, Kerry, Limerick, or any district menaced with disturbance in which the thanks of the resident nobility and gentry have not been voted to the Catholic clergy for their incessant and laborious attention to their duties."[21] The same newspaper was quick to notice the loyal conduct of particular priests, such as Father Prendergast of Ballingarry, Co. Tipperary, who initiated a subscription to rent a barracks for troops in that village, and Father Rochford of Monagay, Co. Limerick, who rushed from his chapel along with some parishioners and assisted in the capture of eight "Lady Rocks" (men dressed in women's clothes) almost red-handed.[22] Individual priests who had been victimized by Rockites for showing hostility to the cause also received publicity.[23]

The sectarian prophecies of Protestant doom in 1825 associated with the name of Pastorini presented a special problem. Many Catholics of standing denied that the country people really believed in these predictions, and scouted the notion that such addled thinking played a significant part in the agrarian strife of the early 1820s. John Dunn, a politically prominent Catholic in Queen's County and a large landholder in the Ballinakill district, who claimed to be well acquainted with the views of the lower orders, was asked about the credit given to Pastorini's prophecies before a parliamentary committee in June 1824. Replied Dunn tersely: "The people laugh at them they meet with; nothing beyond that. The pastoral address of the Roman Catholic bishop of the diocese lately

20. Orpen to Gregory, 6 May 1823 (S.P.O., S.O.C.P.1, 2513/7).
21. *Dublin Evening Post* (hereafter cited as *D.E.P.*), 2 Feb. 1822.
22. *D.E.P.*, 11, 18, 23 Apr. 1822.
23. See, e.g., *D.E.P.*, 26 Jan. 1822, 21 Aug. 1823.

disabused them of any idea that they might have had of their truth."[24] What Dunn was really telling the committee was that no person "of the least respectability" treated the prophecies with anything but ridicule;[25] this threw into question his original assertion.

Newspaper editors sympathetic to the cause of Catholic emancipation seized upon the killing of an "opulent farmer" named Marum in the highly disturbed Kilkenny barony of Galmoy as clear evidence that the Rockites were not motivated by sectarian prejudices. Marum was a brother of the Catholic bishop of Ossory.[26] The "immediate cause" of his murder in March 1824 was his taking of a property which lay under an order of ejectment, but subject to possible redemption. Two months later, when the land was in fact redeemed and restored to the possession of a "kind and indulgent" Protestant gentleman whose family had held it for generations, the tenants reportedly greeted his return with great rejoicing. Here, declared the *Leinster Journal,* was "another decisive proof" that the "vulture press" was lying when it asserted that "the unfortunate disturbances which occasionally occur in this country spring from a belief in Pastorini's prophecies and an union for the destruction of Protestants."[27]

What emerges clearly from the historical record is that politically conscious Catholics of the middle and upper classes found Pastorini's prophecies to be deeply embarrassing at a time when they were giving their wholehearted support to a campaign aimed at gaining admission to Parliament for some of their wealthy coreligionists. This embarrassment was sometimes evident in the proceedings of the Catholic Association in Dublin. At one of its meetings in June 1824 a speaker maintained that the enemies of the Catholics were seeking to poison the minds of the English people by publishing a work entitled *Pastorini* in Ulster and then actively distributing it in England. There, he said, it was represented "as having emanated from the Catholic bishops and the association," though it contained "monstrous calumnies upon the Catholic religion."[28] At another meeting in the following December a speaker claimed to know why "the enemies of peace and good order" were reporting the presence of

24. *Minutes of evidence taken before the select committee appointed to inquire into the disturbances in Ireland, in the last session of Parliament, 13 May–18 June 1824* (hereafter cited as *S.O.I. evidence,* for *State of Ireland evidence*), p. 275, H.C. 1825 (20), vii, 1. For Bishop James Doyle's pastoral address of 1822, see *Report from the select committee on the state of Ireland, ordered to be printed 30 June 1825, with the four reports of minutes of evidence* (hereafter cited as *S.O.I. evidence*), pp. 665–72, H.C. 1825 (129), viii, 455.

25. *S.O.I. evidence,* p. 276, H.C. 1825 (20), vii, 1.

26. *D.E.P.,* 18 Mar. 1824.

27. Quoted in *D.E.P.,* 10 June 1824.

28. *D.E.P.,* 15 June 1824.

"numerous copies of Pastorini" among the peasantry of County Clare. "It was understood," he asserted unconvincingly, "that [Protestant] missionaries were circulating them about the kingdom in cheap pamphlets for sinister purposes."[29]

Daniel O'Connell himself told a parliamentary committee in March 1825:

I think that no effect has been produced upon the lower orders of the Irish Catholics by the book called Pastorini's prophecies. That book was written by an English bishop . . . ; and it would not have been heard of in Ireland if it had not, as we understand, been spread very much by persons inimical to the Catholic claims. There was a considerable number of copies of it printed in Dublin, and certainly not printed with the assent of any Catholic. . . . As to the book itself, it is a book very likely to excite very little attention in Ireland; it is not written with virulence so as to gratify the vulgar; it is not written with taste or talent so as to please the educated; and it has been condemned by the highest authorities in the Catholic church from the moment it [was] issued.[30]

Concluded O'Connell, "What we call the Orange party have put forward Pastorini on all occasions."[31] A more remarkable series of half-truths has not often been uttered.

III

Contrary to the implications of O'Connell's tendentious statement, the so-called prophecies of Pastorini were certainly distributed widely, and also widely believed. There had been numerous Irish editions of Bishop Charles Walmesley's *General history of the Christian church* since the first version appeared in Dublin as early as 1790 under the author's pen name of Signor Pastorini.[32] An edition labeled the fourth was published in Dublin in 1805; another, called the sixth, was printed in Belfast in 1816; and still another, also labeled the sixth, appeared in Cork in 1820.[33] The work was essentially a commentary on the Book of Revelation, for

29. *D.E.P.*, 11 Dec. 1824.
30. *Minutes of evidence taken before the select committee of the House of Lords appointed to inquire into the state of Ireland, more particularly with reference to the circumstances which may have led to disturbances in that part of the United Kingdom, 18 February–21 March 1825* (hereafter cited as *S.O.I. evidence*), p. 167, H.C. 1825 (181), ix, 1.
31. Ibid., p. 168.
32. [Charles Walmesley], *The general history of the Christian church from her birth to her final triumphant state in heaven, chiefly deduced from the Apocalypse of St. John the apostle, by Sig[nor] Pastorini* (Dublin, 1790).
33. Copies of these editions are available in the National Library of Ireland, Dublin.

centuries a favorite of those who believed that the second coming was an event to be expected and rapturously welcomed in their own lifetime. Walmesley's reading of the Apocalypse led him to assert, among other things, that God's wrath would be poured out to punish heretics about fifty years after 1771, thus initiating the sixth age of Christ's church, the last before the second coming.[34] This vague assertion led others to place a definite term to the existence of Irish Protestantism. By most the limit was fixed eventually at 1825, though some put it at 1821.[35]

Copies of Walmesley's ponderous and expensive pseudoscholarly tome were generally to be found in the libraries of curious Protestant gentlemen rather than in the cabins and farmhouses of Irish country people, schoolmasters apart.[36] Roadside inns, however, often kept copies of the book, and if the story recounted by the earl of Rosse in April 1822 is at all representative, the work was much in demand: "Mr. Daly of Castle Daly . . . told me that, travelling some time ago, he was at the inn at Loughrea, and having asked for a book to read, the waiter brought him Pastorini, supposing from his name that he was a Catholic; and that the 8th chapter was so much dirtied by reading that it was scarcely legible."[37]

But it was in the form of small tracts and handbills that Pastorini's prophecies penetrated countryside and town over much of Ireland. Exactly when and where this began to happen is something of a mystery. No reference to an acquaintance with Pastorini at the popular level has been discovered for any year before 1817. The agrarian rebels who staged the Caravat movement from 1813 to 1816 were apparently altogether innocent of Pastorini, though not necessarily of millenarian predictions in general. One piece of evidence points to the calamitous famine and typhus epidemic of 1817 as the time when short printed condensations of Pastorini's predictions reached certain rural districts of Munster. In his book, *Captain Rock detected*, published in 1824, the Rev. Mortimer O'Sullivan, sometime Protestant curate and schoolmaster in Tipperary town, recalled:

Anyone who has been a resident in the country parts of Ireland may have observed that about seven years since, a considerable change began to take place in the

34. Walmesley, *General history* (6th ed., Cork, 1820), pp. 477–8.

35. [Mortimer O'Sullivan], *Captain Rock detected, or the origin and character of the recent disturbances, and the causes, moral and political, of the present alarming condition of the south and west of Ireland, fully and fairly considered and exposed by a Munster farmer* (London, 1824), p. 284.

36. "I have no occasion for the book [Walmesley's *General history*] I sent you; I have another copy, printed in 1810 in Dublin, being the 4th edition," the earl of Rosse informed Lord Redesdale on 3 May 1822 (P.R.O.N.I., Redesdale papers, T.3030/C.34/13/3).

37. Earl of Rosse to Lord Redesdale, 19 Apr. 1822 (ibid., T.3030/C.34/13/2).

nature of the little penny tracts and ballads with which the itinerant pedlars were supplied. . . . The fact is certain that love songs and stories were no longer the principal wares of the book venders; and that stories of martyrs' deaths, and judgments and executions of obstinate heretics, and miracles performed in the true church were now in very general circulation. By one class of these productions the animosity of the faithful was whetted against the b— — —y Protestants; in another, they learned how heretics ought to be treated; and the miracles . . . sustained them by a hope that at last God would fight for them and exterminate their oppressors. At the same time prophecy, the constant resource of a depressed people, afforded them its consolations. Pastorini, circulated in various forms . . . , became a favourite study.[38]

Although north Munster was affected as early as 1817, the new stream of millenarian ideas apparently had its source not there but rather in the west midlands. In August of that year an informer told a magistrate that while traveling from Birr to Mohill, he had stopped at the house of Andrew Murray of Highstreet in northeast Galway. Murray reportedly produced a "prophecy book" from which he sought to demonstrate that "all Protestants were to be murdered within the year 1817"; he also contended that nine counties of Ireland (meaning apparently the Protestants in these counties) were to be consumed in a single night, and that this massacre would be followed by a six-day war in England.[39] A few other scraps of evidence, somewhat later in date, also point to the west midlands as the original fount of the Pastorini cult. In June 1819 a Catholic inspector of yarn at Mullingar, Co. Westmeath, speaking of "the different counties around this," called attention to the growing popular conviction that the Protestant church and state were to be overthrown "in the year of twenty-five."[40] Though this informant did not mention Pastorini by name, a retrospective comment by the earl of Rosse in the spring of 1822 was quite specific in its attribution of the millenarian notions which had taken root by 1819 among the country people of King's County and east Galway. On a visit in April 1822 to a relative living 12 miles from Birr, Lord Rosse discovered that "Pastorini had been in circulation among the lowest orders in that neighbourhood for three years,

38. O'Sullivan, *Captain Rock detected*, pp. 282–3.
39. Information of Patrick McKeen, 21 Aug. 1817 (S.P.O., S.O.C.P.1, 1830/13). McKeen, it seems, was some kind of itinerant worker and (despite his name) a Protestant; Murray was apparently a Catholic and perhaps the keeper of an alehouse. Besides introducing the "prophecy book," Murray also produced a Bible, probably for the purpose of tendering an oath to McKeen. I owe this reference and others for the years 1817–20 to the kindness of Paul E. W. Roberts.
40. Information of Charles Farrell, [?] June 1819 (S.P.O., S.O.C.P.1, 2079/12).

and that [since] last year a small book, being an extract from it, has been in circulation among them."[41]

There was a striking congruity between many of the districts in which the cult of Pastorini first flourished and the areas in which agrarian rebels calling themselves Ribbonmen staged a brief revolt in late 1819 and early 1820. This movement began and was strongest in Roscommon and east Galway, but it also spread to adjacent parts of Mayo, Westmeath, King's County, and Clare.[42] It was specifically concerned with the grievances of conacre rents, laborers' wages, tithes, taxes, and priests' dues, especially the first three; the participants were drawn almost exclusively from the ranks of the poor having little or no land.[43] Of the oaths used by the Ribbonmen to bind people (often "whole villages") to their cause, some called for a general and "undefined obedience,"[44] but others were sectarian, at least to the point of demanding loyalty to the Roman Catholic church, that is, invoking solidarity among Catholics.[45] Moreover, the movement was stimulated by, and no doubt helped to spread, Pastorini's millennial vision. Writing of the Oranmore district near Galway town in February 1820, at the height of the disturbances, one observer declared, "It is prophesied all the world are to be of *one religion* in the year 1825 or 1826."[46] It was from the west midlands, then, that the Pastorini cult penetrated into the province of Munster.

As Pastorini had become practically a household name throughout much of the south by 1822 or 1823, the diffusion of his prophecies there seems to have occurred suddenly and rapidly in the few years before and after 1820.[47] The extraordinary spread of Pastorini's millennial speculations over the area affected by the Rockite movement is revealed in the explicit language of threatening notices and in the often-alarmed remarks of those in authority. The active magistrate Andrew Batwell of Bowen's

41. Earl of Rosse to Lord Redesdale, 19 Apr. 1822 (P.R.O.N.I., Redesdale papers, T.3030/C.34/13/2).
42. For the spread of the movement, see *D.E.P.*, 26 Oct., 6, 11 Nov., 2, 11, 24 Dec. 1819; 13, 18, 22, 25 Jan., 10, 26 Feb., 2, 7, 9 Mar. 1820.
43. *D.E.P.*, 2 Dec. 1819; 13 Jan., 24 Feb., 2, 7, 16 Mar. 1820.
44. *D.E.P.*, 11 Dec. 1819.
45. *D.E.P.*, 9 Mar. 1820.
46. Rev. John Burke to [?], 23 Feb. 1820 (S.P.O., S.O.C.P.1, 2171/74). See also S.P.O., S.O.C.P.1, 1820/2173/11.
47. *S.O.I. evidence*, pp. 279–80, 311, 323, H.C. 1825 (20), vii, 1; *Minutes of evidence taken before the select committee of the House of Lords appointed to examine into the nature and extent of the disturbances which have prevailed in those districts of Ireland which are now subject to the provisions of the insurrection act, and to report to the House, 18 May–23 June 1824* (hereafter cited as *S.O.I. evidence*), p. 82, H.C. 1825 (200), vii, 501.

114 THE TRADITION OF VIOLENCE

Court in northeast Cork received a letter from "John Rock" in June 1822 telling him plainly that if he should manage to escape death now, "the year 1825 will surely come, when the fate of all your sort will be decided, so [be] advised once for all by your friend."[48] In the following October a "respectable" Catholic involved in the collection of tithes near Kanturk received a notice which said: "You are not to join these bloody Protestants, for you know there [sic] time is expired. I will slatar [i.e., slaughter] them like dogs." Subjoined to this notice when it was submitted to Dublin Castle was a brief and almost nonchalant explanation of its first sentence: "The writer here alludes to a notion now universal in the County Cork among the lower classes that a certain prophecy in the Book of Rev[elation] commenced being fulfilled in the year 1821 and is to end in the universal dissolution of all Protestant establishments in 1825."[49] And early in 1823 a military officer stationed in north Cork attributed the recent increase in outrages there to a prophecy "greatly believed in by the credulous and uninformed peasant," namely, that in that year "'there will be general war by land and sea.'"[50]

In north Kerry and in Clare as well Protestants lived in dread because of the credence given by Catholic peasants to Pastorini's hopeful vision. A Tarbert gentleman reported in January 1822 that Pastorini's book (probably an extract) was "in private circulation amongst the lower orders of the Roman Catholicks, who, according to its prophetical doctrine, expect to have the Prodestants [sic] exterminated out of this kingdom before the year 1825."[51] Intoxication with Pastorini may well explain two sectarian incidents which took place in the following month. In one case a band of Rockites "visited every Protestant family of the lower class in this neighbourhood [i.e., Kilflyn parish near Tralee] and, after treating them in the most unmerciful manner, *ordered* that they should immediately leave the parish," or else they would forfeit their lives.[52] In the other incident Rockites in the Ardfert district apparently threatened to destroy the ancient diocesan cathedral. For in a memorial to the government entreating the speedy dispatch of troops to the town, the Protestant in-

48. Threatening notice, 28 June 1822, enclosed in Major Samson Carter to William Gregory, 29 June 1822 (S.P.O., S.O.C.P.1, 2345/86). Another notice posted in June 1824 on one of the gates at the entrance to Bowen's Court proclaimed: "Capten Rock is going to comence to kill all the Protestants the [i.e., he] will find and . . . burn them alive in their houses" (Threatening notice, 9 June 1824, S.P.O., S.O.C.P.1, 2615/47).
49. Threatening notice, 29 Oct. 1822 (S.P.O., S.O.C.P.1, 2347/23).
50. Colonel Sir Hugh Gough to Major J. Finch, 11 Feb. 1823 (S.P.O., S.O.C.P.1, 2511/27).
51. William Lindsay to Henry Goulburn, 23 Jan. 1822 (S.P.O., S.O.C.P.1, 2345/19). Lindsay named the author of the book as "Pasterina," whom he called a Roman cardinal!
52. Rev. James P. Chute to Bishop Thomas Elrington, 13 Feb. 1822 (S.P.O., S.O.C.P.1, 2348/47).

habitants of Ardfert protested, "The venerable cathedral built above 800 years [ago] must, it seems, be demolished to satiate their fury. . . ."[53]

Unlike certain parts of the south, such as north Kerry, where Orangeism in Protestant circles helps to account for the currency of Pastorini,[54] Clare was free at this time from overbearing Protestantism. And yet its Catholic inhabitants had also become conversant with the new brand of millenarianism. Few elite observers were better qualified than Major George Warburton to say how much credence was accorded to the "emissaries" who circulated Pastorini's wisdom there. A high-ranking police officer, Warburton's duties brought him into frequent contact with all classes of the peasantry, and he was permanently resident in Clare from mid-1816 to early 1824. His view was categorical: "Upon my word, generally speaking, I do not think there is an individual of the lower orders that is not aware of this prophecy, and that is not very strongly impressed with the belief of them [sic]."[55] In fact, the country people of Clare spoke openly of Pastorini "in their common conversation, at their work and on other occasions when they are assembled together." One gardener was said to have told the gentleman who employed him that "there would be bloody work" in 1825, and that "he had the word of God for it."[56]

Though millenarian beliefs were also reportedly widespread in Tipperary, Kilkenny, and King's County,[57] it was in Limerick that the prophecies attributed to Pastorini enjoyed perhaps their greatest vogue during the early 1820s. This was the view of the able and exceptionally well informed police officer Major Richard Willcocks; it was shared by the king's counsel Francis Blackburne, who was appointed in April 1823 to administer the insurrection act in parts of Clare and the whole of Limerick. After spending a year there, Blackburne became convinced that millenarian literature could hardly be more pervasive. As he informed a parliamentary committee in May 1823, "When I went to Limerick, I made it my business . . . of inspecting every notice and every publication dispersed through the country and connected with seditious subjects, from which distinct evidence of what was operating on the minds of the people might be collected; and I do not think that in a single instance has one of those papers been produced to me that there was not a distinct allusion to the prophecies of Pastorini and the year 1825."[58]

53. Memorial of the Protestant inhabitants of Ardfert, n.d., but Feb. 1822 (S.P.O., S.O.C.P.1, 2348/66).
54. *S.O.I. evidence*, pp. 116–17, H.C. 1825 (129), viii, 1.
55. *S.O.I. evidence*, p. 142, H.C. 1825 (20), vii, 1. See also ibid., p. 124.
56. Ibid., p. 145.
57. Ibid., p. 93; *S.O.I. evidence*, p. 103, H.C. 1825 (200), vii, 501.
58. *S.O.I. evidence*, p. 7, H.C. 1825 (200), vii, 501. See also ibid., p. 59.

Blackburne might have spared himself all the trouble of inspection there; for over a year before his arrival Dublin Castle had been receiving accounts of Pastorini's renown, especially in west Limerick. In February 1822, a few days after the burning of the Protestant church of Killeedy near Newcastle, a local Protestant exclaimed, "This Pastorini is doing a great deal of mischief in the country."[59] Even more emphatic was the anonymous report submitted by a resident of Adare. Pastorini, he declared grandly, "has done more towards the subversion of the British empire than Bonaparte with all his legions." This writer had conversed with some of his Catholic neighbors about Pastorini's millennial certitude and was struck by their replies. One frieze-coated countryman told him: "You know, sir . . . , it must be so; the prophecys [sic] must be fulfilled; Pastorini was no liar." Another asserted, "I w[oul]d believe Pastorini sooner than the Bible; the date of the Protes[tan]ts is out." A third man, said to be sympathetic to the Whiteboys, when taxed with the tragic fate of the rebels in 1798, retorted: "The devil mend the scoundrels; they began 25 years before it was the will of God they should."[60] Significantly, Limerick was the only Catholic diocese, apart from Kildare and Leighlin, in which the bishop issued a pastoral letter controverting the doctrines associated with the name of Pastorini. In this address, read from the altars of all the chapels in his diocese on St. Patrick's Day, 1822, Bishop Charles Tuohy declared, "I have reason to know that even under the pretext of religion the poor credulous people are led astray by these wicked advisers, telling them prophecies of wonderful events to happen in the years 22, 23, and 24."[61]

Other predictions besides those attributed to Pastorini were also current in parts of Munster during the early 1820s. Among them were certain ancient prophecies generally ascribed to Colum Cille, versions of which had been widespread among Catholics, especially in Ulster and Connacht, during the revolutionary upheavals of the 1790s.[62] A variant of the old story of the "black militia," usually a reference to bloodthirsty Orangemen, was circulated in the Borrisokane district of north Tipperary early in 1824. Its propagator "declar'd that the time had arriv'd when they [i.e., the Catholics] would have possession of this island, as an ancient prophecy foretold that they should conquer when the black people came to Ireland." Asked who these black people were, he replied that "the police were the people so designated, as the dark colour of their clothing sufficiently proved."[63] This particular adaptation of a hoary anti-

59. F. Hacke[?] to Rev. Edward Geratty, 11 Feb. 1822 (S.P.O., S.O.C.P.1, 2350/60).
60. "Indigator" to [?], 29 Jan. 1822 (S.P.O., S.O.C.P.1, 2350/30).
61. S.O.I. evidence, p. 26, H.C. 1825 (20), vii, 1.
62. Donnelly, "Propagating the cause of the United Irishmen," pp. 19–20.
63. Rev. J. Conolly to Henry Goulburn, [?] Jan. 1824 (S.P.O., S.O.C.P.1, 2621/2).

Protestant revelation was in fact a matter of common notoriety. The prominent Catholic barrister and politician Richard Lalor Sheil was asked whether the low proportion of his coreligionists serving in the police, about which he had complained to a parliamentary committee in March 1825, could not be explained by the fact that "they looked upon the police as the realization of some old prophecy about a black militia which was to arise at this period and to kill all the Roman Catholics."[64]

Another prediction, reminiscent of the millennial hopes of foreign invasion current among United Irishmen and Defenders in the late 1790s, was heard again in the Adare district of Limerick early in 1822:

The children of God are to be defeated with great loss in the 2 first battles; before the 3[r]d, on their march, they are to meet with a white horse [a symbol of the Jacobite cause]. They are then to come victorious and to chase the locusts to the north. A man with 4 thumbs is to hold the horses of 4 kings or great generals at the battle, which is to be fought at Singland near Lim[eric]k. . . . 2 brothers, McDonnells by name, of Scotch extraction, are to come to the relief of Ireland with their fleets; one is to land at the north, the other at the west. When all is over, the Spaniards are to settle a frame of government. Ireland was to be in after times in the possession of the Spaniards.[65]

Similar prophecies circulated in County Cork. Whiteboys in the Liscarroll district were said to believe that "though they may be beaten back twice or thrice by the army, yet when having turned, they will meet a man in the way who comes from heaven, and [he] having sprinkled them with holy water, they will turn round again and the army will fly before them, though they (the Whiteboys) should hold up but straws."[66] The landowner and magistrate Justin McCarthy related to a parliamentary committee in June 1824 a striking instance of this type of millennial wisdom in his district, south of Mallow. From one of his demesne workers McCarthy had obtained a copy of a prediction attributed to Colum Cille, according to which "the Irish power" under General O'Donnell was to annihilate the English under the marquis of Abercorn. Then, he said: "Two days before I received the order of the House of Commons, I was passing through one of my own fields and heard some persons talking. I found my own mason reading to my gardener. They appeared exceedingly confused; the man thrust the manuscript into his pocket and told me he was reading some accounts to the gardener. The gardener is a very faithful, confidential fellow; I ascertained from him that it was the very same prophecy that I had a copy of before."[67]

64. *S.O.I. evidence*, p. 101, H.C. 1825 (129), viii, 1.
65. "Indigator" to [?], 29 Jan. 1822 (S.P.O., S.O.C.P.1, 2350/30).
66. *S.O.I. evidence*, p. 311, H.C. 1825 (20), vii, 1.
67. Ibid., p. 324.

Of course, not every report of the propagation of millenarian ideas is to be accepted unreservedly. There were hoaxes, such as the enterprise of the man armed with prophecies who went into the parish of Kilmoe near Skull in southwest Cork, "pretending that he was an agent of the Whiteboys, to stimulate the people to rebellion." The gentlemen who apprehended him must have been embarrassed to discover that he was a government spy.[68] There were also millenarian notices issued in the name of Captain Rock which expressed nothing more than the personal feelings of the individuals who composed them. For example, an announcement echoing Pastorini and posted in the town of Clonakilty in May 1823 declared menacingly: "This is to let the Protestants know there is a scourge over them from the almighty God. I am the man . . . that will give it. Jack Rock."[69] The authorities were mildly relieved to find that the writer of this notice was only an adolescent journeyman weaver of Clonakilty who had "not long left school." Still, there was the worrisome implication that boys learned at "those seminaries something else besides their grammar." Moreover, even if this particular notice was simply the product of one misguided youth's infatuation with the writings of Pastorini, it was also true, as Lord Carbery lamented, that "many, very many" Catholics of the lower classes were equally taken with them, if only by indirect contact. "That diabolical book," he railed, "has poisoned the minds of thousands and tens of thousands of those wretched beings."[70] Clearly, the government spy in the parish of Kilmoe knew what he was doing when he equipped himself with prophecies.

IV

Millenarian ideas in printed form circulated in a variety of ways. The most common vehicle was the penny handbill, or broadsheet. In the counties of Limerick and Clare handbills containing brief extracts from the speculations in Pastorini's tome, along with "observations trying to inculcate the probability of their being fulfilled," were distributed by the thousands.[71] One of these broadsheets, submitted to parliamentary committees in May 1824 by the police inspector Major George Warburton, bore the name of Thomas Conolly, printer and stationer of Camden Street, Dublin. It purported to explain why the persecution of Catholics, begun by the Protestant reformers in 1525, could last only until 1825, when the

68. Ibid., p. 379.
69. Threatening notice, [?] May 1823, enclosed in Rev. John Townsend to William Gregory, 27 May 1823 (S.P.O., S.O.C.P.1, 2513/43).
70. Lord Carbery to William Gregory, 24 June 1823 (S.P.O., S.O.C.P.1, 2513/78). See also S.P.O., S.O.C.P.1, 1823/2513/87.
71. *S.O.I. evidence*, p. 298, H.C. 1825 (20), vii, 1.

300-year "reign of the locusts" would be succeeded by the restoration to unchallenged supremacy of "the great, the only organized body of Christians, the Catholic church." "What a happiness," it declared, "if during this short remaining interval some part of them [i.e., the Protestants] would submit to see their errors and the great mischief that has been done to the church by their revolt against it! It is full time to lay down all animosities against their ancient mother, think of a reconciliation, and ask to be received again into her bosom."[72] The Dubliner Thomas Conolly had apparently acquired a considerable reputation in the south for such penny productions. For Warburton acknowledged that the expression "a Conolly" was used familiarly by peasants to denote his millenarian broadsheets.[73]

Other printers at Limerick and Cork furnished similar wares to chapmen who attended fairs and markets in the country.[74] It was hardly unknown for the chapmen to become lecturers. Peddlers "with light parcels or packs" were said early in 1824 to have recently dispersed "a large supply" of millenarian literature in the Borrisokane district of Tipperary. According to the Protestant clergyman who reported their doings to Dublin Castle, these peddlers also took it upon themselves to "dilate much on the pretended prophecys of Pastorini . . . and others."[75] For those with more expensive tastes and an appreciation for visual demonstration, chapmen also offered what Warburton described as "a sort of scale or map and something in the way of the stream of time; it purported to be a history of the progress of the church of Christ, and the various schisms which have taken place were marked in different columns. I recollect particularly the Protestant was supposed to end [in] 1825."[76]

Protestant proselytizers also helped unwittingly to spread or deepen millenarian consciousness among the deluded papists whom they hoped to win to reformed evangelical Christianity. In the belief that Irish Catholics were deliberately kept ignorant of the Holy Scriptures by their priests, the proselytizing organizations flooded the country with Bibles and Testaments in both the English and Irish languages. During the year ending in February 1823 the London Hibernian Society distributed gratis 13,000 Testaments and Bibles, "making a total of 92,600 since the institution of the society" in 1806.[77] A second body, the Hibernian Bible Society, established in Dublin in the same year, was even more enterprising in

---

72. Ibid., pp. 143–4. See also *S.O.I. evidence*, pp. 82–4, H.C. 1825 (200), vii, 501.

73. *S.O.I. evidence*, p. 144, H.C. 1825 (20), vii, 1.

74. Ibid., pp. 23, 325; *S.O.I. evidence*, p. 7, H.C. 1825 (200), vii, 501.

75. Rev. J. Conolly to Henry Goulburn, [?] Jan. 1824 (S.P.O., S.O.C.P.1, 2621/2). See also *S.O.I. evidence*, pp. 141–2, H.C. 1825 (20), vii, 1.

76. *S.O.I. evidence*, p. 84, H.C. 1825 (200), vii, 501.

77. *The treble almanack for the year 1824* . . . (Dublin, 1824), i, 195.

this direction. By 1823 some 218,000 Testaments and 104,000 Bibles had been issued from its depository.[78] Other organizations added to the inundation, though in smaller quantities. This outpouring was not always as unwelcome in the Catholic countryside as one might imagine, for it helped to make possible animated fireside discussions of St. John's Apocalypse. Recalling his days as a Protestant curate and schoolmaster in Tipperary town, the Rev. Mortimer O'Sullivan remarked that "those who could not procure the book [i.e., Pastorini's *General history*], but who were instructed in the principles of it, often gave the members of the Bible society hope of making converts from the readiness with which they received the Testament, of which they scarcely read any part but the Revelations. I remember when a house at my gate was a place of rendezvous for numbers to meet together and read."[79] The Catholic clergy were right after all. As they repeatedly insisted, it was indeed positively dangerous to allow the laity to construe the divine word without theological guidance.

To the circulation of millenarian ideas in oral form schoolmasters made a major contribution. Schoolmasters, in fact, played an important role in the Rockite movement, as they did in other popular political and agrarian agitations before and after 1800. Many rural schoolmasters as a matter of course carried "articles," the cant term for the Whiteboy oath and regulations, and presumably those of Captain Rock, which they used to enlist recruits as the occasion arose.[80] To the schoolmaster, as the general scribe of the village or parish, repaired all those who had petitions or letters that needed to be written,[81] including during times of agrarian rebellion the innumerable threatening letters and notices which gave impetus to the movement. Schoolmasters were also invariably well versed in the millenarian prophecies attributed to Colum Cille and Pastorini.[82] Witness the case of Charles McCarthy Considine, a Clare native who had come to take charge of a school at Glenville near Cork city. Toward the end of 1824 he found himself standing before a bench of magistrates convened at Fermoy under the insurrection act. Besides being faced with the usual charges (absence from his dwelling during the hours of curfew, idle and disorderly conduct), he was accused of delivering threatening notices concerning the purchase of gunpowder. But what must have been most damning in the eyes of the magistrates was the testimony of one laborer against him: "Prisoner talked of Pastorini and said that next year

78. Ibid., i, 191–2
79. O'Sullivan, *Captain Rock detected*, p. 283.
80. William Carleton, *Traits and stories of the Irish peasantry* (London, n.d.), pp. 240–1.
81. Ibid., p. 258.
82. Ibid., pp. 241, 262.

would be a *year of war.* He talked of many other things and said that the price of labour was too low." Considine was sentenced to be transported for seven years.[83]

Some schoolmasters traversed the countryside, stopping for short periods of teaching in different places. When Edward Connors, "an aged itinerant schoolmaster and land surveyor," died suddenly in a cabin near Kanturk in June 1824, certain millenarian documents were found on his person.[84] One of these papers suggests that for Connors the mundane tasks of surveying land or teaching the three Rs were often subsidiary to the exercise of a higher calling:

I am commissioned to unfold unto thee in part the secrets of futurity; pay attention to my relation and profit by my discourse. Know then, O Catholics, that the present captivity which will shortly determinate is but a just punishment for the cruelty of many of thy actions and the insatiable ambition of thy restless disposition. Yet it is likewise a preparatory measure towards the future exaltation and agrandizement [*sic*], for those shall be recalled from banishment [apparently, the Irish soldiers, or "wild geese," serving in foreign armies] and mayest again reign, and thy posterity in future inherit greatness. Yet before that comes to pass, many strange occurrences shall take place and wonderful events be accomplished.[85]

A properly suspicious police officer pointed out that Connors had come to the Kanturk district from the village of Banemore near Newcastle West in County Limerick, "which at the commencement of the disturbances in this county [i.e., Cork] was, from its remote situation, the resort of many of the disaffected leaders."[86] Indeed, what eventually became the Rockite movement had originated on Viscount Courtenay's estate around Newcastle.[87]

Connors's circuit was narrower than that of the traditional "prophecy man," the bounds of whose travels, according to William Carleton, "were those of the kingdom itself." A "rare character" in the Irish countryside by the early 1840s, when Carleton sketched him censoriously, the prophecy man had been a common figure forty or even twenty years before. Unlike those itinerant schoolmasters and peddlers for whom the circula-

83. *D.E.P.*, 2 Nov. 1824.
84. Major Samson Carter to William Gregory, 12 June 1824 (S.P.O., S.O.C.P.1, 2615/42).
85. Enclosed in the letter cited in fn. 84.
86. Carter to Gregory, 12 June 1824 (S.P.O., S.O.C.P.1, 2615/42).
87. William Gregory to Charles Grant, [?] Nov. 1820 (S.P.O., S.O.C.P.1, 2185/51); Major Richard Going to Charles Grant, 19 Nov. 1820 (S.P.O., S.O.C.P.1, 2185/51); Report of Richard Willcocks and George Warburton to Charles Grant, 23 Oct. 1821 (S.P.O., S.O.C.P.1, 2296/24); *D.E.P.*, 25 Oct. 1821.

tion and explanation of millennial wisdom constituted only part of their work, the prophecy man was a person "who solely devotes himself to an anxious observation of those political occurrences which mark the signs of the times as they bear upon the future, the principal business of whose life it is to associate them with his own prophetic theories." He usually practiced his art at night, in the house of some countryman with whom he happened to be staying, when after the labor of the day the neighbors would crowd around the fireside to listen respectfully to his address, or his harangue, as it must have frequently seemed. The prophecy man enjoyed perhaps his greatest prestige during the French wars, when talk of the liberation of Ireland through foreign invasion and the revered name of Bonaparte were constantly on his lips. Bonaparte's downfall and especially his death somewhat diminished the stature of prophecy men. So did the accession of George IV to the English throne, contrary to a well-known Irish prediction. But with the sudden rage around 1820 for Pastorini's speculations, prophecy men obtained a further extension of credit until the failure of Protestantism to vanish in 1825 "nearly overturned the system and routed the whole prophetic host," at least as Carleton viewed the matter sixteen years later.[88]

Another important vehicle for the transmission of millennial hopes, and an outlet for sectarian feeling as well, was the broadside ballad or the somewhat more elaborate and expensive garland (a small booklet of eight pages, containing from two to six songs). Both of these were sold for a halfpenny or a penny by the professional ballad singers and the peddlers who thronged to fairs, race meetings, and other large public gatherings.[89] Many broadside ballads of the early nineteenth century proclaimed political prophecies.[90] Some songs during the years of the Rockite movement endorsed in vulgar terms the abstruse speculations ascribed to Pastorini, as illustrated by the following Limerick ballad of 1821:

> Now the year 21 is drawing by degrees,
> In the year 22 the locusts will weep,
> But in the year 23 we'll begin to reap.
> Good people, take courage, don't perish in fright,
> For notes will be of nothing in the year 25;
> As I am O'Healy, we'll daily drink beer.[91]

88. William Carleton, "The Irish prophecy man" in *Irish Penny Journal*, i, no. 50 (12 June 1841), pp. 393–4.

89. Georges-Denis Zimmermann, *Songs of Irish rebellion: political street ballads and rebel songs, 1780–1900* (Dublin, 1967), pp. 22–3.

90. Ibid., pp. 28–31, 198–9, 206–7.

91. Ibid., p. 30.

Other ballads sung in the early 1820s, though they belonged to the older millenarian and sectarian tradition of the 1790s, accurately reflected the current popular mood. Two men were tried under the insurrection act at Fermoy in January 1824 for disorderly conduct and violation of curfew at a public house in nearby Kildorrery on the day after Christmas. One of them had sung on that occasion an old Irish ballad learned twenty years before, whose words were more or less these: "Ye sons, arise and take up arms, and join if only three remain; they shall have from Dingle to Carrick-on-Suir as a property to be happy with; tear Orangemen and Protestants to pieces; dethrone King George, and his own soldiers shall rebel and join the rebels." Since the prisoners had been drunk, the court was lenient and simply admonished them, but it would perhaps be too charitable to conclude that what came from the throat did not also come from the heart.[92] The same might be said of the five men whom a police constable overheard singing mightily in a public house at Rathkeale, Co. Limerick, in November 1824. Among their "seditious songs" was one whose verses concluded with the well-known words, "We will wade knee-deep in Orange blood and fight for liberty."[93]

V

Why was there such a great upsurge of millenarianism and anti-Protestant feeling at this particular time—the early 1820s? Though numerous factors were at work, the social consequences of the economic crisis, and especially the dread of famine after the harvest failure of 1821, played a crucial role. Some elite contemporaries took this view. When reporting the circulation in north Kerry early in 1822 of Pastorini's supposed prediction of the demise of Protestantism by 1825, William Lindsay of Tarbert remarked, "Numbers and myself suppose it is encouraged by distress, the principal cause of the disturbances."[94] But it is unnecessary to rely on such evidence alone. The connection between millenarian hopes of salvation and fear of imminent famine was clearly expressed in the exhortation and lament of a manifesto posted in County Limerick in January 1822:

Hearken unto me, ye men of Ireland, and hear my voice! Arise, O! Melesians [*sic*]; the day of our deliverance is coming, when the trumpet beats to arms. . . . Your eyes shall have no pity on the breed of Luther, for he had no pity on us.

92. *D.E.P.*, 20 Jan. 1824.
93. William Smith to Henry Goulburn, 19 Nov. 1824 (S.P.O., S.O.C.P.1, 2619/48).
94. William Lindsay to Henry Goulburn, 23 Jan. 1822 (S.P.O., S.O.C.P.1, 2345/19).

Behold, the day of the Lord cometh, cruel both with wrath and fierce anger, to lay the land desolate. . . . Their children also shall ye dash to pieces. Before their eyes their houses shall be spoiled, and their wives ravished. . . . You see misery upon misery is come upon us. Seldom a day passes that our cattle is [sic] not canted by the roguery and oppression of our landlords. We have nothing left but to die valiantly or starve. We are the most miserable people on the face of the earth, while the sons of perdition are satisfying their appetite, luxury, and gluttony abroad. . . . Oh! when their belly is full and warm, what a feeling they have for the poor. . . . Lament and mourn, ye hereticks, for the day of your destruction is come.[95]

A widespread readiness to die if necessary in order to bring the millennium closer was reportedly manifest among the thousands who engaged in the abortive insurrection of late January 1822 in northwest Cork. Many of the "prophetic gentry," said a sarcastic Protestant clergyman at the beginning of February, "who marched to the attack on Newmarket on the 25th ult[im]o previously went to the priests to confess & get absolution, & what they called to prepare for death."[96] To the depth of the Rockites' millenarian convictions — "a spirit both political & religious" — another Protestant attributed the failure of government repression to destroy the movement. "The cause the wretched people have espoused appears in their eyes so praiseworthy," he declared in May 1823, "that neither the prospect of utter death [n]or banishment seems to have the desired effect."[97] The most unshakable millenarians were apparently the laborers, whose economic and social condition was least amenable to improvement. A rise in agricultural prices was thought to have brought about by early 1824 a much more law-abiding disposition among farmers in the Pallaskenry district of Limerick. But since prophecies of Protestant doom were still rife, laborers could "only be kept down by force" until the haven of 1826 was reached.[98]

Also contributing to the upsurge in millenarianism and sectarian hatred during the early 1820s were the extraordinary intensity of the tithe grievance and the provocative activities of Protestant proselytizers. Conflict over tithes in the past had not always led to a heavy accumulation of sectarian spleen. Indeed, the issue had come to sharply divide upper-class Protestants. On the one side were the nobility and gentry, who generally

95. Manifesto "published by Capt[ain] Storm and Steele," 5 Jan. 1822 (S.P.O., S.O.C.P.1, 2350/5).
96. Rev. John E. Orpen to Emanuel N. Orpen, 2 Feb. 1822 (S.P.O., S.O.C.P.1, 2344/8).
97. Jemmett Browne to William Gregory, 3 May 1823 (S.P.O., S.O.C.P.1, 2153/2). See also S.O.I. evidence, p. 86, H.C. 1825 (200), vii, 501.
98. John Waller to Francis Blackburne, 5 Feb. 1824 (S.P.O., S.O.C.P.1, 2618/27). See also S.P.O., S.O.C.P.1, 1823/2513/62; S.O.I. evidence, p. 227, H.C. 1825 (200), vii, 501.

embraced the solution of a commutation of tithes; on the other side were the bishops and many of the clergy, who rejected such a solution.[99] But now the popular demand, or at least the ultimate popular aim, was often the complete abolition of tithes, and not simply their reduction, as heretofore.[100] With this shift the mixing of economic and religious objections to the system became much more prevalent. Thus the millenarian manifesto from County Limerick quoted at length above, which heralded the impending massacre of Protestant "hereticks," also declared: "Now, brethren and fathers, it is your duty not to pay tythes or taxes, for before full six months is over, I will be at the head of an army of two hundred and forty thousand men."[101] A placard appearing in March 1822 in the Tramore district of Waterford called upon all Catholics aged sixteen to fifty to muster in support of Captain Rock; they were to pay no tithes and "to fight for their religion."[102] A similar blending of motives was evident in the menacing notice sent to the Rev. Patrick Kennedy, the resident parson of Templetouhy parish near Thurles. This notice, which threatened Kennedy with murder and his daughters with rape, proclaimed, "You are doubly hateful to us for having been a tithe proctor" as well as for being a clergyman of the wrong church.[103] It is also difficult to believe that those Rockites who burned or set fire to a half-dozen Protestant churches in Limerick, Kerry, and Cork were giving expression only to their detestation of tithes or church rates.[104] Tithes had been an important issue in every major agrarian rebellion in the south since 1760, but (apart from the events surrounding 1798) the burning of churches was a novelty introduced by the Rockites. As the king's counsel George Bennett put it in May 1824, the Catholic lower orders had come to believe both that "they are oppressed by those who profess the religion of the established church," and that "there is likely to be soon a great change on that subject."[105]

99. *D.E.P.*, 22 Aug., 21 Sept. 1822, 1 May 1823; *S.O.I. evidence*, pp. 776–7, H.C. 1825 (129), viii, 455; Angus Macintyre, *The liberator: Daniel O'Connell and the Irish party, 1830–1847* (London, 1965), p. 172; D. H. Akenson, *The Church of Ireland: ecclesiastical reform and revolution, 1800–1885* (New Haven and London, 1971), pp. 105–6.

100. *D.E.P.*, 24 Nov., 1, 11, 15 Dec. 1821, 5 Feb. 1822; S.P.O., S.O.C.P.1, 1822/2342/33; 1822/2348/15.

101. Manifesto, 5 Jan. 1822 (S.P.O., S.O.C.P.1, 2350/5).

102. *D.E.P.*, 14 Mar. 1822.

103. Threatening notice, n.d., enclosed in Edward Wilson to Henry Goulburn, 11 Dec. 1822 (S.P.O., S.O.C.P.1, 2356/79).

104. For the burning of Protestant churches, see *D.E.P.*, 1 Dec. 1821; 12 Jan., 12, 26 Feb., 2 Mar. 1822; 20 Sept. 1823; S.P.O., S.O.C.P.1, 1822/2344/22; 1822/2348/3, 5, 12; 1822/2350/39, 53–4, 60, 73, 93–4; 1823/2515/21, 27, 30.

105. *S.O.I. evidence*, p. 28, H.C. 1825 (200), vii, 501.

Compared with tithes, Protestant proselytism was less significant in stimulating popular Catholic sectarianism, but not much less. Indeed, the Rev. Mortimer O'Sullivan seemed inclined to believe that the striking change which he had observed around 1817 or 1818 in the subject matter of the penny tracts and ballads sold in the countryside was a direct response to "the attempts at proselytism" by Protestant "missionaries."[106] The proselytizers certainly became more aggressive after 1815 in circulating the Scriptures, in distributing anti-Catholic literature, and in establishing schools aimed at the children of the Catholic poor. The Religious Book and Tract Society for Ireland claimed in 1823 to have issued over 1,160,000 tracts and 86,000 books since 1819 alone.[107] Some of its productions were simply "dropped by people travelling in gigs and picked up on the road by countrymen."[108] Formal schooling, however, was a far more serious and contentious affair. The controversies that raged after 1819 at the national level about schools under Protestant auspices, their management and funding, and the use of the Scriptures within them were in part a reflection and in part a cause of strife at the local level.[109]

In Munster and Connacht Catholic clerical opposition was focused primarily on the schools founded by the Baptist Society, which proselytized openly, and by the London Hibernian Society, whose inspectors required that children in its schools recite the Scriptures from memory. Repeated denunciations of these missionary academies from the altars of Catholic chapels, accompanied by orders that Catholic children be withdrawn from them, served to sharpen sectarian consciousness.[110] In February 1822 a cottage school sponsored by the London Hibernian Society on the outskirts of Tipperary town was burned to the ground.[111] Though this incident remained a singular one in the south until later in the decade, there were other manifestations of the grass-roots Catholic reaction raised by Protestant evangelism, such as the stoning of a Methodist preacher in the streets of Kilrush, Co. Clare,[112] and the circulation of ballads scorning the efforts of the Protestant missionary organizations. One songster was jailed in Limerick city in November 1824 "for singing and vending in the streets an impious halfpenny ballad." His broadside, declared a deeply offended observer, "purported to turn into ridicule not only the

106. O'Sullivan, *Captain Rock detected*, pp. 282–3.

107. *Treble almanack for the year 1824*, i, 190–1.

108. *S.O.I. evidence*, p. 379, H.C. 1825 (20), vii, 1.

109. D. H. Akenson, *The Irish education experiment: the national system of education in the nineteenth century* (London and Toronto, 1970), pp. 80–94.

110. *S.O.I. evidence*, pp. 326–8, 391–3, H.C. 1825 (20), vii, 1.

111. S.P.O., S.O.C.P.1, 1822/2355/55; *D.E.P.*, 28 Feb. 1822.

112. *D.E.P.*, 14 Dec. 1824.

Bible but all Bible societies"; it also sought "to convey the idea that aid from foreign powers would ultimately crush the system in these countries."[113] With the beginning of the long round of so-called Bible discussions in late 1824, religious controversialism and sectarian animosity entered upon a new phase.[114] As an editorial writer in the *Dublin Evening Post* colorfully if extravagantly expressed it in November of that year, "The country is converting into an immense theological arena, and polemics are likely for some time to usurp the place of politics, if indeed they will not be mixed together and form that delightful compound, the fermentation of which produced such remarkable consequences in the reign of Charles I."[115]

VI

Well before religious controversialists and the crusade for Catholic emancipation raised the heat, sectarian fires were already burning brightly for another reason: the popular identification of Protestantism with the various forces — yeomanry, police, and regular troops — used to suppress the Rockite movement. The association was strongest in the case of the yeomanry. This was an overwhelmingly Protestant armed force which had originated in the counterrevolutionary frenzy of the mid-1790s. Two-thirds of the 31,000 yeomen in Ireland in 1821 were concentrated in Ulster; in all of Munster they numbered fewer than 2,400.[116] But their unpopularity in the south was far out of proportion to their strength. Just how unpopular they were is suggested by the frantic plea of one north Kerry gentleman to the head of his brigade in October 1821: "For God's sake, my dear major, get arms and ammunition for the corp[s] and don't let a body of loyal men be murdered who have brought down on themselves the vengeance of the insurgents by their exertions to save their country."[117] The past history of yeomen as superloyalists and their local knowledge of the workings of agrarian combinations made their Catholic neighbors especially hostile toward them. Anticipating government reluctance to comply with his request for the raising of a new yeomanry

113. *D.E.P.*, 13 Nov. 1824.
114. Desmond Bowen, *The Protestant crusade in Ireland, 1800–70: a study of Protestant-Catholic relations between the act of union and disestablishment* (Dublin and Montreal, 1978), pp. 98–104.
115. *D.E.P.*, 13 Nov. 1824.
116. *A return of the number of troops or corps of effective yeomanry . . . , so far as relates to Ireland*, pp. 3–10, H.C. 1821 (306), xix, 177.
117. William Sandes to Brigade-Major Daniel Mahony, 27 Oct. 1821 (S.P.O., S.O.C.P.1, 2296/26).

corps in the Borrisokane district of Tipperary, the Rev. Ralph Stoney declared in March 1822: "I know that the yeomanry are unpopular, but so is everything that is constitutional and loyal. They saved the nation in the year 1798, and the disaffected dread them more than they do the regulars because they are well acquainted with their characters and know their haunts."[118]

Dread there may have been, but there was also loathing. For the yeomanry were used in ways that were bound to inflame popular feeling, as, for example, in their seizure of illicit stills and their distraining of tenants for nonpayment of rent or tithes, not to mention their searches for illegal arms and for suspected agrarian rebels. When opposed in the performance of their duties, yeomen were more likely than better-disciplined soldiers to fire upon menacing or stone-throwing crowds, as illustrated by the lethal clashes with country people near Ballybunnion, Co. Kerry, in late 1821 and near Clonakilty, Co. Cork, in early 1822.[119] Rarely were yeomen punished for employing excessive force or for engaging in unprovoked violence, a circumstance which naturally intensified the hatred of the local population. An outrage by members of the Nenagh corps in January 1822 put the Catholic inhabitants of that Tipperary town into a frenzy. "If you were to hear the language of them," exclaimed one gentleman, "as they now think they can get no law [i.e., no justice]; what a town to live in!"[120]

The Protestant triumphalism of many yeomanry corps was yet another source of Catholic irritation. There was no exact parallel in the south to the annual yeomanry and Orange festival on 21 June at Enniscorthy, Co. Wexford, where a symbolic tree of liberty was burned to celebrate the retaking of that town from the rebels in 1798.[121] But yeomen of course joined lustily in the Orange celebrations of the anniversary of the Boyne which occurred in some southern towns and which occasionally led to serious confrontations. In July 1821 the Bandon Orangemen, marching in procession, fired a fieldpiece loaded with stones at an opposing party of Catholics, killing one woman. A few days later at the fair of nearby Timoleague, a crowd of Catholics in reprisal murdered a Protestant identified as "one of the Bandon Orangemen."[122] Apart altogether from annual processions, almost any occasion was good enough for the playing of loyalist tunes by the yeomanry bands of Munster and Leinster: "The

118. Rev. Ralph Stoney to Henry Goulburn, 4 Mar. 1822 (S.P.O., S.O.C.P.1, 2355/43).
119. D.E.P., 15 Dec. 1821, 22, 29 Jan. 1822; S.P.O., S.O.C.P.1, 1822/2342/54, 66.
120. D.E.P., 26 Jan. 1822.
121. D.E.P., 24, 26 June 1823.
122. S.O.I. evidence, p. 379, H.C. 1825 (20), vii, 1. See also S.P.O., S.O.C.P.1, 1821/2293/6.

Boyne water" by one corps at Freshford in Kilkenny, "The Protestant boys" and "Croppies lie down" by others at Dunmanway and Bandon in Cork.[123] It was perhaps significant that John Walsh, an Adare yeoman murdered by a party of Rockites in October 1821, had served as the fifer of that corps.[124]

The most dramatic example of a Rockite onslaught against yeomen largely motivated by bitter sectarian feeling was the burning of Glenasheen near Kilmallock by a large band of over 100 men in April 1823. Like its sister village of Ballyorgan, Glenasheen was inhabited almost exclusively by Palatines, whose ancestors from the German Palatinate on the Rhine had settled on advantageous terms as tenants in various parts of County Limerick at the beginning of the eighteenth century.[125] Because of their Protestant heritage and the favor shown them by local landowners, the Palatines identified themselves wholeheartedly with the Protestant ascendancy, and adult males in their communities usually belonged to units of yeomanry or volunteers.[126] In the attack on Glenasheen the Rockites succeeded in destroying three houses and set fire to four others. A local proprietor noted that "the object of the rebels (as they frequently declar'd) was to get possession of the arms & murder the 'Protestant Palatine devils.'"[127] The Palatine schoolmaster, whose dwelling the Rockites set alight, heard them shout that "he was a Protestant devil and that not one should be spared."[128] Palatines in other districts of the county also suffered at Rockite hands. Two who belonged to the Adare yeomanry corps were assaulted and robbed of their arms early in 1824; the house of a third was burned near Shanagolden; and a fourth was

---

123. *D.E.P.*, 5 Feb. 1822, 6 Mar., 17 May 1823.

124. S.P.O., S.O.C.P.1, 1821/2296/25; *D.E.P.*, 20 Oct. 1821. The sergeant of the Ballylongford yeomen infantry received a Rockite notice in February 1822 ordering him to surrender his farm within nine days, or else his house and cattle would be destroyed (S.P.O., S.O.C.P.1, 1822/2348/65).

125. S.P.O., S.O.C.P.1, 1823/2517/27. To some degree the Palatines intermarried with the local Catholic population, and a number of their communities had lost their distinctiveness by the early nineteenth century, but certain others retained it. See Lecky, *Ire.*, i, 351–2.

126. *S.O.I. evidence*, p. 576, H.C. 1825 (129), viii, 455. The Tarbert corps of yeomanry was considered a nest of Orangemen by Catholics; Palatines brought from County Limerick constituted a significant element within it. Daniel O'Connell pointed to this circumstance in explaining why Rockite oaths administered in north Kerry displayed strong anti-Protestant animus (*S.O.I. evidence*, pp. 116–17, H.C. 1825 (129), viii, 1; *S.O.I. evidence*, pp. 141–2, H.C. 1825 (181), ix, 1).

127. Charles D. Oliver to William Gregory, 1 May 1823 (S.P.O., S.O.C.P.1, 2517/26). See also S.P.O., S.O.C.P.1, 1823/2517/25, 32–3; *S.O.I. evidence*, pp. 7–8, H.C. 1825 (20), vii, 1.

128. *D.E.P.*, 3 May 1823.

murdered after taking a farm on Lord Courtenay's estate around New-castle West from which tenants had been dispossessed.[129] Along with other Protestants, Palatines emigrated from County Limerick in considerable numbers during the early 1820s, and among the reasons commonly as-signed for their departure was the sectarian animosity of the surround-ing Catholic population.[130]

Though the police establishment was not as overwhelmingly Protes-tant in its composition as the yeomanry, it was by no means free in Cath-olic eyes from the stench of Orangeism. Even the new constabulary force established in 1822 leaned heavily to the side of the ascendancy. In a total body of slightly more than 2,700, there were fewer than 850 Catholics. In the eight counties comprising the province of Leinster, Protestants out-numbered Catholics in the new force by nearly three to one. In the prov-ince of Munster the religious balance was less lopsided, with Catholic constables actually constituting a large majority in Kerry and a small majority in Waterford. On the other hand, in Limerick and Tipperary the proportions were fairly close to those prevailing in Leinster.[131]

Yet even if Catholic constables had been far more numerous, the nature of police work in many areas of the south during the early 1820s was such that the establishment could not have avoided the enormous popular hostility which it aroused. Nor can it be claimed that the opprobrium attaching to the police stemmed mostly from Catholic sectarianism. The ways in which the police earned hatred among the country people were numerous. Their anti-Rockite activities altogether apart, members of the constabulary interfered with many traditional folkways. They dispersed country dancers, scattered mourners at wakes, and drove bowlers from the roads. They seized the fishing nets of boatmen along the river Suir to prevent their taking salmon fry, killed the dogs of peasants by the road-side, and cleared public houses of their patrons, sometimes at bayonet point.[132] After sunset, dances, wakes, and public-house drinking were violations of the insurrection act in those counties or baronies declared subject to its provisions, and the police were routinely the enforcers of this draconian law.

129. *D.E.P.*, 3 Feb. 1824; *S.O.I. evidence*, pp. 85, 88, H.C. 1825 (200), vii, 501; *S.O.I. evidence*, p. 576, H.C. 1825 (129), viii, 455.

130. *S.O.I. evidence*, pp. 7–8, H.C. 1825 (20), vii, 1; *S.O.I. evidence*, pp. 88, 191, H.C. 1825 (200), vii, 501.

131. *Abstract of returns relative to magistrates, constables, and subconstables appointed under the constables' act for Ireland*, pp. 1–4, H.C. 1824 (257), xxii, 405.

132. *D.E.P.*, 11 July 1822; 19 Aug., 2 Sept., 2 Dec. 1823; 6, 20 Jan. 1824; *S.O.I. evidence*, p. 177, H.C. 1825 (20), vii, 1.

To these sources of irritation must be added numerous instances of the unauthorized use of firearms or bayonets by members of the constabulary.[133] After a series of such cases the *Dublin Evening Post* was provoked to remark in February 1824, "There is scarcely a day in which we do not hear of some outrage committed by these preservers of the peace; and, we confess, we are too often disappointed in not hearing of their punishment."[134] On top of everything else, the police were the main auxiliaries of the regular army in the repression of the Rockite movement — seeking informers, setting spies, arresting suspects, coaching witnesses for the crown, and testifying for the prosecution themselves, both under the insurrection act and under the ordinary criminal law. It therefore comes as little surprise to find, for example, that after some constables intervened to stop a faction fight at the fair of Abbeyfeale in July 1824 and tried to take two ringleaders off to the guardroom, they were stoned by members of both factions, who "called out several times that 'Captain Rock was alive, murder the Peelers.'"[135]

Yet even if it must be acknowledged that the nonsectarian sources of popular hatred for the police were many, it should also be recognized that the Catholic country people often viewed them through sectarian eyes. A County Limerick notice of January 1822 screamed its vengeful message: "Those dog teachers, the police, have no mercy on them, for it is no sin to kill hereticks. It was never so easy to masacre [*sic*] them as now. There shall be one conflagration made of them from sea to sea."[136] This effusion is perhaps to be explained by the well-attested fact that the Orange Order had penetrated into the police establishment in County Limerick. Major Richard Willcocks admitted to a parliamentary committee in May 1824 that soon after his appointment in late 1821 as head of the constabulary in that county, he had found it necessary to suppress the Orange system among his men.[137] Blame for this state of affairs attached to Willcocks's predecessor, Major Richard Going, whose sorry fate owed much to his presumed Orange proclivities.[138]

Going had permitted one or more Orange lodges to be formed within

133. *D.E.P.*, 19 Aug., 9 Sept., 2, 4, 6, 9, 11, 23, 30 Dec. 1823; 6 Jan., 10 Apr. 1824.

134. *D.E.P.*, 12 Feb. 1824. At the spring assizes of 1824 in Leinster alone, twenty-two policemen stood trial, nine of them for murder (*D.E.P.*, 6 May 1824). Six policemen were convicted of manslaughter in the killing of a man in Queen's County and were sentenced to be transported (*D.E.P.*, 13 May 1824).

135. *D.E.P.*, 6 July 1824.

136. Threatening notice, n.d., but ca. Jan. 1822 (S.P.O., S.O.C.P.1, 2350/5).

137. *S.O.I. evidence*, p. 49, H.C. 1825 (200), vii, 501; *D.E.P.*, 1, 5 June 1824.

138. *D.E.P.*, 2 Feb. 1822; *S.O.I. evidence*, p. 107, H.C. 1825 (20), vii, 1.

his police establishment, a circumstance which became publicly known and helped to make the corps "much disliked," to put it mildly.[139] But what greatly intensified popular hatred for Going and his constables was their association with a notorious tithe affray near Askeaton in mid-August 1821 as well as the events and sectarian rumors that followed from it. In this affray a large force of over 200 Whiteboys who had attacked the house of a tithe proctor were surprised by a much smaller party of police numbering fewer than twenty men. In the ensuing exchange of fire the police shot two Whiteboys dead on the spot, mortally wounded a third, and took several prisoners; a subconstable was also killed.[140] When the bodies of the insurgents were brought to Rathkeale, Going arranged — as a terror to Whiteboys in general — that they should be buried in quicklime, with their captured associates digging the grave, instead of allowing the families and friends of the deceased to claim the corpses.[141]

What made this affront to popular custom far worse was the coupling of a rumor, apparently baseless, with an undisputed fact. According to the rumor, "universally believed among the lower orders," one of the Whiteboys shot by Going's police had been put under ground while still alive. The undisputed fact was that the bodies had been "committed in the good old style of ninety-eight to a croppy-hole, which the prisoners were compelled to dig."[142] Within two months of this episode, which at once acquired a sectarian aura in the popular Catholic mind, Going himself was killed. A small party of men waylaid him as he was riding one evening from Limerick city to Rathkeale; they fractured his skull and shot him five times.[143] His death was proclaimed by "a joyous shout through the country, which reechoed from place to place; lighted heaps of straw were also at night exhibited on the different hills in triumph" over the accomplishment of the deed.[144] To beware the fate of Going became thereafter a stock reference in Rockite threatening notices in numerous parts of the south.

Limerick was not the only county affected by the Rockite movement in which members of the constabulary were associated in the public mind with Orangeism. In May 1823, when the yeomanry and Orangemen of

139. Report of Richard Willcocks and George Warburton to Charles Grant, 23 Oct. 1821 (S.P.O., S.O.C.P.1, 2296/24).
140. *D.E.P.*, 23 Aug., 22 Dec. 1821.
141. *S.O.I. evidence*, pp. 104–7, H.C. 1825 (20), vii, 1.
142. *D.E.P.*, 8 Nov. 1821. See also *S.O.I. evidence*, pp. 49–50, H.C. 1825 (200), vii, 501.
143. *D.E.P.*, 16, 18 Oct. 1821; S.P.O., S.O.C.P.1, 1821/2296/21; Galen Broeker, *Rural disorder and police reform in Ireland, 1812–36* (London and Toronto, 1970), pp. 122–3.
144. *D.E.P.*, 20 Oct. 1821. See also S.P.O., S.O.C.P.1, 1821/2296/21.

Bandon buried a comrade in the local churchyard, they paraded from the Orange lodge through the streets of that town, carrying Orange flags, playing loyalist tunes, and sporting the full insignia of the Order. Along with them the police quartered at Bandon marched openly.[145] At the assizes in County Cork, according to Daniel O'Connell, police magistrates were accustomed to interfere in the selection of petty juries in criminal cases by "attending particular prosecutions, setting aside the Catholic jurors, and endeavouring to pick out, as much as possible, a Protestant jury, some of them Orangemen."[146] And a resident of Freshford, Co. Kilkenny, reported at the end of 1823 that "with few exceptions" the police stationed there were Orangemen; they belonged to a lodge established in the town, whose head was notorious for having killed a local farmer, and one of whose patrons was a local magistrate.[147] Senior police officials were certainly conscious of the need to purge the constabulary of the discrediting odor of Orangeism, and serious steps were taken in the early 1820s to rid the force of Orange lodges and other flagrant displays of anti-Catholic bigotry among some of its members.[148] But as demonstrated by the widespread currency of the prophecy identifying the police with the "black militia," it was no easy task to eradicate the sectarian image of the constabulary implanted in the minds of many Catholic country people in the south.

Like the police, the regular army also gave a fillip to Catholic sectarianism. The great military buildup in Munster and adjacent parts of Leinster that began toward the end of 1821 was largely achieved by transferring to the Irish establishment regiments from Britain and some of its overseas possessions. After modest reinforcement from abroad the army in Ireland reached a level of 16,000 men by mid-1822; it was further increased to about 21,000 during the following year.[149] English or Scottish cavalry units like the Rifle Brigade were especially prominent in military operations directed against the mobile and stealthy followers of Captain Rock. Catholics in disturbed districts were reminded of the religious allegiance of many of these new troops when the soldiers marched on Sundays to what had once been sparsely attended services in the local Protestant church. The filling of Protestant churches with soldiers sometimes elicited a Catholic sectarian response, as indicated, for example,

145. *D.E.P.*, 17 May 1823.

146. *S.O.I. evidence*, pp. 117–18, H.C. 1825 (129), viii, 1.

147. *D.E.P.*, 20 Dec. 1823. See also *D.E.P.*, 30 Dec. 1823.

148. S.P.O., S.O.C.P.1, 1821/2296/24; *D.E.P.*, 29 June, 10 July 1824; *S.O.I. evidence*, p. 107, H.C. 1825 (20), vii, 1.

149. Broeker, *Rural disorder*, pp. 121, 157–8.

by Rockite notices ordering Protestant clergymen to discontinue the holding of divine service for troops stationed in their parishes.[150]

A common Rockite view of the army (and of the police as well) was to see it as a force designed especially for the protection of Protestants and Orangemen. In a notice posted on the door of a Catholic chapel at Killaloe, Co. Clare, in November 1821, Captain Rock offered to "promote & reward" anyone who would shoot eight named persons, apparently all Protestants. On the back of this notice were scribbled the words, "With this + we will conquer any reg[imen]t [of] cavalry; it is fixed to begin to end in the year 25."[151] Even plainer was the attitude toward soldiers and police expressed in another notice which a body of Rockites left behind for a Protestant resident of Pallaskenry, Co. Limerick, after burning his out-offices in June 1823: "This is to show all hereticks the way that we will serve them, and to show them that they are not to put their trust in the Peelers or army, for when they are asleep, we will be awake, and let all the bloody Orangemen of Pallas know that we are preparing for them against the first of July, and let them not boast of the forty thousand, for this is the death they may all expect."[152] What helped to solidify such views of the army was the fact that temporary barracks for troops, especially those stationed in dispersed rural outposts, were usually provided by Protestant gentlemen or clergymen. To those Rockites who burned buildings that served or were capable of serving as makeshift barracks, it must have seemed more than a coincidence that their owners were so often members of the established church.[153]

One notorious incident which underscored the depth of Rockite hostility toward the army, and which seems to have had sectarian overtones, was the raping of certain women whose husbands belonged to the 1st Rifle Brigade. This episode occurred near Kildorrery, Co. Cork, in mid-February 1822. A group of women traveling with children in three cars or wagons in advance of their soldier husbands was stopped by a band of about forty men after passing through Kildorrery on their way to new quarters. According to the earliest reports of the incident, seven or nine of the dozen women in the group were taken from the cars and violated in what amounted to a series of gang rapes.[154] From the account of a later trial of three men accused of participating in this brutal assault, it appears that fewer women than originally reported may have been

150. S.P.O., S.O.C.P.1, 1823/2513/7.
151. Threatening notice, 19 Nov. 1821, enclosed in Ensign Connop to Lieutenant-Colonel Creagh, 30 Nov. 1821 (S.P.O., S.O.C.P.1, 2296/48).
152. D.E.P., 24 June 1823.
153. S.P.O., S.O.C.P.1, 1822/2343/44; 1822/2347/28, 40; 1823/2511/41, 44.
154. D.E.P., 21, 23 Feb. 1822; S.P.O., S.O.C.P.1, 1822/2345/32.

abused, and that in each of the rapes only two or three men were in-volved, though others assisted in holding down the victims. Clearly, the assault was intended as an act of Rockite vengeance against the absent husbands of these women. (Rape as punishment was not unknown in other contexts at this time.[155]) In fact, one of the assailants boasted to his victim that "he would let the Riflemen know that it was *Captain Rock's* men" who did the deed.[156] Whether these self-proclaimed Rockites were also prompted by sectarian animus is not absolutely certain, but a number of circumstances raise the possibility of sectarian motivation. First, the Rockites reportedly threatened to kill every English or Scottish woman in the group. Second, a woman who was ravished testified that one of her attackers had specifically asked if there was an officer's or a sergeant's wife riding on her car, a question perhaps designed to isolate a Protestant victim.[157] The talk in some millenarian notices of ravishing the wives of heretics could also be taken to lend support to this conjec-ture. But whatever was in the minds of these Rockites, there can be no doubt that the great influx of Protestant soldiers into the disturbed southern counties during the early 1820s thickened the strands of millenarianism and sectarianism in popular Catholic culture.

VII

One final aspect of the intriguing subject of Catholic millenarianism — an epilogue to its role in the Rockite agitation — should be treated here. As the Rockite movement faded almost everywhere in the south during the second half of 1824, the O'Connellite campaign for Catholic eman-cipation began to take firm hold at the grass roots. Despite certain quali-fications which should be made, the newfound position of priests on the popular side being the most important, there is much to be said for the view that energies previously channeled into a great clandestine move-ment, mostly agrarian in its objectives and quite violent in its tactics, now came to be funneled into an open, nonviolent crusade for political rights. What is significant for our purposes is that millenarianism con-tinued to be a factor of some weight in the new political agitation as it had been among the Rockites. Catholic priests and bishops might dismiss millennial predictions as a heap of "unintelligible farrago,"[158] while middle- and upper-class supporters of the Catholic Association might

155. For the raping of a servant girl whose sister had been a crown witness, see *D.E.P.*, 12, 14 Mar., 25 Apr. 1822. See also S.P.O., S.O.C.P.1, 1823/2513/62.

156. *D.E.P.*, 11 Apr. 1822.

157. *D.E.P.*, 23 Feb., 11 Apr. 1822.

158. *S.O.I. evidence*, p. 379, H.C. 1825 (20), vii, 1.

attribute their persistence to the schemes of Protestant proselytizers and Orangemen.[159] Nonetheless, the transition of 1824 was considerably facilitated by this cultural continuity between the two movements.

Most, though not all, of the evidence for this interpretation comes from members of the Protestant elite or from those in positions of authority. Some reported that a general rising in the near future was being planned or at least feverishly discussed; others observed that Pastorini's prophecy about the destruction of heresy in 1825, which had subsided for a time, had once again been revived.[160] No doubt a certain discount must be made for the nervousness or paranoia of numerous Protestants as the year of their long-heralded doom finally approached.[161] But to dismiss this evidence out of hand as the product of overwrought imaginations would be a serious mistake. The villains of the piece were Daniel O'Connell and the priests, especially the latter, who were so assiduously directing the collection of the so-called Catholic rent, the already-famous penny a month.[162] The gravamen of the charges against the clergy, apart from their alleged use of spiritual terrors to enforce payment, was that their personal assistance in the collection of the rent, accompanied by "inflammatory harangues" and a decided reticence about how the money would be employed, contributed to a climate thick with talk of Pastorini and revolution.[163]

O'Connell appeared to be the chief political beneficiary of all this ferment. With some reason Protestants believed that in spite of his repeated condemnations of Ribbonism and Whiteboyism, the peasantry flocked to the standard of his Catholic Association believing that he was about to lead an armed revolt.[164] That some country people saw O'Connell in this light is not really surprising. After all, no other contemporary barrister defended half as many accused Whiteboys, or saved half as many from the gibbet. No Rockite brief was so atrocious that O'Connell refused to take it, not even the case of those charged with raping the women

159. See section I above.
160. S.P.O., S.O.C.P.1, 1824/2619/55–6; S.O.I. evidence, pp. 14–15, H.C. 1825 (181), ix, 1.
161. S.O.I. evidence, pp. 279, 379, 440, 501, 839–40, H.C. 1825 (129), viii, 173, 293, 455; S.O.I. evidence, pp. 14, 17, 19, 25, H.C. 1825 (181), ix, 1.
162. S.P.O., S.O.C.P.1, 1824/2615/49, 52; S.O.I. evidence, pp. 6–7, 13–16, H.C. 1825 (181), ix, 1.
163. S.P.O., S.O.C.P.1, 1824/2619/51, 56; S.O.I. evidence, pp. 13–16, H.C. 1825 (181), ix, 1.
164. S.P.O., S.O.C.P.1, 1824/2621/64. "I beg to mention one of the many reports in circulation amongst the lower classes, which is that the [Catholic] rent *is to pay a police which Mr. O'Connell is going to raise*" (George M. Drought to Henry Goulburn, 11 Nov. 1824, quoted in S.O.I. evidence, pp. 13–14, H.C. 1825 (181), ix, 1).

of the Rifle Brigade.[165] Far more of the peasantry envisioned O'Connell as the deliverer who would fulfill the prediction of the destruction of Protestantism, or who would at least accomplish its abasement in Ireland. One of the best-known songs composed by the blind County Galway poet Raftery, "The Catholic rent," places O'Connell in exactly this position — the scatterer of heretics, as revealed by Pastorini.[166]

165. *D.E.P.*, 11 Apr. 1822. O'Connell was also a counsel for the defense in trials arising from the murder of Thomas Hoskins, the burning of Churchtown barracks (three policemen were killed in this incident), the abduction and rape of Miss Honora Goold, and the slaying of the Franks — all notorious crimes connected with the Rockite movement (*D.E.P.*, 20 Sept. 1821; 6, 8, 27 Aug. 1822; 15, 17 Apr., 28 Aug. 1824; S.P.O., S.O.C.P.1, 1822/2354/8).

166. This ballad, probably written in 1828, was sung to the air of "St. Patrick's Day." See Douglas Hyde, *Songs ascribed to Raftery, being the fifth chapter of "The love songs of Connacht"* (Irish University Press, Shannon, 1973; originally published 1903), pp. 113–23. See also Gearóid Ó Tuathaigh, *Ireland before the famine, 1798–1848* (Dublin, 1972), pp. 66–8.

BIBLIOGRAPHY

Contemporary sources

Manuscript material
Public Record Office of Northern Ireland, Belfast
  Redesdale papers (T.3030/C.34/13/2,3).
State Paper Office, Dublin
  State of the country papers, series 1.

Contemporary publications
I. Parliamentary papers (in chronological order)
  A return of the number of troops or corps of effective yeomanry . . . , so far as relates to Ireland, H.C. 1821 (306), xix, 177.
  Abstract of returns relative to magistrates, constables, and subconstables appointed under the constables' act for Ireland, H.C. 1824 (257), xxii, 405.
  Minutes of evidence taken before the select committee appointed to inquire into the disturbances in Ireland, in the last session of Parliament, 13 May–18 June 1824, H.C. 1825 (20), vii, 1.
  Minutes of evidence taken before the select committee of the House of Lords appointed to examine into the nature and extent of the disturbances which have prevailed in those districts of Ireland which are now subject to the provisions of the insurrection act, and to report to the House, 18 May–23 June 1824, H.C. 1825 (200), vii, 501.
  Report from the select committee on the state of Ireland, ordered to be printed

138 THE TRADITION OF VIOLENCE

30 June 1825, with the four reports of minutes of evidence, H.C. 1825 (129), viii, 1, 173, 293, 455.

Minutes of evidence taken before the select committee of the House of Lords appointed to inquire into the state of Ireland, more particularly with reference to the circumstances which may have led to disturbances in that part of the United Kingdom, 18 February–21 March 1825, H.C. 1825 (181), ix, 1.

II. Newspapers
Dublin Evening Post.

III. Other contemporary publications
Carleton, William. "The Irish prophecy man" in *Irish Penny Journal*, i, no. 50 (12 June 1841), pp. 393–6.
Carleton, William. *Traits and stories of the Irish peasantry* (London, n.d.).
[O'Sullivan, Mortimer]. *Captain Rock detected, or the origin and character of the recent disturbances, and the causes, moral and political, of the present alarming condition of the south and west of Ireland, fully and fairly considered and exposed by a Munster farmer* (London, 1824).
The treble almanack for the year 1824, containing (I) John Watson Stewart's almanack; (II) the English court registry; (III) Wilson's Dublin directory, with a new, correct plan of the city; forming the most complete lists published of the present civil, military, and naval establishments of Great Britain & Ireland (Dublin, 1824).
[Walmesley, Charles]. *The general history of the Christian church from her birth to her final triumphant state in heaven, chiefly deduced from the Apocalypse of St. John the apostle, by Sig [nor] Pastorini* (Dublin, 1790).
[Walmesley, Charles]. *The general history of the Christian church . . .* (4th ed., Dublin, 1805).
[Walmesley, Charles]. *The general history of the Christian church . . .* (6th ed., Belfast, 1816).
[Walmesley, Charles]. *The general history of the Christian church . . .* (6th ed., Cork, 1820).

Later works

Writings in Irish studies
Akenson, D. H. *The Irish education experiment: the national system of education in the nineteenth century* (London and Toronto, 1970).
Akenson, D. H. *The Church of Ireland: ecclesiastical reform and revolution, 1800–1885* (New Haven and London, 1971).
Bowen, Desmond. *The Protestant crusade in Ireland, 1800–70: a study of Protestant-Catholic relations between the act of union and disestablishment* (Dublin and Montreal, 1978).
Broeker, Galen. *Rural disorder and police reform in Ireland, 1812–36* (London and Toronto, 1970).

Donnelly, J. S., Jr. "Propagating the cause of the United Irishmen" in *Studies*, lxix, no. 273 (Spring 1980), pp. 5–23.

Hyde, Douglas. *Songs ascribed to Raftery, being the fifth chapter of "The love songs of Connacht"* (Irish University Press, Shannon, 1973; originally published 1903).

Lecky, W. E. H. *A history of Ireland in the eighteenth century*, 5 vols. (London, 1892).

Lee, Joseph. "The Ribbonmen" in T. D. Williams (ed.), *Secret societies in Ireland* (Dublin and New York, 1973), pp. 26–35.

Macintyre, Angus. *The liberator: Daniel O'Connell and the Irish party, 1830–1847* (London, 1965).

O'Farrell, Patrick. "Millenialism, messianism, and utopianism in Irish history" in *Anglo-Irish Studies*, ii (1976), pp. 45–68.

Ó Tuathaigh, Gearóid. *Ireland before the famine, 1798–1848* (Dublin, 1972).

Zimmermann, Georges-Denis. *Songs of Irish rebellion: political street ballads and rebel songs, 1780–1900* (Dublin, 1967).

Other writings in social science

Adas, Michael. *Prophets of rebellion: millenarian protest movements against the European colonial order* (Chapel Hill, N.C., 1979).

Cohn, Norman. *The pursuit of the millennium: revolutionary millenarians and mystical anarchists of the middle ages* (rev. ed., New York, 1970).

Harrison, J. F. C. *The second coming: popular millenarianism, 1780–1850* (London and New Brunswick, N.J., 1979).

Thrupp, S. D. (ed.). *Millennial dreams in action: studies in revolutionary religious movements* (Schocken Books paperback ed., New York, 1970).

Worsley, Peter. *The trumpet shall sound: a study of "cargo" cults in Melanesia* (2nd ed., New York, 1968).

II

LAND AND RELIGION IN ULSTER

The Province of Ulster

CARTOGRAPHIC LABORATORY, UNIVERSITY OF WISCONSIN – MADISON

Introduction

Ever since the seventeenth century the north of Ireland has been different from the rest of the country. What initially set the north apart was of course the early seventeenth-century plantations of Ulster from Scotland and England. As a result, the Gaelic order was overthrown and replaced by a new society in which the ruling class of mainly Anglican landowners stood in a special political relationship with those sections of the lower classes who were either Presbyterians or members of the Church of Ireland. Fear of a Catholic political and economic recovery solidified this bond. The relationship was to be severely strained at a few points in succeeding centuries, usually when the economic interests of the landed elite and those of the Protestant lower orders sharply diverged. But the Protestant lower classes never became so thoroughly alienated from their betters that they were prepared to unite wholeheartedly with Catholics in dismantling the traditional political and social structure.[1]

Also setting the north dramatically apart was its precocious industrial development, at first in a rural setting and subsequently in an urban

1. For the Ulster plantations, see especially Moody, *Londonderry plantation;* Michael Perceval-Maxwell, *The Scottish migration to Ulster in the reign of James I* (London, 1973); Aidan Clarke (with R. D. Edwards), "Pacification, plantation, and the Catholic question, 1603–23" in T. W. Moody, F. X. Martin, and F. J. Byrne (ed.), *A new history of Ireland,* vol. iii: *early modern Ireland, 1534–1691* (Oxford, 1976), pp. 193–205, 222–4; A. T. Q. Stewart, *The narrow ground: aspects of Ulster, 1609–1969* (London, 1977), pp. 21–41. The special relationship between the mainly Anglican landowners and the Protestant "lower orders" is a recurrent theme of D. W. Miller's recent book, *Queen's rebels: Ulster loyalism in historical perspective* (Dublin and New York, 1978).

environment. For most of the seventeenth century, Ulster, along with Connacht, was economically the least developed of the provinces of Ireland. Beginning in the 1680s and 1690s, however, the expansion of the linen industry transformed the character and economy of the countryside, especially in the counties of Antrim, Armagh, Down, Londonderry, and Tyrone. The phenomenal growth in exports of linen cloth during the eighteenth century tells the story in a nutshell. In 1700 fewer than half a million yards of Irish linen were exported to England, whereas in 1800 Britain took more than 38 million yards. Even though the linen industry had spread by the latter date to parts of north Leinster and Connacht, the weaving of cloth, as distinct from the spinning of yarn, was heavily concentrated in east Ulster. Particularly in this region of the province, the relative economic importance of agriculture substantially declined, and the quality of the farming there scandalized agricultural improvers like Arthur Young.[2]

As in other parts of Europe, so too in the north of Ireland, protoindustrialization acted as a spur to demographic expansion, especially in the second half of the eighteenth century. In those areas where weaving flourished, farmer-weavers were easily persuaded to divide their holdings with their sons when the latter were still comparatively young, since fathers and sons both won their livelihood far more from their looms than from agriculture. The hand-spinning of yarn also encouraged relatively early marriages by providing young women with a source of income that made them more attractive as nuptial partners. Such conditions almost certainly increased marital fertility; the prosperity associated with the linen industry in the late eighteenth century probably also raised life expectancy by reducing infant and child mortality. To this combination of factors may chiefly be attributed the doubling of the population of Ulster from some 600,000 or 700,000 in 1753 to more than 1,400,000 in 1791. Had it not been for emigration, which was heaviest from the northern province throughout the eighteenth century, the increase would have been greater still.[3]

2. On the development of the linen industry in the late seventeenth and the eighteenth centuries, see Gill, *Ir. linen industry*, pp. 6–220; Cullen, *Anglo-Ir. trade*, pp. 58–66, 107–10; Cullen, *An economic history of Ireland since 1660* (London, 1972), pp. 24–5, 59–64; W. H. Crawford, *Domestic industry in Ireland: the experience of the linen industry* (Dublin, 1972), pp. 1–37.

3. For the most recent estimate of the increase in the population of Ulster during the late eighteenth century, see Stuart Daultry, David Dickson, and Cormac Ó Gráda, "Eighteenth-century Irish population: new perspectives from old sources" in *Journal of Economic History*, xli, no. 3 (Sept. 1981), p. 624. On emigration from Ulster during the eighteenth century, see Dickson, *Ulster emig.* For the positive correlation between the development of protoindustrialization and population growth, see E. L. Almquist, "Mayo

Introduction

Swelling population and growing rural wealth brought about an especially steep rise in land values in the northeast between 1750 and 1800. This development obviously strengthened the economic position of the landed elite, but the rapid advance of the linen industry also created at least two major problems for the gentry. First, their monopoly of political power was threatened by the rise of a thrusting textile and mercantile elite, mainly Presbyterian in religion, radical in political outlook, and prepared to seek allies even among Catholics in the struggle for reform. Second, strain and even open conflict replaced the high degree of harmony which had previously characterized relations between the gentry and the Protestant lower orders.[4]

The most serious manifestation of this second problem before 1790 was the formidable Steelboy movement of 1769–72. The Steelboys' principal aims were to reduce rents and to stop evictions. Theirs was essentially a protest against the landlord elite for appropriating too large a share of the rural surplus. That the movement coincided with a series of poor harvests was not accidental. The effect of reduced crop yields on tenant incomes was equivalent to a sudden and dramatic increase in rents. But what energized the Steelboys' protest was the fact that even before the bad harvests, land values had been rising swiftly for over two decades. Tithes and grand-jury cess also contributed to agrarian turmoil at times. Yet the overall record of rural protest in Ulster between 1760 and 1790 is strikingly meager by comparison with the repeated Whiteboy outbreaks in Munster and parts of Leinster. Apparently, the scope for agrarian rebellion was significantly reduced by two factors: first, the progressive improvement in rural living standards (except during the 1770s, when linen production temporarily stagnated); and second, the lower intensity of the tithe grievance in Ulster, where a clerical tax on potatoes was largely unknown.[5]

On the other hand, industrial expansion helped to create favorable conditions for institutionalizing the sectarian consciousness of the Protestant lower orders. As David Miller argues in the first essay in this sec-

and beyond: land, domestic industry, and rural transformation in the Irish west" (Ph.D. dissertation, Boston University, 1977).

4. Miller, *Queen's rebels*, pp. 49–55. As a body, Presbyterians were divided in their attitudes toward relieving Catholics from the remaining penal laws. Even in the 1790s only a minority of northern Presbyterians supported the United Irish demand for what was called Catholic emancipation (Stewart, *Narrow ground*, pp. 101–10).

5. For agrarian protest in late eighteenth-century Ulster, see Lecky, *Ire.*, ii, 45–51; F. J. Bigger, *The Ulster land war of 1770 (the Hearts of Steel)* (Dublin, 1910); W. H. Crawford and Brian Trainor (ed.), *Aspects of Irish social history, 1750–1800* (Belfast, 1969), pp. 25–48; W. A. Maguire, "Lord Donegall and the Hearts of Steel" in *I.H.S.*, xxi, no. 84 (Sept. 1979), pp. 351–76.

tion, the emergence of the Protestant Peep-of-Day Boys in the mid-1780s should be seen as a product of structural changes in the linen industry, first manifested in County Armagh, coupled with divisions among the northern Protestant gentry on the Catholic question. The main structural change was the proletarianization of a significant section of the predominantly Protestant weavers of north Armagh. Many of them ceased to be independent artisans, buying yarn and selling cloth on their own account; they became instead the employees of a draper or bleacher, who supplied yarn and took their cloth while paying them a wage. Over such linen workers, as Miller explains, the landed elite could exercise little social control of a traditional kind.

In addition, numerous members of the northern Protestant gentry had ceased by about 1780 to consider Catholics a grave menace to the security of the established political and social order. To be sure, the events of the 1790s were to reconfirm the validity of the Catholic threat for Irish Protestants generally, but around 1780 there seemed to be good reasons to discount the danger. At that time it no longer appeared necessary or desirable to many of the northern gentry to choose tenants on religious grounds, to restrict Catholics to the less lucrative branches of the linen industry, or even to preserve inviolate that fundamental legal distinction by which Protestants alone enjoyed the privilege of bearing arms.

But this was heresy to the Protestant lower orders of County Armagh. The intrusion of Catholics into all branches of the linen industry, the increased ability of Catholics to compete for land, and especially the arming of some Catholics through the Volunteer movement all seemed to point ominously in the same direction: the abandonment by the landed elite of the meaning of Protestant ascendancy as that was understood by the Protestant lower orders. The Peep-of-Day Boys were determined on their own to reassert the customary meaning of Protestant hegemony. Miller shows that in north Armagh the gentry were often able to regain control over rebellious Protestants by incorporating them within new or revived Volunteer corps. But he also emphasizes that in south Armagh and elsewhere, this tactic contributed in a major way to the vigor of the Catholic response, institutionalized in the Defender movement. The aggressiveness of the Catholic Defenders by the end of the 1780s impelled the gentry toward the new role that a section of their class would assume in the Orange Order beginning in 1795.

If the decade of the 1790s was a great watershed in Irish history, it was even more of a turning point in the history of Ulster. Under the impact of the French revolution the political, economic, and religious tensions of the preceding half-century came to a head. Members of the chiefly Presbyterian textile and mercantile elite, joined by Presbyterian professional men, sought to break the monopoly of political power exercised by the Anglican aristocracy and gentry. To the Protestant lower orders the middle-class Presbyterian radicals appealed for support mainly by exploiting the traditional agrarian grievances of rents, tithes, and taxes. To the Catholics they appealed partly on the same grounds but mostly by embracing the cause of full civic and political equality for all members of that religious persuasion.

As long as the United Irishmen demanded only reform, however radical (as they did until 1795), they could rely on the backing of most middle-class Presbyterians. But once the commitment to revolution was made, much of this support fell away. The commitment to revolution, predicated as it was on a French invasion, also weakened the effectiveness of the United Irish appeal to the Protestant lower orders. This was especially true of those areas of the province containing either a Catholic majority or a large Catholic minority. In such areas the United Irishmen did make some inroads among Protestants. But fear and hatred of Catholics usually prevailed over agrarian grievances, particularly when the local gentry mobilized and led the Protestant lower classes in the Orange Order and the yeomanry. Outside Antrim and Down (which were the two Ulster counties with the smallest proportions of Catholics), the great bulk of the Protestant country people rallied in the end to the side of order, thus helping to defeat the forces of revolution.[6]

The resounding confirmation of the special relationship between the landed elite and the Protestant lower classes in the 1790s was to remain valid until the 1870s. One of the most striking features of early nineteenth-century Ulster was the comparative rarity of agrarian turmoil (though not of rural sectarian violence). Except for the protracted struggle of the illicit distillers of Inishowen in County Donegal against revenue officials, and some sporadic collective action against landlords and parsons in a few counties during the early 1830s, specifically agrarian movements were conspicuous by their absence. Indeed, all types of agrarian violence and intimidation were relatively uncommon in Ulster. In 1844 its nine counties had only 5.1 agrarian crimes for every 100,000

6. For the United Irish movement in Ulster and the loyalist reaction, see especially Rosamund Jacob, *The rise of the United Irishmen, 1791–4* (London, 1937); Charles Dickson, *Revolt in the north: Antrim and Down in 1798* (Dublin, 1960); Senior, *Orangeism, 1795–1836*, pp. 22–117; Peter Gibbon, *The origins of Ulster unionism: the formation of popular Protestant politics and ideology in nineteenth-century Ireland* (Manchester, 1975), pp. 22–43; R. B. McDowell, *Ireland in the age of imperialism and revolution, 1760–1801* (Oxford, 1979), section III; N. J. Curtin, "'Traitors, miscreants, and wicked men': mobilization, social composition, and aims of the United Irishmen in Ulster, 1791–8" (M.A. thesis, University of Wisconsin-Madison, 1980).

persons recorded in the 1841 census. The corresponding rates for the other three provinces were much higher: 11.3 in Leinster, 15.6 in Connacht, and 18 in Munster.[7]

The distinctiveness of Ulster in this respect is all the more remarkable because the rural areas of the province were subjected to a series of rude economic shocks in the early nineteenth century. Like farmers elsewhere in Ireland, those of the north were hit hard by the postwar deflation, particularly by the severe price declines of 1813–16, 1819–22, and the early 1830s. What made the picture even bleaker was the faltering of the rural linen industry and then the growing deindustrialization of the countryside. This latter process was painfully apparent all over Ireland, but its social implications were greatest in Ulster. As the export figures plainly show, linen production stagnated during the first fifteen years of the nineteenth century. The competition from cotton textiles seriously undermined the demand in Britain for Irish linens, especially the coarse varieties, and prices declined sharply as a result.

When output expanded again during the 1820s and 1830s, it did so under increasingly novel conditions. First, there occurred a switch from hand to machine, and from countryside to town, in the spinning of linen yarn. The availability of cheap rural female labor delayed the change-over in the earliest decades of the century, but the balance shifted deci-sively in favor of machinery soon after the invention of the wet-spinning process in 1825. By making it possible for even fine linens to be spun in the mills, the new process laid a firm basis for the concentration of the industry in Belfast and its vicinity. Domestic hand-spinning in the Ulster countryside, already weakened by the spreading use of mill yarn between 1800 and 1830, was almost completely destroyed in the course of the following decade.

Second, the position of the independent male weavers deteriorated, partly on account of falling prices for their cloth and also because of the entry of lower-paid women and boys into the weaving branch of the industry after the introduction of mill yarn. Since linen manufac-turers in and around Belfast offered their employees wages that were relatively higher than the earnings of independent producers, many rural handloom weavers migrated there and surrendered their independence. In fact, by the early 1840s most Ulster weavers had become the employ-ees of a manufacturer. Weaving itself continued to be a handicraft until the general adoption of the power loom in the 1850s and 1860s. Long before then, however, living standards had seriously declined. As the

7. J. S. Donnelly, Jr., *Landlord and tenant in nineteenth-century Ireland* (Dublin, 1973), p. 35.

prices of linen cloth fell sharply during the 1830s and early 1840s, so too did the earnings of handloom weavers, especially those who remained in the countryside.[8]

In view of these severe blows to the rural economy, the comparative rarity of agrarian violence and the maintenance of the special relationship between the landed elite and the Protestant tenantry require some explanation. Economic and political factors were both important. As already noted, the general absence of a clerical tax on potatoes, that perennial source of discord and basis of collective action in Munster and parts of Leinster, softened popular antagonism toward tithes in the north.[9] Also significant in Ulster was the relatively small number of graziers and substantial dairy farmers, groups which in other parts of Ireland protested vociferously when liability to tithe was increasingly extended to grassland after the passage of the tithe-composition acts of 1823–4. In Munster and Leinster large farmers with pastoral interests furnished numerous leaders to the tithe war of the early 1830s.[10] In Ulster, however, where tillage greatly predominated and large holdings were rare, the movement was weaker than in any of the other provinces.[11] No doubt the anti-Protestant overtones of the tithe war in the south helped to isolate northern Presbyterian and Anglican tithe payers from the agitation. But material differences in their situation go a long way in explaining their aloofness.

Most historians have regarded the general recognition of tenant right by Ulster landlords as the principal reason for the comparative tranquillity of the north in the early nineteenth century. Tenant right or, as it came to be called, the Ulster custom was not in fact homogeneous throughout the province, but the kernel of the practice was the acknowledged right of an outgoing tenant (usually a bankrupt or failing tenant) to sell his interest to a solvent successor. This interest was conceived as the value of the unexhausted improvements or, more properly, as the value of the occupancy right. An unlimited right of sale (i.e., by auction to the highest bidder, without any need for landlord approval of the purchaser or the price) may have become standard by 1815. But the desire to check

---

8. On the linen industry in Ulster during the early nineteenth century, see Gill, *Ir. linen industry*, pp. 221–334; Green, *Lagan valley*; Cullen, *Economic history*, pp. 119–21; Crawford, *Domestic industry*, pp. 38–71.

9. Potatoes were liable to tithe only in Londonderry, Tyrone, and parts of Donegal (Patrick O'Donoghue, "The tithe war, 1830–1833" [M.A. thesis, University College, Dublin, 1961], p. 3).

10. For the effects of the tithe-composition acts, see Patrick O'Donoghue, "Causes of the opposition to tithes, 1830–38" in *Studia Hib.*, no. 5 (1965), pp. 13–19.

11. The movement was also weak in Connacht (O'Donoghue, "Tithe war," pp. 143–6).

subdivision and to promote consolidation of holdings subsequently led numerous Ulster proprietors and their agents to impose certain restrictions on sales. On the other hand, even when a landlord prohibited an auction and circumscribed the range of potential buyers or limited the purchase price, the intent and the usual result was still to leave the departing tenant with a substantial sum of money after his arrears of rent had been paid.[12]

The Ulster custom, however, would have been a far less effective device for peacefully removing tenants had not the willingness to accept emigration become so rooted a feature of northern life during the early nineteenth century. It was in general his readiness to board an emigrant ship that allowed the northern tenant to contemplate the sale of his holding with relative equanimity. The opportunity for internal migration to Belfast also existed, but despite the speed with which this town grew between 1790 and 1850, its attractiveness was distinctly inferior to the lure of North America. Relatively light in the first fifteen years of the century, emigration increased enormously during the thirty years before the great famine. It has been estimated that roughly one million people left Ireland for the United States and Canada between 1815 and 1845, and over the same period several hundred thousand more took up residence in Britain. Ulster's share of this exodus cannot be computed precisely. But the available evidence indicates that the province supplied at least 40 percent and perhaps as much as 50 percent of all Irish emigrants to North America — a total of 400,000 or 500,000 people — in the thirty years before the famine. Almost certainly, the general level of agrarian violence and intimidation in the north would have been much closer to that of the other provinces if emigration had not served as a great safety valve.[13]

If tenant right and emigration together helped to prevent any serious deterioration in the special relationship between the landed elite and the Protestant lower orders in the countryside, events in the political sphere invested that relationship with added significance. The recoil of

12. On northern tenant right in the late eighteenth and early nineteenth centuries, see W. A. Maguire, *The Downshire estates in Ireland, 1801–1845: the management of Irish landed estates in the early nineteenth century* (Oxford, 1972), pp. 138–47; W. H. Crawford, "Landlord-tenant relations in Ulster, 1609–1820" in *Irish Economic and Social History*, ii (1975), pp. 5–21.

13. For estimates of emigration from the Ulster counties between 1815 and 1845, see W. F. Adams, *Ireland and Irish emigration to the new world from 1815 to the famine* (New Haven and London, 1932), passim. See also Connell, *Population*, pp. 27–9; S. H. Cousens, "The regional variation in emigration from Ireland between 1821 and 1841" in *Transactions and Papers of the Institute of British Geographers*, no. 37 (Dec. 1965), pp. 15–30.

most northern Protestants of all classes from the ideals of the United Irishmen — ideals perverted by Catholic atrocities in the south — was strengthened by the revival of the Catholic "menace" in new forms under Daniel O'Connell. His crusade for Catholic emancipation in the 1820s, accompanied by fierce denunciations of the Orange Order, rearoused in most Ulster Protestants the old fears of Catholic political domination. One result was that sectarian clashes between bodies of Orangemen and Catholic Ribbonmen intensified in the north. In addition, following O'Connell's famous by-election victory in County Clare in 1828, Protestant Brunswick clubs, dedicated to resisting Catholic claims by preparing petitions and holding public meetings, sprang up all over Ulster. Led by members of the upper class, but with the rank and file drawn chiefly from the lower orders, more than 100 such clubs were established within three months — vivid testimony to pan-Protestant solidarity. And a similar reaction greeted O'Connell's repeal movement in the early 1840s. His theatrical protestations of loyalty to Queen Victoria were lost on northern Protestants, who generally regarded this movement as even more subversive than the last. For in their view the repeal of the act of union would immediately open the way to a Catholic-controlled parliament in Ireland. The association of Irish nationalism with Catholicism, evident in both of these mass movements, was an unintended prescription for the longevity of the special interclass relationship in Ulster, despite all the pain of agricultural slumps and rural deindustrialization.[14]

Although at midcentury northern politics thus seemed to be firmly locked into a predictable mold, the unpredictable happened between 1870 and 1881: the landed elite was challenged at the polls as it had never been before. From somewhat different perspectives the two remaining essays in this section — one by Brian Walker, the other by Paul Bew and Frank Wright — deal with this extensive erosion of landlord hegemony as well as with its restoration (at least over the Protestant country people) during the political crisis of 1885-6. Before 1870 any objective observer of the political situation in Ulster would have concluded that agrarian radicals had little prospect of drawing votes from Catholic and Protestant tenants in numbers sufficient to secure more than a few seats in parliamentary elections in rural constituencies. The scope for the development of agrarian radicalism as a political force then appeared to be narrowly limited, even among enfranchised Catholics. In only three northern counties (Donegal, Monaghan, and Cavan) did Catholic voters equal or exceed the number of enfranchised Presbyterians and Angli-

14. Senior, *Orangeism, 1795–1836*, pp. 204–34; Robert Kee, *The green flag: a history of Irish nationalism* (London, 1972), pp. 207–8, 213–15.

cans. And before the advent of the Home Rule party many Ulster Catholic farmers backed Conservative rather than Liberal candidates when such a choice was presented to them. Protestant tenants did the same on an even greater scale. The results of the six general elections between 1847 and 1868 in the nine Ulster counties should have been enough to discourage even the most fanatical opponents of the Tory landlord elite: of the 108 candidates returned, only 7 were Liberals. Admittedly, the great majority of the Tories were elected without a contest, but the outcome of contested elections in the northern counties between 1847 and 1868 augured ill for the Liberals, since 15 of their candidates were defeated. Even in the early 1850s, when agricultural prices were depressed, Ulster Liberals were unable or unwilling to capitalize on agrarian discontent among farmers. In the 1852 general election the Tories captured every seat but one in the northern county constituencies.[15]

As Bew and Wright argue, the problem with the Ulster Liberals was that they lacked any meaningful agrarian program. The idea of fixity of tenure as long as rent was paid, and that of the limitation of rents by public tribunals, were generally anathema to these Liberals. Given the social background of the Ulster Liberal leaders, this negative attitude is scarcely surprising. The party was controlled by urban (chiefly Belfast) business and professional men, joined by a relatively small number of Liberal landowners. Though the Liberals hoped to build an urban-rural coalition embracing at least the more substantial (and mainly Protestant) farmers, they had no realistic notion of how even this limited goal might be accomplished. Economic conditions between 1854 and 1876 did not stimulate creative thought on this problem. Apart from the agricultural depression of 1859–64, which affected Ulster least of all, the northern countryside had never known greater prosperity.

But grievances can be nourished even in prosperous times, and as the authors of these two essays show, Gladstone's land act of 1870 gave northern farmers much cause to complain. This fact is not well appreciated by scholars.[16] What grievances could northern tenants possibly have had after Gladstone's act invested their cherished Ulster custom with the force of law? There were two in particular. One stemmed from a circumstance already mentioned: a variety of customs affecting the sale of a tenant's right of occupancy prevailed on different northern estates. Directly or indirectly, these usages restricted the purchase price of tenant right. Land-

15. B. M. Walker (ed.), *Parliamentary election results in Ireland, 1801–1922* (Dublin, 1978), pp. 248, 250, 259, 267–8, 281, 297, 305, 316.

16. A rare exception is R. W. Kirkpatrick, "Origins and development of the land war in mid-Ulster, 1879–85" in F. S. L. Lyons and R. A. J. Hawkins (ed.), *Ireland under the union: varieties of tension: essays in honour of T. W. Moody* (Oxford, 1980), pp. 201–35.

holders had come to regard such restrictions as infringements on the full-blown right of free sale. But the 1870 land act gave legal recognition to prevailing usages, and the courts therefore treated well-established landlord restrictions as inherent in local custom. The second grievance concerned leasehold tenancies and constituted a profound source of dissatisfaction among large farmers. By a notorious court decision leaseholders were debarred from exercising a right of sale at the expiration of their current agreements.

Walker in particular stresses that discontent over these two issues led to the formation of numerous tenant-right associations among farmers in the northern counties during the 1870s. He shows how these organizations became electoral arms of the Liberal party in rural constituencies. But Bew and Wright emphasize that Ulster Liberals were slow to accept the full demands of the tenant-right bodies for legislative redress of their grievances, and that the Liberals persisted until the end of the 1870s in taking a sectional, or Ulster-centered, approach to the land question. As a result, some Protestant votes which might otherwise have gone to Liberals were lost to Conservative candidates, who had begun to make suitable noises about the shortcomings of Gladstone's act as it affected Ulster. And some Catholic votes were lost to Home Rule nominees, whose agrarian and political objectives harmonized with the interests of Catholics in the north as well as the south.

Nevertheless, under the impact of agricultural depression and the rise of the Land League, Ulster Liberals finally abandoned their moderate and sectional approach in 1880 and espoused the "three Fs" (fair rents, fixity of tenure, and free sale), plus the gradual establishment of peasant proprietorship. This shift in policy, together with the growth of inter-denominational voting, set the stage for the capture by Liberals of eight Ulster county seats out of eighteen in the general election of that year. The authors of both essays agree that political cooperation between Protestants (even some Orangemen) and Catholics, and between Ulster Liberals and the Land League, continued until Parnell refused to endorse the land act of August 1881 and was clapped in jail along with several of his lieutenants.

Henceforth, for a variety of reasons, interdenominational political cooperation began to disintegrate. Some differences in emphasis appear in the explanations offered for the onset of this development. Walker stresses the general satisfaction of the northern tenant-right associations with the new law as well as the revulsion of Ulster Protestant farmers over agrarian violence in the south and over the Phoenix Park murders in Dublin. Focusing on the eclipse of northern liberalism, Bew and Wright attach special significance to the so-called nationalist invasion of Ulster; they believe that it polarized politics along denominational lines outside the Liberal strongholds of Antrim and Down.

Polarization was dramatically registered in the general elections of 1885 and 1886, which Walker examines at length. In these campaigns, waged on a new and greatly extended franchise, the Liberals were squeezed out of political existence in the north by the changed nature of the dominant issues and by the altered social composition of the electorate. Almost effortlessly, the tide of nationalism swept up the Ulster Catholic community without distinction of class. Catholic farmers and laborers voted for Home Rulers (or in some cases in 1885 for Tories, in order to punish the Liberals). The creed of unionism galvanized northern Protestants, but on this side the electoral outcome was largely determined by what happened to the new Protestant laboring vote. As Walker demonstrates, Protestant farm workers were safely mobilized by the Orange Order behind the Tory landlord banner. But perhaps this would have occurred even without the Orange Order, for as Bew and Wright suggest, the legacy of northern liberalism as a farmer-based party was in conflict with the class consciousness of many rural laborers, whose experience with farmers often inspired a hearty dislike. Moreover, since the Liberals were perceived as less sound on the constitutional issue, which had almost shoved the land question offstage, many Protestant farmers preferred the Conservatives as well.

Nothing has been or is so durable among all classes of northern Protestants as the fear of Catholic political domination. Time and again since the seventeenth century, it has reduced economic interests to political irrelevance. Long after the forces of nationalism had shattered the political power of the landed elite in the rest of Ireland, the aristocracy and gentry preserved a preeminent place in the intractable political environment of Ulster.

4 *David W. Miller*

The Armagh Troubles, 1784–95

The sectarian conflict in County Armagh between Protestant bands called Peep-of-Day Boys and Catholic bands styling themselves Defenders is known to students of Irish history primarily because of its apparent impact on larger historical developments. Defender societies arose in numerous parts of Ireland during the 1790s and figured prominently in events leading to the 1798 rebellion. The Peep-of-Day Boys have often been seen as precursors of the Loyal Orange Order, founded after a celebrated skirmish in north Armagh in 1795 known as the battle of the Diamond. After a sketch of the economic and social background of the troubles and a review of the principal recent efforts to explain them, I shall try to do two things in this essay. First, I will offer a new explanation of the troubles, and, second, I shall suggest how an understanding of these local events can give us new insight into the high politics of the age. In both these tasks I will make critical use of some explanations which contemporaries themselves offered for the troubles.

Economic, Social, and Political Background

It was the age of improvement in County Armagh. "I walked over the fine improvements which the primate has made near his lodge," John Wesley noted in his diary when he visited the town of Armagh in 1773. "He intends also to improve the town greatly and to execute many other grand designs."[1] Wesley was referring to Richard Robinson, Anglican

1. *The journal of the Rev. John Wesley, A.M.*, ed. Nehemiah Curnock (8 vols., London, 1938), v, 511–12.

archbishop of Armagh, afterward created Lord Rokeby, who by the time he died in 1794 could take credit for the establishment of a public library, a classical school, an observatory, barracks, a public infirmary, and a county jail as well as an archepiscopal palace and improvements to the cathedral. Under his auspices and influence Armagh was transformed from an array of mud cabins into the splendid ornament of the Ulster countryside which it is today.[2] Robinson also interested himself in improving the breed of cattle by bringing a bull and several cows "of the true Teeswater breed" from England.[3] The archbishop in fact set the tone for the whole gentry of the county. Arthur Young noted with pleasure in 1776 the "very great improvements" which William Brownlow, who owned the northeastern corner of the county from Lurgan almost to Portadown, had made in his demesne: a temple, a greenhouse, and a lake flanked by well-planned walks to vantage points from which to view Lough Neagh and the surrounding countryside.[4] On the other side of the county Young visited Elm Park, home of Maxwell Close, and was shown several other gentlemen's seats nearby, including that of a certain Mr. Leslie (just over the border in County Monaghan), whose "great improvements" included not only aesthetic developments but also the systematic draining, fertilizing, and fencing of his demesne. Having converted "a poor waste tract of little value . . . to a very fine grass land," he had "found the business of improvement profitable."[5]

If such agricultural improvements did not always extend beyond the landlords' demesnes to their tenants' holdings, this was, paradoxically, not so much a sign of the tenants' impoverishment as of their affluence, at least relative to tenants in other parts of Ireland. The real source of wealth for tenants (and, ultimately, for improving landlords) was the domestic manufacture of linen — so much so that tenants often neglected their little patches of agricultural land not out of laziness but because their looms were so much better sources of income. Linen had been the mainstay of the growing Irish export trade since the 1730s, and despite a setback in the 1770s, the linen industry was about to experience, in the late 1780s and early 1790s, the most rapid expansion in its history.[6] In 1784 almost 49 million yards of linen were produced in Ireland, of

    2. Gilbert Camblin, *The town in Ulster* (Belfast, 1951), pp. 92–3; *D.N.B.*, sub Robinson, Richard.
    3. *Arthur Young's tour in Ireland (1776–1779)*, ed. A. W. Hutton (2 vols., London and New York, 1892; reprinted Shannon, 1970), i, 119.
    4. Ibid., p. 127.
    5. Ibid., pp. 124–5.
    6. L. M. Cullen, *An economic history of Ireland since 1660* (London, 1972), pp. 51, 62.

which at least 15 million were brought to market within a 20-mile radius
of Portadown.[7]

The organization of linen manufacture was also becoming more complex. Earlier in the century weavers had ordinarily been independent
entrepreneurs, buying yarn and selling cloth in the open market. By the
1760s, however, weavers increasingly found themselves dependent upon
wealthier drapers, who would issue yarn to a weaver unable to buy it
on his own account and would then pay for the resulting cloth by the
piece. As the weaver was drawn into this system, he lost his independence
and became an employee even though his home might continue to be
his workplace.

How many weavers were there in County Armagh? Some 12,000 weavers would have been required simply to produce the amount of brown
linen sold at public markets in the county in 1784. An estimated one-
quarter of the linen manufactured in Ulster was woven by wage earners,
however, and did not pass through the public markets.[8] The proportion
was probably higher in areas such as north Armagh where fine linen was
made. Therefore, there were probably between 16,000 and 20,000 weavers in the county in the 1780s. Since the county contained, according to
the hearth-money returns, only some 22,000 houses in 1790,[9] there must
have been an average of almost one weaver per household. Many households, however, probably had two or more weavers each, while others
had none. In 1821 (after the textile industry had begun to shift from the
countryside to Belfast) a survey of Lord Gosford's Baleek manor, south
of Markethill, revealed 311 weavers among 278 families. But only 173
of these weavers were the landholders themselves, the remainder being
male children.[10] In the 1780s, particularly in north Armagh, some of the
wage-earning journeymen weavers may have resided with their parents,
and others may have had living arrangements which would not have
counted as separate households.

The volume of trade passing through the linen markets serving County
Armagh is depicted in figure 4.1. Most commercial linen production took
place in the northern half of the county, where, as shown by figure 4.2,
the population was predominantly Protestant. Although Catholics were
beginning to take it up, linen production for the international market
(as opposed to the weaving of narrow "bandle linen" for local consump-

7. Gill, *Ir. linen industry*, pp. 160–1; *Aspects of Irish social history, 1750–1800*, ed.
W. H. Crawford and Brian Trainor (Belfast, 1969), pp. 72–4 and pl. vii.

8. Gill, *Ir. linen industry*, p. 152.

9. Charles Coote, *Statistical survey of the county of Armagh* (Dublin, 1804), p. 246.

10. William Greig, *General report on the Gosford estates in County Armagh, 1821*,
intro. by F. M. L. Thompson and D. J. Tierney (Belfast, 1976), pp. 41–5.

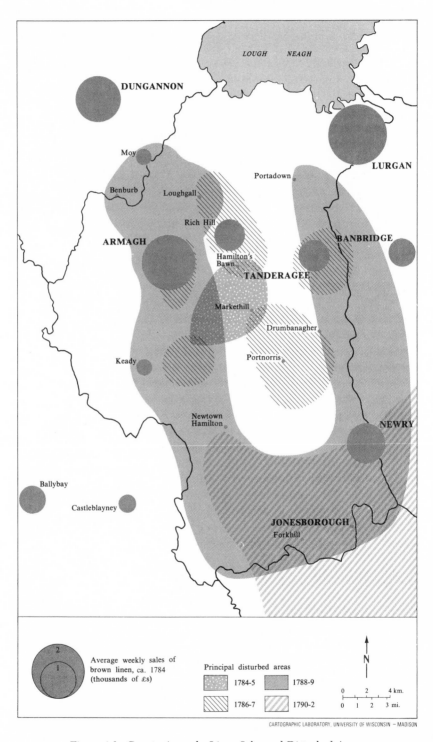

Figure 4.1. County Armagh: Linen Sales and Disturbed Areas

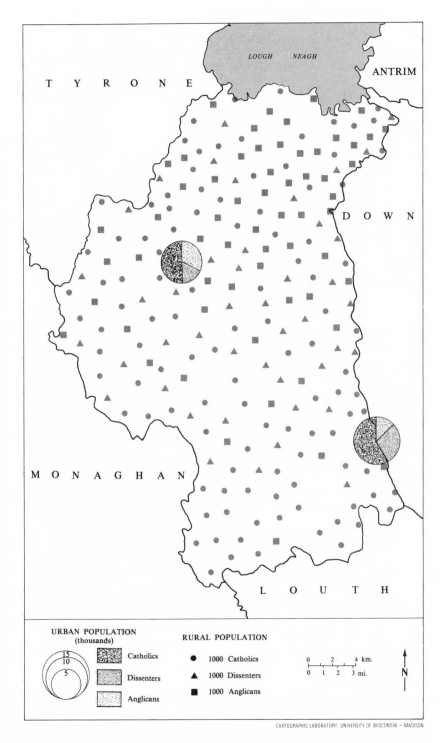

LOUGH   NEAGH

ANTRIM

T Y R O N E

D O W N

M O N A G H A N

L O U T H

URBAN POPULATION
(thousands)

RURAL POPULATION

15
10
5

Catholics

Dissenters

Anglicans

● 1000 Catholics

▲ 1000 Dissenters

■ 1000 Anglicans

0   2   4 km.

0 1 2 3 mi.

N

CARTOGRAPHIC LABORATORY, UNIVERSITY OF WISCONSIN – MADISON

Figure 4.2.   County Armagh: Distribution of the Population by Religious Affiliation, 1834

tion) had originally flourished in the Protestant colony in Ulster. In north Armagh and west Down linen had become so profitable that weavers whose grandfathers had acquired looms to supplement their income from farming now cared little for agriculture. "I am now got into the linen country, and the worst husbandry I have met with," Young declared as he approached Markethill on the road from Newry.[11] Since land had ceased to be the principal means of production, tenants were quite prepared to subdivide their holdings to enable their sons to set themselves up as weavers too. Of the "manufacturer" with a 10-acre holding, Young remarked, "When his son grows up and marries, he universally divides his farm with him, building a new mud cabbin; thus farms are constantly growing less and less."[12] So also did population density in north Armagh soar.

Since figure 4.2 is based on a census taken in 1834, it shows population densities somewhat greater than those which obtained in the 1780s. Correlation of these data with partial returns of a religious census in 1766, however, reveals that figure 4.2 is a reasonably good guide to the Protestant-Catholic balance in different portions of the county during the late eighteenth century.[13] The concentration of Anglicans in the northeast corner of Armagh reflects the fact that this district had been set aside for English settlement in the original scheme for the Ulster plantation in the early seventeenth century. Another district, the Fews in the southwest of the county, had been earmarked for Scottish settlement, but as figure 4.2 reveals, that aspect of the plan was a failure. The distribution of Presbyterians, who were spread fairly evenly through the middle third of Armagh, probably reflects eighteenth-century westward migration by descendants of earlier Scottish settlers in Down and Antrim.

As demonstrated by figure 4.2, Catholics were at least a substantial minority nearly everywhere in County Armagh. Descendants of the population displaced by the seventeenth-century plantations, Catholics were especially numerous on less desirable land, such as the boggy south shore of Lough Neagh and the hilly terrain between Newry and Keady. Where they were truly isolated from British settlers, the Catholics tended to retain another sharp cultural difference: the Irish language. In the two southernmost baronies of the county, Upper Orior and Upper Fews, the 1851 census found that 45 percent of those seventy years of age or older could speak Irish. Since these persons were the survivors of the younger generation of the 1780s, and since no doubt a higher proportion

11. Young, *Tour*, i, 116.
12. Ibid., p. 120.
13. R = 0.883 for nineteen observations.

of the older generation alive at that time were Irish-speaking, probably well over half the Catholics in the extreme south of Armagh still retained the old language in the 1780s.

Prior to the 1740s, it was said, Catholics had refrained from commercial linen weaving, considering it "as a manufacture introduced by the Protestants or Huguenots tending to change their religion."[14] By the last quarter of the century, however, Catholics were definitely engaged in weaving, though probably seldom as employers. While traveling between Newry and Armagh, Young noted: "Religion mostly Roman, but some Presbyterian and Church of England. Manufacturers generally Protestants."[15]

Predominantly Catholic sections of the county were prime targets for "improvement." Around 1750 "some enterprising Englishmen" took advantage of waterfalls near Keady to start a bleaching establishment there, thus promoting the linen trade, "previously to which the whole surrounding country was little better than an uncultivated heath."[16] Similarly, the town of Newtown Hamilton had been founded as recently as about 1770, "previously to which time the whole district was a dreary, wild, and uninhabited waste." Quickly, lands were brought under the plow, roads were built, an Anglican church was erected and its living endowed by the ubiquitous Primate Robinson, and significantly, "great numbers of persons were induced to settle" under the terms of advantageous leases.[17] By the 1790s the town had been drawn into the linen economy.[18]

The role that County Armagh played in national politics was also probably seen by contemporaries as a reflection of the spirit of "improvement." Throughout most of the eighteenth century the Irish polity had consisted essentially of a narrow elite of landed Protestants represented in a Parliament which lacked effective powers to make policy independently of the British government. In the early 1780s, however, a "Patriot party" in the Irish Parliament achieved its goals of legislative autonomy and commercial concessions (known, somewhat misleadingly, as free trade). These measures had been wrested from a reluctant British government by the threat of force on the part of paramilitary bodies called the Volunteers.[19]

14. W. H. Crawford, *Domestic industry in Ireland: the experience of the linen industry* (Dublin, 1972), p. 36, quoting Robert Stephenson (1795).

15. Young, *Tour*, i, 117.

16. Lewis, *Topog. dict. Ire.*, ii, 34.

17. Ibid., pp. 400–1.

18. W. H. Crawford, "Economy and society in south Ulster in the eighteenth century" in *Clogher Rec.*, viii (1975), p. 247.

19. For an excellent recent account of the Volunteers, see P. D. H. Smyth, "The

The Volunteers were an unauthorized Protestant militia formed in 1778 at a time of alarm over possible French invasion. That threat evaporated, but the movement flourished and became a tool in the hands of gentry who supported Patriot goals.

County Armagh was very much involved in these developments. Lord Charlemont, who owned extensive property in the county, became the commander-in-chief of the Volunteers, and it was a meeting at Armagh of officers and delegates of the first Ulster regiment that summoned the famous Volunteer convention of 15 February 1782 at Dungannon.[20] Resolutions were there adopted asserting that "a claim of any body of men, other than the king, lords, and commons of Ireland, to make laws to bind this kingdom is unconstitutional, illegal, and a grievance," and that "the ports of this country are by right open to all foreign countries not at war with the king." These resolutions formed the basis of the new constitutional settlement which the Patriot party achieved later that year. When added to the repeal of certain of the penal laws which had been enacted to exclude Catholics from the polity, and to the fact that some Volunteer units soon began to make conciliatory gestures toward Catholics, these developments seemed to mark a new era both for Armagh and for the whole of Ireland.

Recent Explanations

In recent historiography two explanations of the troubles stand out. Hereward Senior suggests that land hunger and insecurity were fundamental realities "nearly everywhere" in eighteenth-century Ireland.[21] In response, from about 1760 on, the peasantry organized oath-bound secret societies such as the (Catholic) Whiteboys of the south, and the Oakboys and Steelboys, who included many northern Protestant tenants. The Steelboys, though they directed their protest largely against landlords rather than Catholics, were nevertheless "potential agencies of denominational strife," for one of their grievances was the eviction of Protestant tenants in favor of Catholics willing to pay higher rents. Thus, Senior argues, when the Volunteer movement "disturbed the balance of forces" in the countryside by, for example, causing widespread distribution of arms, local brawls assumed added importance. Hence, a fight at Markethill in July 1784 between two Presbyterians, in which a Catholic incautiously took the side of the winner, prompted the loser to form out

---

Volunteers and Parliament, 1779–84" in Thomas Bartlett and D. W. Hayton (ed.), *Penal era and golden age: essays in Irish history, 1690–1800* (Belfast, 1979), pp. 113–36.

20. Lecky, *Ire.*, ii, 282.

21. Senior, *Orangeism, 1795–1836*, pp. 1–21.

of "Steelboy elements" a band known as the Nappach Fleet. This band's searches for arms in Catholic hands became a pretext, Senior implies, for driving Catholics out of Ulster because of the threat they posed to Protestant living standards, though he cites no evidence of such expulsions in the 1780s.[22]

Peter Gibbon, on the other hand, realizes how unsatisfactory it is to attribute the Peep-of-Day Boy violence of the 1780s to an imminent threat posed by Catholic weavers to Protestant living standards.[23] After all, these were years of rapid expansion in the linen industry; there was no shortage of employment. Instead, Gibbon argues that Armagh Protestants perceived a generalized threat to the system of social inequality from which they had hitherto benefited. Since the dominant economic activity in north Armagh was linen manufacture, not commercial farming, and since domestic weaving required only a trivial amount of land, he maintains that population pressure upon the land could not have been the main source of the troubles. Gibbon analyzes the problem by contrasting the experience of those Presbyterian areas of Down and Antrim where the United Irish movement flourished in the 1790s with that of north Armagh and its environs, where the Orange Order got its start at the same time. In the relevant parts of Down and Antrim, he argues, large-scale commercial farming survived, and weaving remained in the hands of independent small entrepreneurs. But in north Armagh virtually all Protestant tenants had been reduced to holdings too small to support commercial farming and had become virtual employees of bleachers and other putters-out.

Therefore, Gibbon argues, farmers and weavers in Antrim and Down could and did organize in the United Irishmen to redress their grievances, but the Protestant population in County Armagh had been so "homogenized" that they could develop no effective revolutionary leadership. Instead, Armagh landlords were "cast in the role of tribune" for Protestant weavers. In order to cope with "the vicissitudes of submission to free-market forces," these weavers linked arms with those landlords who would accept such a role in reasserting the settlement of 1691 as they under-

---

22. Byrne does speak of some "well-disposed people" near Tanderagee being compelled, apparently temporarily, to flee "the county" in 1787, but massive forced migrations to Connacht seem not to have occurred until the mid-1790s. See [J. Byrne], *An impartial account of the late disturbances in the county of Armagh, containing all the principal meetings, battles, executions, whippings, &c. of the Break-o-Day-Men and Defenders since the year 1784 down to the year 1791, with a full and true account of the nature of the rising of both parties* (Dublin, 1792), pp. 28–9 (hereafter cited as *Impartial account*).

23. Peter Gibbon, *The origins of Ulster unionism: the formation of popular Protestant politics and ideology in nineteenth-century Ireland* (Manchester, 1975), pp. 22–43.

stood it, that is, the maintenance of Protestant ascendancy. In this arrangement, actualized in the formation of the Orange Order, landlords
were compensated for their loss of economic power (to a new elite of
drapers, bleachers, and eventually factory owners) with renewed political power. And weavers were compensated for their proletarianization
by the confirmation of their superiority over Catholics, who had previously been moving into the Protestant preserve of linen weaving.

   A rigorous evaluation of the explanations offered by Gibbon and Senior
should entail some consideration of general theories as to why outbreaks
of violence occur. Much, though by no means all, systematic thought on
collective violence can be divided into breakdown and solidarity theories.[24] Breakdown theories, of which the classic exponent is Durkheim,
generally envisage pervasive social change as dissolving the mechanisms
of society for controlling behavior, thus allowing considerable violence
and protest to grow and persist until a new, stable social order emerges.
Solidarity theories, the most notable being that of Marx, conceive of society as composed of well-defined groups with common interests. When
social change operates to some group's detriment or creates a new disadvantaged group, that segment of society naturally and understandably
resorts to violence to defend its interests.

   The explanations of both Senior and Gibbon rest on solidarity theories.
Even though Senior does not consciously advance any general theory of
conflict, his explanation relies heavily on the preexisting solidarities within
Irish society: "In Ireland . . . quarrels, no matter what their origin,
tended to divide along religious lines." He thus produces an explanation
which accords with a widespread current belief about Irish history: that
in the realm of sectarian relations nothing much ever changes. Gibbon,
on the other hand, sets out to discover change within the apparent continuity of Irish sectarian hostility. A new group — a rural proletariat — was
formed as a result of the increasingly sharp differentiation of functions
within linen manufacture. To protect themselves against falling to the
lowest possible status, its Protestant members sought to "enforce" the penal
code against Catholics. Landlords, who had also been losing status relative to linen bleachers, assumed the leadership of this rural proletariat
by avowing solidarity with it in the Orange Order.

   The basic weakness of the two explanations is the same: neither Senior
nor Gibbon seeks to discover the reasons for the Armagh troubles per
se. Each is really trying to explain the rise of an important manifestation
of solidarity in modern Ireland: the Loyal Orange Order. Both therefore

   24. I follow here the typology proposed by Charles Tilly, Louise Tilly, and Richard
Tilly in *The rebellious century, 1830–1930* (Cambridge, Mass., 1975), pp. 3–11.

rely on solidarity theories. As an explanation of the rise of the Orange Order, Gibbon's theory in fact works fairly well. But should the evolution of the Orange Order from 1795 be viewed simply as a continuation of the Peep-of-Day Boy phenomenon? Senior himself observes that the troubles which began in the mid-1780s seem to have ended in County Armagh in 1791.[25] Perhaps it is more accurate to say that sectarian violence in *north* Armagh virtually ended by early 1790, though Defenderism persisted in the predominantly Catholic southern quarter of the county even after 1791 and spread to neighboring Louth and Down as well.

Since the contemporary evidence so clearly suggests that the troubles, at least in north Armagh, went through two distinct phases, a satisfactory explanation must take account of that chronological pattern. Perhaps these two phases represent, respectively, the breakdown of previous forms of social control (up to 1790) and the creation of a new solidarity group (from 1794). If so, what is really needed is a synthesis of two theories: a breakdown theory to account for the first phase of the troubles and a solidarity theory to explain the origins of the Orange Order. Because Gibbon's solidarity theory is basically satisfactory for the latter purpose, this essay concentrates on reconstructing and explaining the initial phase, up to 1790 or so.

Toward a New Explanation

In trying to formulate a new explanation, I have found it useful to look carefully at the ways in which four contemporaries who wrote narrative recollections of the troubles tried to explain them. The most extensive of these narratives is a pamphlet by J. Byrne entitled *An impartial account of the late disturbances in the county of Armagh*, which was published in Dublin in 1792. Several early nineteenth-century historians, notably Sir Richard Musgrave, relied heavily on this work of fifty-seven pages. But its inaccessibility (apparently only one copy survives in a public repository in Ireland) has meant that later scholars have not fully exploited it. Byrne described himself as "a dyer and publican" and "an inhabitant of the town of Armagh." His name does not appear in the list of Armagh householders compiled for Primate Robinson in 1770. He has been tentatively identified, however, as the John Byrne elected by Armagh Catholics in 1790 as their representative on the Catholic Committee. Byrne claimed that he had kept a journal beginning around 1784, and though he could not have been an eyewitness to many of the events

---

25. Senior, *Orangeism, 1795–1836*, p. 12. But in this passage Senior wrongly follows Blacker in dating the battle of Lisnagade in 1791.

he recounts, he clearly made a habit of seeking the facts from those in a position to know them.[26] Supplementing Byrne's account are two long, reflective letters by other local observers. One was written in 1796 by John Ogle of Newry, the sheriff of County Armagh, and the other in 1797 by Dr. William Richardson, a Church of Ireland clergyman whose parish lay near the Armagh border in County Tyrone.[27] Finally, we have an unpublished memoir written after 1840 by Colonel William Blacker, an eyewitness to events surrounding the battle of the Diamond and a member of a prominent Orange family.[28]

The arguments of these four contemporary explanations can be divided into the *underlying causes* which are adduced and the *precipitating incidents* which are alleged to have triggered the Armagh unrest. I propose to deal in this section with the underlying causes identified by contemporaries because I have found some of their suggestions helpful in formulating my own explanation. In a subsequent section I shall deal with precipitating incidents.

Whereas both Senior and Gibbon posit underlying causes that one would associate with solidarity theories, three of the four contemporary explanations may be classified as breakdown theories. It might be supposed that this fact reflects only the nostalgic conservatism of literate, propertied people at the end of the eighteenth century — a hankering for the "good old days" of deference which neither Gibbon nor Senior could be expected to share. Ironically, however, it is the most certifiably reactionary of our contemporary observers — William Blacker — who makes assumptions which can be associated with solidarity thinking.

According to Blacker, the underlying cause of conflict was a fundamentally continuous Catholic conspiracy against Protestants, virtually unbroken since the age of religiodynastic wars. The Defenders were merely a "ramnification" [sic] of the Whiteboys. Blacker subscribed to the widespread belief among Irish Protestants that the initial Whiteboy rising was deliberately timed to coincide with the attempted French invasion of 1759.[29] In fact, the Whiteboy outbreaks began only after the defeat of

26. T. G. F. Paterson's notes on Byrne's pamphlet (hereafter cited as Paterson's notes), preface (P.R.O.N.I., T.1722); Crawford and Trainor, *Irish social history*, p. 175, citing P.R.O.I., M.238a. See also R. J. Hayes (ed.), *Manuscript sources for the history of Irish civilization* (11 vols., Boston, 1965), i, 453.

27. John Ogle to Edward Cooke, 15 July 1796 (S.P.O., Rebellion papers, 620/24/37); Dr. William Richardson to marquis of Abercorn, 14 Feb. 1797 (P.R.O.N.I., Abercorn papers, T.2541/IB3/6/4).

28. Extracts from the Blacker memoir in a lecture by T. G. F. Paterson (hereafter cited as Paterson lecture), pp. 3–14 (P.R.O.N.I., T.2595/4).

29. Paterson lecture, pp. 3–4 (ibid.). See also Young, *Tour*, i, 81.

the French fleet. As the years passed, however, Protestants telescoped into one grand conspiracy their memories of the diverse alarms at that time, and of the shudder which must have passed from one big house to the next when a French privateer actually took Carrickfergus briefly in 1760. This notion survived, in the teeth of the evidence, because before the 1770s the basis for solidarity among Catholics was assumed to be their loyalty to the alternative dynasty sponsored by France and their interest in recovering forfeited estates. Of course, even in the early eighteenth century the attachment of most Irish Catholics to the Stuart cause had been tenuous: the lead of the Scottish highlanders in 1715 and 1745 was not followed in Ireland. Not until the 1770s, however, did educated Irish Protestant opinion decisively, if not unanimously, accept the fact that Catholics had lost whatever basis for solidarity they may once have found in hopes for a Stuart restoration. This fact was being confirmed by Catholics who took the oath of allegiance and made other gestures of acquiescence in the status quo.[30]

The most celebrated feature of the Volunteering episode—the willingness of a large segment of the Protestant elite to turn their armed retainers against the government—is inconceivable without a conviction on the part of this elite that a new era had commenced. Solidarity with the government against the Catholic-Jacobite menace no longer seemed essential to Protestant survival.[31] John Ogle's explanation of the Armagh troubles turned on the second thoughts which he and no doubt other members of the elite had come to have about that conviction by the 1790s. The underlying cause of the troubles, in Ogle's view, was the Volunteers' challenge to established authority, a challenge which "promised general confusion." The particular form taken by this "confusion" was the willingness of popular Protestant forces to accept Catholic assistance. Thus the troubles derived from a breakdown in the assured dominance of the Protestant elite over the Catholics.

In the Rev. William Richardson's view the underlying cause of the troubles was a gradual breakdown of the Armagh gentry's control over their Protestant tenantry.[32] The process began in 1753 when a particular magistrate, trying to avoid giving offense, took no action to suppress the "party strife" which arose in a "bitterly contested" local election. The consequence was popular "insubordination," to which Richardson attrib-

30. John Brady, *Catholics and Catholicism in the eighteenth-century press* (Maynooth, 1965), pp. 191–5, 197–202, 204–5.
31. This point is developed further in my *Queen's rebels: Ulster loyalism in historical perspective* (Dublin and New York, 1978), pp. 37–9.
32. Rev. William Richardson to marquis of Abercorn, 14 Feb. 1797 (P.R.O.N.I., Abercorn papers, T.2541/IB3/6/4).

uted both the Oakboy and Steelboy risings of the next two decades. The "gentlemen of property and magistrates" were further divided by another electoral contest in 1776. In addition, "the progress of American doctrines" excited popular discontent, and the raising of the Volunteers enhanced popular hopes not only of redress of constitutional grievances but also of the lowering of rents. Richardson apparently regarded the emergence of a Patriot party in the Irish Parliament as a fatal break in the ranks of the governing class.

Byrne identified an entirely different underlying cause of breakdown, namely, the prosperity of the linen industry: "The great influx of cash and plentiful markets of provisions among the lower orders of the people, and so many young men taken at a short apprenticeship to the linen business [that] they get the handling of cash before they know its real value, prompts them to intoxication and riot before they have well digested their mother's milk."[33] Though this passage certainly reflects socially conservative and moralistic values, it also suggests some significant social processes likely to occur in a protoindustrial setting. As linen manufacture flourished, no doubt it did become possible for males to achieve economic independence of their parents at an earlier age than was possible in a predominantly agricultural economy. A father's ability to control the behavior of his adolescent and young adult sons was probably diminished as the supreme prize in his gift — inheritance of the family's holding — ceased to be as economically attractive as a loom and a cottage, though perhaps with no more than a vegetable garden attached to it.

Regrettably, little evidence has survived besides Byrne's word on the social composition of the Peep-of-Day Boys. There is, however, a fairly detailed list of alleged members of a crowd which killed one Cornelius Kearney at Rathfryland, Co. Down, in December 1785. The offense seems to bear so close a resemblance to Peep-of-Day Boy raids upon Catholic houses in Armagh, a few miles to the west, that the characteristics of the participants are worth mentioning. Eight of the eleven men named were described as weavers; the other three were a horsebreaker, a sawyer, and a laborer. Their ages ranged from twenty to thirty years.[34] While we cannot be certain how closely this crowd resembled those which were active in County Armagh, it does tend to corroborate Byrne's account of the sort of persons involved.

For Byrne, the crucial breakdown occurred at the level not of the ascendancy's dominance over the Catholics, as Ogle would assert, nor of the

33. Byrne, *Impartial account*, p. 27.
34. *B.N.L.*, 23–27 Dec. 1785.

local gentry's control over their Protestant tenantry and retainers, as Richardson would have it. Rather, it took place at the level of the family's control over its adolescent and young adult sons, particularly among Protestant families. This interpretation is consistent with Gibbon's picture of the socioeconomic structure of County Armagh in contrast to those parts of Antrim and Down which became United Irish strongholds. It has the further merit of recognizing, rather than lamely trying to explain away, the fundamental fact that linen weaving was a lucrative occupation in these years. Indeed, it provides a more satisfactory account of the role of economic change in these events than Gibbon's attempt to discern class formation in them.

What Happened: A Reconsideration

Figure 4.1 depicts the changing geographical extent of the troubles from 1784 to 1791. In 1784-5 the unrest reported by Byrne seems to have spread from Markethill no further than about 5 miles to the north, west, and southwest. Then calm apparently returned to the immediate Markethill vicinity, though it was encircled in 1786-7 by new disturbed areas: the neighborhoods of Tanderagee, Portnorris, Granemore, Armagh town, Rich Hill, and Loughgall. For 1788-9 little is heard of disturbances in the belt of territory from Portnorris to Markethill and northward through Hamilton's Bawn to Rich Hill. Rather, the serious troubles of these two years are found in a U-shaped band along the borders of the county: from Portadown through Tanderagee almost to Newry, and then across a broad stretch of mainly Catholic territory in the southern quarter of the county to Crossmaglen, and then north to Newtown Hamilton, Keady, Armagh, and Moy. There was some recrudescence of trouble near Markethill, where a murder occurred in 1790, but otherwise in 1790-1 disturbances apparently disappeared almost entirely from the northern half of the county. Violence continued in south Armagh, however, and spilled over into Down and Louth.

Generally, violence seems to have spread in concentric circles. As a new "circle" experienced violence, the previous circle within it calmed down. Each circle apparently experienced a violent phase of one to three years, except that in the southern sector of the outermost circle the violent phase lasted longer. These crude generalizations from the evidence would be consistent with a "breakdown" model in which the local sources of authority are caught unawares by the challenge to their authority but manage eventually to regain a semblance of control over their own dependents, though not before the disorder has spread to areas outside their own immediate influence. To the extent that such a breakdown may have occurred within the family, as Byrne suggests, this hypothesis is difficult to test, but it is possible to evaluate breakdown at other levels by studying the behavior of the Protestant gentry in both of their authority roles: landlords and magistrates. The persistence of unrest for a longer period of time in south Armagh might have been due to the very sparseness of gentry there. In 1783 only sixteen out of sixty-six County Armagh gentlemen's seats shown on *Taylor and Skinner's maps of the roads of Ireland* lay south of Markethill.[35] It is therefore appropriate to look closely at the gentry's response to the troubles.

To judge from Byrne's narrative, the gentry early recognized the Peep-of-Day Boys as the aggressors. Eight of the latter were brought to trial and convicted at the spring assizes of 1785, but William Richardson, M.P., owner of the Rich Hill estate, interceded with the court to have their fines and jail sentences remitted.[36] Richardson apparently hoped that leniency would have a good effect, but, on the contrary, within a few weeks he and two other gentlemen found themselves intervening to prevent a pitched battle between hundreds of Defenders and Peep-of-Day Boys. He managed to cajole the Defenders into leaving the field by promising not to repeat his mistaken leniency at the assizes and by providing beer in nearby Hamilton's Bawn. He then persuaded the Peep-of-Day Boys to disperse, apparently by gently threatening another prosecution.

In the face of mounting Peep-of-Day Boy violence in 1786 against the houses and other belongings of Catholics, Byrne recorded that many of the gentry lent arms to Catholics or advised them to purchase weapons. Since it was still technically illegal for Catholics to bear arms, such a policy must have given further color to the pretext which Peep-of-Day Boy apologists advanced for their behavior, namely, that they were enforcing the penal laws by disarming Catholics. Furthermore, when gentlemen armed their Catholic tenants, they were implicitly admitting that, notwithstanding their own good intentions, they could not protect those tenants. The essence of the gentry's weakness was revealed at the summer assizes of 1786, when they indicted the captain of the Nappach Fleet as well as four Defenders accused of a riot at Tanderagee. The captain was acquitted, while the Defenders were convicted and punished, and the Peep-of-Day Boys held "a kind of triumph."[37] Only rarely over the

35. *Taylor and Skinner's maps of the roads of Ireland* (2nd ed., London, 1783), pp. 4, 16, 22–7, 262, 265–7, 286, 288. Small areas of south Armagh are not covered by these maps, but they are not sufficient to account for the large disparity between north and south Armagh.

36. Byrne, *Impartial account*, p. 10. For the identity of this "gentleman of fortune and humanity," see ibid., p. 12.

37. Ibid., p. 22.

next few years did it prove possible to obtain convictions of Protestant rioters.[38] To maintain a semblance of evenhandedness, the authorities were reduced to preventing prosecutions of accused Catholics or, in one case, to obtaining a royal pardon for a Catholic believed to have been unjustly convicted.[39] People began to say that they had "popish g[rand] juries and Protestant petit juries."[40]

Thus in the first three or four years of the troubles, landlords generally sympathized with Catholic victims of the Peep-of-Day Boys. Determined landlords could and did restrain their Protestant tenants somewhat. William Richardson eventually managed to quiet the Rich Hill estate, partly by threatening not to renew the leases of rioters,[41] and it has been argued that William Brownlow was instrumental in keeping Lurgan and its vicinity calm during the 1780s.[42] If this was true, it may have been because Brownlow had become involved in the linen business himself. His rent books show that he would sometimes supply his small tenants with a loom,[43] and this fact no doubt enhanced the dependence of the tenants upon him. But landlords who stood outside the linen nexus may have found that the traditional sanctions which Irish landlords used to control their tenants' behavior were ineffective. The tenant may have been a wage earner who, if deprived of his cottage and tiny garden plot, could easily obtain the equivalent on another estate nearby. Land might well have ceased to be his principal source of support, and even if tenure of a small bit of land was essential, there was no incentive to retain an attachment to a particular family holding. If the threat of eviction could thus be ignored, and if the threat of prosecution was rendered empty by the refusal of juries to convict, the gentry might have to turn to coercive force.

The force at their disposal was quite limited. Officially, the magistrates were supposed to rely upon the local constabulary, which, if Armagh resembled other Irish counties in this respect,[44] would have been a worthless collection of old retainers. If these constables were insufficient for the task, the normal recourse was to call upon the government for troops,

38. E.g., in 1788, when for the first time sentences (of fine and imprisonment) were actually carried out against two Peep-of-Day Boys (ibid., p. 33).

39. Ibid., pp. 33, 43; Rev. William Campbell to Rev. Benjamin McDowel, 18 Aug. 1788 (P.R.O.N.I., Bruce papers, T.3041/1/E53).

40. Campbell to McDowel, 18 Aug. 1788 (P.R.O.N.I., T.3041/1/E53).

41. Byrne, *Impartial account*, pp. 23–4.

42. Paterson's notes, no. 14 (P.R.O.N.I., T.1722).

43. See entries for the townlands of Ballynamony, Clanrolla, and Cornakinnegar in the Brownlow rentals for 1787–90 (P.R.O.N.I., Brownlow papers, D.2667/1).

44. See Galen Broeker, *Rural disorder and police reform in Ireland, 1812–36* (London and Toronto, 1970), p. 29.

and this in fact was occasionally done.[45] A more usual strategy at this time, however, was to employ the local Volunteers. In County Armagh it seems to have been common to use parties of Volunteers even for such routine law-enforcement duties as serving warrants, making arrests, and carrying out evictions.[46] On at least three occasions they were deployed to prevent or stop rioting: on a fair day in 1786 by Richardson at Rich Hill, in November 1786 by a Captain Patten at Tanderagee, and in the late spring of 1788 by Thomas Macan and Joshua McGeough at Lisnadill.[47]

There was another way in which the Volunteer movement might be used to restore tranquillity: Protestant rioters might be co-opted to the side of "order" by enrolling them in the Volunteers. Indeed, in the spring of 1788, first at Benburb and then at several other locations, new companies of Volunteers were raised, drawing recruits from among the Peep-of-Day Boys. In Byrne's view this development stopped the "nocturnal depredations," for "such of the Peep-of-Days as had a thirst for arms were now to be supplied with new ones, so that what they could plunder from the papists were of no value in the Volunteer ranks, nor would the Volunteers suffer any of their members to be guilty of this practice."[48] Certainly, the raising of these new companies of Volunteers in 1788 was an important turning point, the significance of which we can best grasp by looking for patterns in the incidents reported during the years 1784–91.

Though the approximately 100 separate incidents between 1784 and 1791 mentioned in the sources are not amenable to rigorous statistical analysis, they can be divided into three broad categories: (1) combat between organized bands or between persons identified as having engaged in antecedent acts of violence; (2) attacks on "innocent" victims; and (3) demonstrations, together with any violent acts apparently precipitated by them. From an analysis of attacks on "innocent" victims, it emerges that incidents of searching for arms in Catholic houses were reported frequently for the years 1784–7, but ceased to be mentioned after early 1788.[49] Furthermore, there appears to have been a definite shift begin-

45. See, e.g., Byrne, *Impartial account*, p. 22.
46. *B.N.L.*, 10–14 Mar., 28 Apr.–2 May 1786, 19–22 Aug. 1788.
47. Byrne, *Impartial account*, pp. 24, 34; Rev. William Campbell to Rev. Benjamin McDowel, 18 Aug. 1788 (P.R.O.N.I., Bruce papers, T.3041/1/E53); Rev. William Campbell to earl of Charlemont, 9 Feb. 1788 (James Caulfield, first earl of Charlemont, *The manuscripts and correspondence of James, first earl of Charlemont* [2 vols., London, 1891–4], comprising Historical Manuscripts Commission, *12th report*, appendix, pt. x, and *13th report*, appendix, pt. viii [hereafter cited as *H.M.C., Charlemont MSS*], ii, 69–70).
48. Byrne, *Impartial account*, pp. 32–3.
49. Byrne's own house was raided in February 1789, and there were some attacks on

ning in 1788 from combat in the context of fairs, markets, race meetings, or arranged battles[50] to demonstrations which asserted, or were taken to assert, the local dominance of either Catholics or Protestants. On the Catholic side the demonstrations included celebrations of traditional holidays (Old May Day, St. John's Eve), which Protestants construed as threatening, as well as large gatherings of Defenders which no doubt really were intended to overawe nearby Protestants. On the Protestant side they consisted mainly of parades and maneuvers by local Volunteer units which Catholics regarded as provocative. Such demonstrations entered the record as occasions for contention during 1788,[51] and the first one to produce fatalities involved, significantly, the earliest of the new companies, the Benburb Volunteers. On 23 November 1788, as this company, playing "The Protestant boys" and "The Boyne water," marched to Sunday worship at Armagh cathedral, there was a minor confrontation with some Catholics along their route. Upon arriving at Armagh the company altered its original plan to return by another road, armed themselves more thoroughly, and returned by the same road, spoiling for a fight. They were not disappointed. Larger crowds of Catholics had gathered, stones were thrown, and the Volunteers opened fire, killing two persons and wounding several others. This incident was only one of a number of similar encounters, each of which touched off further violence in the surrounding countryside.

The significance of this shift around 1788 in the character of the most dramatic incidents of violence can be seen in the following mortality figures:[52]

Year	Slayings	Executions
1784	0	0
1785	0	0
1786	2	0
1787	0	0
1788	3	0
1789	3	0
1790	1	6
1791	2	1

Catholic dwellings near Tanderagee in reprisal for the battle of Lisnagade in July 1789 (ibid., pp. 3, 44). Neither of these incidents is a clear case of a search for weapons.

50. Byrne described a skirmish between Peep-of-Day Boys and Defenders on the night of 1 January 1789 as the Nappach Fleet's "last appearance in this county" (ibid., p. 39).

51. Ibid., pp. 34-9.

52. These figures were obtained by searching Byrne, *Impartial account*, and all other available sources for these disturbances. Items not cited elsewhere in this essay are: earl of Charlemont to [?], Aug. 1788 [draft]; Rev. Edward Hudson to Charlemont, 11 Aug.

The conflict clearly became more deadly around 1788. Not all of the slayings occurred in clashes directly precipitated by demonstrations, but contemporaries no doubt blamed the highly charged atmosphere created by some of the well-publicized demonstrations for many of the more obscure acts of violence. The practice of enrolling Peep-of-Day Boys in the Volunteers certainly exacerbated the situation in the short run. Yet the gentry leadership of the Volunteers probably did manage within a year or two to gain control over the new companies and over any Peep-of-Day Boys who had found their way into the old units. This would account for the virtual ending of disturbances in north Armagh by early 1790.

Meanwhile, however, Catholics were confirmed in the belief that the Protestant rabble was being deliberately set upon them. By 1788 Catholics were already losing some of the sympathy which they had hitherto enjoyed from the Protestant gentry. The earliest indication in the sources of this loss of sympathy is Byrne's remark that at the assizes in 1787 it was rumored that some Catholics had accepted bribes not to press charges against Peep-of-Day Boys. "This gave great umbrage to some of the magistrates that spared no trouble to bring those rioters to a due course of law," Byrne recalled, "and indeed it helped to cool the very great exertions of the magistrates that espoused the peace and welfare of the county."[53] In his account of events in 1788 Byrne noted that Defenders had adopted the tactic of refusing to purchase goods from Protestants who supported the Peep-of-Day Boys. This practice of exclusive dealing "turned many well-disposed Protestants against them, that hitherto espoused their cause."[54]

Probably the main reason why the Catholics were losing the sympathy of the Protestant elite, however, was the change which occurred around 1788 in the character of the violence. The ending of searches for arms in Catholic houses early in that year meant that the Catholics were no longer cast so unambiguously in the role of victims. Moreover, the shift from combat between communal bands to incidents arising out of demonstrations no doubt altered the perspectives of many gentlemen on the troubles. Public brawls and faction fights were, after all, a common occurrence throughout Ireland which the gentry customarily treated as a politically harmless form of recreation. Demonstrations, however, were another matter. Then as now, parades in the north of Ireland were often

1789; Hudson to Charlemont, 10 Jan. 1790; Hudson to Francis Dobbs, 29 Jan. 1791 (R.I.A., Charlemont papers, MSS 12 R 21, no. 109; 12 R 15, no. 61; 12 R 16, nos. 37, 51); Thomas Prentice to Charlemont, 28 Nov. 1788; Robert Livingston to Charlemont, 17 Dec. 1788; Hudson to Charlemont, 11 July 1789 (H.M.C., Charlemont MSS, ii, 79–81, 83, 102–3).
    53. Byrne, Impartial account, pp. 28–9.
    54. Ibid., p. 31.

not merely recreation, but also serious ritual assertions of dominance by parading groups over the territory along their route. A successful Catholic attack upon a Volunteer procession or other Protestant parade would betoken Catholic ascendancy in the territory in question. Many landlords believed that Catholics were entitled to the quiet enjoyment of their lives and possessions, but few could contemplate with equanimity a challenge to the proposition that all of Ireland was Protestant territory. For upon this proposition their moral claim to their own landed possessions rested.

The shift in landlord attitudes can be illustrated by the case of John Moore, whose Drumbanagher estate, east of Portnorris, lay on the fringe of an area where attacks on Catholics and their property were occurring in 1786 and 1787. In February 1787 Moore received a threatening notice from "the lads for justice, vulgarly call'd the Break-of-Day Boys," apparently because he had threatened to discipline a servant whom he suspected of being one of "the lads." In transmitting the document to Lord Gosford, Moore declined to ask for military assistance and expressed confidence that he could handle the situation with "my own people."[55]

Two years later, however, Moore's attitudes had changed. On St. John's Eve (23 June) 1789, Catholics near Drumbanagher held a traditional celebration which Peep-of-Day Boys construed as a gathering of Defenders. Moore, accompanied by both a contingent of Volunteers and a large Protestant crowd, arrived unexpectedly at this scene of pipers, fiddlers, and dancers. For reasons that are obscure, he demanded a large garland of flowers which was part of the festivities. Perhaps the Catholics invested the garland with some sectarian meaning, or the Protestants believed that they did so.[56] In any event, the Catholics surrendered the garland without resistance. Nevertheless, shots were then fired, apparently not by the Volunteers, but by members of the Protestant crowd, some of whom later claimed that Moore had ordered them to fire. At least two Catholics were wounded, and the incident triggered disturbances over a wide area. "This whole country for ten mile[s] round is in absolute rebellion and confusion," Moore told Lord Charlemont on 15 July.[57] Bodies of 1,000 to 6,000 Catholics assembled in various places at night,

55. John Moore to Lord Gosford, 23 Feb. 1787, enclosing threatening notice from "John Tormentor," 15 Feb. 1787 (R.I.A., Charlemont papers, MS 12 R 14, nos. 84–5).
56. One can see how sectarian meaning can become attached to practices seemingly unrelated to religious division in the following incident: in 1950 at Portnablagh, Co. Donegal, observers asked some children on St. John's Eve why bonfires were lighted on the hilltops; the children replied that "they were burning the Protestants' bones" (Kevin Danaher, *The year in Ireland* [Cork, 1972], p. 139).
57. R.I.A., Charlemont papers, MS 12 R 15, no. 56. See also Rev. Edward Hudson to earl of Charlemont, 11 July 1789 (*H.M.C.*, *Charlemont MSS*, ii, 102–3).

engendering in Protestants, including Moore himself, the traditional fears of massacre so often aroused since 1641.

The most celebrated incident sparked by the affray near Drumbanagher took place on 12 July — the anniversary of the battle of the Boyne — at Lisnagade, the site of an old fort, just across the boundary in County Down. Accounts of this clash differ,[58] but apparently a local Volunteer unit proposed to celebrate the twelfth in the fort, which required that they march through the field of a tenant who naturally objected to their treading on his crop. A group of Defenders occupied the fort, swearing to keep the Volunteers out. Magistrates arrived with Volunteers and a small detachment of regular troops. An arrangement was made under which the Defenders were to go home and the Volunteers were not to trespass in future. But just as the Volunteers were withdrawing, someone fired upon them, a pitched battle ensued, and the Defenders were routed, apparently without any serious injuries on either side. Exaggerated accounts of the incident were soon in circulation: Moore heard that the Defenders had been armed with cannon and that many had been killed or wounded. In sharp contrast to his cool disregard of danger in 1787, he begged Charlemont to have the government send ammunition, "otherwise we may all fly the country." Meanwhile, he had decided "to arm those under me, of the Protestant boys that have none." Concluded Moore, "For heaven's sake, don't forget the powder & ball with all expedition."[59]

It is fortunate that so much is known of Moore's changing predicament, for his location in the transitional zone between predominantly Protestant and overwhelmingly Catholic territory means that his own experience probably reflected especially well the dilemmas of the Armagh gentry as a whole. Having developed policies to deal with the misbehavior of some of their Protestant dependents toward Catholics, whom they presumed to be mainly passive victims, they found that partly as a result of those policies Catholics had become much more assertive.

If, like Colonel Blacker, we were to ignore the mainly Protestant aggressions of 1784–8, then indeed the Defenders would appear to be a ramification of the Whiteboys. In south Armagh from 1789 Defenderism probably resembled rather closely the Whiteboys, the Rightboys, and other agrarian secret societies.[60] A document found in the possession of a sus-

58. John Moore to earl of Charlemont, 15 July 1789 (R.I.A., Charlemont papers, MS 12 R 15, no. 56); Byrne, *Impartial account*, pp. 43–4; Paterson lecture, p. 4 (P.R.O.N.I., T.2595/4).

59. John Moore to earl of Charlemont, 15 July 1789 (R.I.A., Charlemont papers, MS 12 R 15, no. 56).

60. J. S. Donnelly, Jr., "The Whiteboy movement, 1761–5" in *I.H.S.*, xxi, no. 81 (Mar. 1978), pp. 20–54; idem, "The Rightboy movement, 1785–8" in *Studia Hib.*, nos. 17–18 (1977–8), pp. 120–202.

pected Defender leader arrested near Jonesborough gives a few clues about their organization. The document, signed by fifty-one Defenders at Drumbanagher and dated 24 April 1789, conveyed to a new Defender lodge in a part of County Louth the oath required of members and the rules of the society. To judge from this evidence (which, of course, may represent only the practice of a single lodge), members were required to observe strict secrecy about Defender affairs, to submit themselves to the local committee "in all things that are lawful," and, curiously, to obey George III and his successors "for this present year 1789 . . . and also while we live subject to the same government." They were to refrain from drunkenness, profanity, and loud talk at lodge meetings. Each member was to supply himself with a gun and bayonet, but no group of members was to "go to a challenge" without permission from three members of the committee. This local committee called its lodge "no. 18" and sent its missive to "the committee of Carrickarnan, body of Defenders no. 1 for the county of Louth."[61] If, as seems likely, lodges were numbered consecutively within each county, then these facts suggest that formal Defender organization was already extensive in Armagh by early 1789, but that it was only getting started in Louth. This is consistent with what is known from other sources about the spread of the unrest.

A major focus of discontent in south Armagh during the years 1789–92 was the Forkhill estate. In his will the late landlord, Richard Jackson, had established a trust providing, among other things, for clothing and educating Anglican children and for giving to each, at the age of twenty-five, "five pounds and a loom, and a small holding in preference to other tenants who may offer."[62] The main burden of implementing the terms of the will fell upon one trustee, the Rev. Edward Hudson, rector of Forkhill. Whatever Jackson's purposes may have been in setting up the trust, Hudson had a clear vision of what he wished to accomplish: "I hope to make our savages happy against their will by establishing trade and industry amongst them." To the south and east of Forkhill, Hudson reported to Lord Charlemont in December 1789, a great expanse of country was controlled by the Defenders, who could assemble "almost in an instant" on signals given by whistle. But despite some intimidation of Protestants who had taken land under the trust, things were now quiet at Forkhill, thanks to a detachment of troops supplied by the government.[63] Less than

---

61. Sir Richard Musgrave, *Memoirs of the different rebellions in Ireland* . . . (2nd ed., Dublin, 1801), p. 57, and appendix, pp. 8–9 (hereafter cited as *Rebellions*). See also Byrne, *Impartial account*, p. 42.

62. Coote, *Armagh*, p. 363n.

63. Rev. Edward Hudson to earl of Charlemont, 7 Dec. 1789 (R.I.A., Charlemont papers, MS 12 R 15, no. 67).

two weeks later, however, Hudson's horse was shot out from under him.[64] During the succeeding year unrest continued in the Forkhill vicinity. Apparently, part of the trust fund was applied to furnishing primary education for Catholic children, but Hudson forfeited whatever goodwill this gesture might have gained when he dismissed a schoolmaster who had promised to teach Catholic prayers in the Irish language. It was rumored that the new schoolmaster, Alexander Barkely, would refuse to teach "anything but the Protestant prayers."

In these events we see an isolated local community, which no doubt had an elaborate set of social relationships little understood by outsiders, being threatened with "improvement." Hudson believed that fewer than ten families in Forkhill parish were not related to all the rest, and that the parish had remained such a backwater partly because for thirty-five years the estate had been owned by "the most indolent man on earth," who kept more than half of it in waste ground.[65] Under these circumstances, improvement meant not merely the physical displacement of Catholic squatters on the waste land, but the potential disruption of the whole social order of the local Catholic community.

Late in January 1791 the Forkhill unrest reached a climax when a party of men broke into Barkely's house and cut out his tongue as well as that of his wife. They also cut off his wife's thumb and four fingers, one by one, and cut out the tongue and sliced off the calf of the leg of his wife's brother, who happened to be visiting. Mrs. Barkely died from her injuries. Not surprisingly, this incident achieved great notoriety. In loyalist retelling, the already repugnant facts were apparently embellished with a story that one of Mrs. Barkely's breasts had been cut off.[66] The government offered a reward of £500 for each of the first five of the perpetrators to be apprehended and convicted.[67] And Forkhill came to be seen as the fount of discord. At the spring assizes of 1791 the grand jury of Louth issued a proclamation which traced the widespread unrest in that county specifically to the "many tumultuous and illegal assemblies in the neighbourhood of Forkhill."[68] It was again the troubles at Forkhill which the Armagh grand jury singled out at the summer assizes of 1791 as a rationale for offering a reward of 5 guineas each for the conviction of the first twenty Catholics charged with illegally assembling in arms.[69] Even

64. Paterson's notes, no. 28 (P.R.O.N.I., T.1722).

65. Rev. Edward Hudson to earl of Charlemont, 7 Dec. 1789 (R.I.A., Charlemont papers, MS 12 R 15, no. 67).

66. Musgrave, *Rebellions*, p. 61, makes this allegation in a footnote to a contemporary account which details the mutilations without mentioning this most sensational one.

67. *B.N.L.*, 8–12 Apr. 1791.

68. Ibid.

69. *B.N.L.*, 20–23 Sept. 1791.

though the gentry seem to have regained control over the Protestant rioters in north Armagh, they could do little to stem the unrest in south
Armagh on the part of Catholics enraged by the physical and cultural
encroachments of an improvement scheme.

The spread of the Defender movement in the early 1790s to neighboring counties — indeed the growth throughout Ireland of unrest in various
forms which the authorities were apt to lump together as "Defenderism"
— meant that, even if County Armagh itself became relatively calm for
a year or so, local Protestants were very much aware of an organized
Catholic threat. That awareness was heightened by the outbreak of war
with France in 1793 and by the decisions of the government to extend
the franchise to Catholics, raise a mainly Catholic militia, and dissolve
the Volunteers. The decision to disband the Volunteers was made to keep
that movement from falling under the sway of the Jacobin radicalism
which had appeared in Belfast and elsewhere, while the concessions to
Catholics were intended to retain their allegiance in time of national
crisis. Sensible as these measures may have seemed in a national context,
they were quite unsettling in areas containing significant numbers of
lower-class Protestants. Since Defender cells soon infiltrated militia ranks,
and since the protection of the Volunteers had been removed, poorer
Protestants often felt deserted by the state.[70]

In the summer of 1794 General William Dalrymple reported to the
government about the intimidation of Catholics near the town of Armagh: "Many of them are preparing for flight the moment their little
harvests are brought in; some are gone to America, others to Connaught.
Their houses are placarded, and their fears excessive."[71] Significantly,
Dalrymple found the magistrates unwilling to act. The extent of disturbances in 1794 is unclear, but beginning in the spring of 1795 a well-
documented cycle of troubles started near Loughgall.

The troubles of 1795 recapitulate those of 1784–8, though with crucial
differences. In June there was a fight at the Diamond, a crossroads near
Loughgall, between two men. Rival bands assembled, but an armed confrontation was averted by the timely intervention of magistrates. Major
combat was forestalled for only a few months, however, and in September bands of Protestants and Catholics began to gather near the Diamond and made threatening gestures toward one another. Senior suggests that perhaps both sides expected to exchange shots at a safe distance
until magistrates and troops came and ended the affair. Indeed, that is
what seemed to be happening, but the local gentry and Catholic clergy

70. Senior, *Orangeism, 1795–1836*, p. 13.
71. General William Dalrymple to Thomas Pelham, 9 Aug. 1794 (P.R.O.N.I., Calendar of Pelham papers, T.755/2/94–6). For the original document, see B.L. Add. MS 33,
101, ff. 144–5.

lost control of the situation probably because the confrontation had lasted for days, with participants being drawn from farther and farther away. In particular, some Defenders from south Armagh arrived and did not feel bound by a truce which had been arranged earlier. On 21 September Defenders attacked a local inn occupied by well-armed Protestants, and a battle ensued in which the Defenders suffered heavy casualties; estimates of Defender deaths ranged from sixteen to forty-eight. Protestants followed up their victory with a series of raids on Catholic homes over the next few months, which had the purpose of driving Catholics out of the county. Meanwhile, Protestants who had fought at the Diamond organized the society which came to be known as the Loyal Orange Order.[72]

What had changed since the 1780s? Clearly, the Catholics had lost the sympathy extended to them earlier by many of the Protestant gentry. Moreover, the conflict had assumed more than a local dimension. Those gentry who sought to end the Diamond affair, much as William Richardson had prevented an impending battle nearby a decade earlier, found their efforts undone by the fact that the participants were drawn from an area much wider than their own influence. Even if the Armagh magistrates had possessed the will to control disorderly Protestants, at this point their difficulties were only part of a vast national crisis about which they could do little. Many of the gentry, however, apparently agreed with Richard Jephson, who advised Charlemont, shortly after the battle of the Diamond: "It is impossible for the Protestant gentry to keep up the farce of impartiality between the parties or to disavow the absolute necessity of giving a considerable degree of support to the Protestant party, who . . . have got the name of 'Orange boys.'"[73] Within the next year or so the Orange society began receiving the patronage or encouragement of several influential Armagh gentlemen.[74]

In 1796 the government obtained some lists of Catholic refugees in Mayo who had been expelled from their homes in Ulster. Schedules containing the names of 359 householders are extant, but the earliest of the lists, identifying 72 householders who arrived in Mayo between May 1795 and May 1796, fails to indicate their former residences.[75] It is reasonable to suppose that many of these 72 families had come from the areas near the Diamond. Interestingly, however, the refugees whose previous residences are known included significant numbers from districts which had been remarkably quiet in the 1780s. Several of these localities fell within the spheres of influence of gentry who were early sponsors or friends of

72. Senior, *Orangeism, 1795–1836*, pp. 14–19.
73. Quoted ibid., pp. 19–20.
74. Ibid., pp. 37–47.
75. Patrick Tohall, "The Diamond fight of 1795 and the resultant expulsions" in *Seanchas Ardmhacha*, iii, no. 1 (1958), pp. 36–50.

the Orange Order: near Lurgan, William Brownlow (son of the William Brownlow who had apparently prevented trouble in the 1780s but died in 1794); south of Portadown, the Blackers of Carrickblacker; and along the southwest shore of Lough Neagh, the Verners of Churchill.

Beginning with these events in 1795, Gibbon's contention that a section of the Armagh gentry established ties of solidarity with rebellious Protestants by becoming their tribunes is well founded. This aspect of the disturbances, however, is not a point of continuity with the troubles of the 1780s. Rather, in those earlier troubles the gentry tried to cope with a breakdown of authority — certainly their own authority and perhaps also that which was exercised within the Protestant family. Social changes promoted by linen manufacture seem to have been the principal causes of this breakdown: neither fathers nor landlords could so easily control disorderly postadolescents when the customary basis of their previous domination — land — lost much of its former economic significance. Nevertheless, even though by 1789 the gentry had begun to lose patience with the Catholics whom they had previously sought to protect, they did attempt with some success to regain control over Protestant rioters. By the way in which they did so, they contributed to the spread of unrest among Catholics far beyond County Armagh. Thus it happened that in 1795, in the context of revolutionary threats far more menacing than anything the Armagh Catholics could muster, a section of the Armagh gentry stopped trying to be masters of the Protestant rabble and settled for the role of tribunes instead.

What the Troubles Explain

Let us return to the four explanations by contemporaries and look this time at the precipitating incidents which they identified in their efforts to make sense of the troubles. To be sure, contemporary perceptions on this point may tell us little about why the disturbances actually occurred. But by critically assessing their perceptions, we may learn something of the significance of the troubles for larger issues in Irish history.

Blacker chose his precipitating incident in a transparently partisan way. Though he believed that the underlying cause of the troubles was an ancient conspiracy, he had to fix a starting point for this particular phase of the eternal hostility of Catholics toward Protestants. He asserted that "one of the first open demonstrations" of that revived antagonism was the notorious battle of Lisnagade in 1789. In this incident, significantly placed by Blacker in "1791 or 92 — I forget which,"[76] Defenders

76. Paterson lecture, p. 4 (P.R.O.N.I., T.2595/4).

fired upon a twelfth of July procession of Volunteers and were thereupon routed by an intrepid Protestant counterattack. By making this the precipitating incident in his explanation, Blacker not only depicted the Catholics as cowardly aggressors but also conveniently avoided perhaps five years of violent clashes, in many of which the Protestant side can hardly be represented as innocent victims.

Richardson and Ogle differed over whether the underlying cause of the troubles was a breakdown of the ascendancy's dominance over Catholics or over humbler Protestants, but they identified precipitating incidents which seem closely related to one another. According to Ogle, when the Volunteer leaders found that they could not achieve all their objectives, they "desperately invited the papists to add their weight to embarrassing the state" by joining Volunteer corps. Once armed, the Catholics became the prey of recently demobilized Protestant Volunteers, who "had no other object to divert their attention" and "discovered that it was illegal that papists should possess arms," without recollecting that it was equally illegal for them to take the law into their own hands.[77]

According to Richardson, the unrest began when Patriot leaders raised a following among lower-class Protestants and obliged the government to make conciliatory gestures toward Catholics, or so at least it was believed. In Armagh this belief exacerbated Protestant resentment over recent instances in which Catholics had bid up the price of land. Trouble broke out, Richardson reported, when Lord Gosford tried to prevent theft from his orchards by posting armed guards who happened to be Catholics. Seizing upon the fact that it was unlawful for Catholics to bear arms, Protestants under the name of Break-of-Day Boys attacked Catholics in their homes on the pretext of searching for weapons. These disturbances continued for years, "the magistrates little troubling themselves, each having his neighbour's conduct to plead in his own excuse."[78]

Thus both Richardson and Ogle saw Protestant attempts to disarm Catholics as the precipitant of the troubles. Contemporary correspondence proves that such raids for weapons were widespread from 1786 to 1788, and Byrne asserted that they had occurred as early as 1784.[79] Indeed, it was believed that the term Peep-of-Day Boys stemmed from the Protestant practice of surprising Catholics at daybreak in their "searches."

77. John Ogle to Edward Cooke, 15 July 1796 (S.P.O., Rebellion papers, 620/24/37).

78. Dr. William Richardson to marquis of Abercorn, 14 Feb. 1797 (P.R.O.N.I., Abercorn papers, T.2541/IB3/6/4).

79. Lord Gosford to Arthur Acheson, 8 Feb. 1788 (N.L.I., Gosford papers, MS 8018/4); Rev. William Campbell to earl of Charlemont, 9 Feb. 1788 (H.M.C., Charlemont MSS, ii, 69); Campbell to Benjamin McDowel, 18 Aug. 1788 (P.R.O.N.I., Bruce papers, T.3041/1/E53); Byrne, Impartial account, p. 6.

A local Orange gentleman made an amusing attempt in 1835 to represent the etymology of the label in a more favorable light: the Defenders "were in the habit of taking arms from the houses of Protestants, and bodies of men called Peep-of-Day Boys went generally early in the morning for the purpose of recovering their arms, and from that circumstance derived their name."[80] The Rev. William Campbell, Presbyterian minister of Armagh, stated explicitly in 1788 that Peep-of-Day Boys was "the name given to the Protestants who more than a year ago took the arms from Roman Catholics, in doing which, for want of knowledge of the law, they thought they acted legally."[81]

Byrne also mentioned raids for weapons, but in asserting that the troubles originated in 1784, he selected a different sort of precipitating incident: a sequence of faction fights which came to be polarized along sectarian lines. Senior repeats many of the details which Byrne provided of this faction fighting, and Gibbon attempts to incorporate it in his explanation by conceptualizing it as a local kind of "recreational" violence prevalent in County Armagh. Types of violence which struck elite observers as recreational were no doubt common among the journeymen weavers of Armagh, as they were in many other parts of Ireland with very different local economies.[82] As suggested earlier, a highly significant feature of the Armagh troubles was the shift in violence from one sort of recreational context to another: faction fights and pitched battles being supplanted by confrontations at demonstrations around 1788. Indeed, combat of the former sort was so endemic in the mid-1780s that it is difficult to decide when the troubles as such began.

Byrne is the sole source of the story repeated by Senior and many others of the fight between two drunken Protestants at Markethill on 4 July 1784. According to Byrne, the friends of the loser in the townland of Edenknappagh, under the leadership of "Captain Whiskey," organized as the Nappach Fleet. They plundered the houses of the victor's friends in the name of searching for arms and deliberately arranged a race meeting for the purpose of provoking a faction fight. Among the victor's friends

80. Evidence of Lieutenant-Colonel William Verner in *Report from the select committee . . . to enquire into . . . Orange lodges*, p. 4, H.C. 1835 (377), xv, 1.

81. Rev. William Campbell to earl of Charlemont, 9 Feb. 1788 (*H.M.C., Charlemont MSS*, ii, 69). In fact, the term cannot have originated with these troubles, for Arthur Young, writing in 1780, mentioned Peep-of-Day Boys, along with the Steelboys and the Oakboys, as groups of "insurgents" composed of "manufacturing Protestants in the north" (Young, *Tour*, ii, 55). Young made no reference to sectarian clashes.

82. Gibbon's assertion (*Origins*, p. 37) that by the 1770s this violence had taken the form of regular mock battles between vengeance groups which had been organized in "almost every parish in Armagh" seems to be founded on extremely slender evidence.

were several Catholics, including one who had incautiously given the victor some helpful advice on the occasion of the original brawl. Accordingly, these Catholics were singled out as special targets of the Nappach Fleet, but faction fighting persisted throughout 1785 without the two sides polarizing solely along sectarian lines. In 1786, however, a pamphlet controversy between Catholic and Protestant clergymen in the town of Armagh allegedly produced "a thorough reformation from a drunken war to a religious one."[83] As there exists no strictly contemporary corroboration of any detail of Byrne's account for some two years after July 1784, it is reasonable to query the significance which he accorded to these occurrences.

For the events of late 1786 in and around Tanderagee there survives at least Campbell's version, recorded in general terms fifteen months later and subsequently elaborated.[84] Since the earliest contemporary document on the troubles is a threatening notice emanating from somewhere near Tanderagee and dated 15 February 1787, and since Byrne himself used the term Peep-of-Day Boys only once in his narrative before 1786, it is reasonable to ask whether he exaggerated the connection between the brawls and faction fights of 1784–5 and the well-attested sectarian violence beginning in late 1786. Could Byrne have been one of those of whom the Rev. Campbell complained when he told Lord Charlemont that "every drunken quarrel, or rescue of cattle, or unfortunate accident that happens is immediately ascribed to these parties, though in no sort connected with them"?[85]

Such suspicions are enhanced by Byrne's desire to write with a literary flair. "Not being versed in the thorny paths of literature,"[86] he anticipated in his preface the criticism of better-educated writers "who could set off my materials in . . . fanciful dress." Perhaps significantly, it was chiefly in the chapters covering the years 1784–6 that Byrne indulged his literary pretensions. For example, leaders of the opposing groups are identified as Captain Whiskey and Captain Fanatic, and the reader is left to puzzle out for himself whether these are personifications or the pseudonyms of actual individuals. In treating events after 1786, the narrative assumes a more straightforward, matter-of-fact tone, leading one to ask whether the story of earlier occurrences might not indeed contain fanciful elements.

Why Byrne chose the fight at Markethill to begin his account can per-

83. Byrne, *Impartial account*, pp. 1–25.
84. Rev. William Campbell to earl of Charlemont, 9 Feb. 1788 (*H.M.C., Charlemont MSS*, ii, 68–9); Campbell to Rev. Benjamin McDowel, 18 Aug. 1788 (P.R.O.N.I., Bruce papers, T.3041/1/E53).
85. Campbell to earl of Charlemont, 9 Feb. 1788 (*H.M.C., Charlemont MSS*, ii, 70).
86. Byrne, *Impartial account*, p. 4.

haps be appreciated by considering one explanation of the troubles with which he explicitly disagreed. This was the explanation of J. Blackhall, agent for the Cope estates of Loughgall and Portnorris. Only Byrne's word exists for what Blackhall said, but Byrne cited Blackhall in order to challenge him, and Blackhall died in 1787. Thus the few sentences in Byrne's pamphlet recounting Blackhall's explanation of the unrest can be thought of as a separate contemporary account of events prior to that date, albeit one transmitted to us by Byrne. According to Byrne, Blackhall had maintained that "the Portnorris men were the first and principal abettors of the disturbances in this county."[87] Byrne paid his respects to this late "worthy magistrate" but rejected his assertion. Who were these "Portnorris men"? From the context it appears that many of them were "the tenants of the late unfortunate George R. Fitzgerald" who "returned to this county after the unhappy exit of that gentleman." Byrne here alluded to circumstances which he assumed were familiar to his reader but which now are somewhat obscure.

George Robert Fitzgerald ("Fighting Fitzgerald") was the flamboyant nephew of the equally eccentric Frederick Augustus Hervey, earl of Bristol and bishop of Derry. The "unhappy exit," to which Byrne referred, took place in June 1786, by hanging, for a murder which Fitzgerald committed while attempting to ambush a personal enemy. Though Fitzgerald owned no property in the Portnorris area,[88] he had been actively soliciting tenants in Ulster to migrate to his estate in County Mayo. Catholic tenants were displaced to make room for these Protestants, and, though the details are unclear, the local priest and his parishioners on the Mayo estate apparently took action against Fitzgerald's grandiose schemes to promote agricultural and industrial improvement at their expense.[89] Thus, it seems, a group of Protestants from the Portnorris district had responded to Fitzgerald's offer of land in Mayo only to find their position there untenable. It is easy to imagine how such a group, arriving back at Portnorris to find that their former holdings had been let to others, would be especially angry and might identify the local Catholics with those whose wrath they themselves had aroused in Mayo.

Thus there may be an important sense in which "improvement" was a catalyst, if not exactly a precipitant, of the troubles. At the point when the initial faction fighting polarized along sectarian lines in 1786, peculiar ferocity was imparted to the conflict apparently by Protestants who had been lured to the wilds of Mayo by an improving landlord, only to

87. Ibid., p. 14. See also ibid., pp. 21–3.
88. Paterson's notes, no. 7 (P.R.O.N.I., T.1722). For a report on Fitzgerald's solicitation of tenants in Ulster, see *B.N.L.*, 27–30 July 1784.
89. "George Robert Fitzgerald – part I" in *Dublin University Magazine*, xvi, no. 91 (July 1840), p. 17.

be driven out by Catholics. Moreover, four years later, just when the gentry seemed to have regained control over the situation in north Armagh, disturbances in south Armagh, as previously noted, were being sustained by the effects of an "improvement" scheme at Forkhill.

The difference between Blackhall and Byrne is of interest partly because it serves as a reminder that among the very confused events under scrutiny here, a contemporary might fasten on a point of departure in accordance with his own perceptions and biases. Even though they lived only a few miles apart, Byrne and Blackhall had different views of the origins of the disturbances. In both cases the troubles "began" with the events leading up to the first occasion on which the observer found them impinging on his own life. For Byrne this happened in 1784, when some victims of the Nappach Fleet straggled into Armagh town and perhaps into Byrne's own public house: "It was lamentable to see poor, quiet peasants coming to Armagh every day with grief painted in the emaciated figure of a poor old man, making a complaint against his neighbour, with whom he lived in peace and quietness since the days of his nativity."[90] For Blackhall it probably happened when he had to deal with the behavior of his employer's former tenants, returned from Mayo.

Though both men exercised selective perceptions, they may unconsciously have had a common purpose in doing so. The Loughgall Volunteer unit which Blackhall commanded was one of the first in the country to invite Catholics to enlist. If Ogle and Richardson typified local gentry opinion in their belief that Catholic possession of arms triggered the unrest, it seems likely that poor Blackhall spent many of his last unhappy days taking the blame from his neighbors for the turmoil occurring around them. Byrne, as a loyal Catholic, would largely have shared the attitudes of a liberal Protestant like Blackhall. His choice of a fight between two Protestants as his beginning point was a way of implying that conflict in Armagh did not have to be sectarian. Both Byrne and Blackhall would have welcomed the gestures of goodwill toward Catholics which various liberal elements in the Volunteers were making around 1784. Both sought to account for the outbreak of the troubles in a way which avoided the most obvious coloration which local experience placed on these events — that they represented the souring of the high hopes of the Volunteer movement.

Conclusion

Thus when we really understand what contemporaries were saying, and what they avoided saying, we penetrate the romantic haze with which the Volunteers were suffused by nationalists in the nineteenth cen-

90. Byrne, *Impartial account*, p. 6.

tury. The myth that the Volunteers were precursors of modern Irish nationalism has obscured the reality that to contemporary Catholics they more closely resembled the "B" Specials than a nationalist movement. At a meeting in Eglish during the mid-1860s a young man reciting the famous lines of Thomas Davis—"Ireland awoke, Dungannon spoke / With fear was England shaken"—was interrupted by an octogenarian. The Volunteers, he objected, were a pack of murderers who shot innocent people. Though not taken seriously, he mentioned details which accord with what is now known of the incident of 23 November 1788 on the road from Armagh town to Benburb.[91]

Senior, then, was quite right to call attention to the destabilizing impact of the Volunteer movement on social relations in County Armagh. That impact occurred not merely because the movement resulted in the widespread dissemination of arms, but also because it seemed to portend profound and contradictory changes in the distribution of power. The central issue in Irish politics between 1770 and 1829 was the readmission of Catholics to membership in the polity. That process had only just begun when, in the early 1780s, a section of the Protestant gentry allied themselves with their Protestant retainers, who were only marginally within the polity, against the government. Although this Patriot party seemed to have achieved its principal aims with the granting of legislative autonomy and commercial concessions in the early 1780s, their methods had the effect of seriously dividing the polity. A substantial group within the Volunteers wanted to press forward toward the goal of parliamentary reform, which would have made humbler Protestants, as well as their landlords, full members of the polity.[92] At the same time some Volunteer units were making gestures which seemed to invite Catholics to combine with them in the democratic cause. Under these revolutionary conditions—a group within the polity seeking allies outside it—contention was perhaps inevitable: hence the turmoil of the 1790s throughout Ireland. In this light the Armagh troubles may be considered the first phase of that upheaval.

Why were the members of the Patriot party so stupid as to split the polity and thus lay up for their class such a store of tribulation in the future? From the vantage point of 1779 it was difficult for liberal-minded Protestants to imagine that Catholics might find a basis for solidarity against them. Many intelligent observers believed that Catholicism was then on its last legs throughout Europe, and in Ireland educated Catholics were availing themselves of the opportunity to renounce Jacobite

91. Tohall, "Diamond fight," p. 17.
92. Interestingly, Blackhall was also prominently involved in this effort (*B.N.L.*, 2–5 Mar. 1784).

sympathies by taking the oath of allegiance. Mass nationalism — the eventual nondynastic alternative to the old basis of Catholic solidarity — would not become a dominant and lasting feature of Irish political culture until several decades later.[93] Consequently, the risk entailed by threatening armed collective action against the government in 1782 seemed minimal to influential Protestants. They failed to realize that the mere absence of the traditional Catholic menace did not make it safe for them to turn their retainers against the administration. By the mid-1780s that course of action had exposed the anomalous structure of the Irish polity in the north. Whereas in most of Ireland governmental functions — especially the use of force to maintain order — were exercised through and for the benefit of a small landed class of Protestants, in many parts of Ulster the Protestant population included a significant lower class as well. Members of this class had been encouraged to believe that they possessed a special role in the maintenance of order and were fully part of the polity. In the past, however, they had been called to play that part only during brief periods of alarm over threatened invasion or insurrection. Now for several years in succession they were constantly reminded of their proconsular role.

What made Armagh different from many other parts of Ulster was a class of Protestants too humble to be considered fit material even for the Volunteers in the early 1780s. Forming an important element in this class were young weavers whose position in the peculiar protoindustrial economy of Armagh rendered them unamenable to traditional family constraints on their behavior. Their exclusion from the Volunteers was bound to prompt a sense of relative deprivation, and their jealousy can be seen in Byrne's account of a speech purportedly made by a Nappach Fleet captain in 1785, a few months after Blackhall's Volunteer unit invited Catholics to enlist: "I have got information from a friend . . . that there are many papists in the place where he lives, who have taken the oath of allegiance, having got long leases, and of course [they] must have arms to shoot the sparrows from their grain, and not even that, but the perfidious Volunteers have taken them into their ranks."[94]

93. The United Irishmen of the 1790s did of course use nationalist rhetoric in the service of their republican objectives (in contrast to much later Irish radicalism, which adopted a republican strategy to obtain nationalist objectives). The solidarity for which they called, however, was between Catholics and Protestants, not among Catholics alone. Furthermore, I suspect that few Catholic peasants (and few Presbyterian peasants) who were "out" in 1798 were motivated mainly by nationalist ideology.

94. Byrne, *Impartial account*, p. 9. For the action of the Loughgall unit on 5 June 1784, see Rev. Patrick Rogers, *The Irish Volunteers and Catholic emancipation (1778–1793): a neglected phase of Ireland's history* (London, 1934), p. 154.

Today we are accustomed to think of the franchise and the right to be elected to legislative bodies as the key to membership in the polity. In a predemocratic age, however, the crucial distinction between members and nonmembers of the polity was not the franchise but the right to raise and deploy physical force. When French peasants in 1789 demanded, as they often did, the right to carry guns to protect their crops from the nobles' pigeons, they, like the Armagh Catholics, were implicitly demanding membership in the polity. However squalid the events described in this essay may seem, the issues at stake were not so remote from the major themes of European history in this period. Some members of the Armagh gentry, like their counterparts elsewhere in Ireland, clearly understood that the polity would have to be expanded. Nevertheless, improvement and that great engine of improvement, the loom, had given them a county in which they could not control that expansion.

BIBLIOGRAPHY

Contemporary sources

Manuscript material
National Library of Ireland, Dublin
  Gosford papers (MS 8018).
Royal Irish Academy, Dublin
  Charlemont papers.
Public Record Office of Northern Ireland, Belfast
  Abercorn papers (T.2541).
  Extracts of Blacker memoir in T. G. F. Paterson, "The battle of the Diamond"
    (T.2595/4).
  Brownlow papers: Rentals for Brownlow's-Derry estate (D. 2667/1).
  Bruce papers (T.3041).
  Transcript of J. Byrne, *An impartial account of the late disturbances in the
    county of Armagh . . .* , with notes by T. G. F. Paterson (T.1722).
  Calendar of the Pelham papers (T.755/2).

Contemporary publications and published contemporary sources
Belfast News-Letter.
Brady, John. *Catholics and Catholicism in the eighteenth-century press*
  (Maynooth, 1965).
Byrne, J. *An impartial account of the late disturbances in the county of Armagh,
  containing all the principal meetings, battles, executions, whippings, &c. of
  the Break-o-Day-Men and Defenders since the year 1784 down to the year*

1791, with a full and true account of the nature of the rising of both parties (Dublin, 1792).

Caulfield, James, first earl of Charlemont. *The manuscripts and correspondence of James, first earl of Charlemont*, comprising Historical Manuscripts Commission, *12th report*, appendix, pt. x, and *13th report*, appendix, pt. viii, 2 vols. (London, 1891–4).

Coote, Charles. *Statistical survey of the county of Armagh* (Dublin, 1804).

Crawford, W. H., and Trainor, Brian (ed.). *Aspects of Irish social history, 1750–1800* (Belfast, 1969).

"George Robert Fitzgerald – part I" in *Dublin University Magazine*, xvi, no. 91 (July 1840), p. 17.

Greig, William. *General report on the Gosford estates in County Armagh, 1821*, with introduction by F. M. L. Thompson and D. J. Tierney (Belfast, 1976).

Lewis, Samuel. *A topographical dictionary of Ireland . . .* , 2 vols. (London, 1837).

Musgrave, Sir Richard. *Memoirs of the different rebellions in Ireland from the arrival of the English . . .* (2nd ed., Dublin, 1801).

Report from the select committee appointed to enquire into the nature, character, extent, and tendency of Orange lodges, associations, or societies in Ireland, with the minutes of evidence and appendix, H.C. 1835 (377), xv, 1.

Taylor and Skinner's maps of the roads of Ireland (2nd ed., London, 1783).

Wesley, John. *The journal of the Rev. John Wesley, A.M.*, ed. Nehemiah Curnock, 8 vols. (London, 1938).

Young, Arthur. *Arthur Young's tour in Ireland (1776–1779)*, ed. A. W. Hutton, 2 vols. (London and New York, 1892; reprinted Shannon, 1970).

Later works

Writings in Irish studies

Broeker, Galen. *Rural disorder and police reform in Ireland, 1812–36* (London and Toronto, 1970).

Camblin, Gilbert. *The town in Ulster* (Belfast, 1951).

Crawford, W. H. *Domestic industry in Ireland: the experience of the linen industry* (Dublin, 1972).

Crawford, W. H. "Economy and society in south Ulster in the eighteenth century" in *Clogher Record*, viii, no. 3 (1975), pp. 241–58.

Cullen, L. M. *An economic history of Ireland since 1660* (London, 1972).

Danaher, Kevin. *The year in Ireland* (Cork, 1972).

Dictionary of national biography, ed. Sir Leslie Stephen and Sir Sidney Lee, 66 vols. (London, 1885–1901).

Donnelly, J. S., Jr. "The Rightboy movement, 1785–8" in *Studia Hibernica*, nos. 17–18 (1977–8), pp. 120–202.

Donnelly, J. S., Jr. "The Whiteboy movement, 1761–5" in *Irish Historical Studies*, xxi, no. 81 (Mar. 1978), pp. 20–54.

Gibbon, Peter. *The origins of Ulster unionism: the formation of popular Protestant politics and ideology in nineteenth-century Ireland* (Manchester, 1975).

Gill, Conrad. *The rise of the Irish linen industry* (Oxford, 1925).

Hayes, R. J. (ed.). *Manuscript sources for the history of Irish civilization*, 11 vols. (Boston, 1965).

Lecky, W. E. H. *A history of Ireland in the eighteenth century*, 5 vols. (London, 1892).

Miller, D. W. *Queen's rebels: Ulster loyalism in historical perspective* (Dublin and New York, 1978).

Rogers, Patrick. *The Irish Volunteers and Catholic emancipation (1778–1793): a neglected phase of Ireland's history* (London, 1934).

Senior, Hereward. *Orangeism in Ireland and Britain, 1795–1836* (London and Toronto, 1966).

Smyth, P. D. H. "The Volunteers and Parliament, 1779–84" in Thomas Bartlett and D. W. Hayton (ed.), *Penal era and golden age: essays in Irish history, 1690–1800* (Belfast, 1979), pp. 113–36.

Tohall, Patrick. "The Diamond fight of 1795 and the resultant expulsions" in *Seanchas Ardmhacha*, iii, no. 1 (1958), pp. 36–50.

Other writings in social science

Tilly, Charles; Tilly, Louise; and Tilly, Richard. *The rebellious century, 1830–1930* (Cambridge, Mass., 1975).

5 Paul Bew and Frank Wright

The Agrarian Opposition in Ulster Politics, 1848–87

At what point did a pan-Protestant opposition to Irish self-government become inevitable? There exists a tradition in popular historiography which claims that the critical period is 1879–82, when Michael Davitt's National Land League failed to establish itself as a major force among the Ulster Protestant tenantry, the only important section of the non-Catholic population which might have embraced Irish nationalism. The Land League, so it is argued, won southerners to the associated causes of nationalism and agrarian revolution, while at the same time it left northerners cold. This same historiography goes on to assert that the tradition known as the Ulster custom (which gave tenants the right to sell the interest in their holdings when they gave them up, and which was allegedly the basis of northern prosperity and the greater privileges of northern tenants) was the obstacle to the expression of solidarity embracing both Ulster Protestant tenants and their southern Catholic counterparts.[1]

Sophisticated modern scholarship is highly suspicious of this last notion, which certainly exaggerates the significance of the Ulster custom. As Barbara Solow observes, "There is nothing *in the institutional arrangement* called Ulster custom that guarantees a fixity of tenure."[2] The alleged relationship between Ulster custom and superior economic con-

---

1. John Healy, "Land as north's political dynamic," *Irish Times*, 22 July 1978, is a good summary of this popular historiography.
2. B. L. Solow, *The land question and the Irish economy, 1870–1903* (Cambridge, Mass., 1971), p. 25.

ditions, though not without some foundation, must therefore be treated cautiously. Not only was the Ulster custom found in areas of the north which could hardly be described as models of agricultural prosperity, but aspects of the custom were found outside the province. A writer for the *Irishman* in 1875 was properly skeptical about the validity of drawing sharp contrasts between north and south: "The radical error of all orations on the important question of landholding is the assumption that a broad and deep distinction must be made between the province of Ulster and all the other provinces of Ireland."[3] Though payments per acre were generally lower and usually made secretly in the south, tenants there did often sell the interest in their holdings.[4] Thus if the Ulster custom represented a degree of de facto security and capital accumulation among northern tenants, it cannot be supposed that there existed in the south, especially in the more prosperous parts, a uniformly contrasting situation. It is therefore not surprising that on the eve of the agitation of 1880–1 in the north, T. A. Dickson, one of the leading northern agrarian reformers, stressed the community of interest between the farmers of Ulster and those of Munster.[5] The collapse of agricultural prices, which threatened tenant-right values, had the effect of universalizing demands for rent reductions.

Far from leaving the Protestant farmers of the north cold, the land war had important consequences in Ulster. Ulster liberalism became a substantial political movement, giving the Protestant tenant farmers the means and opportunity to further their interests by independent action within the metropolitan political system of the United Kingdom. Yet it did so at precisely the same moment when Parnell managed to make the hitherto emotive unity of Catholics in Ireland a practical reality for Catholics in the north. Parnell demonstrated to them that they could participate in a national movement, and finally undermined the practice of clerical accommodation with northern Liberal elites. Thus at the very moment when a type of unionism which contradicted the previously dominant pan-Protestant form of unionism began to mature, the ground was laid for the first home-rule crisis of 1886, which made sectarian head-counting the principal concern of northern political life.

3. *Irishman*, 23 Oct. 1875. This argument by the writer in the *Irishman* was based explicitly on George Sigerson, *History of the land tenures and land classes of Ireland, with an account of the various secret agrarian confederacies* (Dublin and London, 1871).

4. For an interesting discussion, see J. S. Donnelly, Jr., *The land and the people of nineteenth-century Cork: the rural economy and the land question* (London and Boston, 1975), pp. 210–18.

5. *B.F.P.*, 29 Jan. 1880. The occasion of Dickson's speech was a meeting at Ballymoney of the Antrim Central Tenants' Defence Association.

Nevertheless, the responses of Protestants and Catholics to the Land League experience, as distinct from what came later, were not so starkly different. The Land League and the Ulster Liberals effectively, even if only tacitly, cooperated with each other in the north.[6] Protestants joined the Land League in significant numbers and Catholics participated in Ulster liberalism. The story can best be summarized by saying that the years 1879–81 saw the lowest ebb of northern agrarian sectionalism and the most effective undermining of landlord hegemony in the north. Yet cooperation between Catholics and Protestants was destined to be short-lived. This essay seeks to offer some explanation for this fact.

Agrarian Radicals and Whigs, 1848–52

When agrarian agitation revived in Ulster in the later years of the great famine, it contained discernibly different tendencies. Dr. James Mc-Knight, editor of the *Derry Standard* (1846–9 and 1853–76) and the *Banner of Ulster* (1849–53), was the undisputed leader of the radical tendency from 1846 until his death in 1876. The center of his influence lay in east Donegal, where he fought a running battle with the singularly unpleasant earl of Leitrim,[7] and in Derry, which was the only county in the north before the passage of the ballot act of 1872 to elect a Liberal M.P. supporting tenant right.

McKnight argued that the original undertakers of the Ulster plantation were trustees rather than feudal proprietors. He also claimed that the tenants had an interest in the soil which landlords were bound by the terms of the royal land grants to respect. Having established both the restrictions imposed on the rents that landlords might legally charge, and the fact that the tenants had carved out virtually all the farms from uncultivated wastes, he maintained that the current proprietors were drawing enormous revenues from these reclaimed estates, created exclu-

---

6. R. W. Kirkpatrick, "Origins and development of the land war in mid-Ulster, 1879–85" in F. S. L. Lyons and R. A. J. Hawkins (ed.), *Ireland under the union: varieties of tension: essays in honour of T. W. Moody* (Oxford, 1980), pp. 201–35. Kirkpatrick acknowledges the League's impact in outer Ulster but ignores its role in the interior of the province. For a valuable critique, see J. R. B. McMinn, "The Reverend James Brown Armour and Liberal politics in north Antrim, 1869–1914" (Ph.D. dissertation, Queen's University, Belfast, 1978), pp. 239 ff.

7. On the occasion of Lord Leitrim's murder, the *Londonderry Standard* (3 Apr. 1878) showed scant remorse: "He had one remedy for the peccadilloes of his tenants — eviction. If they took seaweed — eviction. If they refused to give up a field which he capriciously wanted to give to somebody else — eviction. If they contested his right to take the pick of the family into his domestic service — eviction. If they controverted his decision about an easement or right of way — eviction."

sively by tenant capital and tenant labor.[8] The thrust of McKnight's thesis was that a large part of landlord rent was in effect confiscatory of
tenant property. In its bluntest form this thesis came close to the proposition that as tenant labor had created present agricultural capital, the
landlords were entitled only to the rent of the "raw earth." McKnight
claimed that the landlord was entitled to an essentially residual rent:
"the philosophy of rent being the clear profit remaining after all costs
of production and the interest on the farmer's capital have been deducted,
ought to be kept habitually in view." And when certain Presbyterian
clergy enunciated this doctrine in 1849 and 1850, a howl of execration
from Conservatives, supposedly Liberal landlords, and moderate tenant-
right supporters alike denounced them for preaching communism.[9]

In practice the central differences between the agrarian radicals and
their adversaries revolved around three issues: fixity of tenure, the principle of "authoritative limitations on rents," and the participation of the
northern tenant-right associations in the nationwide Tenant League. The
importance of fixity of tenure was paramount: "All legalisation of tenant
right is *delusive* without fixed tenure, secured occupancy so long as the
rent is paid, and an independent tribunal for limitation of rents."[10] Although McKnight had argued from explicitly sectionalist assumptions relating to the Ulster plantations, his program was the three Fs of the Tenant League: fixity of tenure at fair rents, with the right of free sale. This
had important consequences. First, it implied that the demands of the
northern and southern tenants were harmonious rather than sectionally
differentiated. Instead of making a local fetish of the Ulster custom, Mc-
Knight was demanding its legal confirmation in Ulster and its extension
to the whole of Ireland. Second, the raw-earth thesis involved an explicit
defense of marginal tenants on reclaimed mountain lands.

8. James McKnight, *The Ulster tenants' claim of right, or landownership a state trust;
the Ulster tenant right an original grant from the British crown, and the necessity of extending its general principle to the other provinces of Ireland demonstrated in a letter
to Lord John Russell* (Dublin, 1848), p. 50.
9. Lord Londonderry, who was being courted by the *Northern Whig*, asked the Whig
viceroy Lord Clarendon whether it was possible to employ the government stipend paid
to the Presbyterian clergy (*regium donum*) as a means of disciplining the offending ministers (*Banner of Ulster*, 8 Mar. 1850). It appears that Lord Londonderry later required
two outspoken clergymen to "give up all connexions with his property" (*B.N.L.*, 17 Dec.
1850). When the synod of Belfast discussed a tenant-right petition, the Rev. Henry Cooke
boasted of his support for tenant right, but he refused to endorse an approving resolution
because it would have associated him with the proponents of "socialism" and "communism"
(*Banner of Ulster*, 17 May 1850).
10. See the *Banner of Ulster*'s little pamphlet, *A catechism of tenant right* (Belfast,
1850), para. 3.

Many of these landholders, either themselves or their recent ancestors, had indeed reclaimed their holdings from raw earth. Usually, they were given some waste land at a nominal rent, but several years after they had created the farm, a valuer arrived to impose a significant increase. The typical manner of respecting tenant interest was for the landlord to tell assessors to value the land "as they found it," but to ignore farm buildings. The obvious consequence was that for lowland farmers tenant right was reflected in valuation practices, whereas it was quite otherwise for mountain tenants.[11] In this way, then, McKnight's position spoke not merely to the wider Irish context but also to the largely Catholic mountain tenantry within Ulster.[12]

In the late 1840s and early 1850s, however, McKnight's position was by no means politically dominant even within the opposition to the Conservative bloc.[13] The northern Whigs were the main opposition, but they continued to function according to political methods which were becoming increasingly inadequate. As the *Vindicator*, the Catholic organ in Belfast, declared, because "Whig, in those days of [aristocratic] clanship, meant civil and religious liberty, [while] Tory meant exactly the reverse," Catholics "as a body bound themselves to whiggery, and Protestants, with some honourable exceptions, to toryism."[14] The Whigs in the north tended to consist of urban businessmen and professionals together with a small group of Liberal landlords whose unity had been forged during the reign of the Whigs in Britain from 1830 to 1841. But given their lack of locally rooted power, their strength tended to be a function of the credibility of the Whig party as a whole, and that sank to its lowest ebb during the Russell ministry and the great famine. Practical political activity for them meant exercising influence with the Whig bloc in Britain[15] and building up a local basis of support for that party. As the existing adherents comprised a substantial part of the Belfast middle class and some influential landlords, it appeared altogether practical to persevere in this course. And the chance of securing the backing of the Peelite marquis of Londonderry, whose territorial power in County

---

11. See ibid., para. 14, for a case of this kind on Lord Londonderry's Donegal estate.
12. See F. S. L. Lyons, *Culture and anarchy in Ireland, 1890–1939* (Oxford and New York, 1979), p. 139.
13. In 1850 the circulation of the Ulster newspapers was: *Northern Whig*, 285,500 (three days); *Banner of Ulster*, 123,400 (two days); *Belfast Chronicle*, 90,000 (three days); *Belfast Newsletter*, 72,500 (two days); *Belfast Weekly Vindicator*, 54,750. See *Banner of Ulster*, 10 Oct. 1851.
14. *Vindicator*, 16 Aug. 1851.
15. *Northern Whig*, 28 Mar. 1848.

Down amounted to virtual proprietorship of one of the parliamentary
seats, was not to be missed.[16] Yet there was the obvious political corollary that any extension of the popular base of whiggery would have to
be founded upon an explicit compromise between "good" (i.e., Whig)
landlords and responsible tenants. An antilandlord agitation led by Whigs
was most unlikely.

In 1848 the Whig government put forward a manifestly unsatisfactory
land bill at a time when clearances were proceeding apace. At a meeting
of tenant farmers of Antrim and Down held in Belfast, the Rev. Henry
Montgomery, leader of the Unitarian remonstrants, outlined the need
for "an honest law of tenant right." He thought that landlords would
"act wisely" by replacing "pauper cottiers" with "respectable tenant
farmers and well-paid labourers." But what alarmed him was the possibility that the clearances of small tenants without adequate compensation would put an enormous burden on the poor law. He wanted to
discourage landlords from engaging in wholesale clearances and to insure that those who were dispossessed had the wherewithal to migrate
or emigrate. Montgomery saw the need for greater security if the remaining larger tenants were to invest more, to practice "high farming,"
and thereby to be able to pay greater rents than the present occupiers
could generally afford.[17] But as the Belfast meeting resolved, "We dis-
claim all right on the part of tenants to absolute fixity of tenure, or to
interfere unreasonably with the landlord's letting of his land. . . ." The
assembled farmers did not demand a general procedure for restricting
rents, but only a system of arbitration designed to resolve particular
disagreements. In this respect they echoed the *Northern Whig*, which
declared in April 1848, "To attempt authoritatively to limit rents would
be as clearly in opposition to principle as to attempt to prevent a merchant from getting what he could for a hogshead of sugar, or a farmer
what he could for a quarter of wheat."[18]

Finally, the Whigs, far from attacking the institution of the landlord,
positively affirmed it. "It is good for men to have something to look up
to—the gradations of rank are a social benefit," declared Montgomery.
In a moment of irritation he revealed his feelings about the radicals:
"We have nothing to do with what the *Whig* or the *Standard* says, or
with the amount of falsehood which Mr. McKnight may write in the

16. Ibid., 21 Mar. 1848. At a dinner for his tenants Lord Londonderry expressed regret
that the land question "has lately been worked up to a sort of second repeal question and
was improperly used by persons of dangerous character."
17. Ibid., 4 Mar. 1848.
18. Ibid., 1 Apr. 1848.

Standard, for neither the statements in it [n]or the individual could receive from me further notice."[19]

It is certainly true that neither Montgomery nor McKnight were nationalists, and that McKnight developed his thesis out of the principles he derived from the royal grants to the original undertakers of the plantation. In this sense it is necessary to acknowledge the difference between McKnight and nationalist writers on the land question who regarded the land as stolen by the English crown from the native Irish. After the escalation of the national conflict in the 1880s, these opposed perspectives were frozen within antagonistic national traditions. But the central fact to notice here is that McKnight called for an all-Ireland assault on landlord power and spoke for those in the north who shared the temper of the island as a whole at the end of the famine. Montgomery by contrast sought to create a new legal accommodation between "good" landlords and their more viable tenantry. Politically, he sought to extend the local Whig alliance, which, given its existing composition, had necessarily to speak a political language and to articulate local demands that ignored the sentiments of the bulk of the tenants of Ireland and of marginal farmers in Ulster.

The intervention of the Tenant League in the election of 1852 was the first major challenge to Conservative landlord control in northeast Ulster. The nearly complete failure of the League in the north is the most obvious contrast between north and south. But it is also important to stress the observation of Dr. John Whyte that "the issue of independence versus whiggery had not been so clearly presented in Ulster as elsewhere."[20] The extent to which the opposition to conservatism remained internally ambivalent is reflected in the candidacy of William Sharman Crawford in County Down.

Crawford, who had sat at Westminster for Dundalk and Rochdale, had declared in 1848 that one of the main enemies in the struggle for legal recognition of the tenant right of Ulster was "the Irish landlord interest, which includes the government, who appear to be under the thraldom of that power."[21] Tenant leaders like McKnight trusted him and accepted that the compromises implicit in Crawford's bill of 1850 were aimed at securing the support of "honest friends." Though Crawford did not support fixity of tenure, his proposals were designed to deter landlords from evicting all but the least viable tenants.

The Whigs were far from enthusiastic in their support for Crawford,

19. Ibid., 4 Mar. 1848.
20. Whyte, *Indep. Ir. party,* p. 85.
21. *Northern Whig,* 28 Mar. 1848.

but they found themselves in an increasingly untenable position around midcentury. Not only did their courtship of Lord Londonderry backfire on them,[22] but the ecclesiastical-titles bill of 1851 caught them badly off-guard. This bill reinforced the prohibition under which territorial titles already used by Protestant dignitaries could not be assumed by any other ecclesiastics, and it also voided any bequests made to such persons under illegal designations. In Ireland, of course, the measure was strongly denounced by Catholics as penal legislation. Both Crawford and McKnight opposed the bill from the beginning,[23] but the Catholic *Vindicator* did not fail to notice that R. J. Tennent, Liberal M.P. for Belfast, had opposed only the third reading, after the measure had been amended by an ultra-Tory motion. On balance, the Whigs were probably thankful for the opportunity to shelter behind Crawford in 1852, all the more so as erstwhile Liberal landlords faced with agrarian agitation tended to line up with Tories.[24]

But if the Whigs were unable to dominate the opposition, the radicals found it increasingly difficult to preserve the commitment of northern tenant-right associations to the Tenant League once the agitation about "papal aggression" broke out in 1850. After the introduction of the ecclesiastical-titles bill and the formation of the Catholic Defence Association, the Tenant League found itself committed to a de facto alliance with the C.D.A. Crawford, the obvious titular head of the League, thrashed out a bill with the League's leaders and then secured the ostensible adhesion of the C.D.A. to the measure.[25] As the ties between the C.D.A. and the League in the south seemed to grow closer, northern tenant-right candidates who were already ambiguous on the question of the League began to speak more of the need for Presbyterian parliamentary representation plus support for Sharman Crawford's bill.[26] Only one Presbyterian tenant-righter was elected in Ulster, William Kirk for Newry, and he was not a League supporter but rather a Whig without the opprobrium attached to the Russell era. Whyte's thesis is that in the end the League of North and South was a southern body with some northern allies.[27]

22. See fn. 9.

23. For McKnight's views on the ecclesiastical-titles bill, see *Banner of Ulster*, 11 Feb. 1851.

24. "We know landed proprietors of Tyrone who at home are professed radicals, and yet they employed their feudal influence over their tenants in favour of the Tory candidates" (*Banner of Ulster*, 30 July 1852).

25. Whyte, *Indep. Ir. party*, p. 31.

26. Ibid., p. 44.

27. Ibid., p. 159.

The 1852 election highlights a number of important features of Ulster society and the shape of political forces within it. It is true that the landlords employed "No popery" slogans to discredit popular candidates, but if these were efficacious, it was only because other factors worked in their favor. Having survived the famine without the debasement of their ostensible social functions, northern landlords were able to use their considerable following of dependents to make coercion in a system of public voting very real. Furthermore, the tenant's interest in his property — the salable value of his tenant right — was entirely dependent on landlord grace and favor. Any ambivalent feelings about sectarian issues might provide the source of uncertainty required to insure reluctant compliance at the polls with landlord dictates.[28]

Since the success of landlordism in the 1852 election was so great in Ulster, the opposition to toryism retreated to the boroughs, where the weight of whiggery against the radicals was considerably stronger. Thus, for the most part, the Whigs remained after 1852 the dominant opposition to landlordism, but their strategy of building a "respectable" farmer, Liberal landlord, and urban middle-class coalition was now more a matter of form because efforts to make it substantial in the countryside were fairly hopeless.

Liberals and Catholics, 1852–74

In fact, the post-1853 agricultural revival in the countryside relieved the pressures which had made the Tenant League-McKnight agitation so threatening. Tenant-right values recovered and evictions became rare. Under these conditions the adjustments which Montgomery was seeking were more or less brought to pass by the operation of impersonal economic forces rather than by political and legal intervention. Landlords could now, to their advantage, allow sales of tenant right and relative security of tenure, but with this important qualification: both were by grace. Efforts to create political opposition to landlords would now have either to revitalize radical agrarian demands or, employing the desire for Presbyterian parliamentary representation, to promote the issue of political independence as a goal in itself. But either way the creation of rural opposition would be even harder work than in 1852, when it was backed by circumstances of some urgency.

If the land question was ever to be a solvent for national and religious antagonism in Ireland, at least one necessary condition had to be present.

---

28. "In Ulster . . . a tenant voter is his landlord's slave in exact proportion to the amount of unlegalized tenant right which he possesses, so that if the Ulster custom has improved the physical condition of the population, it has at the same time reduced them to the lowest degree of political bondage . . ." (*Banner of Ulster*, 3 Aug. 1852).

There had to be some common perception of what the problem was. We do not wish to argue that the land question actually had such a potential, but this much at least can be said: McKnight's participation in the Tenant League was an important effort to lay the foundation. If, however, the foundation, so laid, was profoundly to modify the ultimate shape of the national question, then it had to endure in some recognizable form. That is precisely what did not happen.

The uneven development of the Irish economy was reflected in certain key political developments. First, the dominance of industry in the north had the paradoxical effect of insuring that local landlords and their institutions of local government survived the famine without experiencing the complete breakdown of credibility of their counterparts elsewhere. Landlord hegemony over the countryside was sustained by more than simple pan-Protestantism. Second, the dominance of industry expressed itself in the central role of the urban middle class within the opposition Liberal movement. The Whigs remained very much in control of liberalism, which came to express their vision of the world, a vision divorced from the realities that stimulated agrarian radicalism. Thus it was not just Whig dispositions on religiopolitical issues, such as education, which emphasized their local peculiarity. The very least that can be said of the northern Whigs is that if the land question was the best material available for forming a mass base for any movement opposed to pan-Protestantism in the north, they used it very ineffectively until the crisis of 1879–81 turned northern liberalism into a qualitatively different sort of movement.

When Gladstone won the 1868 election, his program for Ireland included the disestablishment of the Irish Anglican church and the solution of the land question. With a newly extended urban franchise, Liberal M.P.s were returned for Belfast, Derry, and Newry, and independent Orange M.P.s for Belfast and Carrickfergus. But when the land bill was published, tenant dissatisfaction with the measure brought to the surface the unresolved tensions within northern liberalism. The somewhat radical Catholic *Northern Star* took issue with "pretentious advocates of the tenants' cause" who counseled against demonstrations "calculated to embarrass the government." Such people, it suggested, thought that "the first consideration should be government, and the last, those principally concerned — the tenant farmers," and it complained that certain Liberals regarded the bill as important "only in so far as it tends to keep the Whigs in and the Tories out of office."[29]

Nor was the *Northern Star* alone in thinking this. From an Ulster standpoint the prime weaknesses of the land bill were three in number. First,

---

29. *Northern Star*, 14 Apr. 1870.

the bill did not clearly define the Ulster custom but ominously referred to "customs and usages," which, as later court decisions showed, were to include every well-established infringement of the custom. Second, the measure was marred by cumbersome and potentially very expensive procedures for claiming compensation; these could swallow up a substantial part of any award made. Third, the bill contained no protection against the raising of rents. The first of these problems was the subject of an amendment moved by William Johnston, independent Orange M.P. for Belfast. His amendment sought to characterize the Ulster custom as it was defined by James McKnight and widely understood by tenants, but the proposal received no support from northern Liberal M.P.s.[30] As a result, a meeting was convened at Ballymoney in April 1870 to discuss the bill. McKnight intended to introduce resolutions covering all three difficulties, but as Samuel McElroy later recalled, "some people thought these resolutions too strong and feared to embarrass the government."[31] Because of this caution even at the relatively independent Ballymoney meeting, the proceedings aroused real disappointment with the Liberal M.P.s and produced a sense that William Johnston was the tenants' only ally. The Rev. J. B. Armour expressed this sentiment in such strong terms that McKnight felt the need to compliment Thomas McClure, Liberal M.P. for Belfast, for attempting to "get the government to consent to the imposition of restrictions on the landlords' power of rackrenting."[32]

The mainline Whigs suffered a considerable loss of popularity over this issue. Such was the insensitivity of Thomas MacKnight, editor of the *Northern Whig* and a Gladstonian, that in the month preceding this incident the newspaper expended political capital defending the rather peculiar and unpopular leases of the Whig Lord Dufferin. Gladstone had managed to generate considerable support in Ulster agrarian circles, and a delegation which met with him in March 1870 reported glowingly that he had "displayed an amount of local knowledge not a little remarkable."[33] The Ulster Liberal leaders made less than effective use of the opportunity so presented to them. And they were soon to discover that they had forfeited their monopoly of agrarian political influence.

A new source of political confusion appeared in the working of the land act. That measure contained separate provisions for Ulster and did

30. Ibid., 15 Apr. 1870.

31. *Report of her majesty's commissioners of inquiry into the working of the Landlord and Tenant (Ireland) Act, 1870, and the acts amending the same*, vol. ii: *Digest of evidence; minutes of evidence*, pt. i, p. 397 [C 2779-I], H.C. 1881, xviii, 73 (hereafter cited as *Bessborough comm. evidence*).

32. *Weekly Northern Whig*, 20 Apr. 1870.

33. *Londonderry Standard*, 18 Mar. 1870.

not attempt to extend free sale southward. Not only did it legalize a distinct system for Ulster, but as its inadequacies became evident, it created a situation in which any future northern agitation was likely to be explicitly sectionalist because it would be concerned with the defects of the law as it affected Ulster. The weaknesses of the act, anticipated by the McKnight resolutions, were soon exposed in the courts, and many observers began to feel that the law had actually diminished the custom. One particularly glaring case was the ruling that at the termination of a lease the occupier had no claim to tenant right. This decision was in flagrant conflict with actual practice on tenant-right estates and had no foundation in pre-1870 realities. In this context Liberal caution could be swamped by the promises of independent Orangemen or even Conservative landlords to support amending legislation that would rectify the injustice. The danger was that if the Liberals' position on the land question became indistinguishable from that of other candidates, their capacity to build up a coherent following would be seriously diminished. Not only would they lose Protestant farmers to independent Orangeism, but Catholic support for liberalism would remain highly conditional.

To secure election in almost any constituency in the north, Liberals of every variety required Catholic support. With perhaps only one exception, every Liberal candidate nominated in Ulster before 1874 was a Protestant.[34] This circumstance often rankled Catholics, especially in places like Newry, where they provided nearly all the Liberal votes.[35] In fact, the same difficulty recurred right up to 1886.[36] Moreover, the education question, which was always festering not far below the surface, erupted in June 1870, when the Powis commission recommended meeting Catholic demands for denominational education. The northern Catholic press was delighted. But a largely Presbyterian group, including some prominent urban Whigs, such as Thomas Sinclair, the Rev. John MacNaughton, and the Rev. John Scott Porter, organized the National Education League, which opposed the commission because it

34. The only exception known to us occurred at the 1872 by-election in Derry city, when the Catholic solicitor-general for Ireland, Christopher Palles, was put forward by the Liberals. At that time Palles was working on the prosecution of certain priests in County Galway arising out of the disputed by-election there earlier in the year. As the *Examiner* (2 Nov. 1872) put it, "If there were no other circumstances at all to tell against Mr. Palles, the fact of the Belfast 'Liberal' Association being in his favour should be sufficient to secure his rejection." Thus far had relations fallen between the Liberal elite and the main northern Catholic journal.

35. See *Northern Star*, 29 Dec. 1870. A vacancy at Newry appeared owing to the death of William Kirk, the Liberal M.P. The seat was filled by his previous Tory opponent, Lord Newry, after a pact with the tiny Protestant Liberal group had been concluded.

36. Charles Russell's report to W. E. Gladstone, 17 Mar. 1886 (B.L., Add. MS 56447).

"aimed at the substitution of purely denominational teaching for that nonsectarian system whose retention and purification our league has been formed to secure."[37] In December 1871, when the National Education League invited Orange leaders to its meetings (in Cookstown they actually appeared in sashes), the temper of the Belfast Catholic press rose. "The Orange sashes," declared the *Examiner*, "will carry this question beyond the domain of nonsectarianism, exposing as it does the real feeling which animates the Presbyterian and Unitarian ministers on the subject."[38]

The education question had always been the most divisive issue within northern liberalism. The dominant place of the Presbyterian view of that issue in Liberal programs had always irritated Catholics. The internal cohesion of liberalism was a direct function of its credibility on the land question and an inverse function of the profile of educational controversy. What aggravated matters was that northern Catholic politics tended to reflect political developments in the rest of the island and did so in proportion to Catholic disenchantment with northern liberalism. In 1872 in Derry city a Home Rule candidate polled poorly at a by-election, with most of the Catholic vote going to the Liberal nominee. But there were some signs nonetheless that the support for home rule was rising in the north. Catholic political influence in the north was to be deployed with increasing effectiveness to promote candidates according to their positions on particular questions, regardless of the long-established practice of supporting Liberals.

In the first northern contest after the introduction of the secret ballot, J. W. E. Macartney stood at the 1873 Tyrone by-election as an independent Orange candidate. Despite his avowed opposition to home rule and denominational education, and his published address to the "Protestant county," the Catholic *Examiner* supported him. This was largely owing to his position on the land question—which was not easily distinguishable from that of the Liberals.[39] Although the *Examiner* said that it would have preferred a candidate espousing fixity of tenure and fair rents, the point was clear. If Catholics were prepared to support a candidate of this kind, what role would be left for Liberals? The Liberals might have been equally alarmed by the attitude of the *Londonderry Standard* to Macartney's now successful candidacy for Tyrone in 1874, which it declared "had far outstripped the triumphal glories of Down," where the son of William Sharman Crawford had just been elected as a Liberal.[40]

37. *Weekly Northern Whig*, 23 July 1870.
38. *Weekly Examiner*, 9 Dec. 1871.
39. *W.E.U.O*, 5 Apr. 1873.
40. *Londonderry Standard*, 14 Feb. 1874.

If in their common disappointment with liberalism Protestant land reformers and Catholics were prepared to support independent Orangemen or even Conservatives who said the proper things about leasehold
tenant right, then liberalism was in deep trouble. It is in fact an open
question what might have happened if William Johnston, who was still
fondly remembered for his abortive amendment to the 1870 land act,
had not made an alliance with Belfast toryism and jettisoned his earlier
radicalism on the agrarian question. Johnston's defection weakened the
otherwise potentially large rural Protestant support for independent
Orangeism. Liberalism's increased strength in the countryside in the 1874
election depended heavily on the legacy of past conflicts,[41] but it was
far from having the success which the coming of the secret ballot might
have been expected to yield. The Liberals' other asset was the perception
that Gladstone was more likely to deliver the requisite improvements
in land legislation than Disraeli.

The Crisis of Northern Liberalism

Attention must now be directed to the crisis that developed in the
relations between the Liberals and their Catholic and Protestant land-
reforming supporters. This crisis was a consequence of both the limited
nature of their agrarian program in relation to Ulster and the fact that
the program reflected a sectional or Ulster-centric approach. It would
be wrong to say that northern Catholic farmers lived on the mountains,
for large areas of the Ulster lowlands contained substantial percentages
of Catholics. Nevertheless, the largest territorial expanses that were heavily Catholic (over 75 percent) stretched along the mountainy frontiers
of the province, and the areas within "Protestant Ulster" of similar composition included the Sperrin mountains in Tyrone and Derry as well
as the Glens of Antrim. In these districts, where much of the land had
been recently reclaimed, the McKnight thesis described actual experience. Whig liberalism was wide of the mark. In the absence of a vigorous land-reform option some of these areas began to show visible signs
of supporting home rule and impatience at clerical accommodation with
Whig leaders.[42]

Frustration with the operation of the 1870 act had become evident
before the 1874 election. Isaac Butt's land bill of 1875, supported by the

41. This was especially true of County Derry, the scene of battles in the 1850s, and
of County Down, where the name of William Sharman Crawford had a powerful appeal.

42. Particularly important in this respect was the central Tyrone area, where home-
rule meetings were held at Carrickmore, Lower Bodoney, and Cappagh (*W.E.U.O.*, 1
Feb., 29 Mar., 20 Sept. 1873).

southern Home Rule M.P.s, was a comprehensive measure designed to
secure the three Fs throughout Ireland. But James Sharman Crawford
brought in another measure aimed principally at protecting leasehold
tenant right in the north, and most Liberal M.P.s supported this measure instead of Butt's.[43] The more radical wing of the northern Liberals,
particularly those connected with the Route Association in the Ballymoney
district, were alarmed at this development, and their opposition to
Crawford was based both on the inadequacy of his bill to secure its intended objective and on his failure to endorse Butt's bill. As the radicals
put it, following McKnight's position in the old Tenant League, they
wanted to extend Ulster tenant right to the rest of the island.[44]

The Ballymoney group outdistanced the main Ulster Liberals in a
number of respects. Paradoxically, they came from an area where the
Ulster custom was about as fully recognized as anywhere in the province.[45] The key figures of the group were Thomas McElderry, chairman
of the Ballymoney town commissioners and lessee of the town markets;
and Samuel McElroy, editor of the *Ballymoney Free Press* and an auctioneer. While both had a very direct interest, as did the town of Ballymoney generally, in the prosperity of the surrounding countryside, they
also expressed the aspiration of urban and rural middle-class elements
to establish their political independence as effectively as they had already
achieved their economic independence. They are perhaps among the best
examples of northern Protestants who looked upon liberalism as standing for freedom from the dead hand of landlord power, precisely because
their area had, in a manner of speaking, already outgrown it.[46] They
tended to take a wide view of politics, and it is probably significant that,
together with nearby Coleraine, Ballymoney was one of the first northern towns to elect a genuinely representative Catholic to its town com-

43. *W.E.U.O.*, 11 May 1878.
44. The Route Tenants' Defence Association supported Butt's bill from the start, see-
ing in it the means of extending tenant right to the rest of Ireland (*B.F.P.*, 16 Mar. 1876).
The association opposed Crawford's bill in 1876 because it included a provision which
would have allowed leaseholders to sign away their tenant right; the bill was accepted
only in 1877, when it was amended to prevent such alienation (*B.F.P.*, 1 Mar. 1877). But
many other tenant-right organizations did not adopt the so-called Ballymoney program
until early 1878.
45. *Bessborough comm. evidence*, pt. i, p. 380. The Route district appears to have
been the most notable for the practice of selling tenant right by auction, a method which
virtually precluded any kind of landlord interference with the purchaser or purchase
price.
46. *B.F.P.*, 14 Sept. 1876. Ballymoney, despite its size, was one of the first towns to
hold a meeting to condemn the Turkish atrocities in Bulgaria. The meeting featured a
stellar performance by the Rev. J. B. Armour.

mission on the strength of essentially Protestant votes.[47] At this time, however, Ballymoney was to play a part in pushing liberalism in a more advanced direction.[48]

At least one of the Liberal M.P.s was aware of the possible damage done by the nonreciprocation of Isaac Butt's support for the Crawford bill. Professor Richard Smyth, M.P. for County Derry, who had himself supported Butt's bill, insisted that "a separate bill did not imply that northern men wanted to sail in a boat by themselves," and he reassured southerners of northern readiness to help them "extricate themselves out of the difficulties which, I am bound to say, are greater than our own."[49] But Smyth notwithstanding, James Daly, a leading figure in Connacht agrarian politics, was soon sharply to say: "What is Ulster tenant right this year?"[50] Nor was the time far off when Parnell and thirty-five Home Rule M.P.s would feel free to abstain from supporting the Ulstermen's cause, and when Mitchell Henry, an opponent of Parnell's noncooperative policy, would observe: "To the great delight of those who fully appreciate the value of the policy of *divide et impera*, the southern and western farmers are ostentatiously divorced in their tactics from the northern farmers."[51]

While the division at the national level was becoming increasingly apparent, it began to have a direct impact within Ulster itself. In 1876 the *Weekly Examiner* urged Catholic voters in County Donegal to ballot at a by-election for the Tory candidate.[52] But the *Examiner*'s point was made with far more devastating effect in the County Down by-election of 1878, caused by the death of James Sharman Crawford. The Liberals confidently expected to retain the seat. And because over 80 percent of the electorate was Protestant, they made little effort to conciliate Catholic voters. The Conservative candidate, Lord Castlereagh, heir to the marquisate of Londonderry, did not make the same mistake. As the *Ballymoney Free Press* was to remark after the election, the Liberal could be judged better than the Conservative only "by inference."[53] And the *Examiner* dwelled on the fact that Lord Londonderry's tenants were considerably more comfortable than farmers in other parts of the island, so what was all the Liberal talk of tenant right about?[54] More significantly, however,

47. *W.E.U.O.*, 25 Oct. 1879.
48. For the authoritative account, see McMinn, "Armour."
49. *Irishman*, 13 Nov. 1875.
50. *Connaught Telegraph*, 5 Mar. 1879.
51. *Nation*, 23 July 1878.
52. *W.E.U.O.*, 24 Aug. 1876.
53. *B.F.P.*, 23 May 1878.
54. This assertion was coupled with an interesting claim to the effect that Catholic

Lord Castlereagh, unlike his Liberal opponent W. D. Andrews, gave un-
dertakings to support the intermediate-education and Irish-university
bills, both of which the Catholic clergy wanted, and a further undertak-
ing to endorse a motion to set up an inquiry into Irish home rule.[55]

The *Examiner*'s message was quite clear: by voting for Andrews, "you
sever the ties between north and south."[56] When Castlereagh won, the
newspaper hailed it as "a victory the most glorious on record" since the
famous election of Daniel O'Connell in Clare. The contest proved once
and for all that northern Catholic voters "would not for selfish purposes
sever their fortunes from that of their suffering brethren, the tenant
farmers of the [other] three provinces."[57] By 1878 there were in effect
two agrarian movements in Ireland, and sections of the Ulster Catholics
were refusing to support the northern agitation, which seemed relevant
neither to their condition nor to that of the island as a whole.

The County Down by-election constituted an important demonstration by northern Catholics of their independence of whiggery. They had
served notice that if Liberals wanted their support, they must take a more
militant position on the land question and relegate educational concerns
to a subordinate place.[58] On educational issues they were to get their
answer quickly. In August T. A. Dickson, M.P. for Dungannon, clashed
publicly with the Belfast presbytery, a stronghold of the National Education League, on the intermediate-education bill. The Rev. John Mac-
Naughton had insinuated that the Tory Presbyterian M.P.s, C. E. Lewis
of Derry city and J. P. Corry of Belfast, had better expressed Presbyterian feeling on the matter by their opposition than had Dickson by his
support. Dickson pointedly told the opponents of the bill that the main
ground of their objection was that "there must be in it or under it some
hidden snare, or it would not have received the hearty support of Mr.
Butt and the Roman Catholic M.P.s and the Catholic press."[59] The *Ulster Weekly News*, which had always been impatient with educational
questions, said that if the bill established denominational education, what
a pity this was not known earlier, because it was a good bill: "We have

---

priests seeking sites for churches and schools found that Conservative landowners were
"immeasurably better in their dealings with them than the land-jobbing Whigs" (*W.E.U.O.*,
18 May 1878).

55. What Lord Castlereagh actually promised is not altogether clear. But this set of
propositions is as close as possible to the opposing suggestions made by the *Examiner* (18
May 1878) and to his own later statements. It is not likely that he undertook to support
home rule itself.

56. *W.E.U.O.*, 18 May 1878.

57. *W.E.U.O.*, 25 May 1878.

58. Ibid.

59. *B.F.P.*, 15 Aug. 1878.

a strong opinion that there is no ecclesiastical organisation which would not desire to have denominational teaching imposed on the country, if only it were possible for each sect to have an advantage over all the others."[60] Such a public rupture between Liberals over the education question began to clear the air.

The agricultural crisis was also beginning to bite. As prices fell in the summer of 1878,[61] farmers were slow to discharge their debts. "Shopkeepers find it extremely difficult," noted the *Ballymoney Free Press*, "to collect their country accounts, not from any unwillingness on the part of the people to pay, but they hesitate to sell in a low market."[62] The full meaning of this development was not spelled out until June 1879, when the recognition dawned that Irish agricultural prices were unlikely ever to regain their former standard. In that event all values — fee simple, tenant right, and rents — would decline.[63] In August 1879 an entirely spontaneous demonstration at Toome near Ballymena called for rent reductions and land reforms virtually embodying the three Fs.[64] The crisis seemed to be propelling farmers beyond the positions hitherto taken by the Ulster Liberals. But temporarily the Toome meeting stood out as an isolated occurrence. In general, the *Examiner*'s comment on the tenant-right advocates was justified: "Now a real crisis has come, they are utterly silent."[65] Ominously, the public row between the *Examiner* and the *Ballymoney Free Press*, in which the former revealed its ignorance of the advanced position assumed by the Route Association in support of Isaac Butt's bill, demonstrated the enormous political costs thus far of the sectional policies of Ulster liberalism.[66]

The Impact of Parnell and the Land League

It is against this background that the visit of Parnell to Belfast and Newry in October 1879 must be viewed. The resolutions at both meetings called for an Irish parliament, rent reductions, and peasant propri-

60. *Ulster Weekly News*, 17 Aug. 1878.
61. *B.F.P.*, 22 Aug. 1878.
62. *B.F.P.*, 26 Sept. 1878.
63. *B.F.P.*, 19 June 1879.
64. *B.F.P.*, 14 Aug. 1879.
65. *W.E.U.O.*, 27 Sept. 1879.
66. *B.F.P.*, 30 Oct. 1879; *W.E.U.O.*, 1 Nov. 1879. The *Examiner* and the *Free Press* fell into a nasty row over a proposed land meeting at Ballymoney which was canceled. The *Examiner* described the resolutions to be offered there as "vague, lengthy, and irresolute," and referred to the inclusion of the "rest of Ireland" in the program as an "advance." Naturally, these remarks irritated the Ballymoney group, whose policy from the very beginning was to support Butt's bill. Quite clearly, the *Examiner* knew nothing about the

etorship. The main lesson intended to be drawn was that in Ulster there
had been no agitation. But an important feature of Parnell's visit was
that under his umbrella gathered priests, Home Rulers, agrarian revolutionaries, separatists, and proponents of the three Fs. Some of the hitherto
minor figures of northern Catholic politics openly clashed with the priests.
Dr. John C. Quinn, secretary of the Ulster Home Government Association, who had taken a hand in the County Down by-election of 1878,
rattled Father Patrick O'Neill, parish priest of Rostrevor, by saying that
he would not vote for a Whig "even though the priests told them they
should put in a Whig [for Newry] instead of a Home Ruler." And in Belfast Quinn declared: "Talk to me no more of tenant right, of fixity of
tenure, etc. The whole thing [i.e., landlordism] is rotten from its very
roots, and the tree is rapidly falling of its own decay." Parnell studiously
avoided taking sides between Dr. Quinn and some of the more conservative priests, permitting all to remain under his banner and thereby implicitly shifting the previous balance in an anticlerical direction.[67]

In the aftermath of this visit even the *Northern Whig* allowed that
peasant proprietorship might be a good thing. And the *Coleraine Chronicle* urged the necessity of rent reductions.[68] In January 1880, at a meeting
of the County Antrim Tenants' Defence Association in Ballymoney, resolutions were passed in favor of the three Fs (though the magic words
"fixity of tenure" were not used, the definition of "firm tenure" amounted
to the same thing) and in support of the gradual establishment of peasant proprietorship. T. A. Dickson expressed the hope that "Liberal Irish
members of Parliament will, in the spirit of true patriotism, put aside
points on which they differ, and unite heart and hand about the land
question." Referring to the resolutions of the farmers' clubs of Munster,
Dickson asserted, "We have a common platform on which Ulster and
Munster can join hands." And taking a leaf out of Parnell's book, he talked
of the evils of emigration and the adverse effects which large grazing
farms would have on northern towns.[69]

With Disraeli's government now pushing toward a policy of coercion
in Ireland, and with the agricultural depression acting as a radicalizing
force, northern agrarian liberalism at last confronted the cautious sectionalism of its earlier positions.[70] The way was now open for firm
cooperation between Catholic and Protestant tenant farmers behind the

role of the Route Association in attempting to persuade Ulster Liberals to transcend the
sectionalism of their position.
67. *W.E.U.O.*, 18 Oct. 1879.
68. Both quoted in *B.F.P.*, 23 Oct. 1879.
69. *B.F.P.*, 29 Jan. 1880.
70. Paul Bew, *Land and the national question in Ireland, 1858–82* (Dublin, 1978), p. 218.

Liberal banner, even though it was a cooperation based upon putting very real differences aside in order to agree on the one common point. The 1880 Ballymoney program had at least the important virtue of distinguishing the land policy of Ulster Liberals from the various sectionalist noises of independent Orangemen and moderate Conservatives. At last Dr. James McKnight's position was becoming the dominant current in northern liberalism, four years after his death. In the 1880 election the Liberals lost all their borough seats, but alongside near-misses in counties Antrim and Down, they secured both seats in Derry, Monaghan, and Donegal as well as one seat each in Armagh and Tyrone.[71] The Ulster Liberals had become an unambiguously rural party. Now that they had adopted a program more or less identical to that of certain farmers' clubs in Munster and Leinster, they too were about to face the initiative mounted by the Parnellite Land League.

The principal strategy of the Land League in the south was to call for Griffith's valuation as a basis of rent and to resist paying the usual rents until the last possible moment, a policy known as paying "rent at the point of a bayonet." Otherwise, the League sought to maintain a united front against coercion. The most attractive feature of this strategy was the low risk of martyrdom.[72] Ulster tenants, however, were peculiarly situated with respect to this strategy. First, Griffith's valuation in the north was much higher in relation to the rent actually charged because the valuation had been carried out last in Ulster, after flax prices had risen dramatically. To insist that Griffith's valuation be the criterion for fixing rents was therefore to make a fairly modest demand. Second, the effectiveness of many strategies of resistance to rent depended on the absence of landlord allies and retainers in the area, who could weaken boycotts of the sale of farms or goods. Thus, however keen farmers might have been to engage in resistance, the attractive element in the south — low risk of martyrdom — was absent in the north, where the position of landlords was much stronger.[73] Third, the individuals who were the

71. B. M. Walker (ed.), *Parliamentary election results in Ireland, 1801–1922* (Dublin, 1978), pp. 122–7.

72. See Bew, *Land*, pp. 121–6.

73. Resistance to the payment of rent did occur in the north. In November 1880 some south Armagh tenants started to battle for rent reductions (*W.E.U.O.*, 18 Nov. 1880). In other places petitioning for abatements was common, as, for example, in Montiaghs parish in north Armagh (*W.E.U.O.*, 27 Nov. 1880). Newspaper reports of such activity were sometimes unclear as to whether tenants were actually resisting the collection of rent. On the duke of Manchester's Portadown estate a petition for a reduction of 50 percent was organized. At Land League meetings in December 1880 at Ballycastle and Dungiven, resolutions were passed, in the first case to pay no more than Griffith's valuation, and in the second to refuse the Skinners' company any rent until its intended increase was withdrawn

direct objects of government coercion were the representatives either of western separatist radicalism or of militant Parnellite constitutional nationalism. Thus, once the Land League got under way, the practical contribution that northern tenants could make to it was to voice opinions that lent strength to the cause. It is vital, however, to stress the fact that in certain periods of the Land League's activity, supporters of quite divergent strategies and ultimate objectives could coexist and cooperate with each other. Differences between Irish revolutionaries and reformers were often obscured.

As the decade of the 1880s opened, tenant organizations in the north waited for the Bessborough commission to report, while the Land League came no further than the Ulster frontier. Initially, the *Ballymoney Free Press* diagnosed the situation thus: "Instead of demanding a reform of landlordism, the demand in the south of Ireland and even some parts of Ulster is the abolition of landlordism."[74] Extreme Protestants took alarm. In County Antrim the twelfth of July Orange meeting in 1880 denounced early moves by the Liberal government to placate the Land League,[75] and Orangemen shot dead two people at Dungannon in what the *Witness* described as a nationalist demonstration.[76] Such ultraloyalists as the Rev. R. R. Kane stomped the countryside trying to whip up Protestant opposition to the League, and contingents of Orangemen went to the assistance of Captain Charles Boycott in County Mayo.[77]

The nature of the Protestant opposition is most instructive, for it took hold of James McKnight's plantation thesis and turned it to sectarian account. McKnight had argued firmly that all tenants, without regard to differences of race or religion, were entitled to what he saw as plantation rights.[78] McKnight had employed a liberal view of historical evolution to affirm a lasting basis for peace between the descendants of Protestant settlers and Catholic natives. But T. G. Peel, an Orange leader in County Armagh, now viewed the history of the plantation from a different angle: "Rents as a rule are too high, and the people meet with little or no encouragement from the landlords and the agents. . . . It was a condition [imposed on the undertakers] that they should encourage English and Scottish tenants, but they violated the condition and let their lands at high rents to any and every man who would pay those

(*B.F.P.*, 2 Dec. 1880). A clear case of a rent strike was the campaign for a reduction of 25 percent by tenants of Edmund McNeil at Portglenone (*B.F.P.*, 30 Dec. 1880).
74. Quoted in *B.F.P.*, 7 Oct. 1880.
75. *B.F.P.*, 15 July 1880.
76. *Witness*, 20 Aug. 1880.
77. *B.F.P.*, 4 Nov. 1880.
78. McKnight, *Ulster tenants' claim of right*, pp. 18–19.

rents [i.e., the native Irish]. They sowed the wind and now they reap the whirlwind. . . . The Protestant people of Ireland have been sat upon."[79] The history of the plantation was being remolded into a weapon of sectarian war. Antilandlord sentiment (coupled, incidentally, with support for some kind of agrarian reform) was now to be subordinated to a campaign against the papists.

It seemed in November 1880 as if there was a real danger that the land agitation in Ulster would take this form. Although in that month the League managed to hold an undisturbed meeting at Dungannon, bothered only by a counterdemonstration outside the town, the Liberal newspapers in the north showed signs of quavering before threatened confrontation. The Land League was now seen as a menace to the act of union. As the *Ballymoney Free Press* lamented, "Much as we dislike toryism, we would prefer it to connivance at revolution."[80] The danger was great that liberalism would feel forced to make this choice and would wholly abdicate its position on land reform. If it were to survive, it had to act at once.

Liberalism Finds a Popular Base

On 21 November 1880 the Liberals and the tenant-right associations made their intervention at Monaghan. William Ancketel, a Liberal landed proprietor who had given trenchant testimony to the Bessborough commission about the workings of the 1870 land act, declared that he knew of no county where land legislation had failed so signally as in Monaghan. He was backed by an Orangeman, Henry Overend of Carrickmacross, and by Canon Patrick Smollen, parish priest of Clones, who recounted the sufferings of the Farney tenantry. What was the purpose of the meeting? T. A. Dickson observed that the three Fs and peasant proprietorship were now accepted as safe solutions in quarters where until quite recently they had been regarded as visionary. (One suspects that he was thinking of some of his Liberal colleagues, such as those with whom he had clashed over intermediate education.) The coming land act, however, would face opposition. Meetings like that at Monaghan were necessary to show that the measure was essential and to prevent disastrous attempts to conciliate opposition, such as had occurred in connection with the 1870 act. But, Dickson insisted, to strengthen the hand of the Liberal government, "keep the peace." And, as if to hold out an olive branch to the Land League, the County Monaghan

79. *B.F.P.*, 21 Oct. 1880.
80. *B.F.P.*, 4 Nov. 1880.

M.P., William Findlater, spoke of the forthcoming land bill as one which would provide fixity of tenure, "with such improvements as the more advanced views of land reformers might command."[81] In other words, the Liberals were going to join the agitation, but with a strategy quite at variance with Parnell's: the lawful agitation was to be a weapon to strengthen the forces seeking a constitutional settlement of the question on the best possible terms for the tenants; it was not to be part of an agrarian revolution. Parnell's strategy was designed specifically to create ambiguity about whether he was after a constitutional settlement or something more extreme. So long as he preserved that ambiguity, the Liberals and the Land League might act in apparent alliance.

The immediate result of the Liberal intervention was that it weakened decisively the Protestant opposition evident at Dungannon and stole the initiative from the extreme forms of Ulster loyalism. Joseph Biggar was able to advance Land League doctrines before an audience of largely Protestant farmers at Ballycastle, Co. Antrim, a few days later. The Liberal demarche also pushed the more temporizing supporters of tenant right off the stage. For example, at Cookstown, Orangemen organized a meeting at which the attendance was almost exclusively Protestant. Addresses were given by E. F. Litton, Liberal M.P. for Tyrone, T. A. Dickson, and John Givan, and resolutions were passed, stating that there could be no final solution to the land question without the three Fs and a scheme for peasant proprietorship. Calls for rent reductions were coupled with pledges to remain on the side of law and order. Most significantly, J. W. E. Macartney, the independent Orange M.P. who had originally secured election in 1874 by appropriating the Whig position on land reform, refused to come, and mention of his name drew groans from the assembled Protestant tenant farmers.[82]

A general pattern was now unfolding. As events at Dungannon in August and November showed, the Land League was able to hold meetings in the north with increasing ease and against declining ultraloyalist opposition. After the Monaghan meeting the agitation spread across the north, with a tacit division of territory between the Land League and the Liberals, the latter often allied with large bodies of Orangemen, as at Cookstown. It is true that the Order was now joined by a few frightened landowners,[83] but this was little compensation for the disorientation of a large section of its tenant-farming members. As the agi-

81. *W.E.U.O.*, 27 Nov. 1880.
82. *W.E.U.O.*, 4 Dec. 1880.
83. For example, Lord Hill-Trevor and Lord Castlereagh joined at this period (*People's Advocate*, 25 Dec. 1880).

tation gained momentum in late 1880, the majority of Ulster Conservatives apparently decided to cut their losses and to support the constitutional settlement of the land question devised by Gladstone.[84] As the year came to a close, the *Witness*, which had previously explained the differences between the north and the lawless south in terms of the impact of popery, changed its tune:

The threat of Mr. Parnell and his friends has been fulfilled. . . . For a while they were content to hover upon the borders of the northern province. . . . But the flag of the Land League is now unfurled in the very heart of the Protestant north, and the standard bearers are now busy beating up recruits amongst the loyal men of Down [at Mayobridge] and Antrim [Ballycastle and Toomebridge]. . . . The invasion of Ulster by these enemies of landlordism and all its works was to be the signal for civil war. But these sanguine and sanguinary prophecies remain unfulfilled predictions. The Land League is with us, yet Ulster is at peace. . . . Instead of pouring forth a flood of execration to drown the pernicious eloquence of the agitators, the voices of the Orangemen have actually been heard commending from Land League platforms the programme of Parnell. . . . Who can doubt that after this Ulster is fairly given over to the enemy? . . . Surely our landlord friends may say the Philistines are upon us.[85]

The editorial writer, however, rejected the hysterical responses which he had so brilliantly conjured up. The threats of the Protestant ultras had been revealed as so much hot air. In fact, said the *Witness*, the Land League invasion could only bring good in its wake. Ulster farmers were not so easily swayed by demagogy as those of the other Irish provinces. They were also more deeply committed to the Ten Commandments. In consequence, the Land League agitation would be forced into a "moral and constitutional" path.

In a way the *Witness* was correct to observe the likely constitutional outcome. Agrarian meetings in the north tended to be organized by tenant-right associations in principally Protestant areas and by the Land League in mainly Catholic districts. But this is only a rough approximation of reality, for the Land League sponsored an assembly at Maghera, definitely Catholic territory, but still an area where an Orange counter-demonstration might have been anticipated if the political climate of

---

84. As Lord Derby stated explicitly at the time, there was a danger that Ulster would merge with the other disloyal provinces (J. L. Hammond, *Gladstone and the Irish nation* [London, 1938], pp. 216–17). See also A. B. Cooke's invaluable "A Conservative party leader in Ulster: Sir Stafford Northcote's diary of a visit to the province in October 1883" in *R.I.A. Proc.*, lxxv, sec. C, no. 4 (1975), passim.

85. *Witness*, 3 Dec. 1880.

August 1880 had not changed in the way that it had by December of that year. More important, even Land League meetings in the north showed the same ambiguity about ultimate objectives which had allowed reformist southern farmers' clubs and agrarian revolutionaries to coexist under the same umbrella. The fundamental difference between the Land League and tenant-right associations in the north was not so much over agrarian aims as over wider political questions, and even here the division was murky.

When Gladstone's bill became law in August 1881, and Parnell decided to "test the act," ties between the Land League and the tenant-right associations became strained. A new line of demarcation appeared. Was Parnell, in adopting the policy of testing the act, to be regarded as sincere, or was he now a disruptionist? In the end, whether one was a member of Parnell's following depended on whether one disapproved of his imprisonment by Gladstone when he refused to sanction the act or to call off the agitation. This was a very different matter from a test of membership based on what one thought of the new law itself. If the land act alone had been the issue, large parts of Leinster and Munster would have sided with most of Ulster in supporting the new law. But when the question was whether Parnell or Gladstone was to be thanked for the act, the issue assumed a quite different shape. And Parnell, by focusing the issue around Gladstone's coercive measures, insured that it took this shape.

For Ulster Catholics, particularly the mountain tenantry whose distance from Ulster liberalism was most pronounced, Parnell and the Land League had broken the hitherto established patterns of Ulster politics. There was now an alternative strategy to clerical accommodation with Protestant Whigs. Parnell had shown that progress in their part of Ireland depended on the progress of the country as a whole. He had shattered their subordination to the northern Liberals more decisively than they could have done by voting Tory merely to punish local Whigs and to secure from them a more acceptable basis of cooperation.

The overall effects of the Land League experience were crystallized in the Tyrone by-election of September 1881. The Liberal candidate, T. A. Dickson, had been closely associated with the shifts of Ulster liberalism toward a more radical agrarian position. His Conservative opponent was Colonel W. S. Knox, a long-established Orange deputy grand master and for many years M.P. for Dungannon in the Ranfurly interest. Initially an advocate of confrontation with the Land League, Knox now claimed to have supported the 1881 act. Also contesting the seat was a Home Rule candidate, the Rev. Harold Rylett, who had been active in the Land League. At the 1880 election the Catholic vote had gone almost 100 percent Liberal, while the Protestant vote had been two-thirds Conservative and one-third Liberal, including about 7 percent who divided their votes between the independent Orangeman and the Liberal. But at the 1881 by-election the Catholic vote was split two ways, with the Liberal and the Home Rule candidates getting about equal shares, while the Protestant vote was divided again, this time with 44 percent for the Liberal and 56 percent for the Conservative. The final tally was: Dickson, 3,168; Knox, 3,084; and Rylett, 907.[86]

The Tyrone result was a success for Parnell in that half the Catholic vote had gone to a Home Rule candidate contrary to clerical direction and in a manifestly hopeless constituency for that cause. But it was also a coup for Ulster liberalism to have collected just under half the Protestant vote in a frontier constituency where pan-Protestantism had previously sustained landlord hegemony or been able to appropriate the land question on its own terms.

Though this election was of considerable significance, the interpretation given to it by public figures of that period was almost the reverse of our own. If, as Gladstone thought, it proved the satisfaction with which the land act was greeted by Catholics,[87] that inference would have had to rest on the fact that only half the Catholics had voted against the Liberal. If, as Parnell thought, the defeat of Rylett gave the government the courage to lock him up,[88] was he perhaps anticipating Protestant support for home rule? Parnell's aide, J. J. O'Kelly, asserted that Rylett's candidacy was a mistake which "alarmed and angered the whole Presbyterian body and split Ulster once more into two distinctly hostile camps of Protestant and Catholic."[89] If this assessment is correct, then the most novel feature of the Protestants' hostility toward Catholics was that nearly half of them chose to express it by voting Liberal!

These changes in electoral fortunes were perhaps not as dramatic as

86. The calculations here are based on the estimate given in the *Examiner* that "nearly one-quarter" of the Tyrone electorate was Catholic (*W.E.U.O.*, 17 Apr. 1880). The *Examiner* was unlikely to underestimate this figure, since the newspaper had every reason to stress the importance of the Catholic vote. It can be stated with near-certainty that no Catholic voted for J. W. E. Macartney in 1880 (he had endorsed the inspection of Catholic convents). A few Protestant Liberals probably split their votes between E. F. Litton and Macartney, but most Liberals plumped for Litton. All of Lord Claud Hamilton's votes are treated as split with Macartney since, according to the *Examiner*, there was some kind of alliance to that effect. The results of the 1880 general election were: J. W. E. Macartney (independent Conservative), 3,829; E. F. Litton (Liberal), 3,511; Lord Claud Hamilton (Conservative), 3,470. At the 1881 by-election (one vote for one candidate) the results were: T. A. Dickson (Liberal), 3,168; Colonel W. S. Knox (Conservative), 3,084; the Rev. Harold Rylett (Home Rule), 907 (Walker, *Election results*, pp. 124–6).

87. W. E. Gladstone to Lord Cowper, 9 Sept. 1881 (B.L., Add. MS 56453).

88. Katharine O'Shea, *Charles Stewart Parnell: his love story and political life* (2 vols., London, 1914), i, 122.

89. J. J. O'Kelly to John Devoy, [21 Sept. 1882], in *Devoy's post bag*, ii, 142–3.

LAND AND RELIGION IN ULSTER

they might have appeared to be to Gladstone, who presumably thought that there were more Catholic electors in County Tyrone. Nor were they much of a boost to Parnell if he was reckoning on securing substantial numbers of Protestant Home Rule votes. In general, the election registered an increased Protestant Liberal vote and a falling Catholic Liberal vote, on account of the possibility of voting for a Parnellite. But even if Protestants did not vote by the thousands for home rule, it would nevertheless be wrong to underestimate the significance of the Land League's ability actually to attract Protestants, not merely from the tenant-right associations but even from the Orange Order. In County Fermanagh, for example, where the tenant-right associations had never been well organized, they were unable to stimulate much agitation. In this county, where a significant number of Orangemen joined the League, the Order felt compelled to use the sanction of expulsion against League members, a course often threatened but rarely employed for fear of provoking internal dissensions.[90] The more usual response of Orange farmers was to support revived or existing tenant-right associations. But even these bodies went through crisis, as Samuel McElroy observed of the Route district. Farmers there thought that "the tenant-right associations were too moderate, and that the best thing to do was to throw in one's lot with those demanding too much, to get what we want. . . . They said that the Land League had accomplished more in 12 months than the tenant-right associations had done in 11 years."[91]

The extent of the Land League's achievement in Ulster can now be summarized. It began the process of integrating northern Catholics into the organized body of Irish nationalism and freed them from political dependence on northern liberalism, in the process disrupting somewhat the pattern of clerical political discipline and accommodation with Protestant Liberal elites. It also created the political space which simultaneously drew Ulster liberalism away from its cautious sectionalism toward a more radical position on the land question and allowed the Land League and the agrarian Liberals to establish an agitational position which temporarily destroyed landlord hegemony and extreme loyalist reaction. But the chief beneficiaries within Ulster were the agrarian Liberal supporters of Gladstone.

The Land League era helped to build up liberalism among Ulster Protestant farmers, displacing the various local competitors for their sup-

90. We are indebted to Pádraig McGuiness for information on the Land League in Fermanagh. See also Peadar Livingstone, *The Fermanagh story: a documented history of the County Fermanagh from the earliest times to the present day* (Enniskillen, 1969), pp. 259–61.
91. *B.F.P.*, 27 Jan. 1881.

port and driving liberalism toward a stronger critique of landlordism. Yet the Land League itself had shown Ulster Catholics a practical way of participating in a wider Irish agitation and accelerated the process of their divorce from Ulster liberalism. It had also encouraged farmers generally to adopt a calculating approach to the most effective agrarian strategies, which unquestionably weakened the hegemony of pan-Protestantism. These last two phenomena were clearly illustrated in the Monaghan by-election of 1883.

The Nationalist candidate, Tim Healy, was the initiator of a famous clause in the land act of 1881 which prohibited the raising of rents on account of tenant improvements, however long ago they had been carried out.[92] But this legislative sanction of McKnight's raw-earth thesis had been overturned by the chief land commissioners in the case of Adams versus Dunseath. Parnell declared that the Monaghan by-election would "reopen the land question."[93] Healy won the whole Catholic vote and a few hundred Protestant votes, while the Liberal vote collapsed.[94] The *Times* remarked of these Protestant farmers that "no political or religious presuppositions have availed to restrain them from sharing in the spoil and aiding the spoilers."[95] On all sides this interpretation was widely accepted. W. C. Trimble, a local Liberal journalist, observed: "While many [Protestant] Liberals dislike the tactics of the Parnellites and have no sympathy for their hostility to England, they hate toryism more and will even unite with a party they do not agree with against a common enemy."[96] He also acknowledged that the Ulster Catholic habit of support for liberalism had been decisively broken.[97] He watched the polarization of feeling with gloomy apprehension.[98]

Healy's victory set the stage for the nationalist "invasion" of Ulster, as a local Orange grouping, the Dungannon Volunteer Committee of Watchfulness, first described the attempt to capitalize on the Monaghan election.[99] In September it was announced that Parnell himself was to speak in Tyrone. Trimble nervously noted: "What brings Mr. Parnell to Tyrone is not clear; what good he can hope to effect we do not know; but it is evident that he has roused the Orange blood of the county."[100]

92. Bew, *Land*, p. 183.
93. Idem, *C. S. Parnell* (Dublin, 1980), p. 63.
94. Peter Gibbon, *The origins of Ulster unionism: the formation of popular Protestant politics and ideology in nineteenth-century Ireland* (Manchester, 1975), p. 108.
95. *Times*, 3 July 1883.
96. *Impartial Reporter*, 5 July 1883.
97. Ibid., 8 Nov. 1883.
98. Ibid., 12 July 1883.
99. *Tyrone Courier*, 10 Nov. 1883.
100. *Impartial Reporter*, 27 Sept. 1883.

A local Orange notable, D. J. Matthews, printed an appeal to his brethren: "Are you prepared to allow Parnell, the leader of the enemies of our united empire, the champion of the principle, Ireland for the Irish . . . , meaning Ireland for the Romanists . . . , [his] boasted triumphant march through Ulster, commencing with your loyal and peaceful county? Are you prepared to accept the doctrine of the English radicals that the Protestants of Ireland are aliens in their land and should be swept out of it by fair means or foul?"[101] Although T. P. O'Connor and Tim Healy, standing in for Parnell, extolled the benefits conferred on Orange farmers by the Healy clause, they were given an unpleasant reception in Dungannon.[102] The *Fermanagh Times* gleefully described how the nationalists had been excluded from the market square by the Orangemen and the soldiers.[103] The right to hold an undisturbed meeting in the center of Dungannon, as the Land League had done in November 1880, clearly did not extend to this explicitly nationalist gathering.

Later in the month, a further confrontation took place at Rosslea involving Tim Healy and Lord Rossmore as leaders of the opposing bands. Trimble claimed that the Orange Order had to import trainloads of militants for the occasion because local Orange farmers, though opposed to nationalism, were not prepared to be mobilized behind the landlords.[104] The Liberals of the border regions desperately hoped that the government would ban further such meetings, and at the beginning of November the administration took this step. Trimble was delighted, as it put a stop to further collisions. In 1880 he had been hailed by Andrew Kettle as a "dashing recruit" to the Land League.[105] But he was now very obviously a critic of both Parnellism and Orangeism.

It is not difficult to understand Trimble's evolution. He had been deeply shocked by the Phoenix Park murders and by what he saw as attempts to excuse this crime by nationalist leaders. But more important, he resented the descent of the border regions of Ulster into unmitigated sectarianism, brought about by the clashes between Orange and nationalist demonstrators. He was fully aware that the Orange leaders were attempting above all to undo Healy's electoral triumph. Nevertheless, the nationalist meetings had allowed them to create confrontations. The result was a decline in the political significance of the land question.

101. Ibid.
102. Ibid., 4 Oct. 1883.
103. *Fermanagh Times*, 4 Oct. 1883.
104. *Impartial Reporter*, 18 Oct. 1883.
105. A. J. Kettle, *The material for victory, being the memoirs of A. J. Kettle*, ed. L. J. Kettle (Dublin, 1958), p. 38.

That the Land League era had reduced the credibility of pan-Protestantism is indisputable, but Healy's attempt to capitalize on this by pushing nationalist mobilization northward was based upon dubious assumptions about the political potential of the land question, the error of which he recognized too late.[106] In the classic period of fenianism, which culminated in the abortive rising of 1867, land was relegated to a subordinate place in militant nationalist thought. The abolition of landlordism was advocated, to be sure, but this was to take place after the revolution. Following the defeat of the insurrection, there was a gradual upgrading of the land question. It began to be said — by all sections of nationalist thought in different ways — that resolution of the land question held the key to nationalist advance. The problem was that this rethinking did not go far enough. In a curious way it merely inverted the assumptions of the sterile revolutionary nationalism of the 1860s. The land question, which had previously been underestimated, was now made a fetish and given a potential which it did not possess. To adapt a phrase from Andrew Kettle, the land question did not and could not provide the material from which victory was to be made, if by victory is meant a united and independent Ireland. Failure to grasp this truth condemned even so thoughtful a nationalist as Michael Davitt in the years 1879–82 (though not later) to a conspiratorial mode of politics. For the neo-Fenian group of which Davitt was leader, the problem of politics during the Land League period was to keep the agitation against landlordism alive in the hope that in the face of British obduracy this agrarian campaign would become a movement for national independence.

The Land League's success in the north had rested precisely on the fact that it could accommodate a wide range of implicit strategies. The Liberal strategy of keeping up the agitation to strengthen Gladstone's hand was not clearly distinguishable from the Parnellite strategy of forcing Gladstone's hand, until the conflict over Parnell's refusal to sanction the act and his subsequent imprisonment. The neo-Fenian manipulation of the agrarian agitation lent credibility to the claim of Lord Enniskillen that "the Land League is essentially a disloyal organisation, and although landlordism may be the immediate object of its attack, the ultimate separation of the two countries is its aim."[107]

So long as the ambiguities of the land agitation were maximized, Protestant support for the Land League, even though mostly of a calculating kind, was also enhanced. And by the same process pan-Protestant opposition and capacity for disruption of meetings were minimized. But the

106. *Nation*, 19 Dec. 1885.
107. *Fermanagh Times*, 20 Jan. 1881.

effort to subordinate agrarian issues to the extension of nationalism northward reversed both tendencies. Tim Healy's belief that adept exploitation of the land question would allow him to launch a nationalist invasion of Ulster compounded Davitt's original error.

Yet the restoration of sectarian forms of political life in the outer areas of Ulster had relatively few consequences for inner Ulster. The County Down by-election of November 1884, the only one for which there survives a detailed breakdown by area of the votes cast, shows that in the solidly Presbyterian farming districts of Ards and Castlereagh the Liberals secured large majorities. They were at their weakest in south Down, including the Mournes and the area around Newry, where the effects of the nationalist "invasion" and Orange revival were stronger.[108] And in 1885, in the last contest under the old franchise, the Liberals won a by-election in County Antrim for the first time ever.[109] Quite clearly, the Presbyterian farming districts distant from the frontier were solidly Gladstonian. Ulster liberalism, stripped very largely of its urban base by 1880 and of its rural Catholic support by Parnell, had become a party of Protestant tenant farmers, mostly concentrated in inner Ulster.

As such, it was highly vulnerable. Residual in Belfast and squeezed in the frontier areas, its relatively recent development was reflected in the latent power of the pan-Protestant opposition in the inner Ulster countryside. The relationship between farmers and agricultural laborers illustrated several aspects of the weaknesses of rural liberalism. "It is well known that the farmers were hostile to the labourers getting the franchise; again and again I heard them say, 'Gladstone was a grand man, he set the farmers free, but he made the huge mistake of giving labour a vote,'" recalled Hugh Morrison in 1920.[110] Though written long

108. *Northern Whig*, 5 Dec. 1884. This report on the County Down by-election of 1884 is the only post-1870 detailed result known to survive; it gives the number of electors of different religions and the number of votes cast for each candidate by polling districts, of which there were twenty-six. Of the Catholic voters, 81 percent were concentrated in ten districts. The *Whig* claimed that the Tory victory was a product of Catholic support for the Tory candidate. Perhaps this was true, but what interests us here is that in the solidly Protestant farming district of northeast Down, where Catholic electors nowhere exceeded 6 percent of those polling, the Liberal candidate secured 91 percent of the vote in Donaghadee, 80 percent in Greyabbey, 76 percent in Killyleagh, 73 percent in Saintfield, 72 percent in Bangor (partly urban), and 61 percent in Newtownards (also urban). In the still more urbanized area toward Belfast (Holywood, Newtownbreda, and Hillsborough), where Catholics formed less than 6 percent of the electorate, the Liberal vote was between 45 and 53 percent.

109. Walker, *Election results*, p. 129.

110. Hugh Morrison, *Modern Ulster: its character, customs, politics, and industries* (London, 1920), p. 50.

after the collapse of rural liberalism and no doubt tainted by a sense of despair, this statement underscores a central issue.

The Bessborough commission received much testimony about the difficulties which farmers experienced in attracting and keeping labor. In a society in which Belfast and British cities provided alternative employment for Ulster's rural workers, farmers found that they had to choose between providing year-round subsistence for laborers tied to their farms and employing workers in the busy seasons at daily rates which reflected a relative labor shortage. Almost certainly, the costs of both options were greatest precisely in those areas of inner Ulster closest to Belfast, though the custom of rural weaving there made keeping year-round workers slightly easier than elsewhere. The very proximity to the urban core tended to sharpen the class differentiation between farmer and laborer, which was blurred in varying degrees elsewhere. Thus, while Parnell attempted with some success to sustain the support of laborers for the Land League,[111] Ulster Liberals never made any serious attempt to integrate rural workers into the agrarian movement. Even after its switch to a more radical position in 1880 at Ballymoney,[112] liberalism made only sympathetic noises on behalf of agricultural labor. Objective conditions and traditional political loyalties closed off this possibility.

Explicit indications of the resentment of laborers against farmers are rare before the 1885 election, but one interesting example during the Land League period occurred in the Coleraine district. After a Land League meeting took place at nearby Ballycastle, the Coleraine Orangemen indicated that they intended to prevent any League assembly in their area and only called off their opposition to a land meeting once it became clear that it would be a Liberal rather than a Land League affair. When the gathering finally convened, it not only condemned "the wicked and senseless programme of the Land League" and the British government's apathetic folly in "permitting a reign of terror," but it also expressed the hope that "in the event of any legislation for improving the condition of the inhabitants of Ireland, the grievances of the labouring classes and cottier occupiers will not be overlooked."[113] Though the meeting visibly lacked the presence of Orange gentry, the Orange Order was clearly attempting at the base of society to integrate laborers' resentment against farmers with opposition to the Land League. How successful this effort was is hard to gauge, but one witness before the Bess-

111. Bew, *Land*, p. 186.
112. See the speech of the Rev. J. B. Armour and the eighth resolution calling for landlords, town commissions, and boards of guardians to undertake public works in order to alleviate the distress of laborers, reported in *B.F.P.*, 29 Jan. 1880.
113. *B.F.P.*, 30 Dec. 1880.

borough commission spoke of a system in which farmers were spied upon by the laborers in their employ, who reported to bailiffs at Orange lodge meetings.[114] The conflict between laborers and farmers only compounded the strength of the landlord's position. Frequently, landlords employed laborers all year round on their own farms and estates at rates of pay substantially above those given by tenant farmers, and in their capacity as magistrates they often settled disputes between farmers and cottiers.[115] The overall picture is clear.

The dominance of industry over agriculture in inner Ulster can again be seen expressing itself in a paradoxical strengthening of landlord hegemony in the hinterland of the city. The accentuation of class differentiation between farmer and laborer in the inner Ulster countryside, itself a product of the position of labor in a largely industrial context, made the laborer a potential supporter of the landlord-dominated pan-Protestant bloc, in opposition to farmer-based Ulster liberalism. Protestant agricultural workers, once armed with the ballot in 1885, retaliated by voting solidly Tory, thus striking a blow against the pretensions of both the farmers and the invading nationalists. The 1885 general election also saw northern Catholics — following Parnell's instructions — voting Conservative in straight Liberal-Tory clashes. The outcome was the starkest possible polarization: out of a total of thirty-three Ulster seats, seventeen went to the Home Rulers, sixteen to the Tories, and none at all to the Liberals.

Ulster liberalism paradoxically came to life as a serious effort to participate in metropolitan political life independently of pan-Protestantism just before the necessary conditions for its survival, let alone growth, were cut off by the rising significance of the national question. Gladstone had already decided that, taking Ireland as a whole, Liberals were an insignificant presence.[116] They were in fact the Protestant tenant farmers, particularly those in areas where the national conflict lacked an inescapable local immediacy, as it did in the Ulster border regions after the "invasion" of 1883. This large-scale Protestant tenant-farmer liberalism has often been underestimated. It was indeed an indigenous Irish party. Given the power of landlords in the north, such a party could only become a serious entity when it locked independent political activity into a viable metropolitan political alliance. It began to do this just

114. *Bessborough comm. evidence*, pt. ii, p. 1086 [C 2779-II], H.C. 1881, xix, 1.

115. John Young, who owned land near Ballymena, said of tenants in relation to undertenants: "There is no greater tyrant than the tenant farmer when he becomes a landlord himself" (*Bessborough comm. evidence*, pt. i, p. 435).

116. O'Brien, *Parnell*, ii, 104.

before the basis for that alliance was broken in a decisive way. If Gladstone dismissed liberalism as a politically negligible force in Ireland as a whole, his assessment may have been fair, but it does not undermine the fact that the Liberals had started to attack the hegemony of landlordism in inner Ulster. His comments, made after Gladstone had decided for home rule, to the effect that an implicit contract had been broken, do not detract from the fact that these Liberals made a serious effort to break pan-Protestantism as the dominant political voice of unionism.

Because the growth of agrarian liberalism among northern Protestants depended ultimately on its being part of the wider liberalism of the United Kingdom, Gladstone's conversion to home rule forced them to decide whether they intended to accept his repudiation of them or not. Alone among the Protestant Liberal newspapers, the *Ballymoney Free Press* urged loyalty to him and acquiesced in the anticipated Parnellite takeover.

The capacity of the land issue to win Protestant tenants to home rule was scarcely tested. Despite the suggestion of Charles Russell, a distinguished attorney and leading northern Catholic Liberal, Gladstone did not link his home-rule measure to a generous land-purchase bill. Both Parnell and Gladstone regarded the acquiescence of the Irish landlords as the key objective of any such measure and no doubt were skeptical of the value of Russell's proposal.[117] The *Free Press* was exceedingly disappointed with the 1886 land bill: "As a matter of fact, the farmers of Ulster are not much in favour of the establishment of an Irish parliament. Coupled with compulsory sale of the landlords' property at moderate interest, equal to about half of the present judicial rents, those farmers might have accepted this parliament with equanimity, but the proposal to make them buy at twenty years' purchase, the landlords to get only about sixteen years', the balance to be kept by the Irish parliament, is repugnant alike to their sense of justice and loyalty."[118]

The July 1886 election in Antrim North revealed just how thoroughly Gladstonian Protestant liberalism had collapsed. Samuel McElroy, who stood as a Liberal, received five fewer votes than the candidate of the Land League had attracted in 1885.[119] The Liberals who polled in 1885 had either voted Conservative or stayed at home. McElroy felt compelled to ask publicly, "Is Mr. Gladstone's home-rule policy so objectionable as to warrant the Liberal Unionist farmers of north Antrim in repudiating

117. On this subject, see Bew, *C. S. Parnell*, pp. 78–84.
118. *B.F.P.*, 29 July 1886.
119. Walker, *Election results*, p. 130.

his land policy and electing a supporter of Lord Salisbury . . . ?" Yet
he affirmed that "the welfare of the farming class is bound up with
the fortunes of the Gladstonian Liberal party."[120] McElroy's affirmation
was also a Unionist fear. Thomas MacKnight, editor of the *Northern
Whig* and an erstwhile Gladstonian sycophant, described the efforts of
the National League to secure Protestant tenants with promises of the
forcible reduction of rents and the eventual abolition of landlordism.
MacKnight at least was not certain that the land question was a useless
bait for nationalism: "They who had good opportunities of knowing what
was passing in the minds of some of the Unionist tenant farmers felt
much anxiety. . . . There was undoubtedly some hesitation even among
the northern tenants who, as Unionists, had no sympathy with Irish
nationalism."[121]

The anxieties of Unionists on this score were real. This was demonstrated by the importance which they attached to the speech of Joseph
Chamberlain in October 1887 at Coleraine. "I am speaking not to those
who cheer the members of the National League," declared Chamberlain, "but I am speaking to honest men — (cheers) — and I expect to express your sentiments when I say that, although you intend to look after
your own interests, you do not intend to rob anybody else."[122] He was
careful to point out the role already played by Liberal Unionists in shaping the impending land bill and to add that "the Conservative members
from Ulster . . . used in private their influence [on the government] with
the most beneficial effects."[123] The style of Chamberlain's intervention
was at least implicitly undoing the work of the Liberals of 1880–1. It
was not necessary to engage in autonomous activity: "Your landlords
are on your side." In this matter the coalescence of Whig liberalism and
conservatism synthesized one common quality — their determination to
restore undiluted elite initiative. Gladstone's conversion to home rule
might destroy the basis of Ulster liberalism as a strategy, but the destruction of autonomous political activity was a wider problem. It was essential to promote the coming land scheme, with all its likely weaknesses,
in order to fend off any agrarian resurgence. Chamberlain therefore
warned his audience of the "universal protest on the part of the British
taxpayer against risking his capital for the purpose of purchasing Irish
land."[124]

120. *B.F.P.*, 29 July 1886.
121. Thomas MacKnight, *Ulster as it is, or twenty-eight years' experience as an Irish
editor* (2 vols., London, 1896), ii, 205.
122. *Coleraine Constitution*, 15 Oct. 1887.
123. Ibid.
124. Ibid.

The measure was designed to provide a security which was as good as British consols but based on Irish resources. In nationalist Ireland the scheme was regarded with contempt — equivalent to feeding a dog on its own tail, it was widely said. Even the *Times* was skeptical.[125] But Thomas MacKnight was ecstatic. He concluded that the effect of Chamberlain's speech "could scarcely be exceeded. It was not momentary: it has continued long: it has not ever yet lost its force. 'There is a more excellent way,' said one Presbyterian farmer to another. 'Ay, maun,' was the reply, 'Sure this is better than the Land League.'"[126] And the *Londonderry Standard* (Dr. James McKnight's paper until his death in 1876) observed that if Chamberlain's visit was of so little consequence, why were nationalists so keen to belittle it? "If we have been relieved of one form of slavery [i.e., to landlordism], what service would it be if that relief was only given to impose a system a thousand times more intensely abhorred? The object of Irish nationalists, which they support with undying fervour, is to extinguish the right of the minority to any representation whatever, whether municipal or parliamentary."[127] That this paper in particular should adopt such a bitter tone toward Parnellism is a tragic epitaph on the collapse of Protestant agrarian radicalism as an independent political force.

125. In the view of the *Times*, the British taxpayer had a moral responsibility to rescue Irish landlords (*Times*, 14 Oct. 1887).
126. MacKnight, *Ulster as it is*, ii, 208.
127. *Londonderry Standard*, 31 Oct. 1887.

BIBLIOGRAPHY

Contemporary sources

Manuscript material
British Library, London
    Gladstone papers (Add. MSS 56447, 56453).

Contemporary publications
I. Newspapers
    Ballymoney Free Press.
    Banner of Ulster (Belfast).
    Belfast Newsletter.
    Belfast Weekly Vindicator.
    Coleraine Constitution.

Connaught Telegraph (Castlebar).
Fermanagh Times (Enniskillen).
Impartial Reporter (Enniskillen).
Irishman (Dublin).
Irish Times (Dublin).
Londonderry Standard.
Nation (Dublin).
Northern Star (Belfast).
Northern Whig (Belfast).
People's Advocate (Monaghan).
Tyrone Courier (Dungannon).
Ulster Weekly News (Belfast).
Weekly Examiner (Belfast).
Weekly Examiner and Ulster Observer (Belfast).
Weekly Northern Whig (Belfast).
Witness (Belfast).

II. Other contemporary publications

A catechism of tenant right (Belfast, 1850).

McKnight, James. *The Ulster tenants' claim of right, or landownership a state trust; the Ulster tenant right an original grant from the British crown, and the necessity of extending its general principle to the other provinces of Ireland demonstrated in a letter to Lord John Russell* (Dublin, 1848).

MacKnight, Thomas. *Ulster as it is, or twenty-eight years' experience as an Irish editor,* 2 vols. (London, 1896).

O'Shea, Katharine. *Charles Stewart Parnell: his love story and political life,* 2 vols. (London, 1914).

Report of her majesty's commissioners of inquiry into the working of the Land-lord and Tenant (Ireland) Act, 1870, and the acts amending the same, vol. ii: *Digest of evidence; minutes of evidence,* pt. i [C 2779-I], H.C. 1881, xviii, 73; vol. iii: *Minutes of evidence,* pt. ii; *appendices* [C 2779-II], H.C. 1881, xix, 1.

Sigerson, George. *History of the land tenures and land classes of Ireland, with an account of the various secret agrarian confederacies* (Dublin and London, 1871).

Later works

Writings in Irish studies

Bew, Paul. *Land and the national question in Ireland, 1858–82* (Dublin, 1978).

Bew, Paul. *C. S. Parnell* (Dublin, 1980).

Cooke, A. B. (ed.). "A Conservative party leader in Ulster: Sir Stafford Northcote's diary of a visit to the province in October 1883" in *Proceedings of the Royal Irish Academy,* lxxv, sec. C, no. 4 (1975), pp. 61–84.

Donnelly, J. S., Jr. *The land and the people of nineteenth-century Cork: the rural economy and the land question* (London and Boston, 1975).

Gibbon, Peter. *The origins of Ulster unionism: the formation of popular Protestant politics and ideology in nineteenth-century Ireland* (Manchester, 1975).

Hammond, J. L. *Gladstone and the Irish nation* (London, 1938).

Kettle, A. J. *The material for victory, being the memoirs of A. J. Kettle*, ed. L. J. Kettle (Dublin, 1958).

Kirkpatrick, R. W. "Origins and development of the land war in mid-Ulster, 1879–85" in F. S. L. Lyons and R. A. J. Hawkins (ed.), *Ireland under the union: varieties of tension: essays in honour of T. W. Moody* (Oxford, 1980), pp. 201–35.

Livingstone, Peadar. *The Fermanagh story: a documented history of the County Fermanagh from the earliest times to the present day* (Enniskillen, 1969).

Lyons, F. S. L. *Culture and anarchy in Ireland, 1890–1939* (Oxford and New York, 1979).

McMinn, J. R. B. "The Reverend James Brown Armour and Liberal politics in north Antrim, 1869–1914" (Ph.D. dissertation, Queen's University, Belfast, 1978).

Miller, D. W. *Queen's rebels: Ulster loyalism in historical perspective* (Dublin and New York, 1978).

Morrison, Hugh. *Modern Ulster: its character, customs, politics, and industries* (London, 1920).

O'Brien, R. B. *The life of Charles Stewart Parnell, 1846–1891*, 2 vols. (London, 1898).

O'Brien, William, and Ryan, Desmond (ed.). *Devoy's post bag, 1871–1928*, 2 vols. (Dublin, 1948, 1953).

Solow, B. L. *The land question and the Irish economy, 1870–1903* (Cambridge, Mass., 1971).

Walker, B. M. (ed.). *Parliamentary election results in Ireland, 1801–1922* (Dublin, 1978).

Whyte, J. H. *The independent Irish party, 1850–9* (Oxford, 1958).

6 *Brian M. Walker*

The Land Question and Elections in Ulster, 1868–86

Many commentators on nineteenth-century Ulster drew attention to the divisions between Protestants and Catholics in the province. Some, such as William Sharman Crawford, argued that political differences between the denominations were unnecessary and wrong, and that the question of agrarian reform provided a common ground on which they could unite.[1] Political events of the 1870s and 1880s were in fact to bring about a substantial realization of this argument. By 1881 there was a greater degree of interdenominational voting at elections in the northern counties than there had ever been before, thanks to the land question. Yet by the general elections of 1885–6, this cooperation had largely vanished, and never again has there been such a close political alliance between Protestant and Catholic in the Ulster countryside. This study of county elections in Ulster from 1868 to 1886 examines the impact of the land question on electoral politics, assesses the shifting pattern of denominational voting, and evaluates some of the striking social changes of these years.

Characteristics of the Electoral System

For a proper understanding of these subjects, however, certain preliminary comments are in order concerning the electoral system in

1. B. A. Kennedy, "Sharman Crawford, 1780–1861" (Ph.D. dissertation, Queen's University, Belfast, 1953).

the period under review.[2] Prior to the general election of 1885 each of the nine Ulster counties returned two M.P.s; from 1885 these counties were arranged into divisions, roughly equal in population, with one M.P. being returned for each of the twenty-seven divisions. There were also eleven borough seats before 1885 and six afterward. Between 1850 and 1885 the county franchise was confined to adult males occupying property with a ratable valuation of at least £12 and to some categories of leaseholders and freeholders. Beginning in 1885 all adult male householders were entitled to the vote.

In practice, the electoral qualifications meant that in 1881 the vote in the Ulster counties was restricted to 18 percent of the adult males, most of whom were tenant farmers. Some county electors lived in towns within the county, but such voters were not numerous, except in Down and Antrim.[3] We can therefore say that roughly 40 percent of those adult males classified as farmers in the 1881 census were electors.[4] There was, however, some variation among counties in the proportion of farmers possessing the vote. As a result of the franchise changes of 1884–5, all constituencies witnessed an increase in the proportion of males having the vote; the average was now sixty-four electors for every hundred adult males in the population. In social terms the electorate was expanded to include small farmers and agricultural laborers (cottagers only).

These franchise changes affected the religious composition of the electorate, as also did variations in denominational distribution between counties and differences in the social and economic positions of the denominations. Of all male farmers in 1881, 56 percent were Catholic and the remainder were Protestant, but Protestants, especially Presbyterians, tended to own the larger farms.[5] Agricultural laborers (cottagers) were

2. See B. M. Walker (ed.), *Parliamentary election results in Ireland, 1801–1922* (Dublin, 1978); idem, "The Irish electorate, 1868–1915" in *I.H.S.*, xviii, no. 71 (Mar. 1973), pp. 359–406. All the election results cited in this essay have come from the above volume, hereafter cited as *Election results*.

3. In Down and Antrim they were around 5 percent in 1874. County Antrim also contained many voters belonging to the Belfast district; in 1880 the figure was put at 1,472 out of 11,701 electors (*B.N.L.*, 6 Apr. 1880).

4. Information on the social and religious composition of the Ulster population has come from the county tables in *Census Ire., 1881*, pt. i, vol. iii, *province of Ulster* [C 3204], H.C. 1882, lxxviii, 1.

5. See J. D. R. Johnston, "The Clogher valley as a social and economic region in the eighteenth and nineteenth centuries" (M.Litt. thesis, University of Dublin, 1974), pp. 151–62; Stephen Gwynn, *Experiences of a literary man* (London, 1926), p. 19; T. W. Freeman, *Ireland: its physical, historical, social, and economic geography* (London and New York, 1950), p. 173.

divided in the same year in similar proportions, but there was a slightly higher proportion of Catholics among indoor farm servants. Prior to the reforms of 1884–5, Catholics were usually considerably underrepresented in the electorate, in relation to their numbers in the population. Protestants, especially Presbyterians, were overrepresented. From contemporary analyses it is possible to gain important information on comparative denominational voting strengths.

In the 1870s and early 1880s the electors in counties Donegal and Monaghan were divided equally between Protestant and Catholic, and in Cavan Catholics were a slight majority of the electors,[6] although in all three counties Catholics were substantially more numerous than Protestants among the population. There were few Presbyterians in Fermanagh, while in Donegal and Cavan there were probably equal numbers of Presbyterians and members of the Church of Ireland in the electorate. In 1881 the voters of County Tyrone could be divided approximately as follows: 26 percent Catholic, 32 percent members of the Church of Ireland, and 42 percent Presbyterian. Of the electors in County Londonderry in the same year, Catholics comprised about 24 percent, Church of Ireland members 30 percent, and Presbyterians 46 percent.[7] Catholics were slightly more numerous than Protestants in the Tyrone population, while in Londonderry Protestants constituted the larger group by a small margin.

Denominational figures are unavailable for the Armagh electorate, though Protestants held a narrow majority in the population, or for Fermanagh, where Catholics possessed a slight majority, but in both counties Protestant voters were undoubtedly more numerous than Catholics. There were fewer Presbyterians in Armagh than in Tyrone and hardly any in Fermanagh. In Down and Antrim, where Protestants constituted a sizable majority of the population, Catholics were 22 percent of electors in the former county in 1878 and 19 percent in the latter in 1880; the figures for Presbyterians at the same time were 52 percent and 65 percent respectively, while for members of the Church of Ireland they were 25 percent and 16 percent respectively.[8]

After the reforms of 1884–5 the denominational breakdown of the electorate was similar to that of the population. Catholics comprised about

6. This information has been taken from various newspaper reports. For Donegal and Monaghan, see *Ulster Examiner* (hereafter cited as *Ulster Ex.*), 29 Jan. 1874; *People's Advocate*, 7 July 1883. For Cavan, see *Cavan Weekly News*, 9 Apr. 1880.

7. For Tyrone, see *Armagh Guardian*, 9 Sept. 1881; *B.M.N.*, 9 Sept. 1881. For Londonderry, see *B.M.N.*, 1 Dec. 1881.

8. For Antrim, see *Northern Whig* (hereafter cited as *N.W.*), 1 Apr. 1880; *Witness*, 15 May 1885. For Down, see *B.M.N.*, 4 Mar. 1880.

60 percent or more of the electorate in twelve county divisions, while Protestants constituted around 60 percent or more in ten, leaving five where Protestants and Catholics were fairly evenly balanced. Presbyterians and members of the Church of Ireland were variously distributed among the constituencies.[9] Two other significant changes in the electoral system were the ballot act of 1872 and the corrupt-practices act of 1883, the second of which severely limited election expenditure.

Electoral Politics, 1868–9

The land question aroused little interest in the Ulster countryside during the general election of 1868. All the counties, apart from Monaghan, were uncontested, and in every case except Cavan, Conservative M.P.s were returned. The Liberal candidate for Monaghan came far at the bottom of the poll, but another Liberal was elected unopposed for Cavan. As the election addresses show, the main issue was the disestablishment of the Church of Ireland, which the Conservatives opposed and the Liberals supported.[10] Two Conservatives only, the marquis of Hamilton in County Donegal and R. P. Dawson in County Londonderry, drew attention to the land question. They urged that tenants be compensated for improvements. Sir F. W. Heygate, incumbent Tory M.P. for Londonderry, called for amelioration of the condition of laborers. Both Liberals endorsed agrarian reform: William Gray in Monaghan advocated fair rents and fixity of tenure as well as compensation for improvements. A few other candidates mentioned the land question in speeches on the hustings, but it caused little stir.

At this stage agrarian reform was clearly not an important issue, and the existing social and political structure of the countryside went unchallenged. To the bulk of the electorate the views of M.P.s were acceptable or at least not so unacceptable as to arouse serious opposition. All the county representatives, including the one Liberal, either owned land themselves or were the relatives of proprietors of substantial estates in the constituencies for which they were returned.[11] Every one of them belonged to the Church of Ireland. Usually, electoral matters were arranged in the first instance by the leading landed families in each county,

9. *Return showing the religious denominations of the population, according to the census of 1881, in each constituency formed in Ulster by the redistribution of seats act, 1885,* p. 1, H.C. 1884–5 (335), lxii, 339.

10. See contemporary newspapers.

11. This information on the background of M.P.s has been taken from David Thornley, "Isaac Butt and the creation of an Irish parliamentary party, 1868–74" (Ph.D. dissertation, University of Dublin, 1959), pp. 591–5 (hereafter cited as "Irish party").

though secondary landlords and important local interests were also consulted. Generally, tenants voted with their landlords, a consequence mostly of the dominant role of the landlords in society. Besides owning nearly all the land, these men occupied an important social position in the countryside. They acted as magistrates, were members of grand juries as well as boards of guardians, and often presided over local societies and organizations. Contemporary critics regarded the landlord-tenant relationship in electoral matters as including a strong coercive element,[12] but in fact, coercion played only a minor part in the ascendancy of the gentry in the county constituencies of Ulster.

This relationship is well illustrated by the Antrim by-election of August 1869. The contest was caused by the death of Rear Admiral G. H. Seymour, a member of the Hertford family which owned 66,000 acres in Antrim, on which there lived at least 1,000 voters out of a total county electorate of 11,715.[13] The Hertfords put forward a younger member of the family, Captain H. de G. Seymour, as their candidate. His Liberal opponent, Sir R. S. Adair, a landowner from Ballymena, was selected at a meeting of the Liberal Registration Society in Belfast.[14] Seymour arrived in County Antrim from England at the beginning of August, by which time he had already sent letters to the leading local landlords seeking their support.[15] The possibility of another proprietor coming forward as a Conservative candidate was averted, partly through fear that the Liberal would win the seat and partly in acknowledgment of the dominant position of the Hertfords in the county.[16] Seymour proceeded to canvass local landlords and to address gatherings of supporters as well as public assemblies. Adair also held meetings. The election ended in a sizable victory for Seymour, who received 5,588 votes as against Adair's 2,294.

Subsequently, this election was cited as an example of the coercive electoral power of the landlords. Thomas MacKnight, editor of the *Northern Whig*, described it in 1896 as showing "the utter want of independence on the part of many of the sturdy tenant farmers of Ulster."[17] But in 1872, when members of the Stannus family filed suit against the *Northern Whig* for its allegations that they had used their position as

12. See *Londonderry Standard* (hereafter cited as *Lond. Stand.*), 5 Sept. 1868; Thomas MacKnight, *Ulster as it is* . . . (2 vols., London, 1896), i, 54–96.
13. *N.W.*, 19, 20 Dec. 1872.
14. *B.N.L.*, 3 Aug. 1869.
15. Sir C. F. Seymour to F. H. Seymour, 3 Aug. 1869 (P.R.O.N.I., Hertford papers, CR114A/538/4).
16. Sir Edward Macnaghten to Sir C. F. Seymour, 4 Aug. 1869 (ibid.).
17. MacKnight, *Ulster as it is*, i, 211.

the principal agents of Lord Hertford for improper political purposes over the previous twenty-two years, the judgment went in favor of the Stannuses. Only a small number of examples were cited in court for the whole of this period in which coercion had been used. No such evidence could be furnished for the 1869 by-election.[18]

At the same time, the election showed the influential role played by landlords in politics. During the Antrim by-election of 1869 W. T. Stannus denied in a speech at Lisburn that coercion was employed, but then went on to say: "Is it to be counted a crime, in the nineteenth century, for a landed proprietor who is supposed to have an interest in the welfare of his tenants, when he knows a person whom he thinks would make a suitable representative, to use all his legitimate influence on his behalf?"[19] The attention paid by Seymour to the gentry during the campaign was an acknowledgment of their position and power. The proprietors expected to give a lead and the tenants accepted their right to do so, mainly, it seems, in recognition of the social and political role of the landlords.

It would be wrong, nonetheless, to dismiss entirely the coercive element in landlord-tenant relations. During the 1872 court case, though no examples were given of coercion in 1869, it was pointed out that all the Hertford bailiffs canvassed actively for Seymour. Witnesses claimed that it was generally understood that tenants would vote for the estate-office candidate. One person who testified made the valid point that the support for Seymour of all but 14 out of the 940 voters from the Hertford property constituted an abnormally high preference for one candidate. Even if the bailiffs did not threaten prospective voters, tenants may well have feared adverse consequences if they defied their landlord's wishes. One witness, a Hertford tenant, gave evidence of this feeling in court: "At the last County Antrim election I voted for Seymour, and I would rather have not gone, for I was not fit. I have got some notices to quit. I would have voted for a Liberal man if I durst [*sic*], but I was afraid to do it for fear Mr. Stannus would throw me out of my wee place."[20] The absence of the secret ballot did produce a degree of subservience, but it was not a major factor; even after 1872 there was not complete secrecy of voting. In addition, of course, the landlord party could afford a large electoral organization; in fact, Seymour spent just over £9,000 in 1869. But more important still was the deferential type of society which existed in the countryside.

18. *N.W.*, 19–30 Dec. 1872.
19. *B.N.L.*, 13 Aug. 1869.
20. *N.W.*, 28 Dec. 1872.

The Antrim by-election also illustrates, however, that even a well-financed candidate benefiting from extensive landlord influence usually could not ignore the particular concerns of the electors whose votes he sought. There had to be a certain identity of political interest between candidates and the electors. Captain Seymour was new to the Irish scene when he arrived in County Antrim. His opening address was that of a moderate English Conservative, but by nomination day he had moved in response to local political feeling to make strong declarations of support for Protestantism and to promise backing for agrarian reform.[21] The latter issue had become an important one during the election. Because of his soundness in these matters, together with his elaborate organization, considerable landlord support, and distinctive family background, Seymour easily captured the seat.

Thus in County Antrim, which seems to have been fairly typical of most Ulster counties, landlords in this period enjoyed considerable influence over their tenants. This influence was a result of their social position and economic power, but it was also dependent on an identity of political interest between landlords, tenants, and the candidate and his policies. This was now to be challenged. Over the next ten years the basis of landlord power was undermined and the political interest between them and their tenants collapsed.

The Land Question, 1869–73

Beginning with the Antrim by-election of 1869, the question of agrarian reform increasingly became a matter of concern on the hustings. The principal reason for this lay in underlying sources of conflict in landlord-tenant relations. The traditional picture of those relations in the period 1850–79 as one of landlord oppression has been shown to be false. A number of scholars have recently demonstrated that evictions were infrequent, that rents were neither high nor often raised, and that most tenants were not impoverished but enjoyed growing prosperity.[22] At the same time, however, the tenant's position was not a secure one because tenure was vague and ill-defined. In the north of Ireland tenants had certain long-standing rights known collectively as the Ulster

21. *B.N.L.*, 5–17 Aug. 1869.
22. See W. E. Vaughan, "Landlord and tenant relations in Ireland between the famine and the land war, 1850–1878" in L. M. Cullen and T. C. Smout (ed.), *Comparative aspects of Scottish and Irish economic and social history, 1600–1900* (Edinburgh, 1977), pp. 216–26; B. L. Solow, *The land question and the Irish economy, 1870–1903* (Cambridge, Mass., 1971); J. S. Donnelly, Jr., *The land and the people of nineteenth-century Cork: the rural economy and the land question* (London and Boston, 1975).

custom, but as these were not defined by law, the resulting insecurity was a potential source of conflict.

In the late 1840s and early 1850s the land question had aroused interest among the electorate, but growing prosperity after 1853 relegated the issue to the background (except in County Londonderry, where attempts by the London companies to control sales of tenant right led to political unrest).[23] From 1853 to 1868 it aroused little comment at elections in the Ulster counties, which were mainly uncontested. The reasons for this were probably twofold. First, rising prosperity tempered criticism, and second, there seemed little chance of change. Beginning in 1867, however, tenant-right meetings took place in various parts of Ulster, perhaps as a result of John Bright's speech on the Irish land question in the previous year. This unrest continued to grow, slowly at first and then more quickly after the general election of 1868. At least in part, the revival of interest was attributable to knowledge of Gladstone's intention to reform the land laws after dealing with the question of disestablishment of the Church of Ireland. Paradoxically, the weaknesses of his land act dashed expectations and added significantly to the growth of the agrarian movement. The act sought to provide legal recognition of the Ulster custom and to establish the right of tenants to compensation for improvements. But as early as April 1870, James McKnight, editor of the *Londonderry Standard,* informed Gladstone: "Already the notable deficiencies of the bill, as contrasted with popular hope, . . . have begun to excite amongst the people a spirit of embittered controversy."[24] Problems arose over the fact that there was no uniform Ulster custom. Attempts to define it in the courts only acerbated landlord-tenant relations, since each of the parties had different views of what their rights were. Moreover, the act did not protect leaseholders. As noted by Samuel McElroy, a prominent north Antrim tenant righter, the failure of the new law "brought rights more prominently to the footlights."[25]

On 19 November 1869 the Route Tenants' Defence Association was formed at Ballymoney,[26] and it was followed in the early 1870s by a number of other tenant organizations, such as the Down Farmers' Union,

23. Olive Robinson, "The economic significance of the London companies as landlords in Ireland during the period 1800–70" (Ph.D. dissertation, Queen's University, Belfast, 1957), hereafter cited as "London companies."
24. James McKnight to W. E. Gladstone, 2 Apr. 1870 (B.L., Gladstone papers, Add. MS 44426/68). See also E. D. Steele, *Irish land and British politics: tenant-right and nationality, 1865–1870* (Cambridge, 1974), pp. 312–15.
25. S. C. McElroy, *The Route land crusade* . . . (Coleraine, n.d.), p. 30.
26. Ibid., p. 31.

238

LAND AND RELIGION IN ULSTER

established in May 1872.[27] By October 1873 there were at least five tenant-right associations in County Londonderry,[28] probably as a direct result of renewed efforts by certain London companies to limit tenant right on their lands in the 1860s and early 1870s.[29] In January 1874 delegates from twenty-nine tenant-right organizations, nineteen of them based in Ulster, attended a national conference in Belfast. The delegates heavily criticized the 1870 land act and passed resolutions which defined the Ulster custom as embracing continued occupancy at a fair rent as well as free sale, and which called for its full legalization throughout the country. Farmers were urged to elect M.P.s who supported these demands.[30]

Several points are worth noting about these Ulster tenant-right associations. First, they appear to have been composed of fairly well-to-do farmers. Describing events after the inaugural meeting of the Route association, Samuel McElroy noted: "In the evening a great soirée was held in the town hall . . . ; the assemblage embraced the flower of the middle classes."[31] Second, in their origins they were essentially moderate bodies which accepted the right of landlords to own land and to profit from it. A public letter setting forth the aims of the Down Farmers' Union in 1872 indicated that this organization sought to improve the position of the tenant and "at the same time to secure to the landlord well-paid rents and create over the country a prosperous tenantry."[32] And third, most of the associations had close links with the Liberals.[33]

The first political demonstration of this growing tenant-farmer protest came at the Tyrone by-election of April 1873, caused by the death of H. T. Lowry Corry, a member of the Belmore family, who were principal Tyrone landowners. After discussion among the leading county gentry, another member of the Belmore family, Captain H. W. Lowry Corry, was put forward as the Conservative candidate. About the same time the county grand Orange lodge of Tyrone, meeting privately at Killyman, selected J. W. Ellison Macartney, a minor landowner, as a nominee for the seat. This selection came about partly, it seems, because of Orange dissatisfaction with gentry domination of parliamentary representation, but mostly because of unrest over the land question, which was the ma-

27. Circular from W. J. Moore, secretary of Down Farmers' Union, May 1872 (P.R.O.N.I., Moore papers, D.877/27A).

28. *Lond. Stand.*, 15 Oct. 1873.

29. Robinson, "London companies," p. 301.

30. *N.W.*, 21, 22 Jan. 1874.

31. McElroy, *Route land crusade*, p. 31.

32. Circular from W. J. Moore, secretary of Down Farmers' Union, May 1872 (P.R.O.N.I., Moore papers, D.877/27A).

33. See, e.g., McElroy, *Route land crusade*, pp. 23–7, 31.

jor topic of discussion at the Killyman meeting.[34] In his election address Ellison Macartney pledged that as a staunch Protestant, he would give general support to the Conservatives, and then declared his enthusiasm for amendments to the land act of 1870.[35] In response, and not to be outdone, Corry published an address in which he promised to maintain the "glorious revolution" and proclaimed his intention to secure the interests of both yearly tenants and leaseholders.[36] In the heavily fought contest which followed, both candidates emphasized their desire for land reform. The impact of the agrarian issue on the election and on landlord-tenant political relations was graphically described by the earl of Belmore's land agent in a letter to his lordship written just prior to polling: "I sincerely wish Monday's election was over. . . . Several land cases and acts that would better have been left alone for some little time have in these Dungannon three baronies aroused a feeling of democratic antagonism to landlord influences I hardly expected had taken such deep and decided root."[37]

The result, however, was a narrow victory for Corry, who secured 3,139 votes against his opponent's 3,103. Nonetheless, the figures showed that considerable support for the tenant-right candidate had come from both Catholic and Protestant quarters. This development no doubt stemmed partly from the recent ballot act, although that law did not bring complete secrecy; the system was adopted by Corry's assistants, and subsequently by others, of issuing tally cards and asking supporters to return them after the polling, thus allowing party organizers to obtain a rough record of friends and foes.[38] Much more important, this political protest was the result of the way in which rising feeling over the land issue had upset traditional social and political relations in the countryside. Clearly, the identity of interest between the dominant Conservative families and the electorate was coming under strain.

The Rise of Interdenominational Cooperation, 1874–80

The growing political excitement was strongly reflected in the general election of 1874. In sharp contrast to 1868, contests occurred in all the Ulster counties. In Antrim, Down, and Armagh two Conservatives and

34. *B.N.L.*, 14 Mar. 1873; James Greer to earl of Belmore, 14 Mar. 1873 (P.R.O.N.I., Belmore papers, D.3007/P/20).
35. *Tyrone Constitution*, 14 Mar. 1873.
36. Ibid., 21 Mar. 1873.
37. R. C. Brush to earl of Belmore, 5 Apr. 1873 (P.R.O.N.I., Belmore papers, D.3007/P/106).
38. Draft copy of instructions for agents, n.d. (P.R.O.N.I., Carleton, Atkinson, and Sloan papers, D.1252/42/2).

one Liberal fought for each constituency, while in Londonderry, Fermanagh, and Donegal two Conservatives and two Liberals contested the poll. In Tyrone the two sitting Conservative M.P.s were challenged by Ellison Macartney, campaigning on an independent Protestant and Conservative tenant-right platform. In Cavan two Home Rulers faced a Liberal, while in Monaghan one Home Ruler opposed two Conservatives. All the Liberals were supporters of Gladstone except Captain E. J. Saunderson in Cavan and the two Fermanagh Liberals; the latter two were really independent Protestant candidates who advocated land reform.

In their election addresses the Conservatives sometimes referred to defense of the union or of Protestantism, but more often they mentioned the land question. In some cases, as in Tyrone, the Tory candidates made specific recommendations (such as tenant right for leaseholders at the expiration of their current agreements), but usually they contented themselves with general comments, referring perhaps to good relations with tenants on their own estates.[39] During the election campaign itself, however, they found it necessary to assure voters of their determination to back land reform. In customary fashion the Conservatives relied heavily on landlord assistance and expensive organization. Local proprietors and agents canvassed their tenants in the Tory cause.[40] For the three Home Rule party candidates, home rule was the main issue in their addresses, but the land question also featured prominently and became even more important during the election.[41] In Cavan and (to a much lesser extent) in Monaghan, they had the help of local Home Rule associations and the Catholic clergy.[42]

Among Liberals the agrarian issue was clearly the principal topic in their addresses and election campaigns. With the exception of Captain Saunderson, all the Liberal candidates were outspoken in their demand for reforms, which they usually specified as fair rents and free sale.[43] Tenant-right associations played an important part in the Liberal cause; they selected candidates, assisted with election expenses, and helped with canvassing. Catholic priests and Presbyterian ministers were present at some Liberal meetings,[44] and the Ulster Liberal Society based in Belfast rendered further aid.[45]

The Liberals' biggest success came in County Londonderry, where their

39. *B.N.L.*, 28 Jan.–5 Feb. 1874.
40. For such canvassing in County Antrim, see *B.N.L.*, 5 Feb. 1874.
41. *Northern Standard*, 31 Jan. 1874; *F.J.*, 3 Feb. 1874.
42. *Cavan Weekly News*, 13, 20 Feb. 1874.
43. For election addresses in 1874, see S.P.O., Official papers, 1874/11.
44. *N.W.*, 31 Jan. 1874; *Lond. Stand.*, 4 Feb. 1874.
45. *B.N.L.*, 25 Feb. 1874; *B.M.N.*, 4 Mar. 1874.

two candidates easily defeated the Conservative nominees. They also narrowly captured one seat in Down, while in Antrim the Liberal candidate was barely defeated by the Conservatives. In Donegal the two Liberal nominees also lost, but again the contest had been very close. In Tyrone Ellison Macartney now topped the poll with 4,710 votes, as against only 3,171 and 2,752 for his two rivals, while in Fermanagh the two Conservatives were elected without any difficulty. In Armagh as well the Tories won easily, while in Monaghan they left the Home Ruler at the bottom of the poll. Finally, in Cavan the two Home Rule candidates comfortably defeated their Liberal opponent.

With respect to denominational support for the different parties, newspaper reports indicate that apart from Cavan, Monaghan, and Tyrone, most Catholics backed the Liberals, and most members of the Church of Ireland the Conservatives, though there were significant exceptions in some areas. The Presbyterians were divided, but large numbers of them joined Catholics in voting for Liberal candidates, as the results in Antrim, Down, and Londonderry clearly show. Ellison Macartney in Tyrone received substantial support from both Catholics and Protestants.[46] In Cavan the Home Rule candidates apparently obtained only Catholic backing, but in Monaghan the Home Ruler seems to have secured some Protestant support as well, perhaps because of his Orange background.[47]

Thus important shifts of opinion were occurring among the Ulster county electorate, with considerable effect on the parliamentary representation of the province. There were now only thirteen Conservative M.P.s, all of whom were landed gentry and members of the Church of Ireland. There were two Home Rulers and three Liberals, of whom four were professional men and one was a merchant.[48] Two Liberals and one Home Ruler were Presbyterian; one Home Ruler was a Catholic and one Liberal a member of the Church of Ireland. The Conservative M.P.s had managed to hold their seats by endorsing land reform and by relying on their existing organization, but their whole position was now coming under increased social and political threat. An anonymous correspondent in 1875 warned a friend of the Belmores in Tyrone of the changing mood: "The people in this county are at present undergoing a sort of educational process to the effect that 'the Belmore family take no interest in the people of their county,' and this is forced on them as a reason not to support Col. Corry at the next election for the county."[49]

46. *N.W.*, 10 Feb. 1874.
47. John Madden to Isaac Butt, 23 Feb. 1874 (N.L.I., Butt papers, MS 831).
48. Thornley, "Irish party," pp. 591–5.
49. [?] to J. S. Galbraith, ca. 1875 (P.R.O.N.I., Belmore papers, D.3007/P/168).

Following the elections the land question remained in the forefront of northern politics. New tenant-right associations were formed. In County Antrim the various tenant-right bodies joined together in the Antrim Central Tenant Right Association in June 1876.[50] Significantly, the president of this new organization was Lord Waveney, head of the Ulster Liberal Society; in fact, the Liberals had close connections with many of the tenant-right bodies, especially in Down and Antrim. In several areas, however, Conservative associations were also set up, whose aims were to maintain the union, support the Tory cause, and bring farmers and gentry closer together.[51]

The movement for reform was given fresh impetus by the agricultural depression which struck the Irish countryside beginning in 1877. A decline in farm prices and a series of poor harvests resulted in considerable distress. Though not as seriously affected as Connacht, Ulster did not go unscathed. In County Donegal the situation was most serious, while in Cavan, Fermanagh, Monaghan, and Tyrone, certain areas were hard hit.[52] Elsewhere conditions were better, but all over the province farmers experienced falling incomes.[53] The Land League was formed in Dublin in October 1879, but it had little impact in Ulster before mid-1880. Tenant-right associations, however, continued to swell in number.

By-elections in the north between 1874 and 1880 reflected this growing unrest. The Conservatives narrowly held a seat in County Donegal in 1876, when their candidate made strong declarations in favor of land reform.[54] In May 1878 Viscount Castlereagh regained a seat in County Down for the Tories, but only after he had spent £14,000, pledged support for agrarian reform, and gathered endorsements from Home Rulers in the county by leading them to think that he approved of home rule.[55] But in December of the same year a Liberal held a seat in County Londonderry with an increased majority, which caused the local Conservative newspaper to declare that the Tory defeat resulted from "the prejudice of tenant farmers, who have been instilled with the belief that Liberal legislation alone will grant a satisfactory settlement of the land question."[56] This identification of the Liberals with the pressing issue of re-

50. McElroy, Route land crusade, p. 61.

51. B.N.L., 20 July 1874; Ulster Ex., 17 Jan. 1876.

52. Tyrone Constitution, 5 Mar. 1880; Impartial Reporter, 11 Mar. 1880; Weekly Freeman's Journal, 6 Mar. 1880.

53. See editorial of N.W., 15 Mar. 1880.

54. B.N.L., 16 Aug. 1876.

55. N.W., 15 May 1878; Account of expenses of Viscount Castlereagh at the County Down by-election (P.R.O.N.I., Downshire papers, D.671/614/15).

56. Londonderry Sentinel, 21 Dec. 1878.

form was also cited as the main reason for a Liberal victory in County Donegal in December 1879.[57] The urgency of the land question for so many voters had not gone unnoticed by Ulster Conservative M.P.s. From 1874 on, through private correspondence and in Parliament, they tried to promote various moderate measures of reform, but none of their efforts met with success.[58] This left them in a difficult position, which the marquis of Hamilton described in January 1880 to Montague Corry, one of Disraeli's secretaries.[59] Hamilton severely criticized the government for doing nothing and then declared: "There is only one subject that these tenant farmers in the north of Ireland at the present time care about, and that is the land question." He forwarded to Corry a letter from a Donegal proprietor, who asserted that this issue was bridging the traditional denominational cleavage: "Day by day that fear of popery which alone kept the Presbyterians loyal is decreasing; you are now losing them by the hundred, for they now consider the land question the all-important one."[60] The dire political consequences of this major shift alarmed the marquis of Hamilton: "It makes me very unhappy and uneasy, as the whole political aspect of these northern parts is gradually altering." In a belated attempt to stem the tide, the government announced its intention of giving Ellison Macartney's land bill a second reading, but this step had little or no effect, as the general election of April 1880 was to show.

The General Election of 1880 and Its Aftermath

All of the Ulster county seats were contested in 1880. In Cavan two Home Rulers opposed a Conservative; in Antrim, Down, Fermanagh, and Tyrone two Tories stood against one Liberal; and in Monaghan and Londonderry two Conservatives confronted two Liberals. In Armagh three Conservatives faced one Liberal, and in Donegal one Conservative opposed two Liberals. One of the Tories in Tyrone and another in Armagh stood on tenant-right principles, independently of the main Conservatives. Selection procedures differed considerably between parties. The Home Rule candidates in Cavan were chosen at a meeting of the

---

57. Ibid., 18 Dec. 1879.

58. For information on the attitude of Conservative M.P.s toward the land question, see A. B. Cooke (ed.), "A Conservative party leader in Ulster: Sir Stafford Northcote's diary of a visit to the province in October 1883" in *R.I.A. Proc.*, lxxv, sec. C, no. 4 (1975), pp. 61–84.

59. Marquis of Hamilton to Montague Corry, 13 Jan. 1880 (Hughenden Manor, Buckinghamshire, Disraeli papers, B/xxl/H/42).

60. T. G. Hamilton to marquis of Hamilton, 8 Jan. 1880 (ibid., B/xxl/H/42a).

Catholic bishop, clergy, and laity of the county.[61] Among the Liberals
the usual procedure was for tenant-right associations to nominate candidates, often with the aid of the Ulster Liberal Society.[62] In most cases
Tory candidates were designated at private meetings of the leading local
gentry, but in a few instances, notably in Down, county Conservative
associations took part in the selection process.[63]

In the address of every candidate the land question was the primary
issue. The two Home Rulers in Cavan renewed their pledge to support
fixity of tenure at fair rents and the principle of peasant proprietorship
as well as home rule and denominational education.[64] In their manifestos
the Conservatives usually endorsed the government's foreign policy, but
all of them except one dwelt at length on their desire for agrarian reform.[65]
They often urged greater security for the tenant farmer and expressed
approval for Ellison Macartney's bill. Four Tory candidates even advocated improving facilities for land purchase.[66] Some Liberals attacked
the government's foreign policy, but all of them concentrated on the
agrarian issue. They called for the three Fs and some demanded peasant
proprietorship.[67] During the election itself the Conservatives once again
enjoyed the aid of many landlords, who either personally or through
agents canvassed their tenants for support.[68] In some constituencies, especially in Antrim and Down, the Tories also had the help of local Conservative associations.[69] The Liberals benefited greatly from the assistance of tenant-right organizations.[70] Catholic priests and Presbyterian
ministers were much in evidence in the Liberal camp.[71] In the one constituency where Home Rulers were standing, Catholic clergymen promoted them.[72]

61. *Nation*, 20 Mar. 1880.
62. McElroy, *Route land crusade*, pp. 60–5; S. C. McElroy to Lord Waveney, 5 Feb.
1879 (P.R.O.N.I., Adair papers, D.929/HA 1a/F4, 14).
63. *B.N.L.*, 13 Mar. 1880.
64. *Nation*, 20 Mar. 1880.
65. The exception was S. H. Maxwell in County Cavan (*Cavan Weekly News*, 26 Mar.
1880).
66. They were Sir William Verner (Armagh), Edward Macnaghten and James Chaine
(Antrim), and S. M. Alexander (Londonderry). For the addresses of these and other Conservatives, see *B.N.L.*, 12–22 Mar. 1880.
67. *N.W.*, 12–20 Mar. 1880.
68. Anthony Traill to Edward Gibson, 9 Apr. 1880, in A. B. Cooke (ed.), *The Ashbourne papers, 1869–1913* (Belfast, 1974), p. 182; *Copy of the shorthand writer's notes
of the judgment and evidence on the trial of the Down county election petition*, p. 42,
H.C. 1880 (260-sess. 2), lvii, 567 (hereafter cited as *Down petition*).
69. *Down petition*.
70. *People's Advocate*, 20 Mar. 1880; *N.W.*, 20 Apr. 1880.
71. *Derry Journal*, 7 Apr. 1880; *N.W.*, 10 Apr. 1880.
72. *Cavan Weekly News*, 2 Apr. 1880.

The results dramatically demonstrated how much the land question had upset the usual pattern of parliamentary representation. The Home Rulers captured both seats in Cavan, while the Liberals won both seats in Donegal, Monaghan, and Londonderry as well as one seat in Armagh and Tyrone. The Conservatives secured the two seats in Antrim, Down, and Fermanagh as well as one seat in Armagh. The independent tenant-right Conservative was defeated in Armagh, but Ellison Macartney topped the poll in Tyrone. The successes of the Tories in Antrim and Down were in some ways surprising, but they had the advantages of active constituency associations,[73] high election expenditure,[74] and the presence in the electorate of numerous Belfast voters, who were mainly Conservative.[75] Efficient election management[76] and especially harmonious relations between the Tory candidates and their tenants were also important.[77] In Fermanagh the eccentric character of the Liberal nominee and the virtual absence of Presbyterians facilitated the double victory for the Conservatives.[78]

Thus in the Ulster counties the Home Rule party had won two seats, the Liberals eight, and the Conservatives eight. The Liberal M.P.s consisted of merchants, manufacturers, and professional men; among them were four Presbyterians, two members of the Church of Ireland, one Congregationalist, and one Quaker. All the Conservatives were landowners, and, except for one Presbyterian, all belonged to the Church of Ireland. Both Home Rulers were merchants and Catholics.[79] Clearly, significant political, social, and religious changes had occurred by 1880 in Ulster's parliamentary representation. Important alterations had also taken place in the patterns of electoral behavior in the northern counties. Numerous contemporary reports indicate that the Liberals secured the support of most Catholics and many Presbyterians.[80] The Conservatives must therefore have done especially well among Church of Ireland voters and, to a lesser extent, among Presbyterians. Election results

73. *N.W.*, 15 Apr. 1880.

74. *Return of charges made to candidates at the late elections by returning officers . . . ; also the total expenses of each candidate . . .*, pp. 36–43, H.C. 1880 (382-sess. 2), vii, 1.

75. *N.W.*, 12, 15 Apr. 1880; *B.M.N.*, 8 Apr. 1880.

76. *Down petition.*

77. *Report of her majesty's commissioners of inquiry into the working of the Landlord and Tenant (Ireland) Act, 1870, and the acts amending the same*, vol. ii: *Digest of evidence; minutes of evidence*, pt. i, p. 164 [C 2779-I], H.C. 1881, xviii, 73.

78. *B.M.N.*, 12 Apr. 1880.

79. C. C. O'Brien, "The Irish parliamentary party, 1880–90" (Ph.D. dissertation, University of Dublin, 1954), pp. 399–403.

80. *B.M.N.*, 27 Mar. 1880; *N.W.*, 12 Apr. 1880; *Derry Journal*, 12 Apr. 1880; *People's Advocate*, 17 Apr. 1880.

depended largely on the relative distribution of the denominations in different constituencies.

The interesting question of the extent of Presbyterian support for the Liberals can best be answered by examining the electoral outcome in more detail.[81] In the case of County Londonderry, if one assumes that there was no differential turnout between denominations, and if one ignores cross-party voting, which was insignificant, then it is clear that Catholics (23 percent of the electorate) could have contributed only 40 percent of the Liberal vote. Thus about 60 percent of the Liberal vote had to come from Presbyterians, or up to 80 percent of the Presbyterians who cast ballots. Taking the same approach to other county constituencies, it seems that in Down approximately 51 percent of Presbyterian votes went to the Liberals, while in Antrim the corresponding figure was around 45 percent. In both cases, especially Antrim, the percentage of Presbyterian tenant farmers who were Liberals was actually higher because the constituencies contained a high proportion of town and Belfast dwellers, most of whom were Conservatives. In Monaghan the proportion was roughly 23 percent and in Donegal it was probably similar.[82] Taking the cross-voting in Tyrone into account,[83] 27 percent of Presbyterians plumped for the Liberal, while 26 percent gave one vote to the Liberal and their other vote to the independent Conservative.

Clearly, in many areas in the countryside there was active political cooperation between Catholic and Presbyterian electors. Some northern Catholics may have supported the Liberals through lack of a Home Rule alternative, but most seem to have accepted the Liberal cause. John Harbison, a prominent Catholic Liberal and tenant righter from Cookstown, remarked that Catholics in Tyrone and Londonderry had "wrought with extreme warmth and zeal" on behalf of the Liberals;[84] the Catholic *Belfast Morning News* backed the Liberals and disparaged Parnell as an agitator.[85] In the common interest of land reform differences between Presbyterians and Catholics in other matters were relegated to the background.

81. Where there were two candidates for a party in a constituency, the combined total of their votes has been divided by two to determine the number of electors supporting that party. For the sources relating to denominational strengths in the electorates, see fn. 6–8 above.

82. Incorrect election results are given by Peter Gibbon, *The origins of Ulster unionism: the formation of popular Protestant politics and ideology in nineteenth-century Ireland* (Manchester, 1975), p. 108 (hereafter cited as *Ulster unionism*).

83. For information on voting in Tyrone, see *Tyrone Courier*, 17 Apr. 1880.

84. John Harbison to Lord O'Hagan, 25 Apr. 1880 (P.R.O.N.I., O'Hagan papers, D.2777/7/Q/23).

85. *B.M.N.*, 13 Apr. 1880.

The termination of the general election brought no abatement in agrarian agitation. Not only did the tenant-right organizations continue to demand fair rents, free sale, and fixity of tenure,[86] but the Land League also spread to many parts of the province beginning in the autumn of 1880. Though the League was strongest in Catholic areas of Ulster,[87] there is evidence that large numbers of Protestants joined it as well. It is also apparent that in the whole movement for land reform, including both tenant associations and Land League branches, there was considerable cooperation between Catholic and Protestant tenant farmers. Shortly before his arrest early in 1881, Michael Davitt spoke at a Land League meeting in County Armagh to a religiously mixed audience; a local correspondent later noted that "Orangemen that day joined the League in vast numbers."[88] This was not an isolated incident. "One of the signs of the times," the *Impartial Reporter* of County Fermanagh remarked in December 1880, "is the union of Orangemen, Protestants, and Catholics in accepting the League in Derrygonnelly."[89] Two Fermanagh Orange lodges had their warrants canceled because of Land League activity by their members.[90] The correspondence of landlords, agents, and their partisans underscores the pervasive reality that farmers of all religions and political backgrounds were uniting behind the banner of agrarian reform. Sir Thomas Bateson, a prominent northern landlord and a leading Conservative, informed Lord Salisbury in late December 1880: "A few weeks since, the Land League invaded Ulster. Up to that moment rents were well and cheerfully paid without even a murmur. Now all that is changed. The League operates in concert with the Central Radical Tenant Right Association, and the result is a general strike on the part of the tenants; men who voted for the Conservatives last April are now openly fraternising with democrats whom six weeks ago they would not have touched with a long pole, and the wave of communism has spread like wildfire. The demand is 25, 30, and in some cases 50 percent permanent reduction of rents, on the plea of low prices caused by American importation."[91] Writing of County Monaghan earlier in the same month, the Rev. D. C.

86. J. L. McCracken, "The consequences of the land war" in J. C. Beckett and T. W. Moody (ed.), *Ulster since 1800: a political and economic survey* (London, 1955), p. 62.

87. Ibid., p. 61.

88. [?] to Francis O'Neill, 19 Jan. 1882 (P.R.O.N.I., O'Neill papers, D.1481).

89. Quoted in Peadar Livingstone, *The Fermanagh story* . . . (Enniskillen, 1969), p. 260 (hereafter cited as *Fermanagh*).

90. Aiken McClelland, "The later Orange Order" in T. D. Williams (ed.), *Secret societies in Ireland* (Dublin and New York, 1973), p. 130.

91. Sir Thomas Bateson to marquis of Salisbury, 30 Dec. 1880 (Hatfield House, Hertfordshire, Salisbury papers).

Abbot remarked, "Most of the Presbyterians, the younger Methodists, and I may say all the Romanists go in the 'whole length of the unclean animal' with the Land League."[92]

At public meetings in the north in late 1880 and during the first half of 1881 the speakers, including Home Rulers, dealt almost exclusively with the land question.[93] Throughout this period Liberal and Nationalist politicians cooperated in the tenant-right movement, though there were certain signs of tension.[94] Demonstrations were organized, sometimes by landlords, against the Land League, which was accused of being tainted with republicanism, but even these gatherings could not entirely ignore the agrarian issue.[95] An assembly held in County Monaghan in December 1880 to protest against Land League activities was described by one of its supporters as a "tenant-right, anti-Land League, Orange meeting."[96]

These developments redounded to the political credit of northern Liberals. A by-election in County Londonderry in May 1880 resulted in the unopposed return of a Liberal. More dramatic was the outcome of the Tyrone by-election of August 1881. The Liberal nominee T. A. Dickson declared his approval of the recently passed land act.[97] His Tory opponent, Colonel W. S. Knox, uncle of the earl of Ranfurly and a prominent Orangeman, stood on Conservative and strong Protestant principles.[98] At the last moment, in response to a move by Parnell in Dublin, the Rev. Harold Rylett, a Unitarian minister with advanced agrarian views, entered the contest as a Home Ruler.[99] The campaign proved a very bitter one. Knox's supporters charged that Parnell's object of "the land for the people" meant the displacement of Ulster Protestants,[100] and Parnell himself for the first time in the north linked demands for land reform with self-government.[101] The final result was: Dickson, 3,168; Knox, 3,084; and Rylett, 907. Since about half of the 1,800 Catholics who voted supported Dickson while the other half backed Rylett,[102] at least 2,200 Prot-

92. Rev. D. C. Abbot to H. de F. Montgomery, 18 Dec. 1880 (P.R.O.N.I., Montgomery papers, D.627/428/7).

93. For a speech by Parnell in County Fermanagh, see *Ulster Ex.*, 11 Nov. 1880. For speeches by Michael Davitt and John Dillon in County Down, see *B.N.L.*, 24 Dec. 1880.

94. *Ulster Ex.*, 2 Nov., 10 Dec. 1880.

95. *Ulster Ex.*, 11 Nov. 1880.

96. Rev. D. C. Abbot to H. de F. Montgomery, 18 Dec. 1880 (P.R.O.N.I., Montgomery papers, D.627/428/7).

97. *N.W.*, 22 Aug. 1881.

98. *B.N.L.*, 23 Aug. 1881.

99. *B.M.N.*, 26 Aug. 1881.

100. Election leaflet, Tyrone by-election, 1881 (P.R.O.N.I., Greer papers, T.2642/8/22).

101. *Ulster Ex.*, 1 Sept. 1881.

102. *N.W.*, 9 Sept. 1881; *Ulster Ex.*, 10 Sept. 1881.

estants must have polled for the Liberal, and these included Orangemen. Parnell believed that 500 Orangemen had voted Liberal. The continuing growth of Protestant and even Orange support for the Liberals and against landlord representatives was ruefully acknowledged by James Crossle, a Tyrone land agent, shortly after the election: "It is too bad that what was once called Protestant Tyrone could not return a Protestant member. That low fellow Dickson was returned by Protestants, and I believe numbers of Orangemen voted against their grand master. The fact is, the Protestants as well as the Roman Catholics do not want an Orangeman or even a Fenian if he is a gentleman or a landlord. I look upon the event of this election as a death blow to Protestantism."[103]

The Decline of Interdenominational Cooperation

By the end of 1881, however, serious divisions had appeared within the ranks of the tenant-right movement, the result of which was that the northern tenant-right associations and the Land League each went their own way, and much of the previous Catholic-Protestant cooperation ended. The connection of the tenant-right bodies with the Liberals and of the Land League with the Nationalists was an important factor in this development. Gladstone's agrarian legislation of 1881, which enshrined the three Fs as the law of the land, met with divergent responses. Northern tenant-right organizations expressed their approval of it, as did the Ulster Liberal Society and the Ulster Liberal M.P.s.[104] But the Parnellite leadership of the Home Rule party and the Land League assumed a different stance. Partly because of anger over other government measures and partly to appease his more revolutionary wing, Parnell adopted a hostile attitude toward both the land act and the Liberals.[105] At the Land League convention in September 1881 the new law was heavily criticized, and the League persisted in its struggle against the collection of the usual rents. As a result, Parnell and other Land League leaders were arrested and the organization was banned. Eventually, after his release from prison, Parnell and others formed the Irish National League in October 1882. The main object of this new body was national self-government; further agrarian reform now became a subsidiary aim.

By this time cooperation between northern Catholic and Protestant farmers in the work of the Land League and tenant-right associations had largely disappeared. The change of attitude on the part of many

103. James Crossle to Sir William Verner, 8 Sept. 1881 (P.R.O.N.I., Verner papers, Out-letter book of James Crossle, D.236/488/2).
104. MacKnight, *Ulster as it is*, i, 398–9; *N.W.*, 21 Nov. 1881.
105. O'Brien, *Parnell and his party*, pp. 36–79.

Protestants toward the Land League was reflected in the columns of the *Impartial Reporter* of Enniskillen. Under the editorship of W. C. Trimble, a strong supporter of tenant right, the paper expressed considerable sympathy with the Land League movement in Fermanagh prior to August 1881. But on 11 August, in response to a violent speech by a prominent member of the League at a meeting in the county, the paper asserted that the Land League in Fermanagh had always followed the old lines of tenant right, and warned that it should not advance beyond them. A week later, the paper welcomed Gladstone's land act and henceforth became increasingly critical of Parnell, his advocacy of agrarian reform and self-government openly on the same platform, and his increased militancy, as shown by the "No-rent manifesto."[106] In late December Trimble chaired a meeting at Enniskillen to revive the Fermanagh Farmers' Association, which had lapsed in the face of the Land League.[107] By the end of 1881 Protestant support for the League in the county had vanished almost entirely.[108]

In the rest of Ulster as well, Protestants seem to have left the Land League by late 1881, and they also shunned the new National League. In June 1882 Sir Thomas Bateson gave Lord Salisbury a very different account of the situation from that of eighteen months earlier:

I have just come back from the north of Ireland. There has been a considerable change in the feelings of the better class of Liberal Presbyterians since the Kilmainham treaty and the Dublin assassinations. The same applies to the democratic Presbyterian farmers. They approved . . . of the spirit of communism which transferred 25 percent of the landlords' property to the tenant farmers, but they are greatly alarmed at the nationalisation scheme of Mr. Davitt and his confederates. They think that confiscation should not be extended to their class, or rather in favour of the class below them. They hold that communism has been pushed far enough, and there seems to be a growing feeling that the policy of the National party is to stamp out the English garrison and make Ireland a purely R[oman] Catholic country. There is throughout Ulster a growing distrust of the R[oman] Catholics on the part of the Protestant farmers, and with the exception of the ruinous cutting down of rents by the land commis[sion], things are, from what I can gather, better than they were a few months ago. I speak of the Protestant districts of Ulster only.[109]

There is no other evidence that fear of land nationalization was a potent factor in the collapse of support among Protestant farmers for the Land

106. *Impartial Reporter*, 11 Aug., 27 Oct. 1881.

107. Ibid., 29 Dec. 1881.

108. Livingstone, *Fermanagh*, p. 261.

109. Sir Thomas Bateson to marquis of Salisbury, 27 June 1882 (Hatfield House, Hertfordshire, Salisbury papers).

League and the National League. But the close association of these bodies with nationalist aims, together with the wave of agrarian violence in the south and the west, resulted in the thorough alienation of northern Protestant tenants.[110]

Nevertheless, concern with the land question remained very much alive in rural Ulster. In spite of the 1881 land act and some improvement in the condition of agriculture, dissatisfaction persisted. In the years that followed, tenants sought rent reductions in the new land courts, and peasant proprietorship along with the exclusion of leaseholders from the benefits of the 1881 land act became salient issues. Organization continued among Ulster farmers to promote their demands, though clearly at a slower pace because some of the most important aims had already been achieved. In January 1883 the Ulster Land Committee was formed as a central body representing the various tenant-right associations in the province.[111] The National League sponsored a campaign in the north in 1883, and a number of branches were set up, but rapid growth did not come until 1885 and 1886.

The Ashbourne act of 1885 gave important new facilities for land purchase, but many regarded them as inadequate. From their inception the Ulster tenant-right organizations had tended to be more moderate than the Land League, but by 1886 both supported the compulsory sale of estates. The northern tenant righters, however, saw peasant proprietorship as a long-term process, and in the meantime they intended to advance the farmers' interests. In its memorial to Gladstone in 1886 the Antrim Central Tenant Right Association declared: "The terms of the Ulster plantation settlement were intended to secure to the tenants the occupation of their holdings at easy rents."[112] The National League, on the other hand, demanded an immediate end to landlordism, saying that the landlords had stolen the land from the people. One speaker at a meeting of the Donoughmore branch of the National League in November 1885 assured his listeners that "the land they lived on once belonged to their ancestors, free of rent and free of burden, possessed in joint ownership with the chiefs of Donegal."[113]

Yet in spite of organizational fissures and ideological differences among northern tenants, their relations with landlords everywhere underwent dramatic change in this period. The position of the gentry in society had been challenged. H. H. McNeile, a County Antrim proprietor, lamented their lost status to Lord Cairns in February 1882. "Where a year ago there

110. *N.W.*, 26 June 1883; MacKnight, *Ulster as it is*, ii, 17; *Lond. Stand.*, 3 July 1883.
111. *Lond. Stand.*, 27 Jan. 1883.
112. *B.N.L.*, 6 Feb. 1886.
113. *Derry Journal*, 4 Nov. 1886.

was good feeling and courtesy," he observed, "there is now a defiant take-what-you-can, you-are-lucky-to-get-anything sort of feeling, even among the best of the tenantry."[114] On boards of guardians the exclusive leadership of the gentry was questioned and the right of farmers to a share of power asserted. Landlords still retained prominent positions on these boards and in local affairs generally, but the extent of their dominance had been irrevocably questioned by the farmers, Catholic and Protestant, who had developed a new political and social consciousness of their own, with profound consequences, thanks to the agrarian issue. In Fermanagh, for example, according to a recent county history, the activity of the Land League aroused Catholics to a new level of political awareness and enthusiasm for the Nationalists.[115]

The changing importance of the land question, the growing rivalry between Liberals and Nationalists, and the widening split between Presbyterians and Catholics were reflected in by-election results between 1881 and 1885. In the County Londonderry by-election of November 1881 a Liberal defeated the Conservative even though some formerly Liberal Catholics voted Tory on advice from Home Rule quarters so as to defeat the government candidate.[116] In 1883 Tim Healy stood for County Monaghan as a Nationalist against Liberal as well as Tory opposition. He was returned with the backing of most Catholic electors and some Presbyterians, the latter apparently won over to Healy because of his well-publicized contribution to the 1881 land act.[117]

Though the Liberal candidate in Monaghan came far at the bottom of the poll, the future status of liberalism in rural Ulster was as yet unclear. Thus in January 1884 a Liberal was elected unopposed for Londonderry. On the other hand, in November of the same year a Conservative defeated a Liberal in a straight fight in Down. In 1885 two by-elections occurred, the first in Antrim, won narrowly by the Liberals, and the second in Down, secured by the Conservatives. The evidence of these last three elections indicated that the Liberals still enjoyed considerable Presbyterian backing, while the Conservatives were at least maintaining their electoral support of 1880. The Nationalists, though still weak, were gaining influence over the Catholic vote. Nationalist interventions in Antrim and Down had been important, helping the Liberals in the first case and the Conservatives in the second.[118]

114. H. H. McNeile to Lord Cairns, 4 Feb. 1882 (P.R.O., Kew, Cairns papers, 30/51/16f/102).

115. Livingstone, *Fermanagh*, pp. 258–64.

116. *B.M.N.*, 28 Nov. 1881.

117. See John Magee, "The Monaghan election of 1883 and the 'invasion of Ulster'" in *Clogher Rec.*, viii (1974), pp. 147–66.

118. *B.M.N.*, 28, 29 Nov. 1884; 23 May, 4 July 1885.

Challenge and Response: The General Election of 1885

The general election of 1885 posed a great challenge for all three parties. The tripling in the number of rural constituencies, the enormous expansion of the electorate, and the new rules which severely restricted election expenditure presented great problems for the party organizations. The altered social and religious composition of the electorate resulting from the enfranchisement of most laborers and from shifts in denominational strength, along with the changing relative importance of contemporary political issues, meant that the parties had to cope with new dangers as well as new opportunities. They responded in different ways and with varied measures of success.

During 1885 existing Conservative bodies set up new local committees, associations were established where there had been none before, and the social base of these associations and committees was extended. This reorganization was most successful in Antrim, Down, Armagh, and Tyrone, less successful in Fermanagh, Londonderry, and Monaghan, and largely ineffective in Cavan and Donegal.[119] The associations and committees held conventions to select candidates, looked after the registration of voters, and provided volunteers to conduct the campaigns.

Especially important in this reorganization was the role of the Orange Order. Though it embraced only a minority of Protestants in 1885, this institution included within its membership a large and growing proportion of the newly enfranchised laborers. In Antrim, Down, and (to a lesser extent) Armagh, the Orange Order received a formal place in the Tories' new electoral structure. Speaking at Ballynahinch in May 1885, E. S. Finnigan, the leading Conservative organizer in northeast Ulster, explained how the Tories proposed to set up new committees for each polling district, with representatives drawn from the old county associations and the new electors. "The Orange Order," he declared, "would have a well-defined position. The district master and district officers, together with the master of each of the lodges in the district, would be appointed . . . upon each committee."[120] A similar structure was established in many parts of these three counties.[121]

Elsewhere in the north the Orange Order was apparently not accorded a formal place in these associations, but laborers, including Orangemen,

---

119. The extent of this reorganization, especially as it affected registration activities, is discussed in B. M. Walker, "Party organisation in Ulster, 1865–92: registration agents and their activities" in Peter Roebuck (ed.), *Plantation to partition: essays in Ulster history in honour of J. L. McCracken* (Belfast, 1981), pp. 191–209.

120. *Weekly News*, 9 May 1885. For comment on the successful appeal of the Orange Order to laborers, see *Weekly Whig*, 18 June 1885.

121. See, e.g., *B.M.N.*, 19 May 1885; *Weekly News*, 8, 22 Aug. 1885.

did play a significant role in the new bodies. Though this role differed
in degree from one area to another, in most places it was an effective,
not a token one. Where laborers were ignored, they altered things to their
own liking. In the constituency of Armagh North, local Orangemen, who
believed that they had not been properly consulted in the selection of
a candidate, put forward their own nominee, Colonel E. J. Saunderson,
whom the official Conservatives eventually had to accept.[122] In County
Londonderry several meetings of Protestant laborers finally persuaded
apathetic Conservatives to advance a Tory candidate.[123]

At the beginning of 1885 the Liberal organization in rural constituencies depended on the tenant-right associations, composed very largely
of farmers. Attempts were subsequently made to install new Liberal associations and to expand existing bodies so as to embrace laborers and
others recently enfranchised. These efforts met with some success in Antrim, Down, and Tyrone, though even in these counties the Liberals were
unable to attract many laborers or Catholics into their organizations.
This difficulty led to a disastrous split in the main Liberal association
in Antrim North, where John Pinkerton stood as an independent after
refusing to allow his name to be placed in nomination at a meeting which
he said represented the Presbyterian farmers, but did not "adequately
represent the Roman Catholics or the labourers."[124] Complacency or
worse characterized the Liberal organization elsewhere in the north. In
County Londonderry the main activity flowed from the Central Liberal
Union, which drew traditional support from tenant-right associations
but apparently made no special effort to reorganize for the election, instead depending on its previous structure. In Armagh North and Donegal East there was some Liberal activity, but in other constituencies there
was none. In those areas where they were active, however, conventions
were held to choose candidates, and the associations helped to manage
the campaigns. Fewer Presbyterian ministers than before and no Catholic priests were in evidence at Liberal meetings.

Only a year before the general election, the Nationalists possessed little organization in Ulster. But from the beginning of 1885, under leadership from headquarters in Dublin, many National League branches were
formed in the north; they provided the electoral structure of the Nationalist party there and embraced farmers as well as laborers.[125] Frequently,

122. P. J. Buckland (ed.), *Irish unionism, 1885–1923: a documentary history* (Belfast, 1973), pp. 110–20.
123. *Londonderry Sentinel*, 1, 24 Oct. 1885.
124. *Weekly Whig*, 28 Aug. 1885.
125. R. E. Beckerson to earl of Carnarvon, with report on the progress of the Irish National League, 1 Jan.–30 June 1885 (S.P.O., C.S.O., Police and crime records, Irish National League proceedings, 1883–90).

these branches were coterminous with Catholic parishes, and the local
Catholic clergy played an important part in them, just as they did in
the county conventions held to select candidates under the chairmanship
of a representative from the Dublin headquarters of the National
League.[126] Valuable assistance in such matters as registration was provided to the new nationalist movement by former northern Liberal supporters and by volunteers from Dublin. Nationalist organization was
notably weak in Antrim and Down, effective only in parts of Armagh
and Londonderry, but widespread and efficient in Donegal, Tyrone, Fermanagh, Monaghan, and Cavan.

During the campaign the parties advertised their policies and at the
same time maneuvered with each other for political advantage. In sharp
contrast to 1880, the land question was no longer the overriding issue.
Among both Liberals and Conservatives the principal subjects of election addresses were maintenance of the union, and only secondarily
agrarian reform and better conditions for laborers, though the two parties put different emphases on these issues. The Conservatives gave the
prime place to maintenance of the union between Britain and Ireland
as well as to the integrity of the empire, both of which they saw threatened by home rule.[127] The next most important issue in Conservative
addresses was the condition of laborers, for whom many candidates advocated better housing. Farmers were reminded of the Tory government's
land-purchase act of 1885 and given promises that Conservative candidates would support necessary amendments to the land laws, though
these were rarely specified. Some Tory nominees were critical of the principle of free trade associated with liberalism; others sought to rally all
supporters of the union.

In their addresses the Liberals also endorsed the union strongly, though
not usually in such outspoken terms as the Conservatives.[128] Addressing
the land question in considerable detail, Liberal candidates urged that
even judicial rents be reduced and that leaseholders be admitted to the
benefits of the 1881 land act. Most demanded better housing for laborers
and stated their approval of free trade. In their speeches they appealed
often to all creeds and classes.[129] The Nationalist candidates did not
publish addresses, but in their speeches they repeated the main points
of the Nationalist party's platform.[130] They castigated the union, saying

126. *B.M.N.*, 2, 18 June 1885; *Derry Journal*, 28 Aug. 1885.
127. For Conservative addresses, see *B.N.L.*, 27 Oct.–21 Nov. 1885.
128. For Liberal addresses, see *N.W.*, 30 Oct.–21 Nov. 1885.
129. *N.W.*, 28 Nov. 1885.
130. See the speeches by William O'Brien and W. J. Reynolds in *B.M.N.*, 25, 26 Nov.
1885.

that it had brought ruin to Ireland, and proclaimed their total opposition to landlordism, which they blamed for terrible past sufferings. Like the candidates of the other parties, Nationalists often declared their concern for the interests of laborers, and like many Liberals, they urged all denominations to support them.

Negotiations between the parties immediately before the election vitally affected the eventual outcome. Early in 1885 Liberals and Conservatives decided to cooperate in certain areas — Tyrone and Donegal East — in order to avoid splitting the pro-union vote. As a result, Liberal candidates withdrew from Tyrone, leaving Conservatives straight fights against Nationalists, while in Donegal East no Tory appeared and a Liberal opposed a Nationalist.[131] But many in both Liberal and Conservative camps objected to this alliance. The presence of large numbers of supporters of all three parties in many electoral divisions created considerable possibilities for cross-voting in those constituencies where only two parties offered candidates; and since the Nationalists contested only divisions having a sizable Catholic electorate, Liberal and Conservative candidates were left to fight a considerable number of seats. Late in October Parnell offered Nationalist support to the Liberals in certain constituencies uncontested by Nationalists in return for a Liberal seat for Captain W. H. O'Shea, but when this overture came to nothing, Parnell and the Nationalists turned against the Liberals.[132]

Conservative and Nationalist party organizers secretly combined to prevent Liberal candidates from running against Tories in Mid Armagh as well as Down East, and to keep a Liberal or independent Home Ruler from opposing Nationalist candidates in Armagh South and Newry.[133] On 24 November Parnell published an address to Nationalists in those Ulster divisions where there were no Nationalist candidates.[134] The address was hostile to the Liberals and urged electors in Londonderry North to vote for the Conservative there unless Liberals backed the Nationalist in Derry city. In addition, Parnell endorsed John Pinkerton, the independent candidate in Antrim North, and said that Nationalists should support the Liberals in Down North and Antrim East only if they opposed coercion. Yet in two of the four Antrim divisions, South and Mid, Parnell urged Nationalists to back the Liberal nominees.

131. D. C. Savage, "The origins of the Ulster Unionist party, 1885-6" in *I.H.S.*, xii, no. 47 (Mar. 1961), pp. 185–208.

132. Katharine O'Shea to Lord Richard Grosvenor, 28 Oct. 1885 (B.L., Gladstone papers, Add. MS 44316/63).

133. For Down East and Newry, see Michael McCartan to Timothy Harrington, 12 Nov. 1885 (U.C.D., Archives Department, McCartan letter book, P11/B). For the Armagh divisions, see T. M. Healy, *Letters and leaders of my day* (2 vols., London, 1928), i, 231–2.

134. *Weekly Whig*, 28 Nov. 1885.

The order in which the elections occurred was also important to their final outcome. The Derry city contest on 26 November resulted in a Tory victory when the few Liberals of that borough supported the Conservative. The first county elections were those in Tyrone North and Antrim North two days later. In the former Lord E. W. Hamilton (Conservative) defeated John Dillon (Nationalist). Most Catholics voted for Dillon, and most Protestants, including Presbyterian Liberals, for Lord Hamilton.[135] In an angry speech after the results were announced, Dillon declared that since Liberal votes in this division had largely been cast against the Nationalist, then Catholic votes in Londonderry North and Mid Antrim should be cast against the Liberal.[136] This advice was to cost the Liberals dearly. In Antrim North the Conservative received 3,233 votes, less than half the ballots cast, but the Liberal, with 2,149 votes, and the independent, with 1,915 votes, split the rest of the ballots sufficiently to allow the Conservative to win. Endorsed by Parnell, the independent here, John Pinkerton, secured most Catholic and some Presbyterian votes.[137] Two days later, the Liberals also lost Londonderry North to the Tories, mainly, it appears, because Catholics supported the Conservative. In this contest the Conservative obtained 5,180 votes and the Liberal 3,017. Since roughly 2,850 Catholic electors voted, and since most of them backed the Conservative,[138] the Liberal received a majority of the Protestant ballots, but this was simply not enough to win.

This pattern of voting prevailed as the election continued. Where a Liberal and a Conservative were the only candidates, the Catholic vote usually went to the Conservative.[139] The Liberals increased their supporters, mostly among farmers; the Conservatives also boosted theirs, chiefly among laborers, but in addition they enjoyed vital Catholic backing.[140] In the Antrim by-election of 1885, before the county was split into four divisions, the victorious Liberal received 3,971 votes, while at the general election in the county the four Liberal candidates secured a total of 10,647 votes, but they won no seats, probably because in four of the divisions Catholic support went to either the Conservatives or the independent. Thus in Mid Antrim the Tory captured 3,832 ballots and defeated the Liberal with 2,713. As the Catholic electors, estimated at 2,300, seem mostly to have voted Tory, this probably tipped the balance in the

135. Ibid., 5 Dec. 1885; *F.J.*, 9 Dec. 1885.
136. *Weekly Examiner*, 5 Dec. 1885. This view was also shared by an editorial writer in *B.M.N.*, 28 Nov. 1885.
137. *N.W.*, 1 Dec. 1885.
138. *N.W.*, 3 Dec. 1885; *Weekly Whig*, 5 Dec. 1885; *F.J.*, 9 Dec. 1885.
139. *United Ireland*, 5 Dec. 1885; *Weekly Whig*, 12 Dec. 1885.
140. *Weekly Whig*, 5 Dec. 1885; Thomas MacKnight to W. E. Gladstone, 17 Dec. 1885 (B.L., Gladstone papers, Add. MS 56446).

Conservative's favor.[141] In perhaps as many as six constituencies Liberals could have defeated Tories if only they had enjoyed extensive Catholic support.[142]

In the remaining constituencies most Catholics voted Nationalist and most Protestants voted either Conservative or Liberal. Departures from this pattern were minimal. The Nationalist William O'Brien in Tyrone South believed that he had received forty to fifty Protestant votes, but that seventy or eighty Catholics had "deserted" him.[143] In a few areas, namely Fermanagh and Cavan, some Protestants abstained or voted Nationalist because they objected to Conservative candidates who were landlords.[144] In Londonderry South some hundreds of Protestants supported the Nationalist Tim Healy.[145] Why they did so is not exactly clear. Perhaps Healy benefited among Protestant voters not only from his agrarian radicalism but also from the fact that there was less Catholic clerical intervention in the county than elsewhere. Indeed, one County Londonderry parish priest refused to attend the inaugural meeting of a National League branch in order to avoid giving it a sectarian image.[146]

The net result of the general election in the county divisions of Ulster was that the Nationalists captured sixteen seats, while the Conservatives took eleven and the Liberals none at all. The victorious Conservatives consisted of one professor of law and ten who were, or were related to, prominent landowners; of the latter, a few were also in professions. All were adherents of the Church of Ireland except for one Presbyterian. Among the Nationalist M.P.s were seven who belonged to the legal profession, two merchants, two journalists, a shopkeeper, a tailor, a private secretary, and a rentier. Only eight of these sixteen had family connections with Ulster; all were Catholics. As for the defeated Liberals, every one was a Presbyterian, and all were merchants or manufacturers, apart from one small landowner.[147]

141. *United Ireland*, 12 Sept. 1885; *N.W.*, 4 Dec. 1885. For the contests in Antrim North and South, see *N.W.*, 1, 9, 11 Dec. 1885.

142. In Londonderry North and Mid Antrim the Liberals probably enjoyed a considerable majority of the Presbyterian vote and could have won easily with Catholic support. In Antrim North and East, and Down North they secured more than 50 percent of the Presbyterian vote and could also have won with Catholic backing. In Mid Armagh and Down East and West a Liberal alliance of over 50 percent of Presbyterians and most Catholics could possibly have brought Liberal victories.

143. For an account of denominational voting in Tyrone South as well as the other divisions in that county, see *Weekly Examiner*, 12 Dec. 1885.

144. *Cavan Weekly News*, 30 Oct., 11 Dec. 1885; *Impartial Reporter*, 3 Dec. 1885.

145. *Weekly Examiner*, 12 Dec. 1885.

146. *Derry Journal*, 7 Oct. 1885.

147. O'Brien, "Irish parliamentary party," pp. 414–20. Local newspapers and directories provided information on the Liberals.

In comparison with the electoral outcome in 1880 striking changes had occurred in the parliamentary representation of the Ulster counties. Perhaps most startling was the collapse of the Liberal party. There were several reasons for this collapse. First, the Liberals were outmaneuvered by the Conservatives and Nationalists in a number of divisions, and they neglected to establish effective local organizations in others. Second, they failed to win the Orange laboring vote, partly because of their organizational weaknesses and their concentration during the election on farmers' interests. Protestant laborers also shunned liberalism because to them and to many farmers, especially in areas where there was a strong nationalist movement, the Conservatives seemed sounder on the constitutional issue, which had now become highly significant. Finally, the Liberals were no longer capable of enlisting the Catholic vote, which went Nationalist or, for tactical reasons, Conservative. This loss of Catholic support stemmed partly from the Liberals' failure to give Catholics a larger role in their associations, but more important was the great attraction which the nationalist cause now possessed for Catholic voters.

The Conservatives emerged from the election as the exclusive representatives of nonnationalist opinion in Ulster, and, surprisingly in the light of social developments over the last decade, the Tory M.P.s were drawn almost entirely from the gentry. Assessing the new political situation for Lord Salisbury in April 1887, Lord Deramore (formerly Sir Thomas Bateson) commented: "In 1885, under the lead of the resident gentlemen, the labourers and artisans swept every so-called Liberal from the different hustings in Ulster and sent 16 members to support your government, the bulk of the farmers going for the Gladstone candidates in hope of securing more plunder. It is not the farmers who hold Ulster for the queen, but the labourers and artisans, officered by the landlords."[148] Though Deramore underestimated the importance to the Tories of support from farmers, his statement was otherwise accurate enough. Protestant laborers had indeed rallied to the Conservative party, whose leaders, the gentry, had successfully adapted to the new political circumstances of the day by reorganizing and expanding their local associations as well as by showing concern for the laborers' material interests. The alliance of the Conservatives with the Orange Order at the local level had been vital to their success. Although constituting only a minority of the electors, the Orange laborers were an important addition to the conservative cause. But the Tories had also retained considerable support among Protestant farmers, no doubt because of their advocacy of land reform and their renovation of constituency associations. Finally, in the chang-

148. Lord Deramore to marquis of Salisbury, 29 Apr. 1887 (Hatfield House, Hertfordshire, Salisbury papers).

ing climate of opinion the Conservatives' strong views on the sanctity of the union greatly assisted their cause among Protestant voters of all social classes.

The degree of success achieved by the Nationalists in 1885 was even more striking than that of the Conservatives because Home Rulers had held only three seats in Ulster before the general election. Like the Tories, the Nationalists benefited from efficient organization on a broad social basis and from an increase in the proportional strength of their supporters in the electorate as a result of franchise reforms. More important, however, was the overwhelming appeal of the nationalist cause among northern Catholics, farmers and laborers alike. But if the nationalist cause galvanized Catholics in one direction, it propelled Protestants in another. That very few Protestants were attracted to it was due in part to its organizational structure, but more significantly it was because Protestants perceived in this cause no advantages and grave dangers.

Enduring Alignments: The General Election of 1886

The emergence of the Conservatives as the principal party among the Ulster Protestant community was graphically demonstrated by the Mid Armagh by-election of February 1886. The contest resulted in a resounding Conservative victory over the leading northern Liberal, T. A. Dickson, who tried unsuccessfully to focus attention on the land question. Soon after Dickson's defeat his brother-in-law, Robert MacGeogh, sadly admitted that the Liberal party had collapsed in rural Ulster, and that Liberal voters, frightened by home rule, had given their support to the Conservatives. "The home-rule scare carried the election," declared Mac-Geogh, "and every other consideration will be regarded as of secondary importance in every Protestant household in Ulster until this bogey is laid."[149]

Gladstone's introduction of a home-rule bill in the Commons early in April 1886 quickly led to a split in the Ulster Liberal party. The vast majority of northern Liberals repudiated the measure. Henceforth Liberals opposed to home rule were usually called Liberal Unionists, while the Conservatives were often referred to simply as Unionists. The northern Liberal Unionists established the Ulster Unionist Committee in June to promote the united action of all Liberal opponents of home rule in the province; after the general election in July this body became the Ulster Liberal Unionist Association.[150] The small number of Liberals who sup-

149. Robert MacGeogh to James Bryce, 5 Feb. 1886 (Bodl., Bryce papers, J1/3).
150. N.W., 1, 30 May, 15 June 1886.

ported Gladstone were known simply as Gladstonian Liberals, and some of them now formed the Irish Protestant Home Rule Association.[151]

The general election of July 1886, which followed the defeat of Gladstone's government of Ireland bill in the Commons, saw the completion of the realignment of political forces in Ulster, an event of lasting significance. The overriding issue was of course the question of home rule. In Londonderry South, Donegal East, Down South, and the four divisions of Tyrone—all constituencies in which the Nationalists had slightly more or fewer supporters than their opponents—Liberal Unionists and Tory Unionists combined their organizations to support candidates of either party. Liberal Unionists won seats in Tyrone South and Londonderry South, while a Tory Unionist took Tyrone North. In the remainder of Down as well as in Antrim, Armagh, and Londonderry North, there was no such cooperation, and the Liberal Unionists had virtually no influence over electoral affairs. In these constituencies the former Conservative organizations controlled the proceedings, with the backing of the Orange Order,[152] and would continue to do so in future elections.[153] The Tory Unionists won ten seats altogether in these divisions. Elsewhere in Ulster they controlled the party organization but obtained no seats. The social and religious character of Tory Unionist M.P.s was unchanged from 1885, except that one Presbyterian merchant had replaced a Church of Ireland law professor. The Liberal Unionist M.P.s consisted of a Presbyterian temperance official and a Congregationalist merchant. Subsequently, Liberal Unionists played only a minor role in northern politics and in 1912 finally merged with the Conservatives.

The Nationalist party used the same organization and nominated mostly the same candidates as in the previous general election. In a number of constituencies which they had not contested in 1885, however, there were candidates of the Irish Protestant Home Rule Association as well as some Gladstonian Liberals. In other divisions special efforts were made to woo Protestant support for Nationalist candidates. W. J. Reynolds, the incumbent Nationalist M.P. for Tyrone East, sought support from prominent Protestant Home Rulers and asked party headquarters in Dublin for suitable election literature for Protestants. His correspondence also shows that he relied on local Catholic priests for information about absent voters and for the gentle guidance of their parishioners: "I think it would be well to give a few hints to the people on Sunday how to mark their

151. *Weekly Examiner*, 29 May 1886.

152. For the role of the Orange Order in constituency associations and at nomination meetings, see *B.N.L.*, 21, 23 June 1886.

153. J. F. Harbison, *The Ulster Unionist party, 1882–1973: its development and organisation* (Belfast, 1973), pp. 6–21.

votes."[154] The Nationalists won fourteen seats but gained very little Protestant backing. The Gladstonian Liberals and Protestant Home Rulers met with insignificant support.[155] The social and religious composition of the Nationalist parliamentary contingent from Ulster was the same as in 1885.

When the 1886 general election concluded, almost all Protestant electors in the countryside, former Liberals and Conservatives alike, were in one political grouping, the unionist movement, which was dominated by the Conservatives. Nearly all Catholic voters, former Liberals and Nationalists alike, were in another political grouping, the nationalist movement. This state of affairs has proved to be of enormous durability. Over the next three decades some mixed denominational voting still took place for Liberal Unionists or Gladstonian Liberals. Divisions also occurred within the ranks of the unionist movement on a few occasions, as in the first decade of the new century, over surviving agrarian tensions, but fundamental political alignments had now been firmly established among the rural population of Ulster which have remained to this day.

Conclusion

This survey of northern electoral politics from 1868 to 1886 has demonstrated how important the land question became at the polls, and how the urgency of the agrarian issue before 1885 led to dramatic changes in the parliamentary representation of rural Ulster. At the beginning of this period elections were dominated by the Conservative gentry, not by means of coercion, but through their generally accepted social and economic place in society, combined with a sense of political identity between them and the electorate. Subsequently, the growing unrest over the land question thoroughly disrupted all of this, so that by the early 1880s the gentry's position had been seriously undermined. But in 1885, reversing previous trends, and contrary to some recent comment on the matter,[156] they regained much of the ground which they had lost in the parliamentary representation of the province, though under entirely new circumstances. The constitutional issue was now of surpassing impor-

154. W. J. Reynolds to James Dickson, 25 June 1886; Reynolds to secretary of National League, 2 July 1886; Reynolds to Father Montague, 2 July 1886; Reynolds to Rev. McAleavey, 9 July 1886 (P.R.O.N.I., Donnelly and Duffy papers, Out-letter book of W. J. Reynolds, 1885–6, D.1813/1/2).

155. P. J. O. McCann, "The Protestant home-rule movement, 1886–95" (M.A. thesis, U.C.D., 1972), p. 44.

156. Gibbon, *Ulster unionism*, pp. 143–6.

tance, and party organization on a broad social basis formed an essential part of electoral politics. To be sure, over the next few decades, owing partly to their social and economic decline, the gentry's role in Unionist politics would diminish,[157] but they retained an important place in local Unionist associations and among the parliamentary contingent until recently.

For much of the period before the cataclysmic events of 1885–6, a relaxation of denominational barriers took place among the rural electorate. By 1881 a substantial section of northern Protestants, mainly Presbyterian, were voting together with Catholics for Liberal candidates. The degree of this Presbyterian Liberal support ranged from about 50 to 70 percent of Presbyterian electors in Tyrone, Londonderry, Antrim, and Down, to about 23 percent in Monaghan and Donegal. The extent of this phenomenon varied from one constituency to another, depending on the relative strength of the denominations in the electorate. Political cooperation reached a climax in August 1881, after which it began to disintegrate. By 1885 it had almost entirely disappeared, though during the general election of that year a different type of mixed voting by Conservatives and Nationalists did occur for tactical reasons. In 1886, however, Protestants and Catholics were clearly divided into opposing political camps.

The nature of the electoral system strongly shaped these developments. The composition of the electorate, which vitally affected the outcome of elections, was the result of the combined effect of the franchise laws together with geographical differences in denominational distribution and disparities in the social position of the denominations. The ballot act gave rise to some changes in voting patterns, but it did not insure complete secrecy in voting because of the widespread adoption of the tally-card system. In any case, coercion was not a serious matter before 1872, and when tenants turned against landlords beginning in the early 1870s, it was primarily because of the new climate of political opinion. The corrupt-practices act of 1883, by limiting election expenditure, was a relevant factor in the emergence by 1885 of the new, voluntary-type political organizations with a broad social basis. To some extent, however, the political events of the 1870s had already caused a move in this direction, even among the Conservatives.

In all the political changes of this period the organizational structures of the parties were of considerable importance. The Liberals drew valuable assistance from the tenant-right movement before 1885, but their reliance on this source proved disadvantageous in the general election

---

157. See the names of Ulster M.P.s, 1886–1922, in Walker, *Election results.*

of that year. The Conservative apparatus which existed in 1868, with its heavy reliance on canvassing by landlords and their agents, was incapable of meeting the tenant-farmer challenge of the next thirteen years. But its subsequent renovation in 1885 and 1886 through the formation of broadly based local associations, backed by the Orange Order, turned out to be effective, indeed much more so than has been conceded by some recent commentators, who have tended to concentrate on the Conservatives' ramshackle organization in Fermanagh rather than on their well-oiled machinery in east Ulster.[158] This new Unionist structure, of course, repelled Catholics and many Liberal Protestants by its association with Orangeism. The Nationalists obtained assistance from the National League and were helped by the local Catholic clergy. These aids made possible their successes of 1885–6 but also restricted their appeal among Protestants.

Differences in the efficiency of party organizations undoubtedly influenced election results, but electoral issues were of greater importance. The growing urgency of the land question significantly affected the outlook and behavior of voters after 1868. In rural constituencies the agrarian issue caused the extensive interdenominational cooperation which boosted the fortunes of northern liberalism in 1874 and 1880. In the boroughs some Presbyterians and Catholics joined forces on certain issues, particularly disestablishment, bringing some Liberal gains in 1868, though this mixed voting declined thereafter in the absence of unifying issues.[159] The land question, however, was replaced in the mid-1880s by the constitutional issue as the matter of overriding importance in the minds of the country people of Ulster. The electorate now divided, with most Protestants of all social ranks in the countryside, both Liberals and Conservatives, coalescing in the unionist movement, and with most Catholics of all social ranks, both Liberals and Nationalists, gathering under the banner of home rule.

A final point worth considering is the extent to which the unionist movement which emerged in the years 1885–6 was influenced by the rise of nationalism. Though many features of the movement were already evident before 1885, the behavior of Nationalist leaders strongly shaped its particular form. This is especially true of the decision taken by Parnell, Dillon, and other Nationalists in 1885 to collude with the Conser-

158. See Savage, "Ulster Unionist party," pp. 185–6; Buckland (ed.), *Irish unionism*, pp. 99–100, 106–10.

159. During this period the Conservatives held all eleven Ulster borough seats, except for three in 1868 and one in 1874 and 1880, which went to the Liberals. Of the six new urban divisions created in 1885, Conservatives won five in that year and four in 1886; the remainder were taken by the Nationalists.

vatives in some constituencies and to have the Catholic vote in others
cast for the Tories and against the Liberals. This decision may have possessed short-term tactical or personal advantages for the Nationalist
leadership, but it shifted the balance in the pro-union movement at both
local and central levels away from Protestant Liberals, who had been
and were willing to cooperate politically with Catholics, to Conservatives who, backed by the Orange Order, were hardly prepared to do
so. The structure of power in the unionist movement which emerged
from the electoral turmoil of 1885–6 has been of lasting importance for
subsequent Ulster and Irish politics.

BIBLIOGRAPHY

Contemporary sources

Manuscript material
Public Record Office of Northern Ireland, Belfast
    Adair papers.
    Belmore papers.
    Carleton, Atkinson, and Sloan papers.
    Donnelly and Duffy papers.
    Downshire papers.
    Greer papers.
    Hertford papers.
    Montgomery papers.
    Moore papers.
    O'Hagan papers.
    O'Neill papers.
    Verner papers.
Collections in other depositories:
    Bryce papers: Bodleian Library, Oxford.
    Butt papers: National Library of Ireland, Dublin.
    Cairns papers: Public Record Office, Kew, Richmond, Surrey.
    Disraeli (Hughenden) papers: Hughenden Manor, Buckinghamshire.
    Gladstone papers: British Library, London.
    McCartan papers: Archives Department, University College, Dublin.
    Salisbury papers: Hatfield House, Hertfordshire.
    Chief Secretary's Office, Official papers, Notebook on election addresses, 1874:
        State Paper Office, Dublin.
    Chief Secretary's Office, Police and crime records, Irish National League pro-
        ceedings, 1883–90, R. E. Beckerson's reports on the progress of the Na-
        tional League, 1885: State Paper Office, Dublin.

Contemporary publications
  I. Newspapers
  Armagh Guardian.
  Belfast Morning News.
  Belfast Newsletter.
  Cavan Weekly News.
  Derry Journal.
  Freeman's Journal (Dublin).
  Impartial Reporter (Enniskillen).
  Londonderry Sentinel.
  Londonderry Standard.
  Nation (Dublin).
  Northern Standard (Monaghan).
  Northern Whig (Belfast).
  People's Advocate (Monaghan).
  Tyrone Constitution (Omagh).
  Tyrone Courier (Dungannon).
  Ulster Examiner (Belfast).
  United Ireland (Dublin).
  Weekly Examiner (Belfast).
  Weekly Freeman's Journal (Dublin).
  Weekly News (Dublin).
  Weekly Northern Whig (Belfast).
  Witness (Belfast).

  II. Parliamentary papers (in chronological order)
  Return of charges made to candidates at the late elections by returning offi-
      cers . . . ; also the total expenses of each candidate . . . , H.C. 1880
      (382-sess. 2), vii, 1.
  Copy of the shorthand writer's notes of the judgment and evidence on the
      trial of the Down county election petition, H.C. 1880 (260-sess. 2), lvii, 567.
  Report of her majesty's commissioners of inquiry into the working of the Land-
      lord and Tenant (Ireland) Act, 1870, and the acts amending the same, vol. ii:
      Digest of evidence; minutes of evidence, pt. i [C 2779-I], H.C. 1881, xviii, 73.
  Census of Ireland, 1881, pt. i: Area, houses, and population; also the ages,
      civil or conjugal condition, occupations, birthplaces, religion, and educa-
      tion of the people, vol. iii, province of Ulster [C 3204], H.C. 1882, lxxviii, 1.
  Return showing the religious denominations of the population, according to
      the census of 1881, in each constituency formed in Ulster by the redistribu-
      tion of seats act, 1885, H.C. 1884–5 (335), lxii, 339.

  III. Other contemporary publications
  Gwynn, Stephen. Experiences of a literary man (London, 1926).
  Healy, T. M. Letters and leaders of my day, 2 vols. (London, 1928).
  McElroy, S. C. The Route land crusade . . . (Coleraine, n.d.).
  MacKnight, Thomas. Ulster as it is, or twenty-eight years' experience as an
      Irish editor, 2 vols. (London, 1896).

Later works

Writings in Irish studies

Buckland, P. J. (ed.). *Irish unionism: a documentary history* (Belfast, 1973).

Cooke, A. B. (ed.). *The Ashbourne papers, 1869–1913* (Belfast, 1974).

Cooke, A. B. (ed.) "A Conservative party leader in Ulster: Sir Stafford Northcote's diary of a visit to the province in October 1883" in *Proceedings of the
Royal Irish Academy*, lxxv, sec. C, no. 4 (1975), pp. 61–84.

Donnelly, J. S., Jr. *The land and the people of nineteenth-century Cork: the
rural economy and the land question* (London and Boston, 1975).

Freeman, T. W. *Ireland: its physical, historical, social, and economic geography*
(London and New York, 1950).

Gibbon, Peter. *The origins of Ulster unionism: the formation of popular
Protestant politics and ideology in nineteenth-century Ireland* (Manchester,
1975).

Harbison, J. F. *The Ulster Unionist party, 1882–1973: its development and
organisation* (Belfast, 1973).

Johnston, J. D. R. "The Clogher valley as a social and economic region in the
eighteenth and nineteenth centuries" (M.Litt. thesis, University of Dublin,
1974).

Kennedy, B. A. "Sharman Crawford, 1780–1861" (Ph.D. dissertation, Queen's
University, Belfast, 1953).

Livingstone, Peadar. *The Fermanagh story: a documented history of the County
Fermanagh from the earliest times to the present day* (Enniskillen, 1969).

McCann, P. J. O. "The Protestant home-rule movement, 1886–95" (M.A. thesis,
University College, Dublin, 1972).

McClelland, Aiken. "The later Orange Order" in T. D. Williams (ed.), *Secret
societies in Ireland* (Dublin and New York, 1973), pp. 126–37.

McCracken, J. L. "The consequences of the land war" in J. C. Beckett and T. W.
Moody (ed.), *Ulster since 1800: a political and economic survey* (London,
1955), pp. 60–9.

Magee, John. "The Monaghan election of 1883 and the 'invasion of Ulster'" in
Clogher Record, viii (1974), pp. 147–66.

O'Brien, C. C. "The Irish parliamentary party, 1880–90" (Ph.D. dissertation,
University of Dublin, 1954).

O'Brien, C. C. *Parnell and his party, 1880–90* (Oxford, 1957; corrected impression, 1964).

Robinson, Olive. "The economic significance of the London companies as
landlords in Ireland during the period 1800–70" (Ph.D. dissertation, Queen's
University, Belfast, 1957).

Savage, D. C. "The origins of the Ulster Unionist party, 1885–6" in *Irish Historical Studies*, xii, no. 47 (Mar. 1961), pp. 185–208.

Solow, B. L. *The land question and the Irish economy, 1870–1903* (Cambridge,
Mass., 1971).

Steele, E. D. *Irish land and British politics: tenant-right and nationality,
1865–1870* (Cambridge, 1974).

Thornley, David. "Isaac Butt and the creation of an Irish parliamentary party, 1868–74" (Ph.D. dissertation, University of Dublin, 1959).

Vaughan, W. E. "Landlord and tenant relations in Ireland between the famine and the land war, 1850–1878" in L. M. Cullen and T. C. Smout (ed.), *Comparative aspects of Scottish and Irish economic and social history, 1600–1900* (Edinburgh, 1977), pp. 216–26.

Walker, B. M. "The Irish electorate, 1868–1915" in *Irish Historical Studies*, xviii, no. 71 (Mar. 1973), pp. 359–406.

Walker, B. M. (ed.). *Parliamentary election results in Ireland, 1801–1922* (Dublin, 1978).

Walker, B. M. "Party organisation in Ulster, 1865–92: registration agents and their activities" in Peter Roebuck (ed.), *Plantation to partition: essays in Ulster history in honour of J. L. McCracken* (Belfast, 1981), pp. 191–209.

III

CHANGING LINES OF CLEAVAGE AND COHESION

Introduction

In the same decade that the landed elite regained political hegemony in the Protestant-dominated areas of Ulster, resurgent nationalism and agrarian radicalism were fundamentally recasting the established political and social order in the remainder of the country. By 1886 the political power of the landlord class had been severely curtailed. In the general election of that year Nationalist candidates swept to victory in every parliamentary constituency outside Ulster, with the exception of the two seats assigned to the University of Dublin. Even in Ulster, Nationalists captured as many as sixteen seats, one short of a majority in that province.[1] Less successful was the assault on landlord power at the level of local government, but here too the ground gained was impressive, especially in Munster and Connacht. By 1886 effective control of half the poor-law boards in the country had passed into tenant hands.[2]

The landed elite, however, was still pugnacious and not without resources. Its political power at the parliamentary level was not simply a function of the number of Irish M.P.s prepared to protect its interests at Westminster. Many British M.P.s and the great bulk of the peers in the House of Lords could be trusted to take its side in a crisis. And in local government the landlord class still controlled half the poor-law

---

1. B. M. Walker (ed.), *Parliamentary election results in Ireland, 1801–1922* (Dublin, 1978), pp. 136–41.

2. W. L. Feingold, "The Irish boards of poor-law guardians, 1872–1886: a revolution in local government" (Ph.D. dissertation, University of Chicago, 1974), p. 219. See also idem, "The tenants' movement to capture the Irish poor-law boards, 1877–1886" in *Albion*, vii, no. 3 (Fall 1975), pp. 216–31.

boards and remained until 1898 thoroughly in command of the grand juries, which exercised wide fiscal and administrative as well as judicial responsibilities.

This picture of retreat without collapse also applies to the economic power of the landed elite during the 1880s and 1890s. The landlord class was compelled to endure substantial reductions in rental income as a consequence of a combination of agricultural depression, mass agrarian agitation, and the policy of rent control embodied in the land acts of 1881 and 1887. For that unfortunate minority of landowners who entered this period of crisis already saddled with unusually heavy debts, the loss of 20 to 30 percent of their customary revenues often forced them to sell all or part of their estates. Even for those proprietors whose incumbrances were less burdensome, retrenchment in expenditure became an absolute necessity.[3]

The impact of financial adversity, however, was not geographically uniform. On the whole, the landlords of Leinster and Ulster appear to have fared considerably better than those of Munster and Connacht; the difference mostly reflected marked regional variations in the intensity of the agrarian upheaval.[4] Moreover, the goal of peasant proprietorship, which the Land League had proclaimed as the solution to the land question in 1879, was still far from realization over twenty years later. As late as 1903, before passage of the important land-purchase act of that year, less than 15 percent of the tenant occupiers of agricultural land in Ireland had taken the steps necessary to convert themselves into owners of their holdings.[5] After 1885 or 1890 there was no doubt a certain inevitability about the transfer of ownership from landlord to tenant. Even British Conservatives were ready to facilitate the growth of peasant proprietorship.[6] To many politicians, and not just to Nationalists, the question was not whether the landlord class would be extinguished, but how soon and on what terms. Yet it has been forcefully argued that it was not the economic and political decline of the landed elite that undermined the will of its members to resist extinction, but

---

3. On the declining economic power of the landed elite, see J. E. Pomfret, *The struggle for land in Ireland, 1800–1923* (Princeton, 1930), pp. 196–202; B. L. Solow, *The land question and the Irish economy, 1870–1903* (Cambridge, Mass., 1971), pp. 168–84; L. P. Curtis, Jr., "Incumbered wealth: landed indebtedness in post-famine Ireland" in *A.H.R.*, lxxxv, no. 2 (Apr. 1980), pp. 332–67.

4. Curtis, "Incumbered wealth," p. 343.

5. J. S. Donnelly, Jr., *Landlord and tenant in nineteenth-century Ireland* (Dublin, 1973), pp. 94–5.

6. For the terms and results of Tory land-purchase legislation, see Pomfret, *Struggle for land*, pp. 220–314; Curtis, *Coercion & conciliation*, pp. 343–55.

rather their increasing cultural alienation produced in the decade or so before the first world war by the strident "Irish Ireland" movements of the time.[7] Still, the origins of this crisis of identity and confidence can be traced back at least to the 1880s.[8] And after all the appropriate qualifications have been made, there is ample reason to insist that a great turning point in modern Irish history was reached when the forces of political nationalism and agrarian radicalism coalesced in a new form beginning in 1879.[9]

The apparent suddenness of this conjuncture has impressed some scholars, while others, taking careful note of the political implications of broad economic and social developments in the postfamine period, have shown much less surprise. Certainly, the dominant patterns of Irish politics in the 1850s and much of the 1860s gave no hint of the great antilandlord mobilization that was to occur during the 1880s. As Theodore Hoppen has demonstrated, the landed elite made a substantial political comeback in parliamentary elections after 1850. Ground surrendered to the O'Connellite repeal movement in the 1840s was recovered. This political revival of the landlord class was in part simply a reflection of the disintegration of the repeal movement, its electoral machinery, and the strong ideological commitments it had evoked. In a real sense the Tenant League of the 1850s constituted an ideological alternative to the laissez-faire principles of the landed elite. The League challenged the idea that the relationship between landlord and tenant was a strictly private affair. But the social base of the League was confined to large farmers, and even that base quickly evaporated when agricultural prices rebounded after 1853.

In the absence of strong ideological attachments, public politics reverted to older patterns in which local issues and loyalties frequently determined electoral outcomes. This was most clearly visible in borough constituencies, but the counties manifested it as well.[10] The politics of localism was a game that the landlord class could play with skill and

7. L. P. Curtis, Jr., "The Anglo-Irish predicament" in *Twentieth Century Studies*, no. 4 (Nov. 1970), pp. 37–63.

8. J. S. Donnelly, Jr., *The land and the people of nineteenth-century Cork: the rural economy and the land question* (London and Boston, 1975), pp. 382–3.

9. The nature of this turning point has given rise to scholarly debate. See T. W. Moody, "The new departure in Irish politics, 1878–9" in H. A. Cronne, T. W. Moody, and D. B. Quinn (ed.), *Essays in British and Irish history in honour of James Eadie Todd* (London, 1949), pp. 303–33; T. N. Brown, *Irish-American nationalism, 1870–1890* (Philadelphia, 1966), pp. 85–98; T. W. Moody, "Irish-American nationalism" in *I.H.S.*, xv, no. 60 (Sept. 1967), pp. 438–45; Paul Bew, *Land and the national question in Ireland, 1858–82* (Dublin, 1978), pp. 46–73.

10. K. T. Hoppen, "National politics and local realities in mid-nineteenth-century Ire-

advantage. To espouse local causes which in no way threatened vital class interests was perfectly painless and might even be pleasurable. More important, the nonideological character of the game allowed proprietorial influence and the coercive resources of the landed elite to be used to maximum effect.

As several scholars have recently shown, however, there was in fact a distinct transition in the late 1860s and the 1870s from the politics of localism to the mass antilandlord mobilization of the 1880s. Its chief manifestations were the post-1867 Fenian movement and the farmers' clubs. In the period before the abortive rising of 1867, the Fenians drew their recruits in the main from shop clerks, urban artisans, and nonfarm laborers. Indeed, Fenian support was much stronger in the towns than in the countryside, though some farm servants, agricultural laborers, and cottiers did join the movement. Farmers, whether large or small, generally held aloof. Doctrinaire revolutionary republicans who were unwilling to soil their hands with agrarian issues before the armed overthrow of British rule left the great bulk of farmers quite cold. Large farmers in particular were socially repelled by a movement whose principal rural appeal was to groups they tended to despise. But British repression and the cause of the Fenian prisoners after 1867 reintroduced the ideological element into Irish politics. The demonstrations organized by the Fenian Amnesty Association in the late 1860s collectively attracted hundreds of thousands. This outpouring of patriotic sentiment was testimony not to the strength of republicanism, but to the power of a national issue, suitably presented, to evoke an enormous popular response. The remarkable by-election victory of the Fenian prisoner Jeremiah O'Donovan Rossa in County Tipperary in 1869 showed that many comfortable farmers admired the idealism and self-sacrifice of the Fenian cause, even if they considered it misguided.[11]

Still more significant was the election in 1874 of John O'Connor Power as M.P. for County Mayo. Though he stood not as a Fenian but rather as a Home Ruler, O'Connor Power was a member of the supreme council of the Irish Republican Brotherhood. How widely his Fenian connections were known to the voters is unclear. But some local Fenians promoted his candidacy, and his victory was another sign of the growth of nationalist sentiment among the rural electorate. O'Connor Power's triumph was significant for three reasons. First, it pointed toward the

land" in Art Cosgrove and Donal McCartney (ed.), *Studies in Irish history presented to R. Dudley Edwards* (Dublin, 1979), pp. 198–213.

11. Joseph Lee, *The modernisation of Irish society, 1848–1918* (Dublin, 1973), pp. 62, 118–20; Bew, *Land*, pp. 38–45; Hoppen, "National politics," pp. 214–23; Samuel Clark, *Social origins of the Irish land war* (Princeton, 1979), pp. 200–9.

emergence of a mass nationalist consciousness in Connacht, a region in which all previous nineteenth-century popular political movements had been notably weak. Second, it provided the occasion for the formation of a corps of leaders who would soon help to direct the agrarian and nationalist upheaval in Mayo and adjacent counties. And third, it was early evidence of the willingness of at least some Fenians to alter their tactics by engaging in constitutional politics and by giving uncharacteristic emphasis to the land question. When two years later the Ballinasloe Tenants' Defence Association was established, the chief organizer of the new body was Matthew Harris, a Fenian who had served as O'Connor Power's campaign manager in 1874.[12]

The Ballinasloe Tenants' Defence Association was a relative latecomer in the proliferation of farmers' clubs on the Irish political scene after 1868. The earliest of the new clubs had generally been formed in hopes of influencing land legislation sponsored by the Liberals under Gladstone. Profound dissatisfaction with the land act of 1870 primarily explains the spread of such organizations in the prosperous years before 1877. Although Ulster accounted for more tenants' defense associations, or farmers' clubs, than any other province, similar bodies were scattered across the rest of the country, including Connacht. On the whole, the membership of these organizations, like that of the defunct Tenant League, was drawn from the class of large farmers. Their major demands, now denominated as the three Fs, also closely resembled those of the Tenant League. In Ulster the main stress was on free sale, but elsewhere the principal emphasis was on fair rents, or the limitation of rents through arbitration. The relationship between the farmers' clubs and the home-rule movement was troubled throughout the 1870s because club members resented the tendency of the national question to overshadow agrarian issues. Nonetheless, these organizations repeatedly intervened in electoral politics on behalf of Home Rule candidates (or Liberal nominees, as in Ulster). Thus when the onset of a severe agricultural depression created the opportunity for mass political mobilization in the countryside at the end of the 1870s, a foundation for a new breakthrough had already been laid.[13]

The home-rule movement under the leadership of Isaac Butt was itself a clear indication of the increasing fluidity of Irish politics during the 1870s. By allowing disagreement on all subjects of political controversy except home rule, Butt hoped to reconcile Irish Protestants to conservative nationalism. (His federalist scheme called for a parliament with

12. Lee, *Modernisation*, pp. 67–9; Clark, *Social origins*, pp. 205–7.
13. Clark, *Social origins*, pp. 214–20; Hoppen, "National politics," pp. 220–1.

limited powers in Dublin and an imperial parliament at Westminster.) Though Butt's early efforts to gain Protestant support eventually foundered, he did win a wide measure of approval from Catholic tenant farmers and priests by endorsing land reform and denominational education. These issues along with that of home rule provided the material for a remarkable degree of success at by-elections in the early 1870s and at the general election of 1874. Nationalists claimed that in 1874 almost sixty Home Rulers had been returned. This figure has been shown to be misleading. Only about one-third of that number proved dependable followers of Butt in Parliament. Yet even if the conversion of many victorious candidates to home rule lacked sincerity, their positive declarations on the hustings showed that the electoral pressure for patriotic conformity was exceptionally strong. After the 1874 election Butt might have concentrated his energies on creating a political machine in the constituencies which would have enabled him to gather a larger band of resolute, disciplined adherents for the next Parliament. By choosing instead to labor (not even on a full-time basis) in the current House of Commons with an inadequate, halfhearted, undisciplined contingent, he and his cause rapidly lost credibility and popular influence in Ireland. By the end of 1877 Butt had ceased to be the undisputed leader of Irish constitutional nationalism. Yet in its prime his movement had demonstrated the existence of a vast reservoir of nationalist feeling which bolder, more radical politicians were soon to tap.[14]

The origins of the land war, however, are to be discovered not only in the political realm but also in the economic and social changes that had occurred during and since the great famine. Three developments deserve to be singled out. First, there was the extraordinary decline in the population. Between 1841 and 1851 it fell from 8.2 to 6.6 million, or by almost 20 percent; by 1881 it had dropped to 5.2 million, a further decrease of 21 percent. Starvation, disease, and emigration were responsible for the initial decline; continuing emigration and, in certain districts, lower fertility accounted for the fall thereafter. Regionally, the demographic contraction between 1841 and 1881 was greatest in Munster and Connacht, lower in Leinster, and least in Ulster. Second, partly because of population decline and partly in response to relative price movements, the uses to which the land was put shifted increasingly from tillage to pasture. Already by 1851 grassland and meadow comprised 68 percent of the land in use (probably a substantial increase since the early 1840s), and by 1876 the proportion had risen to 79 percent. Third, while rents and the cost of labor increased after 1850, both rose far less

14. McCaffrey, *Ir. federalism*; Thornley, *Isaac Butt*.

than the value of agricultural output. Hence the profits of farming grew dramatically. According to the calculations of one scholar, gross farming profits soared by as much as 77 percent between the early 1850s and the early 1870s.[15]

The social and ultimately the political consequences of these developments were far-reaching. The catastrophe of the famine and the flood of emigration brought about a transformation of the agrarian class structure. Laborers declined substantially, not only in absolute numbers but also (more significantly) as a proportion of the agricultural work force. Between 1841 and 1881 the laborers' share of the adult-male work force in agriculture is estimated to have fallen from 56 to 38 percent, while that of farmers rose from 28 to 40 percent. What these trends also meant, as in many other countries at this time, was that after the famine a greater proportion of all agricultural labor was performed by farmers' offspring; while laborers were declining, farmers' sons rose from an estimated 14 percent to 20 percent of the labor force. At the same time, farm workers who were not the offspring of farmers were becoming more dependent on money wages and may also have occupied less land than prefamine laborers.[16] Regionally, the shift in the rural class structure was most extensive in Connacht, where the laborers' share of the adult-male work force in agriculture plummeted from roughly three-fifths in 1841 to only about one-quarter by 1881.

As John Boyle shows in his contribution to this volume, the increasing scarcity of rural laborers led to improvement in their material welfare (especially higher wages and more regular employment), but it also contributed to their political weakness vis-à-vis farmers. The amelioration of the laborers' economic condition occurred slowly, particularly in Connacht and Donegal, where the opportunities for employment were so limited that seasonal migration to Britain long remained a grim necessity for thousands. The lag in improvement was especially pronounced in the matter of housing. Even after the passage of the laborers' act of 1883, which was supposed to provide agricultural workers with a decent

15. W. E. Vaughan and A. J. Fitzpatrick (ed.), *Irish historical statistics: population, 1821–1971* (Dublin, 1978), pp. 3, 15–16; Clark, *Social origins*, pp. 107–12; W. E. Vaughan, "An assessment of the economic performance of Irish landlords, 1851–81" in F. S. L. Lyons and R. A. J. Hawkins (ed.), *Ireland under the union: varieties of tension: essays in honour of T. W. Moody* (Oxford, 1980), p. 187.

16. Clark, *Social origins*, pp. 113–19. David Fitzpatrick has shown that after 1861 landholding by laborers increased, but the trend from 1841 to 1861 remains unclear. Different results are obtained depending on whether one uses the number of holdings as given in the 1841 census (Fitzpatrick) or as given in the poor-law return of 1844 (Clark). See David Fitzpatrick, "The disappearance of the Irish agricultural labourer, 1841–1912" in *Irish Economic and Social History*, vii (1980), pp. 76–7.

cottage and a little land, building proceeded at a snail's pace for fifteen years, owing largely to the monumental disinterest or active opposition of farmers. Meaningful progress did not take place until after 1898, when responsibility for the construction of cottages was transferred to the new rural-district councils and laborers received the right to vote for members of these bodies. Even then, the advance was modest and regionally unbalanced, Connacht and Ulster (each for different reasons) trailing far behind the other two provinces.

That laborers had grievances was clear. But by comparison with the prefamine period, when violent conflict between laborers and large farmers was commonplace in numerous districts, the three decades after the famine saw a great diminution in this type of class warfare. Boyle examines the breaking of farm machinery by harvest workers in certain southeastern counties in 1858, and laborers were presumably involved in the destruction of graziers' property in Mayo and Galway in the years 1879–80. Though such outbreaks were exceptional, relations between laborers and substantial farmers were still acrimonious. After 1870 class consciousness among laborers provided a plausible basis for a whole series of efforts (mostly local but sometimes more ambitious) to organize rural workers into unions. Boyle's survey of these activities indicates that while important local gains could occasionally be realized, the unions tended to be small, ineffective, and ephemeral.

The role of laborers in the land war of 1879–82 furnishes additional evidence of their general inability to exploit what limited political leverage they possessed. The Land League frequently needed the support of farm workers in order to make its policy of boycotting effective against landlords and land grabbers. And as Boyle demonstrates, laborers generally cooperated with the League in its use of this weapon. Yet as Boyle also shows, concrete reciprocation by the League was less than generous. At the local level the farmers who dominated League branches were long on words about the plight of agricultural laborers but short on remedial action. And the national leaders of the movement, with a few honorable exceptions, were not much more energetic. Inevitably, many farm workers became apathetic toward the League. Politically, laborers were the least influential part of the Land League coalition.

Even without the full participation of farm workers, the Land League and the National League were able to wage a highly effective agrarian and political campaign chiefly because they drew so many large farmers, small tenants, and middle-class townsmen into the coalition against the landed elite. Though it would surely be erroneous to claim that anything like a perfect identity of interests had come to prevail among the elements of this coalition by the late 1870s, the degree to which their

concerns harmonized had increased greatly since 1850. Of major importance in unifying the interests of large and small farmers were certain
features of the gradual reform of estate administration before, during,
and after the famine — reform facilitated by demographic changes and
the shift toward pasture. Middlemen were largely eliminated and the
practice of subletting was severely curtailed. Consequently, an ever-
increasing proportion of landholders became direct tenants of the proprietor. A sizable majority had acquired this status by the late 1870s.
No longer did the issue of rent sharply divide different categories of tenants, as it had persistently done in the late eighteenth and early nineteenth centuries; now it united tenants against landowners. Another
harmonizing influence, up to a point, was the common involvement of
large and small farmers in pastoral agriculture. Prior to the famine large
farmers had been clearly differentiated from small ones by the strong
orientation of the latter toward tillage. But after 1850 small farmers,
even those in the west, became more fully integrated into the expanding
and lucrative livestock economy.[17]

The increased wealth of country people was reflected in the growing
prosperity of those town dwellers who served rural needs, especially
shopkeepers, publicans, provision merchants, and other traders. As a
proportion of the total population, these urban groups increased in size,
and in a variety of ways their links with the countryside were strengthened. Between 1850 and 1880 the commercial ties in particular became
much tighter, as rural dwellers marketed more of what they produced,
and as they purchased a great deal more of what they consumed. These
commercial links were often reinforced by kinship bonds between farm
families and the small businessmen of the towns, and by the special role
of certain townsmen in purveying political information to the countryside. Thus when the agricultural depression struck in the late 1870s, many
small businessmen perceived their own interests as closely corresponding
to those of their rural customers. Reductions in rents such as the Land
League demanded would not only bolster the falling incomes of tenant
farmers but would also shore up the sagging fortunes of shopkeepers,
publicans, and other traders.[18]

Yet if the new challenging collectivity embraced townsmen as well
as large and small farmers, it cannot be assumed that support for the
Land League was universal within these social groups, not even in the
west or the south. As William Feingold shows in his analysis of the poor-
law election of 1881 at Tralee, Co. Kerry, less than 60 percent of the

17. Clark, *Social origins*, pp. 108–13, 119–20.
18. Ibid., pp. 122–38.

shopkeepers who voted were willing to back the local Land Leaguers seeking to capture control of the board of guardians. And the same was true of the farmers who participated in this hotly contested election. Slightly more than 40 percent of them either voted for the Conservative nominees or split their ballots evenly between the two sides, thereby indicating a neutral stance. To determine whether relative wealth influenced the way in which farmers and shopkeepers behaved in this election, Feingold used the valuation records to classify both groups of voters into three economic categories. Among the shopkeepers no meaningful differences in voting preferences could be discerned, but among the farmers some striking variations emerged. The largest farmers registered exceptionally strong support for the League, and a clear majority of the small farmers were also of the same mind. But only about two-fifths of the middling group backed the Land League candidates. Unfortunately, the size of the sample in each of the subgroups of farmers is too small to permit firm conclusions to be drawn about the relationship between wealth and support for the League.

The class alliances on which the Land League was built — between large and small farmers, and between farmers and urban traders — did not endure after 1890. Divergent economic interests led to a breakdown of the temporary coalition of the late 1870s and early 1880s. In the case of the traders and farmers, as Líam Kennedy shows in his contribution to this volume, it was the movement for agricultural cooperation that pitted the two groups against one another. Traders generally saw the cooperative movement as a serious menace to their interests. It is easy to appreciate why butter merchants should have been gravely alarmed by the growth of cooperative creameries, since the new methods of production and marketing constituted superior alternatives to the traditional ways of doing business. It is also easy to understand why shopkeepers and other traders might have taken umbrage at the establishment of cooperative credit institutions, since such societies provided credit on terms better than those offered by numerous traders.

But what caused the greatest anxiety among the small businessmen of the towns was the possibility that the cooperative movement would venture into the field of retailing, as had happened on an extensive scale in Britain. Even though the leaders of the Irish cooperative movement soon abandoned their ambition to promote cooperative retailing because of the fierce opposition it aroused, they were unable to allay the fears of traders that this self-denying ordinance would be only temporary. As a result, the battle lines drawn between cooperators and traders in the early 1890s long persisted as significant political divisions. The fact that the leaders of the cooperative movement, especially in its early days, were often closely associated with the ascendancy class and the unionist political position allowed their opponents to portray their activities as antinationalist. But the conflict was essentially one between two groups of nationalists.

Kennedy's analysis of this conflict leads him into a general consideration of the relative strength of traders and farmers in the Irish political system during the late nineteenth and early twentieth centuries. Other scholars have already pointed to the importance of traders in the nationalist seizure of control of the poor-law boards, especially in the northwest, and to their prominence in the Land League's campaign, particularly in Connacht.[19] Kennedy broadens this perspective by showing that, relative to their share of the population, traders were overrepresented in an array of political organizations: the Irish parliamentary party and especially its local apparatus, the elected membership of the Council of Agriculture, the county committees of agriculture, and the county councils. Farmers, on the other hand, tended to be underrepresented in all these bodies, and small farmers markedly so. This pattern, well established before independence, was to persist after it. In seeking to explain why traders possessed disproportionate political power, Kennedy rejects as simplistic the theory of debt bondage. Instead, he offers a sociological explanation which stresses the strategic position of traders at the interface between town and country, and their heightened consciousness of the political opportunities conferred by this positioning.

Farmers, by contrast, besides suffering from locational and occupational disadvantages which restricted their ability to become political actors in formal and routinized settings, were also a much less coherent social group. As long as the landed elite conveniently provided a compelling focus for opposition on both economic and political grounds, farmers of different socioeconomic status could more easily preserve a united front against the common landlord enemy. But once this foe had been defeated or at least thrown onto the defensive, the divergent economic interests of certain categories of farmers were likely to find independent political expression. In fact, the character of the agrarian reforms of the late nineteenth and early twentieth centuries brought into bold relief the enduring conflict between wealthy graziers and poor peasants.

This conflict was concentrated in Connacht, north and east Leinster, and north Munster, that is, in those regions where cattle and sheep ranches had become a prominent feature of the rural landscape. Although the

19. Samuel Clark, "The social composition of the Land League" in *I.H.S.*, xvii, no. 68 (Sept. 1971), pp. 447–69; Feingold, "Boards of guardians," pp. 82, 267.

geography of the problem had shifted somewhat since the 1840s, its essence had remained unchanged. A relatively small group of individuals — the graziers — possessed vast quantities of land, while a great number of other people had very small amounts of land (or, as with many laborers, none at all). This gross inequality had long been a powder keg, and one of the most surprising nonevents of the land war of 1879–82 was that it did not explode at that time. Popular hopes of breaking up the ranches did help to stimulate Land League mobilization in Connacht in late 1879 and early 1880.[20] But it seems that the political weight of large farmers, graziers, and traders (many of them doubling as graziers) in the Land League coalition prevented the issue of land redistribution from finding a place in the League's program. Whether the peasants of the west and certain other districts outside Connacht viewed rent control and peasant proprietorship as anything more than palliatives is doubtful, but the palliatives helped to reduce the pressure for breaking up the ranches during the 1880s and early 1890s.

The expansion of ranch farming, its economic characteristics, and the belated rise of organized, systematic opposition to it are central concerns of David Jones's essay in this section. The association between the growth of ranching and the mass evictions of the late 1840s and early 1850s has long been recognized; Jones documents the strength of this correlation through an analysis of the geographical incidence of evictions. What is much less well known is the variety of ways in which the amount of untenanted land (i.e., nonresidential holdings let for less than a year) increased significantly after the 1850s. Particularly important was the forfeiture of large farms by tenant graziers or the nonrenewal of their leases during the 1880s and 1890s. As Jones points out, proprietors had a strong incentive to expand the amount of untenanted land because it was exempt from the provisions of the agrarian legislation of 1881 and 1887; hence the rent of such land was determined by open competition rather than by the land courts. By letting tracts of pasture to graziers for eleven months, landowners were partly able to offset the financial losses arising from agrarian reform.

Ranchers had perforce to accept the eleven-month system, since alternative supplies of pasture were contracting. The prohibition of free sale by many branches of the National League after 1885 and the improving prospects for owner-occupancy after 1890 meant that the number of holdings voluntarily surrendered by tenants declined. Graziers made a virtue of necessity by dominating the annual auctions of eleven-month land through their vastly superior financial resources. Initially, graziers

20. Bew, *Land*, p. 88.

had supported moderate agrarian reform, and the principle of free sale most of all, because sales of tenant interest enabled them to acquire additional grassland. But if reform were pushed beyond the three Fs, the ranchers were certain to become losers. Consequently, Jones argues, they tended after the early 1880s to see their interests as coinciding with those of the landed elite, with whom they increasingly identified both politically and socially.

This shift in the orientation of the graziers was not lost on the peasantry, but it was the land-acquisitive character of the ranchers, living often in the midst of land-starved smallholders, that constituted the primary motor of collective action against them. Twice within roughly a decade — between 1898 and 1902, and again from 1906 to 1908 — the peasants pushed the issue of land redistribution into the forefront of politics under the aegis of the United Irish League, which after 1900 was the premier nationalist organization. On neither occasion, however, did the small farmers and their allies achieve a decisive political breakthrough. On the first occasion the leaders of the League became preoccupied with gaining a comprehensive measure of tenant land purchase that would be compulsory for Irish landlords. On the second occasion, during the so-called ranch war of 1906–8, as Jones points out, the League faced serious objections within its own ranks to the dominant strategy of agitation (cattle driving) and allowed itself to be diverted by other issues. Not enough is yet known about the internal dynamics of the United Irish League at either the national or the local level.[21] But it may be provisionally suggested that the balance of political forces, already weighted against the radical ambitions of the western smallholders in the days of the Land League, had become even more antithetical to their claims in the years since then. The fate of similar movements of smallholders in 1918 and 1920, largely at the hands of revolutionary nationalist leaders, seems to support this hypothesis.[22]

21. See, however, F. S. L. Lyons, *John Dillon: a biography* (London, 1968), pp. 181–4, 201–2, 210–11, 222–7; D. W. Miller, *Church, state, and nation in Ireland, 1898–1921* (Dublin and Pittsburgh, 1973), pp. 17–27, 214–17.

22. Dorothy Macardle, *The Irish republic* (Corgi ed., London, 1968), pp. 224–5, 322–4; Erhard Rumpf and A. C. Hepburn, *Nationalism and socialism in twentieth-century Ireland* (New York, 1977), pp. 21, 53, 55; David Fitzpatrick, *Politics and Irish life, 1913–1921: provincial experience of war and revolution* (Dublin, 1977), pp. 156–7, 174–84, 267–8.

7 *William L. Feingold*

Land League Power:
The Tralee Poor-Law Election of 1881

I

Historians are familiar with the Land League agitation of 1879–82 as
one of the major landmarks in modern agrarian protest, a movement
which not only figured prominently in Irish history but was also one
of the most effective of its kind in nineteenth-century Europe. Consequently, considerable scholarly attention has been devoted to studies of
the League, and much more is known about it today than was known
even a decade ago. One area of inquiry, however, has received much
less attention than it deserves: the actions and attitudes of those people
at the grass roots who made the League a mass movement.

Earlier treatments of the League emphasized the more prominent
figures who formed the national leadership of the movement. Charles
Stewart Parnell, Michael Davitt, John Dillon, and the others who
walked the halls of Parliament or toured the countryside as agitators
tended to monopolize the limelight, leaving the impression that the
masses below them were mere passive players responding to the actions
and ideas of those at the top. This impression was of course only partly
true. In recent years, thanks largely to the efforts of social and economic
historians who have studied the objective forces behind the agitation,
the tenant masses have come into focus as an important force in their
own right. Studies of rents, price movements, and social conditions before and during the agitation have suggested that the principal impulse

The collection of data for portions of this essay was made possible by a grant-in-aid
from the American Council of Learned Societies, to which I wish to express my gratitude.

came from the tenants themselves, whose enhanced standard of living in the decades prior to the economic depression of the late 1870s had raised their expectations of improvement.[1] But while such studies have supplied a valuable corrective to the former overemphasis on prominent leaders, they still do not deal sufficiently with the people who actually participated in the movement at the base—those who joined or supported the local branches of the League, or who, for various reasons, refused to give their allegiance.

Historians of the League are thus left with numerous unanswered questions. How influential was the Land League among the people it purported to represent? From which social groups did it draw its main support, and which groups shunned it? Who were its local leaders, what were their aims, and what did they contribute to the agitation? Did their goals coincide with the objectives of those at the top? And were there significant regional variations in any or all of the above? Answers to such questions as these would obviously enhance our understanding of the Land League as a mass movement. But they can only come through concentrated inquiry into the local and regional aspects of Irish politics during the period. This essay is offered as a contribution in that direction.

Among the thousands of obscure local actions which contributed to the effectiveness of the Land League, one event in County Kerry offers an excellent basis for scrutinizing the Land League's impact at the grass roots. This event was a poor-law election held in the town of Tralee in March 1881, when the movement throughout the country was at a high-water mark. In that contest the local branch of the Land League nominated a list of candidates for election to the board of guardians against another list supported by the landowners of the district. The League's objective was to win a majority of seats at the board and to take over its executive offices, thereby gaining control of the body. The contest in Tralee was not an isolated event; it formed part of a systematic campaign by the Land League to seize control of poor-law boards throughout the country. The movement to capture the boards was publicly endorsed by the national leadership, including Parnell, and was widely reported in the national press. From all indications, however, it was in Tralee that the response was greatest and the electoral result most impressive. The proceedings in Tralee therefore provide an absorbing illustration of Land League influence in a local community. A brief digression for some essential background will set the scene for an examination of that contest.

---

1. See, e.g., J. S. Donnelly, Jr., *The land and the people of nineteenth-century Cork: the rural economy and the land question* (London and Boston, 1975), pp. 251-2; Joseph Lee, *The modernisation of Irish society, 1848-1918* (Dublin, 1973), pp. 80-4.

II

When the Land League emerged in 1879, the boards of guardians had been in operation for about four decades. They had been founded in 1838 as part of the administrative machinery designed to implement the well-known Irish poor law of that year. Under the provisions of this legislation Ireland was divided into 130 new territorial units known as poor-law unions, each having a workhouse for the maintenance of paupers and a board of guardians with power to levy and expend the tax known as the poor rate.[2] In a reorganization of the system in 1847 the number of unions was increased to 163, at which it remained until after the Land League agitation. The system was completed in the early 1840s, just in time to undergo an initiation by fire in the great famine. During and immediately after the famine the boards developed into an important administrative network, to which Parliament assigned numerous new functions in areas related to poor relief, public health, the care of orphans, voter registration, and emigration.[3] By the 1870s the annual budget of the poor-law administration surpassed those of the two other major elements of local government, the county and municipal authorities, and the guardians had a considerable amount of patronage at their disposal. By the local-government act of 1872 the poor-law commission, which had been the original supervisory body, was converted into the local-government board. The new board retained direct control over poor-law administration and was given additional powers, largely aimed at coordination, over all other local authorities as well.[4]

The composition of the boards of guardians is of primary interest, mainly because it explains why they were so enmeshed in the politics of the period. Constitutionally, they could be termed quasi-representative, since they included both elected and appointed members. On each board there were a number of seats (about twenty per board on the average) whose holders were chosen in annual elections by the ratepayers of the union. Since the owner and the occupant of a landholding each contributed to the poor rates in equal amounts, both were entitled to vote in elections. Occupiers of holdings valued at less than £4, however, were exempted from the tax and consequently excluded from the voting. Thus the franchise, which was exercised by more than a half-million voters

---

2. The best source for information about the origins and early operation of the poor-law administration is Sir George Nicholls, *A history of the Irish poor law in connexion with the condition of the people* (London, 1856).

3. Richard O'Shaughnessy, "Local government and taxation in Ireland" in J. W. Probyn (ed.), *Local government and taxation in the United Kingdom* (London, 1882), pp. 328–31.

4. For the growth of the fiscal and administrative functions of the poor-law administration, see McDowell, *Ir. administration*, pp. 181–8.

nationally, extended to all landowners and all occupiers of holdings valued at £4 or more. Guardians had to meet a property qualification that was somewhat higher and differed from union to union, but it was set low enough to insure the representative character of the elected membership (as low as £6 in some poorer unions of the west). A multiple-vote system was used in which owners or occupiers of larger holdings were entitled to additional votes (up to six for a tenement valued at £200 or more). Though there was no limit to the number of votes that an occupier could accumulate for different holdings, landowners were restricted to a maximum of eighteen votes in any poor-law union.[5] The appointed element, known colloquially as ex-officios, consisted of justices of the peace, equal in number to the elected guardians but holding seats permanently in their official capacity. The law stipulated that they should be residents of the union, and that they should be drawn from the local magistracy in descending order of the amounts which they paid in poor rates.[6]

The existence of these different types of members made for a potentially explosive social admixture at the boards. The elected guardians, chosen by an electorate in which the votes of landholders far outweighed those of landowners, were almost always members of the rent-paying classes. The ex-officios, on the other hand, were invariably landowners, partly because most justices of the peace were landowners, but mainly because those who paid the highest rates were inevitably landlords with large estates and pedigrees which placed them among the gentry.[7] The constitutional arrangements, in short, brought together as poor-law guardians representatives of both landlords and tenants, the two classes which, in nineteenth-century Ireland, stood opposed on practically every substantial issue of the day.

The fact that the two elements were equal in number should have insured an equilibrium between them in the distribution of power. Indeed, such an equilibrium had been intended by the framers of the poor law.[8] But the intention did not accord with current political realities, which dictated that in public affairs the landlords, not the tenants, should have the prevailing voice. Consequently, for the first forty years the

5. An excellent brief description of the functions and constitutional structure of the various local-government authorities at the time of the Land League may be found in W. F. Bailey, *Local and centralised government in Ireland* (London, 1888). The boards of guardians are treated on pp. 18–30.

6. Ibid., pp. 29–30.

7. The social character of board members is treated in W. L. Feingold, "The Irish boards of poor-law guardians, 1872–1886: a revolution in local government" (Ph.D. dissertation, University of Chicago, 1974), especially chapters 1 and 6.

8. Nicholls, *Irish poor law*, p. 208.

elected guardians generally deferred to the ex-officios in all matters. The strength of the landlords' influence can be judged from the extent to which they monopolized the board offices. Three officers were elected annually by the whole board: a chairman, vice-chairman, and deputy vice-chairman, the two latter being alternate chairmen who presided in the event of the absence of the other officers. As late as 1877 no less than 99 percent of the 163 chairmen in Ireland were ex-officios, while 93 percent and 69 percent of the two lower offices respectively were also held by nonelected members.[9]

Deference, however, is only part of the explanation for the monopoly. The landlords were too intelligent to trust their fortunes to this factor alone. To fortify their position, they took pains to see that the elected membership was composed of men favorable to a continuance of their power. Many of those who sat as elected guardians were land agents, bailiffs, or other functionaries whose principal purpose in becoming guardians was to uphold the interests of their landlord patrons. The leading landowners in every poor-law union inserted such men among the elected membership, and these clients gave them a numerical as well as a deferential mandate.[10]

The presence of clients on the boards reveals still another of the landlords' powers—their ability to control elections. The manner in which poor-law elections were conducted offered large scope for direct or indirect intimidation of voters. They were conducted by a system of "open voting-papers" brought to the homes of electors. The voter indicated his choice of candidates on the voting paper, signed it, and returned it to the clerk of the union. The process usually took several days, and in the interim there were many opportunities for interested parties, including landlords and their agents, to see how people had voted. Intimidation could of course be applied from either side. But before the advent of the Land League and its use of the boycott, the landlords, through their control over the disposal of land, had the power to do the greater damage; and when they made their wishes known to the tenantry in poor-law elections, as they often did, the tenants usually complied. A poor-law election was not sufficiently important to risk the loss of one's farm or shop, or the right to cut turf on the landlord's estate, even if such implied penalties were rarely carried out.[11] These were the chief factors underlying the landlords' supremacy at the boards. It was

9. See W. L. Feingold, "The tenants' movement to capture the Irish poor-law boards, 1877–1886" in *Albion*, vii, no. 3 (Fall 1975), p. 224.

10. Feingold, "Boards of guardians," pp. 50–2.

11. Ibid., pp. 59–60.

this supremacy which the Land League challenged and in most places destroyed.[12]

The challenge actually began a few years earlier, in the 1870s, when elected guardians connected with tenant-right and home-rule organizations in some parts of the country decided to publicize their causes by introducing political resolutions at board meetings. Ex-officio chairmen who tried to block such motions often found themselves confronted by procedural obstruction and by demands from the militant guardians for a greater voice in the proceedings of the board. Sometimes the tenants demanded the right to share in the board offices, and in rare cases that right was conceded to them in the lower offices, but never in the chairmanship. The demands, however, became more widespread and more forceful over time, so that by the end of the decade the question of the ex-officios' control had become a significant issue in localities where tenants' organizations were active.

With the emergence of the Land League in 1879 the issue rapidly assumed national proportions. The tenants' opposition, which had previously been a halfhearted challenge, now escalated to a full-scale confrontation. Each year from 1880 to 1882, when the poor-law elections occurred in March, Land League branches in widening circles of poor-law unions offered candidates to oppose the ex-officios. Their first objective was to take control of the elected seats, for they could not hope to break the ex-officios' grip on the offices so long as these seats were monopolized by landlord partisans. Wherever the League was successful in winning a majority strong enough to overcome the combined force of ex-officios and their elected clients, they proceeded to seize the offices. The achievement of such majorities was simplified by a high rate of ex-officio absenteeism at most boards, resulting from the fact that many ex-officios were absentee landlords. The new officers were usually Land Leaguers, many of them presidents or secretaries of League branches.

The attack was most vigorous in those regions where the Land League was strongest — in the three provinces of the south where Catholics constituted a large majority of the population. The Land League was, after all, predominantly a movement of Catholic tenants. In these districts boards fell to the tenants in increasing numbers. From 7 to 10 percent of the offices changed hands annually between 1880 and 1882. After the Land League's demise the campaign was continued by its successor, the National League, so that by 1886, the last year of intensive activity in poor-law elections, the tenants controlled a majority of the chairman-

12. An account of the Land League's attack on the ex-officios is given in Feingold, "Tenants' movement."

ships, vice-chairmanships, and deputy vice-chairmanships in the three southern provinces. In Munster and Connacht, where tenant radicalism was most prevalent, the monopoly of power which the landlords had previously exercised was transferred almost entirely into the tenants' hands. Ulster, the center of Protestant power, witnessed little change.

III

This brief recounting of the tenants' movement to seize control of the boards of guardians brings us to the poor-law elections of 1881 and to the contest in Tralee. The elections that year were exceptional because of the extraordinary amount of attention given to them by the central organization of the Land League. This was not the first time that Parnell or other national leaders had shown an interest in capturing control of local government. It was a pet project of Michael Davitt, one of the founders of the Land League and its chief moral force. Davitt had advocated a tenants' movement to secure the elected seats on poor-law boards and town councils in public addresses as early as 1878.[13] And a tentative plan for such a movement was incorporated in the famous "New Departure" scheme discussed by Davitt, Parnell, and the American Fenian John Devoy.[14] At a meeting of the central branch of the Land League in December 1880, just three months before the elections of 1881, Davitt bemoaned the appalling apathy of some Leaguers toward poor-law elections and stressed that the executive of the Land League was "desirous of having these positions contested throughout the country."[15] The interest is understandable, for the movement to capture the poor-law boards offered all of the major factions which constituted the Land League coalition something attractive. The defeat of the ex-officio party could easily be viewed by agrarian reformers as a blow struck against landlordism, and by Fenian nationalists as a victory over British authority in Ireland; the Parnellite nationalists, who sought home rule through constitutional means, could find much to praise in any campaign which developed the electoral consciousness of the masses and emphasized peaceful rather than violent forms of protest.

Furthermore, specific political conditions at the time of the elections seemed — to the Parnellites at any rate — to warrant closer attention than usual to the poor-law elections. The autumn of 1880 and the following winter were one of the most turbulent periods of the Land League agi-

13. Davitt, *Fall of feudalism*, p. 133.
14. John Devoy, *Recollections of an Irish rebel* (New York, 1929), p. 314.
15. *Irish Times* (hereafter cited as *I.T.*), 22 Dec. 1880.

tation, with acts of violence and evictions reaching high levels. In December the British government announced its intention to introduce a coercion act which would enable the authorities to imprison suspected agitators without trial. The measure was passed in March 1881, but even before then the League's leaders were thrown into turmoil over the question of how to respond to it. Those on the left wing favored a plan which included a rent strike and secession of the Irish party from Parliament — acts which, if carried out, were bound to generate even more violence in the countryside and the intervention of British troops. Parnell and his moderate followers viewed such proposals with disdain, but they knew that some show of defiance was needed if the League was not to disintegrate. It had to be an action which, while giving the impression of carrying the movement forward, would avoid further provocation. Parnell's announced solution, which he developed during a brief sojourn in Paris in February 1881, was a plan to "widen the agitation" to include the English masses.

Meanwhile, the impending poor-law elections, which some local nationalist newspapers had already begun to publicize, were brought to Parnell's attention, presenting him with a useful if temporary means of diverting attention from extremist proposals. In an open letter to the branches of the Land League, which appeared in the *Freeman's Journal* on 1 March 1881, he reminded Leaguers about the approaching elections: "It is of the highest importance that the people should be encouraged to wrest the local government of their country from the landlord classes. I trust, then, that the local branches of the League will everywhere see that all exertions are made to secure the return of Land League candidates as poor-law guardians, and to drive from office the agents, bailiffs, and landlord nominees who have hitherto been allowed to fill these important positions."[16] Two days later, John Dillon dispatched a circular letter to all branches instructing them to convene special meetings in order to make arrangements to nominate and secure the return of Leaguers as guardians.[17]

Parnell's letter and Dillon's circular struck a responsive chord in countryside and town. During the next three weeks the poor-law elections became the focus of attention, as Land League branches held special meetings and nominating conventions to choose their candidates and to plan the campaigns.[18] The local and national press on both sides of the political divide covered these proceedings as though the contests were

16. *F.J.*, 1 Mar. 1881.
17. *I.T.*, 3 Mar. 1881.
18. According to the *Nation* and certain provincial newspapers, nomination meetings were held in Mitchelstown and Cork city (Cork), Clonaslee (Queen's County), Tullamore

for parliamentary seats. Land Leaguers pursued the business, the *Irish Times* observed, "with quite as much energy as if they were repealing the union."[19]

In the elections themselves the Land League met with mixed results. The most spectacular victory was in the Tralee union, where the North Kerry Land League contested seventeen of the forty-one seats and won thirteen of the contests. There were other, less dramatic successes but many disappointments as well. Focusing on the latter, the Conservative *Irish Times* noted, "It is enough to say that the effort to carry in Mr. Parnell's nominees universally and with a marked superiority was not successful."[20] But the *Nation*, the chief organ of the League, in reviewing the results, highlighted the conspicuous victory in Tralee and congratulated the Irish people on their bold achievement. "In the south and west," the editor declared, "the L.L. candidates have been very successful — indeed, in Kerry the national organisation has swept everything before it, showing pretty plainly what Kerry would do in a parliamentary contest if only one arose."[21]

IV

The League's success in Tralee was the product of vigorous campaigning by its principal local organ, the North Kerry Land League. This branch owed its effectiveness to the organizational talent of Timothy Harrington, who eighteen months later would move to the center of Parnell's inner circle as one of the two secretaries of the National League. A former schoolteacher, who had left teaching in 1880 to become a publisher, Harrington had been a home-rule supporter in the 1870s. In the spring of 1880 he helped to set up the North Kerry branch of the League, assumed its presidency, and rapidly became one of the principal organizers in the southwest.[22] The *Kerry Sentinel*, which he founded with his brother Edward, was the voice of the Land League in the district.

Under Harrington's leadership the North Kerry Land League, with its headquarters in Tralee, had by 1881 extended its ambit northward in Kerry to the banks of the Shannon and southward to the borders of

(King's County), Manor Hamilton (Leitrim), Dromore (Tyrone), Drogheda (Louth), Tulsk, Knockcroghery, and Roscommon (Roscommon). The last-mentioned meeting was an open, popularly attended nominating convention.

19. *I.T.*, 3 Mar. 1881.
20. Ibid.
21. *Nation*, 2 Apr. 1881.
22. Paul Bew, *Land and the national question in Ireland, 1858–82* (Dublin, 1978), pp. 104, 124, 127.

the Killarney union — an area comprising roughly half of the county. The Tralee union, which occupied the central portion of Kerry, had long been a scene of popular protest. The town itself had been the headquarters of an active Fenian organization in the 1860s and of a tenant-right society in the 1870s. The county had been among the first to return a Home Ruler to Parliament and had warmly received Isaac Butt on his visits there. The spirit of the Kerry voters was always high during elections. As Samuel Hussey, the well-known land agent to Lord Kenmare, once observed wryly, "An election in most places is an occasion for breaking heads, abusing opponents, and other demonstrations of ardent philanthropy. Such opportunities are never lost on Kerrymen, whose wits are sharper and whose heads are harder than the average run of humanity."[23] The Kerry poor-law electorate, however, had never attempted to displace the ex-officio party, which had governed the boards of guardians in the county since their inception. Harrington's accomplishment in the election of 1881 was to convert this raw material into a constitutional weapon for the reform of the Tralee board.

Prior to 1881 there were only seven Land Leaguers among the forty-one elected members of the board. In November 1880 the League had lost the opportunity to augment its strength by one, when a vacancy occurred through the death of an old member. In the ensuing by-election the landlords' candidate was victorious in spite of the League's effort to place one of its own men in the seat. Intimidation may have contributed to the outcome. The landlords, according to one account, "went in a body and brought their tenants to vote against the popular candidate."[24] The incident was not forgotten by the Leaguers, who eagerly seized the next opportunity to oust their enemies. Their principal target in 1881 was the board chairman, Major William Rowan, an ex-officio who was faultless in his attendance at its meetings and who never allowed a political resolution to be introduced by its members. As the chief obstacle to the Leaguers' ambition to win control of the board, Rowan clearly had to be removed. But before he could be driven from the chair, the League needed greatly to expand its strength on the board so as to neutralize the large ex-officio force that was bound to turn out for the election of officers. This expansion Harrington set as his first objective.

Before the Land League could hope to make any substantial electoral gains, however, the threat of reprisals by landlords had somehow to be countered. This could be done in two ways: by building up the voters'

---

23. S. M. Hussey, *The reminiscences of an Irish land agent, being those of S. M. Hussey,* compiled by Home Gordon (London, 1904), p. 93.

24. *Kerry Sentinel* (hereafter cited as *K.S.*), 15 Mar. 1881.

confidence and instilling in them a readiness to set the landlords at defiance, and by threatening them with reprisals from the Land League's side. The usual form of popular reprisal was the boycott. Beyond that stood the possibility of violence against the offending person or his property, of which there were examples enough in every community, though League branches rarely condoned such activities openly. Given the fanaticism of some of their supporters, it was hardly necessary for local branches to spell out the possible consequences of unfriendly action. The specter of a boycott or a menacing visit from Captain Moonlight could be as intimidating as the landlord's threat of a notice to quit or his systematic denial of favors. Harrington's strategy called for the use of both methods.

During the two weeks before the election on 21 March, Harrington organized a series of demonstrations in different parts of the Tralee union. In his speeches he emphasized the need for tenants to stand fast against landlord intimidation. The landlords, he told one audience, had sent out "whips" to canvass for their candidates. But, he cried, "the people have at length learned to disregard such whips and such attempts at intimidation, and have determined to look after their own interests and the interests of their country in all future struggles."[25] At another meeting, repeating the imagery, he chided his listeners for their previous submission, declaring that the landlords' candidate for the division had been "so long playing the whip" on them that he believed they "would again be obedient to the lash." This feigned slur on his countrymen's courage brought cries of "No! No!" from the crowd.[26] Taunts and words of encouragement constituted the persuasive portion of Harrington's campaign.

The coercive portion involved the use of his newspaper in an unusual way for reporting the election. All poor-law unions were subdivided for electoral purposes into smaller components called electoral divisions. Each division sent one or more representatives to the board of guardians. There were eighteen such divisions in the Tralee union. In the 1881 election the most hotly contested division was the town of Tralee, where eight candidates contended for four seats. Four of the aspirants were Land League nominees; the other four were landlords' candidates. At a meeting of the North Kerry Land League during the week before the election, Harrington's chief aide John Kelly (who was an elected member of the Tralee board) secured the passage of a resolution that "any man who voted for candidates outside of those nominated by the League should be held up to opprobrium." The threat of reprisal was

25. Ibid.
26. Ibid.

clearly implied in the motion, and in order to give it added force Harrington published the resolution in the next edition of the *Sentinel*.[27] But he did not stop there. In the following edition, which appeared after the election had taken place, he published a list of all voters and how they had cast their ballots. The open voting-papers made such an action possible. There is no way of gauging the impact which publication of the poll made on the electors generally. But the next edition carried a letter from one alarmed voter begging in urgent tones to inform the *Sentinel* that it had misrecorded his votes, and that he had in fact cast all four of them for Land League candidates![28]

In the election two Land Leaguers and two Conservatives were returned for the Tralee division. This represented an increase of two seats for the League in the division, since all of the vacant seats had previously been held by Conservatives. In the other electoral divisions of the union the League secured eleven additional seats; after the election six more were gained by the apparent conversion of a number of guardians who had not run as Land League candidates. These additions raised the League's strength on the board to twenty-six elected guardians.[29] The League was now ready to confront Major Rowan in the officers' election at the first meeting of the new board.

It was to be, as the *Sentinel* described it, "the most exciting contest since the establishment of the workhouse." On 28 March, one hour before the meeting was scheduled to begin, Harrington and twenty-five Land League guardians met in caucus at O'Sullivan's Hotel to nominate three candidates to oppose Rowan and the two other ex-officios currently occupying the board offices. The general feeling of this caucus, the *Sentinel* reported afterward, was that Rowan should be opposed for the chairmanship by Patrick Kenny, a popular Land League guardian who had been a longtime spokesman for tenants' causes at the board. But Kenny was in prison, having been arrested only a few days earlier under the coercion act. The group decided that to nominate a "suspect" for chairman was unwise, since it would offer the ex-officios a pretext for

27. *K.S.*, 22 Mar. 1881.
28. *K.S.*, 1 Apr. 1881.
29. Reports in the *Sentinel* prior to the election estimated the number of Land Leaguers on the board at seven. Just after the election the *Nation* reported that the League had won thirteen new seats in the Tralee union. These additions brought the League's total to twenty. But at a party caucus following the election there were twenty-five League guardians present, and one other, who was absent because he had been arrested during the intervening week, should be counted. Hence there were six more League guardians at the time of the caucus than were numbered in the election reports. Unless these reports were erroneous, the six additional members converted to the League side after the election.

calling on the local-government board to invalidate the election. John Kelly was therefore selected to contest the chairmanship, Kenny the vice-chairmanship, and a third guardian who had also previously served on the board, the deputy vice-chairmanship.[30]

Full unity on the side of the Land League, however, was lacking at the board meeting. Major Rowan had been busy himself during the week gathering supporters for the contest. He was normally the only ex-officio who attended regularly, but for this particularly important meeting the erstwhile major had been able to marshal twenty-six justices. A head count of the two parties yielded twenty-six for the ex-officios and twenty-five for the Land League. Four other guardians who were present were so far uncommitted, and the future of the board seemed to hinge on their votes. The meeting opened and each side nominated its candidate for chairman. In the ensuing poll three of the Leaguers who had attended the caucus bolted, while three of the four uncommitted guardians voted for Kelly. The major thus won the election by a vote of twenty-nine to twenty-six.[31] The defectors had cost the League control of the executive!

A less accomplished politician than Harrington might have sought reprisals against the renegades. Indeed, at the meeting of the North Kerry branch immediately following the election, one member did propose that they be expelled from the League. But Harrington halted the action. He argued that "while it is the duty of every member to urge his brothers to work and keep up the rules," he disapproved of "the system of bringing forward charges against members at meetings of the League very often on slight pretext."[32] The pretext, of course, was not slight. But Harrington perhaps had in mind the impression that dictation might leave among people not yet fully committed to the League, and the recent poor-law election had shown clearly that there were numerous such people in the town. He might have calculated, moreover, that the League no longer needed the chairmanship, since it now possessed enough votes to control regular business meetings of the board. Major Rowan would never succeed in attracting ex-officios to regular meetings in numbers sufficient to overcome the new League majority.

Indeed, the major himself seems to have put that construction on the outcome. For at the next meeting of the board at which a Land League resolution was introduced, instead of refusing, as he had done in the

30. *K.S.*, 1 Apr. 1881. The account of the officers' election which follows appeared in the same edition.
31. The fourth uncommitted guardian abstained in the voting.
32. *K.S.*, 8 Apr. 1881.

past, to entertain the motion, Rowan offered to step down from the chair after the board's usual business was concluded so that the resolution could be passed with someone else in charge. The Leaguers refused to accept this conciliatory gesture on the grounds that they had every right to raise such questions as part of ordinary business.[33] Thus the struggle between Leaguers and landlords continued in Tralee until the elections of 1883, when the local branch of the National League finally won enough additional seats to evict the major from the chairmanship.[34]

V

It is normally difficult to make generalizations about voting behavior in poor-law elections. Though local newspapers often gave the names of candidates, their party affiliations, and the total number of votes they received, the press almost never reprinted the actual polls or analyzed their content. And none of the pollbooks themselves have been discovered. Consequently, there is no way to correlate the votes of individuals with social or occupational data.

The single known exception is the poll of the Tralee electoral division which Harrington published in the *Kerry Sentinel* in order to "inform the public who their friends and enemies" were. For a number of reasons historians could hardly have asked for a better record to have been preserved. The election took place in a predominantly urban electoral division rather than a rural one. Voters in rural divisions consisted almost entirely of farmers and landowners. Urban divisions such as Tralee incorporated both the town and a portion of the farmland surrounding it. This circumstance permits the historian to study a broader range of social groups, since the inhabitants of the division included people with town occupations as well as farmers and landowners. The town of Tralee was also distinctive in size—large enough to provide a suitable sample for analysis (there were 568 names in the *Sentinel* poll), yet small enough not to be divided into wards, as were such larger towns and cities as Limerick, Dublin, and Cork. In towns having wards, each ward sent one candidate to the board of guardians. In Tralee, where there were no wards, the four seats were contested at large, with each voter casting four votes instead of one. The electors could vote entirely for candidates of one party or the other, or could split their votes between the parties, thus providing the researcher with a measurable index of the strength of their commitment to either side. It is therefore fortunate that Har-

33. *K.S.*, 6 May 1881.
34. *K.S.*, 30 Mar. 1883.

rington chose to use this particular method of electoral intimidation, and the opportunity to take advantage of his inadvertent contribution to scholarly research ought not to be missed.

The 568 names in the *Sentinel* poll[35] represented all enfranchised persons in the division of Tralee, in the order that their names appeared in the pollbook and in the valuation records used to compile it. That is to say, they were listed in the order of their townland lot numbers or addresses. Next to each name on the list, four numbers between one and eight were assigned, each representing a different candidate for whom the elector voted. When an elector cast all four votes for the landlords' candidates (nos. 1–4), who for the sake of convenience are here called Conservatives, the *Sentinel* listing stated "four old" rather than the numbers of the candidates. When an elector voted for all four Leaguers (nos. 5–8), the listing stated "four new" rather than the numbers. The designations "old" and "new" were used because all the Conservatives were incumbents and all the Leaguers were insurgents. When an elector split his votes between the parties or voted for fewer than four candidates, the actual numbers of the candidates for whom he had voted were given. Finally, when an elector did not vote, the words "not vote" appeared, and when an elector committed a procedural error which caused his ballot to be invalidated, the word "informal" appeared. The election itself had been extremely close, with only 102 votes separating the most popular candidate (378 votes) from the least popular one (276 votes). Both were Land Leaguers. Two Conservatives and two Leaguers were elected.

For the analysis which follows, an attempt was made to discover, for each voter on the list, the principal occupation from which the voter derived his or her income, and the valuation of the land and building which he or she occupied or owned. A variety of sources were employed in combination.[36] By these means a usable sample of 413 voters was compiled. These individuals were then assigned to six occupational categories: (1) landowners; (2) professionals, that is, physicians, dentists, apothecaries, barristers, solicitors, teachers, journalists, and land or business agents;

35. *K.S.*, 29 Mar. 1881.

36. Landowners were identified through *Copy of a return of the names of proprietors and the area and valuation of all properties in the several counties in Ireland, held in fee or perpetuity, or on long leases at chief rents, prepared for the use of her majesty's government and printed by Alexander Thom, 87 and 88 Abbey-street, Dublin, by the direction of the Irish government and at the expense of the treasury*, H.C. 1876 (412), lxxx, 395. Occupations of nonlandowners were identified through *Slater's royal national commercial directory of Ireland* (Manchester, 1881), pp. 270–4. And the valuations of holdings were ascertained from the General Valuation Office, Dublin, Valuation records (1881), Tralee union, Tralee electoral division.

(3) clergymen; (4) manufacturers, including owners of goods produced by manufacturers outside the district, and builders; (5) tenant farmers; and (6) shopkeepers, including merchants, publicans, and operators of shops in the town.[37] There were few artisans and no laborers on the list, since members of these classes usually failed to meet the £4 property qualification required for the vote.

Table 7.1 shows the number and proportion of Tralee electors in each of the six occupational categories.

TABLE 7.1
Occupations of Eligible Voters in the Tralee Divisions[a]

Occupation	Number in sample	Percent of sample
Shopkeepers	236	57
Farmers	69	17
Landowners	48	12
Professionals	36	9
Manufacturers	16	4
Clergymen	8	2
TOTAL	413	

[a]There were 150 additional voters whose occupations were not identified.

It is safe to assume that the great majority of voters in this election were aware of the central issue at stake. Whatever the long-term goals or ideological positions of the candidates, the single issue on which the election was fought was whether the old guardians who favored control of the board by the ex-officio party should be retained, or whether they should be replaced by new guardians favoring control of the board by the Land League. It is therefore reasonable to conclude that persons who cast all four votes for Land League candidates were full supporters of the League, and that those who cast all four for Conservatives were

37. The shopkeeper category is an eclectic one, including retailers of all kinds, such as bakers, grocers, drapers, spirits merchants, butter merchants, and so forth; it also comprises publicans, innkeepers, and other persons who do not fit reasonably into any other category. A few artisans who were on the list were included in the shopkeeper category because they all had shops in the town. Persons who appeared in the sources as both farmers and members of a town occupation were counted in the town occupation, for it was thought best to consider as farmers only those voters who earned their livelihood almost entirely from agriculture. The classification system therefore contains a slight bias toward the town occupations, and within the town occupations, toward the shopkeeper class. But the number who appeared in two or more occupational categories was small and insufficient to distort the overall results of the survey.

full supporters of the ex-officio party. By the same logic those who cast three votes for Land Leaguers or three for Conservatives may be said to have demonstrated qualified support for that side, even if they cast their fourth vote for the other side or did not use it at all. Finally, those who divided their votes evenly between the two camps may be assumed to have been neutral in the contest, regardless of whether it was a consciously intended neutrality or the product of votes cast on the merits of the candidates. If one accepts these modest assumptions, it becomes possible to use the distribution of votes between parties as an index of a voter's commitment to the one party or the other, and to correlate the degree of commitment with the social data.

Table 7.2 summarizes the votes of the participating electors by occupation, with the electors placed in five voting categories. Category "0" contains those electors who cast no votes for Land League candidates. Category "1" signifies one vote for a Leaguer and the remainder for Conservatives; and so on down to category "4," which signifies four votes for Leaguers and none for Conservatives. Those who did not vote or whose ballots (in a few cases) were deemed informal, and those who cast only one or two votes were not included in the sample. Such votes were deemed insufficient to indicate either a party preference or neutrality. With these eliminated, the sample of participating voters was reduced to 319. Table 7.2 may be regarded as a statistical index of the party preference of the voters in different occupations. It shows the number and percentage of each occupational group who were committed fully to the landlords' party ("0"), partially to the landlords' party ("1"), were neutral ("2"), committed partially to the Land League ("3"), or fully to the Land League ("4").

TABLE 7.2
Distribution of Votes by Occupation

Voting category	Farmers No. %	Shopkeepers No. %	Manufacturers No. %	Clergy No. %	Professionals No. %	Landowners No. %	Total No. %
Conservative							
0	9 16	26 14	6 46	2 29	12 57	29 83	84 26
1	7 13	22 12	1 8	2 29	4 19	5 14	41 13
Neutral							
2	8 14	31 17	2 15	1 14	2 10	− −	44 14
League							
3	10 18	41 22	2 15	1 14	− −	1 3	55 17
4	22 39	67 36	2 15	1 14	3 14	− −	95 30
TOTAL	56	187	13	7	21	35	319

Participation in the election was high: fully 82 percent of enfranchised persons actually voted. This turnout contrasts sharply with that of pre-Land League elections, when few seats were contested and voter apathy was prevalent throughout Ireland.[38]

As table 7.2 indicates, the voters were strongly motivated by partisan considerations. If voters had been concerned primarily with the personal merits of the candidates, one would expect to find a fairly arbitrary distribution among the five categories (0–4). But that was clearly not the case. Only a small minority of voters took a neutral stance (14 percent), while roughly the same numbers were partially Conservative (13 percent) or partially supportive of the League (17 percent). A majority of voters gave full backing to one or the other party, with Conservatives securing all of the votes of 26 percent and the Leaguers receiving all of the votes of 30 percent. The pattern revealed in table 7.2 is that of an electorate whose members were divided by party into two camps of almost equal strength. Almost half of the electors fully or partially supported the Land League, and a slightly smaller proportion endorsed the Conservatives.

The voting preferences of some groups were predictable, and for them table 7.2 simply confirms expectations. One would expect landowners to vote for the Conservative candidates, and so they did. Fully 97 percent of the participating landowners voted in the two Conservative categories; 83 percent cast all four votes for Conservatives. The professional group might also be expected to have shown a preference for the ex-officio party, since their incomes and education placed most of them closer to the landed class than to the tenants. Again, this presumption is confirmed. Of the twenty-one professionals who participated, sixteen showed a preference for the Conservative side, twelve of them voting fully Conservative. Only three professional men, in fact, supported the League. One was Timothy Harrington, the second was his brother Edward, and the third was a solicitor who handled Land League litigation. Clearly, the League could not expect much endorsement from physicians, lawyers, or other professionals.

The manufacturers and clergy were small groups, composing together a mere 6 percent of the electorate. The seven clergymen in the sample represented only a fraction of the dozens of priests, nuns, and ministers in the union, most of whom lived and worked on church-owned land

38. In 1878 only 235 contests were held in the 3,044 electoral divisions, most of them in urban divisions. See *Report from the select committee on poor-law guardians, &c., together with the proceedings of the committee, minutes of evidence, and appendix*, p. 209, H.C. 1878 (297), xvii, 263.

and were therefore ineligible to vote. Even if these two groups had acted in unison, they could not have had much impact on the outcome. As it happened, their votes were dispersed, the participating manufacturers leaning slightly toward the Conservative side, and the clergy following the dictates of their religious backgrounds. The four on the Conservative side were all Church of Ireland ministers; and the two in the Land League camp were Catholic priests.

The groups mentioned thus far constituted only 24 percent of the electorate. The remaining 76 percent consisted of shopkeepers and tenant farmers. The commitment of these two classes to the Land League is less impressive than might be expected. A slim majority of the farmers (57 percent) and of the shopkeepers (58 percent) registered qualified or full support for the League. In both cases those who gave full backing outnumbered those who gave partial endorsement. At the other end of the spectrum, however, a considerable number of farmers and shopkeepers voted against the Land League candidates. Twenty-nine percent of the farmers and 26 percent of the shopkeepers were in the two Conservative categories, about half as many in each case as were in the Land League categories.

The figures in table 7.2 do not tell us anything about the kinds of farmers and shopkeepers who supported the League or opposed it. Did poorer farmers or shopkeepers vote any differently from prosperous ones? Did Catholics vote differently from Protestants? From which groups among the tenants and shopkeepers did the League and the landlords receive their principal support? To answer these questions it is necessary to focus on voting patterns within the farming and shopkeeping classes.

VI

Tables 7.3 and 7.4 contain the same analysis for shopkeepers and farmers as did table 7.2 for the entire electorate, except that the two classes are here subdivided according to the valuation of their holdings into "small," "middling," and "large" shopkeepers and farmers. Valuations are not an accurate index of the actual wealth or income of an occupier, but since they were used for purposes of taxation and were based on the estimated income which a holding produced in a year, the valuations are a satisfactory guide to relative wealth. The designations "small," "middling," and "large" were often used by contemporaries to describe their neighbors. I have attempted here to develop ranges of valuations for the subgroups which approximate contemporary definitions.[39]

39. The ranges of valuations for shops differ widely from those for farms. Hence, for

TABLE 7.3
Distribution of Shopkeepers' Votes by Valuation of Premises

Voting category	Small shopkeepers		Middling shopkeepers		Large shopkeepers		Total	
	No.	%	No.	%	No.	%	No.	%
Conservative								
0	11	*13*	10	*17*	5	*12*	26	*14*
1	10	*11*	8	*14*	4	*10*	22	*12*
Neutral								
2	15	*17*	9	*16*	7	*17*	31	*17*
League								
3	16	*18*	13	*22*	12	*29*	41	*22*
4	36	*41*	18	*31*	13	*32*	67	*36*
TOTAL	88		58		41		187	

In considering first the shopkeepers, it should be noted that about half were small shopkeepers, a third were of the middling kind, and slightly more than a fifth were large. All subgroups tended to exhibit the same general pattern of voting. A relatively small portion in each category (12–17 percent) cast all four votes for Conservatives, and still smaller sections (10–14 percent) cast three votes for Conservatives. Then the percentages rise in each category as one moves toward the Land League side, with 16 to 17 percent splitting their votes evenly, 18 to 29 percent casting three Land League votes, and 31 to 41 percent providing four Land League votes. All groups, in other words, were decidedly pro-Land League and antilandlord. If there are any surprises in these figures, they relate not so much to the nature of the political commitment as to the degree of allegiance. More than half (58 percent) of the voting shopkeepers were on the Land League side, as against slightly more than a quarter (26 percent) in the Conservative camp. The Land League enjoyed a majority, but it was perhaps not so large as the rhetoric of Land League leaders would suggest. When neutral votes are included, it is clear that almost half the Tralee shopkeepers were not ready to throw their weight behind the League.

Within the three subgroups of shopkeepers there were some differences in the degree of commitment to each party, though these were marginal. Between 53 percent and 61 percent of each group voted on the Land League side, with the large and the small shopkeepers registering slightly more support than the middling ones. The most zealous sup-

shopkeepers, small includes business premises valued at £4 to £9; middling, premises valued at £10 to £19; and large, premises valued at £20 or more. For farmers, small includes holdings valued at £4 to £19; middling, holdings valued at £20 to £49; and large, holdings valued at £50 or more.

TABLE 7.4
Distribution of Farmers' Votes by Valuation of Holding

Voting category	Small farmers		Middling farmers		Large farmers		Total	
	No.	%	No.	%	No.	%	No.	%
Conservative								
0	4	17	3	18	2	13	9	16
1	2	9	5	29	–	–	7	13
Neutral								
2	4	17	2	12	2	13	8	14
League								
3	5	22	1	6	4	25	10	18
4	8	35	6	35	8	50	22	39
TOTAL	23		17		16		56	

porters of the League were the small shopkeepers, of whom 41 percent gave all four of their votes to Leaguers, as against 31 or 32 percent for the two other subgroups. But these variations are inconclusive and do not establish any significant differences in the degree of support offered to the League by shopkeepers of varying size.

With regard to the farmers, attention must be called to the restricted size of the sample. It contained fifty-six voters, about 40 percent of whom were small holders, 30 percent middling, and 30 percent large. It is possible that this limited body of voters was not representative of farmers in the region as a whole. Generalizations based on their voting behavior must therefore be approached with caution. As a body, the farmers tended to distribute their votes like the shopkeepers. Fifty-seven percent gave full or qualified support to the Leaguers, and 29 percent gave full or qualified support to the Conservatives. These proportions varied from those of the shopkeepers hardly at all. But substantial differences appeared in the voting patterns of the three subgroups. A slight majority of the small farmers (57 percent) voted in the two categories on the Land League side. A strong majority of the large farmers (75 percent) cast their votes this way. But only a minority of the middling group (41 percent) voted on the Land League side, while a larger section of the middling group (47 percent) gave three or four votes to Conservatives. In other words, middling farmers appear to have been more conservative in their voting preferences than either small farmers, whose commitment to the League was similar to that of shopkeepers, or large farmers, whose allegiance was exceptionally strong.

This interesting contrast, particularly between middling and large farmers, might reflect an element of discord among farmers of varying wealth. But the sample is far too small to allow any such generalization without further investigation. The number of middling farmers who voted on the Conservative side was only eight, while the number of large farmers who voted on the Land League side was only twelve. There is always the possibility in such small groups that voting behavior was influenced by personal or other considerations not related to party. Recent research, however, has indicated a growing division of opinion between small and large farmers during the Land League years.[40] Moreover, this division broadened into an open schism during the later stages of the land war, when small farmers founded their own organization, the United Irish League.[41] Where did the middling farmers stand in this dispute? Were their loyalties divided between the two sides or did they constitute a coherent faction among the tenantry? Further research into the relationships among farming groups will be needed before firm conclusions about the meaning of these data can be drawn.

Religious issues did not enter into the election campaign in Tralee. Nevertheless, it is common knowledge that the Land League was predominantly a Catholic-based organization, and that Protestants often tended to shun or oppose it. Was this division reflected in the voting of the Tralee electors? With the assistance of Professor Maurice O'Connell, a Kerryman and historian who is familiar with the religious backgrounds of most families in the Tralee region, I was able to identify the probable religious affiliation of 120 Tralee voters. There were sixty shopkeepers and sixty farmers in the sample, all chosen at random. An analysis of the sample, which I have documented elsewhere,[42] showed that there were just eight Protestants among the sixty farmers, of whom only three supported the Conservatives. Three others did not vote, one was neutral, and one cast four votes for the Land League party. There were fourteen Protestant shopkeepers, of whom two were neutral, six did not vote, and six voted on the Land League side. Not one of the Protestant shopkeepers backed the Conservative party! Perhaps as Protestants, they considered themselves exceptionally vulnerable to boycott and did not want to tempt the fates any more than was necessary. Clearly, religious affiliation was not a factor in the Tralee election.

VII

For about one month during the agrarian agitation, the Leaguers in Tralee were absorbed in their exciting quest for control of the poor-law board. Does their brief experience shed any light on the nature of the

40. Bew, *Land*, especially chapters 5 and 8.
41. F. S. L. Lyons, *Ireland since the famine* (London, 1971), pp. 216–17.
42. Feingold, "Boards of guardians," pp. 170–1.

Land League or on other broad themes relating to the period? Though this local event may not reflect conditions elsewhere, a few aspects of that experience, together with other data discussed in this essay, lend themselves to generalization. The discovery that the middling farmers tended toward the Conservative side in their voting behavior, while large farmers overwhelmingly supported the Land League, could be peculiar to Tralee alone or to only a few communities in Ireland. On the other hand, the finding that little more than half of the participating shop-keepers and farmers supported the Land League party, and that the other half either opposed it or remained neutral or uncommitted, almost certainly has national implications. Great emphasis was placed on the poor-law elections by the League executive, and the Tralee contests were depicted by Nationalists themselves as the most extensive of the Land League incursions in 1881. The results therefore suggest that the League was not overwhelmingly effective in marshaling popular backing. The reasons for this relative lack of effectiveness deserve further exploration.

The study of the election campaign mounted by the North Kerry Land League also provides insights into the operations of local political and agrarian bodies. Though the activities of other branches may have differed from those of the North Kerry branch in points of detail, the Tralee experience undoubtedly incorporated many features common to most branches in the poor-law elections of 1880–6. It should be noted, first of all, that the contests for the elected seats and board offices in Tralee and elsewhere were conducted largely by men who were newcomers to official politics. Apart from the few who had held seats on boards of guardians or town councils before 1880, their previous political experience had been largely confined to such partisan organizations as farmers' clubs, Home Rule associations, and Land League branches. As previously noted, only seven members of the branch in Tralee had served on the board before 1881. Nineteen others were added as a result of the 1881 election. Although some of these nineteen may have worked for candidates in earlier parliamentary elections (of which there had been only two in recent years, in 1874 and 1880), none had themselves stood as candidates. The poor-law elections therefore provided most of them with their first opportunity to participate directly in constitutional politics.

The experience in Tralee was, moreover, a valuable one. In the 1881 contest the North Kerry branch served as a party machine. It nominated candidates for the elected seats, conducted the campaign, selected contestants for the board offices, and planned strategies to secure their return. These processes entailed the use of a number of techniques of modern electioneering, such as the canvass of voters, mass demonstrations, the party caucus, and different types of mass persuasion. These activities afforded members of the branch the chance to develop and sharpen their skills in political maneuver. When the experience of the Tralee organization is multiplied by the hundreds of other poor-law elections involving Land League or National League branches, it becomes clear that the local elections of the 1880s were a major instrument in the political education of the tenantry. Though it would be difficult to gauge their importance relative to other sources of politicization during the period, Parnell's sweeping electoral victory in the general election of 1885 was certainly achieved with the assistance of local branches of the National League. By 1885 the branches had already acquired considerable independent experience in conducting political campaigns as a result of their participation in poor-law elections. These facts suggest that it may be necessary to revise the traditional view which gives Parnell and his party almost exclusive credit for educating the Irish masses in the ways of constitutional politics.[43]

It is improbable, however, that many Leaguers embarked on the contests with the principal motive of gaining practice for future parliamentary contests. Their main objective, as the Tralee election indicates, was the more immediate and prosaic one of seizing control of the board from the landlord party. It is in this sense, as a chapter in the tenants' struggle against landlordism, that the poor-law elections may well hold the greatest significance for historians. For as the Tralee contest again illustrates, the tenant party was ultimately successful in its quest. The rapidity of the changeover varied from one poor-law union to another, but by 1886 most of the boards of guardians in the three southern provinces were in the hands of the tenant representatives. What did this change of leadership signify for the structure of local politics?

It signified nothing less than the emergence of a new governing class in the Irish localities. In their role as poor-law guardians the Land Leaguers were more than mere partisans in a political struggle; they were the administrators of a key institution of local government which had formerly been managed by the landlord elite. As such, they were a new elite, one whose claim to power was based on political service to the masses rather than hereditary status. Their ascent to power represented, in short, an important step in the democratization of Irish local government. In every poor-law union there were dozens of men similar to those in the Tralee branch — they might be termed "new politicians" — who had been active in partisan organizations. In democratic societies local political leaders of this kind find their way into various offices of national and local government. In Ireland they were excluded from such

43. See, e.g., O'Brien, *Parnell and his party*, pp. 354–5.

opportunities by property qualifications (one almost had to be rich to be an M.P.) and by landlord manipulation of elections, including real or implied threats of reprisal. These new politicians were would-be governors without institutions to govern. But in the boards of guardians they could now see a government body within their reach and they needed little prodding from above. Parnell's open letter to Land League branches urging them to contest the elections of 1881 may have added impetus to the movement to capture the poor-law boards. But the agitation itself was already under way, and it was rooted to a large extent in the desire of local partisan organizations to find places for their members in public offices and to do so at the expense of landlords in their districts. Their success represented a major contribution to the destruction of the landlords' political power and to the creation of a basis for local self-government by the tenantry.

The democratization of local government in Ireland has often been attributed to the well-known act of 1898. Admittedly, this measure completely reformed Irish local government by replacing the existing structure based on aristocratically dominated grand juries with a new system founded on elected county councils.[44] Historians have traditionally viewed the 1898 act as marking the transition in the locus of power from the landlords to the tenants.[45] But surely the transition began much earlier, in the Land League's struggle to seize control of the boards of guardians during the early 1880s. By the time county councils came into existence at the opening of the twentieth century, there were already thousands of experienced administrators in Irish local communities to continue a smooth transition to tenant rule.

44. The boards of guardians were absorbed into this system as committees of the newly created urban- and rural-district councils.

45. The view of Ernest Barker, stated as long ago as 1917, has never since been challenged: "In 1898 the squirearchy was dethroned, and local self-government, which the local-government act created, took its place. The Irish peasant, as he took over possession of his holding from his landlords, also took over from the same hands the government of his county and rural district" (*Ireland in the last fifty years, 1866–1916* [Oxford, 1917], p. 22).

BIBLIOGRAPHY

Contemporary sources

Manuscript material
General Valuation Office, Dublin
   Valuation records.

Contemporary publications

I. Newspapers
  Freeman's Journal (Dublin).
  Irish Times (Dublin).
  Kerry Sentinel (Tralee).
  Nation (Dublin).

II. Parliamentary papers (in chronological order)
  Copy of a return of the names of proprietors and the area and valuation of all properties in the several counties in Ireland, held in fee or perpetuity, or on long leases at chief rents, prepared for the use of her majesty's government and printed by Alexander Thom, 87 and 88 Abbey-street, Dublin, by the direction of the Irish government and at the expense of the treasury, H.C. 1876 (412), lxxx, 395.
  Report from the select committee on poor-law guardians, &c., together with the proceedings of the committee, minutes of evidence, and appendix, H.C. 1878 (297), xvii, 263.

III. Other contemporary publications
  Bailey, W. F. *Local and centralised government in Ireland* (London, 1888).
  Davitt, Michael. *The fall of feudalism in Ireland, or the story of the Land League revolution* (London and New York, 1904).
  Devoy, John. *Recollections of an Irish rebel* (New York, 1929).
  Hussey, S. M. *The reminiscences of an Irish land agent, being those of S. M. Hussey,* compiled by Home Gordon (London, 1904).
  Nicholls, Sir George. *A history of the Irish poor law in connexion with the condition of the people* (London, 1856).
  O'Shaughnessy, Richard. "Local government and taxation in Ireland" in J. W. Probyn (ed.), *Local government and taxation in the United Kingdom* (London, 1882), pp. 319–83.
  Slater's royal national commercial directory of Ireland (Manchester, 1881).

Later works

Writings in Irish studies

Barker, Sir Ernest. *Ireland in the last fifty years, 1866–1916* (Oxford, 1917).
Bew, Paul. *Land and the national question in Ireland, 1858–82* (Dublin, 1978).
Donnelly, J. S., Jr. *The land and the people of nineteenth-century Cork: the rural economy and the land question* (London and Boston, 1975).
Feingold, W. L. "The Irish boards of poor-law guardians, 1872–1886: a revolution in local government" (Ph.D. dissertation, University of Chicago, 1974).
Feingold, W. L. "The tenants' movement to capture the Irish poor-law boards, 1877–1886" in *Albion,* vii, no. 3 (Fall 1975), pp. 216–31.
Lee, Joseph. *The modernisation of Irish society, 1848–1918* (Dublin, 1973).
Lyons, F. S. L. *Ireland since the famine* (London, 1971).
McDowell, R. B. *The Irish administration, 1801–1914* (London and Toronto, 1964).
O'Brien, C. C. *Parnell and his party, 1880–90* (Oxford, 1957; corrected impression, 1964).

8 *John W. Boyle*

A Marginal Figure:
The Irish Rural Laborer

In 1894 a writer in the *Lyceum* observed that two groups in Irish society could not be ignored or forgotten: the farmer, since "our own prosperity" was bound up with his, and the "sturdy organised artisan," who was quick to rebel when aggrieved. "But of the unskilled agricultural labourer in Ireland," he declared, "comparatively little is heard."[1] There was much truth in this statement, as the woes of the tenant farmer had obscured those of the farm worker, for whom nothing had been done until the modest beginning made with the laborers' act of 1883. The charge of neglect could also be leveled against historians. Long engaged with political issues or with the struggle for the land and its political repercussions, they gave but a passing mention to what was once the most numerous class in rural society. Publications by Lee, Donnelly, Hoppen, Bew, and Clark have paid greater attention to the fortunes of the laborer and his diminishing importance in the Irish economy,[2] Lee

---

Some of the material in this article appeared in my Thomas Davis lecture, "The rural labourer," broadcast by Radio Éireann in 1957. The lecture was published in *Threshold*, iii, no. 1 (Spring 1959).

1. *Lyceum*, vii, no. 77 (Feb. 1894), p. 100.
2. Joseph Lee, *The modernisation of Irish society, 1848–1918* (Dublin, 1973), pp. 92–3; J. S. Donnelly, Jr., *The land and the people of nineteenth-century Cork: the rural economy and the land question* (London and Boston, 1975), passim, but especially chap. 5; K. T. Hoppen, "Landlords, society, and electoral politics in mid-nineteenth-century Ireland" in *Past & Present*, no. 75 (May 1977), pp. 63–5, 92; Paul Bew, *Land and the national question in Ireland, 1858–82* (Dublin, 1978), pp. 42–3, 142–3, 164, 170, 174–5, 185–6; Samuel Clark, *Social origins of the Irish land war* (Princeton, 1979), passim, but especially pp. 36–7, 113–19, 249–52, 374–5.

going so far as to assert that the dispersal and elimination of the only genuine Irish proletariat were set in motion during the great famine at midcentury.[3] The rural proletarian still awaits his Gibbon, but when he appears, he will be greatly aided by the statistical data assembled and analyzed by Fitzpatrick in his recent article, "The disappearance of the Irish agricultural labourer, 1841–1912."[4]

An approximate indication of the numerical decrease is given by the Irish census returns. Between 1841 and 1901 the male population aged fifteen and over fell, in round numbers, from 2,400,000 to 1,500,000, a decline of slightly under 38 percent in sixty years, while the number of rural laborers decreased by 73 percent, from 1,100,000 to 295,000.[5] Since the census authorities were plagued with problems of occupational classification — they had not completely overcome them even in 1901 — the figures for laborers, especially those in the earlier returns, must be regarded with some skepticism. The line of demarcation was less than clear between those who could maintain themselves from the yield of their own holdings and those who gained much of their livelihood by working for others. Were "assisting relatives," frequently the sons of small farmers, to be classed as farmers or as farm workers when they might spend more time elsewhere than on the family holding? How many of the general laborers should have been assigned to agriculture? How many returned as farm workers, or even as farmers, worked as navvies or unskilled assistants in the building trades for much of the year? And what

3. Joseph Lee, "Irish agriculture" in *Agricultural History Review*, xvii, pt. i (1969), p. 65. Professor Lee's actual words are: "The small farmers, and especially the labourers — the real rural proletariat — were decimated by the famine. The rural proletariat was not so much transformed as buried. The majority of the rural bourgeoisie had always been bourgeoisie, who now flourished on the graves of the proletariat."

4. David Fitzpatrick, "The disappearance of the Irish agricultural labourer, 1841–1912" in *Irish Economic and Social History*, vii (1980), pp. 66–92.

5. W. E. Vaughan and A. J. Fitzpatrick (ed.), *Irish historical statistics: population, 1821–1971* (Dublin, 1978), pp. 75–8, 89. The exact figures are 2,432,119 and 1,512,548. Navy and military personnel serving in Ireland were not included in the census returns for 1841 or 1851. The figures for laborers can be only approximations, since the occupational classification was not constant throughout the sixty years ending in 1901. In 1841 there were three categories: 1,105,258 servants and laborers, 59, 692 servants, and 29,064 laborers and porters (*Report of the commissioners appointed to take the census of Ireland for the year 1841*, p. xxiii [504], H.C. 1843, xxiv, 1). I assume that the first category consists of agricultural workers, whether indoor or outdoor. In 1901 agricultural laborers, shepherds, and indoor farm servants numbered 333,192. The 115,540 general laborers were assumed by the census authorities to be almost entirely agricultural workers, and I have included them in the total already given. If the general laborers in the six county boroughs are omitted, the total for agricultural laborers is reduced to 294,522 (*Census Ire.*, 1901, pt. ii: *general report* . . . , p. 119 [C 1190], H.C. 1902, cxxix, 1).

of the case of Thomas Gaughan, cited by Fitzpatrick? Gaughan, partner
with nineteen others in 300 acres of poor land at Glencastle near Belmullet, Co. Mayo, declared in his 1911 census schedule that he was a
"landowner, mason, carpenter also."[6] These questions do not exhaust
the difficulties faced by those responsible for the compilation of census
returns — or by present-day historians. Fitzpatrick has attempted to resolve these difficulties and to restrict his term "farm workers" to those
mainly or wholly engaged in agricultural labor for others. He shows
that the fall in absolute numbers of the Irish population was accompanied by a change in occupational distribution, the proportion of the
total male work force engaged in farming (farmers, assisting relatives,
laborers) declining from 718 per 1,000 in 1841 to 572 in 1901, a decrease
of some 20 percent. During these sixty years there was a notable alteration in the composition of the agricultural work force, for the ratio of
farm workers and assisting relatives per 100 farmers fell from 271 to 146,
a reduction of 46 percent and a clear indication that rural laborers as
a class suffered the heaviest losses. Fitzpatrick's statistics for counties
and provinces reveal marked regional variations throughout the period,
but in no county after 1851 did the laborer-farmer ratio ever return to
that prevailing in 1841.[7]

Though regional and temporal variations make generalizations hazardous, it would appear that the classification of farm workers made
on the eve of the famine still had some validity in the late nineteenth
century. According to the evidence given to the Devon commission, they
could be divided into three categories.[8] The unmarried farm servant lived
with his employer and was at least assured of his food and some wages
in cash; £4 a year was a high wage in County Limerick shortly before
the famine.[9] The married laborer, if he were fortunate, held his cabin
and a small plot of ground from a farmer at a fixed rent, usually payable
in work calculated at the lowest rate of wages prevailing in the district.
Such a man, in spite of his serflike position, was in a sense a subtenant,
though a tenant at will. The married man in the third category had
only a cabin; his position was summed up with absolute simplicity by
Michael Sullivan, a Cork laborer, who began his evidence to the Devon
commission in 1845 with these words: "I hold no ground. I am a poor
man. I have nothing but my labour."[10] A man like Sullivan had no prospect of steady employment and depended on taking a little conacre ground

6. Fitzpatrick, "Disappearance," p. 68.
7. Ibid., pp. 87–8.
8. *Devon comm. digest*, i, 474–5.
9. Ibid., pp. 491–2.
10. Ibid., p. 488.

in the hope of growing on it a crop that would enable him to pay the
rent and secure his food. Some farmers were reluctant to allow him even
this hazard or tried to insist on payment in advance.[11] In desperation
the laborer often replied by intimidation or violence.[12] If he were employed, his daily wage varied from 8d. to 1s., or if with diet, 4d. to 6d.,
but when times were bad, it was even lower, and there were instances
where a man was willing to work for food alone.[13] He belonged to "the
most wretched of the many wretched classes in Ireland."[14] The rural
worker suffered from three evils — unemployment or underemployment,
poor housing, and low wages — that were slow to disappear, and of the
three, unemployment was the most intractable.

The taking of conacre was an attempt on the part of the laborer to
be self-sufficient. Another method often combined with it was the temporary migration that has not completely disappeared, though its scope
and nature have altered. It was of two kinds, internal and external.
Landless men and the sons of small farmers from mountainous or poor
districts moved into the richer plains to work at the busy times of the
year, especially for reaping and potato digging. The custom was long
established. A Kerryman, writing in the eighteenth century, described
in the poem "An spailpín fánach," or "The wandering laborer," the contempt with which he was treated in the hiring fairs of Tipperary and
other counties:

> Go deo deo arís ni raghad go Caiseal
> Ag díol ná ag reic mo shláinte,
> Ná ar mhargadh na saoire in shuí cois balla
> Im scaoinse ar leataoibh sráide —
> Bodairí na tíre ag tíocht ar a gcapall
> Dá fhiafraí an bhfuilim hírálta.
> Ó ! téanam chun siúil, tá an cúrsa fada;
> Seo ar siúl an spailpín fánach.[15]

11. Ibid., pp. 521, 523.

12. Ibid., pp. 491–2; Joseph Lee, "The Ribbonmen" in T. D. Williams (ed.), *Secret societies in Ireland* (Dublin and New York, 1973), p. 29.

13. *Devon comm. digest*, i, 475–6.

14. Ibid., p. 475.

15. Pádraig Ó Canainn (ed.), *Filíocht na nGael* (Dublin, 1958), p. 161. Translation: "I'll never again go to Cashel selling and bartering my health, nor hang about the street at a hiring fair, the boors of the district on their horses asking if I'm hired. Let's start, the journey's long; it's off with the wandering labourer." In a later verse he imagines himself, not with a reaping hook, flail, or spade in his hand, but carrying a pike under the French flag. For hostility on the part of local laborers in Limerick, Tipperary, Kilkenny, and other southeastern counties toward migrants from Kerry and Connacht during the early decades of the nineteenth century, see B. M. Kerr, "Irish seasonal migration to Great Britain, 1800–38" in *I.H.S.*, iii, no. 12 (Sept. 1943), pp. 369–70.

The hiring scene was to be reenacted many times in the following century. External migration was to Great Britain. It too was an established feature of the rural economy and had been noted early in the eighteenth century by Bishop Berkeley, who doubted whether it benefited either country.[16] An incomplete count in 1841 put the number of migrants at over 57,000, about one-seventh being women. Though every county in Ireland contributed some, nearly 80 percent of the total were from Ulster and Connacht, mainly from the western seaboard. Migrants from Ulster usually went to Scotland, and those from Connacht to England, arousing hostility among local laborers in both countries by accepting lower wages. They were assumed to bring back about £5 each after several months' work, an important sum before the famine for rural workers in the infertile regions of the country.[17]

Accounts of the physical condition of Irish migrants suggest that their customary diet before migration was insufficient to render them fit for hard work. The following description by Sir John Macneill, a civil engineer and landowner, is of navvies he employed in the construction of the Dublin and Drogheda railway in the early 1840s, but it is applicable to some external migrants a half-century later: "We find in a month's training, after a man gets sufficiently strong from better meat, he is able to compete with the best in wheeling a barrow, which is the point their companions try him upon. When they first come to work upon scanty food, they have not the physical strength necessary. Sometimes they are knocked up from that and get ill; in other cases where they have the means and eat meat, not being accustomed to it before, they are also made ill; so that in general for a few weeks when they first commence to work, they are unable to do much. This I have observed both in England and Scotland; but they get round and afterwards work exceedingly well."[18]

Though the great famine reduced the number of rural laborers and small farmers by death and emigration, there was no dramatic improvement in the condition of those remaining. In some respects their problems were aggravated. After a brief initial expansion the area under tillage again declined, and the increased acreage of pasture land provided

16. A. A. Luce and T. E. Jessop (ed.), *The works of George Berkeley, bishop of Cloyne* (9 vols., London, 1948–57), vi, 148–9.

17. *Report and tables relating to migratory agricultural labourers [for 1880]*, pp. 3–4 [C 2809], H.C. 1881, xciii, 807. The data for 1841 are reprinted from the 1841 census.

18. *Devon comm. digest*, i, 505. Some 7,000 to 8,000 navvies were employed in the construction of the Dublin-Drogheda line, which opened in 1844. Macneill was also in charge of work on the harbor at Dundalk, on the embankments for Lough Swilly and Lough Foyle, and on the Belfast Waterworks; he served as consulting engineer to the Grand Canal Company.

less employment. Country towns lost population and rural industries decayed.[19] In the north the decline of the domestic system had begun even before the famine. By midcentury the linen industry was mechanized and the day of the handloom weaver, who also cultivated a little ground or worked for a farmer, was ended. Women were employed as outworkers for the hosiery or making-up trades, but the pittance they earned was not sufficient to halt the steady drift from the land to the mills and factories of Belfast and the Lagan valley.[20]

The introduction of agricultural machinery had been one of the sparks that ignited the explosive anger of the English laborers in 1830. Savage sentences were inflicted for machine breaking and other offenses; nineteen persons were executed and 481 transported to Australia.[21] Machinery made its appearance in Ireland about 1850, but its adoption provoked no serious opposition until 1858. In August of that year reaping, threshing, and hay-tedding machines were being used on large farms in King's County, Tipperary, Kilkenny, and Waterford. The seasonal character of agricultural employment meant that the harvest period, when the demand for labor was greatest, offered landless men and cottiers the chance to earn enough to tide them over the leaner months. But use of the new laborsaving inventions was a serious threat to the migrant harvesters. According to a local newspaper, a reaping machine owned by James Walsh, a large farmer at Outrath, Co. Kilkenny, cut 5 acres of corn a day, a task that would have occupied forty men working from 6 A.M. to 6 P.M.[22] The machine, made by a London firm, cost £31, whereas the

19. See table 10 ("Population of towns, 1831–1911") in Vaughan and Fitzpatrick, *Population*, pp. 28–41. Between 1841 and 1861 twenty-one towns dropped below 2,000 in population. For decay in rural industries, see L. M. Cullen, *An economic history of Ireland since 1660* (London, 1972), pp. 147–8.

20. For the mechanization of the linen industry, see R. D. C. Black, "The progress of industrialization, 1850–1920" in T. W. Moody and J. C. Beckett (ed.), *Ulster since 1800: a political and economic survey* (London, 1954), p. 51. An increased demand for flax, consequent on the expansion of the linen industry, gave more seasonal work to rural laborers in some of the preparatory processes, e.g., scutch-milling. For outworkers in the making-up side of the shirt and collar industry, in embroidery, lacework, and hosiery, see F. S. L. Lyons, *Ireland since the famine* (rev. ed., London, 1973), p. 63; "The Londonderry shirt-making industry" in W. P. Coyne (ed.), *Ireland, industrial and agricultural* (Dublin, 1902), pp. 417–19; Elizabeth Boyle, *The Irish flowerers* (Holywood, Co. Down, and Belfast, 1971), passim, but especially pp. 70–3; J. H. Tuke, *Irish distress and its remedies . . .* (London, 1880), p. 21.

21. J. L. and Barbara Hammond, *The village labourer* (2 vols., Guild Books ed., London, 1948), ii, 41–128; E. J. Hobsbawm and George Rudé, *Captain Swing* (Norton Library ed., New York and Toronto, 1975), pp. 308–9. Of those executed, sixteen were charged with arson and three with other offenses. Machine breakers were transported or given short prison sentences.

22. Unless otherwise stated, this account of the disturbances in 1858 is drawn from

day's wages would have amounted to £4 or possibly £6. How quickly the capital outlay could be recovered would depend on the acreage to be cut, but on large farms it could be amortized in a relatively short time. The machine was smashed by angry reapers, who also destroyed another in the same county belonging to a Scottish settler named Harrison, of Pigeonpark near Thomastown. Harrison was injured when he resisted. Three of his neighbors lent him a replacement, but the presence of a large party of police was needed before it could be used. Other machines were broken in Tipperary and Waterford. Machine smashing continued into September, when a thresher lent to a clerical magistrate at Barrons Court in north Tipperary was badly damaged.

Machinery was not the only object of the rural Luddites' wrath. The sickle was being replaced by a scythe to which was fixed a wooden frame known as a cradle. Farmers could now employ one man with a scythe to do the work of six men with reaping hooks. Angry spalpeens in Kilkenny and Tipperary broke scythes and cradles as a protest against their use.[23]

The laborers did not limit themselves to the breaking of machines and implements that deprived them of employment, but in certain instances resorted to a form of strike for higher wages. The most notable example took place at Callan, a small town 10 miles from the city of Kilkenny and close to the Tipperary border. Early in August 1858 there were few reapers waiting to be hired, but they seem to have agreed among themselves to accept only the rate upon which they had decided. The arrival of a very large number, not merely local men and the usual contingent from Connacht, but others from Tipperary and King's and Queen's counties, had little effect on the men's solidarity. Shortly after the middle of the month, between 1,200 and 1,500 gathered for hire at the crossroads. They were offered 2s. a day instead of the 3s. they demanded. Michael Dwyer, a local farmer, persuaded some to accept 2s. after he had treated them to whiskey. The rest seized the sickles, drove the scabs away, and hooted Dwyer. Part of the crowd, angry and starving, went to the house of a police inspector named Cullen, whom they regarded

the Larcom papers, N.L.I. MS 7653 (Constabulary, Queen's County and Kilkenny). These consist of newspaper cuttings from the following papers: *Kilkenny Moderator*, 10 Aug. 1858; *Daily Express* (Dublin), 13 Aug. 1858; *Evening Mail* (Dublin), 18 Aug. 1858; *Evening Packet* (Dublin), 21 Aug., 27 Sept. 1858. I am most grateful to my old friend Thomas P. O'Neill, now of University College, Galway, who first drew my attention to them.

23. According to the Rev. P. S. Dinneen, *Foclóir Gaedhilge agus Béarla: an Irish-English dictionary* . . . (rev. ed., with additions, Dublin, 1927), v. *spailpín*, the word became common in English in the eighteenth century. Dinneen notes amusedly that Arthur Young derived it from *spal*, a spade, and *peen*, a penny, i.e., a worker at a penny a day! It seems more likely that it is a diminutive of *spailp*, a bout or spell, in which case it means a man doing casual work. Spalpeen became a term of abuse.

as a government representative, and asked for bread. But they returned empty-handed, for Cullen was absent and his wife declared that she had none. Troops were dispatched to the disaffected areas and the leading rioters were sent to prison.

The events of August 1858 may not allow confident generalizations about the condition of Irish farm workers, but they do reveal the continued existence of a surplus of casual labor. According to Fitzpatrick, the wage rates for permanent farm workers in Kilkenny and Tipperary were low, as were the laborer-farmer ratios.[24] Both counties, however, had grain-growing areas that required extra hands during the harvest. Low wheat and barley prices in the late 1840s had caused a switch to the rearing of livestock, but the onset of the Crimean war in 1854 brought about an increase in prices and in the acreage under grain that continued for some years.[25] As a consequence, reapers flocked into these areas. Their demand for 3s. a day reflects their expectations, yet even the 2s. offered amounted to at least double the rate prevailing before the famine. But for those who could read it, the *Freeman's Journal* provided, in an editorial written during the disturbances, a sharp reminder of the limitations imposed by the principles of laissez-faire economics: "In this country every man has the right to make the best use of his capital. The farmer has a right to employ reaping or mowing machines if he conceives they will do his work cheaper or better, and the labourer has the right to set any price he pleases on his labour, or not to hire it, except on his own terms. . . ."[26]

The freedom enjoyed by these casual workers was the knowledge of necessity, knowledge that prompted many of them to seek a less overstocked labor market in Great Britain. An article in the *Scottish Farmer*, reprinted in the *Freeman's Journal* (12 September 1862), describes the appearance and living conditions of migrant harvesters who went regularly to Scotland, and suggests that some improvement had taken place since the 1840s, though their lot was still miserable. They were packed into filthy cattle trucks and traveled on board ships crowded to excess. Formerly, the migrants were full-grown or middle-aged men, who wore a scarecrow hat or bonnet and, over a short tattered shirt, a blue dress coat with the armpits and elbows of moleskin and a patch of the same material down the front. Their blue trousers were short, with a large

24. Fitzpatrick, "Disappearance," p. 80 and table 4.
25. Lee, *Modernisation*, pp. 39–40.
26. *F.J.*, 12 Aug. 1858. The *Kilkenny Journal* indicated that reapers were earning from 4s. to 5s. a day in 1857. Though it advised harvesters to refrain from violence, it urged the gentry and farmers to be more generous in future to "the ill-fed, hard-worked, much enduring Irish labourer" (*Kilkenny Journal*, 14 Aug. 1858, quoted in *F.J.*, 16 Aug. 1858).

seat and knees of the inevitable moleskin. By 1862, however, the harvesters were young men; they wore corduroy unmentionables, gray homespun sleeved waistcoats, and bonnets, which in the writer's view made them more workmanlike and respectable in appearance, even though the clothing was still poor enough. But they still persisted in wearing the curling lock, the *glib* noted by Tudor historians, hanging down over the forehead. The Scottish observer commented disapprovingly that they were clean neither in clothing nor in person, that many had only one shirt, perhaps washed but once during the harvest and, if washed by the owner, in cold water without soap, though he admitted that warm water was difficult to obtain. They spent Sunday mornings in the straw barns "examining their shirts," which was no doubt a euphemism for delousing.

These migrants as a class did not drink; they even denied themselves proper food in order to take home a few pounds. It was their practice to gather in a central market town and wait to be hired. Many of them slept on the hard pavement, choosing a dry or sheltered corner, but had scarcely any body clothes to cover them, and used their arm or bundle for a pillow. As few had been able to afford more than their fare, they lived on penny loaves or the porridge given them by charitable farmers until they obtained work. Sleeping quarters were provided by the farmers — usually in barns or in the bothies that were to become the standard accommodation later in the century. Yet they worked well on the whole, and in the field were cheerier than the Scots, whose fierce resentment of the migrants' acceptance of lower wages had provoked frequent clashes in earlier years. The writer concluded by prophesying that the growing use of reaping machines in the Scottish lowlands would lead to the disappearance of the Irish harvesters. This happened eventually, but Irish migrants still made the journey to Scotland for the "tattie-howking" (potato digging) as long as potatoes remained an important crop commercially.[27]

The returns made in 1880 of migratory laborers give not only their numbers, provenance, and destination, but also the proportion of small-holders among them. The total, almost certainly greatly underestimated,[28]

---

27. J. E. Handley, *The Irish in modern Scotland* (Cork, 1947), pp. 166, 169.

28. *Report and tables relating to migratory agricultural labourers [for 1880]*, pp. 5–7, 10–12. There were two estimates, the first (42,272) made up of laborers leaving ports other than Dublin, and of those who bought "harvest men's" through tickets on the Midland and Great Western system. This estimate was too high, since some men made more than one journey. The authors of the report assumed that it should be reduced by 3,000, which would still leave the revised figure about 16,000 greater than the second estimate. The latter was reached early, before the weather prospects were good; it was based on

amounted to 22,900, of whom two-thirds were landless. Together, Leinster and Munster accounted for fewer than 2,000. Over 5,000 were from Ulster (nearly half of them from Donegal), and almost 16,000 from Connacht (Mayo contributing some 10,000). The grand total included both external and internal migrants; the latter made up less than 10 percent of the whole, but proportionately were more important in Leinster and Munster than elsewhere. The impact of this temporary migration, in social and economic terms, is best realized when we reckon the number that left each county as a percentage of its male population over twenty years of age.[29] Mayo led with a staggering 17.3 percent, followed by Roscommon (4.5), Donegal (4.4), Leitrim (4.1), and Galway (3.1). All of the other counties had percentages below 1.7, most of them below 1. It is incorrect to assume that all landholders among the migrants were occupants of 10 acres or less; one man from Connacht held 700 acres and another from Ulster 350. But these "estates" consisted of poor, barren land, with respective poor-law valuations of 2½d. and 2d. per acre, scarcely capable of providing, in the words of a popular ballad ("Three lovely lasses from Banion") more than "the grass of a goat and a cow."

Of the external migrants, almost two-thirds of those from Ulster went to Scotland, many of them sailing from Derry and smaller northern ports. The overwhelming majority of those from the other provinces went to England. For the landless men and for those smallholders who could survive only by working as laborers, the migrant tradition was so persistent as to amount in some cases to a lifetime habit: one Lancashire estate bailiff, giving evidence to a royal commission in 1893, remarked that two Irishmen whom he employed for harvest work had been coming to him for over thirty-three years, while an assistant commissioner described Achill Island as the winter quarters for laborers on Scottish and English farms.[30] The same commission also heard evidence that recalled what Sir John Macneill had told the Devon commission fifty years earlier. A railway foreman said that migrants from Mayo were often fine-looking men but lacked muscle from underfeeding; a Lancashire farmer declared bluntly that no man could work on an empty belly; and a Clare Island smallholder, who by turns had been miner, building laborer, and

returns of those intending to go, collected by the Royal Irish Constabulary and the Dublin Metropolitan Police. It was an underestimation because it was compiled so early; some of those questioned were probably reluctant to give an account of their movements to the police. I have used the lower estimate because of the detailed analysis that accompanies it.

29. Only thirty-five of the migrants were women.

30. *Royal commission on labour: the agricultural labourer*, vol. iv, *Ireland*, pt. iv, pp. 2ln., 57 [C 6894-xxi], H.C. 1893–4, xxxvii, pt. i, 341. The introduction of machinery was reducing the demand for labor and the migrants' earnings (ibid., p. 61).

farm worker, asserted that it took three months and good food before
the Irishman sweated the water out of his body and became the equal
of an English worker.[31]

From Flora Thompson, born in 1876 at Juniper Hill on the Oxfordshire-
Northamptonshire border, comes a less somber account of Irish harvesters in England. In her thinly disguised autobiography, Laura (i.e., Flora)
describes how she met them when she became a youthful assistant to
the village postmistress. The postmistress, taking pity on "the wild-looking
men with tousled hair and beards, sun-scorched faces, and queerly cut
clothes, with coloured shirts . . . sticking out of their trousers," sold them
postal orders for their families after official hours — employed on piece-
work, they could not afford to come during daylight. Laura had seen
them as a child, when some neighbors tried to frighten her when naughty
by threatening to give her to "them old Irishers." The fear did not survive her infancy, "for who could be afraid of men who did no one any
harm, beyond irritating them by talking too much and working harder,
and by so doing, earning more money than they did?" Laura soon became the confidante of the older men, who were illiterate, and wrote
letters to their dictation. Addressed to their wives, they began with inquiries about the health of "herself," the family, relatives, and neighbors, and continued with directions to "pay off [the debt] at the shop,"
to ask a certain price for something they had to sell, and to lay by a
little in the stocking. But they were not to deny themselves anything
they fancied, for if the writer had his way, his wife would live like a
queen. Laura was touched by these letters containing rich, warm phrases
that sounded like poetry, dictated with a fluency that contrasted sharply
with the long hesitations of her own illiterate countrymen. The Irishman
also had better manners, taking off his hat when he came through the
door, saying "please" more frequently than the Englishman, and expressing thanks for even the smallest services. The younger men were inclined
to pay compliments, but in such charming words that no one would
feel offended.[32]

By 1870 the cash wages of agricultural laborers had risen considerably
over the levels prevailing twenty years earlier. One poor-law inspector,
surveying unions covering parts of Cork, Kerry, and Limerick, concluded
that in general wages had doubled, the greatest advances having taken
place during the previous five years.[33] Substantial increases were also
reported from other areas. No attempt was made to calculate an aver-

31. Ibid., pp. 21–2n.
32. Flora Thompson, *Lark Rise to Candleford* (Penguin Modern Classics ed., Harmondsworth, 1973), pp. 470–2.
33. *Reports from poor-law inspectors on the wages of agricultural labourers in Ireland*,
pp. 22–3 [C 35], H.C. 1870, xiv, 1.

age, weighted or unweighted, for the whole of Ireland. One assistant commissioner, however, summarizing returns for unions in south Ulster, Louth, Meath, and County Dublin that recorded increases of 20 to 100 percent, assumed an overall average of 50 percent.[34] Around Dublin, Belfast, and the larger or more prosperous towns, weekly wages were as high as 10s., 12s., or even 14s., but as low as 6s. in poorer districts.[35] The yearly wages of indoor farm servants, generally the only class employed by the smaller farmers, were from £8 to £14 or £15.[36] Servant boys and girls were the most discontented; having no permanent tenure (they were often engaged by the quarter) or local ties, and looking to America as their ultimate destination, they stayed until they had saved enough money to emigrate.[37] Casual workers received from 2s. 6d. to 4s. per day, with the highest wages being paid at harvest time, no doubt a reflection of the growing scarcity of labor in certain areas during the busy season.[38]

Against these increases must be set the higher cost of living. Poor-law officials were confronted not only by widespread variations in prices and wages but by the changes in patterns of consumption that had been taking place over the years. Some concluded that real wages had risen because money wages had outstripped prices, and that an improved diet (more tea, bread, and animal food) was evidence of a higher standard of living.[39] One commissioner, however, considered that in the Kells union in Meath the general advance in the price of all commodities, excepting tea, sugar, and buttermilk, had gone far "to neutralise, if not counterbalance, wage increases."[40] It was the same official who remarked that discontent was most evident in the grazing districts of Meath and other counties in his survey, where employment was not continuous.[41]

The grievances of the married rural laborer were still numerous. They may be summed up as the lack of constant employment and the need to buy such food as Indian meal and flour to offset the diminished yield from potato ground, accompanied by the consequent inability to raise sufficient pigs and poultry for sale. Rents were still high for conacre land, and tenants, often at the bidding of their landlords, refused to sublet ground to them for cabins or plots.[42] Some poor-law officials sympa-

34. Ibid., p. 8.
35. Ibid., pp. 5–7.
36. Ibid., pp. 8, 18–19, 24–5.
37. Ibid., p. 8.
38. Ibid., pp. 6–7.
39. Ibid., pp. 7, 19.
40. Ibid., pp. 10–11.
41. Ibid., p. 9.
42. Donnelly, *Cork*, p. 236.

thized with the laborers: W. P. O'Brien, referring to the refusal to give them ground, remarked that they were "thus led to regard themselves as being treated in some measure as a persecuted race"; Dr. T. Brodie was convinced that only the possession of a couple of acres of land could stem the tide of emigration; W. J. Hamilton, in advocating improved housing for them, declared that "no able-bodied agricultural labourer, who has a house he can call his own, would enter a workhouse if he could avoid it, or remain a day longer in it than he could possibly help."[43] Others, however, while listing such causes of discontent as uncertainty of employment and wretched housing, drew attention to improvident habits, the evil influence of agitators, and the "expectations raised in their minds by popular writers and speakers, which can never be realised so long as there are to be both rich and poor in the land."[44] Dr. John Hill expressed his particular distrust of servant boys who, being young and unmarried, and having little or nothing to do after their day's work, were peculiarly apt to fall into evil courses; from this class came many of the most unruly and dangerous characters to be found in Irish county and borough jails.[45]

Agitators were already at work in 1870. In December 1869 Philip Francis Johnson, owner of a small hotel in Kanturk, Co. Cork, had formed the Kanturk Labour Club, of which he was elected secretary.[46] It issued a manifesto to Irish farm workers, reminding them that legislation in England had regulated the wages and hours of the mechanic and given him a measure of assistance when he was unemployed. In Ireland a minister of agriculture might be appointed who could, through beneficial legislation, enable the laborer to share in the joys of life. It asserted that legislation (i.e., the 1870 land act) was intended to make the tenant farmer "proof against fenianism," and asked why the farm worker should not also be "vaccinated by the state."[47] In June the club held an open-air meeting at which 2,000 people were present; speeches were made denouncing those Irish M.P.s who had failed to support, or even opposed, an amendment to Gladstone's bill that would have given laborers a cottage and a little land at a fixed rent and with tenure.[48]

43. *Reports from poor-law inspectors*, pp. 11, 28–30.
44. Ibid., pp. 1–2.
45. Ibid., pp. 16–17. Dr. Hill based his remarks on incidental information gathered during an inquiry into prison dietaries made in 1868. He asserted that in the Delvin poor-law union laborers were generally contented, but disaffected toward the English government; this is doubtless a reference to the influence of fenianism following the 1867 rising.
46. Donnelly, *Cork*, p. 237, notes that a report of the club's formation appeared in the *Cork Examiner*, 4 Jan. 1870, and that 200 laborers assembled under Johnson's leadership at his hotel early in the same month.
47. *Irishman*, 22 Jan. 1870.
48. Ibid., 11 June 1870.

Public attention was drawn to the club's existence when, after some strikes and rioting in Cork city, farm workers in early July damaged mowing machines and demanded higher wages in several districts near the city and at some remove from Kanturk.[49] In February 1871 one member of the Mallow Farmers' Club made the unfounded claim that militiamen were drilling the laborers, and that Johnson was one of the "Reds of Duhallow," an advocate of physical force to solve the rural workers' problems.[50]

The Cork laborers' movement was given a new impetus when Joseph Arch's National Agricultural Labourers' Union decided to assist it, partly because Irish migrants still tended to compete with English farm workers and had been used, apparently unwittingly, in an attempt to break a strike in Warwickshire.[51] In May 1873 the N.A.L.U. addressed Irish rural workers in a manifesto.[52] It recounted the success of the English union, aided by several M.P.s and by clergy of all denominations, including Archbishop Henry Manning. It emphasized the anomaly of poverty in such a fruitful and fertile land as Ireland. "We have seen you thrown on the shores of England to wander about without a place to lay your head, enduring the greatest hardships and privations, and doing the most laborious work at the lowest rate of wages, simply because you were strangers." The manifesto urged the laborers to unite and referred to the delegate organizers, one of them speaking "your native tongue," sent to assist in the campaign. Its final recommendation was to follow the example of Father Mathew and to abstain from drink and tobacco.

Under Johnson's guidance the two delegates addressed meetings in all six counties of Munster and in Queen's County as well. The high point of the campaign was reached in Kanturk, where a conference was held on 14 August, followed the next day (a holiday) by an open-air meeting that attracted an audience of between 3,000 and 4,000. At this conference an Irish Agricultural Labourers' Union was formed, with the leader of the Home Rule party, Isaac Butt, as president, his fellow M.P., P. J. Smyth,

49. Donnelly, *Cork*, p. 237.

50. Ibid. The International Working Men's Association interested itself in Ireland and opened a Cork branch in February 1872 (J. W. Boyle, "Ireland and the First International" in *Jn. Brit. Studies*, xi, no. 2 [May 1972], p. 53). Though the branch collapsed under attacks within a few months, assertions and denials of membership were being made at laborers' meetings in 1873 (*Irishman*, 26 July, 18, 25 Oct., 1 Nov. 1873).

51. An official of the National Agricultural Labourers' Union, in a letter published in the *Irishman*, 4 May 1872, asked that Irish laborers be prevented from coming to England until the strike ended, and remarked that some had already been "decoyed" over. P. L. R. Horn, "The National Agricultural Labourers' Union in Ireland, 1873–9" in *I.H.S.*, xvii, no. 67 (Mar. 1971), pp. 340–52, deals with the participation of Joseph Arch and his union in the attempt to organize Irish rural laborers.

52. *Irishman*, 10 May 1873.

as vice president, and Johnson as secretary. The meeting of 15 August, with Archdeacon O'Regan, the parish priest of Kanturk, presiding, was addressed by the officials of the new union as well as by Joseph Arch and other speakers. It was not concerned solely with the laborers' cause, for resolutions were passed which in effect called for home rule and tenant right.[53] Later meetings, after Arch had returned to England, paid less attention to the farm workers' claims. At one held in Cork on 12 October — a combined demonstration with the city trades — amnesty for the Fenian prisoners and home rule took pride of place.[54] Embarrassed by the political tone of the new union's proceedings (Arch was a Liberal M.P.), and disappointed by the failure of efforts to dissuade Irish harvesters from flocking to England, the N.A.L.U. quietly ended its connection with Johnson's organization.[55]

The Irish union survived, largely owing to the efforts of Johnson and Peter O'Leary, one of the two N.A.L.U. delegates sent in May, who remained in Ireland even after Arch's union withdrew. But both of them soon became interested, like Arch, in emigration as a partial solution to the laborers' problems, O'Leary traveling to North America and Johnson acting as an emigration agent. Johnson had earlier directed much of his fire against landlords and at first tried to tie the union to the Irish Land League when the latter was formed. But he became so absorbed in the League's activities that the union faded away.[56]

The demise of Johnson's union did not mean the end of agitation by laborers or of attempts to organize rural workers. Kanturk farm workers struck for higher wages during the harvest of 1880, and a negotiating committee representing landowners, farmers, and laborers awarded the strikers an advance of 2s. per week.[57] In 1881, shortly after a Land League convention in Limerick city, where some speakers urged farm workers to follow the example of Arch's N.A.L.U. and to strike for higher wages, laborers became militant and secured increases of 1s. and 2s. weekly.[58] No national union was formed, but local bodies continued to appear during the 1880s and 1890s, especially in those areas where permanent farm workers were numerous.[59] These local laborers' leagues or unions often included other rural workers besides agricultural laborers; they

53. *F.J.*, 16, 18 Aug. 1873; *Irishman*, 23 Aug. 1873.
54. *Irishman*, 18 Oct. 1873.
55. Horn, "N.A.L.U. in Ireland," pp. 346–8.
56. Ibid., pp. 350–1. For O'Leary's emigration activities, see *Irishman*, 16, 30 Aug. 1879.
57. Horn, "N.A.L.U. in Ireland," p. 351.
58. Donnelly, *Cork*, pp. 238–9.
59. Apart from larger organizations, such as the Irish Democratic Trade and Labour Federation and the Irish Land and Labour Association, there were four bodies, not all active, in County Wexford and others in Monaghan and Donegal in the early 1890s.

tended to be ephemeral, dissolving and reforming again. An Irish Labour League, composed overwhelmingly of general workers in town and country, met in Dublin early in 1891. It was addressed by Parnell who, at a time when he was fighting for his political life, confined himself to pleasing generalities. The league had no future since the skilled trades held aloof, but the delegate attendance list confirmed the existence of numerous small rural unions.[60]

Two other organizations were more ambitious. With Michael Davitt's assistance the Irish Democratic Trade and Labour Federation was formed in January 1890 at Cork and enrolled agricultural and other unorganized workers. Its secretary was Michael Austin, an officer of the Cork Trades Council, who became an M.P. in 1892, when Davitt persuaded the anti-Parnellite Nationalists to choose some labor representatives as parliamentary candidates.[61] The federation established branches in a number of southern counties, but it could not retain a major share of Austin's energies, especially after his election to Parliament, and it disappeared later in the decade. The Irish Land and Labour Association was the second body. After a preliminary meeting at Limerick Junction it held a conference at Cork in November 1894; there a resolution was passed, calling on Irish M.P.s to have Parliament extend to Ireland the same facilities to acquire land already enjoyed by English farm workers.[62] It too had its principal strength in Munster. Its patron was William Field, a Dublin cattle dealer and Parnellite M.P., whose influence checked any radical tendencies. In 1900 it became part of the Nationalist machine. The split between the Parnellites and the anti-Parnellites was healed and, by the rules governing the selection of parliamentary candidates, the association was entitled to be represented at nominating conventions.[63] Delegates from both the Land and Labour Association and the Knights of the Plough, a smaller and more ephemeral body, had attended early meetings of the Irish Trades Union Congress, formed in 1894. But Field was soon debarred on the grounds that he was not a qualified delegate according to standing orders, and by the end of the century the association itself had ended its affiliation with congress.[64]

60. *F.J.*, 16 Mar. 1891.

61. T. W. Moody, "Michael Davitt and the British labour movement, 1882–1906" in *R. Hist. Soc. Trans.*, 5th ser., iii (1953), p. 70; idem, "Michael Davitt" in J. W. Boyle (ed.), *Leaders and workers* (Cork, 1966), pp. 52–3.

62. *F.J.*, 12 Nov. 1894.

63. Lyons, *Ir. parl. party*, p. 151.

64. No official report of the first congress of the Irish Trades Union Congress was published, but a lengthy account of its organization and proceedings appeared in *F.J.*, 27, 28, 30 Apr. 1894. The Dublin District Trades Council and Labour League issued an

Of the three evils afflicting the rural worker—unemployment or underemployment, low wages, and poor housing—it was evident by the 1870s that the last was the most grievously felt, to judge by the frequency with which laborers' meetings called for its improvement. Though the number of hovels that continually appalled foreign travelers in Ireland had fallen substantially since the famine, there were still approximately 40,000 one-room cabins inhabited by 41,000 families in 1881.[65] Many were to be seen in the west, but not all rural slums were confined to remote or barren districts. Some were to be found in such fertile counties as Limerick and Meath: in 1884, according to one witness before a select committee on agricultural laborers, half of the 5,000 farm workers in the Limerick poor-law union lived in one-room cottages.[66] If the demand for an adequate cottage and an acre of land at a fair rent and with security of tenure were granted, the rural laborer would be less vulnerable to the evils of unemployment and low wages.

The formation of the Irish Land League in 1879 was the beginning of a successful campaign for the three Fs. The right to a free sale of his holding hardly concerned the laborer, but a fair rent and fixity of tenure certainly did. Farm workers had few direct grievances against landlords, who in general gave steady employment at slightly higher rates than did farmers, and some provided cottages comfortable by the

---

agenda and list of delegates for the congress, together with a program for a May Day demonstration to be held on 6 May 1894 (*Irish Trades Union Congress, April 27th & 28th, "Labor omnia vincit"; Labour Day demonstration, May 6th, Dublin, published by the Dublin District Trades Council and Labour League* [Dublin, 1894], hereafter cited as *Agenda, Irish T.U.C., 1894*). The Irish Land and Labour Association was not represented, since it was not formed until November 1894, but William Field and another delegate represented the central branch (Athy) of the Knights of the Plough, which claimed 500 members (*Agenda, Irish T.U.C., 1894*, p. 43). Other rural workers' organizations represented were the Irish Democratic Labour Federation, with 150 members, the Irish National Labour Association, with 100 members, and the Irish National Labour League, with 300 members (*Agenda, Irish T.U.C., 1894*, p. 41). Delegates were required by standing orders to be working or to have worked at the trades they represented, and to be members of a recognized trade union or trades council. Field ceased to be a delegate after 1896 but continued for some years to attend as a visitor. The Irish Land and Labour Association was represented for the last time at the fifth congress (Belfast, 1898), when its delegate was William Hickey, of Boher, Co. Limerick (List of delegates, *Report of the fifth Irish Trades Union Congress, held in the Exhibition Hall, Belfast, 30th and 31st May and 1st June, 1898* [Belfast, n.d.]).

65. *Census Ire., 1891*, pt. ii: *general report* . . . , p. 10 [C 6780], H.C. 1892, xc, 1.

66. *Report from the select committee on agricultural labourers (Ireland), together with the proceedings of the committee and minutes of evidence*, pp. 62–3, H.C. 1884–5 (32), vii, 559. The witness was Andrew Harte, a poor-law guardian in the Limerick union, a land valuer, and the occupier of some 350 acres on which, he stated, there were six laborers' cottages.

standards of the period. The chief complaints were that not many land-lords took positive steps to expand employment, and that they discouraged subletting by their tenants. Hostility between farmers and their employ-ees had long been evident, especially since it was rarely tempered by kinship or marriage ties.[67] Yet there was no general revolt on the part of the landless men against the farmers during the land war. It is argu-able that, initially at least, farm workers expected to benefit in terms of more employment and higher wages from a victory for the tenant farmers.[68] And that victory, as instanced by the Boycott and Bence Jones cases, could scarcely have been won without the cooperation of the laborers.

Captain Charles Boycott, in addition to acting as land agent for Lord Erne, farmed 1,000 acres which he had leased on Erne's estate at Lough Mask, Co. Mayo. His farm workers, who demanded 9s. to 15s. per week instead of the customary 7s. to 11s., went on strike during the grain har-vest in 1880. After a brief attempt to gather the crops with the help of his family and a few servants, Boycott surrendered to the men's de-mands with ill grace. Then came the tenants' demand for a reduction of their rents by 25 percent, as against an abatement of 10 percent in the previous year. When he stood firm, the tenantry started a boycott and induced the farm workers to follow suit, which they did en masse. A relief expedition of fifty Orange laborers from Cavan and Monaghan, heavily protected by soldiers and police, saved what was left of the har-vest, but Boycott had to leave Lough Mask for nearly a year until the excitement died down and he could return.[69]

William Bence Jones also farmed about 1,000 acres, part of his es-tate near Clonakilty, Co. Cork. The Land League took action against him early in December 1880 when he attempted to raise a tenant's rent, and called on his demesne laborers to strike. This they did. Jones ob-tained other workers, principally from the nearby town of "Orange" Bandon, but a few also from County Cavan. Jones evicted from their cottages all those farm workers who continued the strike, but the League provided twenty-five of them with housing and employment. The ten-ants generally maintained their resistance until well after the passage

67. Clark, *Social origins*, pp. 117–19. The data used by Clark are for marriages re-corded in the Roscommon registrar's district, 1864–80. The social gap between farmer and laborer is the subject of Frank O'Connor's excellent tale, "Legal aid," in *The stories of Frank O'Connor* (London, 1953).

68. Palmer, *Land League crisis*, p. 117.

69. Ibid., pp. 197–210; T. H. Corfe, "The troubles of Captain Boycott, part I: the Land League" in *History Today*, xiv, no. 11 (Nov. 1964), pp. 758–64; idem, "The troubles of Captain Boycott, part II: the campaign," ibid., no. 12 (Dec. 1964), pp. 854–62.

of the 1881 land act, when they could enter the land courts in order to obtain a judicial determination of their rents.[70] The Boycott and Bence Jones cases were followed by many others in which farm workers, willingly or reluctantly, supported the League. In October 1881 the Orange Emergency Committee, created by the Grand Orange Lodge of Ireland in December 1880, reported that it had assisted boycotted landlords in nineteen counties by supplying laborers, mainly from Ulster, to replace those who had deserted their employers. The Property Defence Association, composed of landlords and land agents, was also formed in December 1880. Endowed with ample funds, it organized numerous if expensive relief expeditions, usually consisting of northern recruits, to save crops threatened by the League's activities.[71]

The landlord counteroffensive also included a propaganda war. The Dublin *Evening Mail* endeavored repeatedly to sow dissent between tenants and their farm workers. This was a revived rather than a new tactic, for in midcentury parliamentary elections Tory candidates had used the plight of laborers and cottiers to discredit tenant-right candidates, whom they accused of offering nothing to those who tilled the soil and gathered the harvests.[72] It was not a threat that could be ignored indefinitely.

The month of October 1880 was marked by expressions of laborer discontent and attempts to allay it. Sunday, 3 October, was a day of highly successful and widespread Land League meetings, the most impressive being a huge demonstration welcoming Parnell to Cork city. A more ominous note was struck a week later. League meetings were again numerous, but at Shanagarry, Co. Cork, a crowd of farm workers gathered to protest against the tyranny of farmers and to denounce the Land League.[73] It was, incidentally, at Shanagarry that a landlord had divided up a farm for his laborers, an example not appreciated by the farmers of the area.[74] After the League's first meeting at Barntown, Co. Wexford, inflammatory placards appeared, stating the farm workers' grievances and asserting that they had been neglected by Catholic clergymen and others who took part in land demonstrations. The manifesto denounced the "vile treatment" which the laborers suffered at the hands of farmers, who had no more right to the land than they had, and proclaimed that "the land shall be ours as well as the farmers'."[75]

70. Palmer, *Land League crisis*, pp. 210–15; Donnelly, *Cork*, pp. 272–5.
71. Palmer, *Land League crisis*, pp. 226–31.
72. Hoppen, "Landlords," pp. 63–5, 92.
73. Palmer, *Land League crisis*, p. 163; Donnelly, *Cork*, p. 242.
74. Bew, *Land*, p. 142.
75. Ibid.; *Irishman*, 16 Oct. 1880.

Some conciliatory gestures were made by the Land League. A meeting at Templemore, Co. Tipperary, after adopting a pledge to be loyal to the League and to refrain from taking the farms of evicted tenants, resolved that no settlement of the land question could be final that did not make suitable provision for the welfare of the agricultural laborers.[76] The Limerick League promised them a comfortable house, half an acre of land, and the grass of a cow. The promise might have been more convincing had it not been for the views expressed earlier by the president of the Limerick Farmers' Club. When he had appeared before the Richmond commission in June, he seemed to favor a scheme of internal migration, but on being asked if he personally would give a laborer or cottier 10 or 20 acres of his own 180-acre farm, he replied that it would not be fair or just to deprive any man of his holding.[77]

The role played by the laborers during the land war was on the whole passive rather than active, that is, they generally cooperated in the boycotting campaign by withdrawing their labor, but as Clark has demonstrated, they formed only a small percentage of those arrested for offenses under the act passed early in 1881 for the protection of persons and property.[78] Equally, their interests received comparatively little attention in the shape of resolutions passed at land meetings, to judge from those reported in the *Nation*, which recorded a steady decline in the number of such resolutions between June 1879 and August 1881.[79] Nonetheless, Parnell realized the importance of retaining the support of the rural proletariat while satisfying the varied demands of the farmers, large or small. He spoke of internal migration, of settling the landless men on semiwaste land, or the lighter grazing lands that had been cleared in the late 1840s, but he was careful not to commit himself to detailed proposals that would antagonize farmers. At the land conference of April 1881 in Dublin, held to consider Gladstone's recently introduced bill, the demand on behalf of the farm workers was formulated in very general terms. The national convention in September, after the bill had become law, devoted most of its final session to them. Parnell called upon both groups to stand together, said that there was no need for a separate laborers' movement, and promised to lead one himself if the farmers did not treat them fairly. There were other concessions. Whereas farmers had to pay subscriptions to the Land League in proportion to the valuations of their holdings, rural laborers had to pay only 1s. a year. The final proof of unity was the alteration of the League's name, which

76. *Irishman*, 16 Oct. 1880.
77. Bew, *Land*, p. 142.
78. Clark, *Social origins*, pp. 249–52.
79. Ibid., pp. 297–9.

now became the Irish National Land League and Labour and Industrial Movement.[80]

Rural laborers derived no obvious benefits either from land legislation in 1881 or 1882, or from the agrarian disturbances that brought about the imprisonment of Parnell and the suppression of the Land League. Bitterness between farmer and farm worker continued. In May 1882 a letter in *United Ireland* told of the sufferings of a seventy-year-old cottier. He had held a cabin and a half-acre of land from a Kerry farmer for twenty years, paying for it by ninety days' work a year, the value of the labor being reckoned at 7d. per day. Ill and unable to work, the cottier offered to pay his rent in money provided by his children, but the farmer demanded payment at the rate of 1s. 6d. a day and summoned him twice before petty sessions. He was compelled to pay 9d. a day and also incurred costs of £3 15s.[81] Other farmers were as ready as any landlord to evict.

The farm worker had further causes for complaint against the tenant farmer, who seldom kept his cottage in repair, or grudged him even straw for thatching. Some farmers insisted on exacting labor at the busiest times of the year, reckoning it at 1s. a day or less, and thus preventing the cottier from earning the 2s. or 3s. normally payable for casual harvest labor. Others let mountain or bog land in conacre and, when it had been brought into cultivation, added it to their own farms and forced the laborer to start once again on rough ground. A long-standing complaint was that some farmers made considerable profit from conacre land by charging rates several times higher than the rent they paid to their own landlord.[82]

If farmer tenant right could mean laborer wrong, the system of cottier tenancy stood condemned. As long as the rural laborer remained in a state of virtual peonage, little could be done to improve his lot. The pressing necessity was for legislation that would give him a measure of independence. This had been recognized as early as the 1830s, when an Irish royal commission recommended the building of cottages with a small plot of land attached, the rent, tenure, and other conditions to be fixed by a body to be called the board of improvement.[83] But half a century passed before the first effective steps were taken. The hard

80. Bew, *Land*, p. 186; Palmer, *Land League crisis*, p. 286.

81. *United Ireland*, 1 May 1882, cited by P. H. Bagenal, "Uncle Pat's cabin" in *Nineteenth Century*, xii (Dec. 1882), p. 931.

82. Ibid., pp. 926–7; *Report from the select committee on agricultural labourers (Ireland)*, p. 74; *Royal commission on labour: the agricultural labourer*, vol. iv, Ireland, pt. iii, pp. 13, 48; Donnelly, *Cork*, p. 239.

83. *Report of the viceregal commission on poor-law reform in Ireland*, vol. i, p. 4 [C 3202], H.C. 1906, li, 349.

economic fact that laborers were voting in the only way they could — with their feet — finally convinced their employers that some inducement must be offered them to remain. It was also desirable politically if tenant gains were to be consolidated and nationalist unity strengthened. Parnell kept the promise he had made in September 1881. In August 1882, a few months after his release from Kilmainham jail, the Irish Labour and Industrial Union was formed under his auspices. He used the occasion to praise his proletarian allies for their cooperation in the land agitation and to call for remedial legislation on their behalf. In the following October the laborers' demands were incorporated in the program of the Irish National League. In 1883 the Labourers' (Ireland) Act was passed.

This statute was not the first to deal with the housing of the rural worker, but all previous laws amounted to little more than pious hopes that landlords and farmers would undertake the task. Though some had provided respectable housing for their laborers, the hopes were not generally realized. The act of 1883 recognized this fact, for it transferred responsibility partly to the boards of guardians. Boards with well-to-do farmers as members were, however, reluctant to prosecute fellow farmers who refused to comply with the provisions of the law, or to finance housing schemes out of the poor rates, though assisted by grants from the board of works.[84] The operation of the act also bristled with legal and financial difficulties, and it took some twelve amending statutes from the original date until 1919 to remove them and hasten building. The legal procedure for acquiring land was gradually simplified, the definition of an agricultural laborer (which at first excluded the casual worker, usually the worst housed) was extended to include most rural laborers and fishermen, and financing was made easier by reductions in interest rates and grants-in-aid from central funds.[85]

Each cottage built under the 1883 act was provided with a half-acre plot, increased after 1892 to one acre. The cottages were modest structures, but they set a new standard for rural housing. The Irish local-government board required a minimum of two bedrooms and a kitchen, and laid down certain structural rules that prevented a repetition of the worst features of the old cabins. Perishable materials were replaced by brick or local stone and mortar, and slates were preferred to thatch, as they were more easily maintained. Rents were of necessity low and were

84. See *Report from the select committee on agricultural labourers (Ireland)*, p. 70, for the workings of the act in the Sligo poor-law union. See also Donnelly, *Cork*, pp. 240–2.

85. Unless otherwise indicated, the account in this and subsequent paragraphs of the provisions of the various acts for the housing of rural laborers is based on G. F. E. Johnston, "Irish agricultural labourers, 1881–1921," Moderatorship thesis, University of Dublin, 1954.

subsidized from the beginning. The mean was 1s. a week, but the rents were higher or lower according to the nature of the district and the quality of the cottage provided. Arrears were heavy at first, but declined as wages rose. By 1920 the arrears amounted to less than 4 percent of yearly rents.

The cost of building and acquiring land varied from union to union, but averaged about £105 in the early years; rising prices increased the figure to approximately £180 in 1914, when the outbreak of the first world war brought fresh building to a standstill. A new act was passed in 1919, but inflated prices (£450 was then required to provide a cottage and an acre of land) and the disturbed state of the country discouraged further efforts until after 1921, when such schemes became the responsibility of the two new states.

The rate of building, as opposed to its cost, is of more than economic interest. About 16,000 cottages were completed or authorized by 1900, Munster taking the lion's share with 9,000. Leinster had some 6,500, but Ulster and Connacht possessed only about 300 and 160 respectively.[86] The local-government act of 1898 enabled laborers to take part in the election of the new rural-district councils that replaced the boards of guardians as the authorities charged with rural housing; the new councils more than doubled the rate of construction. The fresh financial provisions of the act of 1900 maintained that rate until 1914. When in 1921 administration of the acts ceased to be a British responsibility, 54,000 cottages had been erected or authorized at a cost of £9 million.[87]

Agricultural laborers are notoriously more difficult to organize than industrial workers, especially in a country of small farms like Ireland. There were consequently no Irish equivalents of the large English and Scottish unions. Yet local organizations that sprang up in a number of areas were not without influence. Wexford and the midland counties of Leinster as well as Cork, Tipperary, and Limerick in Munster were such areas; they were also the counties where cottages were built most quickly and in the greatest number. On the eve of the first world war Cork already possessed as many as the whole of Ulster.[88] Political antagonisms rather than financial or social considerations seem to explain the very low rate of construction in the northern province.

The relatively small number of cottages built in Connacht can be attributed to the poverty of its poor-law unions and to the social position

86. *[Twenty-seventh] annual report of the local-government board for Ireland . . .* , pp. 68–71 [C 9480], H.C. 1899, xxxix, 1.

87. *[Forty-eighth] annual report of the local-government board for Ireland for the year ended 31st March 1920 . . .* , pp. lxxvi, lxxviii [C 1432], H.C. 1921, xiv, 781.

88. *[Forty-first] annual report of the local-government board for Ireland for the year ended 31st March 1913 . . .* , pp. 150–63 [C 6978], H.C. 1913, xxxii, 457.

of its laborers. Many in need of rehousing were, strictly speaking, small tenants who did not qualify under the earlier acts, but who eked out a living as migratory harvesters. Though the total number of external migrants had dropped to under 20,000 by the end of the century, the proportion of those from Connacht remained constant at 80 percent.[89]

The problem in the west concerned a high proportion of the population rather than one class within it. As in west Donegal, the other main center of migratory labor, the land was too poor to support so many people, and a bad harvest, as in 1879, meant acute distress, if not famine. A Congested Districts Board was appointed in 1891 to deal with those poor-law unions having a ratable value of less than 30s. per head. When other areas were added in 1909, the board's operations covered Donegal, all of Connacht, Kerry, and parts of Clare and west Cork. The board devoted most of its financial resources to the consolidation and extension of holdings, thus making it possible for tenants to gain a less precarious livelihood. Until it was dissolved in 1923, the board spent £10 million on the purchase of estates for subdivision. Its officials also encouraged local industries, including fisheries, though with limited success.[90]

What then did the rural laborers gain from the land war and its aftermath? Unlike the tenant farmers, they did not win the land, if we except the 50,000 who ultimately received an acre each. There were not sufficient rural industries to retain them, and a class that had numbered at least 350,000 at the start of the land war shrank within fifty years to 160,000 and was halved again during the following quarter-century.[91]

The history of the Irish rural laborer from 1880 to 1921 is a history of slow and modest progress.[92] His real wages rose, a trend reflected in his food and clothing. Hunger ceased to be inevitable in winter, and if he relied too much on bread and tea, he also had eggs and milk when

89. *Report and tables relating to Irish migratory agricultural and other labourers for the year 1901*, pp. 9–10 [C 850], H.C. 1902, cxvi, pt. ii, 87. Of the 19,732 migrants (622 of them females), 1,238 went elsewhere in Ireland.

90. W. L. Micks, *An account of the Congested Districts Board for Ireland, 1891–1923* (Dublin, 1925), pp. 18, 25, 35–84, 124, 150, 153.

91. Rural laborers numbered approximately 350,000 in 1880, 160,000 in 1930, and 80,000 in 1955. These figures are for the whole of Ireland.

92. Progress was indeed slow for some. James Chambers, poor-law guardian and delegate to the Irish T.U.C. in 1901, reported that a group of agricultural laborers in Wexford were receiving only 4s. a week. He asked how a man could, after paying a rent of 1s. a week for a cabin, support a wife and family on what was left (*Report of the eighth Irish Trades Union Congress held in the Town Hall, Sligo, on Monday, Tuesday, and Wednesday, 27th, 28th, and 29th May, 1901* [Dublin, n.d.], p. 37). My mother, born in 1883 near the Carlow-Kilkenny border and familiar also with adjacent parts of Wexford, Kildare, and Queen's County, confirmed that in these areas 4s. a week with diet was commonly paid at the turn of the century.

they were plentiful, "yalla male" (Indian meal) as a standby, and at times meat in the shape of American salt bacon, known as "lad" in some areas. Cheap ready-made clothing enabled him to present a more cheerful appearance, while his children, if still barefoot and liable to be "delicate,"[93] no longer went practically naked during their childhood. His wages rose to between 20s. and 30s. during the first world war, when he had the protection of minimum wages until peace returned. If he still suffered from unregulated working hours and spells of unemployment, he was less vulnerable than in earlier years, for he was acquiring a scarcity value. But for some, seasonal migration was still a necessity, while for others emigration was the preferred and final solution. Only in east Ulster was there an industrial area of sufficient consequence to absorb many. As the Lagan valley continued to grow in economic importance, more and more Ulster farm workers abandoned agriculture for the factories and workshops of Belfast.

Thus the marginal man, the rural laborer, left field and farm and passed into history and song. The degrading hiring fair where, as in County Down at the beginning of this century, the laborer in search of a job stood with a straw in his mouth,[94] disappeared with the coming of the first world war. But it survived in the book of the people. Nearly two hundred years after the Kerry spalpeen expressed bitter resentment at the treatment he received from his boorish employers, the Derry farm servant in the wryly humorous ballad, "The hiring fair," warned his listeners not to work for farmer Brady of Strabane, the Simon Legree of rural Ireland.

93. A euphemism for consumptive, i.e., suffering from pulmonary tuberculosis.

94. Personal interview with the late John Cowser of the Royal Belfast Academical Institution. Mr. Cowser had seen such hiring fairs during his boyhood in south Down.

BIBLIOGRAPHY

Contemporary sources

Manuscript material
National Library of Ireland, Dublin
  Larcom papers: Constabulary, Queen's County and County Kilkenny (MS 7653).

Contemporary publications
I. Parliamentary papers (in chronological order)
  Report of the commissioners appointed to take the census of Ireland for the year 1841 [504], H.C. 1843, xxiv, 1.

Reports from poor-law inspectors on the wages of agricultural labourers in Ireland [C 35], H.C. 1870, xiv, 1.

Report and tables relating to migratory agricultural labourers [for 1880] [C 2809], H.C. 1881, xciii, 807.

Report from the select committee on agricultural labourers (Ireland), together with the proceedings of the committee and minutes of evidence, H.C. 1884–5 (32), vii, 559.

Census of Ireland, 1891, pt. ii: *general report, with illustrative maps and diagrams, tables, and appendix* [C 6780], H.C. 1892, xc, 1.

Royal commission on labour: the agricultural labourer, vol. iv, *Ireland*, pt. iv [C 6894-xxi], H.C. 1893–4, xxxvii, pt. i, 341.

[Twenty-seventh] annual report of the local-government board for Ireland . . . [C 9480], H.C. 1899, xxxix, 1.

Report and tables relating to Irish migratory agricultural and other labourers for the year 1901 [C 850], H.C. 1902, cxvi, pt. ii, 87.

Census of Ireland, 1901, pt. ii: *general report, with illustrative maps and diagrams, tables, and appendix* [C 1190], H.C. 1902, cxxix, 1.

Report of the viceregal commission on poor-law reform in Ireland, vol. i [C 3202], H.C. 1906, li, 349.

[Forty-first] annual report of the local-government board for Ireland for the year ended 31st March 1913 . . . [C 6978], H.C. 1913, xxxii, 457.

[Forty-eighth] annual report of the local-government board for Ireland for the year ended 31st March 1920 . . . [C 1432], H.C. 1921, xiv, 781.

II. Newspapers and periodicals
Freeman's Journal (Dublin).
Irishman (Dublin).
Lyceum (Dublin).
Nineteenth Century (London).

III. Reports, memoirs, travelers' accounts, works of reference
Berkeley, George. *The works of George Berkeley, bishop of Cloyne*, ed. A. A. Luce and T. E. Jessop, 9 vols. (London, 1948–57).

Dinneen, P. S. *Foclóir Gaedhilge agus Béarla: an Irish-English dictionary* . . . (rev. ed., with additions, Dublin, 1927).

Irish Trades Union Congress:

Irish Trades Union Congress, April 27 & 28th, "Labor omnia vincet"; Labour Day demonstration, May 6th, Dublin, published by the Dublin District Trades Council and Labour League [Dublin, 1894].

Report of the fifth Irish Trades Union Congress, held in the Exhibition Hall, Belfast, 30th and 31st May and 1st June, 1898 [Belfast, n.d.].

Report of the eighth Irish Trades Union Congress, held in the Town Hall, Sligo, on Monday, Tuesday, and Wednesday, 27th, 28th, and 29th May, 1901 [Dublin, n.d.].

Kennedy, J. P. (ed.). *Digest of evidence taken before her majesty's commissioners of inquiry into the state of the law and practice in respect to the occupation of land in Ireland*, 2 vols. (London and Dublin, 1847–8).

Ó Canainn, Pádraig (ed.). *Filíocht na nGael* (Dublin, 1958).
Thompson, Flora. *Lark Rise to Candleford* (Penguin Modern Classics ed., Harmondsworth, 1973).
Tuke, J. H. *Irish distress and its remedies; the land question: a visit to Donegal and Connaught in the spring of 1880* (London, 1880).
Vaughan, W. E., and Fitzpatrick, A. J. (ed.). *Irish historical statistics: population, 1821–1971* (Dublin, 1978).

Later works

Writings in Irish studies

Bew, Paul. *Land and the national question in Ireland, 1858–82* (Dublin, 1978).
Black, R. D. C. "The progress of industrialization, 1850–1920" in T. W. Moody and J. C. Beckett (ed.), *Ulster since 1800: a political and economic survey* (London, 1954), pp. 50–9.
Boyle, Elizabeth. *The Irish flowerers* (Holywood, Co. Down, and Belfast, 1971).
Boyle, J. W. "Ireland and the First International" in *Journal of British Studies*, xi, no. 2 (May 1972), pp. 44–62.
Clark, Samuel. *Social origins of the Irish land war* (Princeton, 1979).
Corfe, T. H. "The troubles of Captain Boycott, part I: the Land League" in *History Today*, xiv, no. 11 (Nov. 1964), pp. 758–64.
Corfe, T. H. "The troubles of Captain Boycott, part II: the campaign" in *History Today*, xiv, no. 12 (Dec. 1964), pp. 854–62.
Coyne, W. P. (ed.). *Ireland, industrial and agricultural* (Dublin, 1902).
Cullen, L. M. *An economic history of Ireland since 1660* (London, 1972).
Donnelly, J. S., Jr. *The land and the people of nineteenth-century Cork: the rural economy and the land question* (London and Boston, 1975).
Fitzpatrick, David. "The disappearance of the Irish agricultural labourer, 1841–1912" in *Irish Economic and Social History*, vii (1980), pp. 66–92.
Handley, J. E. *The Irish in modern Scotland* (Cork, 1947).
Hoppen, K. T. "Landlords, society, and electoral politics in mid-nineteenth-century Ireland" in *Past and Present*, no. 75 (May 1977), pp. 62–93.
Horn, P. L. R. "The National Agricultural Labourers' Union in Ireland, 1873–9" in *Irish Historical Studies*, xvii, no. 67 (Mar. 1971), pp. 340–52.
Johnston, G. F. E. "Irish agricultural labourers, 1881–1921" (Moderatorship thesis, University of Dublin, 1954).
Kerr, B. M. "Irish seasonal migration to Great Britain, 1800–38" in *Irish Historical Studies*, iii, no. 12 (Sept. 1943), pp. 365–80.
Lee, Joseph. "Irish agriculture" in *Agricultural History Review*, xvii, pt. i (1969), pp. 64–76.
Lee, Joseph. *The modernisation of Irish society, 1848–1918* (Dublin, 1973).
Lee, Joseph. "The Ribbonmen" in T. D. Williams (ed.), *Secret societies in Ireland* (Dublin and New York, 1973), pp. 26–35.
Lyons, F. S. L. *The Irish parliamentary party, 1890–1910* (London, 1951).

Lyons, F. S. L. *Ireland since the famine* (rev. ed., London, 1973).

Micks, W. L. *An account of the Congested Districts Board for Ireland, 1891–1923* (Dublin, 1925).

Moody, T. W. "Michael Davitt and the British labour movement, 1882–1906" in *Transactions of the Royal Historical Society*, 5th ser., iii (1953), pp. 53–76.

Moody, T. W. "Michael Davitt" in J. W. Boyle (ed.), *Leaders and workers* (Cork, 1966), pp. 47–55.

O'Connor, Frank. "Legal aid" in *The stories of Frank O'Connor* (London, 1953).

Palmer, N. D. *The Irish Land League crisis* (New Haven, 1940).

Other writings in social science

Hammond, J. L., and Hammond, Barbara. *The village labourer*, 2 vols. (Guild Books ed., London, 1948).

Hobsbawm, E. J., and Rudé, George. *Captain Swing* (Norton Library ed., New York and Toronto, 1975).

9 Líam Kennedy

Farmers, Traders, and Agricultural Politics in Pre-Independence Ireland

Introduction

In the last quarter of the nineteenth century Irish political institutions were being recast in a form that brought them into a more sensitive relationship with the body of popular political feeling. The ballot act of 1872, though it did not initiate major new political trends,[1] at least lowered the cost of exercising electoral rights in accordance with the voter's own preferences rather than with those of landlord or priest. As a result of the extension of the franchise in 1884, smaller property holders and laborers participated directly for the first time in the process of returning M.P.s. Prior to 1884 members of these social groups were involved only indirectly in the political system, most effectively when organized into large intimidatory crowds.[2] The electoral process as well as the heads of luckless opponents sometimes bore the clear imprint of their collective action. With the fusion of parliamentary and agrarian struggles during the first phase of the land war (1879–82), a strong countrywide organizational base was grafted onto the structure of parliamentary representation in nationalist Ireland. Such a broadening of the base of the political pyramid necessarily entailed the provi-

---

1. See Michael Hurst, "Ireland and the ballot act of 1872" in *Hist. Jn.*, viii, no. 3 (1965) pp. 326–52.
2. J. H. Whyte, "The influence of the Catholic clergy on elections in nineteenth-century Ireland" in *E.H.R.*, lxxv, no. 295 (Apr. 1960), pp. 244–6; K. T. Hoppen, "Landlords, society, and electoral politics in mid-nineteenth-century Ireland" in *Past & Present*, no. 75 (May 1977), p. 89.

sion of services by an increased number of political figures at the local level. The turn of the century saw further democratization in the Irish countryside, as popular local government, county committees of agriculture, and other administrative innovations were introduced.[3] Thus, in an era of democratic reform, when political opportunities were being opened up on a broad front, the issue of how the chief beneficiaries of these reforms responded assumes major significance. Did the lower and middle strata of Irish society — rural and town laborers, tenant farmers, traders, small businessmen — now come to enjoy political representation and power in rough proportion to their numbers in the population? If not, can deviations from such a distribution be explained? Are the deviations so marked as to suggest varying levels of organizational strength and political awareness within Irish society? In exploring aspects of these and related issues, this essay analyzes the exercise of power by farmers and traders during the late nineteenth and early twentieth centuries.

Social change in the decades of reconstruction after the great famine, signified especially by a reshaping of the occupational structure,[4] strongly influenced the power relationships examined here. In the agricultural sector of the economy the proportion of the work force engaged in farming declined during the second half of the nineteenth century. The more politically significant developments, however, relate to occupational shifts within that sector. The greatest decline occurred among laborers and cottiers, groups whose interests, when not in direct conflict with those of tenant farmers, were less easily harmonized with the concerns of other agriculturalists. By contrast, the middle peasantry consolidated its position, as indicated by the rise in the number of holdings above 15 acres from 276,600 in 1845 to 303,500 in 1910.[5] The postfamine pe-

---

3. An important recent work by W. L. Feingold demonstrates that the boards of poor-law guardians provided an outlet for local political activity throughout the second half of the nineteenth century. But it was not until the 1880s that control of these bodies was wrested from the landlord class and its representatives. See W. L. Feingold, "The Irish boards of poor-law guardians, 1872–1886: a revolution in local government" (Ph.D. thesis, University of Chicago, 1974).

4. A rough summary of occupational trends in postfamine Ireland may be found in Charles Booth, "The economic distribution of population in Ireland" in W. P. Coyne (ed.), *Ireland, industrial and agricultural* (Dublin, 1902), pp. 64–72.

5. The figures for 1845 are taken from P. M. A. Bourke, "The agricultural statistics of the 1841 census of Ireland: a critical review" in *Econ. Hist. Rev.*, 2nd ser., xviii, no. 2 (Aug. 1965), pp. 376–91. For statistics on farm size in 1910, see *Agricultural statistics of Ireland . . . , 1910*, p. 16 [C 5964], H.C. 1911, c, 517. On changes in the rural class structure, see especially Joseph Lee, *The modernisation of Irish society, 1848–1918* (Dublin, 1973), pp. 2–4.

riod also witnessed a strengthening of the class of capitalist farmers, many of whom were graziers.[6] As recent historians have demonstrated, the rise to social and political prominence of this farming elite is crucial to an understanding of agrarian politics in the late nineteenth century.[7] William Feingold has shown that as early as the 1870s strong farmers and graziers were challenging the landowners for control of the poor-law boards.[8] The distinctive contribution of large farmers to the land war must also be noted. Unlike the smallholders in the west of Ireland who sparked off the land war in the spring of 1879, large farmers in some eastern and southern counties had been mobilized in farmers' clubs during the 1860s and the 1870s.[9] Such associations provided an organizational structure through which the land movement in the west was channeled to other parts of Ireland.[10] Equally significant, large farmers were active in shaping the strategy and objectives of the agrarian agitation.[11]

The decline, in both absolute and relative terms, of the numbers working in agriculture was accompanied by an increasing degree of urbanization in Irish society. Whereas a mere 15 percent of the population lived in towns of at least 1,500 inhabitants in 1841, by 1901 the urban share had risen to 32 percent, or roughly one in every three of the population.[12] Development was not limited to numbers alone. Henry Coulter, a correspondent of *Saunders's News-Letter* who toured the west of Ireland in the early 1860s, was deeply impressed by the visible signs of progress which he found in towns and villages there. Of Kilrush, a town

6. This farming elite was clearly visible to a number of contemporary observers. See, e.g., Henry Coulter, *The west of Ireland: its existing condition and prospects* (Dublin, 1862), pp. 44–9; B. H. Becker, *Disturbed Ireland, being the letters written during the winter of 1880–81* (London, 1881), pp. 20, 73; *The Irish peasant: a sociological study* (London, 1892), pp. 95–6; M. J. Bonn, *Modern Ireland and her agrarian problem* (Dublin, 1906), pp. 41–2, 91.

7. The best discussion of the role of large farmers in agrarian politics in the late nineteenth and early twentieth centuries is by D. S. Jones, "Agrarian capitalism and rural social development in Ireland" (Ph.D. thesis, Queen's University, Belfast, 1977). For an incisive analysis of the relationships between different agrarian groups during the early phase of the land war, see Paul Bew, *Land and the national question in Ireland, 1858–82* (Dublin, 1978).

8. Feingold, "Boards of guardians," pp. 80–3, 104–5.

9. On farmers' clubs, see Bew, *Land*, pp. 54–5, 101–3; Feingold, "Boards of guardians," pp. 87–90; Samuel Clark, "The political mobilization of Irish farmers" in *Canadian Review of Sociology and Anthropology*, xii, no. 4, pt. 2 (1975), pp. 494–5. See also R. A. Anderson, *With Horace Plunkett in Ireland* (London, 1935), pp. 63–4.

10. Clark, "Political mobilization," p. 495.

11. Bew, *Land*, pp. 176–9.

12. *Report of the commission on emigration and other population problems* (Dublin, 1954), p. 10.

of some 4,500 inhabitants, Coulter observed: "This town is a remarkable instance of the improvement which has taken place in so many country towns throughout Ireland since 1846. During the interval that has elapsed, the shops in Kilrush have doubled in number and greatly increased in size. For example, in 1846 there was scarcely a shop in the town more than 24 feet in length, and there was not one having a plate-glass window, whereas now there are twelve shops with plate-glass windows, some of 30 feet in front, and over 80 from front to rear. These shops are well stocked with goods varying in value from £1,000 to £7,000. . . ."[13] Even the village of Scariff, which had suffered severely during the famine, and which "in 1846 had only one little shop of the meanest description, now contains several thriving and wealthy shopkeepers, who have set up establishments and made their fortunes within a period of ten or twelve years."[14] Three decades later, another traveler was struck by the wealth of publicans, shopkeepers, provision merchants, and cattle dealers.[15]

The rise of traders — wholesalers, retailers, dealers in agricultural inputs and outputs — was one of the strategically significant features of change in postfamine society. A quantitative impression of these developments is readily conveyed by the occupational statistics. Charles Booth calculated that the proportion of occupations concerned with trading rose from 3.6 percent at midcentury to 5.4 percent in 1891, a relative gain of 50 percent over the period.[16] This upward trend was sustained in subsequent decades.[17] In the thirty years before 1911, for example, publicans, innkeepers, and grocers increased in number from 23,459 to 24,945. In the context of a declining population this small absolute rise represented a considerable relative gain. (Roughly comparable figures for 1841, when 12,369 persons followed these occupations, indicate a lower absolute and much lower relative level of trading activity in prefamine Ireland.)[18] In the countryside this expansion reflected the diffusion of market relationships through the rural economy, in particular the growing commercialization of agriculture. Thus, marketed (but not total) output in Irish agriculture rose between the early 1840s and 1870.[19] The acreage of potatoes

13. Coulter, *West of Ireland*, pp. 56-7.
14. Ibid., p. 30.
15. *Irish peasant*, p. 144.
16. Booth, "Economic distribution," p. 65.
17. Líam Kennedy, "Traders in the Irish rural economy, 1880-1914" in *Econ. Hist. Rev.*, 2nd ser., xxxii, no. 2 (May 1979), pp. 201-10.
18. *Report of the commissioners appointed to take the census of Ireland for the year 1841*, p. 440 [504], H.C. 1843, xxiv, 1.
19. On changes in the value of agricultural output between 1840-4 and 1869-71, see Cormac Ó Gráda, "Agricultural head rents, pre-famine and post-famine" in *Economic and Social Review*, v, no. 3 (Apr. 1974), p. 390. Ó Gráda calculates that over this period the value of agricultural output declined marginally from £49.8 million to £48.6 million.

— the major subsistence crop — declined dramatically, indicating not only a drop in population but also a movement away from domestic consumption of the produce of the land. Increased reliance on the purchase of consumption goods and farm inputs on the one hand, and on the sale of agricultural commodities on the other, immersed the farming population more deeply in the market system. Naturally, this necessitated the services of a larger number of distributors of various kinds.

Increased reliance on the market forged links between town and countryside that were later to prove of critical political importance. Samuel Clark has identified three major strands in the bond that joined farmers to segments of the town population: kinship ties which connected farmers to shopkeepers, publicans, provision merchants, and other townsmen; commercial ties that included a significant credit relationship; and an information network through which traders, by acting as channels of communication between the outside world and the local rural community, further strengthened their relationship with country clients.[20] Certain changes in the economic structure of urban centers reinforced dependence on country trade. The contraction of small industry and crafts in the towns and villages reduced or choked off sources of demand for retail and other services.[21] In short, the economic base of country towns and villages in postfamine Ireland was narrowing, thus inducing increased reliance on the sale of services to the inhabitants of the rural hinterland.

With the onset of agricultural depression after 1876 and the consequent reduced purchasing power of farmers, both farmers and traders had a vital interest in shoring up agricultural incomes.[22] For many traders the situation was all the more acute because during the long period of agricultural prosperity prior to 1877 it had become common commercial practice to extend considerable credit to farmers.[23] The prospect of default on these large outstanding loans spelled business failure. The only course of action that could accommodate the economic interests of both traders and their country clients was one which sought to reduce rent payments to landlords, thus increasing the disposable income of farmers.[24] Such action, necessarily involving confrontation with the land-

20. Clark, "Political mobilization," pp. 490–1.

21. The decline of artisans and related groups is apparent from an inspection of the occupational statistics contained in the censuses of population, 1841–1911. See also L. M. Cullen, *An economic history of Ireland since 1660* (London, 1972), pp. 144–8.

22. Samuel Clark, "The social composition of the Land League" in *I.H.S.*, xvii, no. 68 (Sept. 1971), p. 450; Becker, *Disturbed Ireland*, p. 50.

23. Coulter, *West of Ireland*, pp. 57–8; Becker, *Disturbed Ireland*, pp. 208–10; *Irish peasant*, pp. 41–3; *Report from the select committee on money lending* . . . , p. 156, H.C. 1898 (260), x, 101.

24. The smaller traders clearly recognized that if farmers withheld the rent owed

lord class, had the further merit of being compatible with the height-ened sense of nationalism apparent among townsmen and strong farmers in the 1870s.[25]

It was not only the growing coincidence of interests between certain types of traders and their rural clients that was to prove politically so significant; the increasing numerical and social importance of traders in postfamine society was also accompanied by a developing taste for political power. The electoral influence enjoyed by shopkeepers within borough constituencies in the 1850s and 1860s has been traced in fasci-nating detail by K. T. Hoppen.[26] This influence derived partly from nu-merical strength (in Derry and Galway, for example, shopkeepers made up roughly one-third of the electorate) and partly from the use of social networks centering on retailers, publicans, and other traders. An addi-tional indication of the rising political importance of traders is the prom-inent role which they played in attempts to gain control of the poor-law boards during the 1870s and 1880s. Feingold points out, however, that their political activity was most exuberant in the poorer northwestern counties; elsewhere the leadership role of large tenant farmers was con-siderably more significant.[27] The land war of 1879–82 marked a major stage in the political advance of the trading community. Townsmen par-ticipated prominently along with farmers in the agitation. Indeed, an analysis of the social composition of the Land League reveals that shop-keepers and publicans played a disproportionately large role, relative to their numbers in the population, in organizing and directing the onslaught against landlordism.[28] This alliance of agrarian and urban in-terests was carried over into the National League and the struggle for home rule.

Political Representation

Even by the end of the nineteenth century, Irish parliamentary repre-sentation bore a distorted relationship to numerically significant groups in the population. Nonetheless, the political progress of traders and large

---

to the landlord, then their country customers would be in a better position to pay shop debts (Becker, *Disturbed Ireland*, p. 50).

25. Feingold, "Boards of guardians," pp. 95–6, 103–4; K. T. Hoppen, "National politics and local realities in mid-nineteenth-century Ireland" in Art Cosgrove and Donal McCartney (ed.), *Studies in Irish history presented to R. Dudley Edwards* (Dublin, 1979), pp. 220–3.

26. Hoppen, "National politics," pp. 194–8.

27. Feingold, "Boards of guardians," pp. 270–1.

28. Clark, "Social composition," pp. 455–6. Clark's findings, however, are derived from the study of a social movement strongly associated with the western half of Ireland. To attempt to extrapolate the results to other regions is therefore risky.

farmers was beginning to be reflected at the somewhat rarified level of parliamentary membership.[29] F. S. L. Lyons has examined the social background of Irish M.P.s over the period 1892–1910. From his data on the occupations of Nationalist M.P.s in five parliaments from 1892 to 1910, it emerges that on average 13 percent of the seats went to local merchants ("men owning shops in the country towns").[30] This proportion was practically the same as that of farmers, despite their numerical predominance in the population.

Clearly, parliamentary representation of the tenant masses rested very much with outside groups in the last decade of the nineteenth century and the first decade of the twentieth. Though the stronger farmers had secured a significant minority presence within the parliamentary party, the more interesting feature is their failure to achieve dominance in the representation of the rural electorate. By contrast, traders were considerably overrepresented, and though this does not necessarily mean that the deficit in tenant representation came partly from this source, there is reason to suppose that this was the case. Indeed, if the testimony of a diverse group of contemporaries can be accepted, traders were even more strongly entrenched in political life below the parliamentary level, that is, in the organizational structures of the Nationalist party and in local government. Thus a disgruntled figure in the home-rule movement, who was later a historian of the Irish parliamentary party, complained that the conventions of the United Irish League consisted of "half gombeenmen and half political priests."[31] (The pejorative term "gombeenman" was applied to local moneylenders or, more usually, retailers charging allegedly usurious interest on credit accounts.) The writer T. W. Rolleston echoed this view: parliamentary representation, he declared, was controlled by the "small country publican and gombeenman."[32] Pioneers of agricultural cooperation in Ireland, such as George Russell, Horace Plunkett, and R. A. Anderson, frequently asserted that shopkeepers, publicans, and other traders carried disproportionate weight in the nationalist movement.[33] From a different ideological position the labor leader and Marxist James Connolly, in the course of a blistering

29. Between 1880 and 1885 the number of farmers and shopkeepers rose from two to twenty-two (Lee, *Modernisation*, p. 107). For the social background of parliamentary representatives in the period 1874–80, see O'Brien, *Parnell and his party*, pp. 14–20.

30. Lyons, *Ir. parl. party*, p. 169.

31. F. H. O'Donnell, *A history of the Irish parliamentary party* (2 vols., London, 1910), ii, 464.

32. For the controversy centering on this claim, see *F.J.*, 21, 22, 24, 28 Jan. 1908.

33. George Russell, *Cooperation and nationality* (Dublin, 1912), p. 13; *Irish Homestead*, 5 May, 22 Dec. 1906, 18 June 1910, 18 Nov. 1911; Irish Agricultural Organisation Society, *Annual report, 1907* (Dublin, 1908), p. 68; Anderson, *Horace Plunkett*, pp. 115–21. See also the opinions expressed in *Annual Report, 1909*, p. 76; *Annual report, 1911*, p. 22.

attack on middlemen and dealers in the small country towns, spoke of these figures as "dominant influences in the councils of the local home-rule or other constitutional national organisation."[34] Still another writer commented in more moderate terms: "The members of the Irish party are closely connected with the class of country traders. The country traders are the chief men and the capitalists of their districts; they are strongly represented in the local branches of the United Irish League; and they naturally exercise a considerable influence on the policy of the Irish party."[35] These observations, while suggestive, need to be tested empirically. Specifically, was it true that traders wielded disproportionate power at the local political level? And if so, did this have important implications for the exercise of power by farmers, as seems to be implied? It will be shown later that the situation was more complex than contemporary accounts indicate. In particular, it will be argued that it is just as much a mistake to claim that traders controlled or dominated elected bodies as it is to ignore the political strength of traders and townsmen.

Conflicting Interests

As previously noted, the alliance between farmers and townsmen in the agrarian and political agitations of the late 1870s and the 1880s marked a significant stage in the political advance of certain categories of traders. The fact that the demand for major land reforms was so directly concerned with the welfare of farmers tended to obscure this political advance. The connection between land reform and farmers' interests was easily perceived. Less visible, but no less real, was the benefit which reforms would confer on traders whose fortunes were linked with those of rural dwellers.[36] The mass movement based on this coalition of interests succeeded in wresting substantial concessions from landlords and from the state. But this coincidence of interests, latent in the 1860s and the 1870s, and crystallized with the onset of the agricultural depression, was not to endure indefinitely. Important areas of conflict between farmers and those traders who serviced the rural population opened up toward the end of the nineteenth century.

One major area of tension which revealed a basic divergence of interests centered on access to land. Many shopkeepers, motivated by eco-

34. James Connolly, *Labour in Ire.* (reprint ed., Dublin, 1951), p. 240.
35. Sir Ernest Barker, *Ireland in the last fifty years, 1866–1916* (2nd ed., Oxford, 1919), p. 77. For similar comments, see Bonn, *Modern Ireland*, p. 30.
36. Becker, *Disturbed Ireland*, pp. 50, 109; Clark, "Social composition," p. 450.

nomic and status considerations, competed actively in the land market and secured farms for themselves.[37] In certain parts of the country traders also vied strongly with tenant farmers for tracts of grazing let by landlords on a short-term basis.[38] Smallholders seeking to augment their holdings by adding land rented on the eleven-month system were frequently outbid by shopkeeper-graziers. Thus shopkeeper-graziers (and indeed other graziers) severely restricted the opportunities available to smallholders in their struggle to achieve economic viability.[39] One response to this situation was the agitation, located mainly but not exclusively in the west of Ireland, for the breaking up of the grazing ranches. Agrarian reformers demanded that these lands, customarily let by landlords in large tracts on the eleven-month system, should be divided among smallholders. The popular mood in the west during this movement was well conveyed by a contemporary observer:"Half the social significance of this campaign lies in the fact that here in Iar Connacht the graziers are for the most part shopkeepers. They are not farmers at all, properly speaking. . . . Therefore, the local public feeling, running before the law, proceeds, if it can, to make life disagreeable and unprofitable for the shopkeeper who, instead of confining himself to shopkeeping, takes up land for stock farming in a country where hardly any cottier or tillage farmer has a holding fit to live on."[40]

Relationships between certain farmers and traders were further strained by conflicts stemming from the spread of the movement for agricultural cooperation. The cooperative system began to establish itself in rural Ireland during the early 1890s under the stimulus of a nonfarming elite composed mainly of paternalistic individuals associated with the landed ascendancy.[41] In 1890 there was only one agricultural cooperative in the whole country; by 1914 there were over 1,000 societies with nearly 90,000 members.[42] The strongest arm of the movement, in terms of member-

37. Jones, "Agrarian capitalism," pp. 288–9.

38. "The good meadows of the west are often set for eleven months to the village shopkeeper, the solicitor, or the doctor; even the clergyman himself does not scorn sometimes to increase his scanty income by this means" (Bonn, *Modern Ireland*, p. 41). See also Stephen Gwynn, *A holiday in Connemara* (London, 1909), p. 110.

39. Jones, "Agrarian capitalism," pp. 239–66.

40. Gwynn, *Connemara*, pp. 109–10. See also *Royal commission on congestion in Ireland: appendix to the sixth report*, p. 61 [C 3748], H.C. 1908, xxxix, 701.

41. It has been suggested that organizational skills acquired by farmers in the course of the land war were successfully transposed to the sphere of local cooperative enterprises. See Margaret Digby, *Horace Plunkett: an Anglo-American Irishman* (Oxford, 1949), p. 54.

42. The spread of cooperatives is discussed in detail in Líam Kennedy, "Agricultural cooperation and Irish rural society, 1880–1914" (Ph.D. thesis, University of York, 1978), pp. 20–40.

ship and turnover, consisted of the cooperative creameries, which rooted themselves firmly in the Munster and Ulster counties. Credit societies were particularly linked with the west of Ireland. The Leinster counties, with the exception of Kilkenny, nourished comparatively few societies. Essentially, the originators of the movement sought to organize farmers to take control of three major areas of farm business — the purchase of farm inputs, processing, and the marketing of farm produce. Their efforts immediately brought farmers into conflict with various types of traders, including butter merchants, cattle and pig dealers, and provision merchants.[43] But the extent of the trader reaction was not confined to those directly servicing the requirements of agricultural producers, whether on the supply or the marketing side. General shopkeepers and other retailers, acutely aware of the broad success which the consumer-cooperative movement had achieved in retail trade in Britain, were apprehensive about the possibility of similar developments in Ireland.[44]

Indeed, the form of activity first advocated by Horace Plunkett and his small band of enthusiasts in 1889 was consumer cooperation.[45] But they quickly became aware of formidable barriers in their way and switched the focus of their campaign to the founding of creamery organizations and later credit societies. The report of the Irish section of the British Cooperative Union for 1892 showed a keen appreciation of the difficulties: "Owing to the influence of the village shopkeepers in most places over the farmers and labourers, the spread of distributive cooperation must needs be slow; but having educated the people by showing them the advantages of cooperative production, we believe the starting of stores to be only a question of time. We hold to our firm opinion that it would be extremely unwise and dangerous to the success of our dairying movement to force distribution upon the Irish people for the present."[46]

During the 1890s in such towns as Mallow, Kanturk, Skibbereen, Thurles, Nenagh, Drogheda, and Longford, traders convened meetings to condemn the cooperative system.[47] The traders of Mallow, for exam-

43. Digby, *Horace Plunkett*, pp. 100–2; Kennedy, "Agricultural cooperation," pp. 252–5.
44. Lionel Smith-Gordon and Laurence Staples, *Rural reconstruction in Ireland* (London, 1917), pp. 39–40; Sydney Brooks, *The new Ireland* (Dublin, 1907), p. 44.
45. Horace Plunkett, "Cooperative stores for Ireland" in *Nineteenth Century*, xxiv (Sept. 1888), pp. 410–18; Patrick Bolger, *The Irish cooperative movement: its history and development* (Dublin, 1977), pp. 62–3.
46. Cooperative Union, *Annual congress report, 1892* (Manchester, 1893), p. 63. In Mallow, Thurles, and later Templecrone, traders' defense associations were set up to fight the cooperative system (Kennedy, "Agricultural cooperation," pp. 252–3).
47. Digby, *Horace Plunkett*, p. 102; Kennedy, "Agricultural cooperation," pp. 252–3.

ple, pledged "by every means in our power to help one another to fight the unjust alliance . . . which tried to destroy our trade and will eventually bring ruin to the farmers themselves."[48] Organized opposition to cooperative societies by traders and townsmen also took the form of attacks in local newspapers, boycotting, and occasionally even physical intimidation.[49] A further set of resources available to traders involved the use of their political influence to contain or stunt cooperative evolution. This technique was to assume increasing significance in the new century. Since the exercise of political power by farmers and traders is of central relevance to this essay, developments in this area are examined in some detail. It will be argued that the early years of the twentieth century marked not only a critical stage in relations between traders and certain categories of farmers but also a turning point in relationships among agrarian groups in general.

Agricultural Politics

The Irish nationalist movement, particularly after the reunification of its major segments within the United Irish League in 1900, was generally hostile to the economic reforms embodied in the cooperative program.[50] This position rested in part on the fear that greater prosperity, especially if attributable to a Unionist administration,[51] might sap the desire for political autonomy — the fear (as one unionist derisively put it) that "comfort and prosperity will make you less keen politicians, that — like a pack of hounds — you won't hunt unless you are kept hungry."[52] Apart from political strategy, more mundane considerations guided Nationalist politicians. Traders were no laggards in making representations to political bodies when they felt that their interests were threatened.[53] This fact emerges clearly from a number of controversial debates that surrounded the proceedings of the Council of Agriculture

48. *Cork Examiner*, 4 Feb. 1896.

49. Anderson, *Horace Plunkett*, pp. 20–2; Digby, *Horace Plunkett*, pp. 54–5, 102; Bolger, *Cooperative movement*, p. 67.

50. Digby, *Horace Plunkett*, pp. 100–1, 145; Bolger, *Cooperative movement*, pp. 95–102.

51. Lyons, *Ir. parl. party*, p. 105.

52. Horace Plunkett, *Plain talks to Irish farmers* (Dublin, 1910), p. 16.

53. This type of interest-group activity is clearly illustrated by the action in 1896 of the Waterford Pig Dealers' Association in relation to their local M.P., John Redmond. Redmond, who was then leader of the Parnellite wing of the nationalist movement and a nominal member of IAOS, was obliged to dissociate himself publicly from any attempt to establish bacon-curing stores of a cooperative kind (*Waterford Star*, 1 Feb. 1896). More generally, the success of traders in securing the support of Nationalist M.P.s for their attacks on IAOS testifies to their political influence and alertness.

between 1905 and 1914. The council, which consisted of 104 members, acted as a forum for discussion of matters relating to agriculture and technical education, and it possessed an advisory role in policy-making.[54] It was conceived essentially as a channel of communication between the Department of Agriculture and Technical Instruction (referred to hereafter as DATI) and its clients, particularly those on the land. The representative character of the council should be noted; two out of every three of its members were elected by the various county councils, thus linking it to the recently democratized local-government system.[55]

The main umbrella body for agricultural cooperatives was the Irish Agricultural Organisation Society (called hereafter IAOS). Its primary function was to promote the cooperative system through the provision of expert advice. It also served to defend the interests of cooperatives in the wider political and legal spheres. Because of recurring financial problems it was forced to seek aid from DATI. The issue of subsidizing cooperative organization came to a head within the Council of Agriculture in November 1906.[56] The critics of cooperation were first into the arena with a motion stating that all work connected with agriculture should be carried out directly by DATI. It was "inadvisable to have further moneys expended through any irresponsible society" (i.e., IAOS), according to proponents of the resolution, who sought in effect to terminate the grant.[57] But the council also contained a strong element that supported the cooperatives. After some heated exchanges a motion favoring financial support for cooperative organization was passed by a seemingly comfortable margin, 52 votes as against 25.[58] A look beneath the surface, however, reveals a more complicated pattern. Voting behavior, analyzed according to whether votes for or against the motion came from the elected or the nominated group on the council, is set out in table 9.1.

54. The composition, powers, and objectives of the council are described in Horace Plunkett, *Ireland in the new century* (London, 1904), pp. 232–7. See also *Report of the departmental committee of inquiry into the provisions of [the] Agricultural and Technical Instruction (Ireland) Act, 1899*, pp. 6–9 [C 3572], H.C. 1907, xvii, 799.

55. For the purposes of representation on the council, Cork was treated as two counties and thus entitled to four representatives. The other thirty-one county councils each had two representatives.

56. In the months leading up to the critical debate, Nationalist politicians spoke strongly against any subsidy for cooperative organization. Brooks asserted that in the attack on IAOS "an immense amount of local pressure was brought to bear on the elected members" (*New Ireland*, p. 45).

57. Department of Agriculture, *Journal*, vii (1907), p. 215. The motion was proposed by an auctioneer and publican from County Cavan, T. P. McKenna. It was seconded by another trader, James Donoghoe, of Enniscorthy.

58. Ibid. The *Journal* lists the voters for and against the motion.

TABLE 9.1
Voting Pattern on the Issue of Renewing the Grant to IAOS

	Elected members	Nominated members	Total
Pro	28	24	52
Con	24	1	25
	52	25	77

It is clear from table 9.1 that without the favorable votes of the pha-
lanx of nominated members, mainly chosen by Plunkett, the outcome
would have been much closer.[59] But it is the elected representatives who
are really of interest here, as the behavior of this group offers clues to
the popular political forces at work. The elected members of the council
were not nearly so enthusiastic about renewal of the grant to IAOS. It
is noteworthy that even at this level many of the county-council representatives were prepared to defy the officially endorsed lines of thought
emanating from DATI and the vice-president's office. On the face of
it, many members of the "farmers' parliament" manifested a rather cir-
cumspect view, if not an actual squint, in relation to what constituted
farmers' interests.

Soon after the removal of Plunkett from the office of vice-president
of DATI early in 1907, it became clear that a bleak era was opening
in relations between DATI and IAOS. The new vice-president, T. W.
Russell, in the course of his inaugural address to the Council of Agriculture, remarked pointedly that a delegation of traders had made representations to him before the meeting against the state subsidy for cooperative organization.[60] Accepting the traders' complaints in full, Russell
roundly attacked IAOS, charging it with setting up cooperative shops
in competition with traders.[61] The subsidy, he insisted, must be discontinued. Though the charge that state money was being used to promote
consumer cooperatives was unfounded,[62] the Council of Agriculture recommended that the subsidy be phased out over a period of three years.
Indeed, as many as one-third of the members were in favor of immedi-

59. Plunkett was vice-president and effective head of DATI from its inception in 1899
until the Nationalist party forced his removal from office in 1907.

60. Department of Agriculture, *Journal*, viii (1908), p. 220.

61. Ibid., pp. 221–6.

62. In the very early days of the cooperative movement Plunkett and Anderson had
sought to interest farmers and laborers in cooperative shops, but this effort was quickly
dropped. In the words of one observer, they could not afford "to excite the hostility of
the trading classes" (*Labour Copartnership* [Aug. 1898], p. 125).

ate suspension, though only gradual withdrawal had been proposed by Russell.[63] The issue of the subsidy was brought to a sharp conclusion the following year. In the wake of a public controversy centering on allegations of hostility to the Nationalist party on the part of IAOS and counterallegations of trader dominance in the Nationalist organization, the subsidy was abruptly terminated.[64] Not until the foundation of the Free State did IAOS again receive aid from a department of agriculture.[65]

Having lurched from one financial crisis to another, IAOS perceived an opportunity in 1910 of securing support from an alternative source. A government-sponsored body known as the Development Commissioners had recently been established to channel aid to agriculture. In January 1911, IAOS applied to the treasury for a grant of £6,612 out of the funds of the commission.[66] The matter was then referred to DATI, where T. W. Russell withheld it from consideration until a meeting of the Council of Agriculture in the following November. At this meeting Russell devoted his address to a long attack on the cooperative movement.[67] He warned his listeners: "The Development Commissioners may very easily and with the best intentions land us in very serious difficulties with the traders of the country." Accusing IAOS of being "in effect a gigantic trading body," he claimed that concession of the grant would imply "a cruel war upon the traders and shopkeepers of the country." Any funds available for Irish agriculture should be given to DATI, which would draw up its own scheme of noncontroversial cooperation, this being defined as "every form of cooperation which does not bring us into direct competition and conflict with the ordinary traders of the country." Whether such a pure form of cooperation could exist was not the subject of detailed discussion. (A few years later, it was unkindly suggested that lime-burning societies, of which there were two in 1915, exhausted the official category of noncontroversial cooperatives.)[68] Russell concluded his speech on a humble note: "I have probably done more for the Irish farmer than the whole of the IAOS put together." In view of these services to Irish agriculture it is hardly surprising that the council was happy to reward him with the decision he sought.[69]

63. Department of Agriculture, *Journal*, viii (1908), p. 203.

64. Ibid., p. 623.

65. Horace Plunkett Foundation, *Agricultural cooperation in Ireland: a survey* (London, 1931), pp. 9–10, 15; Digby, *Horace Plunkett*, pp. 145, 259–60.

66. IAOS, *Annual report, 1912*, pp. 62–3; Smith-Gordon and Staples, *Rural reconstruction*, p. 84.

67. Department of Agriculture, *Journal*, xii (1912), pp. 217–31.

68. Smith-Gordon and Staples, *Rural reconstruction*, pp. 171–2.

69. Department of Agriculture, *Journal*, xii (1912) p. 215.

Russell, however, was not alone in giving forethought to the matter of blocking the application of IAOS for the grant. Denis Johnston, secretary of the United Irish League, had circularized members of the council in advance, charging IAOS with ulterior political motives.[70] Following the successful outcome of the meeting, he informed a Dublin newspaper that the cooperative movement wanted to crush the loyal friends of the League among the shopkeepers of Ireland.[71] He also released the following letter from a Macroom trader thanking him for his exertions on the issue: "Of the many services you have rendered in your time to the Irish people, none could have been better than the active part you took in knocking out the grant to the IAOS. We will be sending on a large subscription to the parliamentary fund from here soon. Who are the largest subscribers? Why, the shopkeepers of course, who, as you know, have always been the backbone of nationality in Ireland."[72] The editor of the cooperative paper, *The Irish Homestead*, issued a prompt diagnosis: if this Macroom trader represented the backbone of nationality, then it must be diseased in its spinal column.[73] Eventually, after a long delay of more than two years, the Development Commissioners rejected DATI's program of noncontroversial cooperation and made a direct grant (subsequently renewed) to IAOS.[74] This subsidy, however, was made subject to the strict provision that IAOS confine itself solely to agricultural business.[75]

What light do these tangled episodes shed on the distribution of political power in Irish society? Without seeking to minimize the roles of personal differences, political paranoia, and genuine disagreement over the legitimate spheres of state and voluntary action, one may conclude that traders were especially alert, relative to farming groups, in mobilizing political resources on their own behalf. Even in the realm of agricultural politics, where the voice of farming groups might well have been decisive, the views of traders were not only articulated with vigor (both within and outside formal structures) but actually prevailed.[76] This conclusion

70. Anderson, *Horace Plunkett*, pp. 174–5.
71. *Evening Telegraph*, 18 Nov. 1911.
72. Ibid.
73. *Irish Homestead*, 25 Nov. 1911.
74. IAOS, *Annual report, 1913*, p. 54.
75. *Copy of treasury letter dated 1st April 1913 respecting the conditions on which a grant will be made to the society from the development fund*, p. 2 [C 6735], H.C. 1913, liii, 3.
76. The conflicts discussed here also had their counterparts in the parliamentary sphere, where the Nationalist M.P.s, especially John Dillon, relentlessly attacked the cooperative movement. See, e.g., *Hansard*, 4th ser., clxv, 839–40; 4th ser., clxvii, 366–9; 4th ser., clxx, 876–84; 5th ser., xviii, 1825–54; 5th ser., xl, 1534–65. John Dillon himself had a

is given added point by the fact that trading groups were numerically insignificant relative to the farming population as a whole.[77] If political outcomes had merely been a function of proportional electoral strength, then traders would have had no hope of imposing their views when a conflict of interests arose. Even if one assumes that some farmers were indifferent about cooperation, this result would still have followed from a simple model of the political process.

Social Composition of the Council of Agriculture

In an attempt to resolve this paradox the social composition of the membership of the Council of Agriculture was investigated for 1900.[78] Of the 104 members of the council in 1900, the occupational status of 80 has been traced. Of these 80, 35 were landowners with valuations exceeding £100, the majority of them belonging to what is loosely termed the landed gentry. Ten were farmers whose holdings were valued at less than £100 each. Eleven were connected with trading activity, while 6 clergymen found their way onto the council. Three industrialists, a wide range of professional men, a creamery manager, an auctioneer, a land

---

trading background, but it is difficult to say whether this shaped his views on coopera- tion. His hostility toward Plunkett, for instance, is probably best understood in terms of a general aversion to "constructive unionism," Plunkett being regarded as one of the prin- cipal bearers of this poisoned chalice. See F. S. L. Lyons, *John Dillon: a biography* (Lon- don, 1968), pp. 2, 175–8, 219, 291, 384; Plunkett diaries, 9 Sept. 1897, 7 Jan. 1903 (Plunkett Foundation for Cooperative Studies, Oxford).

77. According to the occupational statistics of the 1901 census, the agricultural cate- gory consisted of 853,000 people. But this is an underestimate, since a considerable num- ber of agricultural laborers were excluded from the agricultural category through classifi- cation as general laborers. The major trader categories of publicans, grocers, general shopkeepers, street sellers, and animal dealers amounted to some 65,000 persons. The addition of other occupations associated with trading would raise this total but would still leave the trader-agriculturalist ratio at less than 10 percent for the country as a whole. For mainly rural Ireland (that is, Ireland exclusive of the half-dozen or so major urban centers) the ratio would be appreciably lower.

78. A variety of sources were used in identifying members of the council, including the records of the Valuation Office in Dublin, newspapers, and other contemporary writ- ings. Works of reference found most useful were Michael Stenton and Stephen Lees (ed.), *Who's who of British members of Parliament*, vol. xi, *1886–1918* (Sussex, 1978); *Thom's Irish who's who* (Dublin, 1923); *Burke's landed gentry of Ireland* (London, 1912); *Kelly's directory of Ireland* (London, 1905); *Thom's directory of Ireland* (Dublin, 1908); *Belfast and Ulster trades' directory* (Edinburgh, 1905); *Return of owners of land of one acre and upwards in the several counties, counties of cities, and counties of towns in Ireland* . . . [C 1492], H.C. 1876, lxxx, 61. In addition, the aid of a number of local informants, who helped to confirm the occupations of members whose addresses were not recorded in sufficient detail, is gratefully acknowledged.

agent, and a newspaper proprietor also appeared on the body. It is important to note, however, the contrasting pathways by which farmers and traders on the one hand and the landowners on the other found places on the council. Farmers and traders were almost exclusively the nominees of county councils; the majority of landowners who have been identified were in fact selected by DATI. Among the elected contingent on the council the presence of traders was marked. Of the 68 elected members, the occupational status of 49 has been traced. Ten of these 49 were involved in various trading activities, ranging from the drink and drapery trades to wholesaling and cattle dealing. (Two others — an apple buyer and cider manufacturer from Dungarvan and a corn miller from Drogheda — while not traders, strictly speaking, may have perceived their interests in somewhat similar terms to those engaged in distributive activities.) Even if there were no traders among the unidentified members, an overrepresentation of traders is still evident.

This analysis of occupations is useful in indicating the minimum presence of particular social categories on the Council of Agriculture. From the figures a number of points emerge clearly. First, a wide range of interests was represented on the council, despite the specialist character of its functions. This was particularly true of the elected members and resulted from the political process whereby county councils appointed them. Second, the political involvement of farmers was rather weak.[79] The presence of clergymen, traders, landowners, and members of the professions obviously limited the number of council places available for farmers. Third, traders had not only established a bridgehead within the council but were in fact overrepresented.

The occupational status of the fifty-two elected members who voted on the issue of cooperation in 1906 has also been examined.[80] It will be

79. A mere 3 percent of the 490,000 landholdings in 1901 had a valuation in excess of £100. The overwhelming majority of farmers lived on medium-sized and small holdings. Even if it were assumed that all the unidentified members of the Council of Agriculture were in fact farmers of the latter type (this was almost certainly not the case), a weak representation is still implied. Another numerically important stratum of rural society, that composed of agricultural laborers, was not directly represented at all.

80. Although the elected and selected members of the Council of Agriculture were clearly distinguished in 1900 (Department of Agriculture, *Journal*, i [1900], pp. 37–40), this practice was subsequently discontinued. Thus it was necessary to use an indirect method in determining the category to which a member belonged in 1906. If a member belonged to the elected category in 1900, it is highly likely that if he appeared on the council again in 1906, he was still an elected member. (There was considerable continuity in the membership of the council over this period.) In addition, it was possible to check each name against the lists of county councillors for 1905. If a member were both a county councillor and a member of the council, then the probability that he belonged to the elected cate-

recalled (see table 9.1) that twenty-eight elected members supported the cooperative system on that occasion. The half-dozen or so members of the landed gentry among the elected members were all favorable, as were a further half-dozen very large farmers (mainly landowners also).[81] The organization of farmers into cooperative societies clearly commended itself to the traditional owners of the soil, perhaps through a sense of paternalism. Some tenant farmers, a land agent, an industrialist, a clergyman, a solicitor, and a number of representatives whose occupations cannot be traced made up the rest of the group. Not surprisingly, representatives with trading interests voted solidly against the proposal to assist cooperative organization. But the influence of traders went further than their numerical representation. Less easily anticipated was the finding that the traders had the support of eight farmers.[82] The residences of these farmers might suggest that a number of them were graziers. But with the exception of one such farmer, there exists no firm evidence of the type of agriculture which they practiced. At least four of them, however, were substantial farmers.[83]

Why the farming vote was split on the issue of cooperation is not immediately apparent. The limitations of the data do not allow the analysis to be pushed further. What is certain, however, and this was of major political significance, is that farmer representatives did not act as a unified group on the council. The absence of unity is especially interesting in that it fits certain political patterns evident in postindependence Ireland, specifically the weak and divided nature of rural interest groups and the nonemergence of a national farmers' party in a strongly rural country.[84] Thus, while the Council of Agriculture provided an institutionalized setting for interest-group politics, in the early twentieth cen-

---

gory is very high. A final and particularly useful check is the knowledge that twenty-four of the twenty-five members named as having voted against the subsidy for cooperative organization were elected members. By combining these overlapping sets of information, it proved possible to allocate members between the elected and selected categories.

81. The average valuation of the holdings of these six farmers was £276. "Gentleman farmer" may be the most apt description for members of this subgroup.

82. The occupations of all but one of the twenty-five voters who opposed the cooperative subsidy have been determined. The remaining one is very unlikely to have been a farmer, as he had a street address in Dublin.

83. These were William Delany, a grazier from King's County and M.P. for the Ossory division of Queen's County; William Corbet, also from King's County, who held a farm valued at £109; David O'Gorman, of Fermoy, Co. Cork, who held a farm valued at £74; and P. J. O'Neill, who resided at Kinsealy House, Malahide, and farmed extensively on the edge of Dublin city. It may be significant that O'Neill's brother, Joseph Anthony, was an agricultural merchant. (I am especially grateful to R. J. Casey, deputy city and county librarian, Dublin, for supplying me with documentation relating to the O'Neill family.)

84. Basil Chubb, *The government and politics of Ireland* (Oxford, 1974), p. 83; Kennedy, "Agricultural cooperation," pp. 268–71.

tury (and in the decades that followed) there did not exist a community of interests sufficiently powerful to bind together different categories of farmers. This lack of solidarity is presumably related to class divisions within the agrarian order itself. Steep gradations of economic and social status separated different strata of agriculturalists. The temporary and sometimes uneasy alliance established between large farmers (frequently graziers) and smallholders during the land war[85] had given way to strong tensions between the two ends of the farming spectrum by the turn of the century. Elements within the United Irish League, particularly in Connacht, articulated bitter antigrazier sentiments.[86] The "ranch war" of 1906–8 marked a high point in the peasant attack on large graziers.[87] It is noteworthy that this agitation coincided with the period of most intense political conflict between cooperators and traders. Thus in the first decade of this century not only did farmers and traders draw apart, but class conflict within the farming sector also intensified.[88] These conditions furnished a poor basis for the development of either solidarity among farmers or effective interest-group politics.

Traders and Local Politics

The significance attached to the overrepresentation of traders on the Council of Agriculture is given additional support by a consideration of lower levels of agricultural decision-making. A priori, there is little reason to expect substantial trader representation on the county committees of agriculture. Yet in 1906 the Gorey district council in County Wexford adopted the following resolution: "It is the opinion of this council that the efficiency of the County Committee of Agriculture and Technical Instruction would be increased by appointing practical farmers on the committee instead of traders, *who are at present appointed* [emphasis added]. . . ."[89] Once the procedure for making appointments to the county committees of agriculture is specified, however, the presence of

85. See especially Bew, *Land*, pp. 177–9; Jones, "Agrarian capitalism," p. 287.

86. For evidence of attacks on graziers and of the related demand for land redistribution, see Gwynn, *Connemara*, pp. 108–13; Bonn, *Modern Ireland*, p. 120; Barker, *Ireland*, p. 61; *Minutes of evidence taken before the departmental committee of inquiry on the Department of Agriculture and Technical Instruction for Ireland*, p. 372 [C 3574], H.C. 1907, xviii, 1; *Congestion comm. evidence*, app. 6th report, pp. 93, 100; *Irish Peasant*, 18 Nov., 9 Dec. 1905. For reports of cattle driving, which was a form of protest against the grazier system, see, e.g., *F.J.*, 23, 24 Jan., 1 Feb. 1908.

87. The only modern study of the "ranch war" is Jones, "Agrarian capitalism," pp. 80–114.

88. This contrasts with the period of landlord-tenant confrontation in the early 1880s, when the broad farmers' alliance was sufficiently robust to contain internal divisions.

89. *Irish Homestead*, 22 Dec. 1906.

traders becomes less surprising. Members of these committees, as of the Council of Agriculture, were selected by county councillors, usually drawing heavily from within their own ranks.[90] That traders were disproportionately represented on county councils was frequently asserted.[91] A seam of trader representation running from the Council of Agriculture and the county committees back to its source in the county councils is therefore not implausible.

But were traders overrepresented on the county councils? The impressionistic views of a range of contemporaries regarding the prominence of traders in local political life, though suggestive, are not in themselves conclusive. To test these assertions, the occupational status of the chairman and vice-chairman of each of the county councils was traced for 1905.[92] The resulting sample of sixty-six persons no doubt includes some of the most influential figures in local political life at that time. No less than 27 percent of this sample, or roughly a quarter, followed trading occupations.[93] The highest proportion of traders occurred in Connacht, the lowest in Munster. The bulk of farmers, that is, those with holdings valued at less than £100, were clearly underrepresented among the officers of the county councils. As a further check, the social composition of the entire membership of six county councils for 1908 was also examined. This exercise revealed both a strong trader presence and also some regional variation in the pattern of representation. The minimum level of trader representation on these county councils is given in parentheses after each county or division thereof: Donegal (28 percent), Cavan (22 percent), Wexford (20 percent), Westmeath (10 percent), Carlow (12 percent), and Tipperary, South Riding (25 percent).[94]

These findings should be related to political patterns evident in postindependence Ireland. A recent survey indicated that shopkeepers,

90. *Committee of inquiry on agricultural and technical instruction*, p. 814.

91. Sydney Brooks, *Aspects of the Irish question* (Dublin and London, 1912), p. 121; Barker, *Ireland*, p. 78; George Russell in *Irish Homestead*, 5 May 1906, 18 June 1910, and in *Cooperation and nationality*, p. 13; *Congestion comm. evidence, app. 6th report*, p. 1001. See also the debate on the representation of farmers in political life at the annual general meeting of IAOS, reported in *Annual report, 1909*, pp. 75–6. According to one speaker, referring to the west of Ireland, "Most of the county councillors were shopkeepers or nonfarmers, with the result that the interests of farmers were neglected."

92. See the sources cited in fn. 78.

93. This may be a slight underestimate, since the occupations of a small number of these officers could not be established.

94. While these are minimum estimates, the actual level of trader representation probably did not deviate markedly from them because the sources used, especially trade directories, give particularly extensive coverage of trading occupations, as compared with certain other occupations, such as farming.

publicans, and other (mainly small) businessmen were strongly overrepresented, relative to their numbers in the population, in the cabinets of successive Irish governments over the period 1922–65.[95] In fact, they had succeeded in filling 20 percent of all cabinet posts since the inception of the state. Similarly, an analysis of the socioeconomic status of a wider sample of politically active persons—public representatives at county, county-borough, and parliamentary levels in the mid-1960s—is also in line with these conclusions.[96] Interestingly, farmers again emerge as underrepresented in political life despite the strongly rural character of the country. For instance, they held less than 8 percent of ministerial posts in the first half-century of independence. Thus inverse relationships between representation and electoral strength in the cases of agriculturalists and traders have been a continuous and striking feature of Irish political life since at least the turn of the century.

Debt Bondage: How Important?

How can these political patterns be explained? One Irish Nationalist M.P. had a ready answer. F. H. O'Donnell charged that countrymen, locked into a system of debt to local shopkeepers, thereby lost both political and commercial independence.

They lose all power of choice, all right of remonstrance, and all liberty of action so long as they are in debt to the gombeenman. Nobody who wants to be anything elective can speak with too much respect of the gombeenman. He is the curse and the vampire of the countryside. He is the most respectable man in the community, if he be vampire enough. . . . About 25 percent of the keepers of drinking establishments, groceries, general stores, etc., are gombeenmen or are trying to be gombeenmen. . . . A country fellow who has run up a bill for a couple of pounds, which he cannot pay at once, has got the hook in his jaw. He will never get loose. . . . All the parliamentarians from Ireland have dozens of gombeenmen among their leading supporters.[97]

This theme—the accumulation of political power through the manipulation of ties based on what is termed debt bondage—has been developed by two recent writers.[98] The simplicity and colorful nature of such explanations of political behavior are intuitively appealing. But on reflec-

95. Chubb, *Government*, p. 95. See also Al Cohan, *The Irish political elite* (Dublin, 1972), pp. 34–5.

96. Chubb, *Government*, pp. 94–6.

97. O'Donnell, *Irish parliamentary party*, ii, 464.

98. Peter Gibbon and M. D. Higgins, "Patronage, tradition, and modernisation: the case of the Irish 'gombeenman'" in *Economic and Social Review*, vi, no. 1 (Oct. 1974),

tion there is something curious about a thesis which suggests in the case of the land war, for example, that many traders used naked coercion against farmers in order to place themselves in the position of local farmers' leaders, articulating essentially farmers' demands. A more fundamental weakness in the crude theory of debt bondage lies in the probable electoral ineffectiveness of such coercive strategies. Necessary conditions for the effective exercise of control would seem to include: an extensive area serviced largely by the trader politician himself or in conjunction with reliable henchmen (otherwise, tied voters would be too few to affect the electoral outcome); the ability to regulate this significant proportion of the total electorate through manipulation of economic ties; and noncompetitive conditions in local markets, with the result that bonds could not easily be dissolved.

The purpose of making these conditions explicit is to reveal the limitations of this explanatory scheme. The economic aspects of credit retailing were frequently misconstrued by contemporary critics. In particular, critics failed to appreciate that trading conditions over most of the country were strongly competitive at the end of the nineteenth century.[99] In addition, electoral reforms had enormously increased the cost of coercive strategies. The cumulative effect of reform acts in 1850, 1868, and 1884 was greatly to swell the number of persons entitled to vote. The reform act of 1884 actually trebled the size of the electorate, bringing it to over 700,000 voters.[100] In the wake of these reforms electoral conditions did not exist for the effective monopolization of political resources in most districts. Consequently, inflated trader representation or other manifestations of trader power cannot be explained satisfactorily by reference to the crude economic mechanism which has been postulated. Undoubtedly, in some isolated instances economic dependence was a decisive influence. But even when confronted with reports of political coercion based on economic power, one needs to distinguish carefully between attempted manipulation of economic ties in order to mobilize political support and actual success in such endeavors. A local election in a remote part of Donegal early in the present century is a case in

---

pp. 27–44; idem, "The Irish 'gombeenman': reincarnation or rehabilitation?" in *Economic and Social Review*, vii, no. 4 (July 1977), pp. 313–20.

99. Kennedy, "Traders and rural economy," pp. 204–8.

100. Lee, *Modernisation*, pp. 108–9. Yet because fewer people were involved in the various stages of organizational activity prior to election day, politically alert groups might enjoy an influence on the electoral process out of proportion to their numbers. This was especially true of the critically important gatherings that selected candidates for political office. and of the informal assemblies and canvassing that frequently preceded a selection meeting.

point. There, a coalition of traders failed to return its nominee despite resorting to economic intimidation.[101]

Bases of Trader Power

If the crude theory of debt bondage is unsatisfactory as a general explanation for the political influence exercised by traders, its corollary that the economic dependence of farmers was primarily responsible for their underrepresentation in political life must be rejected on similar grounds. In this section an alternative explanatory framework is advanced. Two features — the strategic position of traders in the social structure and their consciousness of such status — are especially relevant to the argument. These factors helped to raise the leadership aspirations of traders and to sharpen their perceptions of appropriate opportunities. Shops and pubs are frequently focal points, in spatial and social terms, for life in the countryside. Typically, the local trader is enmeshed in a variety of social and commercial relationships in his own district.[102] To this extent he is closely involved in a traditional and intensely local context. But a necessary implication of his occupational role is the mediation of exchanges between the base of society and higher levels. In other words, the trader is also engaged in a wider set of relationships, mainly of a commercial character, which extend vertically through the society. A Janus-faced figure, the trader is thus both immersed in and transcends his immediate setting. This dual position confers considerable advantages — broader horizons and a clearer perception of opportunities on the one hand, and the ability (gained from a high level of social interaction) to mobilize local support on the other. Consistent with this interpretation is Clark's finding that traders and townsmen played an important mediating role in establishing contact between local activists and national politicians in the early months of the land war.[103]

To insist that relations between traders and farmers should be viewed through a wider focus than the largely economic one employed by such

101. Patrick Gallagher, *Paddy the cope: my story* (rev. ed., Tralee, n.d.), pp. 148–9. Economic intimidation could of course be used in the reverse direction, that is, customers could try to coerce traders into changing their political views. See J. S. Donnelly, Jr., *The land and the people of nineteenth-century Cork: the rural economy and the land question* (London and Boston, 1975), p. 328; Hoppen, "Landlords, society, and electoral politics," pp. 89–90; Becker, *Disturbed Ireland*, p. 49; Gwynn, *Connemara*, p. 113. Over much of Ireland the trader rather than his customers was probably the more vulnerable party in times of divisive political passions. Business sense dictated that he should accommodate himself to major swings in popular opinion.

102. Kennedy, "Agricultural cooperation," pp. 259–61.

103. Clark, "Political mobilization," p. 492.

writers as O'Donnell and, quite recently, Gibbon and Higgins is not to deny that traders were able to accumulate some political power by exerting subtler forms of pressure on customers beholden to them for money and other favors.[104] In other words, political support was one element or commodity in a broader set of social exchanges between traders and their farming clientele. That some farmers were prepared to trade political support for commercial and other benefits is no more mysterious than the observed fact that farmers exchange agricultural for manufactured goods. The economic argument also possesses a measure of validity with respect to other politically aspiring groups and individuals. The creation of political obligations by means of favors was a feature of Irish local politics before and after independence.[105] Other political candidates — for example, members of the professions and large farmers — have also competed in the trade for favors and obligations, thus building up a personal following of voters. One should therefore beware of placing too much emphasis on a feature that is more a description of the conduct of local politics than a specific explanation for the prominence of traders in Irish political life.

The accumulation of power by traders is also a function of the political weaknesses of competing groups. In strongly rural societies, for instance, it is quite usual to encounter rigid, tradition-encrusted power relationships based on steep inequalities in landownership.[106] In Ireland, however, the hegemony of the landed gentry was first challenged in the parliamentary field and later trampled underfoot following the parliamentary and local-government reforms of the late nineteenth century. The northeastern counties represented the only major regional deviation from this pattern.[107] For national and religious reasons, sources of leadership had increasingly to be found below the level of the self-proclaimed natural leaders. Catholic clergymen were obvious centers of political power, but much of their authority had to be exercised indirectly. Clergy-

104. Admittedly, in isolated areas, mainly in the west of Ireland, exploitative relationships existed between some traders and their clients. For further discussion, see Líam Kennedy, "Retail markets in rural Ireland at the end of the nineteenth century" in *Irish Economic and Social History*, v (1978) pp. 49–55.

105. Hoppen, "National politics," pp. 221–4; Cohan, *Political elite*, pp. 63–5.

106. It is therefore interesting to find a clerical spokesman acknowledging that in other countries the landed gentry were the natural leaders of the people, and justifying the priest's political role in Ireland by reference to the unacceptability of the landed elite on religious and national grounds. See John Healy (bishop of Clonfert, 1896–1903), "The priest in politics" in *Record of the Maynooth Union, 1896–1897* (Dublin, 1897), p. 16.

107. For example, the chairmanships of the county councils of Antrim, Derry, Fermanagh, and Tyrone were held by members of the landed ascendancy in 1905.

men were barred from competing for places on local councils,[108] and at a more exalted level they were prohibited from sitting in the House of Commons. Along with other social groups, such as members of the professions (especially lawyers), traders were obvious beneficiaries of these barriers to clerical participation.[109] Still another factor tending to strengthen the political prospects of trader politicians was the marked shift in the balance between urban and rural population during the second half of the nineteenth century. By 1900 an urban base (village or town), with its associated concentration of voters, could be a useful asset to them, especially in view of the strength of localism in determining voting behavior.[110] In other words, the prominence of traders was linked to the spatial arrangement of voters. This argument is buttressed by the fact that no less than 40 percent of the officers of county councils in 1905 were townsmen.[111]

There are even more significant senses in which the factor of location favored townsmen. A recent writer has suggested that channels of political communication in Ireland today are more highly developed in urban than in rural settings.[112] This was even more true of the period before independence and clearly facilitated the perception of political opportunities by townsmen. Furthermore, most formal political activity— meetings of Nationalist organizations, of borough councils, of boards of guardians— took place in urban centers. The creation of new representative units of administration about the turn of the century, notably county councils, district councils, and county committees of agriculture, extended the scope of formal organizations in local politics. Unlike demonstrations and other forms of mass agitation, effective participation in these structures required regular attendance at meetings in the country towns.[113]

108. The Irish local-government act of 1898 provided that "a person being in holy orders or being a regular minister of any religious denomination shall not be eligible as a county or district councillor" (61 and 62 Vict., c. 94, s. 1). This exclusion clause drew a bitter reaction from the professor of Irish at Maynooth College, Dr. M. P. Hickey (*Record of the Maynooth Union, 1897–1898* [Dublin, 1898], p. 30).

109. While the number of lawyers in Ireland increased marginally between 1871 and 1901 (from 2,110 to 2,216), the Catholic share of places within the profession increased appreciably from 35 to 44 percent. The pool of Catholic lawyers was an important source of politicians for the Irish parliamentary party.

110. On localism in Irish politics, see Hoppen, "National politics," p. 224; Cohan, *Political elite*, p. 30; Chubb, *Government*, pp. 157–8.

111. The remainder included not only farmers but also large landowners and persons associated with the landed elite.

112. Cohan, *Political elite*, p. 28. See also Clark, "Political mobilization," p. 491.

113. The organizational and other resources of townsmen could be deployed most

How countrymen might be disadvantaged in relation to these political opportunities is apparent from the testimony of Henry Doran, an inspector for the Congested Districts Board. Doran used the case of the Belmullet representatives on the Mayo county committee of agriculture to illustrate his point. Meetings of the county committee rotated among Ballina, Castlebar, and Claremorris. Members from Belmullet had to travel some 40 miles to the nearest meeting place at Ballina, and a further 20 or 30 miles by train to attend at Castlebar or Claremorris. Doran found that "from January 1904 to the 23rd October 1906 thirty-four meetings were held, and there was not a single member from the Belmullet rural district [who] attended any of these meetings but one."[114] Even though the example is extreme, it is a salutary reminder that the costs of travel and other expenses applied with varying degrees of severity over wide areas of the country in this period.

The work rhythm in trading also permits intermittent absence on political errands. By contrast, the tillers of the soil, though far more numerous, experience severe disadvantages. They are dispersed over the land, caught in the comparative isolation of the farm holding, and fenced into rigid daily and seasonal work routines.[115] While the more substantial traders pushed through the ceiling of local community life, for the ordinary countryman, family, kinfolk, and land absorbed his most passionate energies. Sustained involvement in the affairs of the outside world fitted less than easily into the framework of peasant aspirations.[116] This

---

effectively in small-group situations, such as planning committees or meetings to select candidates for political office. In this type of setting relative numerical strength in the overall voting population counted for little, as compared with political skills and a taste for power.

114. *Committee of inquiry on agricultural and technical instruction*, p. 966. For further evidence on the economic and geographical barriers to participation in committee work, see the comments of another witness before this body (ibid., p. 488).

115. In her sensitive study of the peasantry of Brittany, Suzanne Berger observes that the "seamless workday" of traditional agriculture inhibits regular participation in political and vocational organizations (*Peasants against politics: rural organization in Brittany, 1911-1967* [Cambridge, Mass., 1972], p. 86).

116. Of course, these considerations do not apply to the farming elite which came to social and economic prominence in postfamine Ireland. The consciousness of this stratum of rural society was different from that of the smallholders. The opportunity cost of political activity for members of this class was also lower than for those living close to the margin of subsistence. Somewhat arbitrarily, the figure of £100 valuation has been chosen to mark the dividing line between the farming elite and other farmers. This is a stringent criterion, as the average value of an agricultural holding in 1911 was only £19. One might adopt a lower requirement and say that farmers with holdings valued at £50 or more constituted the elite. By this criterion there was an even greater underrepresentation of ordinary farmers on the political bodies examined here.

limitation was especially evident among the small, impoverished tenants of the west of Ireland. In the course of the land war, for example, traders and other townsmen along with the farming elite played major leadership and organizational roles.[117] Two decades later, western peasants still apparently had difficulty in placing members of their own class in formal positions of power. Of the ten elected members of the Council of Agriculture from Connacht in 1900, only one was a small farmer.[118] The delegation was dominated by townsmen, though some of them had close links with the countryside.[119] When the Council of Agriculture debated the issue of cooperative organization in 1906, the strongest opposition, on a provincial basis, came from Connacht, despite the fact that cooperatives and especially credit societies had spread widely among the western peasantry during the previous decade.[120] The occupational status of officers of county councils confirms the existence of these patterns of representation; townsmen predominated among the officers of Connacht county councils in 1905.

Finally, traders and other townsmen enjoyed an advantage over many rural-based competitors because of the services provided to farmers by towns and villages, and because traders were frequently at the hub of social life there. The point is most obvious in relation to those traders who were heavily involved in servicing the production or consumption needs of agriculturalists. Through their economic contacts traders reached out from their urban base toward a rural clientele. Kinship as well as credit links reinforced such connections. Joseph Lee, for example, draws attention to the close ties between traders prominent as local leaders of the Land League and the farming community. Of the occupations cited, those of provision merchant, cattle dealer, and butcher clearly joined the economic activities of town and country.[121] An analysis of the occupational status of county councillors reveals that corn merchants were prominent politically in a number of east-midland counties; elsewhere, some councillors participated in the cattle trade. The analy-

117. Clark, "Political mobilization," pp. 492–4.

118. The occupations of nine of the ten representatives have been established. It is possible that the unidentified member was a small farmer.

119. P. A. McHugh, M.P. for Leitrim North, was the son of a tenant farmer and owner of the *Sligo Champion*. John O'Dowd, M.P. for Sligo North, was a merchant who held a farm as well. The delegation also contained two traders — one a wool merchant, the other a cattle dealer — whose business links with the countryside are obvious.

120. The three major types of cooperative enterprises were creamery, agricultural, and credit societies. There was an average of thirty-one such societies per county in Connacht in 1910; most of them had been formed prior to 1906. See IAOS, *Annual Report, 1911*, appendix K.

121. Lee, *Modernisation*, p. 98.

sis also confirms the impression of certain contemporaries that retailers associated with the drink and grocery trades enjoyed considerable political influence. Drink and politics mixed well in the Ireland of the new century.

Conclusion

The land war of the late nineteenth century, by drawing vast numbers of rural inhabitants into organized political activity for the first time, effectively marks the politicization of the mass of Irish farmers.[122] It might have been thought that farmers, building on this political education, would emerge in the early twentieth century as a powerful pressure group, alert to their own interests and capable of mobilizing effectively in pursuit of them. But this essay has demonstrated that political involvement by the bulk of farmers in formal structures was weak. Moreover, the controversy within the Council of Agriculture shows that over the period 1906–13 farmers' representatives were successful neither in presenting a united front on the issue of cooperative organization nor in retaining a modest amount of state aid for agricultural cooperation.[123] Ironically, the point most clearly revealed by a study of the agricultural politics of the period is the restricted influence of agriculturalists on questions other than rent control and land purchase. It is sometimes suggested that such anomalies as the underdeveloped state of interest-group politics and the absence of a strong farmers' party in independent Ireland may be explained by the supposed dominance of constitutional and other national issues. The nationalist rhetoric in which attacks on IAOS were couched in Parliament, in the Council of Agriculture, and elsewhere might seem to lend plausibility to this hypothesis for the period prior to 1922. Yet nationalist rhetoric concealed sharp-edged sectional interests, specifically those of traders.

A proper understanding of the role of farmers in the political system during the first decades of this century must rest primarily on a consideration of the rural class structure rather than constitutional or other issues. By 1900 social tensions within the farming population — reflecting both major inequalities in landholding and differences in agricultural systems

122. See, e.g., Lee, *Modernisation*, pp. 72, 89–95; Clark, "Social composition," p. 447. The intermittent character of the interest and participation of smaller farmers in the political process in this and later periods should also be stressed.

123. The lengthy debates and the heat generated over this issue bore little relation to the sliver of expenditure involved. For details of the budget and expenditure of DATI at this time, see *Sixth annual general report of the department . . .* , *1905–06*, pp. 6–10 [C 3543], H.C. 1907, xvii, 241.

— had developed into open conflict. Besides revealing in dramatic fashion the fault lines that ran through rural society, such confrontations exacerbated the difficulties of constructing an enduring agrarian alliance. Furthermore, the declining relevance of antilandlordism in the aftermath of tenurial reforms removed an important unifying cry.[124] It is possible, of course, to exaggerate the extent of overt social conflict within the farming population. The most pervasive effect of rural class divisions was to limit the degree of mutual understanding and solidarity that might have evolved within a less hierarchical social order.

The work of the Council of Agriculture, though less colorful than incidents in the United Irish League campaign or the ranch war, is particularly instructive in illuminating some of the more mundane issues. Thus a Carlow farmer and member of the Council of Agriculture protested strongly that farming conditions differed considerably within Leinster, and argued for wider representation on agricultural bodies to take account of these variations.[125] If farming conditions were perceived as differing so much within Leinster, then presumably there was even greater difficulty in appreciating the condition of smallholders living west of the Shannon. A County Dublin farmer, for example, when questioned about cooperative organization, revealed considerable ignorance of conditions elsewhere in Ireland: "I do not myself profess to be at all familiar with agricultural organisation in its general application to the country."[126] Interestingly, this farmer, who was also a member of the Council of Agriculture, voted against a state subsidy for the development of agricultural cooperatives. More generally, the number and diversity of nonfarming occupations represented on the council bore witness to the fact that the bulk of farmers tended not to place members of their own class in positions of political power.[127] This tendency had definite implications for the divisive issue of agricultural cooperation. Cooperatives were particularly associated with areas characterized by medium-sized holdings.[128] Large farmers, especially graziers, had little personal use for cooperatives. Thus, on this important question as well as on other

---

124. This consideration applies mainly to different categories of farmers. Rural laborers at the bottom of the class structure had played a relatively minor role in the land war. Antilandlord sentiment probably did little to blunt class hostility between farmers and laborers.

125. *Committee of inquiry on the Department of Agriculture and Technical Instruction*, p. 711.

126. Ibid., p. 186.

127. As explained earlier, farmers on the lower rungs of the social hierarchy in rural areas were severely disadvantaged in terms of effective participation in formal political life.

128. Kennedy, "Agricultural cooperation," pp. 185–6.

issues, their interests were not bound up with those of smaller farmers. To the extent that graziers involved themselves directly in the marketing of livestock, there was a conflict of interest. Schemes for the cooperative marketing of livestock, put forward on a number of occasions, threatened existing channels of distribution and were consequently resisted.[129] Significantly, on the issues of cooperative organization and of access to tracts of grazing land there was some overlap between the interests of graziers and traders.

Members of the Nationalist party, with few exceptions, showed persistent hostility toward the cooperative movement, even though most farmer-cooperators were also nationalists. This situation strongly suggests both the political influence of traders and their ability to pursue sectional claims successfully. By contrast, the ineffectual response of agriculturalists points to the difficulty which smaller farmers faced in mobilizing politically. The problem was compounded by the fact that by about 1900 ordinary farmers were denied the support of groups which during the land war had supplied important leadership and organizational resources. The transition from sporadic outbursts of agrarian agitation to systematic interest-group politics was not an easy one.[130]

The central theme of this essay has been the markedly unequal distribution of political power in rural Ireland, despite a radical restructuring of electoral rights in the late nineteenth century. The evidence indicates that traders, unlike smaller farmers and agricultural laborers, enjoyed considerably more political power than their numbers in the population alone warranted. They were overrepresented on certain popularly elected bodies, from county councils to the parliamentary party, in the early twentieth century. These findings help to underscore the essential continuity of political experience in Ireland before and after national independence. For reasons elaborated earlier, the bulk of farmers (those with holdings valued at less than £100) were underrepresented in public life. Even on the Council of Agriculture the presence of a strong nucleus of traders as well as the overrepresentation of large landowners served to narrow the number of farmers severely.

The overrepresentation of traders in public life and the underrepresentation of farmers were closely related phenomena, especially in the west of Ireland. Traders on the Council of Agriculture came mainly from Connacht, while farmers from that province were weakly represented.[131]

129. Horace Plunkett Foundation, *Agricultural cooperation*, p. 7.
130. Only with the emergence onto the national stage of the Irish Creamery Milk Suppliers' Association and, more importantly, the National Farmers' Association in the 1960s, does one find the mass of farmers organized into effective agricultural-interest groups.
131. Four of the thirteen traders on the Council of Agriculture in 1906 came from

KENNEDY: *Farmers, Traders, and Agricultural Politics* 369

But the local political prominence of traders was not confined solely to the poorer agricultural areas. Analysis of the social composition of county councils shows that in such eastern counties as Wexford and Tipperary (South Riding), trader politicians were present in substantial numbers.[132] In Carlow and Westmeath, on the other hand, the situation was quite different. Further investigation is necessary to trace regional variations in detail, but clearly the link between farmer and trader representation was not merely a product of atypical conditions in the west and northwest.[133]

Various factors conditioned the relationship between town and country. Economic and social ties linked villages and towns with their hinterlands, insuring that social contact and mutual understanding did not fall away sharply at the interface. The world of the shop and the world of the farm intersected. Some traders rooted themselves more solidly in the countryside by also engaging in farming.[134] Many traders could trace their origins directly to local rural communities.[135] These considerations, fortified in some poorer areas by the superior status accorded to traders by the farming community,[136] suggest that in the eyes of most country people there was nothing unnatural in the involvement of traders in agrarian agitation or in their prominence as political representatives. Finally, the emphasis of this essay on the overrepresentation of traders in local political life should not be allowed to obscure the equally important find-

---

the northwestern counties of Leitrim, Sligo, and Mayo. Three came from another northern county, Cavan. Of the other council representatives from these counties, it is remarkable that not one was a full-time farmer.

132. There is some contrast here with the findings of W. L. Feingold, who has shown, with respect to the boards of guardians, that trader representation was marked only in some areas of the midwest and the northwest ("Boards of guardians," pp. 269–71).

133. In Tipperary (South Riding), where the average value of a farm was well above the national norm, trader representatives serving on the county council in 1908 were based not only in such towns as Clonmel, Cashel, and Cahir, but also in the tiny country villages of Bansha, Killenaule, and Limerick Junction.

134. Of those combining other occupations with farming in 1901, almost 2,400, or roughly a quarter of those so classified, were shopkeepers or publicans. See *Census Ire., 1901*, pt. 2: *general report*, p. 131 [C 1190], H.C. 1902, cxxix, 1. Probably an even greater number of those whose main occupation was trading also had some farming interests. Too active an involvement in buying or renting land, however, could prompt a hostile reaction from land-hungry farmers.

135. Clark, "Political mobilization," p. 490. See also Kennedy, "Agricultural cooperation," pp. 273–4.

136. At the beginning of this century in many districts it was the country shopkeeper who furnished most technical advice on agricultural matters: "Leaning across his counter, he would discuss all things rural with the omniscience of one who takes in the daily paper" (*Irish Homestead*, 27 Mar. 1909).

ing that traders did not come close to dominating numerically any of
the representative bodies examined here. The study of Irish political
representation about the turn of the century does not lend itself to simple
generalization, the comments of some contemporaries notwithstanding.

BIBLIOGRAPHY

Contemporary sources

Manuscript material
General Valuation Office, Dublin
   Valuation records.
Plunkett Foundation for Cooperative Studies, Oxford
   Private diaries of Sir Horace Plunkett.

Contemporary publications
  I. Newspapers and periodicals
    Cork Examiner.
    Department of Agriculture and Technical Instruction for Ireland, Journal,
      i (1900); vii (1907); viii (1908); xii (1912).
    Evening Telegraph (Dublin).
    Freeman's Journal (Dublin).
    Irish Homestead (Dublin).
    Irish Peasant (Dublin).
    Waterford Star.

 II. Parliamentary papers (in chronological order)
    Report of the commissioners appointed to take the census of Ireland for the
      year 1841 [504], H.C. 1843, xxiv, 1.
    Return of owners of land of one acre and upwards in the several counties,
      counties of cities, and counties of towns in Ireland . . . [C 1492], H.C.
      1876, lxxx, 61.
    Report from the select committee on money lending, together with the pro-
      ceedings of the committee, minutes of evidence, appendix, and index, H.C.
      1898 (260), x, 101.
    Census of Ireland, 1901, pt. 2: general report, with illustrative maps and
      diagrams, tables, and appendix [C 1190], H.C. 1902, cxxix, 1.
    Sixth annual general report of the Department of Agriculture and Technical
      Instruction for Ireland, 1905–06 [C 3543], H.C. 1907, xvii, 241.
    Report of the departmental committee of inquiry into the provisions of [the]
      Agricultural and Technical Instruction (Ireland) Act, 1899 [C 3572], H.C.
      1907, xvii, 799.
    Minutes of evidence taken before the departmental committee of inquiry on
      the Department of Agriculture and Technical Instruction for Ireland [C
      3574], H.C. 1907, xviii, 1.

Royal commission on congestion in Ireland: appendix to the sixth report [C 3748], H.C. 1908, xxxix, 701.
Agricultural statistics of Ireland, with detailed report for the year 1910 [C 5964], H.C. 1911, c, 517.
Copy of treasury letter dated 1st April 1913 respecting the conditions on which a grant will be made to the [Irish Agricultural Organisation] Society from the development fund [C 6735], H.C. 1913, liii, 3.

III. Other contemporary publications

Anderson, R. A. *With Horace Plunkett in Ireland* (London, 1935).
Barker, Sir Ernest. *Ireland in the last fifty years, 1866–1916* (2nd ed., Oxford, 1919).
Becker, B. H. *Disturbed Ireland, being the letters written during the winter of 1880–81* (London, 1881).
Belfast and Ulster trades' directory (Edinburgh, 1905).
Bonn, M. J. *Modern Ireland and her agrarian problem* (Dublin, 1906).
Booth, Charles. "The economic distribution of population in Ireland" in W. P. Coyne (ed.), *Ireland, industrial and agricultural* (Dublin, 1902), pp. 64–72.
Brooks, Sydney. *The new Ireland* (2nd ed., Dublin, 1907).
Brooks, Sydney. *Aspects of the Irish question* (Dublin and London, 1912).
Burke's landed gentry of Ireland (London, 1912).
Connolly, James. *Labour in Ireland* (reprint ed., Dublin, 1951).
Cooperative Union. *Annual congress report, 1892* (Manchester, 1893).
Coulter, Henry. *The west of Ireland: its existing condition and prospects* (Dublin, 1862).
Gallagher, Patrick. *Paddy the cope: my story* (rev. ed., Tralee, n.d.).
Gwynn, Stephen. *A holiday in Connemara* (London, 1909).
Healy, John. "The priest in politics" in *Record of the Maynooth Union, 1896–1897* (Dublin, 1897).
Irish Agricultural Organisation Society. *Annual report, 1907* (Dublin, 1908).
Irish Agricultural Organisation Society. *Annual report, 1909* (Dublin, 1910).
Irish Agricultural Organisation Society. *Annual report, 1911* (Dublin, 1912).
Irish Agricultural Organisation Society. *Annual report, 1912* (Dublin, 1913).
Irish Agricultural Organisation Society. *Annual report, 1913* (Dublin, 1914).
The Irish peasant: a sociological study (London, 1892).
Kelly's directory of Ireland (London, 1905).
O'Donnell, F. H. *A history of the Irish parliamentary party*, 2 vols. (London, 1910).
The parliamentary debates (authorised edition), 4th ser., vols. clxv, clxvii, clxx.
The parliamentary debates (official report), 5th ser., *House of Commons*, vols. xviii, xl.
Plunkett Foundation. *Agricultural cooperation in Ireland: a survey* (London, 1931).
Plunkett, Horace. "Cooperative stores for Ireland" in *Nineteenth Century*, xxiv (Sept. 1888), pp. 410–18.
Plunkett, Horace. *Ireland in the new century* (London, 1904).
Plunkett, Horace. *Plain talks to Irish farmers* (Dublin, 1910).

Russell, George. *Cooperation and nationality* (Dublin, 1912).
Smith-Gordon, Lionel, and Staples, Laurence. *Rural reconstruction in Ireland* (London, 1917).
Thom's directory of Ireland (Dublin, 1908).
Thom's Irish who's who (Dublin, 1923).

Later works

Writings in Irish studies

Bew, Paul. *Land and the national question in Ireland, 1858–82* (Dublin, 1978).
Bolger, Patrick. *The Irish cooperative movement: its history and development* (Dublin, 1977).
Bourke, P. M. A. "The agricultural statistics of the 1841 census of Ireland: a critical review" in *Economic History Review*, 2nd ser., xviii, no. 2 (Aug. 1965), pp. 376–91.
Chubb, Basil. *The government and politics of Ireland* (Oxford, 1974).
Clark, Samuel. "The social composition of the Land League" in *Irish Historical Studies*, xvii, no. 68 (Sept. 1971), pp. 447–69.
Clark, Samuel. "The political mobilization of Irish farmers" in *Canadian Review of Sociology and Anthropology*, xii, no. 4, pt. 2 (1975), pp. 483–99.
Cohan, Al. *The Irish political elite* (Dublin, 1972).
Cullen, L. M. *An economic history of Ireland since 1660* (London, 1972).
Digby, Margaret. *Horace Plunkett: an Anglo-American Irishman* (Oxford, 1949).
Donnelly, J. S., Jr. *The land and the people of nineteenth-century Cork: the rural economy and the land question* (London and Boston, 1975).
Feingold, W. L. "The Irish boards of poor-law guardians, 1872–1886: a revolution in local government" (Ph.D. thesis, University of Chicago, 1974).
Gibbon, Peter, and Higgins, M. D. "Patronage, tradition, and modernisation: the case of the Irish 'gombeenman'" in *Economic and Social Review*, vi, no. 1 (Oct. 1974), pp. 27–44.
Gibbon, Peter, and Higgins, M. D. "The Irish 'gombeenman': reincarnation or rehabilitation?" in *Economic and Social Review*, viii, no. 4 (July 1977), pp. 313–20.
Hoppen, K. T. "Landlords, society, and electoral politics in mid-nineteenth-century Ireland" in *Past and Present*, no. 75 (May 1977), pp. 62–93.
Hoppen, K. T. "National politics and local realities in mid-nineteenth-century Ireland" in Art Cosgrove and Donal McCartney (ed.), *Studies in Irish history presented to R. Dudley Edwards* (Dublin, 1979), pp. 190–227.
Hurst, Michael. "Ireland and the ballot act of 1872" in *Historical Journal*, viii, no. 3 (1965), pp. 326–52.
Jones, D. S. "Agrarian capitalism and rural social development in Ireland" (Ph.D. thesis, Queen's University, Belfast, 1977).
Kennedy, Líam. "Agricultural cooperation and Irish rural society, 1880–1914" (Ph.D. thesis, University of York, 1978).

Kennedy, Líam. "Retail markets in rural Ireland at the end of the nineteenth century" in *Irish Economic and Social History*, v (1978), pp. 46–63.

Kennedy, Líam. "Traders in the Irish rural economy, 1880–1914" in *Economic History Review*, 2nd ser., xxxii, no. 2 (May 1979), pp. 201–10.

Lee, Joseph. *The modernisation of Irish society, 1848–1918* (Dublin, 1973).

Lyons, F. S. L. *The Irish parliamentary party, 1890–1910* (London, 1951).

Lyons, F. S. L. *John Dillon: a biography* (London, 1968).

O'Brien, C. C. *Parnell and his party, 1880–90* (Oxford, 1957).

Ó Gráda, Cormac. "Agricultural head rents, pre-famine and post-famine" in *Economic and Social Review*, v, no. 3 (Apr. 1974), pp. 385–92.

Report of the commission on emigration and other population problems (Dublin, 1954).

Whyte, J. H. "The influence of the Catholic clergy on elections in nineteenth-century Ireland" in *English Historical Review*, lxxv, no. 295 (Apr. 1960), pp. 239–59.

Other works

Berger, Suzanne. *Peasants against politics: rural organization in Brittany, 1911–1967* (Cambridge, Mass., 1972).

Stenton, Michael, and Lees, Stephen (ed.). *Who's who of British members of Parliament*, vol. xi, *1886–1918* (Sussex, 1978).

10 *David S. Jones*

The Cleavage between Graziers and Peasants in the Land Struggle, 1890–1910

Introduction

During the second half of the nineteenth century the commercial sector of Irish agriculture significantly expanded. More and more holdings were run as commercial enterprises with the objective of raising a cash surplus. The essential feature of such enterprises was that the farmer sold for a cash return at least one of his commodities on a regular basis at a recognized market or fair.[1] By 1900 commercial production and a monetized economy were clearly evident even in the remote and infertile areas of the west.

A central feature of this process was the shift in production from tillage to pasture farming and especially to the raising of dry cattle and sheep. A commercial cattle economy had been established as early as the eighteenth century, when "the great proportion of the country was in pasture" and "holdings were of considerable size."[2] Between 1780 and 1812, however, pasture farming experienced a decline as a result of the great increase in cereal prices and the consequent growth of tillage. The prices of all Irish agricultural commodities remained depressed from the

---

1. Some small farmers not involved in commercial production did receive a cash income either through remittances from relatives abroad or by laboring on commercial farms.

2. Lord Dufferin, *Irish emigration and the tenure of land in Ireland* (London, 1867), p. 94. See also R. D. Crotty, *Irish agricultural production: its volume and structure* (Cork, 1966), p. 113; *Minutes of evidence taken before her majesty's commissioners on agriculture*, vol. i, pp. 396–409 [C 2778-I], H.C. 1881, xv, 1 (hereafter cited as *Richmond comm. evidence*, i).

close of the Napoleonic wars until the late 1830s, but after 1842 the market for dry cattle began to recover, allowing a sustained expansion in production at the expense of tillage farming.[3] This expansion assumed increasing significance during the latter half of the nineteenth century. Between 1854 and 1904 the number of dry cattle increased from 1,615,000 to 3,179,000. Thirty-two percent of all dry cattle in 1904 were two years or older, while 33 percent were between one and two years. There was a similar increase in the number of sheep, which rose from 2,122,000 to 4,379,000 between 1851 and 1901.[4]

The basic cause of this expansion was the sustained upward trend of prices. Prices were particularly buoyant from 1865 to 1883 and again between 1900 and 1920, though temporary downturns did occur occasionally. Fluctuations in the demand for store cattle, beef, and mutton are illustrated by Barrington's index of prices for the period 1840–1920 (table 10.1). The trend in the prices of young stores between 1845 and

TABLE 10.1

Index Numbers of the Prices of Irish Beef, Mutton, and Store Cattle, 1840–1920
(base 1840 = 100 for beef and mutton; base 1845 = 100 for store cattle)

Year	Beef	Mutton	Store cattle 1–2 yrs.	Store cattle 2–3 yrs.
1840	100	100	—	—
1845	103	120	100	100
1846–50	96	114	123	164
1851–5	86	98	93	115
1856–60	119	128	150	190
1861–5	126	143	171	204
1866–70	145	146	150	186
1871–5	163	171	221	258
1876–80	147	176	231	247
1881–5	132	162	219	232
1886–90	112	141	230	220
1891–5	113	136	196	209
1896–1900	112	136	227	221
1901–5	115	143	245	236
1906–10	118	114	261	247
1911–15	137	156	318	292
1916–20	272	306	562	559

SOURCE: Thomas Barrington, "A review of Irish agricultural prices" in *Stat. Soc. Ire. Jn.*, pt. ci, xv (1927), pp. 251–3.

3. Crotty, *Agricultural production*, pp. 17–34, 42–3; Dufferin, *Tenure*, pp. 95, 148.
4. Department of Industry and Commerce, Saorstat Eireann, *Agricultural statistics, 1847–1926: report and tables* (Dublin, 1928), table 1, pp. 1–5; table 6, pp. 14–19.

1920 was generally upward, though declines sometimes took place, the most serious being those of 1884–7 and 1891–7. The prices of advanced stores two to three years old followed a similar trend. There was a sustained fall in demand for advanced stores after 1876, but a significant improvement in prices occurred after 1896. The demand for beef rose steadily after 1855 and was particularly strong during the years 1866–78. The price of prime beef reached a peak of 95s. per cwt. in 1873, as compared with only 48s. per cwt. in 1850. A period of low prices between 1879 and 1900 was followed by a sustained recovery.[5]

The upward trend in beef and store-cattle prices stemmed from the growing demand for meat by an expanding urban population in both Britain and Ireland. The ability of Irish graziers to respond to this demand was facilitated by the creation of a railway network after 1845. The importance of the British market for Irish cattle is indicated by the volume of exports to Britain shown in table 10.2. Between the late 1840s and the outbreak of the first world war exports rose more than fourfold. By the first decade of the twentieth century nearly 25 percent of the national herd was shipped to Britain annually.

The increased concentration on pasture farming occurred partly within the peasantry. After the great famine there emerged a sizable stratum

TABLE 10.2

Number of Cattle of All Kinds Exported from Ireland to Great Britain, 1846–1915
(in thousands)

Years	Annual average	Years	Annual average
1846–50	199	1881–5	653
1851–5	202	1886–90	685
1856–60	309	1891–5	713
1861–5	365	1896–1900	750
1866–70	451	1901–5	804
1871–5	604	1906–10	837
1876–80	682	1911–15	829

SOURCES: *Thom's Irish almanac and official directory of the United Kingdom of Great Britain and Ireland* for the following years: 1853, p. 301; 1860, p. 694; 1866, p. 835; 1871, p. 954; 1875, p. 853; 1876, p. 701; 1878, p. 694; 1905, p. 796; 1910, p. 796; 1915, p. 796; 1917, p. 708; *Agricultural statistics of Ireland, with detailed reports on agriculture, for the year 1898*, p. 22 [C 9389], H.C. 1899, cvi, 325.

5. For the prices of Irish agricultural produce, 1830–86, see *Report of the royal commission on the Land Law (Ireland) Act, 1881, and the Purchase of Land (Ireland) Act, 1885: minutes of evidence and appendices*, pp. 960–7 [C 4969-I], H.C. 1887, xxvi, 25 (hereafter cited as *Cowper comm. evidence*). For agricultural price index numbers, 1840–1920, see Thomas Barrington, "A review of Irish agricultural prices" in *Stat. Soc. Ire. Jn.*, pt. ci, xv (1927), pp. 251–3.

of commercial middling tenants. They usually possessed holdings of from 20 to 50 acres and followed a mixed pattern of agriculture in which the rearing of calves and young cattle provided a major source of revenue.[6] But the growth of ranch farming after 1850 was especially important in the process of commercialization. This system of farming, which had little in common with peasant agriculture, involved the grazing of large numbers of dry cattle and sheep over extensive ranges of grassland, and its practitioners were known as graziers or ranchers. The grazier possessed a large expanse of pasture, often in excess of 300 acres.[7] It was rare for him to have all his land in one holding. Normally, the rancher's land consisted of multiple holdings, sometimes scattered throughout a whole county.[8] The grazier was thus for the most part a nonresidential occupier. He dwelt on only one of his holdings or in many cases lived away from his land altogether. The immediate supervision of his cattle and sheep was left to herds or shepherds whom he employed permanently.[9]

It is difficult to give an accurate estimate of the number of graziers at the end of the nineteenth century. In 1901, however, there were 11,338 holdings of over 200 acres, covering about 5 million acres. A high proportion of these holdings were ranches, since dry-cattle husbandry was the predominant activity on farms exceeding 200 acres.[10]

More than any other section of the farming community, ranchers were motivated by a sense of capitalistic enterprise. The overriding aim of the typical grazier was to maximize his net profit. In many cases he was an eager speculator, prepared to assume considerable risk in making investments, particularly in purchasing stock and land.[11] Land was simply an instrument of monetary gain, a profitable outlet for his capital, and was bought and sold in accordance with current and expected returns.

6. George Pellew, *In castle and cabin, or talks in Ireland in 1887* (New York and London, 1888), p. 81.

7. A number of hill graziers in Donegal and west Connacht held over 5,000 acres of mountain pasture.

8. *Royal commission on congestion in Ireland: appendix to the sixth report, minutes of evidence . . . , and documents relating thereto,* p. 57 [C 3748], H.C. 1908, xxxix, 701 (hereafter cited as *Congestion comm. evidence, app. 6th report*).

9. *Congestion comm. evidence, app. 6th report,* p. 57; *app. 10th report,* p. 242 [C 4007], H.C. 1908, xlii, 5.

10. *Census Ire., 1901,* pt. ii: *general report, with illustrative maps and diagrams, tables, and appendix,* pp. 182–5 [C 1190], H.C. 1902, cxxix, 1; *Agricultural statistics, 1847–1926: report,* pp. 5–8. According to the report in *Agricultural statistics, 1847–1926,* for every 1,000 acres of agricultural holdings over 200 acres, there were only 62 acres of plowed land and 34 milch cows as compared with 216 dry cattle and 331 sheep. These figures are for 1926 and apply only to Saorstat Eireann.

11. *Congestion comm. evidence, app. 10th report,* pp. 3, 101.

Unlike the normal tenant farmer, the rancher generally lacked any sense of ancestral or customary ties to the land, and his economic behavior was less constrained by the traditions of rural society. The expansion of ranch farming became especially significant after the great famine, when new opportunities arose for lucrative investment in grazing land and live-stock. On many estates large grazing farms replaced small holdings oc-cupied by subsistence and semisubsistence tenants.[12]

Yet in spite of a favorable long-term price trend for fat and store cattle after 1853, the experience of graziers was one of fluctuating fortunes and uneven success. The upward movement of dry-cattle and sheep prices was broken intermittently by sharp falls. A rush of prosperity for the rancher was all too often followed by serious setbacks when the livestock market temporarily declined. The grazing industry encountered periods of crisis, such as those of 1866–8, 1884–7, and 1891–6, which inflicted severe economic loss. Bankruptcies were then numerous. On his tour through Meath in 1907 the American visitor William Bulfin called at-tention to the toll exacted by earlier crises when he remarked that "many of the big graziers have gone to the wall" and "were obliged to surrender owing to financial straits."[13] One example was Thomas Roberts, who declared to the Morley committee in 1894 that he intended to sell his ranch of 250 acres because he no longer found grazing profitable.[14] A similar predicament faced James Casey, who held 2,000 acres of grass-land near Clifden, Co. Galway, during the downturn of the mid-1880s. In conversation with the visiting English lawyer George Pellew in 1887, he explained: "I have been four years fighting with this depression and am now giving up, as I am losing money. A few weeks ago I brought forty or fifty bullocks and heifers to a large fair near here. I have got twelve and thirteen pounds for worse stock, and was not offered a shil-ling for one of them."[15] But with an upward turn in prices, bankruptcy was followed by a renewed burst of speculation. As one set of graziers went out of business, it was superseded by another group anxious to risk its capital in pasture farming.[16]

Commercial elements in the towns, especially shopkeepers, butchers,

12. Louis Paul-Dubois, *Contemporary Ireland* (Dublin, 1908), pp. 220–2, 299–301; *Richmond comm. evidence*, i, 102, 497–8, 1025; *Congestion comm. evidence*, app. 6th report, p. 137; app. 10th report, pp. 166–7.

13. William Bulfin, *Rambles in Eirinn* (Dublin, 1927; originally published 1907), p. 89. See also A. I. Shand, *Letters from the west of Ireland, 1884* (Edinburgh, 1885), p. 112.

14. *Report from the select committee on land acts (Ireland), together with the pro-ceedings of the committee, minutes of evidence, appendix, and index*, p. 386, H.C. 1894 (310), xiii, 1 (hereafter cited as *Morley comm. evidence*).

15. Pellew, *Castle and cabin*, pp. 180–1.

16. *Congestion comm. evidence*, app. 10th report, pp. 166–7.

and publicans, were often prominent as speculators in livestock and land whenever cattle prices rose steeply. Indeed, shopkeeper-graziers became major figures in the ranching system. Father Joseph Pelly, in evidence given to the Royal Commission on Congestion concerning his own locality of Loughrea in east Galway, claimed that "nine-tenths of the grazing ranches in this part of the country were occupied by the shopkeeper-graziers."[17] Pelly contended that the shopkeepers' ignorance of farming and of the value of land caused them to pay inflated prices for it.[18] On his tour of west Connacht in 1908 Stephen Gwynn made a similar observation: "Here in Iar Connacht the graziers are for the most part shopkeepers." The shopkeeper, instead of attending solely to his business, "takes up land for stock farming in a country where hardly any cottier or tillage farmer has a holding fit to live on."[19]

By the end of the nineteenth century ranching had become prevalent in three broad regions: north and east Leinster, north Munster and east Connacht, and west Connacht and Donegal. In Leinster the grazing region covered an area of fertile grassland stretching from the river Shannon and Lough Ree in the west to the eastern seaboard. The chief ranching counties were Meath, Westmeath, Kildare, and King's County. Large graziers were most conspicuous in Meath, especially in the districts of Kells, Navan, Trim, Oldcastle, and Dunshaughlin. The second region of ranch farming, comprising the plains of east Connacht and north Munster, was demarcated in the west by Lough Mask and Lough Corrib and in the east by the river Shannon. The principal areas of grazing in east Connacht were Loughrea and Ballinasloe in County Galway, the Boyle, Roscommon, and Athlone districts of County Roscommon, the Claremorris area of County Mayo, and the Tobercurry district of County Sligo. In Munster the main ranching counties were Clare and Tipperary. Large grazing farms were also prevalent in the western areas of Connacht and in Donegal. In this western maritime fringe the ranches were composed mainly of large expanses of rough mountain and moorland pasture.[20]

Concomitant with the growth of ranching after 1850, there emerged an intensification of the trade in cattle among the major grazing areas. A significant stimulus to this development was the establishment of a

17. Ibid., p. 170.
18. Ibid., pp. 169–70.
19. Stephen Gwynn, *A holiday in Connemara* (London, 1909), pp. 109–10.
20. T. W. Freeman, *Ireland: its physical, historical, social, and economic geography* (London and New York, 1950), pp. 294–300, 408–33; Bulfin, *Rambles*, pp. 46, 91; Henry Coulter, *The west of Ireland: its existing condition and prospects* (Dublin, 1862), p. 355; Wilfrid Ewart, *A journey in Ireland, 1921* (London and New York, 1922), pp. 124–5.

railway network. The most distinctive feature of the trade was that dry cattle were bought and sold, often several times over, at various stages during their physical growth. Two distinct types of grazier had arisen out of these conditions, namely, the fattener and the store grazier. The fattener (sometimes known as a finisher) specialized in bringing cattle to their full beef potential. His concern was to add flesh to the animal in the final stage before slaughter. The store grazier (sometimes called a middleman grazier) reared cattle in the intermediate stages of growth and concentrated on the development of bone and muscle.[21]

The major store-grazing region consisted of the plains of east Connacht and north Munster. The store graziers of this area procured calves and yearlings from the small farmers of Connacht and Ulster as well as from the dairy farmers of Munster, especially those of east Cork and Limerick. Dairy producers in these two counties also sold their calves to store graziers in east Leinster, especially Kilkenny, Queen's County, and King's County. Though the movement of calves from dairy farms to store pastures constituted an important aspect of the cattle trade, some dairy producers retained their young beef cattle, if they were in possession of sufficient pasture, and reared them as stores. Butter production was often combined with store grazing on the same farm.[22] Certain ranchers with infertile rough pasture specialized in the rearing of young stores up to only eighteen months old. Examples were the hill graziers of west Connacht and Donegal. Other graziers, having richer grasslands, were able to rear advanced stores up to thirty months old.[23] Of course, the ages at which cattle were bought and sold depended also on prevailing market trends as well as the available resources of pasture.

At the end of the store-grazing period the cattle were in some cases purchased by Scottish or English buyers (commonly called shippers) or by a local cattle salesman specializing in cattle exporting, and then shipped directly to Britain.[24] In other cases the store cattle were sold to a fattening grazier in Ireland, who finished them on his own pasture. The major region of cattle fattening comprised the rich grasslands of Westmeath, Kildare, Dublin, and above all Meath. The fattening grazier usually kept his beasts for six to twelve months and sold them for slaughter when they were between three and four years old.[25]

21. Congestion comm., final report, p. 49 [C 4097], H.C. 1908, xlii, 729.
22. Congestion comm. evidence, app. 3rd report, app. 8, p. 345 [C 3414], H.C. 1907, xxv, 337.
23. Ibid.
24. Ibid., pp. 345–7.
25. Ibid., pp. 77, 345; app. 10th report, pp. 102, 176; M. J. Bonn, Modern Ireland and her agrarian problem, trans. T. W. Rolleston (Dublin, 1906), pp. 40–1; Freeman, Ireland, p. 299.

Agitation against Graziers

The growth of ranch farming was strongly resented by the peasant population, especially in the grazing areas of Connacht, north and east Leinster, and north Munster. Conflict between graziers and peasants, though scarcely unknown before the great famine, erupted around 1880, as ranching became an issue of central importance within the wider struggle for agrarian reform. The first signs of conflict were observable as early as the winter of 1879–80 in the western parts of Galway and Mayo. Here an outbreak of violence occurred against the large hill graziers, especially in the Erriff valley, where they suffered extensive injury to their property and livestock.[26] Open hostility between rancher and peasant became evident in other areas after 1885. National League branches then turned their attention to the practice of grass grabbing, or the taking of untenanted pasture for short terms, usually eleven months.[27] Auctions of untenanted pasture were frequently paralyzed by the League's prohibition of such lettings. In addition, those who defied the ban, labeled "grass grabbers," were regularly subjected to rigorous boycotting and other reprisals. The latter included open denunciation by local branches of the National League, the sending of threatening notices, and at times even violent injuries.[28] The purpose of the prohibition was twofold: first, to prevent untenanted grassland from becoming a source of rising rental income during a period when the League was attempting to reduce rents significantly; and second, to stop the landlord from converting evicted lands to profitable use, thus weakening his position further by cutting off a subsidiary source of revenue.[29] At the same time, the ban brought the graziers, who were active bidders for the landlord's pasture, into collision with the land movement.

After the land act of 1903 antagonism between ranchers and peasants became even more acute and prevalent throughout the grazing regions of Connacht, north Munster, and north Leinster.[30] The rising bitterness

26. B. H. Becker, *Disturbed Ireland, being the letters written during the winter of 1880–81* (London, 1881), pp. 20, 74–5, 78–9.

27. "Three months of the National League: proceedings of National League branches: June, July, August 1887" in Irish Loyal and Patriotic Union, *Publications issued during 1887* (Dublin, 1887), pp. 385–448. See also "Ireland in 1887," pt. 2: "proceedings of National League branches," ibid., pp. 219–91.

28. *Cowper comm. evidence*, pp. 40, 45–8, 90, 799, 1002. Denunciation of grass grabbing was in some instances accompanied by the practice of publicly exposing the names of grabbers at National League branch meetings. See, e.g., *Enniscorthy Guardian*, 8, 29 Jan., 12 Feb. 1887; *United Ireland*, 19 Mar. 1887. There was one case at Gorey, Co. Wexford, in which the National League sent letters to grass grabbers, directing them to abandon untenanted grassland (*Enniscorthy Guardian*, 26 Feb. 1887).

29. *Cowper comm. evidence*, pp. 40, 90, 799.

30. *Congestion comm. evidence*, app. 10th report, p. 168; Gwynn, *Connemara*, p. 109.

culminated in a fierce campaign between 1906 and 1909 popularly termed the ranch war. Its beginning was marked by a large public meeting held on 14 October 1906 at The Downs in County Westmeath. The meeting was described as "a demonstration of all who wished to smash and finish ranching and land monopoly and to recover the land for the people."[31]

Public rallies and mass demonstrations became a regular feature of the antigrazier agitation. Such meetings were held throughout the grazing counties of north Leinster and Connacht, and were often addressed by leading figures in the United Irish League. At these gatherings the ranchers were regularly denounced. They were depicted as one of the root causes of the social and economic ills afflicting the peasantry and as props of the landlord system. Resolutions were adopted demanding the expropriation of the graziers, with particular reference to the ending of both nonresidential possession and the eleven-month system. Nonresidential and untenanted land currently in the hands of the ranchers, it was asserted, should be allocated to peasant farmers and their sons as part of a major program of land redistribution.[32] Especially prominent in the antigrazier meetings of Connacht and north Leinster were Lawrence Ginnell, John Fitzgibbon, David Sheehy, and John Hayden. Ginnell, a barrister by profession, was M.P. for Westmeath North; Fitzgibbon was a Roscommon county councillor; Sheehy was M.P. for Meath South; and Hayden was editor and proprietor of the *Westmeath Examiner* and also M.P. for Roscommon South. All four were influential members of the United Irish League and throughout 1907 and 1908 repeatedly addressed large antigrazier gatherings.

A second and far more important tactic employed during the ranch war was cattle driving, in which cattle were illegally removed from the grazier's land at night and then brought to a secret market, placed on the land of neighboring farmers, or most often simply left to wander along country roads.[33] The first reference to cattle driving as a possible weapon of agitation was made by Lawrence Ginnell at the initial public meeting of the ranch war in October 1906:

If the graziers found their ranches empty some fine morning and after six or eight weeks found their cattle not all together, but some in Connaught, some in Munster, and some among the Wicklow mountains, and some in the glens of Antrim; and if this wandering mania became fashionable among ranching cattle all over

31. *Irish Times*, 15 Oct. 1906.

32. For an account of a tenant demonstration on this subject at Cullenagh in the district of Clogheen, Co. Tipperary, see *Leinster Leader*, 25 Jan. 1908.

33. For a description of the effects of cattle driving, see H. B. Leech, *1848 and 1912: the continuity of the Irish revolutionary movement* (2nd ed., London, [1912]), pp. 76, 78.

the country, and if you persisted in it from now until Christmas, the ranchers would lose their taste for the people's land. I would advise you, in language not unknown to my Scotch ancestors, to leave those ranches unfenced, unused, unusable, unstocked, uncut, to bleed and wither and whiten and rot before the world . . . , and so effectively cursed by you, men of the living present, that neither man nor demon would dare to stand another hour between the people and the land that ought to be yours.[34]

Tenants in the ranching areas responded readily to such invocations. During 1907 and 1908 cattle driving became rampant in numerous parts of north Leinster, north Munster, and Connacht. As table 10.3 shows, it reached a peak in the second quarter of 1908, when 297 cattle drives occurred. Indeed, by mid-July 1908 one newspaper account described cattle driving in Meath as an "epidemic."[35] During 1909, however, there were increasingly fewer newspaper reports of cattle driving, and the agitation gradually subsided.

A third aspect of the antigrazier agitation was boycotting. At many antiranch meetings tenants were urged to ostracize the graziers, and the response was again enthusiastic. In December 1905 there were 174 persons boycotted; by February 1909 the figure had risen to 889.[36] Furthermore, the returns for 1909 showed a concentration of boycotting cases in the store-grazing counties of north Munster, Connacht, and east Leinster, though surprisingly little boycotting took place in the fattening

TABLE 10.3

Cattle Drives between 1 January 1907 and 30 September 1908, by Quarterly Periods, for the Whole of Ireland and for Those Counties Most Affected

	1907				1908		
	1st	2nd	3rd	4th	1st	2nd	3rd
Ireland	0	81	62	247	123	297	97
Meath	0	0	27	64	14	19	13
Westmeath	0	0	1	22	28	24	13
Galway	0	53	17	61	15	86	2
Roscommon	0	8	1	46	7	23	2
Clare	0	2	1	5	17	38	41

SOURCE: *A return, by counties and quarterly periods, of the number of cattle drives reported by the Royal Irish Constabulary to have taken place in Ireland from the first day of January 1907 to the 30th day of September 1908*, p. 2, H.C. 1908 (310), xc, 3.

34. *Irish Times*, 15 Oct. 1906.

35. *Leinster Leader*, 18 July 1908.

36. *A return of the number of cases of persons boycotted throughout Ireland on the undermentioned dates* [30 June 1893–28 Feb. 1909] . . . , p. 2, H.C. 1909 (116), lxxiii, 7.

counties of Meath and Kildare.[37] Boycotting was particularly directed against the eleven-month system. Graziers and shopkeeper-graziers who refused to surrender untenanted holdings became targets of organized discrimination.[38] Traders, laborers, artisans, and carters were instructed neither to work for them nor to transact business with them. Such boycotts were in a sense an extension of earlier actions against grass grabbers. Their purpose was to prevent the letting of eleven-month holdings and thus to force landlords to relinquish them to the Congested Districts Board or the Estates Commission.[39]

As with previous rural agitations, the antigrazier movement involved a certain degree of intimidation and violence. Some ranchers surrendered untenanted land as a result of specific threats.[40] Though agrarian violence was generally far below the level of the 1880s, violent clashes between the police and antirancher agitators did occur occasionally. In other instances herds were assaulted and graziers' property was damaged.[41] Hayricks on large grazing farms were sometimes burned.[42] Brougham Leech, registrar of titles and deeds in Ireland as well as a professor of law in Trinity College, Dublin, accurately summarized the range of agrarian outrages perpetrated against the ranchers between 1907 and 1909: "Although cattle driving thus became the most fashionable method of operation, it is not to be assumed that other measures of terrorism and destruction were neglected. Arson, the burning of hayricks, firing into dwelling houses, spiking meadows, the mutilation of horses and cows, the destruction of turf, the damaging of machinery, and various other forms of lawless violence began to increase and multiply."[43] The sharp rise in agrarian crimes from 234 in 1906 to 576 in 1908 testifies to the role of intimidation and violence in the antigrazier agitation.[44]

Opposition to the ranchers was partly articulated by the United Irish League. Unlike the Land League and the National League earlier, the United Irish League stressed the importance of the grazing issue to agrarian reform. This emphasis was reflected in meetings of the national di-

37. *A return showing the number of cases and of persons boycotted in each county in Ireland on the 30th day of November 1905 and the 31st day of January 1909 . . .* , pp. 2–3, H.C. 1909 (57), lxxiii, 3.

38. *Roscommon Journal*, 30 Nov. 1907; E. B. Iwan-Müller, *Ireland today and tomorrow* (London, 1907), p. 85.

39. *Roscommon Journal*, 4 Mar., 9 Nov. 1907.

40. Ibid., 9, 30 Nov. 1907.

41. Ibid., 23, 30 Nov. 1907; *Leinster Leader*, 11 Jan. 1908.

42. *Meath Herald*, 4 Jan., 22 Feb. 1908; *F.J.*, 31 Dec. 1908.

43. Leech, *Revolutionary movement*, p. 78.

44. *A copy of classified return of agrarian outrages of an indictable character reported throughout Ireland in each of the years 1906, 1907, and 1908*, p. 2, H.C. 1909 (70), lxxiii, 1.

rectory of the United Irish League and in those of its branches in the grazing counties. Its policy clearly called for the compulsory expropriation of ranchers and the distribution of grassland among small and middling farmers as well as disinherited sons of farmers.[45] Yet the role of the United Irish League in the ranch war fell short of complete commitment and full-scale involvement. There emerged within its ranks serious objection to certain aspects of the agitation, especially cattle driving.[46] Moreover, the ranching issue became less salient (at the level of both the national directory and local branches) as increased attention was devoted to other issues, such as home rule, the housing of laborers, educational reform, and the tenurial status of urban tenants.[47]

Disillusionment with the United Irish League and continued discontent over the lack of action to confiscate and reassign untenanted and nonresidential holdings led to the formation of another organization called the Associated Estates Committee. Its chief spokesman was Canon T. Cummins, parish priest of Roscommon and Kilteevan in the diocese of Elphin. Thomas Larkin, its secretary, and Hubert Flynn, its treasurer, also played conspicuous parts in its work.[48] The main aim of the Associated Estates Committee was the compulsory acquisition and distribution of untenanted and nonresidential land as well as of residential grazing farms exceeding 300 acres. To create an effective program of land distribution, it strongly urged the passage of legislation conferring compulsory legal powers upon the Congested Districts Board and the Estates Commission in respect of land purchase.[49] In addition, the organization pressed these statutory bodies with some success to take firm action in purchasing untenanted grassland. Indeed, on certain occasions the Associated Estates Committee itself undertook negotiations with landlords on behalf of tenants for the purchase of estates and untenanted land.[50] Though a small elite, the Associated Estates Committee was at times able to mobilize widespread peasant support, especially in Roscommon and east Galway.

The organized opposition to ranching also received considerable backing and direction from the rural labor movement, particularly in Meath and Westmeath. The labor unions of these two counties, representing

45. Minute book of the national directory of the United Irish League (hereafter U.I.L.), 10 Aug. 1904–30 Apr. 1918: 10 Aug. 1904, 24 Jan. 1905 (N.L.I., MS 708).
46. U.I.L. minute book, 15 Jan. 1908 (N.L.I., MS 708); *Westmeath Examiner*, 26 Jan., 2 Feb. 1907; *Galway Observer*, 5 Oct. 1907; *Meath Herald*, 22 Feb. 1908.
47. U.I.L. minute book, 15 Jan. 1908 (N.L.I., MS 708).
48. *Roscommon Journal*, 20 Apr., 20 June 1912.
49. Ibid., 3 Feb., 12 Apr. 1912.
50. Ibid., 20 June 1912.

the interests of both agricultural and general laborers, were prominent allies of the antigrazier movement. In particular, the large public meetings of the Meath Labour Union became in 1907 platforms for the expression of antirancher sentiments. At these gatherings graziers and the whole ranching system were vigorously denounced, and demands were made for expropriation and redistribution.[51]

Other important forums for vocalizing opposition to the graziers were the county and rural-district councils and the boards of guardians. On numerous occasions in Meath and Westmeath the proceedings of these bodies included speeches and resolutions castigating the ranching system and the eleven-month letting, and calling for the surrender and division of grass farms.[52] The Kells rural-district councillors were particularly identified with the antigrazier cause. On one occasion, in September 1907, they demonstrated their support by inviting Lawrence Ginnell to address one of their meetings. His speech was an embittered exposition of the injurious effects of the ranching system.[53] A few days later, Ginnell delivered a vehement attack on commercial ranching before the Trim district council.[54] On another occasion the Kells district councillors sent a strongly worded memorial to the Estates Commissioners demanding the acquisition and distribution of untenanted grass farms.[55]

The emergence of a distinct antigrazier movement was critically linked to the growth of widespread and militant opposition to the landlord system during the days of the Land League and the Plan of Campaign. Although the ranching system had taken shape even before 1850, the appearance of comprehensive opposition to it had to await the mass mobilization of the peasantry against landlord hegemony in the 1880s. The significance of the land war was that it created an elaborate and sophisticated organizational structure within the peasantry, which could be used as a springboard to foment and coordinate opposition to the graziers. Furthermore, as the subject of agrarian reform came to dominate public debate in an increasingly literate and politicized society, the peasantry over the course of time inevitably focused its attention on the ranching issue as an integral part of the land question.

Concern over the ranching system intensified as the long campaign for peasant proprietorship neared its goal. The crucial measure in this respect was the Wyndham land act of 1903. In pursuing agrarian re-

51. *Meath Herald*, 9 Apr., 31 Aug. 1907, 4 Jan. 1908.
52. Ibid., 6 July 1907; 4 Jan., 4 May 1908.
53. Ibid., 4 Sept. 1907.
54. Ibid., 21 Sept. 1907.
55. Ibid., 14 Sept. 1907.

form, peasants gradually began to question the adequacy of their holdings for efficient production.[56] The realization developed that there was
little point in giving tenants the land if the size and fertility of their
farms were insufficient to provide a secure and reasonable livelihood.
Ownership must of necessity be accompanied by measures of land redistribution to allow small and middling farmers an increased opportunity
to earn adequate cash surpluses. This point was forcefully made to the
Royal Commission on Congestion by Father Joseph Pelly, a curate of
Kilcloony parish near Ballinasloe, with specific reference to the rancher-
peasant conflict: "I think it never came to an acute crisis till the Wyndham act. There was no real interference with the graziers until it was
recognised that the act would be futile unless the grasslands were split
up."[57] Consequently, in the words of Stephen Gwynn in 1907, "the same
agencies of pressure as were applied to landlords now begin to be applied to graziers."[58]

The Economic Characteristics of Ranching

Among the interrelated factors contributing to conflict between graziers
and the peasant community, the chief was the land-acquisitive character
of ranch farming. More than any other system of agriculture, its profit-
ability depended on the acquisition of land in quantity. Especially in
periods of marked prosperity, the grazier was constantly engaged in a
quest for pasture. This feature of the ranching system stemmed from
its capital and labor requirements. The ranch enterprise was characterized by: (1) a greater dependence on circulating than on fixed capital;
(2) a high level of liquidity as a result of the importance of circulating
capital; and (3) a small labor input. The distinction between circulating
capital (sometimes called working capital) and the fixed variety is crucial to any analysis of the ranch enterprise. Circulating capital refers
to those assets whose productive potential is maximized or exhausted
within a single production or accounting period.[59] The full value of the
initial capital outlay is therefore recouped within a short time. Fixed
capital, on the other hand, refers to those assets which do not exhaust
their productive potential within a single production or accounting
period.[60] The nature of the capital commitment is essentially long-term.

56. Leech, *Revolutionary movement*, pp. 76–7.
57. *Congestion comm. evidence*, app. 10th report, p. 169.
58. Gwynn, *Connemara*, p. 109.
59. Charles Ritson, *Agricultural economics* (New York, 1977), p. 112.
60. Ibid.

Thus the distinction between fixed and circulating capital rests on the length of time between the initial outlay and the realization of a maximum return.[61]

Within the Irish ranch enterprise the main outlay was in circulating capital, employed to purchase livestock, grass seed, and hay and fodder, and to hire land. The value of these assets could usually be realized within nine to eighteen months, the normal accounting period of the ranch enterprise. The physical development of livestock on open, fertile grazing was rapid enough to allow their profitable sale before the expiration of a single accounting period. As the German visitor Moritz Bonn observed in 1906, "A man buys a beast cheap, lets it graze for a certain time, and sells it off at a higher price in as short a time as possible."[62] William Rochfort, an extensive land agent in Queen's County as well as those of Dublin and Tipperary, also provided evidence of the quick profits to be made in grazing in his testimony before the Fry commission in 1897. He cited the example of the cattle of one rancher having risen in price from £5 13s. to £11 10s. per head over the summer grazing period. Such good returns, according to Rochfort, could also be made over the winter. He quoted an instance in which graziers had paid £4 19s. per head for stores in the autumn and sold them at £10 10s. per head in the following spring.[63] On the other hand, the outlay of the rancher in fixed capital was minimal, confined largely to the provision of horses for the herdsmen, a small number of cows or breeding ewes if the grazier chose to supply his own replacement stock, and quarters for cattle and sheep regularly kept over the winter months. Unlike the commercial tillage farmer, the rancher had little need to invest in such fixed assets as barns, plows and other implements, drainage systems, or manures. He was thus able to maximize or exhaust the value of his capital outlay within a much shorter time.[64]

The distinction between fixed and circulating capital reflected in the difference between grazing and tillage was particularly important in the context of certain forms of land tenure prevailing in nineteenth-century Ireland. Most fixed-capital outlays, especially within a tillage enterprise, involved substantial improvements to the farm, such as new buildings,

61. Ibid.

62. Bonn, *Agrarian problem*, p. 41.

63. *Royal commission of inquiry into the procedure and practice and the methods of valuation followed by the land commission, the land judges' court, and the civil-bill courts in Ireland under the land acts and the land-purchase acts*, vol. ii: *minutes of evidence*, p. 614 [C 8859], H.C. 1898, xxxv, 41 (hereafter cited as *Fry comm. evidence*).

64. Crotty, *Agricultural production*, pp. 60–1; Michael McCarthy, *Land and liberty: a study of the new lords of the soil* (London, 1911), p. 250.

fencing, drainage, or manures. These improvements were immobile; they could not be sold separately from the farm. Landlords throughout most of Ireland, although not formally recognizing tenant interest, or partial ownership by the tenant, before the period of agrarian reform, did allow an outgoing tenant having a yearly tenancy or a tenancy at will to sell on the open market his interest in the farm under certain conditions. This included the right to sell his capital improvements.[65] But there were important exceptions. Such a privilege was frequently not extended to leaseholders, as indicated by witnesses before the Bessborough commission.[66] Moreover, especially in parts of Connacht, the right to sell capital improvements was not even enjoyed by yearly tenants or tenants at will.[67] In such cases the immobile capital outlays embodied in improvements could be appropriated by the landlord. Many leaseholders, and in some instances yearly tenants and tenants at will, who relinquished land were not permitted to sell their immobile assets to the successor. Nor was the landlord in such cases obliged to compensate the departing tenant. Consequently, outgoing leaseholders, yearly tenants, and tenants at will were often unable to redeem losses on most of their fixed assets either by selling them or by claiming compensation.[68]

Even when the departing tenant did enjoy the right to sell his interest, he would still have incurred serious capital losses if the demand for the disposable assets of the farm (for instance, implements and horses) had declined substantially since the initial outlay. Because of the pronounced fall in cereal prices during the second half of the nineteenth century, demand for the disposable fixed capital of the tillage enterprise was also

65. *Reports from poor-law inspectors in Ireland as to the existing relations between landlord and tenant in respect of improvements on farms . . .* , pp. 29, 36, 119–20, 154 [C 31], H.C. 1870, xiv, 37; *Fry comm. report*, p. 24 [C 8734], H.C. 1898, xxxv, 1; *Report of her majesty's commissioners of inquiry into the working of the Landlord and Tenant (Ireland) Act, 1870, and the acts amending the same*, p. 3 [C 2779], H.C. 1881, xviii, 1 (hereafter cited as *Bessborough comm. report*).

66. Seventy-seven witnesses appearing before the Bessborough commission testified to the prohibition of free sale of tenant interest, including capital improvements. Many of these witnesses referred to the prohibition of free sale on leasehold property and especially to the nonalienation clause in standard leases. See, e.g., *Bessborough comm. evidence*, pt. i, pp. 343, 364, 381, 494, 583, 734 [C 2779-I], H.C. 1881, xviii, 73; see also *Bessborough comm. report*, p. 30; *Richmond comm. evidence*, i, 662, 914–15, 918; *First report from the select committee of the House of Lords on land law (Ireland), together with the proceedings of the committee, minutes of evidence, and appendix*, p. 303, H.C. 1882 (249), xi, 1.

67. *Reports from poor-law inspectors*, pp. 52, 58, 60, 63.

68. *Richmond comm. evidence*, i, 398, 403. Unable to sell a right of occupancy, the grazier, especially on a leasehold farm, may have been more inclined to retain his land, even though it was not in his economic interest to do so.

decreasing. Thus the tillage or mixed farmer leaving his holding was frequently unable to recover the full unexhausted value of such assets. Only in circumstances of sustained market demand for capital assets would the tenant who wanted to sell have been able to redeem some or all of his outlay. The difference between ranching and tillage with respect to circulating and fixed capital is therefore especially significant under the following two conditions: (1) the existence of legal or customary restrictions on the sale of part or all of the fixed assets; and (2) a decline since the initial outlay in the market demand for fixed assets. Restrictions on the sale of assets created a degree of capital illiquidity particularly noticeable within large commercial tillage enterprises. On the other hand, the ranch enterprise, with its reliance on circulating rather than fixed capital, remained highly liquid. It was unaffected by the two conditions which often prevented the recovery of capital expenditures on the tillage farm in the event of forfeiture.

Another striking feature of ranch farming was its small labor requirement. The grazier needed to employ only a few herdsmen to supervise the ranch and to tend the cattle. Indeed, two or three herdsmen often had responsibility for over 500 acres of pasture. The main tasks of the herdsmen were to search for stray cattle or sheep, to transfer the stock from one pasture to another, to drive them to and from market, and to distribute hay and fodder during the winter months. For long periods herdsmen were relatively idle. The ranch enterprise was thus free of the labor-intensive demands characteristic of tillage farming, and ranching areas were in fact notorious for the scarcity of opportunity for agricultural employment.[69] The low requirement for labor in ranching meant that any sizable increase in production undertaken by the grazier did not necessitate a significant increase in labor costs — an important consideration in the prevailing situation of a declining supply of agricultural workers.

Measured in monetary terms, the difference between pasture farming and cereal production was amply illustrated by James Wilson. In his article "Tillage versus grazing," written in 1905, during the period of the antigrazier movement, he compared expenditure and net returns in rotational tillage agriculture and dry-cattle farming. Using hypothetical examples, Wilson calculated labor and capital expenditure on a normal acre of tillage over a period of three years. If the alternation was barley, a green crop, and then oats, total expenditure was estimated at between £17 and £22 16s., with the variation depending on the nature of the green

69. *Congestion comm. evidence, app. 3rd report*, p. 345; *app. 7th report*, p. 178 [C 3785], H.C. 1908, xl, 5; *app. 10th report*, p. 21; *Richmond comm. evidence*, i, 403.

crop. These estimates excluded the substantial initial investment in fencing, drainage, implements, and buildings, but they included the costs
of maintenance, interest on capital, rates, taxes, and insurance. Also
included were the costs of manures and labor. On an acre of permanent
pasture for a period of three years, however, expenditure amounted to
only £3 9s., a figure which took into account the cost of laying down
to grass, the labor of two men and one horse for each 200 acres, interest
on capital, rates, and taxes. The purchase price of livestock was excluded.
Thus expenditures in pasture farming were no more than one-fifth of
those in tillage. If hay feeding were taken into consideration, the costs
of one bullock would have increased by £2 10s. over a single year or
by £7 10s. over three years.[70]

The grazier's capacity to recoup quickly the full value of his capital
outlay through his almost exclusive reliance on liquid assets, coupled
with his low demand for labor, enabled him to respond rapidly to price
fluctuations and to vary his acreage accordingly. Thus, if the rancher
decided to cut his losses in a period of low stock prices by decreasing
production and surrendering part of his land, he was not incumbered
by possible losses on his capital outlay. The quick returns characteristic
of grazing insured that there was little irrecoverable investment to prevent him from abandoning some of his land.[71] Conversely, the grazier
was well placed to respond to an upturn in livestock prices by expanding
his acreage. The reason for this was twofold. First, if the rancher wished
to increase production, he did not have to worry about employing much
more labor or about further expenditure on fixed assets. The expansion
of output simply required the acquisition of more land and the purchase
of more stock.[72] Second, the grazier's ability to avoid serious capital losses
in the event of forced or voluntary surrender of his pasture gave him
additional freedom to expand production and to acquire more land. He
did not need security of tenure beyond the length of the grazing season.
Nor did he require the certainty of a sustained market demand for fixed
assets. In other words, by his capacity to realize a quick return on his
capital, the rancher was less likely to be deterred from investment in
land or stock by the possibilities of dispossession or surrender. The first
possibility was more likely to take place in a period of high livestock
prices, while the second was more likely to occur at a time of low prices.

The tendency of graziers to accumulate large acreages of pasture was

70. James Wilson, "Tillage versus grazing" in *Journal of the Department of Agriculture and Technical Instruction for Ireland*, v, no. 2 (1905), pp. 217–35.
71. Crotty, *Agricultural production*, p. 61.
72. McCarthy, *Land and liberty*, p. 250.

increased by their inability to secure a high rate of profit per unit of production. Cattle ranching in late nineteenth-century Ireland was characterized by low output per acre. Since the short-term investments of the grazier were substantial, especially if he purchased rather than bred his replacement stock, his net return per head of cattle and per acre of pasture was usually quite small.[73] One reliable witness before the Royal Commission on Congestion maintained that even "in the good years" the rancher could secure only "a few shillings profit on each acre."[74] Yet he still reaped a substantial gain "because his acres were numbered by the hundred."[75] Thus narrow profit margins impelled territorial expansion. Even in a period of high prices there was little point for the grazier to procure a small acreage if his intention was to maximize his profits.

The Land Market for Graziers

The growth of ranching in the second half of the nineteenth century was made possible by developments in the land market. Graziers were critically dependent on a growing supply of pasture to augment their investments in cattle and sheep. Between 1850 and 1910 significant opportunities arose for ranchers to satisfy their need for more land. The two main sources of supply were evicted holdings and untenanted land. Based on tenurial competition and controlled by landlords, the letting of such land provided graziers with the means to realize their acquisitive ambitions at the expense of the peasant class.

The market in evicted land was especially brisk during the famine and its immediate aftermath (1847–55), as table 10.4 helps to show. The main years for dispossession were 1849 (16,686 families evicted), 1850 (19,949), and 1851 (13,197). Between 1849 and 1856, 25 percent of the families evicted returned to their holdings as tenants or caretakers, although in subsequent years readmissions as a percentage of evictions declined somewhat. The wholesale clearances of the late 1840s and early 1850s allowed commercially ambitious individuals to acquire pasture ground at relatively cheap rates. On many estates the evicted land formerly held by subsistence tenants was consolidated into large pastoral holdings and relet to graziers and other men of capital. In numerous localities tenants were removed en masse, "whole villages being cleared."[76]

73. R. O'Connor, "The small farm" in James Meenan and D. A. Webb (ed.), *A view of Ireland: twelve essays* (Dublin, 1957), p. 115.

74. *Congestion comm. evidence, app. 10th report*, p. 168.

75. Ibid.

76. Shand, *West of Ireland*, pp. 111–14; Becker, *Disturbed Ireland*, p. 20; Sir Ernest

TABLE 10.4
Number of Families Evicted for Each Seven-Year Period between 1849 and 1880
(including cases in which the family was readmitted)

	1849–56	1857–64	1865–72	1873–80
Number of families evicted	68,369	9,477	4,635	7,414
Number of families readmitted	17,427	1,866	979[a]	1,068[a]
Percentage readmitted	25%	20%	21%	14%

SOURCE: *Return by provinces and counties (compiled from returns made to the inspector general, Royal Irish Constabulary), of cases of evictions which have come to the knowledge of the constabulary in each of the years from 1849 to 1880 inclusive*, pp. 3–23, H.C. 1881 (185), lxxvii, 725.
[a]Note that the figures on readmissions between 1870 and 1880 contained in this return refer only to families readmitted as tenants, excluding those readmitted as caretakers.

On a visit to the Westport district of Mayo in October 1880, the English newspaper correspondent Bernard Becker observed that according to local peasants, the greater part of the indigenous population had been "swept away and the country reduced to a desert in order that it might be let in blocks of several square miles each to Englishmen and Scotchmen, who employ the land for grazing purposes only, and perhaps a score or two of people where once a thousand lived — after a fashion."[77] Similar portrayals that linked the development of ranching with the clearances came from other commentators, such as Innes Shand, Henry Coulter, Louis Paul-Dubois, and Ernest Barker. In addition, witnesses appearing before the Richmond commission and the Royal Commission on Congestion frequently mentioned the creation of grazing farms as a result of the evictions. Fairly typical was the testimony of Peter O'Malley, a shopkeeper who served as chairman of the Oughterard district council and board of guardians. Referring to the big grazing farms of Oughterard poor-law union in Galway, he told the Royal Commission on Congestion: "These farms in most cases were occupied by tenants in former times who were obliged to leave through unscrupulous rackrenting landlords or turned out to die or starve by the roadside to satisfy the

Barker, *Ireland in the last fifty years, 1866–1916* (Oxford, 1917), p. 14; Coulter, *West of Ireland*, p. 244; Paul-Dubois, *Contemporary Ireland*, pp. 220–2, 299–301; Hugh Sutherland, *Ireland yesterday and today* (Philadelphia, 1909), p. 67; C. J. Dolan, "The congested districts" in *Irish year book, 1909* (Dublin, 1909), p. 134; *Richmond comm. evidence*, i, 102, 497–8, 1025; *Congestion comm. evidence, app. 6th report*, p. 137; *app. 9th report*, p. 135 [C 3845], H.C. 1908, xli, 487; *app. 10th report*, pp. 8–9.
77. Becker, *Disturbed Ireland*, p. 37.

greed of some covetous neighbour who wanted room for his sheep or bullocks."[78]

The close link between clearances and the development of commercial grazing is also confirmed by the geographical distribution of evictions. During the period 1849–56 the incidence of eviction (standardized by county-population size) was greatest in the regions of north Munster and Connacht. The highest incidence was in fact recorded in north Tipperary, where 194 persons were evicted per 1,000 inhabitants. This was of course a major area for the commercial grazing of store bullocks after the famine. Evictions were also numerous during the years 1849–56 in the ranching counties of north Leinster, though the rate of dispossession there was lower than in Connacht and north Munster. In Meath there were 8,700 persons evicted (62 per 1,000 inhabitants); in Westmeath, 6,400 (58 per 1,000); and in King's County, 11,400 (102 per 1,000).[79]

These patterns persisted in the 1860s and 1870s, even though the rate of eviction sharply decreased. The counties of Connacht remained the chief area of dispossession. For instance, in Mayo there were more than 4,000 persons evicted, and in Roscommon over 2,600, between 1857 and 1864. In both cases the rate of dispossession was 17 per 1,000 inhabitants. The incidence of eviction for the same period was significantly lower in the cattle-fattening counties of Meath and Westmeath (10 per 1,000 and 9 per 1,000 inhabitants respectively), but still above the national average of 8 per 1,000. Between 1873 and 1880, however, the rate of eviction increased to 12 per 1,000 in Meath and 10 per 1,000 in Westmeath, as compared with a national average of 7 per 1,000.[80]

The graziers who took advantage of the market in evicted land were drawn from various social and occupational groups. Some were established ranchers; others were commercial middling tenants intent on expanding their herds and flocks.[81] A large number were townsmen, especially shopkeepers and solicitors.[82] Land agents, bailiffs, and former middlemen, "creatures of the rent office," also seized the opportunity provided by the clearances to secure grazing farms.[83] In west Connacht

78. *Congestion comm. evidence, app. 10th report,* p. 6.

79. *Return by provinces and counties (compiled from returns made to the inspector general, Royal Irish Constabulary), of cases of evictions which have come to the knowledge of the constabulary in each of the years from 1849 to 1880 inclusive,* pp. 3–23, H.C. 1881 (185), lxxvii, 725.

80. Ibid. See also *Meath Herald,* 9 Apr. 1907.

81. Pellew, *Castle and cabin,* p. 81.

82. *Congestion comm. evidence, app. 7th report,* p. 183; *app. 10th report,* pp. 167–8; Palmer, *Land League crisis,* p. 35.

83. *Congestion comm. evidence, app. 10th report,* pp. 167–8. See also Palmer, *Land League crisis,* p. 35.

much of the evicted land, comprising large tracts of upland pasture, was given to Scottish and northern English sheep farmers.[84]

The landlord's motives in replacing small tenants by ranchers were twofold. Some of the new men were prepared to offer much higher rents than could be paid by existing smallholders. But many graziers provided only the same rent per acre as the previous smallholders. Even so, in the landlords' eyes letting to ranchers guaranteed punctual payment of the full rent. Landlords notoriously encountered great difficulty in collecting rents from an impoverished and resentful tenantry scattered in large numbers over an extensive area. The task required that the tenants be constantly harangued and pressured, often through threats of dispossession, by agents, subagents, and bailiffs. Many tenants periodically escaped payment or were allowed to accumulate arrears, especially on overcrowded estates.

Ranchers were a different matter. Since they were far less likely to evade or frustrate the collection of rent, the landlord was sure of his money. In addition, the administrative costs of collection were obviously much reduced among a few large graziers, in contrast to myriads of small tenants. Bernard Becker emphasized these points with respect to Mayo estates:

The best way of effecting [improvement] was thought to be the removal of the inhabitants who paid rent or not as it suited them, and in place of a few hundred of these, to secure one responsible tenant, even if he paid much less per acre than the native peasant. I draw particular attention to the latter fact, as one of the popular grievances sorely and lengthily dwelt upon is that the oppressor not only took the land from the people, evicted them, and demolished their cabins with crowbars, but that he let his property to the hated foreigner for less than the natives had paid and were willing to pay, or promised to pay him. . . . But the fact unfortunately was that Lord Lucan, Lord Sligo, and other great landowners in County Mayo had found it so difficult to get rent out of their tenants that they determined to let their land to large farmers only, at such a price as they could get, but with the certainty that the rent, whatever it was, would be well and duly paid, and there would be an end to the matter.[85]

While proprietors gained definite advantages from letting their estates in large grazing farms in preference to small holdings, the availability of evicted land allowed individuals with capital to invest in dry cattle and sheep. Extensive tracts of territory passed from the hands of the

84. *Richmond comm. evidence*, i, 1025; *Congestion comm. evidence, app. 9th report,* p. 135; Barker, *Last fifty years,* p. 44; Becker, *Disturbed Ireland,* pp. 37–8; Coulter, *West of Ireland,* p. 244; Shand, *West of Ireland,* pp. 111–14.
85. Becker, *Disturbed Ireland,* pp. 38–9.

peasant class into the possession of a growing elite of graziers as a consequence of open competition for this primary resource.

The connection between ranching and eviction was at the heart of
much antigrazier feeling among the peasant communities of north and
east Leinster, Connacht, and north Munster. Though there was little
popular resistance at the time of the clearances, with the exception of
the Donegal sheep war, the bitter memory of mass eviction over the next
half-century fed a lingering sense of rancor against the graziers.[86] The
attitudes of many tenants at the turn of the century were still shaped
by the knowledge that much of the land now held by the ranchers had
once been in the hands of the peasantry.[87] Those peasants too young actually to have seen clearances learned of the brutal experience from their
older relatives. Indeed, one witness before the Royal Commission on
Congestion spoke of the way men over sixty years of age on the Wood-
lawn estate of Lord Ashtown could recall in 1908 the clearance of the
famine years.[88] Such enduring recollections of oppression provided the
United Irish League with an issue to exploit in its campaign against the
graziers. At many public meetings in Connacht, Meath, and Westmeath
the League's spokesmen evoked the ghastly memories of the famine and
its aftermath to inflame small tenants against the ranchers.[89]

The Eleven-Month System

Though the supply of evicted land declined sharply after 1855, landlords extended their control over the market for grazing ground in the
late nineteenth century through the letting of their untenanted pastures.
After 1870 proprietors let their grassland under a short-term arrangement known as the eleven-month system. By 1900 this system constituted the major source of marketable pasture available to the grazier.
Under it, as the highest bidder, he secured the use of the land for only
eleven months, after which it was again put up for auction. At no point
could the holder of such land claim formal tenancy or legal interest.
The landlord always retained possession in law as ratable occupier, and
the user was deemed merely a temporary occupant.[90]

86. Ibid., pp. 20, 36, 73.
87. *Congestion comm. evidence, app. 6th report*, pp. 2, 122, 124, 128; *app. 9th report*,
pp. 135, 147, 153; *app. 10th report*, pp. 6, 29, 198, 202, 208.
88. *Congestion comm. evidence, app. 10th report*, p. 202.
89. *Roscommon Journal*, 18 Mar. 1901; *Roscommon Messenger*, 20 Apr. 1901; *Meath
Herald*, 9 Apr., 7 Sept., 7 Dec. 1907.
90. McCarthy, *Land and liberty*, p. 52; *Congestion comm. evidence, app. 7th report*,
pp. 177, 247; *app. 10th report*, p. 201.

The development of the eleven-month system stemmed from an expansion in the letting of untenanted land, which amounted by 1906 to some 2.6 million acres; valued at over 2s. 6d. per acre were about 1.4 million acres, or 10 percent of all agricultural land. There was considerable variation in the amount and proportion of untenanted land from one county to another. Small acreages and proportions of untenanted land were found in Ulster, Munster, and south Leinster. The highest proportions of untenanted ground occurred in Connacht and north Leinster, especially in Meath (over 21 percent of the total).[91]

During the second half of the nineteenth century proprietors significantly augmented the amount of land in their own possession. This expansion commenced during the clearances of the late 1840s and early 1850s. Not all the land denuded of smallholders was immediately relet. A large portion remained in the hands of the proprietor as untenanted pasture, to be exploited directly by him for profit. Estate owners continued to appropriate considerable tracts even after the famine clearances. This fact emerges clearly from a comparison of the returns of untenanted land in 1906 with Griffith's primary-valuation lists compiled between 1853 and 1865. An analysis was made of four poor-law unions, or rural districts: Kells, Co. Meath; Athlone, Co. Roscommon; Tulla, Co. Clare; and Belmullet, Co. Mayo (see tables 10.5 and 10.6). Each holding returned as untenanted in 1906 was compared with the primary-valuation returns of 1853–65 to ascertain if it was untenanted in this earlier period as well.[92] The results are instructive. In Tulla 33 percent of untenanted land in 1906 had been tenanted at the time of Griffith's valuation. During the interim an estimated expansion of 49 percent took place. Most of the expansion was in untenanted land rated at more than 2s. 6d. per acre. In Athlone 24 percent of untenanted land had previously been tenanted. The interim saw an expansion of 32 percent in the untenanted acreage. This increase was mostly confined to untenanted land valued at less than 2s. 6d. per acre. In Belmullet (an area of poor soil) the untenanted property in 1906 consisted mainly of ground which had been in the hands of tenants at the time of the primary valuation in 1857. The expansion in the untenanted acreage amounted to as much as 377 percent and was particularly noticeable in the case of land rated

91. *Congestion comm. evidence, app. 3rd report,* p. 665.

92. *A return of untenanted lands in rural districts, distinguishing demesnes on which there is a mansion; showing (1) rural district and electoral division; (2) townland; (3) area in statute acres; (4) valuation (poor-law); (5) names of occupiers, as in valuation lists,* pp. 164–6, 225–6, 359–60, 373–4, H.C. 1906 (250), c, 177; Primary-valuation books for the poor-law unions of Kells; Athlone (Co. Roscommon); Tulla; and Belmullet, 1856–8 (General Valuation Office, Dublin).

TABLE 10.5
Acreages of Untenanted Land in 1906 and at the Time of
Griffith's Valuation in Certain Poor-Law Unions

Poor-law union	Total acreage of untenanted land in 1906	Estimated acreage of untenanted land at time of Griffith's valuation	Percentage of untenanted land in 1906 formerly tenanted
Kells	27,932	13,355 (1856)	52
Athlone[a]	15,112	11,439 (1858)	24
Tulla	9,181	6,145 (1856)	33
Belmullet	18,904	3,962 (1857)	79

SOURCE: Primary-valuation books for the poor-law unions of Kells, Athlone, Tulla, and Belmullet, 1856–8 (General Valuation Office, Dublin); *A return of untenanted lands in rural districts, distinguishing demesnes on which there is a mansion, showing (1) rural district and electoral division; (2) townland; (3) area in statute acres; (4) valuation (poor-law); (5) names of occupiers, as in valuation lists*, pp. 164–6, 225–6, 359–60, 373–4, H.C. 1906 (250), c, 177.
[a]Refers only to that part of Athlone union located within County Roscommon.

at under 2s. 6d. per acre. There were correspondingly large increases in the number of untenanted holdings in each of the four unions between the year of Griffith's valuation and 1906.[93] This evidence clearly demonstrates that a significant drive by landlords to bring land into their direct possession occurred during the second half of the nineteenth century. All classes of untenanted property increased — demesne, home farm, out-farms, mountain pasture, and bogland. The expansion took place mainly in two periods: the years 1847–55 and the last two decades of the century.

The revised-valuation books also show that during the latter period many large farms were forfeited by tenant graziers and converted by landlords into untenanted pasture. In numerous cases ranchers were forced to relinquish their holdings because of severe losses during the price slumps of the mid-1880s and the 1890s. Lord Ardilaun was one landlord who acquired large areas of untenanted pasture as a result of bankruptcies among graziers on his estate near Cong in Mayo. As Innes Shand remarked during his tour through the county in 1884, "Lord Ardilaun has a great extent of his hill grazing in his own hands — in fact, pretty nearly the whole of the country between the bridges of Maam and Lough Mask, and in particular the entire estate of Rosshill — owing to large tenants becoming bankrupt and other causes."[94] Another proprietor who increased his untenanted land at the expense of ranchers

93. D. S. Jones, "Agrarian capitalism and rural social development in Ireland" (Ph.D. dissertation, Queen's University, Belfast, 1977), pp. 145–53.
94. Shand, *West of Ireland*, p. 140.

TABLE 10.6
Untenanted Land as a Percentage of Total Land in 1906 and at the Time of
Griffith's Valuation in Certain Poor-Law Unions

Poor-law union	1906	Time of Griffith's valuation	Percentage increase
Kells	27	13	109
Athlone[a]	21	16	32
Tulla	11	7	49
Belmullet	16	3	377

SOURCE: See table 10.5.
[a]Refers only to that part of Athlone union located within County Roscommon.

was John Nicholson of Kells, Co. Meath. A comparison of the returns of untenanted land in 1906 with the primary-valuation lists shows that Nicholson appropriated over 3,000 acres of premium grassland from substantial tenants in the electoral divisions of Boherboy, Ballinlough, and Burry.[95] Forfeitures of large farms may have been particularly frequent among leaseholding graziers. A number of witnesses before the Bessborough and Richmond commissions pointed out the insecurity of tenure among large leaseholders and the unwillingness of landlords to renew agreements unless these tenants consented to steep increases in rent. Thomas Robertson, a Scottish grazier farming in Ireland, declared to the Richmond commission: "Any lease is a lengthened notice to quit." Insisted Robertson: "A 99 years' lease is a 99 years' notice to quit. Any man who takes a lease receives a notice to quit in that lease."[96] The report of the Bessborough commission also stated that in popular estimation, the lease was "not a lengthening of the legal yearly tenancy, but a shortening of the continuous traditional tenancy."[97] Many of the leases taken before 1860 expired during the 1880s, and it appears that renewals were sometimes refused, thus allowing the farms to be converted into untenanted pasture.

The significant growth in untenanted land formed the essential basis of the eleven-month system. After 1870 proprietors increasingly reckoned their untenanted holdings as a commercial resource and decided to let them under the competitive arrangement of the eleven-month system.[98] The eleven-month letting offered distinct advantages to landlords.

95. See Primary-valuation book for Kells poor-law union; *Return of untenanted lands,* p. 177.
96. *Richmond comm. evidence,* i, 390. See also *Bessborough comm. evidence,* pt. i, pp. 364, 381, 734.
97. *Bessborough comm. report,* p. 6.
98. For the commercial value of untenanted land, see *Morley comm. evidence,* pp. 384, 560; *Fry comm. evidence,* p. 681.

It enabled them to escape the main obligations of legislated agrarian reform.[99] Since the land acts applied only to yearly or leasehold tenancies, the eleven-month letting was exempt. As a result, proprietors in such cases were not legally required to recognize the statutory three Fs, and the users of grazing ground could be dispossessed without notice to quit or expensive litigation.[100]

In addition, the rents of eleven-month land were determined competitively, without reference to the tribunals created by the 1881 land act.[101] Thus Arthur White, manager of the Powers and O'Grady estates in Limerick and himself a grazier, informed the Fry commission that the 1,800 acres of untenanted pasture for which he had responsibility as agent were on average let for £3 per Irish acre, whereas the judicial rent for such land was in his estimation 48s. or 50s. per Irish acre.[102] Similarly, Peter Fitzgerald, another Limerick land agent, let 207 acres of untenanted grassland in 1897 at 50s. per Irish acre, as compared with its estimated value of 35s. per Irish acre if it had been subject to a judicial rent.[103] Commercial rents from eleven-month holdings were especially important during a period when the income derived from tenanted farms was declining substantially.[104] Eleven-month land was of course most profitable when cattle prices were buoyant. As Lawrence Doyle told the Morley committee in 1894, the letting value of grazing land in County Meath depended "very much on the state of the market for store cattle."[105]

Thus agrarian reform and the loss of tenurial control by the landlords after 1870 greatly stimulated the development of the eleven-month system. Its value was keenly appreciated both by those who wished to exploit it and by those who wanted to abolish it. As Robert Bedford Daly, a landed proprietor and farmer in Louth, pointed out to the Cowper commission in 1887, "Owners of property now are very tenacious of letting any of the land so held out of their hands and prefer letting it by the year, and another letting is made for the next year; and it is carried on for pasturage only, in order to hold the land in their own hands, to prevent it being taken by people who would bring them into the court and look for a fair rent being fixed."[106] Haviland Burke of the United Irish League put much the same point in a different way when he declared

99. *Congestion comm. evidence, app. 7th report,* p. 247; *app. 10th report,* pp. 138, 168.
100. *Congestion comm. evidence, app. 7th report,* pp. 177, 247.
101. *Congestion comm. evidence, app. 10th report,* p. 138; Gwynn, *Connemara,* p. 110.
102. *Fry comm. evidence,* p. 635.
103. Ibid., p. 702.
104. *Congestion comm. evidence, app. 7th report,* p. 247; Gwynn, *Connemara,* p. 110.
105. *Morley comm. evidence,* p. 384.
106. *Cowper comm. evidence,* p. 728.

in 1907 that "the eleven-month man was the landlord's right-hand man. It was on the ranching system that the landlord fell back against the people of the country; it was the landlord's last line of defence. . . ."[107]

Graziers eagerly seized on the new arrangement. They dominated the auctions of eleven-month pasture, especially when the prices of dry cattle and sheep revived after 1896.[108] Large numbers of ranchers had become heavily dependent on the eleven-month letting by the beginning of the twentieth century. Though it was common for them to pasture stock on ground which they held in formal tenancy or in fee, numerous graziers possessed little or nothing but eleven-month land. By 1910 the eleven-month letting had therefore become a vital feature of the livestock enterprise. Its importance to the grazier stemmed from the economic needs of dry-cattle and sheep production. His liquid assets gave to the grazier the liberty to engage in land transactions in response to price fluctuations. What he needed was a species of tenure which allowed him to secure land at will and also to dispense with it free from complications. The eleven-month system answered this necessity extremely well. The rancher could respond to an upturn in cattle or sheep prices by acquiring pasture without the burdensome expense of purchasing the interest of either tenant or owner. Conversely, when it became expedient for the grazier to contract his acreage during a period of depression, he was absolved under the eleven-month system of any responsibility to find a purchaser for the interest in the holding. The eleven-month arrangement thus offered the grazier maximum flexibility.

Eleven-month lettings also provided members of commercial and professional groups with an easy means of access to livestock farming.[109] The convenience with which eleven-month land could be obtained and surrendered was particularly suited to the speculative enterprise of the commercial townsmen. Shopkeepers with a keen eye for quick profit figured prominently in the taking of eleven-month grazing farms. To the shopkeeper, the eleven-month system was especially attractive because it provided an enriching outlet for his surplus capital.[110]

It is impossible to state precisely what proportion of ranch land was held under the eleven-month system, but the following data relating to the Kells rural district perhaps provide the basis for a rough estimate.

107. See the speech of Haviland Burke to a U.I.L. meeting at Ashbourne, Co. Meath (*Meath Herald*, 7 Nov. 1907).

108. The domination of the eleven-month system by graziers was often mentioned in evidence given before the Royal Commission on Congestion. Indeed, the eleven-month system and ranching were considered synonymous.

109. Many witnesses before the Royal Commission on Congestion pointed to the involvement of shopkeepers in the eleven-month system.

110. *Congestion comm. evidence, app. 7th report*, pp. 161, 187, 247.

Kells was a major ranching area of County Meath noted for the predominance of large grazing farms. In 1901 some 86,000 acres in Kells (84 percent of the land area) consisted of holdings valued at more than £30. An examination of the revised-valuation lists shows that large grazing farms accounted for much of the land in this category. Indeed, holdings of over 200 acres covered 55,000 acres. At the same time almost 28,000 acres were untenanted pasture consisting mainly of large units (the average size of an untenanted farm was 173 acres). Thus it would appear that between 30 and 50 percent of commercial pasture and ranch land was untenanted.[111]

The graziers' dependence on untenanted land increased significantly after 1885 because of the decline in the number of holdings voluntarily relinquished by peasants. At first, the market in such holdings had been stimulated by the land acts of 1870 and 1881.[112] The legal recognition of tenant interest conferred by these reforms created inducements for struggling peasants to surrender their holdings, since they could secure a substantial sum of money by selling their interest in the land.[113] In this way an alternative supply of pasture was created, which, unlike evicted and untenanted property, was controlled by the tenants.[114] There is evidence that during the 1870s, when cattle and sheep prices were high, graziers took advantage of sales of tenant interest to expand their holdings.[115] Their activity helped to create intense competition and led to an increase in the general value of tenant interest. One commentator described the competition for land in the 1870s as a "mania," while another declared that the increase in the value of tenant right was out of all proportion to improvements made and the real level of tenant interest.[116] After 1885, however, the National League resolutely opposed the practice of free sale. The League objected to it particularly because it enabled landlords to recover arrears of rent from the payment which the tenant received on selling his interest and leaving the land.[117] In many areas National League branches prohibited the transfer of occupancy rights.[118] Furthermore, when the 1890s brought enhanced prospects of

111. *Census Ire., 1901*, pt. ii: *general report*, p. 235; *Census Ire., 1881*, pt. ii: *general report, with illustrative maps and diagrams, tables, and appendix*, p. 186 [C 3365], H.C. 1882, lxxvi, 385; *Return of untenanted lands*, p. 177.
112. *Bessborough comm. report*, p. 28; *Richmond comm. evidence*, i, 892, 896.
113. *Bessborough comm. report*, pp. 2–3, 28; *Richmond comm. evidence*, i, 45, 374–86, 463, 892–3, 898.
114. *Bessborough comm. report*, pp. 28, 57.
115. *Richmond comm. evidence*, i, 888, 892, 896.
116. Ibid., i, 896.
117. *Cowper comm. evidence*, pp. 46, 48, 747, 916–17; app. D, p. 971.
118. A large number of witnesses testified before the Cowper commission to the Na-

peasant proprietorship, tenants on their own account became more reluctant to part with their holdings.[119] Antipathy toward sales naturally
increased after so many tenants became owner-occupiers in the wake
of the 1903 land act.[120] As a result, the market in land voluntarily relinquished by peasants increasingly contracted, thus impelling graziers to
look to the landlords for their supply of pasture.

The effect of these developments was to revive and strengthen the
ties between landlords and graziers. As the ranchers became more reliant on the expanses of untenanted grassland, they became increasingly
a party to landlord conservatism and the traditional order of Irish rural
society. Despite their earlier support for the initial land legislation, especially the principle of free sale, graziers were generally hostile to further
and more radical agrarian reform. In particular, they became averse
to a redistribution of untenanted pastures.[121]

At the same time, however, the eleven-month system aroused widespread antagonism to the ranchers. The highly competitive character
of the eleven-month system meant that the peasant, whether commercial or subsistence farmer, had little chance of acquiring such land when
pitted against the grazier. Many ranchers were thereby able to accumulate large reserves of pasture at the expense of the peasantry.[122] A great
number of those who were denied untenanted land were indigent smallholders in the west, living in areas delimited by the Congested Districts
Board.[123] The persistence of rural congestion and poverty in these regions was invariably attributed to the monopolization of land by graziers.
The Royal Commission on Congestion of 1906–8 heard repeated testimony that ranching and especially the eleven-month system were at the
heart of the problem of overcrowding in Connacht and north Munster.[124]
Of course, not all claimants to untenanted land were indigent small-

---

tional League's prohibition on the sale of tenant interest. See, e.g., *Cowper comm. evidence*, pp. 45–8, 116, 449, 564, 673, 916–17; app. D, p. 1002.

119. Ibid., p. 48.

120. Crotty, *Agricultural production*, pp. 88–9, 92–4.

121. Among those testifying before the Royal Commission on Congestion, some witnesses, including large graziers, opposed redistribution of the ranches, especially by compulsory means.

122. It was repeatedly asserted before the Royal Commission on Congestion that the
eleven-month system provided the opportunity for ranchers and shopkeeper-graziers to
accumulate large amounts of land.

123. *Congestion comm., final report*, pp. 4, 39–40.

124. The Rev. James Kelly told the Royal Commission on Congestion that "all over
Connaught the eleven-months' system is a perennial source of social and political inflam-
mation on that problem of congestion" (*Congestion comm. evidence, app. 10th report*,
p. 21). See also Gwynn, *Connemara*, p. 109.

holders. The division and resettlement of untenanted holdings were also demanded by or on behalf of the disinherited sons of commercial middling tenants who could not hope to succeed to the family farm.[125]

The unpopularity of the eleven-month letting was reinforced by its association with eviction. According to popular conviction, well substantiated by historical evidence, many untenanted holdings had once been the homes of evicted tenants. Moreover, in certain localities the eleven-month letting had led to the abrogation of traditional, noncompetitive rights of common grazing (sometimes called agistment) previously enjoyed by small tenants on the untenanted pastures.[126] The violation of these customary entitlements to grassland, together with the evictions already mentioned, strengthened claims for the division and redistribution of the untenanted farms and hardened antipathy to the ranchers.

The eleven-month system also created a perception of graziers as the allies of landlordism. They were considered not only as beneficiaries but also as upholders of landlord hegemony during a period of crisis and change. In particular, the eleven-month system served to perpetuate the old rental regime in spite of agrarian reform and furnished an alternative source of revenue when rents from tenanted holdings were declining. Indeed, the close identification of ranchers with the traditional order prompted Hubert Flynn of the Associated Estates Committee to describe them as "the degenerate offspring of an effete landlordism."[127] Such an identification insured that the struggle against the landlords would eventually be directed against the graziers.

Graziers as Social Climbers

Objections to the ranching system also arose from its disruptive effect on the traditional status order of rural Ireland. The opportunities for investment in land created by the property-owning elite provided a means of status enhancement within agrarian society. The rancher who accumulated pasture and expanded his business was thereby able to solidify his social position within the rural community. For those of lower status, such as middling tenants and commercial townsmen, the acquisition of grazing land, even under the eleven-month system, represented a significant upgrading of social rank within their own localities. Insofar as landlords facilitated free sale and expanded the supply of pasture through

125. For the advocacy of the claims of farmers' sons to untenanted pasture at meetings of U.I.L. branches, see, e.g., *Roscommon Journal*, 9 Mar. 1907; *Munster News*, 1 Feb. 1908.

126. See, e.g., *Congestion comm. evidence*, app. 6th report, p. 154; app. 7th report, pp. 216, 219–20.

127. *Roscommon Journal*, 20 Apr. 1912.

eviction and the letting of untenanted holdings, they stimulated upward social mobility among graziers, land-acquisitive townsmen, and middling tenants. The shopkeeper-grazier often improved his position by "building himself up" at the expense of "the struggling farmers around"; he was able to "make little conquests and aggrandisements and take up patch after patch."[128] Some ranchers were "sons of poor farmers, who have gradually bid in from the landlords farm after farm of their neighbors."[129] Of course, a number of those who undertook commercial grazing already occupied high social positions, such as solicitors, clergymen, and land agents. For such persons speculative ventures in the cattle business further buttressed their social rank.

The status value of ranching derived from the prestige of being a large capitalist and income earner, coupled with the social recognition normally accorded to a substantial landholder. It was this second factor which was especially significant in conferring status in spite of the ascriptive values of traditional rural culture. The possession of a large area of land for commercial grazing, even under the eleven-month system, was in itself sufficiently esteemed to offset the customary emphasis on the status denoted by family name and inheritance. Consequently, with the hegemony of the landlords gone, the grazier "took their place financially, and where his wife and family were in the ascendant, socially also."[130]

The superior social position attained by ranchers of varying origins was indicated by their tendency to adopt many of the norms and habits associated with the gentry.[131] Enjoying the wealth and stature won by his commercial endeavors, the grazier regularly looked to the landlord as a model of social worth. Imitation of the gentry life-style was a central feature of the societal and familial roles performed by the upwardly mobile rancher. Contemporary observers often drew attention to the elitist habits of the graziers. William Bulfin, for example, an American traveler who bicycled through Connacht and Leinster in 1907, heaped ridicule on the rancher stratum for its pretensions to gentility:

This bullockdom was known to the world by Irish names, but it never was more Irish than the cottondom of Manchester or the cutlerdom of Sheffield, and never, never for an hour less un-Irish, purse-proud, and arrogant than they. . . . It would have trampled Irish nationality into the mud ten times within an hour

128. *Congestion comm. evidence, app. 6th report,* p. 61. See also *app. 7th report,* p. 247.
129. Pellew, *Castle and cabin,* p. 56.
130. Lynn Doyle [pseud. for L. A. Montgomery], *The spirit of Ireland* (London, 1935), p. 37.
131. Ibid.; Padraic Colum, *The road round Ireland* (New York, 1926), pp. 241–3; McCarthy, *Land and liberty,* p. 225.

for the sake of a nod of recognition from the hard-up aristocrats of the county club. . . . It called many of its daughters Louise and Charlotte, and Caroline and Alexandria, and Flossie and Gertrude, and sent them to English convents to be "finished" . . . in snobbery and the English accent. It sent its Clarences and Algernons . . . to prepare for the "awmy" or the "baw" and then sent them after the hounds — so that they might all the more surely and rapidly ride to the dogs. It lived above its means did this bullockdom of Ireland, and it made beggared snobs of its Algernons and powerless goddesses of its Charlottes. . . .[132]

Even a generation earlier the elitism of the western grazier had strongly impressed the visiting newspaper correspondent Bernard Becker: "His larder is well supplied with poultry and wildfowl, his cellar contains . . . port and sherry, claret and champagne. His daughters are at the costly training schools of the Sacré Coeur, his lads are studying law in Dublin."[133]

As these descriptions testify, one of the most important means by which the rancher modeled himself on the gentry and enhanced his status was through the education and occupations of his children. It was considered highly desirable for them to attend private boarding schools and, in the case of sons, to enter such distinguished professions as medicine, the law, or the armed services.[134] For the grazier household, private education and professional careers engendered an elitist consciousness and created a prestigious image designed to insure greater acceptability in gentry circles and among the "county set." The desire of ranchers to ape the gentry and professional classes was also reflected in recreational activities. Graziers often identified themselves with such leisure pursuits as horse racing, fox hunting, and game shooting — all characteristic pastimes of the gentry.[135]

The deep impress of high-status culture on the rancher was further shown by the roles of his wife and daughters within the household. The place of females within the household was a significant indicator of the social standing of the family. Among small farmers, wives and grown-up daughters devoted most of their time to physical work, especially domestic chores and such farm labor as butter making and poultry husbandry. But such a role, signifying low status, was eschewed by women in the grazier household. Like the females of the gentry family, their main pursuits were leisure, travel, education, and fashion.[136]

The identification of ranchers with other high-status groups led them

132. Bulfin, Rambles, pp. 90–1.
133. Becker, Disturbed Ireland, p. 192.
134. Colum, Road round Ireland, p. 241; McCarthy, Land and liberty, p. 66.
135. Terence McGrath, Pictures from Ireland (London, 1880), pp. 43–53; McCarthy, Land and liberty, p. 225.
136. McCarthy, Land and liberty, p. 66.

to minimize their links with the peasantry. Interaction between graziers and small farmers was largely restricted to the market or fair, though in the case of the shopkeeper-grazier, contacts with peasants were of course maintained through the shop.[137] Ranchers generally shunned close involvement in the life and routines of the local rural community. Aloofness was especially manifest in their avoidance of forms of nonmonetary cooperation and exchange with neighboring farmers. The grazier's consciousness of superior status in relation to the peasant community was also reflected in the norms governing marital selection. It was almost inconceivable that the children of ranchers would marry into small-farm families.[138] Such constraints on marriage were imposed in the interest of preserving status. Intermarriage between grazier families and those of lower rank could only have resulted in downward social mobility for the rancher. Consequently, grazier families looked to the professions, the minor gentry, or other graziers when arranging marriages for their children. One informed observer asserted in 1911 that the highest ambition of a rancher's daughter was to marry a doctor or a solicitor from a town.[139]

Yet in spite of being upwardly mobile and claiming superior status, graziers often found it difficult to emulate the gentry and professional groups. The landowning and professional elites were reluctant to recognize the status claimed by the ranchers or to accept them fully into their social circles. Even though landlords provided opportunities for upward mobility, they also set limits to the extent of that mobility. These restrictions may be attributed to two factors. First, the ascriptive values of the gentry naturally precluded full admission of the grazier into the circles of the landed elite. Second, within the landlord-grazier economic relationship the rancher inevitably occupied the subordinate place because of his dependence on the landlord for access to pasture. His inferior position, especially under the eleven-month system, may have further lessened his status in the eyes of landowners. Though properly equated with opportunity, dependency was nevertheless a restraint on social mobility. But even if they were not fully accepted in the elite circles of the county set, graziers earned the respect and admiration of some landlords. As one witness told the Royal Commission on Congestion, "by some noble and interested lords the graziers are called the backbone of the country."[140]

137. C. M. Arensberg and S. T. Kimball, *Family and community in Ireland* (2nd ed., Cambridge, Mass., 1968), p. 180.

138. Patrick Noonan, "Why few Irish marry" in J. A. O'Brien (ed.), *The vanishing Irish: the enigma of the modern world* (London, 1954), p. 51.

139. McCarthy, *Land and liberty*, p. 225.

140. *Congestion comm. evidence, app. 10th report*, p. 21.

Thus the rancher's social position was essentially ambiguous and uncertain. His natural response was to achieve a clearer definition of his status. This was perhaps reflected in the adoption of status-earning and status-preserving forms of behavior so as to insure increased acceptance in gentry and professional circles. The uncertainties of their position may have caused among graziers an exaggerated imitation of the gentry lifestyle, an even greater yearning to ingratiate themselves with elite circles "for the sake of a nod of recognition" from the county club.[141] On the other hand, ranchers were equally anxious to avoid forms of behavior which would have suggested a lowering of social rank. Fearful of depreciation in his social standing, the grazier perhaps all the more avoided contact and collaboration with his peasant neighbors.

In addition, there was a certain reluctance among the peasantry itself to acknowledge the social claims of the ambitious rancher. Ascriptive values were as deeply ingrained within the peasant classes as among the gentry. Thus rapid upward mobility was a form of deviance which threatened the established norms and social hierarchy of the rural community. Social controls within a locality operated as strong negative sanctions on the achievement of superior status. For anyone trying to upgrade his social position, but especially for persons seeking to rise above the humble origins of small-peasant or small-shopkeeper background, there was nothing but open disapproval and pronounced contempt. This was particularly true of graziers from modest origins who imitated the life-style of gentry and professional groups, and who in so doing severed their links with the peasant community. For this reason ranchers were commonly reckoned as upstarts and were described in many districts by the term "shoneen," that is, jumped-up small men who had no right to claim a social standing superior to that of the rest of the rural population.[142] William Bulfin gave full vent in 1907 to the popular disapproval attaching to these inveterate social climbers: "The grazierocracy of Ireland was shoneen to the core. There were graziers and there are graziers who were not and who are not shoneens, but they were and are the exceptions. . . . There never was such a nursery of Irish snobbery, and there never will be. . . . It produced the cawstle Cawtholic, the shoneen priest, the shoneen magistrate, the shoneen prelate, the shoneen soldier of England, the shoneen fox hunter."[143] The divergence between his high-blown claims and the limited respect accorded to him by others was yet another reason for the failure of the rancher to legitimize his role within the peasant community.

141. Bulfin, *Rambles*, p. 90.
142. Ibid., p. 178.
143. Ibid., pp. 89–90.

The Price of Aloofness

Though the detachment of the graziers from peasant society was caused in part by considerations of status, it was reinforced by the system of farming and the forms of tenure which they adopted. Detachment was reflected in a general avoidance of contact with the peasant population and particularly in a refusal to participate in the network of mutual aid and cooperation which underpinned peasant farming and community life.[144] The most important manifestation of mutual aid was the tradition of cooring, whereby adjoining farmers regularly exchanged resources and services on a nonmonetary basis.[145] The main form of cooperation was the *meitheal*. This custom involved a group of neighboring men and boys who gave help, on a collective basis and without financial reward, to the farming population of the locality during periods of unusual need, such as sowing, harvesting, or personal crisis.[146]

The failure of ranchers to enter into mutual-aid schemes and cooperative arrangements stemmed partly from the prosaic fact that they had scant need for the services of the community. The small labor requirements of ranch farming meant that the grazier could do without the assistance of local peasants. What little labor he required could simply be hired without having recourse to cooring or the *meitheal*. Moreover, the services provided by the local community in the form of mutual aid and cooperation were essentially nonmonetary and noncompetitive. The rancher, however, was conditioned to apply commercial criteria and to expect a precise and competitively determined reward for activities which entailed expending or transferring personal resources. His commercial mentality and market orientation tended to fix in him an aversion to nonmarket forms of exchange and reward.

The grazier's aloofness from the peasant community must be ascribed to other causes as well, especially his tendency to live away from his land most of the time. As noted earlier, the holding of property on a nonresidential basis was a characteristic feature of ranch farming, attributable to the retail and other business interests of the grazier as well as to the high land and low labor requirements of the enterprise, which allowed "management from a distance."[147] The result was that the

144. Arensberg and Kimball, *Family and community*, pp. 3, 280; C. M. Arensberg, *The Irish countryman* (New York, 1939), pp. 42, 65.

145. Arensberg and Kimball, *Family and community*, pp. 69–75; Damian Hannan, "Kinship, neighbourhood, and social change in Irish rural communities" in *Economic and Social Review*, iii, no. 2 (July 1972), pp. 167–70.

146. Arensberg and Kimball, *Family and community*, pp. 255–6; Hannan, "Kinship," pp. 169–73.

147. T. J. Hughes, "Society and settlement in nineteenth-century Ireland" in *Ir. Geography*, v, no. 2 (1965), p. 91.

nonresidential rancher was rarely in sufficiently continuous contact with a particular locality to become part of its network of mutual obligations or of its other form of social activity.[148] Besides being frequently nonresident, graziers were in many cases only temporary occupants of land. "Migratory in their habits," the ranchers, said one observer, "took great tracts of land here and there."[149] The dependence of the grazier on circulating and liquid capital rather than fixed assets, combined with his speculative outlook within a fluctuating market situation, engendered short-term and ever-changing commitments to his holdings. His unemotional approach was strengthened by a lack of familial or ancestral attachments to the land within his ranching business. Sometimes the pattern of landholding also militated against the integration of ranchers within community life. In many western districts a portion of the land and in a few cases the whole townland was held under joint tenancy even as late as 1900. This fact is evident from the primary- and revised-valuation books. And it also emerges from the valuation books that few graziers in the west held joint tenancies or shared grazing rights with neighboring farmers.[150]

The detachment of ranchers from peasant society contributed to their general failure to become figures of influence or to attain positions of leadership within their localities. This is apparent from their lack of involvement in formal community organizations. In earlier struggles to secure agrarian reform during the 1870s and 1880s, graziers were often members of farmers' clubs, local branches of the Land and National Leagues, and boards of guardians. But after 1900 few graziers appear to have taken prominent parts in the work of boards of guardians, county councils, parish committees, or local political parties and associations.[151] The virtual disappearance of ranchers from community organizations was undoubtedly related to their increasing unpopularity, especially after 1900. As antagonism to the graziers deepened, they became more divorced from the life of the local community, not only through their own volition, but also because they were excluded and ostracized, as the many attempts to boycott them demonstrate.

Two examples are worth citing to illustrate the aloofness of the rancher from peasant society. The first concerns Captain Houstoun, a large hill grazier residing at Westport, Co. Mayo. According to the narrative of his life, as given by his wife Matilda, there was almost complete separa-

148. *Morley comm. evidence*, pp. 386, 524.
149. Ibid., p. 524.
150. See, e.g., Primary- and revised-valuation books for Athlone poor-law union, Co. Roscommon.
151. Jones, "Agrarian capitalism," p. 33.

tion from the local population in the years that he lived there between 1858 and 1879. He remained "isolated and apart from any society and surrounded solely by the peasantry," with whom his personal dealings and day-to-day contact, apart from business, were minimal.[152] Brinsley MacNamara's novel, *Valley of the squinting windows* (1918), set in County Meath, provides the second example. One of its characters is a grazier called Myles Shannon. Described as "the magnate of the valley," he is portrayed as a recluse, socially isolated and eschewing participation in the life of the local village of Garradrimna: "He was serenely independent, exhibiting a fine contempt, as well he might, for the mean strugglers around him. He took his pleasures here by himself in this quiet house among the trees. . . . But who was there to see him or know, since he did not choose to publish himself in Garradrimna."[153]

Their social isolation meant that ranchers could not advance the well-being of peasant society in its traditionally recognized form. By not participating in the customary arrangements of exchange and cooperation, the graziers failed to satisfy certain vital needs in the economic life of the small-farm community.[154] They rendered no personal help, as patronal figures, to small farmers in times of special want and crisis. Nor did ranchers make worthwhile contributions to the social and cultural activities of the neighborhood. Of particular importance was their unwillingness or inability to assume positions of leadership in which they could be seen to be protecting and promoting the interests of the community.

The failure of the grazier to bolster the welfare of the local peasantry was all the more critical in view of his land-acquisitive tendencies, especially his extensive exploitation of local reserves of pasture and meadow. Though this land was privately owned and individually rented, it was nevertheless considered a natural asset of the community itself, to be used for the common good of the local population. The onus was therefore on the rancher to reciprocate the benefits derived from its exploitation and to strike a reasonable balance between rewards and obligations.[155] The more the grazier profited from the natural resources of a

152. Matilda Houstoun, *Twenty years in the wild west, or life in Connaught* (London, 1879), passim. The quotation is taken from the preface, p. v.

153. Brinsley MacNamara, *The valley of the squinting windows* (Dublin, paperback ed., 1964; originally published 1918), p. 95. See also ibid., pp. 21, 43, 117–21.

154. *Congestion comm. evidence, app. 10th report*, p. 198.

155. Barrington Moore, Jr., argues that the peasant's sense of justice and of exploitation depends on "the notion of rewards and privileges commensurate with the services rendered by the upper class." For his discussion of exploitation, see *Social origins of dictatorship and democracy: lord and peasant in the making of the modern world* (London, paperback ed., 1969; originally published 1966), pp. 470–3.

given district, the greater was the expectation that he would enhance its economic and social life.[156] But the services rendered by ranchers to the peasant community were in no way commensurate with the benefits they reaped from utilizing local resources of pasture. As Father John Fallon declared to the national convention of the United Irish League in December 1907, "The vast area of untenanted land in the west and in many other parts of Ireland constitutes a most deadly danger to the general welfare of the country . . . in taking away the natural and economic sources of the agricultural population and sacrificing people for cattle."[157]

In one crucial respect, of course, graziers did contribute to the livelihood of the peasant community. They purchased the young cattle and sheep of small and middling farmers and thus provided them with an all-important cash income. During the period of active opposition, however, there was a general reluctance to admit the value of this service. The enemies of the ranchers were quick to point out that no sacrifice accompanied the contribution. They also contended that the commercial function of the grazier was dispensable if small farmers were given the land to fatten livestock.

Social isolation, however, must have been significantly less among shopkeeper-graziers. Provincial shopkeepers often forged close links with the surrounding peasant community through trade, credit and barter arrangements, and the provision of employment. Assuming a mantle of leadership within their localities, they were "able to impose their wishes and interests upon the community in a fashion as astonishing as it is unwholesome."[158] In particular, shopkeepers often dominated local politics. As a result of his preeminence, the shopkeeper, declared one observer, "overruns the boards of guardians, the rural councils, the district and county councils," and "acts as secretary to the local branch of the [United Irish] League."[159] Shopkeepers who became graziers no doubt found it almost impossible to sever their links with the local peasant population. For instance, James Colvey, a shopkeeper-grazier quoted by

156. *Congestion comm. evidence, app. 7th report*, p. 187; T. O. Russell, *Is Ireland a dying nation?* (Dublin, 1906), pp. 37–42; A. B. F. Young, *Ireland at the crossroads: an essay in explanation* (2nd ed., London, 1907), pp. 43–4.

157. Newspaper cuttings relating to the national conventions of the United Irish League in Dublin (N.L.I., MS 7438).

158. Sydney Brooks, *Aspects of the Irish question* (Dublin and London, 1912), p. 121.

159. Ibid., pp. 120–1. See also *Congestion comm. evidence, app. 10th report*, p. 7; George Birmingham, *An Irishman looks at his world* (London, 1919), pp. 206–7; Colum, *Road round Ireland*, pp. 32–3.

Padraic Colum in his travelogue, was able to retain his shop clientele and continued to play a prominent part in public life and local organizations.[160] Nevertheless, in many districts shopkeeper-graziers risked ostracism as a result of the deep antipathy toward them, and they came under considerable pressure to surrender their agricultural holdings especially during the ranch war.[161]

Conclusion

In summary, there were three major causes of the conflict between ranchers and peasants. The most important was simply the land-acquisitiveness of the graziers and the resulting competition between them and peasant farmers. Because of this collision ranchers were perceived as denying peasants access to land and in some areas as creating or perpetuating the problem of rural congestion and indigence. The second reason for the cleavage between graziers and peasants was the disruption of the status order in the countryside as a result of the growth of ranch farming. Ranching provided an avenue of upward social mobility, one feature of which was the desire of the enterprising grazier to enhance his status within the rural community. His social ambitions were particularly reflected in his tendency to appropriate the life-style of the gentry. But the peasant community was resistant to rapid social advance and contemptuous of ranchers for aspiring so blatantly to elite status.

A third cause of the antagonism to graziers was their failure to bolster the welfare of the peasant community. Their capitalistic values, system of landholding, superior resources, and social status — all helped sharply to differentiate the ranchers from peasant society. Figures of detachment who avoided contact with their peasant neighbors, they contributed little in the way of leadership, patronage, employment, or credit to the life of the community in return for the benefits which they derived from its pastoral resources. Their failure in this respect largely explains their inability to secure even a modest degree of popular acceptance for their self-enriching endeavors.

160. Colum, *Road round Ireland*, p. 33.
161. Iwan-Müller, *Ireland*, p. 85; *Westmeath Examiner*, 9 Mar. 1907; *Meath Herald*, 7 Dec. 1907; *Irish Times*, 28 Sept. 1908.

BIBLIOGRAPHY

Contemporary sources

Manuscript material
National Library of Ireland, Dublin
Minute book of the national directory of the United Irish League, 10 Aug.
1904–30 Apr. 1918 (MS 708).
Newspaper cuttings relative to the national conventions of the United Irish
League in Dublin (MS 7438).
General Valuation Office, Dublin
Valuation records:
Primary-valuation books: poor-law unions of Kells; Athlone (Co. Roscommon); Tulla; Belmullet, 1856–8.
Revised-valuation book: poor-law union of Athlone (Co. Roscommon).

Contemporary publications
I. Parliamentary papers (in chronological order)
Reports from poor-law inspectors in Ireland as to the existing relations between landlord and tenant in respect of improvements on farms, drainage, reclamation of land, fencing, planting, &c. . . . [C 31], H.C. 1870, xiv, 37.
Minutes of evidence taken before her majesty's commissioners on agriculture, vol. i [C 2778-I], H.C. 1881, xv, 1.
Report of her majesty's commissioners of inquiry into the working of the Landlord and Tenant (Ireland) Act, 1870, and the acts amending the same [C 2779], H.C. 1881, xviii, 1; *Digest of evidence; minutes of evidence,* pt. i [C 2779-I], H.C. 1881, xviii, 73.
Return by provinces and counties (compiled from returns made to the inspector general, Royal Irish Constabulary), of cases of evictions which have come to the knowledge of the constabulary in each of the years from 1849 to 1880 inclusive, H.C. 1881 (185), lxxvii, 725.
First report from the select committee of the House of Lords on land law (Ireland), together with the proceedings of the committee, minutes of evidence, and appendix, H.C. 1882 (249), xi, 1.
Census of Ireland, 1881, pt. ii: *general report, with illustrative maps and diagrams, tables, and appendix* [C 3365], H.C. 1882, lxxvi, 385.
Report of the royal commission on the Land Law (Ireland) Act, 1881, and the Purchase of Land (Ireland) Act, 1885 [C 4969], H.C. 1887, xxvi, 1; *Minutes of evidence and appendices* [C 4969-I], H.C. 1887, xxvi, 25.
Report from the select committee on land acts (Ireland), together with the proceedings of the committee, minutes of evidence, appendix, and index, H.C. 1894 (310), xiii, 1.
Royal commission of inquiry into the procedure and practice and the methods of valuation followed by the land commission, the land judges' court, and the civil-bill courts in Ireland under the land acts and the land-purchase acts, vol. i: *report* [C 8734], H.C. 1898, xxxv, 1; vol. ii: *minutes of evidence* [C 8859], H.C. 1898, xxxv, 41.

Agricultural statistics of Ireland, with detailed report on agriculture for the year 1898 [C 9389], H.C. 1899, cvi, 325.

Census of Ireland, 1901, pt. ii: general report, with illustrative maps and diagrams, tables, and appendix [C 1190], H.C. 1902, cxxix, 1.

A return of untenanted lands in rural districts, distinguishing demesnes on which there is a mansion; showing (1) rural district and electoral division; (2) townland; (3) area in statute acres; (4) valuation (poor-law); (5) names of occupiers, as in valuation lists, H.C. 1906 (250), c, 177.

Royal commission on congestion in Ireland: appendix to the third report, minutes of evidence . . . , *and documents relating thereto* [C 3414], H.C. 1907, xxxv, 337; *appendix to the sixth report* . . . [C 3748], H.C. 1908, xxxix, 701; *appendix to the seventh report* . . . [C 3785], H.C. 1908, xl, 5; *appendix to the ninth report* . . . [C 3845], H.C. 1908, xli, 487; *appendix to the tenth report* . . . [C 4007], H.C. 1908, xlii, 5; *final report* [C 4097], H.C. 1908, xlii, 729.

A return by counties and quarterly periods, of the number of cattle drives reported by the Royal Irish Constabulary to have taken place in Ireland from the first day of January 1907 to the 30th day of September 1908, H.C. 1908 (310), xc, 3.

A return showing the number of cases and of persons boycotted in each county in Ireland on the 30th day of November 1905 and the 31st day of January 1909 . . . , H.C. 1909 (57), lxxiii, 3.

A copy of classified return of agrarian outrages of an indictable character reported throughout Ireland in each of the years of 1906, 1907, and 1908, H.C. 1909 (70), lxxiii, 1.

A return of the number of cases of persons boycotted throughout Ireland on the undermentioned dates [30 June 1893–28 Feb. 1909] . . . , H.C. 1909 (116), lxxiii, 7.

II. Newspapers

Enniscorthy Guardian.
Freeman's Journal (Dublin).
Galway Observer.
Irish Times (Dublin).
Leinster Leader (Naas).
Meath Herald (Kells).
Munster News (Limerick).
Roscommon Journal.
Roscommon Messenger.
United Ireland (Dublin).
Westmeath Examiner (Mullingar).

III. Other contemporary publications

Agricultural statistics, 1847–1926: report and tables, compiled by Department of Industry and Commerce, Saorstat Eireann (Dublin, 1928).

Barker, Sir Ernest. *Ireland in the last fifty years, 1866–1916* (Oxford, 1917).

Barrington, Thomas. "A review of Irish agricultural prices" in *Journal of the Statistical and Social Inquiry Society of Ireland,* pt. ci, xv (1927), pp. 249–80.

Becker, B. H. *Disturbed Ireland, being the letters written during the winter of 1880–81* (London, 1881).

Birmingham, George. *An Irishman looks at his world* (London, 1919).

Bonn, M. J. *Modern Ireland and her agrarian problem*, trans. T. W. Rolleston (Dublin, 1906).

Brooks, Sydney. *Aspects of the Irish question* (Dublin and London, 1912).

Bulfin, William. *Rambles in Eirinn* (Dublin, 1927; originally published 1907).

Colum, Padraic. *The road round Ireland* (New York, 1926).

Coulter, Henry. *The west of Ireland: its existing condition and prospects* (Dublin, 1862).

Dolan, C. J. "The congested districts" in *Irish Year Book, 1909* (Dublin, 1909), pp. 133–40.

Dufferin, earl of. *Irish emigration and the tenure of land in Ireland* (London, 1867).

Ewart, Wilfrid. *A journey in Ireland, 1921* (London and New York, 1922).

Gwynn, Stephen. *A holiday in Connemara* (London, 1909).

Houstoun, Matilda. *Twenty years in the wild west, or life in Connaught* (London, 1879).

"Ireland in 1887," pt. 2: "proceedings of National League branches" in Irish Loyal and Patriotic Union, *Publications issued during 1887* (Dublin, 1887), pp. 219–91.

Iwan-Müller, E. B. *Ireland today and tomorrow* (London, 1907).

Leech, H. B. *1848 and 1912: the continuity of the Irish revolutionary movement* (2nd ed., London, [1912]).

McCarthy, Michael. *Irish land and liberty: a study of the new lords of the soil* (London, 1911).

MacNamara, Brinsley. *The valley of the squinting windows* (Dublin, paperback ed., 1964; originally published 1918).

Paul-Dubois, Louis. *Contemporary Ireland* (Dublin, 1908).

Pellew, George. *In castle and cabin, or talks in Ireland in 1887* (New York and London, 1888).

Russell, T. O. *Is Ireland a dying nation?* (Dublin, 1906).

Shand, A. I. *Letters from the west of Ireland, 1884* (Edinburgh, 1885).

Sutherland, Hugh. *Ireland yesterday and today* (Philadelphia, 1909).

Thom's Irish almanac and official directory of the United Kingdom of Great Britain and Ireland: 1853; 1860; 1866; 1871; 1875; 1876; 1878; 1905; 1910; 1915; 1917.

"Three months of the National League: proceedings of National League branches: June, July, August 1887" in Irish Loyal and Patriotic Union, *Publications issued during 1887* (Dublin, 1887), pp. 385–448.

Wilson, James. "Tillage versus grazing" in *Journal of the Department of Agriculture and Technical Instruction for Ireland*, v, no. 2 (1905), pp. 217–35.

Young, A. B. F. *Ireland at the crossroads: an essay in explanation* (2nd ed., London, 1907).

Later works

Writings in Irish studies

Arensberg, C. M. *The Irish countryman* (New York, 1939).

Arensberg, C. M., and Kimball, S. T. *Family and community in Ireland* (2nd ed., Cambridge, Mass., 1968).

Crotty, R. D. *Irish agricultural production: its volume and structure* (Cork, 1966).

Doyle, Lynn [pseud. for L. A. Montgomery]. *The spirit of Ireland* (London, 1935).

Freeman, T. W. *Ireland: its physical, historical, social, and economic geography* (London and New York, 1950).

Hannan, Damian. "Kinship, neighbourhood, and social change in Irish rural communities" in *Economic and Social Review*, iii, no. 2 (Jan. 1972), pp. 163–88.

Hughes, T. J. "Society and settlement in nineteenth-century Ireland" in *Irish Geography*, v, no. 2 (1965), pp. 79–96.

Jones, D. S. "Agrarian capitalism and rural social development in Ireland" (Ph.D. dissertation, Queen's University, Belfast, 1977).

Noonan, Patrick. "Why few Irish marry" in J. A. O'Brien (ed.), *The vanishing Irish: the enigma of the modern world* (London, 1954), pp. 46–53.

O'Connor, R. "The small farm" in James Meenan and D. A. Webb (ed.), *A view of Ireland: twelve essays* (Dublin, 1957), pp. 114–20.

Palmer, N. D. *The Irish Land League crisis* (New Haven, 1940).

Other writings in social science

Moore, Barrington, Jr. *Social origins of dictatorship and democracy: lord and peasant in the making of the modern world* (London, paperback ed., 1969; originally published 1966).

Ritson, Charles. *Agricultural economics* (New York, 1977).

The Unreaped Harvest

If this volume has demonstrated the richness and complexity of agrarian rebellion, rural sectarianism, and popular political unrest in Ireland between the late eighteenth and the early twentieth centuries, it will have served one of its main purposes. But the contributors to this collection as well as its editors are acutely conscious that our joint enterprise, by its particular emphases and omissions, has also exposed much of what still remains undone. Indeed, we hope to have conjured up an image of the abundant harvest yet to be reaped in Irish peasant studies by exploring new fields of inquiry, tapping hitherto neglected sources of information, and adopting sophisticated tools of analysis. In what follows, the editors pass judgment on the gaps (as we see them) in the existing historiography and offer prescriptions as to how they should be filled. To dictate the paths that new investigations should take is not our intention; our aim is only to share our considered reflections on some of the exciting opportunities that deserve to be seized.

Prefamine agrarian unrest had, until recently, received little attention and been the subject of almost no basic research. The articles on the tithe war by the Rev. Patrick O'Donoghue long stood out as the only serious empirical analysis of a prefamine agrarian movement,[1] though

---

1. Patrick O'Donoghue, "Causes of the opposition to tithes, 1830–38" in *Studia Hib.*, no. 5 (1965), pp. 7–28; idem, "Opposition to tithe payments in 1830–31" in *Studia Hib.*, no. 6 (1966), pp. 69–98; idem, "Opposition to tithe payment in 1832–3" in *Studia Hib.*, no. 12 (1972), pp. 77–108.

420   THE UNREAPED HARVEST

the topic of rural discontent was competently treated by several scholars primarily interested in other subjects.[2] Before the 1970s, indeed, the best study by far of agrarian unrest in the prefamine period was still a contemporary analysis by George Cornewall Lewis first published in 1836.[3] A new interest in prefamine agrarian violence was heralded by the appearance in 1973 of a collection on Irish secret societies. Certain perceptive and well-written articles in that work helped to stimulate a fresh concern with this immense subject.[4] Since then, a growing number of publications have focused on popular unrest before the famine,[5] and additional research is now in progress.[6]

The more we learn about the subject, the more evident it becomes that historians have in the past underestimated this unrest. They greatly underrated its magnitude, its frequency, its organizational sophistication, and its importance to the population. They also underestimated its geographical extent; although much of the violence was localized, there were also many regional movements that covered large areas of the country. The Rockites and Terry Alts, for example, were vastly larger movements than the rebellion of 1848 or the Fenian rising of 1867, yet are much less well known to students of Irish history. Moreover, prefamine collective violence, as recent research has shown, was far more complex than had been suspected. It cannot be explained by any single factor or social condition: the demographic expansion, poverty, the defense of a traditional "moral economy," conflicts of interest between laborers and large farmers, the religious cleavage—all of these and still other factors must be taken into account. That there was an inseparable link between this collective action and the structure of Irish peasant society has also become increasingly apparent. So closely related were they that an appreciation of the one is impossible without an understanding of the other. Yet scientific knowledge of Irish peasant society, especially in the eighteenth and early nineteenth centuries, is woefully inadequate.

In approaching the complex problem of unrest in Irish peasant so-

2. Galen Broeker, *Rural disorder and police reform in Ireland, 1812–36* (London and Toronto, 1970); Senior, *Orangeism, 1795–1836*; W. G. Broehl, *The Molly Maguires* (Cambridge, Mass., 1965). See also the works cited in fn. 1 of the introduction to section one.
3. G. C. Lewis, *On local disturbances in Ireland, and on the Irish church question* (London, 1836).
4. See in particular Maureen Wall, "The Whiteboys," and Joseph Lee, "The Ribbonmen" in T. D. Williams (ed.), *Secret societies in Ireland* (Dublin and New York, 1973), pp. 13–35.
5. See fn. 1 of the introduction to section one.
6. Studies are now in progress by M. R. Beames, J. S. Donnelly, Jr., D. W. Miller, and P. E. W. Roberts, among others.

ciety, a logical place to begin, we believe, is with studies providing detailed analysis of specific regional movements and their socioeconomic underpinnings. Such studies will contribute to the development of a common fund of knowledge on all the significant outbursts of protest from the middle of the eighteenth century until the great famine. Most of the larger movements have in fact begun to receive attention; the short-lived or the less geographically extensive agitations, such as the Threshers (1806–7), the Ribbonmen (1819–20), and the Terry Alts (1828–31), are thus especially fertile ground for new research. Only when historians have accumulated a much wider range of such studies will they be able to make general statements with some measure of confidence and to provide tests for many of the hypotheses (such as our suggestion about the varying social composition of agrarian movements) with which they have been working.

Second, the routine, localized violence that was endemic to most parts of Ireland throughout the period we are considering would repay thorough investigation, with the focus either on a specific area of the country or on a certain type of violence. Faction fighting, for example, represents one kind of collective action that is of particular importance. We need to know more about the geographic concentration of factions, their social and political functions, and their eventual decline. What were the reasons for the transformation of factions after 1800 into especially violent collectivities? What was the nature and extent of the overlap between factions and agrarian secret societies, apart from the Caravat-Shanavest feud? What were the reasons for the rather sudden decline of factions, at least as notably violent collectivities, during the late 1830s and the early 1840s? (The common answer, that it resulted from better police activity, does not seem convincing.) What were the special characteristics of Irish society and of the relationship between Irish country people and the state that made faction fighting so much more prevalent in early nineteenth-century Ireland than in most other western European countries. And were there any similarities between Ireland and other societies, such as Corsica or southern Italy, where feuding was also a traditional form of collective action?

Analysis of factions inevitably raises the broader question of the relationship between peasant society and the character of collective action; it is precisely this kind of research that will bear the most fruit. As David Fitzpatrick has argued, Irish scholars should pay more attention to the role of family structure in agrarian collective action.[7] Unlike Fitzpat-

---

7. David Fitzpatrick, "Class, family, and rural unrest in nineteenth-century Ireland" in P. J. Drudy (ed.), *Ireland: land, politics, and people* (Cambridge, 1982), pp. 37–75.

rick, however, we do not feel the need to diminish the importance of agrarian classes in order to recognize that other structures played a role as well. Among them are not only the family but also religion, territorial divisions, and peer groups. Few active collectivities are based entirely on one type of social structure; most are a complex result of the divergent or reinforcing effects of several different sources of cohesion and cleavage. Local studies focusing on the way in which class, religion, territorial divisions, and family structures shaped the character of collective action in particular places are wanted. A longitudinal analysis of how collective action in a certain locality was transformed over time as a result of changes in these social structures would constitute a major contribution to the study of Irish agrarian society.

All this does not mean, of course, that the traditional concerns of Irish historians should be put aside. On the contrary, very often what is needed is more intensive examination of a familiar subject, but from a different perspective. For example, among the volumes that have been written on the rise of Irish nationalism, studies on the development of nationalist consciousness at the popular level are notably scarce.[8] The hypothesis that the Shanavests, and indeed the rural middle class as a group, were strongly imbued with nationalism, but that the poor were apathetic about it before 1815, as Roberts contends, is worth testing. The distinction Roberts draws, between rural middle-class nationalists and lower-class Whiteboys, offers an argument that is provocative, and if not entirely convincing (to us at least), is certainly one that could stimulate further research on an undeniably important subject. It must be explored, of course, with due consideration of the great body of scholarly literature on nationalism and peasants in other lands.

If Irish historians are to trace accurately the development of nationalist consciousness during the nineteenth century, they must face the awesome task of describing and explaining the decay of traditional popular culture in Ireland between 1750 and 1850. No proper understanding of social or political developments in Ireland during the late eighteenth and early nineteenth centuries is possible in the present state of ignorance about popular culture. Here we are referring in particular to a whole complex of traditional practices: patterns (or patrons), wakes, keening, pilgrimages, resort to holy wells, many kinds of popular celebration, the belief in supernatural intervention (including millenarian ideas), and the use of the Irish language — all of which were in serious decline by the early nineteenth century. Even the prophecies ascribed to Pastorini did not retain much credibility after 1825. "The tone of society in Ire-

8. Tom Garvin, *The evolution of Irish nationalist politics* (New York, 1981).

land," remarked one contemporary, "is becoming more and more '*Protestant*' every year; the literature is a Protestant one, and even the priests are becoming more Protestant in their conversation and manners."[9] An entire world of practice and belief was fading away. On this complex topic volumes could be written.

A somewhat less formidable but undeservedly neglected subject is the relationship between the state and the people. Though the topic has received considerable attention in other western European countries, it has been very nearly ignored in Ireland. Dickson's article in our collection is one of the few that consider this issue. Many questions are still waiting to be answered. How effective was the state at controlling the population, and how did its effectiveness change over time? How centralized or decentralized were state functions in Ireland as compared with those in other countries in the same period? What demands were made by the state on the rural population and what were the consequences of these demands? How loyal were local elites to the central state? Merging with this subject is the whole question of the criminal law and its enemies in Ireland during the prefamine period. We need to examine the legal mechanisms devised by elites to control agrarian protest, their implementation, and their effectiveness or lack thereof. At least one major focus of concern should be the instruments of repression and the techniques employed by agrarian rebels to frustrate them.[10]

The studies that we have suggested here by no means exhaust the list of those that are needed to enhance our understanding of prefamine collective action. Antigrazier movements require investigation; the cleavage analyzed by Jones had a long history, stretching back into the eighteenth century, especially in the west midlands. The tithe war, which received scholarly attention before Irish historians began to examine the many other movements, is now due for fresh study. The transformation in the character of rural unrest between the early and the late nineteenth century has recently been analyzed,[11] but there is a clear need to address the transformation in collective action from 1760 to 1845.

Given the prominence of sectarian conflict in Ulster, and given also the prevailing (and quite correct) judgment that this antagonism has

9. W. R. Wilde, *Irish popular superstitions* (Totowa, N.J., 1973; originally published 1852), p. 17.

10. There has been some good work on this subject. See especially S. H. Palmer, "Police and protest in England and Ireland, 1780–1850: the origins of modern police forces" (Ph.D. thesis, Harvard University, 1973); Broeker, *Rural disorder.*

11. Joseph Lee, *The modernisation of Irish society, 1848–1918* (Dublin, 1973); Samuel Clark, *Social origins of the Irish land war* (Princeton, 1979).

deep historical roots, one might expect that there would be numerous
studies tracing the development of rural collective action in Ulster and
seeking to explain why it has so often pitted Protestants against Catholics. Yet the number of such works is remarkably small. Until recently,
there was only one solid book on this question.[12] In the past decade several publications have explored certain aspects of the subject,[13] but we
are still floundering in a sea of ignorance.

For the prefamine period there are several aspects of sectarianism that
call for scrutiny. One is the spread of organized sectarian feuds of the
Armagh type into other counties, both within Ulster and outside it, during the late 1780s and the 1790s. What were the causes of this extension?
How and on what basis did these feuds spread? Related to these questions is the issue of the degree of central organization or at least coordination in the Defender movement that grew out of the Armagh troubles.
Another murky matter is the evolution of what is called Defenderism
in the 1790s into what is termed Ribbonism after 1800. When did this
occur, and why? The whole subject of rural sectarianism in the north
during the early nineteenth century has barely been explored. Once historians know more about it, they will be able to speak more confidently
about its agrarian and political significance. When Ribbonism of the
sectarian type spread from Ulster to other provinces, it was not confined
to the artisans of the towns, though it may have been more vital and
coherent in the urban setting. In his insightful recent book, *The evolution of Irish nationalist politics*, Tom Garvin makes much of the contribution of Ribbonism to the development of popular and party politics
of the nationalist type. This connection deserves closer scrutiny along
the paths suggested by Garvin's pioneering work.

If a subject as important as sectarianism in rural Ulster has been
neglected, it is hardly surprising that little consideration has been given
to the land question in that province. The general assumption has been
that there was no such thing as a land question in Ulster, and only a
few scholars interested in rural unrest have thought it worthwhile to
look closely at the north.[14] Two of the articles appearing in section two
of our collection therefore represent a radical departure from scholarly
tradition; and, as a result, it is no longer possible to dismiss agrarian
collective action in Ulster as minimal and inconsequential.

---

12. Senior, *Orangeism, 1795–1836*.

13. Peter Gibbon, *The origins of Ulster unionism: the formation of popular Protestant
politics and ideology in nineteenth-century Ireland* (Manchester, 1975); D. W. Miller, *Queen's
rebels: Ulster loyalism in historical perspective* (Dublin and New York, 1978).

14. R. W. Kirkpatrick, "Landed estates in mid-Ulster and the Irish land war, 1879–
85" (Ph.D. thesis, University of Dublin, 1976); W. A. Maguire, "Lord Donegall and the
Hearts of Steel" in *I.H.S.*, xxi, no. 84 (Sept. 1979), pp. 351–76.

There are a number of important questions relating to the north for which answers should be sought. First, a study is needed of agrarian violence in Ulster, analyzing its variations over time and from one district to another throughout the nineteenth century. It cannot be denied that agrarian violence in the north was less common than sectarian violence, but nevertheless it should not be overlooked. Where and why did it occur, and who participated in it? In the late eighteenth century it was hardly unknown for Protestants to engage in collective action, the motivation for which was agrarian rather than sectarian.[15] Why was this phenomenon less in evidence during the nineteenth century? And how did agrarian violence in Ulster differ from that in the rest of the country?

Second, the farmers' associations that appeared in the 1860s and 1870s deserve investigation. In their own right they constitute one of the many varieties of protest in nineteenth-century Ireland that must be understood before our picture of agrarian collective action will be complete. In addition, however, they laid much of the groundwork on which the land war was built in both the north and the south. Indeed, this was especially true in the north, where there was a direct organizational link between the activities of the tenant associations of the 1870s and the unrest of 1879–82. The essays in this volume by Bew and Wright and by Walker have introduced the activities of some of these bodies, but the task of studying them has barely begun.

Research must also be undertaken on the long-term consequences in rural Ulster of postfamine economic and social changes, the land agitation, and their relationship to sectarianism. The effects of the various land acts and the evolution of the agrarian class structure in the late nineteenth and the twentieth centuries are in great need of analysis in both the north and the south. How did landlords, farmers, and laborers fare in Ulster as compared with their counterparts in other regions of the country? What difference did the religious cleavage make? Here Irish scholars have a golden opportunity to contribute to a larger academic enterprise, namely, that of understanding the fates of peasantries throughout western Europe in modern times and how their experiences relate to religious and ethnic cleavages.

Agrarian unrest in the second half of the nineteenth century has received more attention than it has in any other period. The Tenant League of the early 1850s, the land war of 1879–82, and to a lesser extent the Plan of Campaign in the late 1880s were all studied by historians before 1970. Recent works on the land war have made it by far the best-

15. Maguire, "Lord Donegall."

known agrarian movement in Ireland.[16] As a result, the conventional notion of the land war as a mass uprising of a homogeneous rural population has given way to a more complex picture of an alliance among a variety of participants, organized in defense of their interests and drawn from a differentiated small-town and rural population. This advance in our understanding, however, has raised as many questions as it has answered.

For the land war we must discover more about how the Land League functioned, how the struggle was waged in various regions, and what happened in different parts of the country during the breakup of the agitation in the winter of 1881-2. Local studies like the one that Feingold contributed to this collection will be essential in providing basic information. It is difficult to draw satisfying conclusions from Feingold's essay (particularly his findings about support for the Land League among farmers) because we have so few works with which to compare it. Were the patterns that he found in the Tralee district typical of other areas? How was the land struggle related to conflicts in local politics and to local lines of cleavage and cohesion? How did local agrarian collectivities become mobilized, what kind of organization did they have, and how did this vary from one part of the country to another?

The entire organizational structure of the Land League from top to bottom might well be made the subject of a book. The functioning of the central executive committee, the operations of local branches, and the relationship between these two levels of organization should be described and analyzed. The Land League courts, at which violators of the League's rules were tried by their fellow tenants, is a fascinating subject that, sadly enough, has been almost completely neglected.

Local studies of the land war, however, cannot be properly carried out before more work is done on local government. The absence of solid research on Irish local government (not one book for any period of the nineteenth century!) is deplorable. Feingold had planned to devote his career to filling some part of this void and was well on his way with his fine study of the boards of guardians in the 1870s and 1880s.[17]

16. Paul Bew, *Land and the national question in Ireland, 1858–82* (Dublin, 1978); Clark, *Social origins*; A. W. Orridge, "Who supported the land war? An aggregate-data analysis of Irish agrarian discontent, 1879–1882" in *Economic and Social Review*, xii, no. 3 (Apr. 1981), pp. 203–33. Other works not exclusively concerned with the land war but making a contribution to its understanding include J. S. Donnelly, Jr., *The land and the people of nineteenth-century Cork: the rural economy and the land question* (London and Boston, 1975); W. L. Feingold, "The Irish boards of poor-law guardians, 1872–1886: a revolution in local government" (Ph.D. thesis, University of Chicago, 1974); T. W. Moody, *Davitt and Irish revolution, 1846–82* (Oxford, 1981).

17. Feingold, "Irish boards of poor-law guardians." See also his "The tenants' move-

Others will now have to take up the challenge. The importance of the subject can scarcely be doubted. For the vast majority of Irish people, local government was more imposing and significant, with greater direct effect on their lives, than many aspects of national politics about which historians have written voluminously. The structure and the operation of Irish local government, and the ways in which they altered over time, should be thoroughly analyzed, as should the relationship of local government to the social and political changes that took place in the Irish counties over the course of the century. What effect did the reform and centralization of local government and judicial administration have on the political strength of the landed class? What were the issues that brought local officials into conflict with the central administration, how were these conflicts resolved, and what relationship did they have to larger political struggles? And how does the study of local government help us to understand the relationship between Irish country people and the state?

Greater knowledge of the workings of local government will prepare the way for studies of the distribution of political power in local communities. This distribution varied greatly from one district to another. There are several obvious questions that need to be answered. How concentrated was power? How did its concentration vary from one community to another and over time? In what kinds of communities was the landed class relatively strong as opposed to the petite bourgeoisie of the towns or the farming population? We also need to examine the roles of personalism, political families, and patron-client ties in local politics, subjects that have been investigated in some depth for the twentieth century, but relatively neglected for the nineteenth.[18] Irish historians, as K. T. Hoppen has argued, have tended to focus principally on national political movements and on periods, such as the O'Connell and Parnell years, when national struggles were at their peak.[19] In the intervals, Hoppen maintains, Irish politics was dominated by local issues and power struggles among local factions and political patrons. These local conflicts are important in themselves. Moreover, a satisfactory understanding of the broader national movements will only be possible when we

---

ment to capture the Irish poor-law boards, 1877–1886" in *Albion*, vii, no. 3 (Fall 1975), pp. 216–31; C. B. Shannon, "The Ulster Liberal Unionists and local-government reform, 1885–98" in *I.H.S.*, xviii, no. 71 (Mar. 1973), pp. 407–23.

18. One article on this subject is that of Peter Gibbon and M. D. Higgins, "Patronage, tradition, and modernisation: the case of the Irish 'gombeenman'" in *Economic and Social Review*, vi, no. 1 (Oct. 1974), pp. 27–44.

19. K. T. Hoppen, "National politics and local realities in mid-nineteenth-century Ireland" in Art Cosgrove and Donal McCartney (ed.), *Studies in Irish history presented to R. Dudley Edwards* (Naas, 1979), pp. 190–227.

learn more about how the national movements were related to local contests.

From this perspective of the interplay between national and local politics, research on fenianism and the agrarian question in Connacht between 1867 and the land war would seem to be especially desirable. The leaders have received due attention, but the secondary figures in town and countryside have not. As we noted in the introduction to section three, there is good reason to believe that the Fenians made considerable advances in this part of the country during the 1870s, and that this progress eventually came to have significant consequences for agrarian politics, especially in Mayo, the cradle of the Land League. The contributions of the various actors and the extent of their cooperation should be explored more fully. Who was important in the Fenian movement in the west in the 1870s, from what social groups were these people drawn, how were they organized, and what precise relationship did this movement have to the land agitation that erupted in 1879?

For the decades after the land war, more information is needed on the Plan of Campaign of 1886–91 and on the United Irish League of 1898–1902. A comparison of these movements with the land war of 1879–82 might help to determine how agrarian collective action changed from one movement to the next. The Plan of Campaign, we suspect, drew its support generally from the same parts of the country as the Land League, but this impression should be verified statistically. Did the Plan of Campaign see a shift in the alliance of small farmers, large farmers, clergymen, and townsmen on which the land war had been built? Some of the strains resulting from this alliance have been analyzed by Paul Bew for the land war. Were similar tensions evident during the Plan of Campaign? Again, research at the local level would help to supply answers to these intriguing questions. One good place to start would be the southwest. The agitation in Kerry was remarkably violent at times, and Clare too witnessed intense landlord-tenant conflict. There is scope here for an illuminating analysis of local leadership and organization as well as for a study of tension between local activists and the national leadership. In the case of Kerry, it would be instructive to determine how the guiding personnel of the old Tralee Land League responded to the new challenges and opportunities of the late 1880s.

The role which tenant farmers played in postfamine collective action has been the focus of almost all the published research on that subject. Yet there were other groups whose parts in the conflict should be examined as well. The response of landlords to the agrarian agitation has long been in need of careful study. Most social movements are considered from a one-sided perspective and the Land League has been no exception.

There is much to be gained by treating the land war as a struggle in which several different parties were engaged — the agitators, the government, and the landlords — and then investigating the interaction among them. Irish landlords did not sit by passively while the League assaulted them. They fought back both individually and collectively. This side of the story deserves to be better known.

Indeed, the landed class has received inadequate treatment from historians for almost any period that one might choose. The way proprietors managed their estates has been carefully studied by a number of scholars, but there has been very little analysis of landowners as a social group. How did the social composition of the landed class change over the course of the century? How much mobility was there into and out of this elite? What were the major divisions within this class? Is it in fact legitimate to refer to it as a class? What was the relationship between the peerage and their families on the one hand and the plain gentry on the other? Whom did landowners and their children tend to marry? What was the content of their social life? In what sorts of economic activities were they engaged, apart from agriculture? How actively did they participate in the political, religious, and cultural institutions of both Irish and English society? Above all, how did the Irish landed class differ from its counterparts in other western European countries? These are questions to which answers are needed.[20]

Laborers constitute another social group about which too little is known. Collective action by laborers is indeed a subject in which new research, building upon the pioneering efforts of Boyle and Horn,[21] could be expected to yield valuable results. The changing social condition of farm workers, as well as their shifting position in the social structure, should also be examined, with the excellent statistical study recently published by David Fitzpatrick serving as an essential foundation.[22] There are still unsettled questions about the relationship between laborers and farmers. How much conflict was there between these two groups, and how did the antagonism evolve over time? The distinction between farmers' offspring and laborers also calls for further investigation. To what extent were these really two separate groups? What was the relationship

20. The best work on this subject has been done by L. P. Curtis, Jr. See his "The Anglo-Irish predicament" in *Twentieth Century Studies*, no. 4 (Nov. 1970), pp. 37–63; idem, "Incumbered wealth: landed indebtedness in post-famine Ireland" in *A.H.R.*, lxxxv, no. 2 (Apr. 1980), pp. 332–67.

21. P. L. R. Horn, "The National Agricultural Labourers' Union in Ireland, 1873–9" in *I.H.S.*, xvii, no. 67 (Mar. 1971), pp. 340–52.

22. David Fitzpatrick, "The disappearance of the Irish agricultural labourer, 1841–1912" in *Irish Economic and Social History*, vii (1980), pp. 66–92.

between these groups? Still another question requiring clarification is the proletarianization of laborers. The vexed issue of whether the proportion of laborers holding land after the famine was greater or smaller than before it may never be resolved conclusively, but it should be possible to determine whether after 1850 laborers as a group became more proletarianized in other ways, for example, by becoming increasingly dependent on wages for their support.

The clergy is yet another body that needs to be studied systematically. The Catholic church as well as the Church of Ireland have both received attention from scholars,[23] but the role of the local clergy in agrarian society has been closely examined only for the prefamine period.[24] The socioeconomic background of the parochial clergy, the character of their seminary education, the role of priests in popular politics and in the shaping of popular culture, and the eclipse of traditional popular religion by institutionalized religious forms, as suggested by Emmet Larkin's "devotional revolution," are all topics that should be explored. Although the importance of religion in Irish society is well recognized, we do not yet possess a thorough analysis of the transformation of this institution in the rural community during the nineteenth century.

The context in which these subjects should generally be pursued is that of a much broader inquiry assessing the overall effect of modernization on Irish peasant society and on rural collective action. In the general introduction we offered some examples of the ways in which the Irish experience was similar to that of peasants in other countries faced with modernization. But a comprehensive empirical study is urgently needed. To what degree did agricultural commercialism pose new threats to the economic security of Irish peasants? Were peasants, as a consequence, worse off or more vulnerable to economic destitution than they had been in earlier centuries? What effects did the decline of domestic industry in the early nineteenth century have on the peasant condition? Did modernization undermine traditional communal ties which had sustained peasant families in hard times? Is it correct to say that relationships between elites and peasants deteriorated steadily from one period to the next as a result of modernization? Did exploitation of the peasantry increase or decrease over time? And finally, what effect did mod-

23. Works on these subjects include D. H. Akenson, *The Church of Ireland: ecclesiastical reform and revolution, 1800–1885* (New Haven and London, 1971); E. R. Norman, *The Catholic church and Ireland in the age of rebellion, 1859–1873* (London, 1965); E. J. Larkin, *The Catholic church and the creation of the modern Irish state, 1878–1886* (Philadelphia, 1975); Larkin, *The making of the Roman Catholic church in Ireland, 1850–1860* (Chapel Hill, N.C., 1980).
24. S. J. Connolly, *Priests and people in pre-famine Ireland, 1780–1845* (Dublin, 1981).

ernization have on the class structure of rural Ireland? The transformation of the class structure between the immediate prefamine period and the postfamine years has received due attention;[25] the results of these inquiries should now be evaluated in a broad analysis extending from the seventeenth century to the present day.

To deepen our current understanding of the transformation of rural collective action is also imperative. We have already pointed out the need to examine how collective action evolved between the eighteenth and early nineteenth centuries. How did it change between the late nineteenth and the midtwentieth centuries? How were newly emerging relationships between different segments of rural society reflected in agrarian politics? Two subjects in particular call for further research. The first concerns the grazier class. In addition to the article here by Jones, a recent essay by Michael Higgins and John Gibbons has addressed this topic.[26] Both contributions could serve as starting points for the work of other scholars. A number of provocative arguments in Jones's article call for verification. Has he perhaps exaggerated the extent to which the grazier class tried to imitate the gentry? Is it true, as Jones maintains, that the grazier class was socially aloof and isolated from the rest of the rural community? And did graziers eventually become inactive in local politics and formal community organizations? There are ways of putting all of these questions to an empirical test. The second of these subjects in urgent need of study is the political slighting of the distinctive interests of small landholders in the west and elsewhere. As we noted in the introduction to section three, it is not yet clear why Irish political leaders and the United Irish League executive failed after 1903 to pay much more than lip-service to demands for the breakup of the ranches and for the redistribution of land. A book similar in its concerns to the stimulating one that Paul Bew has provided on the land war of 1879–82 could no doubt be written about the politics of the ranch war of 1906–8.

Carrying the inquiry one step further, some scholar could render a valuable service through the study of agrarian dissidence after 1910. Gearóid Ó Tuathaigh has provided a number of insights on this subject and has raised some of the important issues.[27] Particularly interesting from our perspective would be research on the relationship of western farmers to the national movement for political independence before 1921, and on the general rebuff given in Dublin after 1921 to western pressures

25. Lee, *Modernisation;* Clark, *Social origins;* Fitzpatrick, "Disappearance."

26. M. D. Higgins and J. P. Gibbons, "Shopkeeper-graziers and land agitation in Ireland, 1895–1900" in Drudy, *Ireland: land, politics, and people,* pp. 93–118.

27. M. A. G. Ó Tuathaigh, "The land question, politics, and Irish society, 1922–1960" in Drudy, *Ireland: land, politics, and people,* pp. 167–89.

432   THE UNREAPED HARVEST

for renewed agrarian reform.[28] As viewed from Dublin, western demands were apparently regarded as archaic survivals of past battles rather than as manifestations of serious problems left unresolved. De Valera would not emerge unscathed from a study of the agrarian policies of his governments; his neglect of the concerns of farmers in the west helps to explain why he and his party eventually began to lose electoral support there.

In all of this research, even that which seems to be most narrowly specialized, due consideration should be given to the larger European and world context. In the general introduction we stressed the need to link the Irish peasant experience to the larger process of the development of world capitalism and its social consequences for rural societies. There are in fact two recommendations here: first, that scholars concerned with Ireland devote more attention to theoretical literature on peasants and to studies of other peasant societies; and second, that they identify the direct connections between forces outside Ireland and the Irish experience. There was a time when historians of Ireland were excessively concerned with external forces. Not long ago, one could legitimately complain that Ireland was largely studied from a British perspective, too much consideration being given to the mutual influences of the two countries on one another (often on the assumption that what was important about Ireland was only what had some connection with England). Recent research on rural unrest in Ireland cannot be faulted for this weakness. Indeed, there has been a conscious attempt to write Irish history from the Irishman's perspective, to the point of neglecting the impact of intersocietal forces.

We need to look again at the effects of the external world on Ireland. These were both economic and ideological. What did it mean for Ireland to be so closely connected to the first nation to industrialize? What special features of English industrialization had distinctive consequences for Ireland? What impact did the special characteristics of the British state have for Ireland and especially for those who were the most alienated from this state — the peasants? What effect did social, ideological, and political developments in Britain, on the continent, and in North America have on agrarian unrest in Ireland? The impact of such external forces on Irish nationalism has been investigated in some depth, but too little attention has been given to their effects on agrarian collective action.

To be sure, impressive strides have been made in some aspects of Irish

28. Further research should build on David Fitzpatrick, *Politics and Irish life: provincial experience of war and revolution* (Dublin, 1977); and Erhard Rumpf and A. C. Hepburn, *Nationalism and socialism in twentieth-century Ireland* (Liverpool and New York, 1977).

peasant studies during the last decade. But there is certainly no cause as yet for complacency or self-congratulation. Too much about the peasants of Ireland — in all their gradations of income and status, in all their modes of thought and action — remains a closed book, or one barely half-open. But if the recent rate of progress in knowledge could be maintained (or better, doubled) during the next decade or two, there may then be reason for celebration.

Index

Abbeyfeale (Limerick), 131
Abbot, Rev. D. C., 247–8
Abercorn, 1st marquis of, 117
Achill Island, 320
Adair, Sir R. A. S., 2nd baronet. *See* Waveney, baron
Adair, Sir R. S., 1st baronet, 234
Adams vs. Dunseath, case of, 219
Adare (Limerick), 116, 117, 129
Aglish (Waterford), 74
Agrarian movements. *See* Peasant movements; Unrest, agrarian
Agriculture: commercialization, 28–31, 374–7, 387–92; effects of mechanization, 316–17. *See also* Prices, agricultural
Agriculture, pastoral: consequences of spread, 279, 281–3, 392–6, 403–4; expansion (1840–1920), 375–7; middle-tenant participation, 376–7, 404; speculative participation, 378–9, 401, 405. *See also* Graziers; Ranching
Agriculture, tillage: investment and profits, 388–90
Alexander, S. M., 244 *n. 66*
Ancketel, William, 213
Anderson, R. A., 345, 351 *n. 62*
Andrews, W. D., 208
Antrim, county of, 144, 154, 160, 163, 169, 211, 222; 1869 by-election, 234–6, 252; 1874 election, 239, 241; 1880 election, 243–4, 246, 263; 1885 by-election, 252; 1885 election, 253, 255, 257, 258 *n. 142*; 1886 election, 261; religious affiliation of electors, 232
Antrim Central Tenant Right Association, 242, 251
Araglin (Cork), 74, 76–8
Arch, Joseph, 324–5

Ardfert (Kerry), 114–15
Ardfinnan (Tipperary), 74, 83, 89
Ardilaun, 1st baron, 398
Ardmayle (Tipperary), 74
Ardmore (Waterford), 74, 77
Ards (Down), 222
Armagh, city of, 156, 169, 173, 178–9, 184, 187
Armagh, county of, 144, 146, 211; Catholic population, 160–3; economy (1770–84), 155–60, 163–4; 1874 election, 239–41; 1880 election, 243–5; 1885 election, 253–5, 258 *n. 142*; 1886 by-election, 260; 1886 election, 261; Orange support for Land League, 247; politics (1780s), 161–3; population increase, 160; proportion of electors, 232; religious affiliation of population, 159; sectarian conflict, 155, 183–4; violence, 15
Armagh troubles: battle of Lisnagade, 176, 181; caused by "improvement," 177–8, 185–6, 189; contemporary explanations, 165–9, 181–6; Drumbanagher incident, 176; Forkhill estate (1789–92), 177–8; geographical extent, 169; Gibbon's and Senior's interpretations, 162–5, 179, 181, 183; methods of control, 171–2, 174, 179; phases, 165, 169; Protestant aggression, 170–1, 176, 180–2; role of Catholics (1788–91), 174–5, 177–9; role of magistrates, 182; role of Protestant elite, 170, 180–1; sectarian violence, 183–4; in 1795, 179–80; types of violence, 172–4; and Volunteer movement, 187
Armour, J. B., 202, 206 *n. 46*
Army: in Ireland (1821–4), 133–5; and Protestants, 134–5
Ashbourne act (1885): and issue of land pur-

Break-of-Day Boys. *See* Peep-of-Day Boys
Brian, John (Captain Wheeler), 80, 81 *n. 69*
Bright, John, 237
Bristol, 4th earl of, 185
British Cooperative Union: report (1892), 348
Brodie, Dr. T., 323
Brownlow, William (father), 156, 171
Brownlow, William (son), 181
Bruff (Limerick), 55
Brunswick clubs, 151
"B" Specials, 187
Bulfin, William, 378, 405, 408
Bunmahon (Waterford), 75
Burke, Haviland, 400
Burry (Meath), 399
Bushe, G. P., 43, 45–6
Butler, 70 and *n. 18*
Butt, Isaac, 205–9, 275–6, 294, 324
By-elections (1870–4): city of Londonderry (1872), 203 *n. 34*; and home-rule movement, 276
By-elections (by county): Antrim (1869), 234–6; Antrim (1885), 222, 252; Armagh (1886), 260; Donegal (1876), 207, 242; Down (1878), 242; Down (1884), 222, 252; Down (1885), 252; Londonderry (1878), 242; Londonderry (1880), 248; Londonderry (1881), 252; Londonderry (1884), 252; Monaghan (1883), 219; Tipperary (1869), 274; Tyrone (1873), 238–9; Tyrone (1881), 216–17, 248
Byrne, J., 165, 168–70, 172, 173 *n. 50*, 174, 182–6, 188

Caherconlish (Limerick), 94
Cairns, 1st earl, 251
Callaghan, Paddy (Captain Cutter), 80
Callan (Kilkenny), 74, 77, 86, 317
Campbell, Rev. William, 183–4
Capital: use in grazing and tillage, 387–92
Capitalism: impact on Irish peasant, 20. *See also* Agriculture: commercialization; Industrialization; Modernization
Cappagh (Tyrone), 205 *n. 42*
Cappaghwhite (Tipperary), 94–5
Cappoquin (Waterford), 74
Cappoquin-Dungarvan district (Waterford), 86
Captain Cutter. *See* Callaghan, Paddy

Captain Fanatic, 184
Captain Flogger. *See* Nowlan, Pierce
Captain Moonlight, 295
Captain Rock, 108, 114, 118, 120, 125, 131, 133–5
Captain Wheeler. *See* Brian, John
Captain Whiskey, 184
Caravat movement: aims, 82–5; aliases, 93 *n. 129*, 96–8; bases, 73–8; causes, 76–7, 81–3; characteristics, 66–7; developments from 1815 to 1845, 94–7; developments after 1845, 98; leaders, 80; map of area of activity, 65; membership, 76–8, 80–1, 93; organization, 78–80; origins, 31–2, 64–6, 68–9; recruiting, 87; and Shanavests, 87–93; suppression, 93–4; tactics, 78, 86–8, 94; territory, 73–6, 92–7; and Whiteboys, 97. *See also* Black Hens; Blue Belt Boys; Bootashees; Coffees; Moll Doyle's Children; Polleens; Ryans; Three Year Olds; Whitefeet
Carbery, 6th baron, 118
Carleton, William, 121
Carlow, county of: Caravats and Shanavests, 93, 96; county-council composition, 358, 369
Carrickarnan (Louth), 177
Carrickbeg (Waterford), 75, 78
Carrickblacker (Armagh), 181
Carrickfergus (Antrim), 201
Carrickmore (Tyrone), 205 *n. 42*
Carrick-on-Suir (Tipperary), 75–6, 86, 89
Carysfort, 1st earl of, 45
Casey, James, 378
Cashel (Tipperary), 68, 73–4, 88
Castlebar (Mayo), 364
Castlecomer (Kilkenny), 98 and *n. 152*
Castlereagh (Down), 222
Castlereagh, viscount (later 6th marquis of Londonderry), 207, 208 and *n. 55*, 242
Catholic Association, 109, 135–6
Catholic clergy: need for research, 430; political role, 276, 302–3, 362–3; role in Ulster elections (1874–86), 240, 244, 255, 258, 261, 264
Catholic Committee, 165
Catholic Defence Association, 199
Catholic emancipation: consolidating effect on northern Protestants, 150–1; effect on Ulster politics, 151; and millenarianism,

440

INDEX

Depression, agricultural. *See* Crisis, agricultural (1877–80)
Deramore, baron. *See* Bateson, Sir Thomas
Derby, 15th earl of, 215 *n. 84*
Derry. *See* Londonderry
Derrygonnelly (Fermanagh), 247
De Valera, Eamon, 432
Development Commissioners: and cooperative movement, 352–3
Devon commission, 313, 320
Devoy, John, 291
Diamond, battle of the, 155, 179–80. *See also* Armagh troubles; Loyal Orange Order
Dickson, David, 9, 34, 423
Dickson, T. A., M.P., 193, 208, 210, 213–14, 216, 248–9, 260
Dillon, John, 257, 264; attack on cooperative movement, 353 *n. 76*; and poor-law elections (1881), 292
Dingers, 96, 98
Dingle (Kerry), 55
Disraeli, Benjamin (1st earl of Beaconsfield), 205, 210, 243
Distillers: resistance to taxation, 54
Donegal, county of, 151, 194, 207, 211, 242; county-council composition, 358; 1874 election, 240–1; 1876 by-election, 242; 1880 election, 243, 246, 263; 1885 election, 253–6; illegal distilling, 54; laborers' condition, 277; living conditions, 334; percentage of migrant labor, 320; ranching, 379–80; religious affiliation of electors, 232; sheep war, 396
Doneraile (Cork), 94–5
Donnelly, James S., Jr., 10, 33–4, 311
Donoughmore (Down), 251
Doran, Henry, 364
Down, county of, 144, 147, 154, 160, 163, 165, 168–9, 176, 196–8, 204, 205 *n. 41*, 207, 210–11, 222; 1874 election, 239–41; 1878 by-election, 242; 1880 election, 243–6, 263; 1884 by-election, 222, 252; 1885 by-election, 252; 1885 election, 253–6, 258 *n. 142*; 1886 election, 261; religious affiliation of electors, 232
Down Farmers' Union, 237–8
Downs, The (Westmeath), 382
Dowsers, 96, 98
Doyle, Lawrence, 400
Drogheda (Louth), 292–3 *n. 18*, 348

Dromore (Tyrone), 292–3 *n. 18*
Drumbanagher (Armagh), 175–7
Dublin, city of, 57–8, 92, 271, 322, 326, 330, 431–2
Dublin, county of: agricultural wages (1870), 322; ranching, 380
Dublin Evening Post, 108, 127, 131
Dufferin, 5th baron (later 1st marquis of Dufferin and Ava), 202
Dundrum (Tipperary), 94
Dungannon (Tyrone), 212–14, 216, 220
Dungannon Volunteer Committee of Watchfulness, 219
Dungarvan (Waterford), 74
Dunmanway (Cork), 129
Dunn, John, 108–9
Dunshaughlin (Meath), 379
Durkheim, Emile, 164
Dwyer, Michael, 317
Dwyers, 96

Ecclesiastical-titles bill (1851), 199
Education: denominational, 203–4, 276; intermediate-education bill, 208; university bill, 208
Egmont, 3rd earl of, 57
Elections: determining factors, 273–4. *See also* By-elections (by county); General elections; Poor-law elections; *entries for counties and provinces*
Eleven-month leases: and expansion of ranching, 396–404; held by graziers and shopkeepers, 347, 400–2; issue in ranch war, 384, 386; as reformers' target (1906–9), 384, 400, 403–4; and rents, 400
Elites, local, 6, 308–9
Elm Park (Armagh), 156
Emigration: effects, 150; from Ulster, 144, 150
Enniscorthy (Wexford), 128
Enniskillen (Fermanagh), 250
Enniskillen, 3rd earl of, 221
Erne, 3rd earl, 328
Erriff valley (Mayo), 381
Estates Commission: and ranch war, 384–6
Evening Mail (Dublin), 329
Evictions: geographical distribution, 394; and graziers, 392–6; link with eleven-month leases, 404

Famine: fear of (1821), 123–4. *See also* Great famine

Farmers: causes of political weakness, 357, 361, 363–9; class divisions, 366–7; conflicts with traders, 346–9; dairy, 380; effect of increased prosperity (1850–80), 279; links with traders, 343, 361–6; parliamentary representation, 345; political support, 242–3, 254; proportion of agricultural labor force, 277; Ulster Catholics, 205, 216; unifying and divisive factors, 281–3; voting patterns in Tralee poor-law election, 280, 305–6. *See also* Graziers; Large farmers; Middling farmers; Small farmers; Tenants

Farmers' clubs: aims, 275; and home rule, 275; need for research, 425; role in land movement, 341. *See also* Tenant-right associations

Feingold, William L., 10, 17, 279–80, 340 *n. 3*, 341, 344, 426

Fenian Amnesty Association, 274

Fenians: and poor-law elections, 291; remaining questions, 428; strategies, 275; supporters, 274

Fermanagh, county of, 218, 242, 250; Catholic support for home rule, 252; 1874 election, 240–1; 1880 election, 243–5; 1885 election, 253, 255, 258, 264; Orange support for Land League, 247, 250; religious affiliation of electors, 232

Fermanagh Farmers' Association, 250

Fermanagh Times (Enniskillen), 220

Fermoy (Cork), 120, 123

Fethard (Tipperary), 73, 86, 89

Fews, Upper, barony of (Armagh), 160

Field, William, 326, 327 *n. 64*

Findlater, William, M.P., 214

Finnigan, E. S., 253

Fiscal policy, 48–50; constraints, 59; effect on county budgets, 50–2, 59; political impact, 52–8

Fitzgerald, George R., 185

Fitzgerald, Peter, 400

Fitzgerald, Thomas Judkin, 91

Fitzgibbon, John, 382

Fitzpatrick, David, 312–13, 318, 421–2, 429

Flynn, Hubert, 385, 404

Foley, Thomas, 80

Food riots, 55

Forkhill (Armagh), 177–8

Foster, John, 47, 59 *n. 72*

Four Year Olds, 96

France: effect of French war (1793) on Ireland, 55; French invasion (1759), 166

Franchise: changes (1850–85), 231; effect of reforms (1884–5), 231–3, 254, 260, 263, 339, 360; for poor-law elections, 287–8

Freeman's Journal (Dublin), 292, 318

Free sale: capital loss, 389–90; and graziers, 282–3, 402–3; and leaseholds, 389 *n. 66*; opposition of National League, 282, 402. *See also* Tenant right

Freshford (Kilkenny), 129, 133

Fry commission, 388, 400

Galmoy, barony of (Kilkenny), 109

Galway, county of, 112, 113, 378–9; attacks on graziers, 381; percentage of migrant labor, 320; political power of traders, 344; ranch war, 385; rural violence, 278

Garvin, Tom, 424

Gaughan, Thomas, 313

Gaultiere, barony of (Waterford), 73, 75, 92

Gaultiere gang, 84

General elections: 1874, 239–41, 274–6; 1880, 211, 216, 243–6, 264; 1885, 224, 253–60, 263; 1886, 260–2, 264. *See also* Elections; Voting, denominational patterns

Gibbon, Peter, 163–6, 169, 181, 183, 362

Gibbons, John, 431

Ginnell, Lawrence, M.P., 382, 386

Givan, John, 214

Gladstone, William Ewart, 201–2, 215–18, 221–2, 224–6, 237, 260–1; and land act (1870), 152–3

Glenasheen (Limerick), 129

Glencastle (Mayo), 313

Glens of Antrim, 205, 382

Glenville (Cork), 120

Going, Major Richard, 131–2

Golden (Tipperary), 88, 94–5

Gombeenmen, 345, 359. *See also* Traders, urban

Gorey (Wexford), 381 *n. 28*

Gorey district (Wexford), 357

Gosford, 1st viscount, 175, 182

Gosford, 2nd earl of: estate of, 157

Industrialization (*continued*)
ster, 144, 316, 335; effect on Ulster econ-
omy, 143–5; effect on Ulster politics, 201,
224; impact on Ulster landlords, 224. *See
also* Linen industry; Rural industry
Inishowen, barony of (Donegal), 147
Irish Agricultural Labourers' Union, 324–5
Irish Agricultural Organisation Society
(IAOS), 350–3, 366
Irish Democratic Trade and Labour Feder-
ation, 325 and *n. 59*, 326
Irish Homestead, The (Dublin), 353
Irish Labour League, 326
Irish Land and Labour Association, 325
n. 59, 326–7 and *n. 64*
Irish language: in Armagh, 160–1; decline,
422
Irishman (Dublin), 193
Irish National Land League and Labour and
Industrial Movement, 330–1. *See also*
Land League, Irish National
Irish parliamentary party, 363 *n. 109*; busi-
ness representation, 281. *See also* Home-
rule movement
Irish Protestant Home Rule Association, 261
Irish Republican Brotherhood. *See* Fenians
Irish Times (Dublin), 293
Irish Trades Union Congress, 326–7 and *n. 64*
Irish-university bill. *See* Education

Jackson, Richard, 177
Jacobites, 167, 187–8
Jephson, Richard, 180
Johnson, Philip Francis, 323–5
Johnston, Denis, 353
Johnston, William, M.P., 202, 205
Jones, David S., 10, 20, 282–3, 423, 431
Jones, William Bence, 328–9
Jonesborough (Armagh), 177

Kane, Rev. R. R., 212
Kanturk (Cork), 114, 121, 323–5, 348
Kanturk Labour Club: aims, 323–4
Keady (Armagh), 160–1, 169
Kearney, Cornelius, 168
Kells, poor-law union of (Meath): unten-
anted land, 397–9, 402
Kells district (Meath), 386, 399; ranch land,
379, 401–2
Kelly, John, 295, 297

Kennedy, Líam, 16, 20, 280–1
Kennedy, Rev. Patrick, 125
Kenny, Patrick, 296–7
Kerry, county of, 130; agricultural wages
(1870), 321; Caravats, 83, 96; Congested
Districts Board, 334; militia-tax burden,
51–2; millenarianism, 123; post-land-war
agitation, 428; Rockites, 108, 114–15, 125;
Shanavests, 93, 96
Kerry Sentinel (Tralee), 293, 296, 298–9
Kettle, Andrew, 220
Kilcloony, parish of (Galway), 387
Kildare, county of, 76, 93; ranching, 379–
80; ranch war, 384
Kildare and Leighlin, diocese of, 116
Kildorrery (Cork), 123, 134
Kilgobnet (Waterford), 80, 87
Kilkenny, county of, 115, 318; Caravats, 73–
4, 76, 86–7, 92–3, 96–8; cattle trade, 380;
cause of rebellion (1769), 30; laborers' vio-
lence, 316–17; Shanavests, 92–3, 96–8
Kill (Waterford), 75
Killaghtee (Donegal), 57
Killaloe (Clare), 93–4, 134
Killarney, poor-law union of (Kerry), 294
Killeedy (Limerick), 116
Killenaule (Tipperary), 74
Killyman (Tyrone), 238–9
Kilmacthomas (Waterford), 75
Kilmaganny (Kilkenny), 74, 86
Kilmanagh (Kilkenny), 74, 86
Kilmeadan (Waterford), 75, 80, 90–1
Kilmeadan gang, 80
Kilmoe, parish of (Cork), 118
Kilrush (Clare), 126, 341
Kilteely (Limerick), 94–5
Kilteevan, parish of (Roscommon), 385
King's County, 112–13, 115, 316–17; Caravats
and Shanavests, 96–7; ranching, 379–80
Kirk, William, M.P., 199
Knights of the Plough, 326–7 and *n. 64*
Knockboy (Waterford), 74, 77–8, 89, 91
Knockboy gang, 74, 77–8, 86, 90–1
Knockcroghery (Roscommon), 292–3 *n. 18*
Knocklong (Limerick), 94
Knox, Colonel W. S., M.P., 216, 217 and
n. 86, 248

Laborers, industrial: wages, 76–7
Laborers, migrant: living conditions, 318–

Longford, town of, 348
Lough Corrib, 379
Loughgall (Armagh), 169, 179, 185–6
Lough Mask, 328, 379, 398
Lough Neagh, 156, 160, 181
Loughrea (Galway), 379
Lough Ree, 379
Louth, county of, 177–8; agricultural wages (1870), 322
Lower Bodoney (Tyrone), 205 *n. 42*
Lowesgreen (Tipperary), 71
Loyal Orange Order, 151; at Bandon, 128, 328; founding, 155, 163–5, 180; membership, 253; members in police force, 131–3; opposition to Parnell's nationalist policies, 219–20, 222; patrons among Protestant elite, 180–1; political candidates, 204; reaction to Land League agitation, 212, 214–15, 218, 223, 247, 328–9; representation of laborers' interests, 154, 223–4; response to Defender movement, 146–7; role in Conservative party (1885–6), 253–4, 259, 261, 264–5; role in Tyrone by-election (1873), 238–9; support for Liberals, 249
Lurgan (Armagh), 156, 171
Lyceum (Dublin), 311
Lyons, F. S. L., 345

Macan, Thomas, 172
Macartney, J. W. E., M.P.: tenant-right candidate, 204, 214, 238–41, 244–5
McCarthy, Justin, 117
McClure, Thomas, M.P., 202
McElroy, Samuel, 202, 206, 218, 225–6, 237–8
MacGeogh, Robert, 260
McGeough, Joshua, 172
McKnight, James: influence on Ulster Liberal policy, 200–3, 205, 211–12, 237; land-reform thesis, 194–9
MacKnight, Thomas, 202, 226–7, 234
Macnaghten, Edward, M.P. (later 4th baronet), 244 *n. 66*
MacNamara, Brinsley, 411
MacNaughton, Rev. John, 203, 208
McNeile, H. H., 251
Macneill, Sir John, 315 and *n. 18*, 320
Maghera (Londonderry), 215
Magpies, 97
Mallow (Cork), 117, 348–9

Mallow Farmers' Club, 324
Maltings: restrictions, 49
Manchester, 7th duke of: estate, 211 *n. 73*
Mandeville, Thomas, 70 and *n. 18*
Manning, Cardinal Henry Edward, archbishop of Westminster, 324
Manor Hamilton (Leitrim), 292–3 *n. 18*
Markethill (Armagh), 157, 162, 169, 183–4
Marum, 109
Marx, Karl, 164
Mathew, Father Theobald, 324
Matthews, D. J., 220
Maxwell, S. H., 244 *n. 65*
Mayo, county of, 113, 180, 212, 393, 395; attacks on graziers, 381; eviction rate (1857–64), 394; Land League and Fenians, 428; migrant labor, 320; Protestant immigrants, 185–6; unrest, 275, 278
Mayobridge (Down), 215
Meath, county of, 396–7, 399, 402; agricultural wages (1870), 322; eviction rate (1849–80), 394; pasture rents, 400; ranching, 378–80; ranch war, 382–6
Meath Labour Union, 386
Meitheal, 409
Members of Parliament, Ulster: denomination and profession, 233–4, 241, 245, 258, 261; landlords' representatives, 271; social characteristics (1892–1910), 345
Middle class, urban: role in collective action, 15–16
Middlethird, barony of (Tipperary), 73
Middling farmers: holdings, 340; voting in poor-law elections, 17, 280, 305–6
Militia: effect on taxes and unrest, 35, 50–2; riots (1793), 54–5; and sectarianism, 179
Militia acts (1793, 1795): effect on taxation, 50–2
Militia-augmentation act (1795), 51
Millenarianism, 104; causes (1821–4), 123–7; and class conflict, 107; and collective action, 102–7; consequences for Catholic emancipation, 135–6; in County Cork, 117–18; diffusion, 115–18; function, 106–7; literature, 118–20; origins, 103–4; and rebellion, 105–6; and Rockites, 33–4, 106–7, 113–14; role in rebellions, 14, 33–4; and tithes, 124–5; types, 102. *See also* Pastorini's prophecies; Rockite movement

448

Newry, viscount (later 3rd earl of Kilmorey), 203 n. 35
Newtown Hamilton (Armagh), 161, 169
Nicholson, John, 399
Northern Star (Belfast), 201
Northern Whig (Belfast), 196 n. *13*, 197, 202, 210, 226
North Kerry Land League, 293–7, 428
Nowlan, Pierce (Captain Flogger), 80

Oakboys, 162, 168, 183 n. *81*
O'Brien, William, 258
O'Brien, W. P., 323
O'Connell, Daniel, 133, 136 n. *164*; effect on Ulster politics, 151; Rockite defense counsel, 136–7 and n. *165*; and Rockite movement, 34, 110, 129 n. *126*, 136
O'Connell, Maurice, 306
O'Connor, T. P., 220
O'Donnell, F. H., 359, 362
O'Donnell, General, 117
O'Donoghue, Rev. Patrick, 419
O'Farrell, Patrick, 104–6
Ogle, John, 166–8, 182, 186
O'Grady estate (Limerick), 400
O'Kelly, J. J., 217
Oldcastle (Meath), 379
O'Leary, Peter, 325
O'Malley, Peter, 393
O'Neill, John, 44
O'Neill, Father Patrick, 210
Orange Emergency Committee, 329
Orange Order. *See* Loyal Orange Order
Oranmore district (Galway), 113
O'Regan, Archdeacon, 325
Orior, Upper, barony of (Armagh and Down), 160
Orpen, Rev. John, 107–8
O'Shea, Captain W. H., 256
O'Sullivan, Rev. Mortimer, 111–12, 120, 126
Ó Tuathaigh, Gearóid, 431
Oughterard, poor-law union of (Galway), 393
Outrath (Kilkenny), 316
Overend, Henry, 213

Paige, J. M., 18
Palatines, 129–30
Pallas (Limerick), 94
Pallaskenry (Limerick), 124, 134

Palles, Christopher, 203 n. *34*
Pan-Protestantism: effect of Land League, 221–2; role in Ulster politics, 201, 217, 219, 221–2, 224–5. *See also* Protestants
Parades: role in sectarian violence, 173–5
Parnell, Charles Stewart, 225, 250; and condition of laborers, 326; impact on nationalism in Ulster, 193; influence on Ulster Liberal fortunes (1879–86), 209–10, 217, 219–20, 224, 248–9, 256–7, 264; influence on Ulster politics (1879–86), 209–10, 219, 224, 248–9, 256–7, 264; and land act (1881), 153, 214–16, 221, 249; and poor-law elections, 286, 291–2, 309; and Ulster tenant right, 207
Pastorini, Signor (Charles Walmesley), 108–11, 116, 120, 122, 136
Pastorini cult: origin, 111–13; spread, 113–16. *See also* Ribbonmen; Rockite movement
Pastorini's prophecies: attitude of Catholic establishment, 108–10, 116; credibility (after 1825), 422; diffusion, 111–16; effect, 115; impact on Catholic emancipation, 34, 136–7; means of circulation, 118–23; role in rural collective action, 105–7. *See also* Prophecies
Pasture: decline (1780–1812), 374; increase (after 1850), 276, 392–404. *See also* Agriculture, pastoral; Graziers; Ranching
Patriot party, 168; achievements, 161–2, 187
Patten, Captain, 172
Paudeen Gar. *See* Connors, Patrick
Paudeen Gar's Boys, 95, 97; organization and membership, 71–2
Paul-Dubois, Louis, 393
Peasant movements: aspirations, 84; character, 10, 15; class participation, 17–18; impact of modernization, 4–8, 11; leadership, 14–16
Peasants: class differentiation, 7–8, 16–18; economies, 18–20; effect of modernization in Ireland, 8–9, 11–12; and population, 11–12; relationship with landlords, 9; revolutionary potential, 7; typologies, 16–20
Peel, T. G., 212
Peep-of-Day Boys, 163, 171, 173 n. *50*, 175; disarming of Catholics in County Armagh, 182–3; forerunners of Orange Order, 155, 164–5; membership, 168; origins,

450

INDEX

Protestants: ascendancy challenged, 16; fear of Catholic domination, 154, 179, 243, 248, 250–1, 260; and Land League, 249–50; proportion in County Armagh, 157–60; support for tenant-right candidate, 239; support for Ulster Liberals, 206, 224–5, 248–9, 254, 257–8; support for Ulster Tories, 196, 224–7; and Ulster Nationalists, 258, 261; voting patterns, 224, 241, 245–6, 252, 257–9, 262; as weavers in County Armagh, 146; in yeomanry, 127–30. *See also* Pan-Protestantism

Quaids, 95
Queen's County, 108; Caravats and Shanavests, 66, 93, 96–7; cattle trade, 380; rural laborers' agitation, 324
Quilts. *See* Knockboy gang
Quinn, Dr. John C., 210

Radicalism, agrarian: in Ulster, 151, 194–205, 227
Radicals, agrarian: policies, 194–5, 198, 206
Raftery, Anthony, 137
Railways: effect on ranching, 376, 379–80
Ranchers. *See* Graziers
Ranching: and agrarian reform, 384–7; as cause of congestion, 403; effect on rural society, 411–13; labor requirements, 20, 390–1; and land clearances, 392–6; profit margins, 388, 391–2; regional distribution, 379; role of capital investment, 387–9, 391, 410; and rural class system, 404–8; use of eleven-month leases, 400–1. *See also* Agriculture: commercialization; Agriculture, pastoral; Graziers
Ranch war (1906–9): aims, 384–6; as continuation of land war, 386–7; organizations opposing graziers, 384–6; role of National League, 381; tactics, 382–4
Rathfryland (Down), 168
Rathkeale (Limerick), 123, 132
Rebellion of 1798, 104; and taxation, 34–5, 37–40
Reform, agrarian: and demands for self-government, 248–51; as election issue (1868–86), 233, 238–9, 244–5, 255–6, 258, 262, 264; and eleven-month holdings, 403–4; and Fenians, 275; and graziers, 282, 347, 381–2, 385–7, 403–4, 410; iden-

tified with communism, 247, 250; identified with Liberals, 242–3; impact of agricultural depression, 209, 242; and independence movement (after 1910), 431–2; interdenominational support, 240–8, 263; and land act (1870) in Ulster, 237; and landlord-tenant relations, 236–9; Ulster Conservative support, 236, 243; and Ulster politics, 237, 247–8, 424–5
Religious Book and Tract Society for Ireland, 126
Rents: as basis for valuation, 196, 211; conacre, 48, 52, 113, 322; demands for control, 195, 197; demands for reduction, 209, 251, 308, 328, 343; effect of reduction, 271–2; graziers', 395, 399–400; laborers', 313, 322, 327, 331; as land-war issue, 279, 282, 328–9; levels, 32, 236, 276–7; as political issue, 209, 211, 275; resistance to payment, 211–12 and n. 73, 247, 252
Reynolds, W. J., M.P., 261
Ribbonmen, 136; character and membership, 113; clashes with Orangemen, 151; and millenarianism, 113; origins, 424
Richardson, Rev. William, 166–9, 182, 186
Richardson, William, M.P., 170–2, 180
Rich Hill (Armagh), 169–72
Richmond commission, 330, 393, 399
Rifle Brigade, 1st, 133–7
Rising expectations: effect on land war, 9; in literature on peasants, 5
Roberts, Paul E. W., 10, 15, 31, 422
Roberts, Thomas, 378
Robinson, Richard, archbishop of Armagh (later 1st baron Rokeby), 155–6, 161, 165
Rochford, Father, 108
Rochfort, William, 388
Rock, Captain. *See* Captain Rock
Rockite movement: ballads, 122–3; and Catholic emancipation, 135–7; Catholic sectarian character, 33, 107–8, 113–14, 125–37; and Daniel O'Connell, 136–7; geographical extent, 103, 420; hostility to army, 133–5; hostility to police, 130–3; millenarian inspiration, 106–7, 113–14, 123–4; origin, 121; and Protestant proselytism, 126–7; role of schoolmasters, 120–1; and tithes, 124–5; violence, 114, 129–30, 134–5; and yeomanry, 127–30. *See also* Millenarianism; Pastorini's prophecies

JACKET DESIGNED BY MIKE JAYNES
COMPOSED BY METRICOMP, GRUNDY CENTER, IOWA
MANUFACTURED BY CUSHING-MALLOY, INC.
ANN ARBOR, MICHIGAN
TEXT AND DISPLAY LINES ARE SET IN CALEDONIA

Library of Congress Cataloging in Publication Data
Main entry under title:
Irish peasants.
Bibliography.
Includes index.
1. Peasant uprisings — Ireland — History — 18th century.
2. Peasant uprisings — Ireland — History — 19th century.
3. Peasant uprisings — Ireland — History — 20th century.
4. Peasantry — Ireland — Political activity — History — 18th
century. 5. Peasantry — Ireland — Political activity —
History — 19th century. 6. Peasantry — Ireland — Political
activity — History — 20th century. 7. Violence — Ireland —
History — 18th century. 8. Violence — Ireland — History —
19th century. I. Clark, Samuel, 1945–   .
II. Donnelly, James S., Jr., 1943–   .
DA948.A2I74   1983   941.608   83-1289
ISBN 0-299-09370-0

DATE DUE

27 Dec 84			